Publications International, Ltd.

TABLE OF CONTENTS

Manufactured in U.S.A.

h g f e d c b a

ISBN 0-88176-663-1

Library of Congress Catalog Card Number 90-61118

ACKNOWLEDGMENTS

You and the Law was written by a wide range of legal experts, including lawyers, law professors, professors from other university disciplines, and legal journalists. The authors and their professional titles and affiliations are listed below by chapter.

The material in each chapter also has been reviewed by various experts. They include the chairpersons and members of American Bar Association (ABA) committees specializing in important legal areas, as well as law professors, university professors, ABA staff, and others with appropriate expertise. These people volunteered their time to review chapters. You will find each of them listed below by chapter.

At the ABA, assigning and reviewing copy was the responsibility of Charles White, Publications Director of the Public Education Division. Providing considerable assistance were the Director of the Division, Norman Gross, and Jane Koprowski, Chuck Williams, and John Paul Ryan of the Division staff.

The "When and How to Use a Lawyer" chapter: Written by Barbara Kate Repa, legal journalist, San Francisco, California. Reviewed by Sherwin M. Birnkrant, Chairman of the Coordinating Committee to the Model Procurement Code of the ABA Section of Urban, State, and Local Government Law; Terry Brooks, Director, ABA Division for Legal Services; and George Kuhlmann, Associate Director and Ethics Counsel, ABA Center for Professional Responsibility.

The "How the Legal System Works" chapter: Written by Ray Reynolds, member of the ABA National Conference of Lawyers and Representatives of the Media. It adapts, with permission, some sections of the book *The Reporter and the Law,* by Lyle Denniston. Reviewed by Shirley Abrahamson, Justice, Wisconsin Supreme Court; Luther J. Avery, Past Chairman-Honorary Member of the Council, ABA Section of Real Property, Probate, and Trust Law; Sherwin M. Birnkrant; Terry Brooks; Edward W. Hieronymus, representative of the ABA Section of Real Property, Probate, and Trust Law to the Uniform Law Commissioners; Larry Ray, Staff Director, ABA Standing Committee on Dispute Resolution; and Wantland Sandel, Director, ABA Division for Judicial Services.

The "Family Law" chapter: Written by Marcia O'Kelly, Associate Professor of Law, University of North Dakota School of Law; Jesse Trentadue, attorney, Hansen & Anderson, Salt Lake City, Utah; Diane Geraghty, Associate Professor of Law, Loyola University School of Law, Chicago; William W. Walker, attorney, Craige, Brawley, Liipfert & Ross, Winston-Salem, North Carolina; Alexander J. Bott, Associate Professor of Law, University of North Dakota School of Law; and Flora Johnson Skelly, legal journalist, Chicago, Illinois; with additional material by Wendy Whicher, mediator, Wheat Ridge, Colorado. Reviewed by Alexander J. Bott; Linda Elrod, Professor of Law, Washburn University School of Law; Doris Jonas Freed, Co-Chairperson of the Research Committee of the ABA Family Law Section; Diane Geraghty; Arnold J. Gibbs, Past Section Chairman-Honorary Council Member, ABA Family Law Section; Marcia O'Kelly; Arnold H. Rutkin, Member of the Council of the ABA Family Law Section and Editor of *Family Advocate* magazine; Donald C. Schiller, Past Section Chairman-Honorary Council Member of the ABA Family Law Section; Philip Schwartz, Chairman of the Committee on Federal Legislation and Procedures of the ABA Family Law Section; Susan Westerman, Chairperson, Committee on Marital Property Issues of the ABA Section of Real Property, Probate, and Trust Law; and Wendy Whicher.

The "Buying and Selling a Home" chapter: Written by Lynn Orr Miller, legal and financial journalist, Boston, Massachusetts. Portions adapted, with permission, from the pamphlet *Buying and Selling a Home,* published by the ABA Standing Committee on Lawyers' Title Guaranty Funds. Reviewed by Stanley B. Balbach, Member of the Council of the ABA Senior Lawyers Division and Vice-Chairman of the Division's Committee on Real Estate Transactions; Sally H. Foote, attorney, Thompson & Foote, Clearwater, Florida; Lynn Orr Miller; Andrea M. Scheiffer, member of the editorial board of *Compleat Lawyer,* a publication of the General Practice Section of the ABA; and Julius Zschau, Chairman of the

Committee on Purchase and Sale of Residential Real Estate, ABA Section of Real Property, Probate, and Trust Law.

The "Renting Residential Property" chapter: Written by Richard E. Blumberg, attorney, Blumberg, Farber, and Smith, Berkeley, California; with research assistance by Daniel Duane. It adapts, with permission, *The Rights of Tenants,* an American Civil Liberties Union handbook written by Richard E. Blumberg and James R. Groh. Reviewed by Richard E. Blumberg; Myron Moscovitz, Professor of Law, Golden Gate University School of Law; Michael Pensack, Executive Director, Tenants Union of Illinois; and Frederic M. White, Professor of Law, Cleveland-Marshall School of Law.

The "Consumer Credit" and "Bankruptcy" chapters: Written by Robert W. Johnson, Director, Credit Research Center, Krannert Graduate School of Management, Purdue University. Reviewed by Nickie Athanason-Dymersky, Deputy Director, U.S. Office of Consumer Affairs; Donald L. Badders, President, National Foundation for Consumer Credit, Inc.; William H. Detlefsen, Manager of Member Services, Associated Credit Bureaus, Inc.; Jim Fine, Project Coordinator, ABA Special Committee on Youth Education for Citizenship; William J. Henderson, President, International Credit Association; Robert W. Johnson; Vicki S. Porter, Vice-Chair, Bankruptcy Committee of the ABA General Practice Section; and Richard C. Sauer, attorney, Division of Credit Practices, Federal Trade Commission. John P. Hennigan, Jr., Professor of Law at St. John's University School of Law, reviewed part of the "Bankruptcy" chapter.

The "Contracts and Consumer Issues" chapter: Written by Ron Coleman, legal journalist, New York, New York. Reviewed by Jim Fine; Harry Haynsworth, David H. Means Professor of Law, University of South Carolina School of Law; Mark R. Lee, Professor of Law, Southern Illinois University School of Law; Frederick H. Miller, Professor of Law, University of Oklahoma College of Law; and Thomas M. Ward, Professor of Law, University of Maine School of Law. Bernard Diederich, an attorney in the Office of the General Counsel of the U.S. Department of Transportation, reviewed the section in this chapter dealing with air travel.

The "Automobiles" chapter: Written by Shel Toplitt and Jill Tapper, both legal journalists, Boston, Massachusetts. Reviewed by John B. Crosby, Chairman, Automobile Law Committee, ABA Section of Tort and Insurance Practice; Jim Fine; James P. Manek, Senior Counsel, Traffic Institute, Northwestern University; and Louis B. Potter, Executive Director, Defense Research Institute. Daniel W. Kummer, Personal Lines Specialist, National Association of Independent Insurers, answered several specific questions.

The "Law and the Workplace" chapter: Written by William F. McHugh, Professor of Law and Director, Center for Employment Relations and Law at Florida State University's College of Law, with the assistance of the Center's staff. Reviewed by Barbara J. Fick, Associate Professor of Law, Notre Dame Law School; Linda H. Lamel, Vice President, Teachers Insurance and Annuity Association; William Levasseur, attorney, Semmes, Bowen & Semmes, Baltimore, Maryland; James B. Lewis, Past-Chair and Honorary Member of the Council, ABA Taxation Section; Adrianne Mazura, attorney, Pope, Ballard, Shepard & Fowle, Chicago, Illinois; Richard G. Moon, Member of the Council of the ABA Section of Labor and Employment Law; Mary-Win O'Brien, Assistant Legal Counsel, United Steelworkers of America; and Theodore St. Antoine, Member of the Council of the ABA Section of Labor and Employment Law and Degan Professor of Law, the University of Michigan Law School.

The "Personal Injury" chapter: Written by Martha Middleton, legal journalist, Chicago, Illinois. Reviewed by Philip H. Corboy, attorney, Corboy & Demetrio, Chicago, Illinois and Jerome Mirza, attorney, Jerome Mirza and Associates, Chicago, Illinois. Thanks to Hervey P. Levin, Committee Chairman, also reviewed by several members of the Workers' Compensation and Employers' Liability Law Committee of the ABA Section of Torts and Insurance Practice: Philip D. Blomberg, attorney, Leonard M. Ring and Associates, Chicago, Illinois; Marvin E. Duckworth, attorney, Hopkins & Huebner, Des Moines, Iowa; Willard J. Gentile, Second Vice President, General Reinsurance Corporation; William Levasseur; Stewart E. Niles, attorney, Jones, Walker, Waechter, Poitevent, Carrere, and Denegre, New Orleans, Louisiana; Stephen I. Richman, attorney, Ceisler Richman Smith, Washington, Pennsylvania; and Mark E. Solomons, attorney, Arter & Hadden, Washington, D.C.

The "Criminal Justice" chapter: Written by Darlene Sordillo, legal journalist, Los Angeles, California. Reviewed by Thomas J. Foltz, Vice-Chair, ABA General Practice Section Committee on Delivery of Legal Services; John Nussbaumer, Associate Professor, Thomas M. Cooley Law School, Lansing, Michigan; Josephine Potuto, Richard H. Larson Professor of Constitutional Law, University of Nebraska-Lincoln, College of Law; Cathryn Jo Rosen, Assistant Professor of Criminal Justice, Department of Criminal Justice, Temple University, Philadelphia, Pennsylvania; Carole Smith, Managing Editor, ABA *Criminal Justice* magazine; and Sarah Welling, Associate Professor of Law, University of Kentucky College of Law.

"The Rights of Older Americans" chapter: Written by Madelyn Iris, Assistant Director of Education, Buehler Center on Aging, McGaw Medical Center, Northwestern University; and Flora Johnson Skelly. Reviewed by Madelyn Iris; Naomi Karp, Assistant Staff Director, ABA Commission on Legal Problems of the Elderly; John Regan, Jack & Freda Dicker Distinguished Professor of Health Care Law, Hofstra University School of Law; and Robin Talbert, Senior Program Specialist, American Association of Retired Persons.

The "Wills, Trusts, and Estate Planning" chapter: Written by Brett Campbell, legal journalist, Austin, Texas; with research assistance by Sandra K. Honath. In part adapted, with permission, from two publications of the ABA Section of Real Property, Probate, and Trust Law: *Planning for Life and Death* and *Wills: Why You Should Have One and the Lawyer's Role in its Preparation.* Reviewed by Alexander J. Bott; Brett Campbell; William D. Haught, Vice-Chair, Committee on Probate and Estate Planning, ABA General Practice Section; Mildred Kalik, Assistant Secretary, Probate and Trust Division, ABA Section of Real Property, Probate, and Trust Law; and Frederick R. Keydell, Liaison from the ABA Section of Real Property, Probate, and Trust Law to the ABA Taxation Section.

Jim Fine wrote various questions and answers added to the chapters entitled "How the Legal System Works," "Contracts and Consumer Issues," "Personal Injury," and "Law and the Workplace." These were reviewed by Howard Davidson, Director, ABA Center for Children and the Law; Harry Haynsworth; Mark R. Lee; Frederick H. Miller; and Thomas C. O'Brien, attorney, O'Brien & Barbahen, Chicago, Illinois.

The Glossary: Written by Ray Reynolds and Brett Campbell. Certain definitions were adapted, with permission, from *The Reporter and the Law,* by Lyle Denniston.

GENERAL INTRODUCTION

Americans have long been fascinated by the law. For years we have been delighted by the courtroom theatrics depicted in television programs and movies. Today we constantly read and hear about the law in the news. Whether it concerns divorce settlements of the rich and famous, troubling disputes over child custody, or controversies between professional athletes and team owners, the law has leapt into the public consciousness.

However, the law does not affect only public figures or notorious characters. It affects each of us in our daily lives—when we make a purchase, start a family, or go to work. To function effectively in our complex society, we must be legally literate.

That is the purpose of *You and the Law*—to explain the law to you in simple, easy-to-understand language. This book uses a straightforward question-and-answer format. It avoids legal jargon and technicalities, explaining in everyday words how the law affects you at home, at work, and at play.

For example, you will learn the legal facts about marriage, separation, and divorce. You will explore the legal aspects of buying or selling a home, and of renting an apartment for yourself or to others. This book offers information on a wide variety of contracts as well as tips on avoiding hassles commonly experienced by consumers. You will see how the law affects older Americans, and get answers to frequently asked questions about major legal topics such as personal injury and wills and estates. There is even a glossary that explains the meaning of commonly used legal terms.

You and the Law is organized so you can easily find information about those areas of law that interest you. The question-and-answer format gives you details about the most common issues raised by each legal topic.

Other features enhance this basic approach. In every chapter, material is highlighted in brief articles that appear alongside the questions and answers. These explanations and examples provide further insights into the legal topics covered. There also are charts, graphs, and maps that provide information about the laws in each state or federal laws that apply across the United States.

However, even a book such as this cannot answer all questions that every person might have on the law. To simplify your search for additional answers, sections at the end of each chapter tell you where to get more information. These sections refer you to many free or inexpensive publications, and suggest government agencies, bar associations, and other groups that can help.

When reading *You and the Law,* there are several important points to keep in mind. First, this book cannot and does not pretend to provide legal advice—only a lawyer who understands the facts of your particular case can do that. In addition, although every effort has been made to present material that is as up-to-date as possible, all laws can and do change regularly. Decisions by state and federal courts, as well as regulations from government agencies at all levels, also can change how laws are interpreted and applied.

Thus, the information included in this book should be considered an introduction to, rather than the final word on, the law in each area. If you are thinking about pursuing any legal action, consult first with a lawyer and/or other expert who is most knowledgeable about the specifics of your legal matters. Armed with the knowledge and insights provided in *You and the Law,* you can have more confidence that the legal decisions you make will be in your best interests.

WHEN AND HOW TO USE A LAWYER

INTRODUCTION

Almost everything we do—from making a purchase, to drivin a car, to interacting with others—is affected by the law in some way. While it often seems hard to live with laws, it would surely be harder to live without them.

In our country, the law is, in a real sense, the people's law. Ou courts are truly open to all, and the law is accessible to everyone It is part of the democratic heritage of Americans.

The availability of the law does, however, reveal a bewilderin variety of choices. When do you need a lawyer? When can (or should) you handle a matter on your own? The purpose of this chapter is to help you make the best choices.

There are many legal situations that you may and should handle on your own, without the assistance of a lawyer. Howeve when circumstances and laws are unique, complicated, or confusing, you may need the advice of a lawyer to guide you. Yo also may need a lawyer's services when you are so close to a personal problem that you are unable to see your way through t a proper solution. This chapter will help you recognize such lega matters, but it cannot examine specific situations. It can, however, help you determine when you should hire a lawyer, what a lawyer can and can not do for you, and what you can d to help.

WHEN YOU NEED ASSISTANCE

Q. Do I need a lawyer for every legal circumstance?

A. Although the law enters into nearly all aspects of daily living, you do not need a lawyer every time you become "involved" with the law. Many Americans have become too inclined to go to court to resolve problems. For example, sports fans have sued to have a referee's controversial decision reversed, or a jilted suitor has tried to recover the cost of an evening's entertainment. Such problems are usually not the best use of the law or our courts.

Q. What should I do if I have an argument with a neighbor over the boundary line between our properties?

A. First attempt to talk to your neighbor. After all, you probably will have to go on living next to each other. If that fails, you may wish to seek legal advice.

Q. If I buy a new stove and it stops working just as the warranty expires, should I contact a lawyer immediately?

A. No, first notify the merchant. If that does not work, contact the manufacturer and, if necessary, the Better Business Bureau. As a last resort, you may file suit in a small claims court. You can do all this without a lawyer.

Q. Should I always wait until a problem becomes serious before I contact a lawyer?

A. No, in serious matters, if you call a lawyer as a last resort, it may already be too late. It is difficult for a lawyer to protect you after you have signed away your rights. Some legal matters are so important or so complex that you must hire a lawyer at the beginning to deal with them effectively.

Q. Why can't legal documents be in a language that I understand?

A. Lawyers and others trained in the law often use legal terms as shorthand to express complicated ideas or principles. The words and phrases, many rooted in Latin, are often jokingly referred to as *legalese.* Although some legalese may be necessary in order to communicate certain ideas precisely, this may not be true for much of it.

In 1978 President Carter ordered that federal officials must be certain each regulation is "written in plain English and understandable to those who must comply with it." Many states also have laws requiring that the authors of insurance policies, leases, and consumer contracts use plain English. It is not likely that legalese will disappear entirely. However, by reading this publication, you may be better able to understand legal documents and how they apply to you.

Help From People Other Than Lawyers

Q. If I do not use a lawyer, who else can help me?

A. Unless your problem is obviously so serious that only a lawyer can resolve it, you should first consider another source of help. If you believe a business has cheated you, help may be obtained from the Better Business Bureau or a consumer protection agency run by your state, county, or city. Many law schools have set up clinics that deal with consumer law. Also, many workplaces, stores, and utility companies have their own departments to help resolve consumer complaints.

Help from the Media

Many newspapers and TV stations offer a "watchdog" service designed to help with consumer problems. Remember that these sources can help only a small number of people. However, when these watchdogs do try to solve a problem, results usually come quickly. When confronted with the possibility that a consumer complaint will be aired in public, most businesses will act quickly to cure the problem. By doing this, the businesses also will boost their own reputations as being fair and dependable.

Q. Are there other professionals who may be of assistance?

A. Yes, there are others who may help you. If you have a problem with insurance, for example, discuss it with your insurance agent. Bankers, accountants, real estate brokers, and stock brokers are others who may be able to help with problems in their specific fields. They may provide free advice that can help you evaluate whether your problem needs the attention of a lawyer.

Q. Can counseling solve some problems?

A. Yes, sometimes problems that seem to be "legal" may be helped or prevented by other means. Several groups offer guidance and counseling for personal problems arising in marriage, child rearing, and managing finances. Private counselors or members of the clergy also may provide such help.

Q. What is a small claims court?

A. Most states have procedures that allow people to represent themselves in court if the total amount of their claim is under a certain dollar amount. Keep small claims courts in mind if your problem is not very complicated and your losses are relatively small (in the hundreds or low thousands).

Q. A friend recommended that I try a local dispute resolution center. What does this offer?

A. For the right kind of case, these centers can be a quick, low-cost (or free) alternative to formal legal proceedings. These will be discussed later in this chapter.

Help From Lawyers

Q. I understand that, under certain circumstances, going to a lawyer may be unnecessary. Are there specific cases when I *should* see a lawyer?

A. Yes, there are times when you should see an attorney. While these matters are sometimes hard to recognize, nearly everyone agrees that you should talk with a lawyer about major life events or changes, which might include:
- Being arrested for a crime or served with legal papers in a civil lawsuit.
- Being involved in a serious accident causing personal injury or property damages.
- A change in family status such as divorce, adoption, or death.
- A change in financial status such as getting or losing valuable personal property or real estate, or filing for bankruptcy.

Q. Is there another way to determine whether I need to hire a lawyer?

A. Yes, by looking at how over 2,000 Americans use lawyers according to a study commissioned by the American Bar Foundation. This study found that the three most common matters taken to lawyers involved real estate, estate planning, and marital problems; see the following chart. (Note that the chart does not specifically mention workers' compensation, which is another major area.)

Q. If it is obvious that I will need a lawyer for a certain circumstance, should I save money and wait until I absolutely need the lawyer's services?

A. No, lawyers should be thought of first as preventers of legal problems. When dealing with legal issues, an ounce of prevention is worth many dollars and anxious hours of cure. Once you have determined that you need professional legal help, get it promptly. You can get the most help if you are in touch with a lawyer as soon as possible.

Q. What exactly is a lawyer?

A. A lawyer (also called attorney, counsel, counselor, barrister, or solicitor) is a licensed professional who advises and represents others in legal matters. When you picture a lawyer, you probably think of an elderly gentleman in a three-piece suit. That picture is no longer accurate. Today's lawyer can be young or old, male or female. Nearly half of all lawyers are under 35; the number of women lawyers has increased more than four times in recent years.

Q. Is most of a lawyer's time usually spent arguing cases in court?

A. No, a lawyer normally spends more time in an office than in a courtroom. The "practice of law" most often involves researching legal developments, investigating facts, writing and preparing legal documents, giving advice, and settling disputes. Laws change constantly, and new cases regularly alter the meanings of laws. For these reasons, a lawyer must put much time into knowing how the laws and the changes will affect each circumstance.

Q. What are a lawyer's main duties?

A. A lawyer has two main duties: to uphold the law and to protect a client's rights. To carry out these duties, a lawyer must have both knowledge of the law and good communication skills.

Q. What are the professional requirements for becoming a lawyer?

A. To understand how laws and the legal system work together, lawyers must go through special schooling. Each state has enacted standards that must be met before any person will be licensed to practice law there. Before being allowed to practice law in most states, a person must:

- Complete four years of college.
- Complete three years at an accredited law school.
- Pass a state bar examination, which usually lasts for two or

(continued)

Distribution of Private Practitioners, by Practice Setting (1980)

	Quantity	Percentage
In firms		
2 lawyers	32,509	8.8%
3 lawyers	22,635	6.1%
4 lawyers	16,233	4.4%
5 lawyers	11,574	3.1%
6-10 lawyers	33,377	9.0%
11-20 lawyers	24,130	6.5%
21-50 lawyers	22,529	6.1%
More than 50 lawyers	27,200	7.3%
Subtotal in firms	190,187	51.4%
In solo practice	179,923	48.6%
Total	370,110	100.0%

Source: Barbara A. Curran *et al.*, *The Lawyer Statistical Report: A Statistical Profile of the U.S. Legal Profession in the 1980s* (Chicago: American Bar Foundation, 1985).

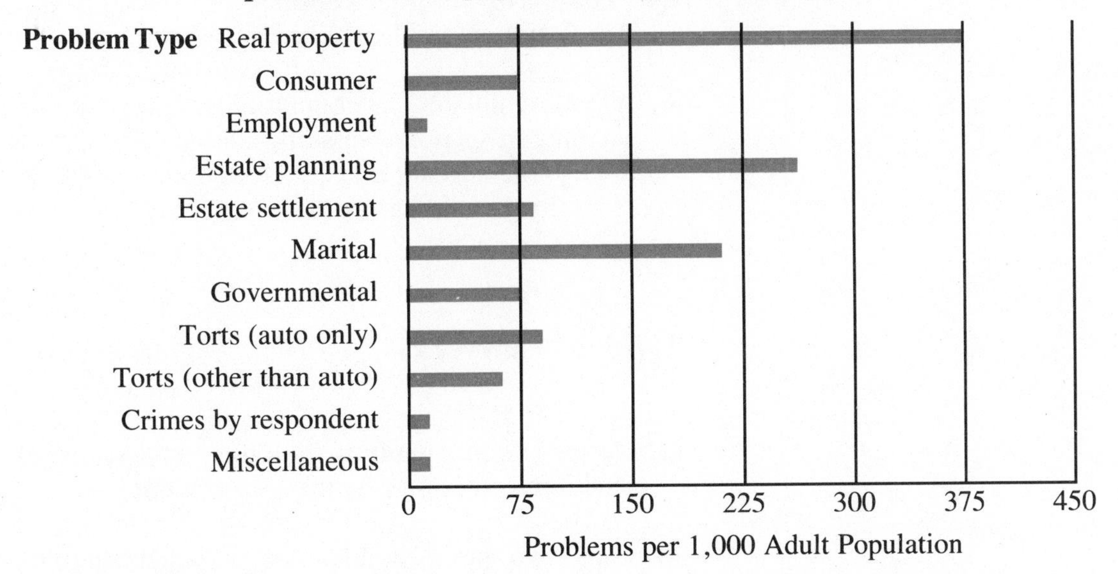

Reprinted with permission from John Flood, *The Legal Profession in the United States* (Chicago: American Bar Foundation, 1985).

three days. It tests knowledge in all areas of law and in professional ethics and responsibility.
- Pass a character and fitness review. Each applicant for a law license must be approved by a committee that investigates his or her character and background.
- Take an oath swearing to uphold the laws and the state and federal constitutions.
- Receive a license from the state supreme court. Some states have additional requirements, such as internship in a law office, before a license will be granted.

Q. Once licensed in one state, is a lawyer automatically allowed to practice law in all states?

A. No, to become licensed in more than one state, a lawyer must usually comply with each state's requirements. Some states, however, permit out-of-staters to practice law if they have done so in another state for several years and the new state's supreme court approves them.

Q. If I have a legal problem, must I always hire a lawyer?

A. Not necessarily. In some specialized situations, such as bringing a complaint before a government agency, nonlawyers or *paralegals* may be qualified to represent you. In addition, their services may cost less than a lawyer's. Ask the government agency what types of legal representatives are available.

Q. I come from another country, and I need to hire a lawyer. Aren't notary publics actually lawyers?

A. A "notary public," "accountant," or "certified public accountant" is not necessarily a lawyer. Do not assume that English (American) titles, such as notary public, mean the same thing as similar words in your own language.

Types of Lawyers

Q. Do lawyers normally work alone, or do most of them work for companies or the government?

A. About two thirds of all lawyers are in private practice; many others work for corporations or the government. Firms of various sizes employ lawyers in private practice. Almost half of the lawyers are *sole practitioners* who work by themselves.

Others join with one or more lawyers in *partnerships.* As the table at the top of page 13 shows, nearly half of the lawyers in partnerships are in firms that have five lawyers or less.

Q. How are lawyers split between rural and metropolitan areas?

A. Eighty-eight percent of American lawyers work in metropolitan areas, and about one third of all lawyers work in large cities. Especially in rural areas and small cities, there are many general practitioners who, by themselves or with the help of other lawyers, handle any type of case. However, the "family lawyer" is becoming harder to find.

Q. On what areas of practice do lawyers normally concentrate?

A. Most lawyers concentrate on one or a few specific areas, including: domestic relations, criminal law, personal injury, estate planning and administration, real estate, taxation, immigration, and intellectual property law (see chart below).

Areas of Legal Practice

Business Law	Advising about starting a new business (corporation, partnership, etc.), general corporate matters, business taxation, and mergers and acquisitions
Criminal Law	Defending or prosecuting those accused of committing a crime
Domestic Relations	Representing individuals in separation, annulment, divorce, and child custody matters
Estate Planning	Advising clients in property management, drawing wills, probate, and estate administration
Immigration	Representing parties in proceedings involving naturalization and citizenship
Intellectual Property Law	Dealing with issues concerning trademarks, copyright regulations, and patents
Labor Law	Advising and representing employers, unions, and employees on questions of union organizing, workplace safety, and compliance with government regulations
Personal Injury	Representing clients injured intentionally or negligently, and those with workers' compensation claims
Real Estate	Assisting clients in developing property; re-zoning; and buying, selling, or renting homes or other property
Taxation	Counseling businesses and individuals in local, state, and federal tax matters

LOOKING FOR A LAWYER

Q. How do I go about choosing a lawyer?

A. The lawyer will be helping you solve your problems. So, you must feel comfortable enough to tell him or her, honestly and completely, all personal facts necessary to resolve your problem. No one you listen to and nothing you read will tell you which particular lawyer will be the best for you; you must judge that for yourself. Most lawyers will meet with you briefly to "get acquainted." This will allow you to talk with your prospective lawyer before making a final decision.

Q. Are there any practical considerations to keep in mind when choosing a lawyer?

A. Yes, the lawyer's area of expertise and prior experience are important. Thirteen states have formed specialization programs. They include Arizona, Arkansas, California, Connecticut, Florida, Louisiana, Minnesota, New Jersey, New Mexico, North Carolina, South Carolina, Texas, and Utah. These programs provide some form of certification for lawyers in those states. A lawyer certified to practice in a specific area of law has shown specific qualifications in that field. In states without certification programs, you may want to ask about your lawyer's areas of concentration. You also may wish to ask about the type of cases your lawyer has handled.

Another consideration is the convenience of the lawyer's office location. Also consider the amount of fees charged and the length of time a case may take. Although they are not always wise guidelines, consider your personal preferences about the lawyer's age, sex, and personality. These preferences may guide you in locating someone with whom you feel most comfortable.

Have Faith

It is important that you trust the lawyer you hire. Furthermore, you should believe that he or she will do the best job possible in protecting your legal rights. However, remember that lawyers cannot work magic. No lawyer can be expected to win every case, and the best legal advice may not be what you want to hear.

Q. Where should I start to look for a lawyer?

A. There are many sources for finding a reliable lawyer. Some of the best are recommendations from a trusted friend, relative, or acquaintance. Be aware, however, that a lawyer who is right for someone else may not suit you or your legal problem.

Q. Are advertisements a good place to look for a lawyer?

A. In some ways, yes, ads are useful. Until recently, the law did not permit lawyers to advertise their services. Today, specific guidelines allow lawyers to advertise. Always be careful about believing everything you read and hear—and nowhere is this more true than with advertisements. Still, newspaper, telephone directory, radio, and television ads may make you familiar with the names of some lawyers. Some ads also will help you determine a lawyer's area of expertise. Other ads will quote a fee or price range for handling a specific type of "simple" case. Keep in mind that the lawyer may not be a "specialist" in the advertised field, and that your case may not have a simple solution. If a lawyer quotes a fee, be certain you know exactly what services the charge does and does not include.

Q. What about a local referral service?

A. Most communities have referral services to help the public find lawyers. These services usually recommend a lawyer in the area to evaluate a situation—often at a reduced cost. Several services offer help to groups with unique problems, such as the elderly, immigrants, victims of domestic violence, or the handicapped. Bar associations in most communities make referrals according to specific areas of law, while considering the areas in which each lawyer concentrates. Many referral services also have competency requirements for lawyers who wish to have referrals in a particular area of law.

Still, these services are not a surefire way to find the "right" or even a "good" lawyer for you. Some services simply refer you to any lawyer who is a member of a particular organization, without any concern for the lawyer's type or level of experience. Most services, however, will refer you to lawyers with experience in the area in which you need help. In the end, you must make your own evaluation in order to feel confident about your selection. To contact a referral service, look in the telephone book's yellow pages under "Lawyer Referral Service," or look under any local or state bar association listing.

Q. My new job offers a prepaid legal services plan. What can I expect?

A. Legal services, like many other things, are often less expensive when bought in bulk. Recently, employers, labor and credit unions, and other groups have formed "legal insurance" plans. Such plans may cover most, if not all, the costs of legal consultation, preparation of papers, and court representation. These group plans follow the same pattern as group or cooperative medical insurance plans. Many employers or unions set up a fund to pay the employees' legal fees, just as they contribute to group insurance plans to cover medical costs. Legal group plans have become much more widespread in recent years. Some department stores even offer such plans to their customers.

Q. I have heard about legal clinics, but I am not sure if I can use their services. What kind of help do they offer?

A. Legal clinics primarily process routine, uncomplicated legal business. These firms often advertise heavily and rely especially on TV ads. They generally use standard forms and paralegal assistants. (Paralegals are those who have received some basic legal training and are certified to help lawyers.) These clinics often charge a small fee for their services. They mainly work on wills, personal bankruptcy, divorces, and traffic offenses. Each clinic office may be small, but clinics often associate with many other offices in a multistate area.

Q. I may want to file a lawsuit, but I do not have much money. Where can I find low-cost legal help?

A. Several legal assistance programs offer inexpensive or free legal services to those in need. Most legal aid programs have special guidelines for eligibility, often based on where you live, the size of your family, and your income. Some legal aid offices have their own staff lawyers, and others operate with volunteer lawyers. To find free or reduced-cost legal services in your area, call the bar association or county courthouse. You also may look in the telephone book's yellow pages under "Legal Aid," "Legal Assistance," or "Legal Services." Sometimes the phone book will list a legal aid office under "Lawyers."

Q. I have been accused of a crime, and I cannot afford a lawyer. What can I do?

A. If the government accuses you of committing a crime, the United States Constitution guarantees you the right to be represented by a lawyer. If you cannot afford a lawyer, the judge handling the case has two options. The judge will either appoint a private lawyer to represent you free of charge, or the government's public defender will handle your case, also at no charge.

Q. Besides court-appointed defenders, is there another form of government assistance available?

A. Departments and agencies of both the state and federal governments often have staff lawyers who may help the general public in limited situations, without charge. The

United States Attorney's Office can provide advice about federal laws. It also can guide you to federal agencies that deal with specific concerns, such as environmental protection problems and discrimination in employment or housing. There is also a program that provides free defense attorneys for qualified indigent persons charged with federal crimes.

The state attorney general also provides guidance to the public, without charge, about state laws. Some states, for example, maintain consumer protection departments as a function of the attorney general's office.

Similarly, counties, cities, and townships often have staff lawyers who may provide the public with guidance about local laws. Some of these local offices also offer consumer protection assistance through their law departments.

However, government lawyers may not, at the government's expense, advise or represent anyone in private legal matters. Assistance from government lawyers must first qualify as being within the areas authorized by laws.

QUESTIONS TO ASK A LAWYER

Q. How will I determine whether I want to hire a specific lawyer?

A. Many lawyers are willing to meet with you briefly without charge so the two of you can get acquainted. During (or soon after) this first meeting, you can decide whether you want to hire that lawyer. Many people feel nervous or intimidated when meeting lawyers. However, remember that you are the one doing the hiring. Most importantly, the lawyer's services should satisfy you, especially when you consider the money you will be paying. Before you make any hiring decisions, you might want to ask certain questions to aid in your evaluation.

Q. What sort of questions should I ask?

A. Ask about the lawyer's experience and areas of practice. How long has the lawyer and the firm been practicing law? What kinds of legal problems does the lawyer handle most often? Are most clients individuals or businesses?

Q. Is it proper to ask the lawyer if anyone else will be working on my case?

A. Since you are the one paying the bill, it is well within your rights. Ask if nonlawyers, such as paralegals or law clerks, will be used in researching or preparing the case. If so, will there be separate charges for their services? Who will be consulted if the lawyer is unsure about some aspects of your case? Will the lawyer recommend another attorney or firm if this one is unable to handle your case?

Q. When I first met with a lawyer, she referred me to another lawyer. Should I be angry?

A. Probably not. Occasionally, a lawyer will suggest that someone else in the same firm or an outside lawyer handle your specific problem. Perhaps the original lawyer is too busy to give your case the full attention it deserves. Maybe your problem requires another's expertise. No one likes to feel that a lawyer is shifting him or her to another attorney. However, most reassignments within firms occur for a good reason. Do not hesitate to request a meeting with the new attorney to make sure you are comfortable with him or her.

Q. What, in particular, should I ask about fees and costs?

A. How are fees charged—by the hour, by the case, or by the amount won? (Different methods of charging and the different types of legal costs will be discussed later.) About how much money will be required to handle the case from start to finish? When must you pay the bill? May you pay it in installments? Ask for a written statement of what will be charged.

Q. When I first meet with my prospective lawyer, should I ask about the possible outcome of the case?

A. Certainly. Beware of any lawyer who guarantees a big settlement or assures a victory in court. Remember that there are at least two sides to every legal issue, and many facts enter into how it will be resolved. Ask for the lawyer's opinion of your case's strengths and weaknesses. Will the lawyer most likely settle your case out of court, or will it go to trial? What kind of experience does the lawyer have in trial work? If you lose at the trial, will the lawyer be willing to appeal the decision?

Q. Should I ask if and how I may help with my case?

A. It is in your best interests for you to ask how you may participate. When you hire a lawyer, you are paying for legal advice. Your lawyer should make no major decision about whether and how to go on with the case without your permission. Pay special attention to whether the lawyer seems willing and able to explain the case to you and answer your questions clearly and completely. Also ask what information will be supplied to you. How, and how often, will the lawyer keep you informed about the progress of your case? Will the lawyer send you copies of any of the documents that have to do with your case?

Q. During our first meeting, should I ask what will happen if the lawyer and I disagree?

A. Yes, your first meeting is the best time to ask about resolving potential problems. Find out whether the lawyer will agree to binding arbitration if a serious dispute arises between the two of you. Most state bar associations have arbitration committees that, for a fee, will settle disputes that you and your lawyer may have, say, over expenses. By agreeing to binding arbitration, both you and the lawyer consent to present your cases to an outside panel and abide by its decision.

LEGAL FEES AND EXPENSES

Q. How can I be sure that my lawyer will not overcharge me?

A. Perhaps the best control for keeping fees from becoming unaffordable is the requirement included in lawyers' ethical codes that all fees must be "reasonable." Of course, what you consider reasonable may not seem so to another person. However, there are some broad guidelines to help in evaluating whether a particular fee is reasonable:

- The time and work required by the lawyer and any assistants, and the difficulty of the legal issues presented;
- How much other lawyers in the area charge for similar work;
- The total value of the claim or settlement, and the results of the case;
- How much time is available to work on the case;
- Whether the lawyer has worked for that client before;
- The lawyer's experience, reputation, and ability;
- The method used to charge fees; and
- The amount of other work the lawyer had to turn down to take on a particular case.

Q. Is it okay if I ask my lawyer what billing method will cost me the least?

A. Yes, there is nothing improper in this. You should do this before you agree to hire him or her.

TALK ABOUT FEES

Although money is often a touchy subject in our society, fees and other charges must be discussed with your lawyer early. You can avoid future problems by having a clear understanding of the fees to be charged. You also can prevent conflicts by getting that understanding in writing—before any legal work has started. If the fee is to be charged on an hourly basis, insist on a complete itemized list and an explanation of charges each time the lawyer bills you.

Legal advice often does not come cheaply. A bill from a lawyer for preparing a "simple" one-page legal document or providing basic advice may surprise some clients. Remember that when you hire a lawyer, you are paying for his or her expertise and time.

WHEN AND HOW TO USE A LAWYER

TYPES OF FEES AND EXPENSES

The method used to charge fees is one of the things to consider in deciding whether a fee is reasonable. For this reason, you should understand the different charging methods before you make any hiring decision. At your first meeting, the lawyer should estimate how much the total case will cost. Also, the lawyer should inform you of the method he or she will use to charge for the work. As with any bill, you should not pay without first getting an explanation for any charges you do not understand. Remember, not all costs can be estimated exactly, because there may be unpredictable changes during the course of your case.

Q. Someone said that I should ask my lawyer to use the billing method that uses contingent fees. What does this mean?

A. A client pays contingent fees to a lawyer only if he or she handles a case "successfully." Lawyers and clients use this arrangement only in cases where money is being claimed—most often in cases involving personal injury. Many states strictly forbid this billing method in criminal cases and in most cases involving domestic (family) relations.

In a contingent fee arrangement, the lawyer agrees to accept a fixed percentage (often one third) of the *recovery,* which is the amount finally paid to the client. If you win the case, the lawyer's fee comes out of the money awarded to you. If you lose, neither you nor the lawyer will get any money. However, you probably will have to pay the basic operating costs and other expenses (such as court filing fees) associated with your case, as discussed later in this chapter.

By entering into a contingent fee agreement, both you and your lawyer expect to collect some unknown amount of money. Because many personal injury actions involve considerable and often complicated investigation and work by a lawyer, this may be less expensive than paying an hourly rate.

Q. Are all contingent fee arrangements the same?

A. No, an important consideration is whether the lawyer deducts the costs and expenses from the amount won before or after you pay the lawyer's percentage.

Example: Joe hires Ernie Attorney to represent him, agreeing that Ernie will receive one third of the final amount—in this case, that amount is $12,000. If Joe pays Ernie his fee *before* expenses, the fee will be calculated as follows:

$12,000	Total amount recovered in case
– $4,000	One third for Ernie Attorney
$8,000	Balance
– $2,100	Payment for expenses and costs
$5,900	Amount that Joe recovers

If Joe pays Ernie *after* other legal expenses and costs, the fee will be calculated as follows:

$12,000	Total amount recovered in case
– $2,100	Payment for expenses and costs
$9,900	Balance
– $3,300	One third for Ernie Attorney
$6,600	Amount that Joe recovers

The above figures show that Joe will collect an additional $700 if the agreement provides that Ernie Attorney collects his share after Joe pays the other legal expenses.

Many lawyers prefer to be paid before they subtract the expenses, but the point is often negotiable. Of course, these matters should be settled before you hire a lawyer. If you agree to pay a contingent fee, your lawyer should provide a written explanation of this agreement that clearly states how he or she will deduct costs.

Q. If my lawyer and I agree to a contingent fee arrangement, shouldn't the method of settling my case affect the amount of my lawyer's fee?

A. Yes, but only if both of you agree beforehand. Lawyers settle most personal injury cases through negotiations with insurance companies; such cases rarely require a trial in court. If the lawyer settles the case before going to trial, this requires less legal work. Insist that the lawyer accept a lower percentage if he or she settles the case easily and quickly. You should make the same demand if the lawyer resolves the case before filing a lawsuit in court.

Q. What billing method do most lawyers use?

A. The most common billing method is to charge a set amount for each hour of time the lawyer works on your case. The method for determining what is a "reasonable" amount depends on several things. More experienced lawyers tend to charge more per hour than those with less experience—but they also may take less time to do the same legal work. Large law firms are often more expensive than smaller ones. Lawyers in big cities usually charge more per hour than those in rural areas. In addition, the same lawyer will usually charge more for time spent in the courtroom than for hours spent in the office or library.

Q. A friend suggested that I might want to have a lawyer "on retainer." What does this mean?

A. A retainer fee is a set amount of money paid regularly to make sure that a lawyer will be available for any necessary legal service. Businesses and people who routinely have a lot of legal work use retainers. Such clients will usually get routine consultation and general legal advice whenever needed. If a legal matter requires courtroom time or many hours of work, the client may need to pay more than the retainer amount. Retainer agreements should always be in writing.

Most clients do not see a lawyer regularly and do not need to pay a retainer fee. Sometimes, however, a lawyer will ask the client to pay some money in advance before any legal work will be done. Although often called a "retainer," this money is a down payment that will be applied toward the total amount owed.

Q. I saw an advertisement from a law firm that charges fixed fees for specific types of work. What does this involve?

A. A fixed fee is the amount that will be charged for routine legal work. In a few situations, this amount may be set by law or by the judge handling the case. Since advertising by lawyers is becoming more popular, you are likely to see ads offering: "Simple Divorce—$150" or "Bankruptcy—from $50." Do not assume these prices will always be the amount of your final bill. The advertised price often will not include court costs and other expenses.

Q. Does the lawyer's billing method influence any other costs and expenses that I might have to pay?

A. No, some costs and expenses will be charged regardless of the billing method. The clerk's office of a court charges a fee for filing the complaint or petition that begins a legal action. The sheriff's office charges a fee for serving a legal summons. Your lawyer must pay for postage, copying documents, telephone calls, and the advice or testimony of some types of expert witnesses such as doctors. These expenses, often called "costs," are not part of a legal fee. You must pay the costs and expenses that relate directly to your case, regardless of the fee arrangement you use. Your lawyer will usually pay these costs as needed, and bill you at regular intervals or at the close of your case.

Q. My lawyer charged me a referral fee. Was this proper?

A. Perhaps. If you go to "Lawyer A," he or she may be unable to help you. Lawyer A may then refer you instead to "Lawyer B," who has more experience in handling your kind of case. Lawyer A will sometimes ask to be paid part of the total fee you pay to Lawyer B. The law often prohibits this *referral fee,* since it will increase the final amount to be paid by a client. Many ethical rules of professional conduct specify that two lawyers may not divide a client's fee unless: (1) the client knows about the arrangement; (2) both lawyers do some actual "work" on the case; (3) they divide the fee to show how much work each lawyer did; and (4) the total bill is reasonable. If one lawyer refers you to another, ask whether there will be a referral fee and, if so, what the agreement is between the lawyers.

Q. Should I "shop around" for the cheapest lawyer I can find?

A. As with other products and services, you often "get what you pay for" when it comes to legal advice. Although you should not expect to get good legal advice without paying for it, you should not pay for more than you get. Examine your bill carefully. If you feel that any charge is too high, or if you do not understand a billed item, ask your lawyer to explain it before you pay.

Q. Is there anything I may do to reduce my legal costs?

A. Yes, there are several cost-cutting methods available to you. First, answer all your lawyer's questions fully and honestly. Not only will you feel better, but you also will save on legal fees. If you tell your lawyer all the facts as you know them, it will save on time that might be spent in later investigations of your case. It also will help your lawyer do a better job.

Remember that the ethics of the profession bind your lawyer to maintain in the strictest confidence almost anything you reveal during your private discussions. You should feel free to tell your lawyer the complete details in your case, even those that embarrass you. It is particularly important to tell your lawyer facts about your case that reflect poorly on you. These will almost certainly come out during trial.

Q. Should I wait for my lawyer to say what he or she needs from me?

A. No, some things should be obvious to you. Before the first meeting with your lawyer, think about your legal problem and how you would like it resolved. If your case involves other people, write down their names, addresses, and telephone numbers. Also jot down any specific facts or dates you think might be important, and any questions you want answered. Bring the information with you to the first meeting, along with any relevant documents such as contracts or leases. By being organized, you will save time and money.

Q. Is it a good idea to limit my contact with the lawyer?

A. To a certain extent, yes, it is a good idea. Keep your phone calls and visits to your lawyer as short as possible—and only

WHEN AND HOW TO USE A LAWYER

phone or visit when absolutely necessary. This should keep a lid on your legal expenses. You will not want to pay for time spent talking about the local basketball team or the weather, so restrict your meetings and telephone calls to business. Remember that you are going to a lawyer only for legal advice. Other matters may be dealt with better by other professionals or groups.

Q. If something related to my case has occurred, should I wait until my next scheduled meeting to tell my lawyer about it?

A. No, situations may vary from one day to the next. Tell your lawyer immediately of changes that might be important to your case. It might mean that the lawyer will have to take a totally different action—or no action at all—in your case. This could greatly affect your lawyer's fee.

Q. Can I reduce my legal costs if I get more involved in my case?

A. Yes, this is often the case. Stay informed and ask for copies of important documents related to your case. Let your lawyer know if you are willing to help out, such as by picking up or delivering documents or by making a few phone calls. You should not interfere with your lawyer's work. However, you can very often help a case move quicker, reduce your legal costs, and keep yourself better informed by doing some of the work yourself. Discuss this with your lawyer.

Expectations About Your Lawyer

You have a right to expect competent representation from your lawyer. However, every lawsuit has at least two sides. You cannot always blame your lawyer if your case does not turn out the way you thought it would. If you are unhappy with your lawyer, it is important that you figure out why. If, after a realistic look, you still believe that you have a genuine complaint about your legal representation, there are several things you may do. The accompanying questions and answers discuss your alternatives.

WHAT TO DO IF YOUR LAWYER DOES NOT SATISFY YOU

Q. I lost my case, and I still had to pay my lawyer's bill and the costs and expenses. I am not very happy with my lawyer. What may I do?

A. First, talk with your lawyer. A lack of communication causes many problems. If your lawyer acted improperly, or did not do something that you think he or she should have done, talk with your lawyer about it. You may be perfectly satisfied once you understand the circumstances better.

Q. I have tried to talk it over with my lawyer. However, my lawyer will not discuss it. Do I have any alternatives?

A. Yes, you may fire your lawyer and hire another. If your lawyer is unwilling to discuss your complaints, consider taking your legal affairs to another lawyer. You decide whom to hire (and fire) as your lawyer. When you fire a lawyer, you may be charged a reasonable amount for the work already done. Most documents relating to the case are yours—ask for them. In some states, however, a lawyer may have some rights to a file until the client pays a reasonable amount for work done on the case.

Q. I am upset with the way my lawyer handled my case. May I file a complaint?

A. Yes, in recent years, it has become easier to get action on a complaint against a lawyer. Ethics codes adopted in many states help guide lawyers in what they may and may not do. Lawyers may be disciplined for violating these guidelines.

Q. Where may I file a complaint against my lawyer?

A. If you believe you have a valid complaint about how your lawyer has handled your case, contact the disciplinary board of the state supreme court. This organization grants or withholds licenses to practice law in your state. Call or write the disciplinary board about your lawyer's suspected misconduct. The board will either investigate the complaint or refer you to someone who can help. In some areas, the state bar association handles this function. If your complaint concerns the amount your lawyer charged, you may be referred to a state or city bar association's fee arbitration service.

Making a complaint of this sort may punish the lawyer for misconduct, but it will not help you recover any money.

Q. Then how may I get money to compensate me for my lawyer's misconduct?

A. You will have to file a malpractice suit against your lawyer. The discussion on medical malpractice that appears in the "Personal Injury" chapter will provide useful information on malpractice in general.

You also might receive compensation from a "client security fund" (see next question and answer).

Q. My lawyer settled out of court and is withholding money from me. What may I do about it?

A. If you believe that your lawyer has taken or improperly kept money or property that belongs to you, contact the state (or sometimes, local) "client security fund." This fund reimburses clients whose lawyers have defrauded them. Fees paid by lawyers maintain such funds, which exist in most states. Some states call this source a "client indemnity fund" or a "client assistance fund." The bar association or the lawyer disciplinary agency can tell you how to contact any such fund in your area.

Q. If I am having a problem with my lawyer, is there any reason that I would want to call the police?

A. Yes, if you believe that your lawyer has committed a crime, such as stealing your money or property, you should report that crime to the police. This is a last resort that should be taken only when you feel certain of your position. However, if you are certain, do not feel intimidated because your complaint is against a lawyer.

LAWSUIT RESOLUTION ALTERNATIVES

Settling Through Negotiation

Q. I am considering filing a lawsuit against someone. Is there anything I may do to avoid this?

A. Yes, you may try to negotiate. Before you even think of going to court, try to talk with the other person in the dispute. Stay calm and reasonable. You may find that, if approached politely, your "opponent" is willing to settle on a friendly basis.

Make certain that person understands why you are unhappy, and what you would consider a reasonable solution to the problem. Making an effort to settle a dispute without a lawsuit is never a waste of time. In addition, many states require by law that an aggrieved party first make a demand for payment or action before filing some types of lawsuits. If you reach a compromise, get the agreement in writing.

LISTEN TO THE OTHER PERSON

Keep an open mind to possible solutions and listen to the other person's side of the story. Remember that, with or without the help of lawyers, most people settle their legal disputes out of court.

Q. I have tried talking it over, but I had no success. What should I do next?

A. The next step is to hire a lawyer to write a carefully thought-out and businesslike letter to the person with whom you have a disagreement. This letter should include a brief factual history of the problem and a date by which you would like a response or settlement. This type of "settle or else" letter has many advantages. It helps you organize the facts and your thoughts logically. Your lawyer can express those thoughts in a way that the other person might not have "heard" when you were talking face-to-face. It also is often just the push needed to get the other person to settle. If the letter sets reasonable time limits, it will often help to encourage settlement of the case. Finally, the demand letter may be used as evidence if the case goes to court. Such a letter will give the judge the background of the legal problem. It also may be evidence that you made the required "demand" for payment or action.

Q. I have already hired a lawyer and filed a lawsuit. Is it too late to negotiate a settlement?

A. No, it is not too late to reduce your expenses (and speed a resolution of the matter) by settling your differences. Judges (and lawyers) usually will encourage those involved in a case to reach an agreement between themselves. If you reach an agreement after filing your case, let the court know you have settled the matter, and the case will be removed from the court's calendar. If you have hired a lawyer, he or she should do this.

After You Settle

It is important to get your settlement in writing, and it is best if you and the other person involved sign the final agreement. Suppose that, after filing a lawsuit, the two of you are able to work out the main problem, such as who owes how much to whom. It still may be necessary to appear before a judge to determine a time schedule or method of payment. It is usually best to get the advice of a lawyer about any settlement before you put it into writing and sign it.

Dispute Resolution Centers

Q. A friend recommended that I try a local dispute resolution center. What does this offer?

A. Nearly all states have established "dispute centers," which some people call neighborhood justice centers, citizens' dispute settlement programs, or night prosecutor's programs. These centers specialize in helping consumers, employers and employees, landlords and tenants, neighbors, and family members with common problems. The centers differ in procedure and degree of success.

Q. My friend mentioned that such centers offer two forms of negotiation: mediation and arbitration. What does each of these methods involve?

A. In mediation, there is usually a neutral person, or mediator. This trained person helps those involved resolve their

(continued)

Advantages/Disadvantages of Dispute Resolution Mechanisms

	Advantages	Disadvantages
Decision Through Court Procedures	• Announces and applies public norms • Follows precedent • Uniformity • Independence • Well-established rules and procedures • Partially funded by state • Decisions act as a deterrence • Decisions are binding • Decisions are enforceable	• Lack of special expertise • Can be confusing • Time consuming • Delays are frequent • Expensive • Requires lawyers • Limited range of remedies • Tends to divide parties • Compromises are not always possible
Arbitration	• Privacy • Parties control forum • Speedy resolution • Tailors remedy to individual problem • Decisions are enforceable	• Lacks precedent • Lacks uniformity • Quality varies • Becoming more structured • Requiring more money and time
Mediation	• Privacy • Reflects concerns of parties • Finds harmonious solutions • Addresses underlying problem • Process educates • Parties control process • Can cost less than decision through court procedures • High rate of compliance • Speedy resolution	• Not binding • Cannot compel participation • No power to induce settlements • No due process safeguards • Lacks enforceability • Reflects imbalance in negotiating skills • Little application/development of public standards • Lacks enforceability • Decision may be unclear

Source: *Paths to Justice: Major Public Policy Issues of Dispute Resolution.*

problems by identifying, defining, and discussing the things about which they disagree. Such a process is informal, and those who use this method for solving their problems need not know the law nor hire a lawyer. Arbitration is a more formal process of resolving disagreements. In arbitration, both sides present evidence and witnesses to a presiding arbitrator. Afterward, the arbitrator most often issues a written decision to resolve the dispute. Most centers offer mediation or arbitration services for free or at a slight cost.

Small Claims Court

Q. What are small claims courts?

A. All states have simplified special courts—most often called small claims courts. The special procedures of the small claims courts (also called magistrates courts, justice of the peace courts, and pro se courts) differ from state to state. These courts are usually a part of the municipal or county court system, and they are available for lawsuits limited to claims for money. (Some small claims courts may evict tenants who do not pay rent.) Every state limits how much you may seek in a small claims court lawsuit. This ranges from a few hundred dollars to thousands of dollars.

Q. May I represent myself?

A. Yes, they allow you to handle your own case.

Q. How does a small claims court work?

A. In the small claims system, there are simple procedures for filing suits. The trials have fewer rules and are less formal. A judge decides the cases; there is no jury. In many states, the court will even arrange to have the trial or hearing after normal work hours. There is very little paperwork involved. The costs of handling the cases are very low, and small claims courts process cases much more quickly than regular courts.

Q. Where can I get more information about small claims courts?

A. There are many good "how-to" books that explain what steps to take to bring a case to small claims court. Look at a few of them if you think you might have such a case, but do not depend on books alone. The laws and rules for small claims

Informal Methods Work (Usually)

These alternatives to the courtroom are quick, inexpensive, and less stressful than more formal methods of handling disputes. However, they will not work for all people and problems. Many forms of arbitration, for example, require the parties to agree in advance to accept the arbitrator's decision as final. Some people are unwilling to agree to such an arrangement, and some cases might be best suited to the regular justice system.

are different in each state. Check with local consumer bureaus, the small claims clerk, and legal aid groups for more information.

Q. It sounds like I will not have to do much in small claims court. Is that true?

A. Not necessarily. Use a small claims procedure only if you are willing to put some time into your case. You will be acting as your own lawyer, so you will be doing research, gathering documents, and investigating factual matters to prepare and present your case.

Q. What are the advantages of filing a lawsuit in a small claims court?

A. First, since you will be acting as your own lawyer, you will not have to locate and pay a lawyer to represent you. Second, the court procedures are simple. You do not need complicated forms or special language, unlike the regular court system. When your day in court arrives, you and your witnesses can talk freely with the judge about what happened. Finally, small claims courts work much more quickly than other courts. It usually takes two or three months to file, argue, and decide your case.

FILING A LAWSUIT

Q. I am thinking about filing a lawsuit against my neighbor. How must I convince the court that I am in the right?

A. If you are suing someone, you are responsible mainly for proving that the other person is liable to you. You may do this in one of three ways, by claiming one of the following "theories of liability":

- Contract liability. You may claim that the person you are suing has broken a valid agreement—either oral or written—which has resulted in a loss of money to you.
- Intentional liability. You may claim that the person you are suing has injured your property intentionally, and as a result you suffered monetary damages.
- Negligence liability. You may claim that the person you are suing has acted carelessly or failed to act when he or she should have done so, and this damaged you.

(continued)

Complaint Verified **(3-81) CCMD-8A**

IN THE CIRCUIT COURT OF COOK COUNTY, ILLINOIS, ... DISTRICT

	Plaintiff. . .	**No.** . . . .
v.		**Contract** . . . .
		Amount Claimed $ . . . .
	Defendant. . .	**Return Date** . . . .

COMPLAINT

The plaintiff. . . claim. . . as follows:

1.

I, ... **on oath state that I am the**. . . . .
plaintiff in the above entitled action. The allegations in this complaint are true.

. . . .

Signed and sworn to before me . . . . **, 19**. . . .

. . . . **.Notary public**

Name
Attorney for
Address
City
Telephone
Atty No.

Sample complaint form used to initiate a lawsuit.

No Small Considerations

Before you decide whether you should take advantage of a small claims court, answer some simple questions. Is your claim one that has only to do with money? If so, is the amount you are suing for within the limit in your state? Is the time and effort you will have to put into learning your state's law and presenting your case worth what you are likely to collect?

Like the regular courts, small claims courts operate according to laws and rules. Even the most careful preparation and the best presentation in court will not help if you cannot prove legally that the other person owes you the money. You must be able to prove "legal liability" in your case—that you have suffered a loss because of someone else's unlawful acts.

Q. What kind of defenses might be employed by the person I am suing?

A. After you claim that someone owes money to you, that person may respond with a "good defense." The defendant may explain that he or she was not at fault or that his or her actions were somehow necessary. If there is a good defense, or you fail to prove your case, the person you sue may be excused from owing you anything.

Q. Is there a time limit for filing a case?

A. Yes, every state has a time limit within which a case must be filed. The logic behind such limits, called *statutes of limitations*, is that most lawsuits are more easily and more fairly resolved within a short time. This is another reason that it is important to act as soon as you and your lawyer feel that you may have a valid legal claim. The time limits vary for different types of cases, but are usually not less than one year after the loss or injury has occurred. To find out what your state's time limit is, check your state's laws under the heading of "Statute of Limitations" (or simply "Limitations") or ask the small claims court.

WHERE TO GET MORE INFORMATION

Many organizations and agencies act as resources for specialized areas. These include national groups, such as the Federal Trade Commission, and local organizations, such as the Better Business Bureau and the consumer protection department of the state attorney general's office or local district attorney's office.

State and local bar associations are also excellent resources for consumers. They can help by providing information about lawyer referral, dispute resolution alternatives, lawyer discipline, and other topics. They also can usually refer you to other legal and nonlegal groups that might help you.

Space prevents us from listing the many helpful organizations or the hundreds of local bar associations across the country. A listing of state bar associations appears near the back of this publication. Check the blue pages of your telephone book for governmental listings; the white pages and the yellow pages can provide additional listings of private and public organizations.

HOW THE LEGAL SYSTEM WORKS

INTRODUCTION

For most people, mystery surrounds law and the courts. Legislators make the law, and judges interpret these laws. Public officials have taken great strides in making the law and its special language easier to understand. How the courts interpret the law, and the courts themselves, however, still confuse the general public.

This chapter tries to clear up some of the mysteries. It introduces you to our legal system and discusses briefly the roles of its key players. This chapter also explains the steps involved in most civil and criminal cases. While it does not cover all kinds of lawsuits, it does try to explain the procedures common to most of them.

This chapter discusses some of the special courts in the American system. It also offers a chart on courts in the federal system and in a representative state. In addition, this chapter explores ways to resolve disputes outside of the court system.

"How the Legal System Works" aims to help you understand the system as a whole. Intended for the general public, it also may serve journalists and any other people who want to become familiar with our legal system. Note that this chapter does not examine practical problems of everyday law. The preceding chapter and those that follow discuss these topics.

LAW AND THE COURTS

Q. What is the function of law?

A. Most people believe the law only forbids or punishes. People think of a police officer arresting a suspect or a judge sentencing a defendant. That may be true of criminal law, at least up to a point. However, the law has a more important role. In the United States, we live by the rule of the law. It provides a logical and civilized way of organizing society. In this sense, the law allows people in this country to enjoy their rights. It also permits Americans to know their duties. And the law allows all this to occur within the structure of an organized society.

In many ways the rule of law is the foundation of our culture. The law provides society with the rules by which all people live. People can know the law and live their lives accordingly. They have the right to rely on the law and be sure of the protection provided by the courts.

The courts have the duty of applying the rules of law to specific facts brought before them. Courts offer one way to resolve disputes between people, legal entities, and units of government. The courts often must uphold limitations on the government and protect against possible abuses by the other branches of government. In addition, courts protect minorities from the majority. They also protect the rights of people who cannot protect themselves.

The law includes the U.S. Constitution and ideas of equal treatment and fair play. Through "due process," no person should be above the law—and no person should be below it. The courts—and the shelters of the law—should be open to everybody.

A recent survey of judges and court administrators revealed agreement about the following basic purposes of courts:

- To do justice in each case.
- To stick to standards of neutrality and fair procedure, so that the public trusts the courts and lawyers can predict the court procedures.
- To provide a nonviolent way to settle disputes. There must be a result and a prompt decision to allow people to get on with their lives.
- To protect the people from the arbitrary use of government power. The U.S. Constitution creates a government of *limited* power. For example, the government must allow most defendants to go free on bail while they await trial. It must not conduct secret trials or carry out unreasonable searches and seizures. It is the courts that enforce these protections of the individual. The courts keep the government's powers within legal limits.

- To make a formal record of legal status. Many court actions record the change of legal status. This includes settlement of estates of people who have died; marriage; divorce; adoption; garnishment; attachment; and transfer of real property. Many court employees, such as court reporters and clerks of courts, keep these records. Courts spend a substantial portion of their budgets on record keeping.
- To deter criminal behavior; to reform persons convicted of crimes; to separate convicted persons from society.
- To inform the public, through court decisions, about what behavior is lawful and what is unlawful.

Lloyd N. Cutler, a former counsel to President Carter, writes of the judiciary:

> It has the greatest respect among the propertied and the underprivileged classes. One, because of all the institutions it has worked the best and, two, because . . . it has upheld the rights of minorities. The judiciary is now looked on as the defender of everyone's rights.

The Adversary System

Q. How does the adversary system promote impartial decisions?

A. There are many examples of court procedures that provide a way to make unbiased decisions. For example, the adversary process forms the basis of our legal system. This process assumes that the best way to find the truth is to let all competitors present their views as adversaries (opponents) to an impartial third party. The adversaries do this under rules that permit the evidence to be given in a fair and orderly fashion. A trial under the adversary process (1) establishes the facts, (2) determines governing law, (3) applies law to the facts, and (4) solves disputes by awarding (or denying) judgment. The impartial third party—the judge or jury—decides the case based on the evidence.

Q. Why does our court system include such ideas as "beyond a reasonable doubt"?

A. To the general public, the adversary system may look like game playing. It includes ideas such as "burden of proof" and standards of proof such as "beyond a reasonable doubt" or "more probable than not." These ideas mean very little to most people. However, they mean everything to an accused person. He or she must be "more probably than not"

Reasons for Rejecting or Dismissing Criminal Cases

There are several common reasons for the rejection or dismissal of criminal cases. One reason involves *insufficient evidence,* resulting from a failure to find enough physical evidence that connects the defendant to the offense. *Witness problems* also influence the dismissal or rejection of criminal cases. These problems include witnesses who fail to appear, who are reluctant to testify, or who are unsure of the identity of the offender. In *the interests of justice,* the prosecutor may decide not to prosecute certain types of cases, particularly those that violate the letter, not the spirit, of the law. One example might involve an insignificant amount of property damage. Other reasons might also play a role in the rejection or dismissal of a criminal case.

guilty of an offense to be charged with a crime. The accused also must be proven guilty "beyond a reasonable doubt" to be convicted.

People often think of the complex nature of the legal process as "legal red tape." Yet this so-called red tape can protect the rights of every United States citizen. It can ensure equal protection under the law and due process of law, both of which are the essence of the American system of justice.

Civil Cases and Criminal Cases

Q. How do civil and criminal cases differ?

A. Civil cases mostly involve the settlement of private conflicts among people or institutions such as businesses. Criminal cases involve the upholding of public or official codes of behavior that society believes necessary to protect its citizens or society itself.

Many civil cases involve domestic relations issues—divorce, child support, custody, and the like. Personal injuries probably account for more claims, called *tort actions,* than any other cause. And businesses often sue each other.

In a criminal case, the government brings charges against the person or business who supposedly committed the crime. In civil cases, the people or businesses involved in the disputes file suits.

Q. Do most civil and criminal cases go to trial?

A. No. Most cases that come to court—about 90 percent—are settled without a trial. Negotiations between the parties account for this, which is as true in civil cases as in criminal cases. Furthermore, many disputes that raise legal issues never result in lawsuits.

State Courts and Federal Courts

Q. How do state and federal courts differ?

A. One of the most confusing aspects of our courts is that we have two distinct, but coexisting, court systems: state courts and federal courts.

The state courts handle most cases. In 1984, for example the most recent year for which complete statistics are available all courts handled about 3,275,000 civil cases. Of this total, state courts received just under three million (92 percent). Federal courts saw about 275,000 (eight percent).

Each state establishes its state courts under the authority of the state constitution. As long as the courts follow the U.S. Constitution, each state may decide its own kind of court structure, under its own constitution and laws. No two states have exactly the same system. However, many state systems are similar. State courts decide almost every type of case. They exist in many towns and almost all counties. State courts are the ones that most citizens use. They handle most of the divorces, probates of estates, and all other matters except those started in or assigned to federal courts. The chart that appears on the following page shows the various state courts of Florida. While no state court system is "typical," Florida's system represents the general structure of state courts in this nation.

There are far fewer federal courts than state courts. Most federal courts are in the larger cities. The chart that appears after the Florida Court System chart shows the general structure of the federal courts. A federal court may hear a case only if a federal law or the U.S. Constitution gives the federal court authority to hear the case. Nevertheless, the federal courts hear some important types of cases, including civil rights, discrimination, antitrust, Social Security, and veteran's affairs. While there are instances of overlapping authority, both state and federal systems usually do not try the same case. Most cases must be tried in one system or the other.

The state courts differ from each other and from the federal courts in many of their methods. That is why general statements about court procedure rarely apply to all courts. Thus the procedures outlined in this publication may not apply to some courts. For an in-depth look at the courts of your state, contact your state bar association, state court administrator, or state supreme court. (A list of state bar associations is provided near the back of this book.)

The Structure of Courts

Q. How are the state and federal courts organized?

A. State and federal courts usually exist in three layers:
- "Limited jurisdiction" or "general jurisdiction" courts, where cases start;
- "Intermediate" (appellate) courts that first hear appeals; and
- "Supreme" courts that have final judicial authority.

(continued)

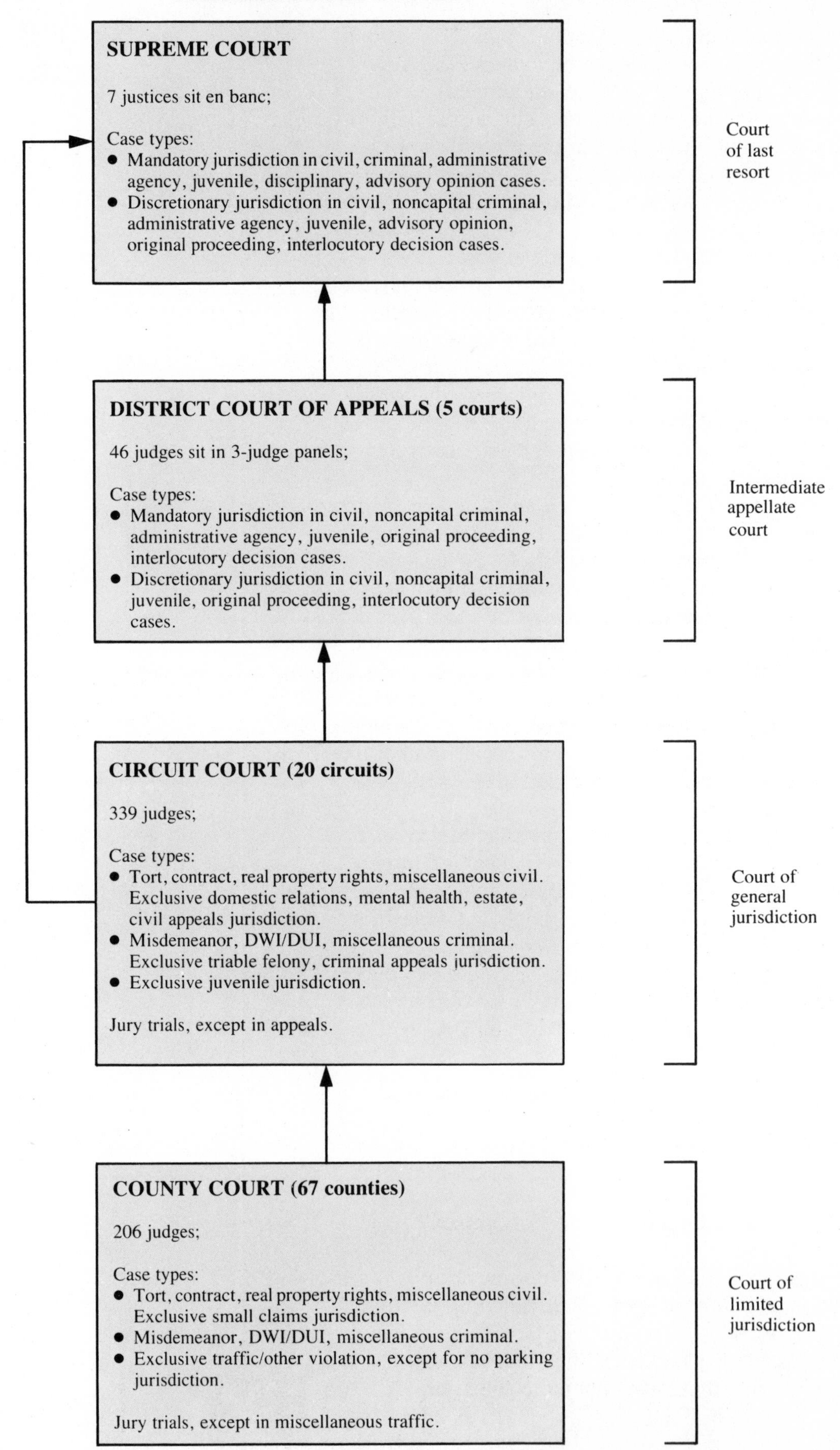

Source: National Center for State Courts, *State Court Caseload Statistics: Annual Report 1984*.

THE UNITED STATES COURT SYSTEM

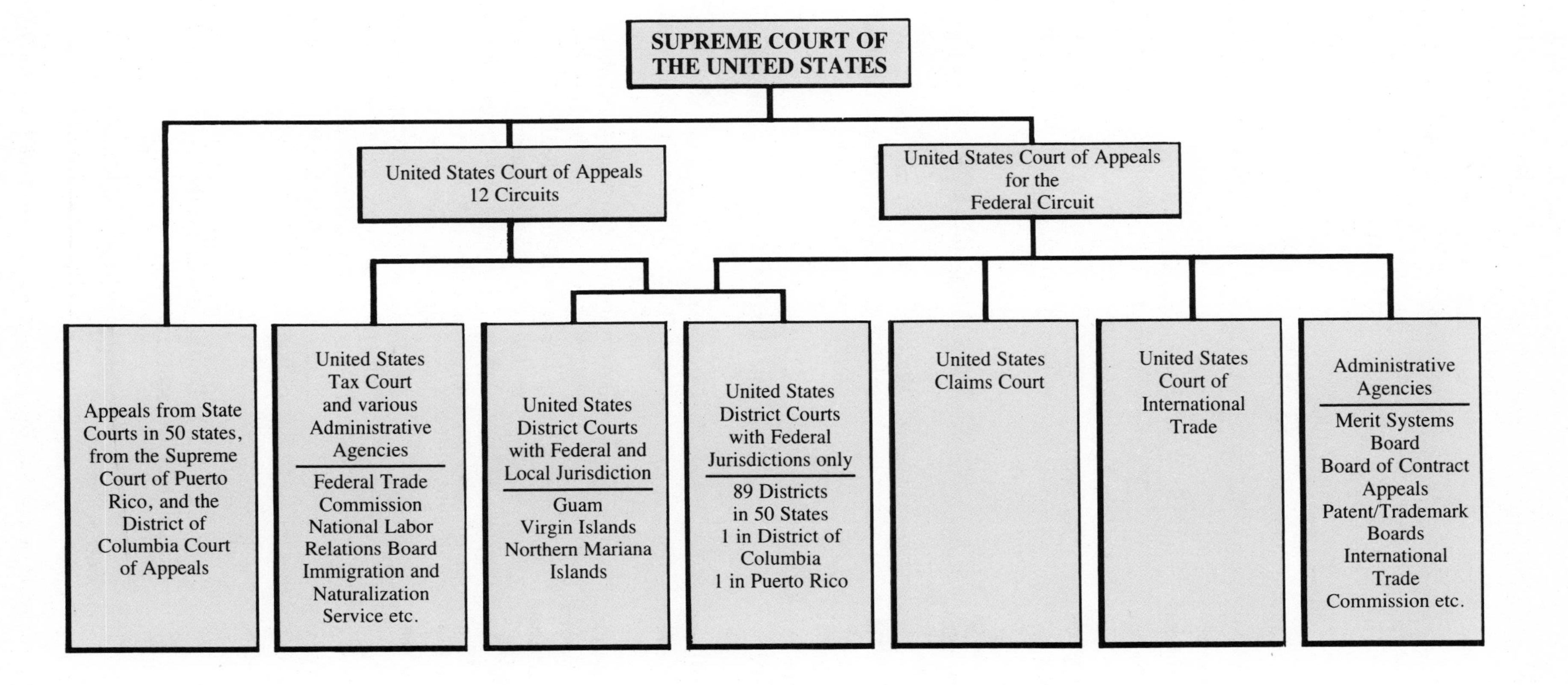

Source: Administrative Office of U.S. Courts, *United States Courts: Their Jurisdiction and Work.*

State Court Organization Varies Greatly

State courts of general jurisdiction are organized by districts, counties, dual districts, or a combination of counties and districts. In some states, the courts established by the state are funded and controlled locally. In others, the court of last resort may have some budgetary or administrative authority over the entire state court system. Even within states, there is considerable lack of uniformity in the roles, organization, and procedures of the courts. This has led to significant momentum among states to form "united" court systems to provide in varying degrees for the uniform administration of the courts and, in many cases, for the consolidation of diverse courts of limited and special jurisdiction.

This country organizes the court systems as hierarchies. Higher courts have the power to review the work of lower courts. However, higher courts use that power only on a small number of cases. Thus appellate courts, and especially supreme courts, deal with only a very small percentage of the total number of cases filed. For example, of the millions of cases handled each year by American courts, the U.S. Supreme Court fully reviews only about 150 cases.

Q. What are trial courts?

A. They are the courts most familiar to the general public, since they are the scene of most courtroom dramas. In trial courts, lawyers present evidence, examine and cross-examine witnesses, and introduce exhibits. The purpose of trials is to determine the facts on which the judge or jury makes decisions. Judges or juries find a defendant "guilty" or "not guilty" in criminal cases and decide liability in civil cases.

Q. Does every state have trial courts?

A. Yes, every state has trial courts of one kind or another. Some exist at the city or town level, and others sit at a county, circuit, or regional level.

Q. Do all state trial courts have the same powers?

A. No, most states have some trial courts with limited jurisdiction, or authority. (A few states—including Massachusetts, Idaho, Illinois, Iowa, and South Dakota—have only trial courts of general authority.) Courts of limited authority are important because they handle up to 90 percent of the cases in the states in which they exist. They process minor criminal cases, such as misdemeanors. These less serious crimes typically have penalties involving fines or jail terms of no more than one year of imprisonment. In most areas, these courts also hold pre-trial hearings in more serious criminal cases. These include preliminary hearings that set bail and obligate defendants to appear at their trials. These courts also handle civil cases with claims up to a certain dollar amount. In some states this may be as low as $500 or as high as $10,000 or more.

Q. Do the state trial courts with limited authority all have the same name?

A. No, their names vary widely. In some states their names come from the official title of the judge: "magistrate courts" and "justice of the peace courts," for example. Some, like "traffic courts," get their name from the nature of their authority. Certain ones have geographic names: "district courts," "municipal courts," or "county courts."

Some of these courts may have simple, informal procedures and very brief hearings. In a traffic court, for example, the entire case may end in a few minutes. It may involve only the police officer reading the charge and a judge asking the accused for a plea. If the plea is "guilty," the judge then passes sentence immediately. Many of these courts, however, use formal procedures and jury trials in civil and criminal cases.

The next group of courts has a variety of names: "district," "superior," or "circuit" courts, or "courts of common pleas." These courts usually have "general" authority. In most states they may try civil or criminal cases without upper limits on the penalties or the amount of money involved. They usually try only the more serious criminal cases or civil cases above a certain dollar amount. Procedures in these courts normally are formal and technical. They also usually keep word-for-word records.

Some states use special trial courts to handle specific kinds of cases. These may include divorce cases, cases involving last wills and other estate matters, child adoption or custody cases, and juvenile crime cases. A later section in this chapter will discuss these special courts.

Q. Which courts have jury trials?

A. Courts of limited jurisdiction generally do not have jury trials, because the matters are relatively minor, such as a traffic ticket. Courts of general jurisdiction do have jury trials. In criminal cases, the defendant can choose to be tried before a jury or a judge. By contrast, in certain types of civil cases, such as domestic relations, jury trials are not available.

Q. Where are most trials held in the federal court system?

A. U.S. district courts hold most federal court trials. The only name they have is United States district courts. The U.S. Constitution and specific federal laws govern the authority and federal rules for the basic procedures in all these courts. There are 94 federal judicial districts in the nation. These federal courts have authority for an entire state or part of a state. None has authority in more than one state.

Each state contains at least one federal district. About half of the states contain only one federal district. Many have two or three districts. California, Texas, and New York each have four districts. Each district has from one to 27 judges, depending on the work load.

Q. What decides whether a federal court (rather than a state court) should hold a trial?

A. No U.S. district court may handle a case unless there is specific legislative authority for that court to decide the case. Not all cases in federal court involve federal law, however. For example, the parties in one case involving state law may come from different states and the dispute may involve $50,000 or more. One of the parties may then demand that a U.S. district court try the case according to the state law governing the dispute. Out-of-state parties may have a better chance for a fair trial in a federal court than in a court of a state where their opponents live.

A federal law gives federal courts authority over some state civil rights cases. Such cases may be transferred to a U.S. district court for trial.

Q. Do federal district courts mostly handle criminal cases?

A. No, federal district courts see more civil than criminal cases because there are fewer crimes under federal law. For example, in the fiscal year that ended June 30, 1985, U.S. district courts saw seven times more civil cases (273,000) than criminal cases (39,000). However, the Speedy Trial Act, which concerns criminal cases, requires a trial to occur in a very short time after indictment. Therefore the federal courts may spend more than one seventh of their time on criminal matters.

Q. Are there any other types of federal trial courts?

A. Yes, besides the district courts, there are a few special trial courts at the federal level:

- Bankruptcy actions filed in the district courts may be sent to federal bankruptcy judges for hearing and decision. There are 232 such judges, who in a recent year received 365,000 bankruptcy petitions.
- Federal magistrates handle smaller civil and criminal matters.
- The U.S. Court of International Trade primarily handles cases involving international trade and customs duties. This court has nine judges.
- The U.S. Claims Court has 16 judges. It hears cases in which a citizen or corporation sues the U.S. government. It also has authority over other special areas.
- The United States Tax Court decides disputes between taxpayers and the Internal Revenue Service. It has 19 judges.

There are also military "courts-martial." The armed services manage these military courts, which are not part of the civilian court system.

Q. May I appeal a decision from one of these federal courts?

A. Yes, but the route of these appeals differs.

- Appeals of district court cases and Tax Court cases go to the various United States courts of appeals;
- Appeals of Court of International Trade cases and Claims Court cases go only to the U.S. Court of Appeals for the Federal Circuit, located in Washington, D.C.
- Appeals of military court cases go to the U.S. Court of Military Appeals.

Other appeals in cases from district court, Tax Court, Claims Court, and Court of International Trade may go to the Supreme Court, with that Court's permission.

Q. If I lose my case at the trial level, may I appeal?

A. Yes, a party who loses at the general jurisdiction trial level may appeal to an intermediate appeals court. The state may not appeal a "not guilty" verdict in a criminal case and obtain a conviction of the defendant. Many times, however, it may appeal the decision on issues of law for use in future cases. The state also may appeal the length of sentence given to a convicted defendant. A defendant in a criminal case usually may appeal a guilty verdict. A defendant who has lost a criminal case and faces a prison sentence may believe that the prosecutor got the conviction by using improperly obtained evidence. The defendant would seek to have the verdict reversed and have the case tried again following the rules. Similarly, someone who must pay money because of losing a civil case may believe that the judge or jury did not apply the law correctly. Both state and federal appeals courts sit to review the procedures of trials held in lower courts.

Q. Will the appeals court try my case again?

A. No, despite popular belief, appeals courts do *not* retry the cases they hear. They also don't hear witnesses or weigh evidence in the same way a trial court does. Instead, the law usually restricts the appeal to questions of law relating to the facts and the record of the case made at the trial level. The role of appeals courts is to make sure that trial courts followed the laws correctly. Appeals courts may decide whether to admit certain facts and how to interpret them. However, they do not search for facts on their own.

Q. What happens after an appeals court makes a decision?

A. If the appeals court decides the lower court did not follow the rules, it will *not* find the defendant innocent. Appeals courts do not deliver new verdicts. They don't find defendants guilty or not guilty. Rather, they (1) agree with or reverse the lower court's judgment, (2) dismiss the appeal, or (3) send the case back to the trial court to determine certain facts. If the appeals court agrees with the verdict, the loser often appeals to a higher court. If the appeals court reverses the verdict, the case returns to a lower court for retrial. The appeals court also may simply reverse the verdict and return the case to a lower court with orders to dismiss it.

Q. Are there intermediate courts of appeals in every state court system?

A. No, about three quarters of the states have intermediate appellate courts. The remaining states, which are usually small, have no courts between trial courts and the highest court in the state.

Q. Does a person always have a constitutional right to appeal a case?

A. No, the right to appeal is not always a constitutional right. However, nearly all state legislatures have adopted a right of appeal by law. Intermediate courts of appeals differ in the range of their authority.

Q. How are the intermediate courts of appeals set up at the federal level?

A. There are 13 intermediate courts of appeals in the federal system. The law has set up 12 of them in different areas. One covers only the District of Columbia; the other 11 cover varying numbers of states. The largest covers nine states, the smallest three. There are 156 judges on these 12 appellate courts. Each court of appeals has between six and 28 judges, depending on the amount of work in the region. The 12 regional courts of appeals receive about 33,000 cases each year. They hear appeals from the district courts, Tax Court, and various federal agencies.

The thirteenth intermediate federal court of appeals—the Court of Appeals for the Federal Circuit—has national authority. Located in Washington, D.C., it has 12 judges. This court hears appeals in patent law from all district courts. The Court of Appeals for the Federal Circuit also hears appeals from the U.S. Claims Court, the U.S Court of International Trade, and some federal agencies.

A decision in one circuit is not binding on any other. Conflicts may be resolved only by the United States Supreme Court.

Q. What are the "highest" courts in the land?

A. At the top of every state court system is the court of last resort—the state "supreme" court. (Not every state calls it that. New York, for example, calls the highest court the Court of Appeals. The New York Supreme Court is actually a trial court.) In all state systems and in the federal system, the highest court has the final authority to interpret the law.

The U.S. Supreme Court may reverse the highest courts of the states, but only on interpretations of the U.S. Constitution or of federal laws. Only the U.S. Supreme Court itself or an amendment to the U.S. Constitution may overrule a decision by the U.S. Supreme Court.

Q. What is the function of the highest state courts?

A. The highest state courts do not conduct trials. They only review the legal procedure and rulings of courts below them.

Like intermediate courts of appeals, the highest state courts do not usually disturb or reconsider the facts of the cases. They review only the law.

State supreme courts have a wide-ranging authority. They usually may review all types of cases from state trial courts. State supreme courts may have only three members, but the more common size is five or seven.

Q. Why does the U.S. Supreme Court exist?

A. In America, there is only one court created directly by the U.S. Constitution. It is the Supreme Court of the United States. The Constitution allows Congress to create, or abolish, any other federal court.

The Supreme Court is one of the three great branches of the U.S. government. As an equal of the presidency and Congress, the Court provides an important function. The Court must interpret and apply the Constitution to cases involving the other branches of government and the states.

Chief Justice John Marshall declared, "It is emphatically the province and duty of the judiciary department to say what the law is." The Court has carried out that duty in deciding whether actions of the executive branch, Congress, the states, and the lower courts agree with the Constitution. This should assure that no party restricts the rights guaranteed to the people by our basic law.

Q. What kinds of cases may the U.S. Supreme Court hear?

A. The laws passed by Congress define the types of cases that the U.S. Supreme Court may hear on appeal (its appellate

Other Court Functions

The courts have several functions in addition to deciding whether laws have been violated. They settle disputes between legal entities (persons, corporations, etc.), and they invoke sanctions against law violations. Courts also decide whether acts of the legislative and executive branches of government are constitutional.

In deciding about violations of the law, the courts must apply the law to the facts of each case. The courts affect policy in deciding individual cases by handing down decisions about how the laws should be interpreted and carried out. Decisions of the appellate courts are the ones most likely to have policy impact.

authority). Over the years, Congress has generally passed laws giving the justices an increasingly wide range of cases for possible review. The Court also has a class of cases that it alone tries (its original authority). The Constitution itself specifies those cases. An example would be a lawsuit filed by one state against another. The Supreme Court is likely to decide only one or two "original" cases each year.

People ask the Court to review thousands of cases each year. Of these, the justices select about 150 cases for full-scale review during each nine-month sitting (term). It decides these cases with written opinions after a full briefing and a public oral argument. As with other appellate courts, if the U.S. Supreme Court refuses to hear a case, the effect is to let stand the lower court's ruling.

Q. How many justices are there on the U.S. Supreme Court?

A. It has nine justices. Federal law sets this figure. Over the years, it has ranged from a low of six, at the beginning, to as high as ten, after the Civil War. At least six of the nine justices must participate for the court to do any business. It takes only four justices to agree to grant full review of a case.

LAWYERS, JUDGES, AND THE COURTS

Lawyers

Q. Where does the legal process begin?

A. The legal process often begins with lawyers and their clients. The previous chapter—"When and How to Use a Lawyer"—discusses how to choose a lawyer. It also talks about how to decide when to take legal action.

Q. Should I always solve a problem by going to court?

A. Lawyers (and clients) who think first of going to court may be doing the client no good. In fact, it may harm the client's interests. A lawyer's role as defender or pleader is important. However, it is no more important than the role as counselor or negotiator. In this latter role, a lawyer often finds that going to court is not the best solution for the client.

Lawyers and their staffs are devoting increasingly more attention to analyzing problems as soon as they are brought to the lawyer's attention. The lawyer or someone on the lawyer's staff will work with the person having the problem to determine the best first step. Some people consider this a case diagnosis. Sometimes the best first step is to go directly to court. Other times it is mediation. The important thing is to take action that matches the problem.

Q. What is a lawyer's role in a civil or criminal case?

A. In a civil case, a lawyer works for one of the parties involved in the suit. A lawyer represents either the *plaintiff* (the party bringing the suit) or the *defendant* (the party being sued). In a criminal case, the *prosecuting attorney* acts for the government, and the *defense attorney* represents a client. Criminal defendants who cannot afford a private lawyer have the right to be defended at no charge by a public defender.

Q. Is every lawyer a government official?

A. Lawyers are not government officials unless they happen to work for the government. Examples include city and county attorneys, prosecuting attorneys, and public defenders. Lawyers are, however, "officers of the court." Society expects lawyers and judges to act in a highly ethical manner. The supreme courts of states have disciplinary procedures that may explore charges of lawyer misconduct. If a client believes that a lawyer acted in an unethical or improper manner, the client may contact this agency. The state bar association should be able to help you contact the state's lawyer disciplinary agency. The previous chapter—"When and How to Use a Lawyer"—discusses legal ethics.

Judges

Q. What is the role of a trial judge?

A. Figures show that few parties appeal the decisions of a trial court. This is especially true in civil cases. In addition, in appeals, decisions of trial courts usually are upheld. This makes it clear that the judge on the trial bench is a key figure, at least for cases that go to trial.

A trial judge most often acts as the umpire in disputes. The judge as umpire must be neutral. A judge's major role is to declare the law and supervise procedures.

Besides managing trials, judges have many other duties. For example, criminal court judges must do several things before a trial begins:

(1) They issue arrest and search warrants;
(2) They make sure defendants know the charge(s) and their right to be represented by a lawyer;
(3) They set and revoke bail;
(4) They hold hearings to determine if the accused person should be held for trial; and
(5) They rule on pre-trial motions (e.g., to exclude certain evidence).

Q. What is one of the most important roles of a judge?

A. Over the past 20 years, judges have become more involved in reducing court delay. To many observers the judge's role as impartial umpire limited his or her power to control the flow of cases. For example, the law usually considered cases ready for trial only when all the parties were ready to proceed. Many observers now agree that the judge must control the speed at which cases move to help reduce or eliminate the backlogs and delays troubling many court systems.

Q. Are court delays and high costs becoming serious problems?

A. Yes, many people believe civil and criminal lawsuits at all levels take too long and cost too much. Many courts and national legal organizations are studying these problems. Because of concern for these problems, more and more people are using dispute resolution options, such as mediation and arbitration.

Q. Can the courts truly reduce costs and delays by managing the speed at which cases move?

A. Yes, many courts have done this without losing the procedures and shelters of the law. This management requires:

- Continual court control of the speed of the legal process, beginning with the time plaintiffs first file cases in the court;
- Time standards for finishing major events in the case;
- Monitoring of intermediate events in the court process to to make sure participants finish them on time; and
- The commitment by participants that trials and hearings will occur when scheduled.

Individual trial courts and entire state trial court systems now use these methods to reduce court costs and delays. A 1986 survey showed that 22 states have statewide time standards for trial courts. Eleven more states have time standards for local trial courts.

UNREASONABLE COURT DELAY DEFINED

The current concern about court delay is not new. As early as 1818 the Massachusetts legislature adopted a system to ease court congestion and delay. Yet, what constitutes unreasonable delay in criminal proceedings has been difficult to define. In *Baker v. Wingo* (1972), the U.S. Supreme Court set down four factors to be weighed in determining whether a defendant had been denied the right to a speedy trial: (1) the length of the delay; (2) the reason for the delay; (3) whether the defendant was responsible for the delay; and (4) whether delay prejudiced the case of the defendant.

Q. Are trial courts the only ones using caseflow management methods?

A. At first the national emphasis on ways to reduce costs and delays was at the trial court level. Now appellate courts are taking steps to reduce the time required to finish cases.

Q. Do cost and delay reduction plans for trial courts include out-of-court programs?

A. Yes, these plans often include court-related mediation and arbitration of civil cases. Courts of appeals also use mediation. The public desires to spend tax dollars in the most efficient manner. Caseflow management methods and the use of mediation and arbitration reflect this desire. Their goal is to allow courts to provide more service without spending much more money. They seek to reduce the time in which courts process cases.

Q. What is a judge's role in a trial without a jury?

A. A judge tries a case without a jury more often in civil and minor criminal cases than in criminal cases involving a felony, which is a more serious crime. In doing so, the judge is the sole "fact-finder." The judge considers the evidence and decides what facts the evidence has established. The judge then draws conclusions from those facts. Finally, the judge bases the legal judgment on the conclusions and facts.

Q. What is a judge's role in a trial with a jury?

A. When a jury tries a case, the judge determines which evidence the jury may consider. The jury is the fact-finder, but it may "find" facts only from the evidence allowed by law. The judge decides, based on law, which evidence the jury may or may not consider. The judge also can influence how the jury analyzes the case. The judge does this by telling the jury which legal rules they must follow in weighing the facts.

Q. What is the role of the appellate judge?

A. Appellate or supreme courts usually do not review or challenge facts that emerge from a trial court. Appeals consider how the trial court applied the laws that governed a verdict. (However, sometimes appellate courts will rule on whether the evidence was sufficient as a matter of law.

(continued)

ROLES OF THE MAIN PARTICIPANTS IN DECIDING CASES

At Trial Level		At Appellate Level	
JUDGE	**JURY**	**JUDGE**	**JURY**
Before trial begins • Issues search and arrest warrants • Sets and revokes bail • Manages speed at which cases move through system		• Main function is to consider how the trial court applied the laws that governed the verdict, which involves interpreting the law • Also reviews procedures followed by trial court, primarily to insure that legal rights of the parties were protected • The facts are usually not reviewed by the appellate court	No jury involvement at appellate level
During trial • Declares the law—judges' primary responsibility • Determines which evidence the jury may consider • Supervises procedures in court (such as ruling on motions by opposing counsel)	Within guidelines set by the judge, the jury: • Decides questions of fact • Evaluates credibility of witnesses • Renders final verdict		

Appellate courts also sometimes will decide whether the trial judge's decision was sustainable as a matter of law.)

The role of the appellate judge or Supreme Court justice, then, mainly involves interpreting the law. He or she primarily reviews and, if necessary, corrects the judgments in law and procedure made by the trial judge.

Selecting and Evaluating Judges

Q. How does someone become a judge?

A. Public officials appoint some types of judges. The voting public elects other kinds of judges. Methods of selection vary greatly among the states and between the states and the federal government.

Public officials appoint all federal judges. For judges authorized under Article III of the Constitution, the President makes nominations. Then the Senate accepts or rejects the nominees. These appointments usually are for life. An exception occurs in very rare instances of misconduct severe enough to result in impeachment.

States select their own way of choosing judges. Most states require general jurisdiction and appellate judges to be lawyers. Public officials appoint some state judges. The voting public elects other state judges. Some states use a mixed system, with judges appointed at first. These judges stay in office only if they win a later retention election.

Two thirds of the states and the District of Columbia select some or all judges by merit. This system began in Missouri. That is why some people call it "The Missouri Plan." Merit selection uses a permanent, impartial commission. It usually contains public officials, lawyers, and private citizens. They locate, recruit, investigate, and evaluate people applying to be judges. The commission then submits the names of the best-qualified applicants (usually three) to the appointing authority (usually the governor). He or she must make a final selection from the list. For later terms of office, either a commission or the voters evaluate the judges to see if they may keep their positions.

Q. Who evaluates state judges?

A. Some state courts have recently begun evaluation programs for judges. These programs help judges improve their on-the-bench performance. The judges get feedback from people who have appeared before them. They include lawyers, jurors, parties in a lawsuit, and other sources. A special committee of the American Bar Association (ABA) has become involved in such programs. Beginning in 1983, this committee developed guidelines to help state courts develop these programs.

SPECIAL TRIBUNALS

Q. On the news I heard about a case going to a "special tribunal." What does that mean?

A. Every lawsuit is, in its own way, special—if for no other reason than the different facts in each. Some jurisdictions have created *tribunals* (judicial courts) to process certain legal actions.

Some jurisdictions created these tribunals because of the type of matters that came before them. The special conditions of these matters, and the know-how they required, called for special courts. That is true of courts for juveniles who get into trouble. The same goes for courts for married couples thinking about separation or divorce. It is also true of disciplinary panels for lawyers or judges.

HOW THE LEGAL SYSTEM WORKS

PUNISHING THE JUDGES

Impeachment is one way of punishing federal judges. It involves the filing of formal charges, followed by a legislative trial. If convicted, the law dictates the removal of the judge from the bench. The law also may apply lesser penalties.

Every state (and the District of Columbia) uses some form of commission that checks into complaints against judges. The most common complaint is "conduct prejudicial to the administration of justice." Others include "willful misconduct" and "violation of the Code of Judicial Conduct." Many states have adopted this ABA code, which covers behavior on and off the bench.

The commissions may recommend to the state's highest court such punishments as reprimand, censure, and suspension. Less severe punishments include forced retirement and removal.

Some tribunals deal with a single branch of the law. An example is the *probate,* or *orphans', court.* This court administers estates, either when a will exists or not. Another type of court only handles lawsuits for money damages against the federal or state government. These are the *claims courts.* Some courts handle simple and low-value money or property disputes between private parties. An example would be a *small claims court.*

Origins of Juvenile Court

Until the late 19th century, juveniles who committed crimes were processed through the criminal courts. In 1899, Illinois established the first juvenile court, based on two concepts. The first concept was that a juvenile was a salvageable human being who needed treatment, not punishment. The second concept was that the juvenile court should protect the child from the stigma of criminal proceedings. Delinquency and other situations, such as neglect and adoption, were deemed to warrant the court's intervention on the child's behalf. The juvenile court also handled "status offenses" (such as truancy, running away, and incorrigibility), which do not apply to adults.

Courts of Special Jurisdiction

Q. Do all states have the same special courts?

A. No, in some states, specially created courts handle the functions discussed below. In most states, the regular trial courts set up by law—courts of limited or general jurisdiction—handle these functions. However, branches of these courts that specialize in these matters often play a major role.

Q. What are "family courts"?

A. Where they exist, family courts are part of a state court system. The federal system has no family courts. The best known branches of family law are domestic relations—divorce, marital separation, child custody. In some states, this also includes problems of juveniles. In other states, juvenile courts handle such problems.

Family courts sometimes try to get family members to negotiate and get back together again. However, these courts also use trial-type procedures when families cannot resolve disputes. They usually follow rules of civil trial procedure. Family courts do not normally use juries. They most often have only judges.

For issues of domestic relations, family courts have the power to arrange or supervise separation agreements. They also may grant divorces. In doing so, the courts will usually divide assets and liabilities. They also will make awards of alimony, child support, and child custody.

Q. How do these special courts deal with juvenile problems?

A. In such cases, family and juvenile courts may hold very informal sessions that only offer advice. Many take more formal steps that are somewhat similar to a criminal trial. Some of these courts have the power to order the trial of older juveniles as adults in regular criminal courts.

Judgments of family or juvenile courts in juvenile cases may confine the youths in special institutions. However, their purpose is to provide treatment, not punishment.

Q. May anyone visit a juvenile or family court?

A. Juvenile cases usually are not open to the public to protect the youths' reputations. Divorce hearings and other family court trials are often open to the public.

Q. Do all states have special courts to administer estates?

A. No, only a few states have these courts. They have such names as *probate court, orphans' courts,* or *surrogate courts.* In other states, general or limited jurisdiction courts handle these matters. Their job is to interpret last wills if there is a doubt or conflict over the will's meaning. These courts also determine the rights to an estate when the deceased person has died *intestate* (without a will). Probate courts manage the distribution of estates. These courts illustrate one of the most important purposes of our courts: They formally record the legal status of property.

Procedures in probate courts may be very brief or summary in form. This is true when wills are "self-executing" and the probate court only has to review them briefly to decide if they are legally proper and authentic. Procedures in probate courts also may develop into full-scale adversary proceedings. Probate courts usually use only judges. However, adversary proceedings may use jury trials.

Q. What happens in a claims court?

A. In a few states, and at the federal level, special tribunals have the power to determine claims for money damages against government agencies. In most states, general or limited jurisdiction courts hear these claims.

A claims court is a form of civil court that uses normal procedures to decide whether the government has wronged a party. The court also decides if the party deserves to recover damages. The party might be a person or company doing business with the government. The party also might be a person who owns property damaged by the government (as in an accident with a government vehicle).

Q. What is a small claims court?

A. Separate small claims courts exist only in a few states. General or limited jurisdiction courts usually apply special procedures to handle small claims. A handful of states do not have any small claims procedures.

Generally, a small claims court is a simple civil court. The law limits its authority to amounts under a specific figure. Usually the amount is not enough to require formal court procedures. Small claims courts save people the expense of a regular civil lawsuit. The claim may involve a dispute over money or property, if the amount is below a specific figure.

In these courts, neither side usually has a lawyer. For this reason, some people call them *pro se* courts. This is from the Latin phrase meaning "for oneself." The judge, acting alone, decides whether the claim is genuine. If so, the judge determines the amount of the claim. The process is normally very informal. Losers usually may not appeal decisions. The popular television program *The People's Court* offers an example of the informal, quick justice provided by these courts.

Q. Are there any other specialized courts?

A. Yes, a few states have workers' compensation courts. In addition, a handful of states have tax courts.

Q. What is an administrative tribunal?

A. Many, if not most, regulatory agencies have these tribunals. They function somewhat like courts in that they apply the policies of the agency on a case-by-case basis.

Administrative tribunals include labor arbitration panels, lawyer disciplinary committees, and commissions on judicial conduct. However, the variety is even greater. It includes state public utility commissions; medical, architectural, and pharmacological licensing boards; contract administration boards; and civil service review boards. Federal agencies include the National Labor Relations Board, Federal Power Commission, Federal Trade Commission, Federal Election Commission, Federal Communications Commission, and Federal Aviation Agency. Others include the Federal Railroad Administration, Interstate Commerce Commission, Civil Aeronautics Board, and Federal Maritime Commission.

The agencies often split their functions between designing specific rules and carrying out those rules on a case-by-case basis. Thus, in some sense they are legislative, judicial, and executive.

Q. Do the administrative tribunals of these agencies act like regular trial courts?

A. Yes, the agencies generally handle cases much as the courts treat civil cases. They follow normal rules of evidence, or something similar. Their proceedings often have "adversaries," with two distinct sides seeking to win.

The regulators must observe the Constitution's guarantee of "due process" as faithfully as judges. Therefore an agency may not remove a privilege or impose a punishment without first giving the person or institution involved notice that it may happen. Then the agency must give the person or institution a chance to argue why it should not happen.

COURT PROCEDURES

Q. How does a civil case begin?

A. A civil case begins with the filing of a *complaint.* After this, the other side files an *answer.* The side filing the suit may then file a *reply.*

A person does not have to prepare a complaint with technical precision to follow the law. Simply put, it should concisely state the claim against the other party. Its aim is to notify the other party of the action. The answer admits or denies the claims made in the complaint. The reply allows the complainer to respond to new matters raised by the defendant's answer.

Q. How does the beginning of a criminal case compare to that of a civil case?

A. The rules are similarly simple in criminal cases. An *indictment* charges a person or institution with a crime. A grand jury may file the indictment. The indictment also may come from a document (called an *information*). The prosecutor files this document in a state that does not routinely use the grand jury to bring charges. The defendant may plead guilty, not guilty, or, if the court permits it, *nolo contendere* (no contest). The defendant may make a motion to ask the court to clarify or dismiss the charges.

Many states have adopted the federal rules. This allows lawyers to follow the same procedures in both state and federal court.

Q. What are "statutes of limitations"?

A. *Statutes of limitations* are laws that set the maximum amount of time a person has to begin a lawsuit. In effect, these *civil* statutes provide a defense for people for wrongful acts they may have committed.

CHECK THE FACTS IN YOUR STATE

This section bases its facts on the Federal Rules of Civil Procedure and the Federal Rules of Criminal Procedure. These rules govern the federal courts. They also are the basis for the rules that many state courts follow. These rules help to ensure a simple and fair trial process. However, not every state court system follows these rules. Statements in this section might not entirely apply to your state's courts. In addition, the procedures in any state may change. For up-to-date information, contact the state bar association or the state court administrator. The latter has an office in the state capital and sometimes in the larger cities.

There also are state and federal *criminal* statutes of limitations. These set a limit to how long prosecutors have to bring charges. The limits vary depending on the crime alleged. They also are different from one state to another, and federal limits may not be the same as state limits.

State and federal tax laws also impose varying statutes of limitations.

Q. What are the time limits for filing a civil lawsuit?

A. Some states may give you ten years to sue for a breach of a written contract. Other states may allow you five years or less, depending on the type of contract. These time limits might differ for oral contracts. Also, sometimes the period in which to file begins when the wrong was committed. An example might be a breach of warranty, which begins when you buy a product. Sometimes it begins when you become *aware* (or should become aware) of the wrong. For instance, in a product liability suit, it may begin when you discover your water heater is defective years after it was installed.

In general, if you think you have a legal case, act *immediately*. This usually means seeing a lawyer. Then you can discuss whether somebody has truly harmed you. You also can find out whether that harm has a legal remedy.

Once you have given your case to an attorney, your lawyer has certain duties. Your lawyer should know the statute of limitations for that specific action and inform you of that time limit. In addition, your lawyer should file the case before the time elapses. If your lawyer does not file on time, you could file a complaint with the bar association or the applicable ethics commission. You also could take other legal action.

The Importance of Statutes of Limitations

If you fail to file a suit within the allotted time, you may face this defense and lose your case. It does not matter how good your case is. You have lost the case before it begins.

Settling Civil Cases

Q. Is it true that very few lawsuits ever go to trial?

A. Yes, many studies have shown that most parties settle their disputes by mutual agreement. They may settle the dispute even before filing a suit. Once they file a suit, they may settle it before or during the trial. They also may settle it while the jury is deliberating, or even after obtaining a verdict.

Q. What is a settlement?

A. A settlement does not usually state that anyone was right or wrong. It also does not have to settle the whole case. It may settle part of a dispute, letting the court resolve the remaining issues.

A settlement may take many forms. It may rest on certain conditions. For example, it may require that the aggrieved party gets his or her job back. The settlement also may require that he or she suffers no permanent disability from an injury. It may be oral or written, although a written settlement is always preferable. A settlement only needs the agreement of all parties.

Q. Do courts encourage the disputing parties to make a settlement?

A. Yes, courts do encourage settlements both outside of and within the court structure. Courts use, and sometimes require, pre-trial settlement conferences. Devices such as court-ordered arbitration and other forms of alternative dispute resolution offer ways to resolve disputes outside of the formal court system.

Q. What types of alternative dispute resolution exist?

A. Alternatives to the traditional court process take many forms. They usually involve impartial decision-makers such as arbitrators or people who try to bring the parties together (mediators). Alternative dispute resolution is rapidly growing, as the following figures suggest:

Number of	1977	1986
Mediation programs	100	410
Community Mediators	5,000	22,000
Jurisdictions Requiring Child Custody and Visitation Mediation	0	36
Bar Association Alternative Dispute Resolution Committees	0	110

Alternative dispute resolution is not a new idea in the judicial system. Most parties settle civil cases before going to trial. Courts use a variety of techniques to bring about voluntary settlements. These techniques include pre-trial settlement conferences, mediation by magistrates, court-related arbitration, and mediation in the judge's chambers.

Q. Do any states require alternative dispute resolution?

A. Yes, in at least 20 states, court-related arbitration or mediation is automatic for many cases. In court-related arbitration or mediation, certain cases *must* start with

MOST PARTIES SETTLE WITHOUT GOING TO TRIAL

This section on pre-trial procedure deals with a typical civil case that proceeds to trial. However, most parties settle their civil suits without a trial. Therefore, it is important to discuss settlements of civil cases first.

arbitration or mediation. Examples include cases under a certain dollar amount. However, sometimes the losing party in arbitration or mediation may appeal. This sends the case back into the court system. In some states a party dissatisfied with the result has a right to a new trial *(trial de novo)* before a judge and jury.

Sometimes the law requires the result of the trial to improve the position of the party who brought the case to trial beyond the award resulting from arbitration or mediation. The improvement must be by a certain amount (often 10 percent). If not, that party will have to pay court costs.

Experimental programs in other communities remove some cases from the courts. Then arbitration or mediation (in places such as neighborhood justice centers) decides the cases.

Q. What types of cases use arbitration most often?

A. Commercial, insurance, and labor-management disagreements widely use arbitration.

Q. What does arbitration involve?

A. *Arbitration* involves submitting the dispute to a third party. He or she makes a decision after hearing arguments and reviewing evidence. Arbitration may be less formal, less complex, and less costly than court cases. In addition, it often ends more quickly than court proceedings. In its most common form—*binding arbitration*—the parties select the arbitrator. They then must obey the decision, either by prior agreement or by law. In *last-offer arbitration,* the arbitrator must choose between the final positions of the two parties.

Q. What is the alternative dispute resolution method known as conciliation?

A. *Conciliation* is an informal process that uses a third party to lower tensions and improve communications. This third party also interprets issues, provides technical assistance, and explores possible solutions. Then the third party tries to help the disputing parties negotiate a settlement. They do this either informally or, in a later step, through formal mediation. People often use conciliation in volatile conflicts. They also use it in disputes where the parties are unable or unwilling to negotiate their differences.

Q. How does mediation differ from arbitration and conciliation?

A. *Mediation* is a bit more structured. It uses a third-party mediator to help the disputing parties negotiate a settlement of their differences. It usually is voluntary and results in a signed agreement. The agreement specifies the terms of the settlement. It also defines the future behavior of the parties. The mediator uses a variety of skills and techniques to help the parties reach a settlement. However, the mediator does not have the power to make a decision.

Q. What is one of the newest ways to resolve disputes?

A. *Med-Arb* is a new way to solve arguments. The disputing parties authorize the med-arbiter to serve first as a mediator. Later the med-arbiter acts as an arbitrator with the power to decide any issues not resolved through mediation.

Q. What is a neighborhood justice center?

A. Many areas have neighborhood justice centers (NJCs). Local or state governments, bar associations, and foundations sponsor these centers. NJCs mainly resolve disputes between people with continuing relationships. Such people include landlords and tenants, husbands and wives, neighbors, and the like. Police, local courts, and prosecutors' offices refer many cases to NJCs. These centers most often settle disputes by mediation and conciliation.

Pre-Trial Procedures in Civil Cases

Q. How does a lawsuit begin?

A. Settlements resolve nearly all civil suits filed. However, very often they occur after a party files a complaint and the court system takes some actions. The remaining cases do go to trial.

An offended person becomes a *plaintiff* if he or she—or a lawyer representing the person—prepares and files a *complaint* in the proper court. The *defendant* is the person or firm against whom the plaintiff files the case.

The complaint states the plaintiff's version of the facts. It also contains the legal theory that forms the basis for the case (negligence, for example). In addition, the complaint asks for certain damages or other relief. The plaintiff also files a request for the court to issue a *summons* (notice) to the defendant. This request goes to the court clerk. In many areas, a deputy sheriff or special process server will serve the summons. In some states, the court will serve the summons

DEFINING THE ISSUE

The *issue* is said to be the disputed point or question to which the parties to a case have narrowed their disagreement. It is a single material point that is affirmed by one side and denied by the other. When the plaintiff and the defendant have arrived at some point that one affirms and the other denies, they are said to be *at issue*. When the defendant has filed an answer denying all or part of the allegations of the complaint, the *issue has been joined* and the case is ready to be set for trial.

by mail. A summons notifies the defendant that the plaintiff has filed a lawsuit against him or her.

After being notified, the defendant has a certain period of time to file an *answer.* This time period is 20 days in federal courts. It varies in state courts.

Q. How does one know where to file a lawsuit?

A. The plaintiff's lawyer must decide where to file the case. A court has no authority to decide a case unless it has *jurisdiction* over the person or property involved. To have jurisdiction, a court must have authority over the subject matter of the case. The court also must be able to exercise control over the defendant, or the property must be located in the area under the court's control. The law sets the extent of the court's control over persons and property. Decisions of the state's highest court in actual cases often explain or clarify the extent of this control.

Q. Does only a local court have jurisdiction in a case?

A. Not necessarily. Certain actions are *transitory*. This means a court may take them in any county in any state where the defendant may be found and served with a summons. However, the jurisdiction must have enough contact with one of the parties and with the incident that led to the suit.

Other actions are *local.* They may be brought only in the county where the subject of a suit resides. An example of a local action is a lawsuit for the foreclosure of a mortgage on real estate.

Q. What does the term "venue" mean?

A. *Venue* refers to the county or district in a state or in the United States where the court will try a lawsuit. The law sets the venue of a lawsuit. Sometimes the court may change the venue to another county or district. If a case has received widespread pre-trial publicity, the judge may grant a motion for a change of venue. This is an effort to obtain jurors who do not already have an opinion about the case. The court also may change the venue for the convenience of the witnesses.

Q. What are motions?

A. *Motions* are requests for the judge to make a legal ruling. They are not pleadings. During a trial, lawyers will make various types of motions. For example, they may question

PLEADINGS

Pleadings are certain formal documents filed with the court that state the parties' basic positions. Pleadings are not the arguments made in court by the lawyers. Common pre-trial pleadings are:

Pleading	Function
Complaint	Probably the most important document in a case. It states the plaintiff's version of the facts and specifies the damages. By doing so, it records the issues of the case.
Answer	A statement by the defendant that responds to the charges in the plaintiff's complaint. It explains why the plaintiff should not win the case. It also may offer other facts or plead an excuse.
Reply	A response to new charges raised by the other party or parties in prior pleadings. Any party in the case may have to file a reply.
Counterclaim	Allows the defendant to sue the plaintiff, and perhaps others, for relief or damages. ("You're suing me? Well then, I'm suing you.") The defendant may file it separately or as part of the answer. If the defendant files a counterclaim, the plaintiff in turn may file a motion to answer the counterclaim.

whether someone may present a specific piece of evidence. Similarly, before the trial, the judge must decide certain kinds of legal questions.

Q. What are some of the most common pre-trial motions?

A. The following are some of the motions most commonly presented before a trial:

- *Motion for Summary Judgment.* This motion asks the court to judge the merits of the case before the trial. A lawyer often makes this motion when there is no dispute about the facts. It only asks the court to decide a question of law.
- *Motion to Discover.* In this common pre-trial motion, one party tries to get information held by the other party.
- *Motion to Dismiss.* This motion asks the court to dismiss the suit because it lacks a legally sound basis. This may occur even if all the alleged facts prove to be true.

Q. Are there any other less common pre-trial motions?

A. Yes, they include:

- *Motion to Quash Service of Summons.* This motion seeks dismissal of the lawsuit because the defendant was not properly served with the summons. There are many other motions to quash (suppress). For example, the defense in a criminal case may make a motion to quash evidence that it believes someone has illegally obtained.
- *Motion to Strike.* This motion asks the court to strike from the plaintiff's petition any irrelevant, biased, or other improper material. The court may order the removal of offending passages.
- *Motion to Make More Definite or Certain.* This asks the court to require the plaintiff to state the facts more specifically, or to describe the injuries or damages more clearly.

Q. How do both sides in a lawsuit prepare for a trial?

A. To begin preparing for a trial, both sides engage in *discovery*. In this formal process the parties exchange information to find out details relevant to the witnesses. It also reveals other evidence each side will present at the trial.

Discovery allows the parties to know before the trial begins what facts the other may present. It aims to prevent *trial by ambush.* This "ambush" occurs when one party discovers evidence or witnesses only when the other party presents it at the trial. This does not give the first party time to gather answering evidence. The most common method of discovery is the taking of depositions.

Q. What is a deposition?

A. A *deposition* is an out-of-court statement given under oath by a witness. The parties use it either at the trial or to prepare for the trial. In most states, any party may take the deposition of the other party, or of any witness. Both sides have the right to be present during oral depositions.

A party takes depositions so it will know in advance what a witness will say at the trial. Another purpose is to obtain the testimony of important witnesses who cannot appear during the trial. Then the party may read the deposition into evidence at the trial.

Often the opposing side will take a deposition from a witness. That party will then use it to discredit the witness's testimony when the trial testimony varies from the deposition.

Usually depositions consist of oral examinations. Cross-examination by the opposing side follows the oral exam. Besides taking depositions, either party may present *interrogatories* (written questions) to the other party, who must then answer the questions in writing under oath.

Q. Are there any other methods of discovery?

A. Other methods of discovery include subpoenaing or requiring the other side to produce books, records, or other documents for inspection. Another method has the other side submit to a physical examination. Yet another involves asking a party to submit a document to determine if it is genuine.

Pre-Trial Procedures in Criminal Cases

Q. Do pre-trial procedures in criminal cases differ much from those in civil cases?

A. No, pre-trial procedures in criminal cases follow the general pattern set up in civil cases. However, there are important differences. We will discuss them in this section.

Q. How are criminal charges brought against someone?

A. A person gets indicted on criminal charges in one of three ways:
(1) Through an *indictment* voted by a grand jury.
(2) Through the filing of an *information* by the prosecuting attorney (also called the county, district, or state's attorney). This alleges that the defendant committed a crime. Sometimes another person presses charges through the filing of a criminal *complaint*. That is a petition to the district attorney asking him or her to initiate charges.
(3) Through a *citation* by a police officer, usually for certain misdemeanors and other minor criminal matters. Examples include minor traffic offenses or violations of local ordinances, such as jaywalking or littering.

Q. What does the charge include?

A. The charge must tell the time, date, and place that the criminal act supposedly took place. It also must state the alleged involvement of the accused and the details of the crime.

Q. What is a grand jury?

A. A grand jury is a body of citizens whom the court summons. Its size varies from one state to another. Grand juries exist in

Defendants and Their Mental Health

In all state and federal courts, defendants may be found incompetent to stand trial on the basis of their mental health if they are found to be unable to understand the proceedings against them or to assist properly in their own defense. Such findings usually follow a court-ordered mental evaluation of the defendant. If found incompetent, a defendant may be committed for treatment until competent to stand trial. Some states set treatment time limits after which defendants must be released. In all states, such defendants may be recommitted under civil commitment laws.

the federal system. However, only about half the states require them. In the other states, they often only investigate public corruption or do such tasks as observing conditions in the jail.

The role of a grand jury usually is to decide whether and against whom it should file criminal charges. This is true in the federal system and in states in which it still serves its traditional function in criminal cases. If a grand jury finds enough evidence that a person committed a crime, it issues an indictment against that person. This is not true in states without grand juries, or in states whose grand juries mainly investigate public corruption. In these states, the prosecutor brings charges by filing an information against the defendant.

Q. May anyone visit a grand jury meeting?

A. No, such proceedings are secret. The public, the news media and the person(s) under investigation have no right to be present. In most areas, people who testify before a grand jury are not permitted to use a lawyer. The proceedings are secret to encourage witnesses to speak freely without fear of retaliation. Another reason is to protect the person(s) under investigation if the grand jury rules that the evidence is inadequate and does not issue an indictment.

In many states it is a crime to reveal information about grand jury proceedings. However, witnesses before a federal grand jury are free to describe their testimony after leaving the grand jury room.

Q. What is the main purpose of a grand jury?

A. The purpose of the grand jury is not to decide guilt or innocence. Instead, it is to determine whether there is enough evidence to bring a person to trial. Anyone indicted by the grand jury has the chance to defend himself or herself at the resulting trial. The judge or jury at the trial will decide whether a person is guilty of the charges.

A grand jury may investigate possible criminal behavior or public corruption. The grand jury has broad investigative powers. It may force witnesses to appear and answer questions or submit records. Besides issuing indictments, a grand jury also may issue a *presentment* detailing the results of its investigation.

Q. How is an arrest made?

A. After a grand jury indicts someone or the prosecutor files an information, the court clerk issues a *warrant* for the arrest of

(continued

GRAND JURY INDICTMENTS

Not all states require a grand jury indictment to initiate criminal prosecutions.

Grand Jury Indictment Required:

All crimes:
New Jersey
South Carolina
Tennessee
Virginia

All felonies:
Alabama
Alaska
Delaware
District of Columbia
Georgia
Hawaii
Kentucky
Maine
Mississippi
New Hampshire
New York
North Carolina
Ohio
Texas
West Virginia

Capital crimes only:
Connecticut
Florida
Louisiana
Massachusetts
Minnesota
Rhode Island

Grand Jury Indictment Optional:

Arizona
Arkansas
California
Colorado
Idaho
Illinois
Indiana
Iowa
Kansas
Maryland
Michigan
Missouri
Montana
Nebraska
Nevada
New Mexico
North Dakota
Oklahoma
Oregon
South Dakota
Utah
Vermont
Washington
Wisconsin
Wyoming

Grand Jury Lacks Authority to Indict:

Pennsylvania

Note: With the exception of capital cases, a defendant can always waive the right to an indictment. Thus, the requirement for an indictment to initiate prosecution exists only in the absence of a waiver.

Source: *Report to the Nation on Crime and Justice*, second edition, U.S. Department of Justice.

HOW THE LEGAL SYSTEM WORKS

PROTECTED BY THE MIRANDA RIGHTS

When a person is in custody, some version of the Miranda rights, such as the following, is read to him or her before questioning: "You have the right to remain silent. If you give up the right to remain silent, anything you say can and will be used against you in a court of law. You have the right to an attorney. If you desire an attorney and cannot afford one, an attorney will be obtained for you before police questioning."

If the arrested person indicates in any manner a desire to consult with an attorney before speaking, there can be no questioning without violating that person's constitutional rights. The law requires police to advise an individual of these rights only when he or she is "in custody" and being "interrogated." Generally that will mean during police questioning after the individual has been arrested.

the person charged. This occurs only if he or she is not already under arrest. An officer then takes the person into custody. Sometimes, for less serious offenses, the court issues citations to the defendants, rather than arresting them.

Q. What are the Miranda rights?

A. When an officer places people under arrest, they must be told that they have the right to remain silent. The officer also must tell them of their right to consult with a lawyer, and that if they cannot afford a lawyer, the court will appoint one. The officer also must warn the people that anything they say may be held against them. The law often refers to these as the *Miranda rights*. This name comes from a 1965 ruling by the U.S. Supreme Court in *Miranda v. Arizona*. It ruled that evidence from an interrogation of people in custody may not be used against them unless the officer revealed the rights mentioned above.

Q. How long may police hold suspects before filing charges?

A. Many states permit law enforcement officers to hold suspects for up to 24 hours without filing a formal charge. Within that time, the officers must either file charges against them or release them.

Q. How soon after the arrest will the suspect see a judge?

A. The court will schedule a *first* or *initial appearance* before a judge soon after the arrest. However, the suspect may waive the right to an initial appearance. (Some courts call this hearing a *preliminary hearing* or *arraignment*. However, most states usually reserve these terms for a later stage of the criminal justice process.)

Q. What is the purpose of an initial appearance?

A. For defendants not indicted by a grand jury, this appearance is like a grand jury. The judge uses the appearance to determine whether there is enough evidence to charge them with a crime. Another purpose is to make sure that the defendants understand the charges against them and that they know their legal rights.

At this hearing the state must show the judge that there is enough evidence, or *probable cause,* to believe the accused persons committed the crime. The accused persons must be present at this hearing. However, they usually do not offer evidence in their defense.

Q. What are the possible results of an initial appearance?

A. A judge might conclude that the state lacks enough evidence to support the charges. If so, the judge will order the charges dismissed. Then the court sets the accused person(s) free.

If the judge believes there is enough evidence, he or she usually will set the amount of *bail*. This is the amount of money that suspects must deposit in order to be released from custody until the trial. Its purpose is to make sure the accused will appear for trial. The court returns the bail to defendants when their trial is over.

Q. How does the judge determine the amount of the bail?

A. When setting bail, the judge regards how likely it is that the suspect will appear for trial. The judge also considers the type of crime, how dangerous the accused seems, and the safety of the community.

Q. What role does a bail bondsman play?

A. Many defendants cannot raise the entire amount of the bail. Therefore, they may arrange for their release through a bail bondsman. The defendant will put up some of the total bond, usually ten percent. In return, the bondsman will guarantee the remaining amount to the court if the defendant does not show up for trial. In many areas, however, bondsmen are becoming obsolete. After defendants pay ten percent of the bail, courts in these areas release the defendants.

The judge may release defendants on their *own recognizance* —that is, on their promise that they will appear for all hearings and for trial. This usually occurs if the defendants have a steady job, roots in the community, or other circumstances suggesting that they will not flee.

Q. What else does the judge do at the initial appearance?

A. Besides setting bail, the judge also will determine if the accused persons have a lawyer. If they cannot afford to hire one, the court will appoint a public defender to represent them at no charge. If there is no public defender's office in the area, the court will appoint a lawyer in private practice to represent them at public expense.

Q. What happens after the initial appearance?

A. Courts then schedule most criminal cases for arraignment. At the arraignment, a court official reads the indictment or information to the defendants and explains their rights. Then the defendants enter their plea. (Some areas, or jurisdictions call this a *preliminary hearing*. These areas refer to the earlier appearance—at which a judge decided whether there was enough evidence to hold the defendant—as a *first* or *initial appearance*.)

Q. Does the defendant's plea affect what happens next?

A. Yes, it greatly affects what follows. If the defendant pleads not guilty, the judge will set a trial date. If the defendant pleads guilty, the judge will set a date for sentencing. The judge, however, will determine probation, fines, or other sentences immediately for some minor crimes.

Sometimes the judge may allow a defendant to plead *nolo contendere* (no contest). In many areas, this plea is just like a guilty plea, except that the defendant does not directly admit guilt.

Some jurisdictions permit a defendant to "stand mute" and not make a plea at all. When asked how the defendant pleads, the defendant's lawyer will say, "My client stands mute." The court then will enter a plea of "not guilty" for the defendant. By standing mute, the accused does not silently admit to the correctness of the proceedings against the accused until that point. This leaves the defendant free to attack all previous proceedings against the defendant that possibly were irregular.

Judges and Plea Negotiations

A major reform has been to increase the responsibility of judges for ensuring fairness in plea negotiations. When someone pleads guilty, the judge does not examine the strength of the case against the defendant. Instead the judge tries to determine if unfair coercion was used to induce a plea. To ensure fairness in plea negotiations, the right to a trial by jury is the right most often explained in open court to a defendant pleading guilty.

Q. Do most criminal cases go to trial?

A. No, most criminal cases never go to trial. Disputing parties resolve many cases without a trial because the accused simply pleads guilty to the original charges. In other cases, the prosecution may drop or reduce certain original charges. Then the defendant may plead guilty to the lesser charges.

Q. What is plea bargaining?

A. Many lawyers and judges would prefer to call it "plea negotiating." Lawyers in civil cases try to negotiate a settlement. Similarly, prosecutors and defense lawyers attempt to resolve the dispute between the state and the defendant through negotiation. The goal is to reach a settlement without a trial.

Q. Does plea negotiating resolve most criminal cases?

A. Probably. However, figures on plea negotiating are hard to get. We do know that most convictions result from the defendant pleading guilty, rather than from convictions after trials. For example, research in 1986 by the Bureau of Justice Statistics showed that over 96 percent of state court convictions resulted from guilty pleas. A study of federal criminal defendants in the fiscal year ending June 30, 1985 produced similar findings. Of the more than 38,000 convicted defendants, trials convicted fewer than 5,000 (less than 15 percent) of them. The rest pleaded guilty.

This suggests that plea negotiations are widespread. However, remember that some defendants plead guilty without negotiations.

Q. Why are plea negotiations so common?

A. Plea negotiations are widespread for practical reasons. Defendants avoid the time and cost of defending themselves at trial. They also escape the risk of harsher punishment and the publicity a trial could involve. The prosecution saves the time and expense of a long trial. This saves tax dollars. Plea negotiations resolve both sides' doubts about whether they would have won the case. They also relieve the court system of the burden of conducting a trial for every crime charged.

Q. What do plea negotiations involve?

A. In return for a guilty plea, the prosecution may drop one or more charges against a defendant. Or the prosecution may reduce the charge, make a recommendation that the judge impose a lesser penalty, or agree to make no recommendation to the judge on punishment.

Plea negotiations require the court's approval. The parties must place their agreement before the judge. Then the judge may accept their agreement or reject it as not in the interests of justice.

Q. What are the objections to plea negotiations?

A. Many victims' rights groups and others claim that plea negotiations result in mild punishments. They say that such negotiations reduce respect for the law and the court system, and put criminals back on the street too soon.

Other observers point out that plea negotiations can put very heavy pressure on defendants to give up their constitutional right to a trial. Some defendants who plead guilty might have won had their case gone to trial. For these defendants, plea negotiations may increase, rather than decrease, their punishment.

(continued)

THE SEQUENCE OF EVENTS IN THE CRIMINAL JUSTICE SYSTEM

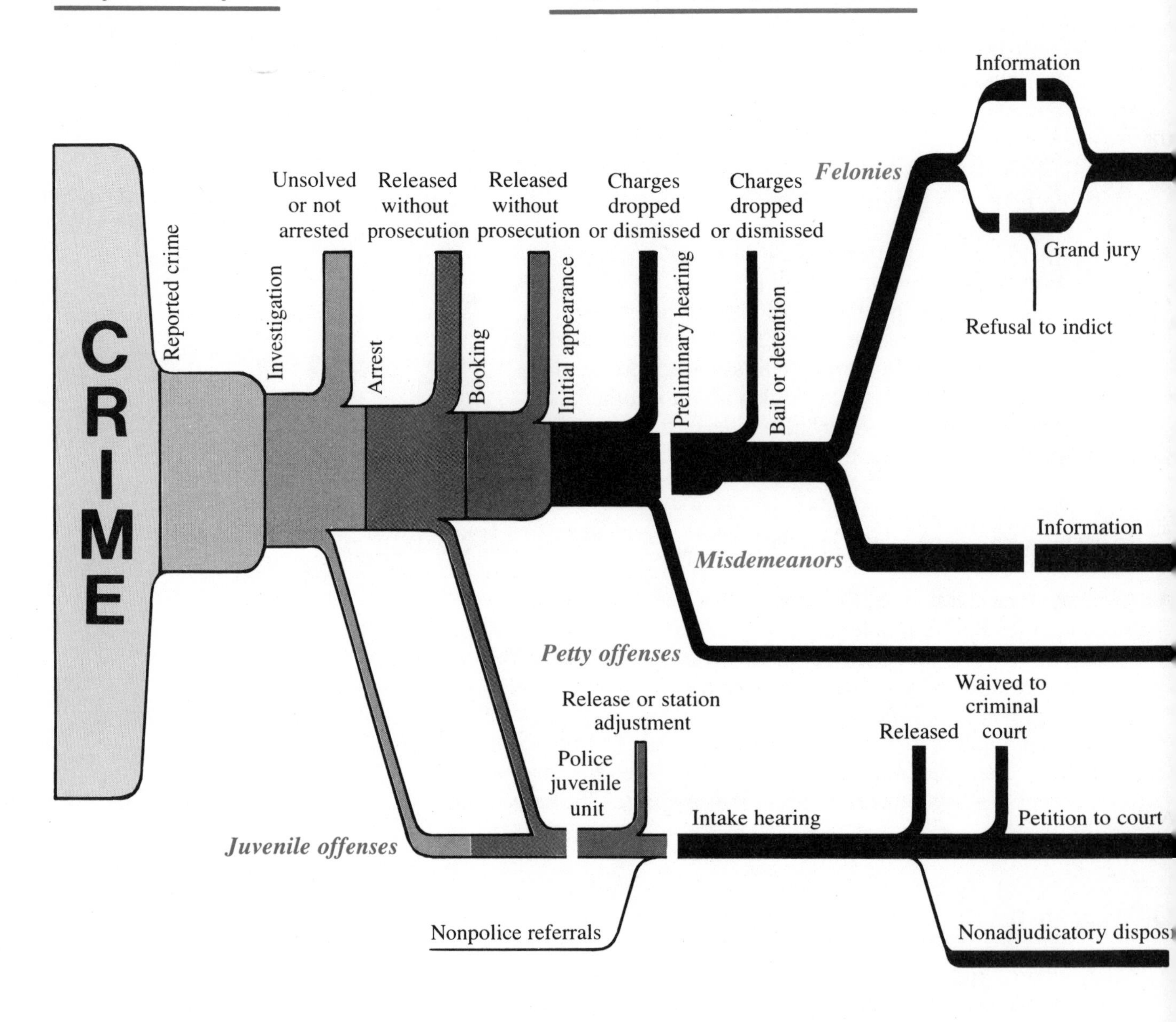

Note: This chart gives a simplified view of caseflow through the criminal justice system. Procedures vary among jurisdictions. The weights of the lines are not intended to show the actual size of caseloads.

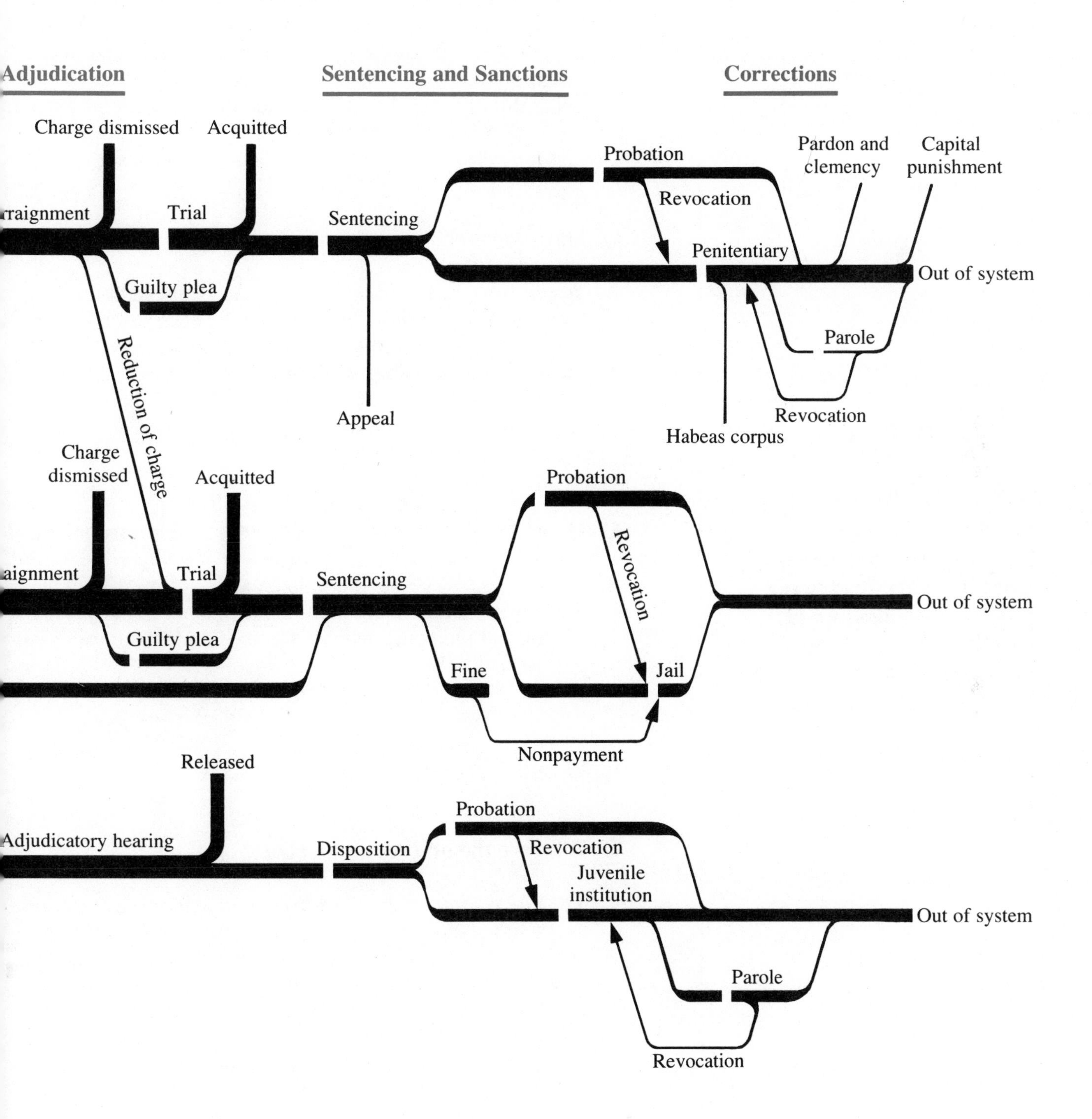

Source: Adapted from *The Challenge of Crime in a Free Society*. President's Commission on Law Enforcement and Administration of Justice, 1967.

Q. Besides plea negotiations, does a defendant have any other choices?

A. Yes. Many states encourage *diversion* programs, which remove less serious criminal matters from the full, formal procedures of the justice system. Typically, this kind of program allows the defendant to agree to probation without going through a trial. If the defendant finishes the probation, the matter will be erased from the records. Probation often involves rehabilitation or making amends for the crime.

Q. Does discovery occur in criminal cases as in civil cases?

A. Yes, in some jurisdictions, discovery is available in criminal cases. In many of these areas, both the prosecution and the defense engage in discovery. Both sides must reveal to each other all witnesses they intend to call to testify at the trial. The prosecution also must reveal all other evidence it will introduce. Some other areas only allow the defense to ask information from the prosecution.

Q. Do criminal cases involve depositions and interrogatories?

A. No, they are very rare in criminal cases. Where they exist, the courts conduct them in the same manner as in civil cases, except that the court may not force defendants to testify against themselves.

Similar But Different

While there are some differences in civil and criminal trials, the basic courtroom procedure is the same. This section discusses civil and criminal trial procedure together, noting the differences where they occur.

Civil and Criminal Trials

Q. Who are the officers of the court?

A. The *judge* controls (presides in) the courtroom. If the court tries a case before a jury, the judge rules on points of law. He or she also informs the jury about the law that governs the case. If there is no jury, the judge determines the facts and decides the verdict. The judge may settle on a finding of guilty or not guilty in a criminal case. In a civil trial, a finding may be for or against the plaintiff or defendant.

The *court clerk* or *bailiff* usually administers the oath to people becoming jurors and to witnesses. The clerk also stores the physical exhibits introduced as evidence. In addition, the clerk has other administrative duties.

The *bailiff* keeps order in the courtroom and calls the witnesses. He or she also leads the jury in and out of the courtroom as directed by the judge. The bailiff makes sure no one outside the courtroom tries to influence the jury.

The *court reporter* records every word spoken as part of the formal proceedings in the courtroom. This includes the testimony of the witnesses, objections made by the lawyers, and the judge's rulings on those objections. A few areas have stopped using court reporters. Instead, they use audio or audiovisual tapes to record the trial.

The *lawyers* for both sides are also officers of the court. Their job is to represent their clients forcefully. The law believes that it can best achieve justice if competent lawyers vigorously present the arguments of each side.

Q. How does the court choose a jury?

A. The court chooses a trial jury at random from a list called a *venire* or *jury pool*. This is true in either civil or criminal cases. The court clerk compiles the list of possible jurors. The method of selecting names for the venire varies. Many states get the names from voter registration lists, driver's license lists, or tax assessment rolls. In federal courts, the court clerk compiles the jury list from the roster of registered voters in the counties in the court's jurisdiction. The presiding judge appoints a jury commissioner to help compile this list.

Q. How does the court screen the list of possible jurors?

A. Most states require a court official to screen the list of potential jurors. This eliminates people who are not eligible under state laws.

The law traditionally exempted many persons from jury duty because of their jobs. Exemptions varied from one state to another. However, the most common exemptions were for lawyers, doctors, dentists, pharmacists, teachers, and the clergy. Some states also exempted nurses, journalists, printers, government officials, fire fighters, and police officers. This was also true of railroad, telegraph, and telephone employees. The law usually exempted people because their jobs were so important to society that they couldn't stop working to attend jury duty.

However, these automatic exemptions are becoming much less common. The American Bar Association says the courts should eliminate all automatic exemptions. In 27 states the courts have sharply cut back or completely done away with them.

On occasion, one side may challenge the qualifications of all the potential jurors. This may be due to a belief that the jury pool—which should represent the whole community—excludes certain groups. The legal term for this is a *challenge to the array*. The contesting party usually claims that court officials compiled the jury list in an illegal manner.

Q. How many people make up a jury?

A. Once the clerk has assembled the jury list, the court selects juries of six to 12 persons from this pool. The size of jury varies from one state to another. Its size depends to some extent on the type of case. In civil cases, especially in courts of limited jurisdiction, the standard size in many areas is becoming six. Both parties may demand a larger jury. Misdemeanor cases sometimes have fewer than 12 jurors. However, serious criminal cases usually require 12 jurors.

In civil cases, the requirement that juries be unanimous is also changing. States are experimenting by permitting verdicts based on the agreement of three fourths or five sixths of the jurors. Unanimous juries remain the rule in criminal cases.

Exemptions from Jury Service

Most states have statutory exemptions from jury service. The most common of these are for undue hardship or public necessity, for personal bad health, or for persons serving as judicial officers. Many states also exempt specific occupations, such as attorneys, doctors, dentists, members of the clergy, elected officials, police officers, fire fighters, teachers, and sole proprietors of businesses.

Q. What is an alternate juror?

A. Courts usually select alternate jurors to take the place of jurors who become disabled during the trial. Alternate jurors hear the evidence just as the other jurors do. However, the alternates do not deliberate the case unless they replace an original juror.

Q. What does jury selection involve?

A. Jury selection begins when the court clerk calls 12 people on the jury list. The clerk asks them to take their places in the jury box. Then the judge usually makes a brief statement. He or she explains the kind of case to be tried. The judge also asks if there is any reason the potential jurors cannot serve. After this, the judge or the lawyers ask them questions. These range from their names, jobs, and residences to whether they know anything about the case. The legal term for this questioning of the potential jurors is *voir dire.*

Q. What happens if a lawyer believes a juror to be biased?

A. Either lawyer may believe that information suggests a juror has a prejudice about the case. If so, the lawyer may ask the court to dismiss the juror *for cause*. For example, the court may dismiss a juror for cause if he or she is a close relative of one of the disputing parties or lawyers. Another reason for dismissal is if the juror works for a company involved in the lawsuit. Each lawyer may challenge any number of jurors for cause.

Q. May a lawyer ask the court to dismiss a potential juror without any special reason?

A. Yes, besides challenges for cause, each lawyer has a specific number of *peremptory challenges*. These challenges allow a lawyer to excuse a potential juror without stating a reason. This allows a lawyer to dismiss a juror because of a hunch. The lawyer may believe that the juror will not be sympathetic to the lawyer's client. The kind of case limits the number of peremptory challenges allowed.

Q. What takes place after the court finishes selecting the jury?

A. When both parties have agreed upon a jury, the court clerk swears in the jurors. The court excuses those not selected from participating as jurors in the case.

Q. Are witnesses always allowed to sit in the courtroom and listen to the proceedings?

A. No, in certain cases, either lawyer may advise the court that he or she wishes to *sequester* the witnesses. This means that all witnesses must stay out of the courtroom until it is time for them to testify. The only exceptions are the plaintiff and the defendant. The idea is that the witnesses will remember events more accurately if they haven't heard the other witnesses. This means their testimony will be more accurate. Another term for sequestering the witnesses is *calling for the rule.*

The judge warns the witnesses not to discuss the case or their testimony with anyone except the lawyers. If neither side sequesters the witnesses, they may remain in the courtroom until they testify.

Q. How does the actual trial begin?

A. A trial begins with the opening statement of the party with the *burden of proof.*

In a criminal trial, the burden of proof rests with the state. It must prove beyond a reasonable doubt that the defendant is guilty.

In a civil trial, the plaintiff has the burden of proof. The plaintiff usually must prove liability by presenting more convincing evidence than the other side offers. Court observers usually call this a *preponderance of the evidence.* Another term for this is the *greater weight of the evidence.* The degree of proof required in a civil case is far less strict than in a criminal case.

The opening statement must stick to facts that the evidence will prove. It may not present an argument.

The defense lawyer follows with his or her opening statement. In some states, the defense may reserve its opening statement until the end of the plaintiff's or state's case. Either lawyer may choose not to offer an opening statement.

Q. What is evidence, and how does either side present it?

A. The heart of the case is the presentation of evidence. There are two types of evidence—direct and circumstantial. They may take either of two forms—oral testimony of witnesses or physical exhibits, including documents. Direct evidence includes eyewitness accounts, confessions, or weapons. Circumstantial evidence usually suggests something by implying it. Examples include how the scene of a crime looks, testimony suggesting a link with a crime, and physical evidence indicating criminal activity. It is very likely that both kinds of evidence are a part of most trials.

Q. What sort of rules affect evidence?

A. Strict rules govern the kinds of evidence that both parties may present and control how they may present the evidence.

Lawyers for the plaintiff or the state begin presenting evidence by calling witnesses. The questions they ask of the witnesses are *direct examination*. Note that direct examination produces not only direct evidence. It also may obtain both direct and circumstantial evidence. Witnesses may testify to *matters of fact*. These are facts that the witnesses determined by using their senses (sight, hearing, and so on). They also may have to identify documents, pictures, or other items presented as evidence.

Q. What is hearsay?

A. *Hearsay* is what the witness says he or she heard another person say. An example would be, "Bill said that John admitted shooting his wife." The witness is repeating a statement made by someone else, not what the witness actually saw or heard. Witnesses usually may not testify to hearsay.

The theory behind this is that hearsay has nothing to do with the reliability of the witness. Hearsay depends mainly on the honesty and awareness of someone who is not in court. That makes this type of evidence very weak. Courts often do not admit hearsay as evidence.

There are, however, exceptions that allow the use of hearsay as evidence. One example is a spontaneous statement made when something startling occurs. Courts allow such statements as evidence. Experience and common sense have shown that one usually can trust them because of their sudden, unplanned nature. Federal and state rules of evidence also recognize other exceptions.

Q. May a witness give an opinion while testifying?

A. Witnesses usually may not state opinions or give conclusions. However, witnesses qualified in a specific field are *expert witnesses*. They are permitted to give their opinion based on the facts in evidence. They also are allowed to give the reason for that opinion. Sometimes lawyers present the facts in evidence in hypothetical questions. At other times lawyers ask experts to state an opinion based on personal knowledge of the facts through their own examination or investigation.

Q. What are leading questions?

A. Leading questions are questions that suggest the answer desired. This, in effect, prompts the witness. An example is, "Isn't it true that you saw John waiting across the street before his wife came home?" Lawyers normally may not ask *leading questions* of their own witnesses.

Q. For what reasons may a lawyer make an objection?

A. The opposing lawyer may make *objections* to leading questions, questions that call for a witness's opinion or conclusion, or questions that require an answer based on hearsay. There are many other reasons for objections.

Most courts require the lawyer to give a specific reason for an objection. Usually, the judge will immediately either *sustain* (uphold) or *overrule* (reject) the objection. If the judge sustains the objection, the lawyer has two choices: The lawyer must either rephrase the question in a proper form or ask another question. If the judge overrules the objection and the witness answers the question, the objecting lawyer may appeal the ruling after the trial ends.

Q. What does cross-examination involve?

A. When the lawyer for the plaintiff or the state finishes questioning a witness, the defense may cross-examine the witness. Cross-examination usually may concern only matters that arose during direct examination. The defense may ask leading questions during cross-examination. The law allows this because cross-examination should test the honesty of statements made during direct examination. Another reason for allowing leading questions is that the lawyer is questioning a witness whom he or she did not originally call.

During cross-examination, the lawyer might try to question the witness's ability to identify or remember. The lawyer also may try to impeach the witness or the evidence. *Impeach* in this sense means to destroy or make the witness or evidence less believable. The lawyer may do this by trying to show bias in the witness. The lawyer may show this by the witness's relationship or friendship with one of the parties. Or the witness may have a personal interest in the result of the case. A lawyer may ask if another court ever convicted the witnesses of a felony or a crime involving bad morals. The lawyer may ask this because it helps determine whether the witnesses are believable.

Opposing lawyers may object to certain questions asked on cross-examination. Opposing lawyers may do so if the questions violate the state's laws on evidence or if they concern matters not discussed during direct examination.

Q. What happens after the lawyer cross-examines the witness?

A. After cross-examination, the lawyer who called the witness has the right to ask more questions on re-direct examination. This allows the lawyer to cover new matters brought out in cross-examination. Re-direct examination usually tries to reinforce a witness's earlier testimony that cross-examination has weakened.

The opposing lawyer may then re-cross-examine. After that, re-re-direct examination may follow. This continues until the lawyers have finished or the judge calls an end to it.

Q. What occurs after the plaintiff or state stops presenting evidence?

A. The lawyer will announce that the plaintiff or state rests.

The defendant's lawyer in a civil case may now make a motion for a directed verdict. (The jury leaves the courtroom when this motion is presented.) This means the lawyer argues that the plaintiff has not proven the defendant's liability by presenting strong enough evidence. In a criminal trial, the defendant's lawyer may ask for a motion to dismiss the charges. This means the lawyer argues that the government has failed to prove its case beyond a reasonable doubt. In both kinds of cases, this means that the lawyer is asking the judge to *direct a verdict* for the defendant. In other words, the lawyer is asking the judge to rule in favor of the defendant, without going to a jury (if one is present). The judge will either grant or deny the motion. If the judge grants it, the case is over, and the defendant wins. If the judge denies the motion, as is the usual case, the court gives the defense a chance to present its evidence.

Q. Does the law require the defense lawyer to present some amount of evidence?

A. No, the defense lawyer may choose to present no evidence. The lawyer may believe that the plaintiff or state did not prove its case. Usually, however, the defense will call witnesses and present other evidence.

Q. Are defendants required by law to testify, even if they do not want to?

A. In a criminal case, the defense does not have to present the defendant as a witness. The Fifth Amendment to the U.S. Constitution protects against self-incrimination. Therefore, the prosecution may not require the defendant to take the stand and explain what happened. In a civil case, however, the plaintiff may force the defendant to testify.

Q. Does the defense present its evidence in the same way that the plaintiff or state did?

A. Yes, the defense presents evidence in the same manner as the plaintiff or state. In return, the plaintiff or state has the right to cross-examine any defense witness. The law also permits re-direct and re-cross-examination.

Q. What happens after the defense ends its case?

A. At the end of the defendant's case, the lawyer for the plaintiff or state may present *rebuttal* witnesses or evidence to contradict the defendant's evidence. This may consist of evidence not presented before. It also may include a new witness who contradicts the defendant's witness.

After rebuttal, the defense then gets to present further evidence.

Q. I've seen lawyers go to the bench to speak softly with the judge. What is the reason for this?

A. Occasionally during the trial the lawyers will ask permission to approach the bench to speak to the judge. Or the judge may call both lawyers to the bench. Court observers call these *bench conferences* or *sidebars.* The court reporter records everything said. During a bench conference the lawyers and the judge speak quietly. The reason for this is that the jurors might become prejudiced by what they hear.

Bench conferences deal with such questions as procedure, the conduct of the trial, or juror misconduct. They also may deal with motions for a mistrial. (These motions ask the judge to end the trial before its normal conclusion because of some unusual event.)

Taking the Fifth

The Fifth Amendment to the United States Constitution involves several important protections. However, the most famous of these allows defendants in criminal trials to refuse to take the witness stand, thus avoiding self-incrimination. This portion of the Fifth Amendment states: "No person . . . shall be compelled in any criminal case to be a witness against himself . . . ."

A bench conference often concerns whether to admit certain evidence. Such questions are for the judge to decide. If the judge cannot make a ruling quickly, the jury leaves the courtroom, and the judge will hear arguments. Whenever the jurors leave the room, the judge warns them not to form an opinion or discuss the case with anyone.

Q. What are the final motions?

A. After both sides present all the evidence and the jury has left the courtroom, either side may again move for a *directed verdict.* If the judge grants the motion, the trial is over. If not, the case is ready to be presented to the jury.

Q. What do the lawyers include in their closing arguments?

A. The lawyer for the plaintiff or state often presents the first closing argument, or *summation.* The lawyer sums up and comments on the evidence in the most favorable light for his or her side. Closing arguments also discuss the facts and properly drawn conclusions. Before closing arguments begin, the judge usually tells the lawyers which instructions he or she will give the jury. It is proper for the closing arguments to comment on the jury instructions and to relate the instructions to the evidence.

During the closing arguments the lawyers may not discuss issues that don't relate to the case. They also may not talk about evidence that neither side presented.

After the plaintiff or state has made its case, the defense presents its closing arguments. The defense lawyer usually answers statements made in the plaintiff's argument and points out defects in the plaintiff's case. In the end, the lawyer sums up the facts favorable to the defendant.

Because the plaintiff or state has the burden of proof, the law allows that side's lawyer to make the *concluding argument.* The lawyer uses it to respond to the defense lawyer and make a final appeal to the jury.

Occasionally the defense may choose not to make a closing statement. If so, the plaintiff or state loses the right to make a second argument.

Q. What happens after the closing arguments?

A. Afterward, the judge instructs the jury about relevant laws that should guide its deliberations. (In some jurisdictions, the court may instruct the jury anytime after the close of evidence. This sometimes occurs *before* closing arguments.) The judge reads the instructions to the jury. Court observers commonly call this the *judge's charge to the jury.*

In the instructions, the judge states the issues in the case. The judge will define terms or words that may not be familiar to the jurors. The judge also will discuss the standard of proof that jurors should apply to the case. These are "beyond a reasonable doubt" in a criminal case and "preponderance of the evidence" in a civil case. The judge may read sections of laws that apply to the case. In addition, the judge will say that the jury is to determine the facts and the believability of the witnesses.

The judge will point out, however, that the instructions interpret the relevant laws governing the case. The judge will order the jurors to stick to these laws in making their decision. In short, the jurors determine the facts and reach a verdict. However, they must do this within the guidelines of the law as interpreted by the judge.

Q. Who decides what instructions the judge will give the jury?

A. The judge makes the final decisions about what instructions the jury will receive. However, many states allow the lawyers to ask the judge to give certain instructions. As noted above, the judge will usually tell the lawyers before the closing arguments what instructions the judge will give the jury. This allows the lawyers to explain the instructions and relate them to the facts.

Q. What is a mistrial?

A. A *mistrial* is a trial that the judge ends and declares void before the jury returns a verdict. If there is no jury, the judge ends the trial and declares it void before he or she has made a decision.

Mistrials occur for a wide variety of reasons. A mistrial might result from a basic error that goes against the defendant and cannot be cured by instructions to the jury. An example of this is a highly improper remark in the prosecutor's summation. If the jury cannot reach a verdict because of a stalemate, the judge also is permitted to declare a mistrial.

Either side is allowed to make a motion for a mistrial. The judge may grant the motion and declare the trial a mistrial. If the judge does not grant the motion, the trial will continue.

A mistrial does not result in a judgment for any of the involved parties. It merely shows the failure of the trial. Because mistrials are not valid trials, the prohibition against double jeopardy (see the "Appeals" section below) does not apply. This means that criminal defendants whose trials result in mistrials may be tried again.

Jury Deliberations and Verdicts

Q. How does a jury deliberate?

A. After receiving the instructions, the jury retires to the jury room to begin deliberating. In most states the first thing done is to elect one juror as the foreman or forewoman.

The bailiff sits outside the jury room to make sure nobody contacts the jury during deliberations.

In some states, the jury may take the exhibits introduced as evidence and the judge's instructions to the jury room. If the jury has a question about the evidence or instructions, the jury gives the bailiff a note to take to the judge, who may respond by writing a note. The judge also may call the jury back into the courtroom for more instructions or to have parts of the transcript read to them.

Usually the court provides the jury with written forms of all possible verdicts. Then when the jury reaches a decision, it only has to choose the proper verdict form.

Q. Does the jury always have to reach a unanimous verdict?

A. The verdict in a criminal case usually must be unanimous. Some states allow a less-than-unanimous decision in civil cases. All federal cases require a unanimous decision.

Q. What happens if the jury cannot reach a decision by the end of the day?

A. The court may *sequester* the jurors, housing them in a hotel. The jurors may not have contact with other people, newspapers, and news reports. Many times, though, the court will allow the jury to go home at night, provided neither party objects.

Q. What takes place if the jurors cannot agree on a verdict?

A. This results in a *hung jury,* which leads to a mistrial. There is no decision in the case. Therefore, it may be tried again later before a new jury. However, if the plaintiff or state decides not to pursue the case further, it is over. Then the defendant is free from civil liability or criminal punishment.

Q. What does a jury do after it reaches a decision?

A. The jury notifies the bailiff, who informs the judge. All the participants gather in the courtroom. Then either the jury's foreman (or forewoman) or the court clerk announces the decision.

Q. What are the possible verdicts?

A. In criminal cases the possible verdicts are "guilty" or "not guilty." In a civil suit, the jury will find for either the plaintiff or the defendant. If the jury finds for the plaintiff, it also will usually set the amount of damages.

Sometimes different verdicts are possible. "Guilty but insane" is a possible verdict in some states. In some very complex civil trials, applying the law to the facts may be too difficult for a jury. In this instance, the judge may simply ask the jury to decide one or more factual questions. Then the judge will apply the law to the facts as determined by the jury. This is a *special verdict*.

Q. May the court ask the jurors what each one voted?

A. Yes, either lawyer may ask the court to *poll* the jury. This request usually comes from the losing party. The court asks each juror if he or she agrees with the announced decision. This helps make sure that the announced verdict is the jury's actual verdict.

Q. What happens after the proper person announces the decision?

A. After the court reads and accepts the verdict, the judge dismisses the jury. Then the trial is over.

Q. What motions does the law allow after the court announces the verdict?

A. The law permits various motions. They differ from one state to another.

A *motion in arrest of judgment* questions whether the indictment or information in a criminal case is sufficient. It then asks the court not to uphold the judgment.

A *motion for judgment notwithstanding the verdict* may be made after the court announces the jury's decision. However, it must be made before the judge enters a judgment. This motion asks the judge to enter a judgment for the losing party despite the decision of the jury.

A *motion for a new trial* asks the judge to grant a new trial based on errors the judge committed during the trial. Some states require the losing party to make a motion for a new trial before filing an appeal.

INSANITY AS A DEFENSE

According to the latest (March 1988) *Report to the Nation on Crime and Justice* from the Bureau of Justice Statistics of the U.S. Department of Justice, only three states—Montana, Idaho, and Utah—have passed laws that abolish the insanity defense. However, in these states, psychiatric evidence is allowed on the issue of whether there is an intent to commit a crime.

In most states, a formal notice of an intent to rely on the insanity defense must be filed by defendants who wish to claim insanity as a defense. Such defendants enter a plea of not guilty at the time of the trial.

Since 1975, 12 states have adopted a verdict of guilty but mentally ill. In these states, this verdict is an alternative to, but does not preclude, a verdict of not guilty by reason of insanity.

Sentencing Alternatives

Several sentencing alternatives may be available to judges. These may include one or more of the following: *incarceration* in a prison, jail, or other facility; *probation,* which allows the convicted person to remain at liberty, subject to conditions and restrictions; *fines,* which primarily are used as penalties in minor offenses; *restitution,* which requires the offender to compensate the victim; and, in rare cases, the *death penalty*.

In many states, the law mandates that persons convicted of certain offenses serve a prison term. Most states permit the judge to set the sentence length within specific limits. However, some state laws stipulate a particular sentence length that must be served and that cannot be altered by a parole board.

Q. How does a judgment differ from a jury's decision?

A. The decision of the jury does not take effect until the judge enters a *judgment* on the decision.

In a civil suit, the judge usually has the power to increase or decrease the amount of damages awarded by the jury. The judge also may make other changes before entering a judgment. In criminal cases, the judge normally may not alter the verdict. He or she must accept or reject it. (The judge rejects it by granting a motion for judgment notwithstanding the verdict.)

Q. What happens if the defendant does not pay the damages awarded to the plaintiff in a civil case?

A. The plaintiff may ask for an *execution* of the judgment. Then the clerk of the court will deliver the execution to the sheriff. The clerk will command the sheriff to seize and sell the defendant's property. The sheriff will apply that money to the amount of the judgment.

Q. If the court convicts a defendant in a criminal case, does he or she go right to jail?

A. No, the judge will set a date for sentencing. At that time, the judge may consider either *mitigating* or *aggravating facts.* Mitigating facts suggest a reason for the judge to show more mercy. An example may be a person provoked into committing a murder in the heat of passion.

On the other hand, aggravating facts suggest a reason for the judge to impose a tougher sentence. An example may be a case in which a gun was used or where the victim was seriously harmed.

To determine the proper sentence, the judge also may use other information from a presentence investigation. The investigation may consider the defendant's criminal record, family situation, health, work record, and other related factors. This information helps the judge find the most fitting sentence.

Q. Is the judge the only person who may decide the sentence?

A. In most states and in federal courts, the judge alone determines the sentence. Some states permit the jury to recommend a sentence. This often happens when the death penalty is a possible sentence. Some states and the federal courts have guidelines to help judges determine fair sentences and to encourage consistency.

Appeals

Q. Who has the right to appeal a case?

A. In a civil case, either party may appeal to a higher court. In a criminal case, only the defendant has this right in most states. (Some states give the prosecution a limited right to appeal to determine certain points of law. These states usually do not allow full appeals by the prosecution. The reason for this is that the U.S. Constitution prohibits *double jeopardy*. This prevents the courts from trying someone twice for the same crime.)

Criminal defendants convicted in state courts also have another appellate safeguard. They may file a *writ of habeas corpus* in the federal courts. This tries to show that someone violated the defendants' federal constitutional rights. The right of a federal review allows the federal judicial system to study abuses that may occur in state courts.

Q. What are the usual reasons that people give for making appeals?

A. People normally make appeals because of errors in trial procedure or errors in the way the judge interpreted the law. Other grounds for appeal also exist.

Q. What makes up the record on appeal?

A. The *record on appeal* consists of the papers filed in the trial court and the court reporter's transcript of the trial. The trial judge must certify the transcript as true and correct. In most states, the appeal includes only the relevant parts of the transcript (those relating to the appeal).

Q. How does the appeal begin?

A. The court refers to the party appealing as the *appellant* or sometimes the *petitioner*. The other party is the *appellee* or the *respondent*.

The appeal starts with the filing of a *notice of appeal*. This begins the time period within which the appellant must file a *brief*. The brief is a written argument containing the appellant's view of the facts. It also includes the legal arguments used by the appellant to try to reverse the trial court.

The appellee then has a specified time to file an answering brief. The appellant may file a second brief answering the appellee's brief.

Q. Do all appeals courts hear oral arguments?

A. No, many state and federal appeals courts base their decision on the briefs, without hearing oral arguments. Or the case may be set for oral argument before the appellate court. Sometimes the court will ask for an oral argument. At other times one of the parties will make the request.

At an oral argument, each side's lawyer has a brief opportunity to argue the case before the court. Each lawyer also may answer questions posed by the judges. The U.S. Supreme Court, for example, sets an hour for oral argument of most cases. This gives each side about half an hour to make an oral argument and answer the justices' questions.

Q. What is the appellate court's purpose?

A. The job of the appellate court is to determine whether the trial court followed the law during the trial. An appellate court normally reverses a trial court only for an error of law.

Not every error of law, however, is cause for a reversal. Some are *harmless errors* that did not affect the rights of the parties to a fair trial. For example, in a criminal case, a higher court may decide that the judge who presided over the trial gave a legally improper instruction to the jury. However, if the mistake was minor and the appellate court thought it did not affect the jury's decision, the higher court may consider the error harmless. It would let the decision stand. However, the appellate court may find an error of law (such as the admission of improper evidence) to be harmful. This *reversible error* would allow the higher court to reverse the trial court's decision.

Q. What happens after both sides orally argue a case or present it in another form to the appellate court?

A. Then the judges meet to discuss the case. The law requires almost all appellate courts to issue written decisions. At the meeting, the court chooses one of the judges to write an opinion. The opinion may go through several drafts before most of the court agrees with it. Judges who disagree with the *majority opinion* may issue a *dissenting opinion*. Judges who agree with the majority decision but disagree with the majority's reasoning may file a *concurring opinion*.

Q. What does an appellate court decision contain?

A. Appellate court decisions begin with a brief summary of the opinion. Then the opening part of the majority opinion usually states the case's facts and the legal issues the court had to decide. The middle part of the opinion states reasons used to reach the decision. It also includes prior appellate decisions supporting that reasoning. The closing part contains the decision and states any further action to be taken in the case.

Q. What occurs after the appellate court hands down the opinion?

A. Nothing happens until the time for a rehearing expires or the court denies a rehearing. Then the higher court sends its *mandate* (order) to the trial court for further action. If the appellate court affirms the lower court's judgment, the case ends, unless the loser appeals to a higher court. If the appellate court reverses the judgment, the mandate may command the lower court to hold a new trial. Or the mandate may order a change or correction of the trial court's judgment. The appellate court also may dismiss an appeal (usually for reasons of jurisdiction). Or it may send the appeal back to a lower court (*remand* it) for review of the facts or for other reasons.

Q. Does an appeal in a civil case prevent the trial court's judgment from being upheld?

A. No, this ordinarily does not stop it from being upheld. The winning party in the trial court may order the judgment executed unless the appealing party files an *appeal* or *supersedeas bond*. The filing of this bond will prevent, or *stay,* further action on the judgment until the appeal ends. This bond guarantees that the appealing party will pay or act on the judgment if an appeal does not reverse it.

WHERE TO GET MORE INFORMATION

The Federal Court System

For details about the U.S. Supreme Court, contact the Public Information Officer, the Supreme Court of the United States, Washington, D.C. 20543. For facts about other federal courts, contact the Public Information Officer, Administrative Office of United States Courts, Washington, D.C. 20544. The Information Service of the Federal Judicial Center is a very useful source of data about federal courts. You can contact it at Dolley Madison House, 1520 H Street, N.W., Washington, D.C. 20005.

The Administrative Office of the U.S. Courts offers several useful, brief handbooks on the federal court system. You can contact it at the address listed above. One example is *The United States Courts: Their Jurisdiction and Work.* In only 23 pages, it quickly compares state and federal jurisdiction. It also examines the work of the various courts. Another useful handbook is *Glossary of Terms Used in the Federal Courts.* It provides a very readable introduction to some of the most common terms and procedures.

Preview of United States Supreme Court Cases is a unique resource. It supplies journalists, lawyers, and other interested parties with up-to-date information on cases the Supreme Court is considering but has not yet decided. This resource analyzes each case's issues, facts, background, and significance. It helps readers understand decisions when the Court makes them. Yearly subscriptions are available from the American Bar Association's Public Education Division, 750 N. Lake Shore Drive, Chicago, Illinois 60611.

Another interesting publication is *Equal Justice Under Law: The Supreme Court in American Life* (Washington: Supreme Court Historical Society, 1982), by Mary Ann Harrell and Burnett Anderson. This lively history of the Court is available from The Supreme Court Historical Society, 111 Second Street, N.E., Washington, D.C. 20002.

The Supreme Court and Its Justices (Chicago: American Bar Association, 1987) includes various articles from the *ABA Journal.* It discusses the Court's internal operation, the appointment of justices, and lawyering before the Court. You can obtain it from Order Fulfillment, order number 299-0013, American Bar Association, 750 N. Lake Shore Drive, Chicago, Illinois 60611.

State and Local Courts

The public information office of the National Center for State Courts provides data on state courts. You can contact it at 300 Newport Avenue, Williamsburg, Virginia 23187-8798. Courts in your locality are a natural, useful source of information. Many courts have handbooks that explain their procedures to the general public. They also often publish materials for jurors, witnesses, and other interested persons. To find out more about your local courts, contact your state court administrator or the state supreme court. Both have offices in the state capital.

Your local or state bar association also can be a good source of information. Bar associations often provide guides to the courts and handbooks for jurors and witnesses. In addition, they offer materials that explain the court system to the general public.

Many bar associations also sponsor bar-bench-media conferences. These meetings improve communication between the press and the courts. Some local and state bar associations offer informative materials that are specially designed for reporters covering the courts in their area.

Explaining the Courts: Materials and Sources (Chicago: American Bar Association, 1983) lists a wide range of publications. It includes various materials explaining state and local courts. You can obtain it from Order Fulfillment, order number 410-0001, American Bar Association, 750 N. Lake Shore Drive, Chicago, Illinois 60611.

Finally, many public libraries have books of state laws and other useful references.

Covering the Courts

Many books discuss reporting on law and the courts. One example is *Free Press and Fair Trial: Values in Concert* (Washington, D.C.: American Society of Newspaper Editors, American Newspaper Publishers Association Foundation, revised edition, 1987). It talks about how the law affects journalists. This book looks at how the First and Sixth Amendments interact. (The U.S. Constitution's Sixth Amendment guarantees a fair trial. The First Amendment ensures the right to a free press. At times, these amendments have conflicted with each other.)

The ABA Standards

The American Bar Association (ABA) has set up standards and guidelines in many areas of court procedure. They guide the work of state and federal courts. However, not every area has adopted them.

Many different ABA standards deal directly with the courts. See *Standards for Traffic Justice, Standards of Judicial Administration, Standards Relating to Appellate Courts,* and *Standards Relating to Court Delay Reduction.* Also see *Standards Relating to Court Organization, Standards Relating to Juror Use and Management,* and *Standards Relating to Trial Courts*. All are available from Order Fulfillment, American Bar Association, 750 N. Lake Shore Drive, Chicago, Illinois 60611.

The ABA Guidelines for the Evaluation of Judicial Performance deals with judicial competence. It is available from ABA Criminal Justice, Evaluation of Judicial Performance Project, 1800 M Street, N.W., 2nd Floor Lobby, Washington, D.C. 20036. The telephone number is (202) 331-2260.

Other Aspects of Law and the Courts

Booklets from many state and local courts explain the role of jurors. For general questions about juries, contact the Center for Jury Studies, 4001 North Ninth Street, Suite 218, Arlington, Virginia 22203.

The National Criminal Justice Reference Service offers information on various matters about criminal procedure. For details, call (800) 851-3420; Maryland residents call (301) 251-5500.

Several publications explore alternative dispute resolution. *Alternative Dispute Resolution: An ADR Primer* (Washington: American Bar Association, 1987) is a useful look at several options. It is available from the ABA's Standing Committee on Dispute Resolution, American Bar Association, 1800 M Street, N.W., Washington, D.C. 20036. Also available from the same committee is a free newsletter, *Dispute Resolution.* It contains news and updates on alternative dispute resolution. Another related publication is *Dispute Resolution in America: Processes in Evolution* (1984), by S.B. Goldberg, E.D. Green, and F.E.A. Sander. You can obtain it from the National Institute for Dispute Resolution, 1901 L Street, N.W., Suite 600, Washington, D.C. 20036.

FAMILY LAW

INTRODUCTION

The government has always had an interest in marriage and families. In addition, today's laws also affect couples who live together outside of marriage.

It is hard to give simple answers to many of the legal questions that the average person may have about marriage, parenthood, separation, or divorce. The reasons for this are that the laws change regularly and vary from one state to another. In addition, judges in different states may decide cases with similar facts in different ways.

This chapter talks about the important laws and court rulings common to most states. If you have other questions, contact a lawyer in your state. Many lawyers work only on family law or make it a large part of their general practice.

DEFINING MARRIAGE LEGALLY

Q. Legally, what is marriage?

A. Most states define marriage as a civil contract between a man and woman to become husband and wife.

The moment a couple marries, their relationship acquires a legal status. Married couples have financial and personal duties during marriage and after a divorce. State laws determine the extent of these duties. In 1888 the United States Supreme Court said about marriage, "[t]he relation once formed, the law steps in and holds the parties to various obligations and liabilities."

The definition of marriage as a personal contract and a legal status shows the two faces of marriage in the English common-law tradition. On the one hand, marriage is a private bond between two people. On the other hand, it also is an important social institution. Today marriage still is both personally and socially important. However, as our society becomes more complex, there is no longer a short answer to the question "What is marriage?"

Today, society also recognizes marriage as:

- A financial partnership in which spouses may choose from a variety of roles. Both spouses may work to support the family, the husband may support the wife, or the wife may support the husband;
- A way to strengthen intimate bonds and mutual support; and
- An arrangement for raising children.

Definitions and opinions of the proper functions of marriage continue to change. The women's rights movement also has changed our ideas of marriage and its legal structure. Marriage will remain, but the role it serves in society will continue to change.

Who May Legally Marry?

In general, any man and woman who are unmarried, over the age of 18, and not closely related by blood to each other may marry. Each state has laws setting the requirements for age, health, and the degree of blood relationship. Some states do not allow people related by marriage to marry each other. Marrying a very close relative (a brother, sister, mother, father, or first cousin) is usually illegal. No state allows a person to marry someone of the same sex. A person also may not marry if he or she already has a spouse. Someone doing this has committed bigamy, which is usually a crime.

Breaking Engagements

Q. What if one person decides to cancel a planned marriage?

A. The law probably would force him or her to return gifts received because of the expected marriage. This includes engagement rings and other gifts between would-be spouses. It also includes shower gifts and wedding presents. However, either person may keep *gifts of pursuit* (those given while courting but before the couple agreed to marry).

Years ago a jilted would-be spouse could sue for "breach of promise" to marry. Many states have abolished or limited this action. Most people think society should not encourage couples to marry when they have serious doubts.

Getting Married

Q. How does one get married?

A. The traditional way to marry is to get a marriage license from a state-authorized official and have a formal wedding ceremony, civil or religious. This creates a *ceremonial marriage*. In 37 states, it is the only way to get married. In the other 13 states and the District of Columbia, a couple also may wed by common law without a ceremony.

Q. What does it take to get a marriage license?

A. One or both partners must apply for a marriage license from a state official and pay a fee. They may have to wait a few days to receive the license. There also may be a waiting period between obtaining the license and getting married.

In some states a couple must show proof of immunity or vaccination for rubella (German measles) or other diseases. Only two states—Illinois and Louisiana—ever required that couples planning to be married take a test for AIDS (acquired immune deficiency syndrome). Both states quickly repealed that law. A few states demand a general physical examination. Many states require a blood test for venereal disease before issuing a marriage license. Some states do not require this test if the couple has lived as man and wife.

If the test shows that a would-be spouse has a venereal disease, certain states may not give the couple a marriage license. Other states will allow the marriage if the couple knows that the test showed the presence of the disease.

Q. What kind of marriage ceremony is necessary?

A. First, a couple must present the marriage license to someone allowed to perform marriages in their state. This person usually is a public official or member of the clergy. The couple must then go through a civil or religious ceremony that follows the state laws. At the very least, the couple must say, before the authorized person and sometimes a witness, that they agree to marry each other. The couple may determine the rest of the ceremony, which may include religious rites.

(continued)

Age Requirements for Marriage

State	Age with parental consent		Age without parental consent	
	Male	Female	Male	Female
Alabama*	14 (a)	14 (a)	18	18
Alaska	16 (l)	16 (l)	18	18
Arizona	16 (l)	16 (l)	18	18
Arkansas	17 (c)	16 (c)	18	18
California	(b)	(b)	18	18
Colorado*	16 (l)	16 (l)	18	18
Connecticut	16 (l)	16 (l)	18	18
Delaware	18 (c)	16 (c)	18	18
District of Columbia*	16 (a)	16 (a)	18	18
Florida	16 (a)(c)	16 (a)(c)	18	18
Georgia*	(b)	(b)	16	16
Hawaii	16 (d)	16 (d)	18	18
Idaho*	16 (l)	16 (l)	18	18
Illinois	16	16	18	18
Indiana	17 (c)	17 (c)	18	18
Iowa*	18 (l)	18 (l)	18	18
Kansas* (j)	18 (l)	18 (l)	18	18
Kentucky	18 (c)(l)	18 (c)(l)	18	18
Louisiana	18 (l)	18 (l)	18	18
Maine	16 (l)	16 (l)	18	18
Maryland	16 (c)(e)	16 (c)(e)	18	18
Massachusetts	18 (d)	18 (d)	18	18
Michigan	16 (c)(d)	16 (c)	18	18
Minnesota	16 (l)	16 (l)	18	18
Mississippi	17	15	21	21
Missouri	15 (d) 18 (l)	15 (d) 18 (l)	18	18
Montana* (k)	16	16	18	18
Nebraska (k)	17	17	18	18
Nevada	16 (l)	16 (l)	18	18
New Hampshire	14 (g)	13 (g)	18	18
New Jersey	16 (c)(l)	16 (c)(l)	18	18
New Mexico (j)	16 (d)	16 (d)	18	18
New York	14 (g)	14 (g)	18	18
North Carolina	16 (c)(f)	16 (c)(f)	18	18
North Dakota	16	16	18	18
Ohio*	18 (c)(l)	16 (c)(l)	18	18
Oklahoma*	16 (c)	16 (c)	18	18
Oregon	17	17	18	18
Pennsylvania*	16 (d)	16 (d)	18	18
Puerto Rico	18 (c)(d) (l)	16 (c)(d) (l)	21	21
Rhode Island*	18 (d)	16 (d)	18	18
South Carolina*	16 (c)	14 (c)	18	18
South Dakota	16 (c)	16 (c)	18	18
Tennessee	16 (d)	16 (d)	18	18
Texas* (j)	14 (g)(h)	14 (g)(h)	18	18
Utah	14	14	18 (i)	18 (i)
Vermont	16 (l)	16 (l)	18	18
Virginia	16 (a)(c)	16 (a)(c)	18	18
Washington	17 (d)	17 (d)	18	18
West Virginia	18 (c)	18 (c)	18	18
Wisconsin	16	16	18	18
Wyoming	16 (d)	16 (d)	18	18

*Indicates 1987 common-law marriage recognized. For example, some states not marked with an asterisk once recognized common-law marriage but have changed their laws and no longer do so. In these states, common-law marriages that preceded the change in law would still be valid.

(a) Parental consent not required if minor was previously married.

(b) No age limits.

(c) Younger parties may obtain license in case of pregnancy or birth of child.

(d) Younger parties may obtain license in special circumstances.

(e) If parties are under 16 years of age, proof of age and the consent of parents in person is required. If a parent is ill, an affidavit by the incapacitated parent and a physician's affidavit to that effect required.

(f) Unless parties are 18 years of age or more, or female is pregnant, or applicants are the parents of a living child born out of wedlock.

(g) Parental consent and/or permission of judge required.

(h) Below age of consent parties need parental consent and permission of judge.

(i) Authorizes counties to provide for premarital counseling as a requisite to issuance of license to persons under 19 and persons previously divorced.

(j) Marriages by proxy are valid.

(k) Proxy marriages are valid under certain conditions.

(l) Younger parties may marry with parental consent and/or permission of judge. In Connecticut, judicial approval.

Source: Gary L. Skoloff, Skoloff & Wolfe, Livingston, New Jersey.

Q. When does a couple truly become married?

A. Most states consider a couple to be married when the ceremony ends. It is true that in some states the lack of sexual relations may allow a spouse to have the marriage annulled (see below). However, in most states this does not affect the validity of the marriage. In all states the proper official must record the marriage license. This acts as proof that the marriage happened.

Name Changes

Q. Does a woman's last name change when she gets married?

A. Only if she wants to change it. The common-law method for changing a name requires simply that a woman use the new name consistently and honestly. In the past, people thought that a woman's last name changed automatically when she married. Now society recognizes a woman's right to choose to change her name or to retain her maiden name.

A woman who marries but wishes to keep the name she used before the marriage should simply continue using that name. In most states a woman who wants to use her husband's last name or a combination of his and her names only has to start using the new name. The same is true of a man who wants to use his wife's last name or a name combining her and his names. If either spouse changes names, he or she should change the name on the driver's license, employment records, Social Security card, bank accounts, credit cards, and other pieces of identification. The spouse also should inform all interested persons.

In many states, people may change names at a time other than at marriage by the common-law method of consistent, honest use. For example, a woman may have used her husband's last name when she married, but now wants to use her old name or a new name. A few states require a court hearing for this change, but in other states, all she has to do is use her new name consistently. All states allow a person to go through a legal name change process.

Premarital Contracts

Q. May a couple define the terms of their marriage?

A. Yes, before they marry, many couples agree to *premarital contracts,* which also are called *prenuptial* or *antenuptial*

Common-Law Marriage

Thirteen states and the District of Columbia allow a common-law marriage to take the place of a ceremonial marriage. In these jurisdictions, a marriage is legal when a man and woman who are eligible to marry agree to be married. They also must hold themselves out to the public as husband and wife. There is a mistaken belief that common-law marriage requires seven years of living together. In fact, a couple probably becomes married from the moment they live as if they are husband and wife.

In states that recognize a legal common-law marriage, that type of marriage creates the same rights and duties as a ceremonial marriage. A legal common-law marriage may end only with a formal divorce. However, it is relatively easy for one partner to argue that the marriage never happened.

ADVANTAGES AND DISADVANTAGES OF PREMARITAL AGREEMENTS

A premarital agreement can help a couple predict and settle possible arguments in advance. Simply working out an agreement can improve communications between two people. It also can help define what they expect of each other. This can be useful even if the courts will not uphold the agreement. Premarital contracts can be helpful in making inheritance plans for children from a prior marriage. When combined with other estate planning, these contracts can help guarantee that children from a previous marriage will receive most of their parent's estate.

Some people argue that premarital agreements make it easier and less upsetting to arrange divorce settlements. When divorcing spouses cannot agree, a judge will decide how to divide property and who is

(continued)

contracts. In the past, courts would not uphold any premarital agreements about a spouse's obligations during marriage or in the event of a divorce. However, state courts sometimes upheld agreements that limited or canceled inheritance claims when one spouse died. Premarital contracts that decide how to divide property after a death became an accepted way to protect the interests of children of first marriages when a parent remarried. Today, many courts uphold certain parts of premarital contracts dealing with divorce. However, such agreements normally must be in written form. Courts rarely uphold an oral agreement.

Prenuptial agreements are not allowed to go against public policy. For example, they may not provide that spouses exchange money or property for sex. Premarital agreements also may not promote a sham marriage—a marriage in name only.

Do not sign any legal document unless you completely understand the terms. Read a premarital agreement carefully and show it to an attorney or financial expert before signing it. No one should be pressured to sign a contract. Courts will usually uphold premarital contracts that were agreed to without the use of force, fraud, or threats.

Q. What kinds of premarital contracts will the courts uphold?

A. Rules differ among the states. Generally, courts will uphold contracts that divide property during a divorce if the couple bargained fairly and if the agreement included *conscionable* conditions. "Conscionable" means that the conditions were fair and reasonable and they did not give one person a much better deal than the other. Some states also require that a property agreement still be fair and reasonable when it is time for the court to decide whether to enforce it. For example, an agreement may have been fair and reasonable when the couple made it, but it may be very unfair five years later. Perhaps the couple's financial state has changed significantly.

Twenty-five years ago, no state upheld a premarital agreement that limited or canceled financial support for a divorced spouse. Many states will now uphold these contracts. In these states, the courts may require that the terms were fair both at the time the couple made the agreement and when the marriage ends. Most courts will refuse to uphold a contract that denies support if, in doing so it would make a spouse eligible for welfare.

The law does not allow premarital agreements to control child custody. Parents may not take away a court's power to decide what is best for the child of divorced parents. Courts also will not uphold an agreement about child support if it reduces a child's right to parental support. Courts might, however, uphold an agreement that provides for more, not less, financial support than the state's child-support guidelines require. (The later "Child Support" section discusses these guidelines in greater detail.)

Courts may uphold provisions of a premarital contract that say who owns what during the marriage. These terms may be used to determine who owns certain funds or assets at the time of a divorce. However, conditions about personal behavior and duties during the marriage, such as who will wash the dishes, will not be enforced by the courts.

Q. What determines whether a couple bargained fairly while writing a premarital agreement?

A. Courts want proof that the agreement was voluntary and made without threats. Some courts say that couples must tell each other how much money and property they own before they can make any enforceable agreement. Timing also may be important. Although some courts have upheld agreements made right before a wedding, it is better to sign an agreement days, weeks, or even months before the ceremony. This makes it less likely that one person pressured the other into signing. A few states require each person to have a lawyer. Even when a state does not require a lawyer, the contract is more likely to be upheld if each party was represented by a lawyer.

Duties of Marriage

Q. What are the duties of a husband and wife?

A. Marriage used to be thought of as a "two-way street," with the husband supporting his wife financially and the wife maintaining the home.

As society changes, so does the law. Today, the wife may be the breadwinner and the husband may be the homemaker. Both spouses often work outside the home. The law makes no assumptions about gender-based roles in marriage. Of course, couples may still choose traditional marriage roles if they wish.

No matter what moral duties one spouse feels he or she owes the other, the courts enforce few legal duties. Each spouse does owe the other financial support, however. As noted above, both spouses may help support the family. However, they may agree that one will maintain the home and raise the children in return for the other's financial support. If so, the spouse providing support must follow their agreement.

(continued)

responsible for financial support. A premarital agreement can reduce financial uncertainties.

On the other hand, some people believe that a premarital agreement may harm one of the divorcing spouses. In some cases, for example, a judge might have awarded the person more than the agreement provides. When people marry, they may not understand the potential financial effects of a divorce many years later. Even if they are realistic, unexpected changes in the law or their circumstances may occur.

Nearly everyone believes that two persons getting married should trust each other. To some people, a premarital contract may reflect a lack of trust. Prenuptial agreements are not very romantic. Finally, it is uncertain whether courts will uphold a contract if the parties' situation differs greatly from the time when the couple made the agreement.

Q. How much financial support do spouses owe each other?

A. In the past, the law required husbands to support their wives. In those days, judges usually allowed husbands to set their families' standard of living. Today, if one spouse is in need, the other must supply such basics as food, shelter, and medical and dental care. However, the husband or wife providing the support may still decide how to meet the family's needs.

When the law used to require that husbands support their wives, courts allowed a wife to use her husband's credit to buy "necessaries." These usually included basic food, clothing, shelter, and medical care. The courts then required the husband to pay the bills. In some states this limited right to use a spouse's credit still exists. These states offer the right to either dependent spouse, male or female.

Invalid Marriages

Q. What if someone thinks he or she has a genuine marriage but it turns out to be false?

A. Sometimes people who live as a married couple learn that their marriage is not legal. For example, one "spouse" may have kept a prior marriage secret. Or both may have falsely believed that a divorce or the death of a spouse had ended an earlier marriage. Or the marriage may be between close relatives, underage persons, or incompetent people. In a few states the *putative* (supposed) *spouse doctrine* offers some protection if the parties went through a ceremonial marriage. A putative spouse may be entitled to the benefits and rights of a legal spouse if, when the putative spouse got married, he or she did not know there was a barrier to the marriage.

In states that reject this doctrine, people who wrongly believe they are married have the same legal status as unmarried couples who live together.

People often discover that their marriage is invalid only when filing for divorce. After a long marriage that a couple believed was valid, a court may refuse to declare the marriage invalid. If so, a divorce is required to end the marriage.

Q. What other legal rules affect invalid marriages?

A. Sometimes the law treats an invalid marriage as valid if one person tricked the other into thinking they are married. If so, a court might not allow the deceiver to declare the marriage invalid. In legal terms, the court *estops* the deceiver from denying that the marriage exists. A court may find that the

Must Both Spouses Work?

The law does not require both spouses to work. Some couples prefer one spouse to earn income and the other to maintain the home. The law no longer assumes that the breadwinner will be male and the homemaker will be female. Also, the courts understand that both spouses may choose to work outside the home.

After a divorce, more courts now expect the "dependent spouse" to become self-supporting in a few years. Two exceptions to this are if the marriage was a long one or if the dependent spouse is disabled. A disabled dependent spouse may have a right to support until he or she dies or is no longer disabled.

doctrine of *laches* (long delay) prevents even the innocent party who originally did not know about the invalid marriage from declaring it invalid.

Another rule sometimes results in treating a technically invalid marriage as valid. This rule is the presumption of the validity of the latest marriage. In other words, if a person married twice, the law assumes the second marriage occurred after a divorce or annulment ended the first. Therefore the person who claims that the second marriage was illegal must *prove* that the first marriage did not end. Because it is difficult to prove the nontermination of the prior marriage, the later marriage usually is upheld.

Living Together Outside of Marriage

Q. What if a couple lives together and chooses not to marry?

A. Some people prefer to live together without marrying. People are starting to treat these relationships as similar to marriages in importance and commitment. This is having serious effects on both society and marriage. It is also causing the law to change. In some states, living together places legal duties on the *nonmarital partners*. The laws governing nonmarital partners, like those for married partners, are changing.

Q. What legal problems may persons who live together experience?

A. For unmarried persons who live together, insurance may be more expensive or harder to find. It also may be more difficult for them to obtain credit, jobs, or housing. In some states, unwed couples risk the right to retain custody of children from a previous marriage or to receive alimony or other payments from an ex-spouse. If one member of an unwed couple needs emergency medical care, a hospital might not consider the other member as "next of kin" who is permitted to give consent for treatment. In addition, an employer's health insurance will usually cover an employee's spouse but not a nonmarital partner.

Q. What duties do live-in couples have to each other?

A. Although the law in this area is evolving, nonmarital partners do have general legal duties toward one another. Most states permit unwed partners to enter into contracts between one another. Some states, such as Illinois, only uphold business

May an Unmarried Couple Live Together Legally?

Most states no longer consider it a crime to live together without being married. In a few states, it still is illegal for unmarried couples to live together. However, in these states, unwed couples may live together without fear of arrest as long as their behavior is not "open and notorious" or "lewd and lascivious."

contracts between nonmarital partners. Most states that allow nonbusiness contracts will uphold only *express contracts*.

In an express contract the couple specifies the terms of the agreement in an oral or written form. State laws differ about what makes a legal contract. Many states require a written contract. The only way to be reasonably sure the courts will uphold an express contract is to write the contract with the help of a lawyer.

Only a few states allow an *implied nonmarital contract*. This is an unwritten contract in which the couple never specified the terms. A court may find that an implied contract exists if a couple's behavior shows that they intended to make a contract. For example: Jane Doe and John Smith decide to live together. Jane leaves a good job in order to care for their home while John pursues a profitable career. After they live together for 15 years, John marries someone else. A court may find that Jane and John had an implied contract to share their resources. Since Jane left her job to be the homemaker and John supported her financially, their behavior suggested that a contract existed. A joint bank account, jointly owned property, or other combinations of resources also may imply a contract to share resources. As a result, the court may rule that John owes Jane part of the money he earned while they lived together.

Unwed partners also may have duties toward each other because of the theories of *equity*. These very old rules allow the courts to settle arguments according to general beliefs of fairness. For this very complex area, you should get the advice of a lawyer.

UNWED COUPLES AND FINANCIAL OBLIGATIONS

An unmarried couple can take some precautions to avoid financial responsibilities to each other. For example, they can avoid making any spoken or written promises about money or property, have separate incomes, and keep the money each earns in separate accounts. They should keep property separate, and they should incur and pay for debts separately. However, a couple may not want to live like that. If the couple wants to buy and own property together, they probably should consider entering into a written contract that states the financial duties they intend to accept and the ones they do not.

THE FINANCIAL SIDE

Property

Q. Which spouse owns what property in a marriage?

A. *Separate property* is property that each spouse owned before the marriage. It also is inheritances and gifts (except those between spouses) acquired during marriage. During the marriage, each spouse usually keeps control of his or her separate property. Each spouse may buy, sell, and borrow money on his or her separate property. This property includes personal effects or other property brought into the marriage. It also consists of profits, rents, or other income obtained from that property. In some community property states (see below) these profits may become marital property.

Property brought into the marriage does not always remain separate. It might be claimed by the other spouse or creditors. Or a couple might combine separate property with property acquired during the marriage. Then the separate property may lose its identity and merge into the marital property. For example, the rent from one spouse's property might go into the couple's joint checking account. If they use this account to pay for the property's upkeep, the rent or even the property may become joint property. Once a spouse's separate property becomes merged, the other spouse may be able to claim part of it upon divorce.

Marital assets also might be used to improve separate property. This may give the other spouse an interest in that separate property. For example, a couple might use their joint checking account to fix up a vacation house left to one of them by a deceased relative. In some states, both spouses may be able to claim that they own the house. In other states, the spouse who did not inherit the property may not get an interest in it. However, that spouse may be able to get back his or her portion of the joint funds spent on the property.

A spouse also might choose to give up control and ownership of separate property. Placing money in a jointly held bank account may create the belief that the money belongs to both partners. Depending on the bank's rules, one spouse might then be able to take this money without the other's approval. Either spouse's creditors may be able to reach this money.

If a couple uses separate money to pay family expenses, the law treats the money as a "gift" to the family. The law does not entitle the spouse donating the money to be repaid without a written agreement or other strong evidence that it was a loan, not a gift.

Q. May a couple own property together?

A. Yes. In community property states this occurs automatically. Eight states—Arizona, California, Idaho, Louisiana, Nevada, New Mexico, Texas, and Washington, as well as Puerto Rico—use the community property system. These jurisdictions hold that each spouse shares equally the income earned and property acquired during a marriage. This is true even if one spouse supplied all the income. Wisconsin laws that took effect in 1986 also treat such income and property as jointly owned. In the other states, spouses probably share property under one of the following three forms of co-ownership:

- *Joint tenancy* exists when two or more people own property that includes a *right of survivorship*. In joint tenancy, each person has an interest in the whole property. This means that each person has the right to possess the property. If one partner dies, the survivor keeps his or her interest in the whole property. Because one spouse died, the

Divorces and Separate Property

During a divorce, courts in some states have the authority to divide separate property. Courts in these states may award part of one spouse's separate property to the other when dividing the marital property. This also may be done to provide support for the minor children.

survivor becomes the sole owner. This is the right of survivorship. Since the survivor keeps his or her prior interest in the property, the law does not probate the property. (Probate is a court procedure that distributes the property of a person who has died.) Any two people—not just spouses—may own property as joint tenants. A creditor may claim the debtor's interest in joint tenancy property.

- *Tenancy by the entirety* is a type of co-ownership of property by a husband and wife. Like joint tenancy, it includes a right of survivorship. Only some states allow a tenancy by the entirety.

  Tenancy by the entirety has features not available to joint tenants. In a tenancy by the entirety, a creditor of one spouse may not "attach" (seize) the property. Each party in tenancy by the entirety usually must consent to the sale of the property. Divorce may result in a partition of the property. Upon the death of one spouse, the property belongs solely to the survivor.
- *Tenancy in common* exists whenever two or more people own property "in common." In a tenancy in common, each person has control over his or her share of the property. Tenancy in common also allows the tenants to own unequal shares. The law does not limit tenancy in common to spouses.

  Tenancy in common has no right of survivorship. When one spouse dies, that spouse's share passes to the heirs, either by will or *intestate succession* (without a will).

Tenancy rules vary from one state to another. Some tenancies are complex and must be created in a precise manner. Otherwise the courts may not enforce them.

Debts

Q. Am I responsible for the debts my spouse brought into the marriage?

A. Not in most states. In states that do not recognize community property, such debts belong to the spouse who incurred those debts. In community property states, a spouse may, under special circumstances, become liable for the other spouse's premarital debts. The money that both spouses earn after marriage also may be applied toward the payment of a spouse's premarital debts. If someone plans to marry a person who owes a lot of money, both people should explore their options. This may include coming up with a long-term plan to pay off the debt. Or it may include premarital bankruptcy or employing other legal procedures to protect separate property from the future spouse's creditors. (For further information, see the "Consumer Credit" chapter.)

Q. May spouses incur debts for each other?

A. Not in most states. In states that do not recognize community property, simply marrying someone usually does not give one spouse the right to burden the other with debts. If one spouse incurs a debt, even under the other spouse's name, the other spouse does not automatically have to pay it. (In community property states, however, both spouses are responsible for debts incurred during marriage.)

However, there are exceptions. For instance, Spouse A may benefit from property or services bought by Spouse B. This may require Spouse A to pay for part of it. If one spouse bought a car but both use it, both may be liable for car payments. Another exception involves *necessaries,* which are food, clothing, shelter, or medical care required for a person's health, safety, and welfare. Marriage brings with it a duty to support the other spouse. If a spouse does not provide support, the other spouse will buy necessities. The law will then require the nonsupporting spouse to pay for them. The couple's standard of living may decide what is a *necessary*.

A spouse also may incur debts in the other's name. For example, if a wife gives her credit card to her husband, she must pay the bills incurred with that credit card. If one spouse pays the other's bills with a specific company on a regular basis, he or she may be forced to continue paying them. To take another example, Spouse A uses Spouse B's property as security for a debt. If Spouse A does not pay back this debt, that property may be taken by the creditor. Finally, if spouses share a credit account, both are responsible for the full debt on that account.

Ending Liability for a Spouse's Debts

It is hard to stop being responsible for a spouse's debts. This is especially true in community property states. In some cases, only a divorce or court order will relieve a spouse of an obligation for debts incurred before the date of separation. After the date of separation, in some states, a spouse may not be liable for the other spouse's necessaries. (It is wise to have a court order establish the separation date. A later section in this chapter discusses this topic further.)

In other states one spouse may be able to stop being responsible for future debts incurred by the other spouse. This requires notifying the merchants or credit card companies, and it does not always work.

Equal Credit Laws

Q. What is the Equal Credit Opportunity Act?

A. Until the 1970s, a wife often "lost" her separate credit rating if her husband died or they got a divorce. She learned that they shared one credit rating, which belonged to her husband. This loss of credit often had disastrous results. A federal law—the Equal Credit Opportunity Act (ECOA)—has solved most of this problem. The law forbids discrimination because of race, color, religion, national origin, sex, age, or marital status when a person applies for credit.

Under the ECOA, a bank or other creditor is not permitted to discourage a spouse from applying for a loan or refuse a loan if the spouse qualifies. In addition, a creditor's terms may not change because of a person's marital status. The law usually does not allow a creditor to ask about marital status when a person applies for an individual, unsecured account.

Examples of this type of account include a bank credit card or overdraft-protected checking account. One exception to this is if the applicant lives in a community property state. Another exception is if the applicant uses property in a community property state as security for the credit.

Q. May a company refuse credit to a woman because she plans to have children?

A. Under the ECOA, a woman may not be asked about birth-control practices or childbearing plans. A creditor is not permitted to reduce her income (and eligibility) for a loan by assuming that because she is a married woman she will have children. On the other hand, a creditor is allowed to ask about children she already has in order to estimate her expenses.

How a Wife May Establish a Separate Credit Rating

A wife should keep a line of credit in a name other than her husband's. This may be her first name and her husband's last name (Mrs. Mary Doe) or any other name except her husband's first name and surname (Mrs. John Doe). The important point is that the credit is "in her name."

Q. Does a woman have to use titles such as "Mrs." or "Ms." on her charge cards or other credit documents?

A. No. Under the ECOA, such titles are unnecessary. Women, married or not, do not have to use a courtesy title.

Q. May a bank refuse to consider a spouse's part-time income?

A. No. Under the ECOA, a creditor must consider a spouse's income when a married couple applies for a loan. This is true even if the spouse only has a part-time job.

Q. May a creditor insist that a wife use her husband's last name on her account?

A. No. A creditor may not refuse to open or maintain an account in the wife's first name and: (1) her maiden name; (2) her husband's last name; or (3) a combined name.

Q. If a married woman applies for a loan, may a creditor ask for information about her husband or insist that he cosign for the loan?

A. A creditor is not permitted to require a cosigner just because a woman is married. The creditor is allowed to require a cosigner when both spouses have vested rights in the security for a loan. An example would be when both spouses use stock that they both own as collateral for the loan.

A creditor is allowed to ask for information about a woman's husband if she uses his income to secure the loan.

This also is true if he will use the account or be liable for it. The creditor is allowed to ask about the husband's record if they live in a community property state or use property in such a state to secure the loan.

Q. May creditors ask a widowed or divorced woman to reapply for credit?

A. If a woman becomes widowed or divorced, a creditor is not allowed to require her to reapply for credit for that reason alone. However, if a widowed or divorced woman used her husband's income to apply for credit, a creditor is permitted to ask her to reapply. In these circumstances, a creditor also is allowed to change the terms of her account or close it. A creditor may not automatically alter or cancel her credit after a divorce or her husband's death unless her ability to pay changes. If she did not use her husband's income to apply for credit, the creditors may not change her credit unless she cannot or will not pay the debt.

Q. If a couple has joint credit, will a credit bureau furnish information on the wife in her name or her husband's?

A. Creditors must supply information in both names to credit bureaus and other creditors about any account used by both spouses or for which both are liable.

Q. If a couple has joint credit, but one spouse wants to establish separate credit, will a creditor consider their shared credit history?

A. Yes, if the creditor looks at credit history, the creditor must consider the history of any joint account. The creditor also must consider facts supplied by the applicant showing that a good history on the spouse's account accurately reflects the applicant's credit history. If the joint account has a bad history, a creditor must consider facts supplied by the applicant showing that the account does not reflect the applicant's credit history accurately.

Taxes

Q. Which spouse is responsible for paying taxes?

A. If each name appears on a state or federal personal income tax return, both parties signing the return are liable for the

Treatment of Married and Single People by Creditors

May a creditor ever treat married people and single people differently? Yes. A creditor may consider the differences in property rights between married people and single people. A person's marital status may have a lot to do with how much he or she owes or owns. It is illegal, however, to base a decision to offer or deny credit *only* on marital status.

taxes. If a couple files jointly, the Internal Revenue Service (IRS) holds each one responsible for the entire debt.

Q. Will getting married reduce a couple's income taxes?

A. Many people believe that to be true. Only an accountant, tax attorney, or other specialist can determine this based on a couple's specific financial situation.

Q. May I make a tax-free gift to my spouse?

A. A person may give his or her spouse any amount of money without paying federal gift taxes if the spouse is a U.S. resident. However, it must be an outright gift or set up as a proper trust (discussed later in this chapter). Most, but not all, state laws do away with taxes on gifts between spouses.

Doing Business Together

Q. Will problems arise if I go into business with my spouse?

A. Today husbands and wives may go into business together much more easily than ever before. However, this causes problems that rarely occur when a spouse is not involved. Part of the problem is that spouses have a unique relationship in the law that requires them to deal honestly and fairly with each other. A person should obtain expert advice before going into any major business with a spouse.

Q. May I allow my spouse to use my property to secure a loan?

A. Yes. A creditor, however, may claim the property if your spouse does not pay the debt. This is true even if you and your spouse get a divorce later.

Q. May I invest in my spouse's business?

A. Yes, but if you are thinking about doing this, you need expert advice, just as you would for investing with someone other than your spouse.

Q. Am I allowed to earn wages while working in my spouse's business?

Using Divorce to Reduce Taxes

Married couples should not use divorce to avoid taxes. In one case, both spouses earned large incomes. Together they paid much more than they would have paid filing separately. So they flew to the Virgin Islands, divorced before December 31, filed as single people, and then remarried the next month. They did this twice. Finally, the IRS objected that their divorce was a sham designed to avoid paying taxes. The tax court determined that their divorce was not recognized in their place of residence and so was not valid. The court made them pay the tax they would have paid had they filed jointly, as well as interest and penalties.

A. Most states allow spouses to pay each other wages. If spouses argue about those wages, however, there may be trouble collecting them.

Q. Does an employee have to pay taxes on money earned when working for a spouse?

A. Yes. If an employee earns wages for working in a spouse's business, those wages are taxable. The law also treats the wages as income to determine whether the employee qualifies for an Individual Retirement Account (IRA).

Q. Does that mean the spouse who stays home has to pay taxes on the support received for doing housework and child care?

A. No. The IRS does not consider homemaking and in-home child care as wage-earning activities. This is true even though the spouse receives financial support for doing those tasks. However, if the spouse does housework or child care for anyone else, the IRS considers the money to be taxable wages.

Bankruptcy

Q. What is bankruptcy?

A. *Bankruptcy* provides relief for people who have more debts than they can pay. When a debtor files for *straight bankruptcy,* a court administers a plan to divide the debtor's property (minus certain exemptions) and money among the creditors. By filing for bankruptcy, people may use federal law to discharge (cancel) their debts. Bankruptcy, however, does not discharge obligations such as taxes, alimony, and child support.

As an alternative, federal law also offers *Chapter 13 bankruptcy*. Sometimes this is called *wage earner's bankruptcy*. This allows debtors to keep their property. However, the court sets up a plan for the debtor to repay creditors over a period of time. Chapter 13 bankruptcy may be used only by people who have regular incomes. (See the "Bankruptcy" chapter for further details.)

Q. May a couple file for bankruptcy together?

A. Yes. The Bankruptcy Reform Act of 1978 allows spouses to file for bankruptcy jointly.

Q. If I want to file for bankruptcy, should my spouse also file?

A. If a couple has no joint debts and does not own any property together, there may be no reason for both to file. The more debts and property held jointly, however, the more likely the couple should file together.

Q. If I file for bankruptcy after a divorce, can it affect my ex-spouse?

A. Yes. By law, bankruptcy does not discharge alimony and child support. However, many other debts are discharged by bankruptcy. Consider the case of a court ordering an ex-spouse to pay for debts incurred jointly during the marriage or to make property settlement payments after a divorce. A bankruptcy may discharge these obligations. The other ex-spouse then would become responsible for paying the creditors. He or she also would lose the property settlement payments. A former spouse's bankruptcy can have serious consequences.

Saving Your Assets by Giving Them to Your Spouse

In general, debtors may not give all their property to their spouses, and then file for bankruptcy. The bankruptcy court probably would reject this as a *fraudulent conveyance*. A creditor or bankruptcy trustee would try to show that the debtor gave away the property to prevent it from being divided among creditors. The court probably would rule that the spouse was only holding the property in trust for the bankrupt spouse. The court then would order the spouse to return the property to a court trustee for division among the creditors.

Pensions and Retirement

Q. Must a working spouse provide a pension for a dependent spouse?

A. No. The law does not force one spouse to provide a pension for the other. Most spouses plan for their retirement with a financial plan. They also provide for each other after death through estate planning. During a divorce, the court divides the marriage property according to state law. The court probably will treat the working spouse's pension and retirement money as part of the marriage property. The court then will divide it between the parties. (For more information, see the chapter entitled "The Rights of Older Americans.")

Q. If only one spouse will receive a pension, how may a married couple be sure that the pension will continue if the spouse receiving it dies?

A. It often depends on whether the spouse has vested pension rights. If the pensioner dies without vested pension rights, the surviving spouse probably will receive nothing. If the pensioner dies after the pension rights become vested, under the Employee Retirement Income Security Act (ERISA), the spouse qualifies for one half of the pension if:

(1) The couple were married for a full year before the pensioner started getting the pension, or they were married a full year before the recipient died; and
(2) The surviving spouse had the right to receive benefits from the recipient's pension.

Q. How much money will a surviving spouse receive from a pensioner's plan after the pensioner dies?

A. The survivor should qualify for at least one half of the benefits the deceased spouse received while alive. This is true only if ERISA governs their pension plan (which it usually does) and if the couple meets the above requirements. Some plans pay more, but that is unusual.

Q. May I receive Social Security benefits as a result of my spouse's disability?

A. Yes. If the spouse of a disabled person meets the requirements for Social Security retirement benefits, he or she also may qualify for disability benefits. A local Social Security Administration office will supply the details for disability benefits and any other benefits.

Q. May a divorced spouse receive retirement benefits from Social Security based on the former spouse's work record?

A. Yes. The nonworking divorced person may qualify for some Social Security benefits from a former spouse. The former spouse must be at least 62 years old; the marriage must have lasted for ten years or more; and the spouse must be unmarried when applying for benefits.

Q. If a spouse dies, will the survivor qualify for Social Security survivor's benefits based on the deceased spouse's earnings?

A. Widows and widowers will get survivor's benefits from Social Security if the following conditions are met:
- Social Security fully insured the spouse at the time of the spouse's death;
- The survivor meets the age requirement;
- The survivor is not married now or has remarried after age 60; and
- The marriage between the survivor and the deceased lasted for at least nine months. There are several exceptions and alternatives to this provision.

Social Security and Your Spouse's Earnings

You may receive Social Security benefits based on your spouse's earnings. However, it will depend on your situation. These benefits may be added to those you receive based on your own work record.

Until recently, a husband who wanted to receive Social Security benefits based on his wife's earnings had to prove that he depended on her support. However, now men or women may receive benefits based on either their spouse's or their own earnings, whichever is larger. (For more information on Social Security benefits, see the chapter entitled "The Rights of Older Americans.")

Younger widows and widowers (under age 60) will get insurance benefits as a parent if the deceased was fully insured under Social Security, and the survivor is caring for the child of the deceased.

Q. May I provide for my own retirement?

A. Yes, but you may not receive any immediate tax relief by doing so. Under the 1981 Economic Recovery Tax Act, anyone with earned income qualified for an Individual Retirement Account (IRA). People funding an IRA did not have to pay tax on this money until they withdrew it after age 59½ or became disabled. Congress later changed the tax laws for IRAs. People may still fund IRAs for their retirement, but contributions to an IRA are not always tax-free. Contact a tax adviser for details. A tax adviser also will be able to advise you on other ways to provide for your retirement. (For additional information on this topic, see the chapters entitled "The Rights of Older Americans" and "Wills, Trusts, and Estate Planning.")

Estate Planning

Q. Should each spouse have a will?

A. Yes. Each person should have a will. It lets each person say how his or her estate will be distributed after death. Without a will, state law decides how to distribute an estate, which may not be what the deceased would have wanted. A later section in this chapter discusses the distribution of property when a spouse dies. (For further details, also see the "Wills, Trusts, and Estate Planning" chapter.)

Q. What if the state law would distribute my estate the way I want?

A. It still is a good idea to have a will. The lack of a will may delay the inheritance for heirs. It also is not certain whom the court will appoint to manage the estate. A carefully drawn will can save the estate (and thus its heirs) money that normally would go to administrative costs. In addition, a carefully drawn will can help avoid or reduce taxes. State laws also might change, and the deceased might own property in another state where the laws are not the same.

If both spouses die without a will and the couple has minor children, the court will appoint a guardian for them. With a will, the couple names a guardian (as long as the court

Using a Lawyer for Writing a Will and Estate Planning

Estate planning and writing a will can be very complex. Most people should not try to do these tasks on their own. It is wise to have a lawyer's help in planning an estate and writing a will. Otherwise the estate may have to pay unnecessary taxes and administrative expenses. If an estate is not very big, having an attorney write a will should not be very expensive.

approves the choice). Without a will, however, the court must make that decision without the guidance of the parents' wishes. If only one spouse dies, and the court appoints the other spouse (or someone else) guardian of the children's inheritances, the court might keep control over the money. This can mean a lot of aggravation. The guardian will have to keep detailed records proving that he or she used all the money for the children's benefit. Sometimes the guardian will have to get the court's prior permission to use the money. Much of this may be avoided with a properly written will.

Q. When should I make a will?

A. You should make a will when you are in good health and not under unusual emotional stress. Waiting and making a "deathbed" will costs more, and it might lead to a long, expensive lawsuit among disputing relatives and potential heirs.

Q. Once a will is made, does it ever have to be changed?

A. A will should be reviewed regularly to decide whether changes in any laws (such as tax law) could affect it. You also should determine if a change in your estate could affect how you distribute it. The family situation also may have changed in a way that would affect the will. People often fail to update their wills to reflect the births of children or grandchildren and even divorce. Failure to reflect these changes can lead to needless and costly lawsuits.

CHILDREN

The Decision to Have Children

Q. Do couples have a right to know about birth-control methods and a right to use them?

A. Yes. Married couples have a right to obtain information about contraceptives and a right to use contraceptives.

Q. Does a woman need her husband's permission to use birth control?

A. No. A woman has the right to control her own body, which includes the right to use birth control. However, if one spouse

Unmarried Couples and Estate Plans

Unwed live-in couples may use wills to leave certain portions of their property to their partner or another person. They should, however, design an estate plan carefully. The law does not protect an unwed couple's property rights the same way it does the rights of married people. For example, the law gives a spouse an automatic share in the marital estate. One spouse's will may not deprive the other of this share. The same, however, is not true for unmarried couples. Unwed couples have no right by law to each other's assets. This means it is even more important for each party in an unmarried couple to express his or her wishes in a will.

wants children and the other spouse refuses, this may show incompatibility and be grounds for divorce. If either spouse failed to disclose his or her reluctance to have children before the marriage, knowing that the other spouse wanted children, that might constitute fraud in some states. The marriage would be subject to annulment.

Abortion

Q. Does a woman have a right to an abortion?

A. Yes. The Supreme Court ruled in 1973 that in the first three months of pregnancy the decision of whether to abort depends on the woman and her doctor. In the second three months, states may regulate the abortion method, but not prohibit it. A woman has no right to an abortion in the final three months of pregnancy unless her life or health is in danger. The Supreme Court has recently upheld some restrictions on abortions and is still considering cases. Therefore, it is possible that the facts in this section will change.

Minors and Abortions

Many people want to know if a pregnant minor needs her parents' consent for an abortion. The U.S. Supreme Court has ruled against state laws giving parents of unmarried, underage girls the power to forbid their daughters' abortions. However, the Supreme Court has upheld a state law requiring a physician to "notify, if possible" the parents or guardian of an unwed minor before performing her abortion. Supreme Court cases awaiting decision may change the law in this area.

Q. Does a woman need her husband's consent to have an abortion?

A. No. A woman may decide whether to bear a child. States may not require a husband's consent. In cases involving hospitals receiving federal funds, courts have struck down hospital rules requiring the father's approval for abortions. Private hospitals not receiving federal funds may set their own rules about abortions.

Q. May public funds pay for abortions that are not necessary for health reasons?

A. The Supreme Court has ruled that this decision is up to the states and localities. They may choose to fund such abortions. However, they will not violate the Constitution if they choose not to do so.

Reproduction and Childbirth

Q. May a wife bear a child against her husband's wishes?

A. Yes. She has the right to decide whether or not to bear a child.

Q. Does the law regarding parentage vary depending on how the parents conceive the child?

A. It may depend on the method used to conceive the baby. The law automatically considers a child conceived by sexual intercourse as the legal offspring of his or her biological parents.

In recent years, however, science has created new ways to conceive children, including artificial insemination, *in vitro* fertilization, and egg donation. The law is changing to reflect these new methods. Most states make the husband who consents to his wife's conceiving by insemination with a donor's sperm the legal parent of that child.

Surrogate Parenthood

In this arrangement, a woman agrees, with or without payment, to bear a child for another couple. This usually occurs when the wife cannot conceive or carry a child to term. In nearly all cases, through artificial insemination, the husband's sperm fertilizes an egg belonging to either the wife or the surrogate mother. This makes the husband the biological father of the child. The surrogate mother agrees to give up all parental rights at birth. Then the wife of the biological father legally adopts the child. A few states outlaw this arrangement when the surrogate mother receives payment. Other states are considering laws that would restrict it.

Q. Does the law regulate where a woman may choose to give birth?

A. The law may limit her choice. For example, some states discourage having a baby at home, with or without a doctor. It may be hard to find a doctor willing to attend a home birth. A couple may face child abuse charges if their infant dies or receives injuries during home delivery. Insurance companies also may refuse to offer malpractice insurance to doctors when they attend home births. Many hospitals have "alternative birth" facilities. These provide a homelike atmosphere and quick access to medical services. Besides hospital-related birth facilities, midwives run maternity or birthing centers in some states.

Q. Does the law govern who may deliver a baby?

A. State laws on who may deliver babies in nonemergency situations vary widely. Only a medical doctor may attend a delivery in some states. In others, nurse-midwives or lay midwives may assist at a birth.

Most states license nurse-midwives, who usually work under the guidance of a medical doctor or in hospitals. Lay midwives deliver babies, but they are neither medical doctors nor nurses. They may face charges of practicing medicine without a license in states that do not permit lay midwives to attend births.

Q. May a husband be present at the birth of his child?

A. If the child is born in a hospital, the hospital will set its own rules. These must meet the requirements of state licensing boards. Expectant parents should check whether a hospital allows the father or siblings or both to be present at childbirth. If not, and if the parents strongly want the husband or siblings to be present, they may consider having the baby in another setting.

Paternity and Support

Q. What may a husband legally do if his wife bears a child that is not his?

A. The law presumes that a married woman's child is her husband's. He must support the child unless he can prove in court that he is not the father. Some states assume the husband is the father no matter what proof he presents. These states do not allow a husband to disprove paternity of a child born during the marriage.

Q. If state law permits the husband to disprove paternity, how may he attempt to do so?

A. State law determines the evidence that the husband may offer at a trial. For example, some state laws provide a husband with only two choices. They permit him to show either (1) that he is impotent or sterile or (2) that blood tests prove he cannot be the child's father.

Q. May an unmarried mother legally force the father of her baby to support the child?

A. In most states, the parents of a baby born out of wedlock have an equal duty to support the child. If the father admits paternity, the mother should have him sign a statement to that effect. Then it will be easier to force him later to help support the child, if necessary. If he does not admit being the father, she may file a paternity suit against him. If this civil action succeeds, the court will force him to provide support. Sometimes the court will require him to pay her pregnancy and childbirth expenses.

Q. How may an unmarried woman prove that a specific man is her child's father?

A. Evidence of paternity traditionally involved proof that the man had sexual intercourse with the woman near the time of conception. Other evidence included witnesses who would swear that the man had admitted that he was the child's father. Or evidence might have included letters that the man wrote to the child as his father.

PATERNITY AND MODERN SCIENCE

Paternity cases increasingly use scientific evidence. The blood tests used during much of this century were useful only up to a certain point. They relied on the man's and woman's blood types. Under the laws of genetics, the mother's and father's blood types limit the child to one of several blood types. Thus, this type of blood test might prove that a certain man could *not* be the child's father. However, it could not prove that he *was* the child's father. Any other male with the same blood type could have fathered the child.

(continued)

To disprove paternity, the man could try to prove that he was out of state for the period during which the couple might have conceived the child. He also could show that the woman had sex with other men near the time of conception.

However, traditional evidence is becoming less popular as new scientific tests are almost always conclusive. (See the accompanying text on "Paternity and Modern Science.")

Q. May anyone besides the mother file a paternity suit?

A. If the mother applies for public aid, the public agency often files a paternity suit to get reimbursed. Under the Uniform Parentage Act, any person may file a suit for the child. A third or more of the states have adopted this act.

Q. If a court decides that a man is a child's father, how much will he have to pay in support?

A. The law requires unwed parents to support their children the same as married parents. Child support guidelines in every state will determine the amount of support. (A later section in this chapter discusses levels of support.) The court often forces the father to pay the legal costs of paternity suits.

Q. How long will such support continue?

A. As with children born in wedlock, the duty of support usually lasts until the child is no longer a minor.

Q. What happens when a court decides a man is a child's father but he still does not provide support?

A. The court may withhold part of his wages and assign them to the child or garnish his wages. The latter automatically transfers the owed amount from his pay. The court also may attach his property or his bank account, or jail him for contempt of court. In some states, the failure of a man to support a nonmarital child is a criminal offense.

Adoption

Q. What is adoption?

A. It is the process by which people become the legal parents of someone who is not their biological child. A single person

(continued)

New tests are changing this. The Human Leucocyte Antigen (HLA) test matches blood type, tissue type, and other genetic factors. Medical experts claim it is 98-percent accurate in determining paternity. Another new tissue-testing procedure is DNA testing. Experts say it is even more accurate. It tests the DNA (genetic material) in cells from the skin or in samples of semen or blood. Experts believe this test is 99-percent accurate in determining paternity. If the results are uncertain, the older blood test and other traditional evidence may play a role.

also may adopt a child. There are three requirements for any adoption to be legal. First, the legal rights of the biological parents must have ended either by a court order or by the death of the parents. Second, the adopting parents must follow the proper adoption procedures for the specific state. Third, a judge must approve the adoption. If the child is ten or older (the age varies with state law), the youngster also may have to consent to the adoption.

Q. If a court order has not ended the biological parents' rights, must both agree to an adoption?

A. If the parents are married to each other and both are alive, they must consent to the adoption of their child. If the parents were not married to each other, the mother must consent. If the father is known, the father also may have to consent. An unwed father who has provided financial support and has had continuing contact with his child probably has the right to give or deny consent to the adoption. On the other hand, a father who has abandoned or neglected his child is entitled only to receive a notice of the adoption.

Adoption vs. Foster Care

Adoptive parents have the same legal rights and duties as biological parents. However, foster parents do not. They usually care for a child for only a limited period of time. Usually, the state that is caring for the child places the youngster with foster parents. The state pays them for the child's care. The child stays in the foster home until the state can arrange a more permanent relationship.

Q. What are the ways of adopting a child?

A. There are three types of adoption: agency, related, and independent (private). Every state permits *agency adoption.* In this type of adoption, a private or public agency has received authority to agree to the adoption of a child in its custody. This authority comes either from the biological parents or the state. The agency interviews potential parents and investigates to decide which applicants will best serve the child's needs. Each agency has its own procedures. Some states limit the fee an agency may charge. Other states leave that decision to the agency and the adoptive parents.

A *related adoption* is one in which relatives, such as grandparents or an aunt and uncle, adopt a child. Another form of related adoption is *stepparent adoption.* It occurs when someone married to the biological mother or father adopts the child. (If the stepparent does not adopt the child, the stepparent has very different legal duties to the child. A later section in this chapter discusses this topic.)

A middleman (such as a doctor or lawyer) who has some contact with the biological parents usually arranges an *independent (private) adoption.* The adopting parents often pay the biological mother's medical and legal expenses. Independent adoptions are illegal in some states.

Q. What criteria do states and agencies use to decide if would-be parents may adopt?

A. All agencies have standards to rate applicants. So do states that require an investigation of private adoptive parents. The best interests of the child form the basis for these standards. The state or agency will make sure the applicants are healthy. They also must be able to afford to care for the child. In addition, their home environment must be good for the child. The state or agency will consider their age, too. They must be mature enough to understand the duties of parenthood, but young enough to handle them.

Q. May single people adopt?

A. Yes. The laws of many states allow single persons to adopt.

Q. Are adoptive parents on probation?

A. Many states require a probationary period for nonrelated adoptions. It usually lasts for six months or one year. During this time, the child lives with the adoptive parents. A state-licensed agency or someone appointed by the court makes sure the family cares for the child properly. If the relationship is acceptable, the agency or the investigator will ask the court to make the adoption permanent. If it is not, the child will be returned to the agency so that the child may be placed in another adoptive home.

Q. Do parents of adopted children have different parental duties?

A. No. Parents have the same rights and duties toward their adopted children as they do to their biological children. The biological parents of an adopted child usually give up all rights of parenthood. In rare cases, a biological parent may have a duty to support the child even after an adoption. In a few states, an adopted child sometimes has a right to inherit from biological parents. However, biological parents have no right to inherit from a child given up for adoption. If the adoptive parents divorce, the law requires the adoptive parents—not the biological parents—to support the adopted child.

Rights and Responsibilities of Children

Q. What are the legal rights of children?

A. Children have a unique status under the law. This chapter cannot explain this special status fully. However, it can point

Black Market Adoptions

In some black market adoptions, the adopting parents pay a sum of money to the biological parent(s) or a middleman. This money is more than the normal costs of the pregnancy and adoption. The law treats this as the buying and selling of a child. Even if the adopting parents do not pay an excessive fee, an adoption is "black market" if it does not comply with state law. Engaging in a black market adoption is a crime in every state. The punishment varies from one state to another, but the laws in some states are getting tougher. In any case, the black market adoption would become void, and the child would become a ward of the state. The same holds true for international black market adoptions.

The Duties of Adult Children Toward Their Parents

Adult children normally have no responsibilities toward their parents. In return, their parents have no duties toward them. However, there are exceptions. In some states, children must support parents who otherwise would be on welfare. The children can avoid paying support if they can show that the parents did not care for them when they were underage. In some states, children may have to contribute to the support of parents in a state hospital or mental institution. However, the children's ability to pay—not the actual costs of the care—usually determines how much they must pay.

out a few of the major differences between the rights of adults and children.

The law defines children as unmarried persons under the age of majority who have not left home to support themselves. Most states set the age of majority at 18 years old. The law protects children from abuse and neglect. It also entitles them to the protection of the state. They may be removed from their home if it is necessary to ensure them a safe, supportive environment. This removal may be temporary or permanent.

The law allows children to make contracts with adults and have them enforced against adults. However, these contracts usually may not be enforced against the children if they are underage or have not left home to support themselves. This protects children from the results of their immature judgment. It means that adults and other children are normally very reluctant to make a contract with a minor. The law allows children to sue. However, an adult legal representative must begin the suit.

Under the law, children accused of committing crimes are subject to the juvenile courts of their state, not the regular criminal justice system. (In some states, children above a certain age—usually 16—may be tried in court as adults.) Juvenile courts entitle children to only some of the due process safeguards that adults receive. In return, these courts have more freedom to deal with juveniles. These courts assume that children are delinquents—not criminals. They also assume that, under the protection of the court, children can be rehabilitated.

Q. What duties do minor children have?

A. Minor children usually must obey parents and submit to reasonable supervision. A parent has the right to punish the child when necessary, but not to use excessive force.

Rights and Responsibilities of Parents

Q. What are the responsibilities of parents toward their children?

A. Parents have certain legal duties toward their children. Whether the parents remain married or not, they must support their minor children. Parents must provide adequate food, shelter, clothing, and medical care. They also must educate their children in a public or private school. Parents have a legal obligation to make sure their children attend school. (Some states allow home schooling.)

Child and Dependent Care Tax Credit

A tax credit for actual expenses incurred for child or dependent care is available to an employed person if the expenditures enable that person to be gainfully employed. The credit is computed at 30 percent for taxpayers with incomes of $10,000 or less, with the rate of the credit reduced one percentage point for each additional $2,000 of income above $10,000. When incomes are over $28,000, the credit is computed at 20 percent. The limits on expenses for which the credit may be taken are $2,400 for one dependent and $4,800 for two or more dependents. The chart below shows the amount of credit that may be taken at various income levels.

		Maximum Dollar Amount of Credit	
Family Income Before Taxes	**Percentage Tax Credit**	**One Dependent**	**Two or More Dependents**
Up to $10,000	30%	$720	$1,440
$10,001 to $12,000	29%	$696	$1,392
$12,001 to $14,000	28%	$672	$1,344
$14,001 to $16,000	27%	$648	$1,296
$16,001 to $18,000	26%	$624	$1,248
$18,001 to $20,000	25%	$600	$1,200
$20,001 to $22,000	24%	$576	$1,152
$22,001 to $24,000	23%	$552	$1,104
$24,001 to $26,000	22%	$528	$1,056
$26,001 to $28,000	21%	$504	$1,008
$28,001 and over	20%	$480	$960

Source: U.S. Department of Labor

Q. How long do parents' legal obligations to their children continue?

A. Parents are legally responsible for their children until they reach the age of majority (usually 18), marry, or have left home to support themselves. In some states, this duty may continue for the child's entire life if the child is disabled. In most states, parents' legal duty to children ends when one of three conditions occurs: (1) the child reaches the age of majority, (2) enters into a legal marriage, or (3) leaves home to become self-supporting.

Who Controls the Money Children Earn or Inherit?

Generally, parents do *not* have direct control over their children's money. If children earn or inherit money, that money must be used for their benefit. Some states require the appointment of a *guardian* under court supervision if a child has money. Unless a court appoints someone else, parents are the guardians of their children's money. The parents are legally responsible for managing it properly and using it for their children's needs.

Q. What are the rights of parents?

A. Parents have a right to direct the care, control, and upbringing of their children. This gives them the power to make various decisions. These include where to live, what school to attend, what religion to follow, and what medical treatment to obtain. Normally the state may not interfere in these decisions. Only in life-threatening or extreme situations will the courts step in to overrule parents. For example, when a child will die without the medical care the parents refuse to obtain, the courts may make the child a ward of the court and order that the care be provided. Parents have even been prosecuted for withholding medical treatment from seriously ill children. There may be certain medical procedures, however, that the law entitles "mature minors" to decide upon for themselves. Such minors may make their own decisions in these matters even if their parents disagree. For example, parents have no veto power over a minor's decision to use contraceptives or to get an abortion.

Parents also have the legal authority to control their children's behavior and social lives. Children have a duty to obey their parents' reasonable rules and commands.

Parents may punish their children appropriately. They may not, however, use cruel methods or excessive force. Child abuse and neglect laws in all states prohibit these forms of punishment.

Q. What if parents cannot control their children?

A. A legal recourse open to parents who cannot control their children is to ask the court to declare the children minors in need of supervision and subject to court authority. This usually is a last resort. Normally courts do not want to get involved in disputes between parents and children.

Q. Are parents responsible for their children's conduct?

A. The answer depends on state and local laws. Parents ordinarily are not responsible for their children's debts—except, perhaps, to the extent that they must provide necessities for their children. Some state laws, however, do make parents liable for their children's debts. If parents cosign a contract with minor children, they are legally responsible for making payments under the contract.

In some communities, parents are liable for damages their children cause if the children acted maliciously. Even in areas without these laws, parents are probably liable if they knew their children behaved illegally or caused damage, and the parents did not stop it. They also may be liable for damage done by children who were acting as their "agent." For example, their children may have been running an errand for them.

Parents also may be liable for damage caused by children if they negligently (carelessly) contributed to that damage (e.g., giving a child a dangerous toy).

Abuse and Neglect Laws

Q. What is child neglect?

A. State laws make it a criminal offense for parents and legal guardians to fail to meet children's basic needs, including food, shelter, clothes, medical treatment, and supervision.

Q. What is child abuse?

A. Special state criminal laws apply to adults who abuse children in their care. Such adults include parents, other adult family members, baby-sitters, and legal guardians. These laws make it a crime to go beyond reasonable physical punishment. For example, adults who beat children so severely that they require medical treatment have violated these laws. Child abuse laws involve other types of cruelty, such as sexual molestation, that endanger children's moral and mental health. The laws also cover emotional abuse, such as subjecting a child to extreme public humiliation.

Q. How are child neglect and abuse detected?

A. The law compels a wide range of people who have contact with children to report suspected child abuse. Such people include doctors, nurses, teachers, and social workers. The law encourages them to do so by granting them immunity from defamation suits by the accused parents. (An exception is if they made the report only to injure the accused.) States often encourage the reporting of suspected abuse through special hot lines. Some states keep central lists of suspected child abuse cases. This helps find parents who take their children to different hospitals so nobody will discover they have repeatedly abused their children.

Q. If the law takes children away from their parents, is the removal temporary or permanent?

A. The goal usually is to reunite the family after correcting the problems that led to the removal. However, this is not always

Taking Children Away from Their Parents

The state may remove children from the custody of their parents if there is reason to believe the parents are physically, sexually, or emotionally abusing the children. The state also may remove the children if the parents are unable or unwilling to provide adequate care, supervision, and support.

possible. For example, the parents may make little or no effort at improving the children's care. Then the state may ask a court to end all parental rights. If this happens, the legal bonds between parents and children are completely and permanently cut. Then another family may adopt the children.

CONDUCT TOWARD EACH OTHER

An early American jurist wrote, "Courts do not go behind the domestic curtain." In fact, a veil of privacy shrouds the family. Courts are unwilling to interfere in the relations between husbands and wives. They usually will step in only if the family is crumbling and there is a tear in the "domestic curtain." Nevertheless, some general statements can be made about the law regarding conduct between marriage partners.

Sexual Relations

Q. May one spouse deny sex to the other?

A. Courts have held that a spouse may not deny sexual relations without good cause, such as illness or abuse. Sexual relations are among the duties married people owe each other. In practice, however, a spouse can do little if the other spouse decides to end the sexual relationship. If a spouse was unable to have sex before the marriage and did not tell the other, the other spouse may be able to get the marriage annulled. If a spouse decides to stop having sex or becomes unable to have sex, the other spouse may have grounds for divorce in some states. In other states, the couple may obtain a divorce on "no fault" grounds. Although courts have held that sexual relations are a marital duty, the only legal remedy to a lack of sex is to end the marriage.

Although husbands and wives have a duty of sexual relations, it does *not* mean that one spouse may use violence to force the other to have sex. A discussion of rape in marriage appears later in this chapter.

Q. May one spouse require the other to engage in distasteful sexual acts?

A. Definitions of "distasteful" will naturally vary. The law does define some aberrant sexual acts as crimes. In practice, judicial discretion could play an important role. Judges tend to consider sexual relations to mean only penetration of the vagina by the penis. The court might not consider any other sex act—for example, oral or anal sex—as one of the sexual duties one spouse owes another.

Since courts rarely interfere in marriages, this is unlikely to be a legal issue. The court will get involved if the couple is dissolving the marriage or if one spouse is using violent physical force resulting in a legal action. Examples include a civil domestic violence action or the filing of criminal charges, such as for assault and battery.

Q. If someone makes a spouse incapable of having sex, may the other spouse sue the person responsible?

A. Yes. The law refers to this as *suing for loss of consortium.* Husbands and wives have the right to expect certain "services" from one another, including sexual services. Therefore, they have a right to sue someone who deprives them of those services. For example, if someone causes an accident that cripples a spouse, the other spouse may sue for loss of consortium. Meanwhile, the injured spouse may sue for medical expenses, suffering, and so on.

Spouse vs. Spouse

Q. How has the law governing the relationship between spouses changed?

A. The common law considered husbands and wives as one entity. As a result, they could not sue or testify against each other in court. Furthermore, a husband had a nearly unlimited right to control his wife and her property. However, a wife could file a criminal charge against a physically abusive husband.

The rules have changed in recent years. Courts now treat husbands and wives as separate but equal entities. And wives now have more remedies against abusive husbands.

Q. May one spouse sue the other for damages?

A. Generally, yes. *Interspousal immunity,* the doctrine that one spouse cannot commit a civil wrong against the other, is being modified. Most states allow a spouse to sue the other for intentional injury (for example, spouse abuse) or for an injury caused by negligence. This can be useful when, for example, one spouse wants to recover damages from the

Is Adultery Illegal?

Most states make it illegal for a married person to have sex with someone who is not his or her spouse. Some states also make it illegal for unmarried people to have sexual relations. The law refers to this crime as *fornication*. However, prosecutors rarely bring charges under these laws. The most serious legal result of an act of adultery is likely to be the end of a marriage. Adultery is a ground for divorce in some states. In other states a couple could obtain a divorce on "no-fault" grounds.

A sexual act cannot be adulterous unless it is voluntary. If a man rapes a woman, she has not committed adultery.

other's insurance company for injuries suffered in an automobile accident. Complete interspousal immunity still applies in a few states.

Q. If one spouse is in an accident while driving the other's car, who is financially liable?

A. In most states, the nondriving spouse has no liability. The car's owner may be liable in the few states that apply the *family car doctrine*. Under this doctrine, the owner is financially responsible for damage caused by a family member while driving the car. The car's owner must have allowed the car to be used as a family car, and certain other conditions must be met. In a few states, the owner may be liable if the driver was acting as the spouse's agent when the accident occurred. For example, the driver may have been running an errand for the nondriving spouse.

Testifying Against a Spouse in Court

One spouse may testify against the other in court if the spouse does so voluntarily. In most states one spouse may not be *forced* to testify against the other. Courts recognize the *marital testimonial privilege*. This rule is based on the belief that it would damage the marriage if a court forced a spouse to reveal marital confidences. The Supreme Court has ruled, however, that this does not prevent one spouse from voluntarily testifying against the other. Such testimony does not require the consent of the other spouse.

Domestic Violence

Q. Is it illegal for one spouse to beat the other?

A. Yes. Beating a spouse is a crime in every state.

Q. What type of treatment makes up a beating?

A. In most states, for the law to step in, a spouse must have inflicted "substantial harm" *(battery)* or threatened "substantial harm" *(assault)*. Threatening words alone are not an assault. However, threats combined with the suggestion that action is about to follow may constitute assault. For example, threats while showing a weapon would be considered assault.

"Substantial harm" is hard to define. The trend is toward less tolerance of any physical violence. An injury serious enough to require a doctor's attention surely constitutes "substantial harm."

Q. Does the law consider treatment less than a beating as abuse?

A. States are passing more protective domestic violence laws. Such laws provide both civil and criminal penalties. Actions may be brought under such laws for abuse that is less than physical violence but causes emotional pain. These could include withholding sleep, disturbances at work, continual spying on a spouse, harassing phone calls, and threats of physical force or confinement.

Q. Can the law force an abusive spouse to leave the home?

A. It is possible in states having expanded domestic violence laws to have an abusive spouse evicted on an emergency basis.

Q. What legal remedies are available to those beaten by their spouse?

A. There are a number of remedies. Unfortunately, several of them have potential drawbacks.

(1) The victim should call the police. While the police may not want to get involved in a domestic dispute, they may provide temporary protection. However, in some states, the police may not be able to remove the physically abusive spouse from the home unless the victim will sign a criminal complaint. In other states, the police officer has the authority to take the alleged abuser out of the house. Calling the police provides immediate protection and makes a record of the beating, which can be useful in a later legal action. (Seeking medical treatment for the beating also will provide a record for later legal action.) In states with expanded domestic violence protection, the police report may lead to an action on the victim's behalf under the domestic violence law.

(2) The victim should seek protection from the abuser. An emergency court order, called a *restraining order* or *order of protection,* requires the abusive spouse not to have any contact with the victim. Many states offer these orders, which are usually temporary. Police enforce these orders. If the abusive spouse violates an order, the victim may take the abusive spouse to court.

(3) The victim can press criminal charges against the spouse. If convicted of assault or battery, the abusing spouse may be sent to jail or put on probation. This may cause other problems, however. A spouse in jail cannot work and provide for the family. Also, a criminal conviction can hurt the spouse's ability to get a job.

(4) The victim can file a civil suit for damages against the abusive spouse in many states. Just as in a criminal case, the victim must prove that the beating occurred and that it was severe. Filing a civil suit costs money and takes time. Unless the abusive spouse has money, property, or insurance, the victim will not be able to collect enough on any judgment to make a suit worthwhile.

(5) The victim can file for a legal separation (available in some states) or divorce (offered in all states). Physical cruelty is a ground for divorce in most

Get Away from the Abuser

The law believes that the victim has every right to leave a physically abusive spouse. This is not desertion, and the abusive spouse still must provide support.

In addition, nearly all experts say abuse victims should leave home and find somewhere safe to stay. Victims who stay risk their health and their lives. If the victim has nowhere to go, the police, churches, and social agencies can help find a shelter. See the reference section at the end of this chapter. It lists a nationwide toll-free hot line offering help to battered spouses.

states. In all states, the victim may obtain a divorce on "no fault" grounds. The victim may be able to obtain "exclusive possession" of the home. However, seeking a divorce may be difficult for a victim of spousal abuse who depends financially on the other spouse. (For a further discussion of divorce, see the "Divorce" section that appears later in this chapter.)

Defenses Against a Physically Abusive Spouse

The victim may use *reasonable force* for self-defense. This means an amount of force that is equal to the danger and is necessary for defense. Thus a court might justify the use of a weapon by a victim if the abusive spouse had one and was advancing. The use of a weapon might be excessive force if the abusive spouse did not have a weapon or if the danger had passed.

Q. How does someone file criminal charges against a physically abusive spouse?

A. The police can provide advice on how to do this. The victim can greatly help the case by providing evidence of the beating and its brutality. Evidence may include a police report, the names and addresses of witnesses who saw or heard the beating, and photographs of scars or marks. It is important to have a medical report showing the severity of the injuries. That is why the victim should go to a doctor or hospital for treatment immediately after the incident.

Q. What may be done to stop one spouse from bothering the other or their children once they have separated and started legal action?

A. A judge may issue one of three orders. These include an *eviction order* (sometimes called a *vacate order*), a *cease and desist order* (occasionally called a *restraining order*), and a *protective order*. These orders require the abusing spouse to stay away from the victim and their children. If the "ordered" spouse does not obey the order, that spouse may be held in contempt of court, subject to a fine and jail. A judge may require the spouse to post a *peace bond*. This is a sum of money that will be forfeited if the spouse does not leave the victim alone.

Q. May a wife charge her husband with rape?

A. It depends on the law in the state where the act occurred. Some states do not recognize spousal rape under any condition. A growing number of states have changed their definitions of rape to allow the state to charge a husband with the rape of his wife. Some of these states allow a rape charge if the spouses are living separate and apart or have a written separation agreement. Other states treat spousal rape as a crime even if the spouses are living together. However, prosecution is usually difficult unless there was some other act (such as a beating) besides the rape. Regardless of the state's rape law, other laws, such as assault and battery, may provide a remedy for a raped spouse.

Any discussion of law and marriage must include the possible results of a failed marriage. Courts usually step in only when a marriage is over.

Ending a marriage can be very complex. For the people involved, it is likely to be very difficult and painful emotionally. Separate maintenance, annulment, or divorce almost always requires a lawyer. Ideally, each person should have a lawyer.

Separation or Separate Maintenance

Q. What is separation?

A. In a *separation,* a couple remains married but stops living together. It is often the first step toward a divorce. However, it does not have to end in divorce. Sometimes people separate when they do not get along but, for religious or other reasons, do not wish to divorce. Separated couples keep many of the rights and obligations of married couples. For example, they may not remarry. In some states, they still may inherit from each other.

Q. What are the types of separation?

A. One form is *desertion.* It occurs when one spouse leaves without the other's consent. The departing spouse does not provide support for the other spouse and children. In many states, a deserted spouse may sue for formal separation. Desertion also is a ground for divorce in some states.

Couples often separate by *mutual consent.* They do this without a formal legal separation. (A separation is legal when it has a formal document stating the spouses' rights and duties toward each other.) Some couples just decide to live apart. However, it is best if they have a separation agreement. In this contract they agree to live apart and end sexual relations. The separation agreement should arrange for finances and child custody. It also should determine any other rights and duties the spouses still owe each other. If either spouse breaks this agreement, the other may sue for breach of contract.

Many states allow formal *judicial separation.* It begins with a lawsuit by one spouse. The other spouse does not have to agree to it. The judge hearing the case decides the terms of the separation. These terms may then be upheld as a court

SEPARATE MAINTENANCE

Separate maintenance is a formal legal separation. If a couple has a formal separation agreement or if a court has entered a formal order of separation (see related question and answer), separation is often referred to as separate maintenance. In separate maintenance, each person should have a lawyer.

order. A judicial separation often awards the same amount of money and custody and visitation rights as a divorce would. However, a judicial separation does not allow either spouse to remarry. Some states allow the courts to convert a judicial separation into a divorce after a certain period of time.

Annulment

Q. What is an annulment?

A. An *annulment* is a court ruling that a marriage is not valid because of a defect at the time of the attempted marriage. The most serious defects are usually bigamy, incest, or marriage to an underage person. These violate state law and usually void the attempted marriage. (In some states, marrying an underage person makes a marriage voidable, not automatically void.) When a marriage is voidable, defects such as fraud (see below) or duress (threats) permit the court, in its discretion, to void the marriage. This means the marriage is valid until the court grants the annulment.

In most states, annulments are not commonly granted for minor reasons. Most often courts award them on the ground of fraud. This means that one party deliberately hid important information from the other before the wedding. The law usually defines this information as facts essential to the creation of a valid marriage. Some courts define the information as facts that, if the other person had known them, would have kept that person from agreeing to the marriage. For example, the court might grant an annulment for fraud if one person hid a prior divorce or an inability to have children or sexual relations. Or that person may have concealed a criminal record or a serious contagious illness.

Q. How common are annulments?

A. They end far fewer marriages than in the past because divorces now are easy to obtain.

Divorce

Q. What is a divorce?

A. A *divorce* is a formal court proceeding that dissolves a valid marriage. After the divorce decree is final, the ex-spouses are free to remarry. Spouses may obtain a divorce in any

ANNULMENTS VS. DIVORCES

In theory, annulment is much different from divorce. Annulment depends on problems at the time the marriage began. Divorce depends on problems arising after the creation of a valid marriage. However, these two methods of ending a marriage may have similar results. The law treats children of parents who get their marriage annulled as legitimate, like those whose parents divorced. People from an annulled marriage are free to remarry. Many states enable courts to distribute property at annulment. Courts also may order support duties after the annulment. Annulment sometimes renews one spouse's rights to money that ended because of the defective marriage. Such money may include spousal support from an earlier marriage. It also may consist of worker's compensation benefits from a prior marriage. This is because the annulled marriage is void, as if it never took place.

state in which one of them lives. A spouse usually must live in a state for six weeks to six months before filing the action for divorce.

Divorce law varies among the states, and it has changed greatly in recent years. Major issues consist of grounds for divorce, division of property, and child custody and support. Methods of negotiating or mediating divorce settlements also have changed and are still changing.

Q. How have attitudes toward divorce changed?

A. Courts formerly granted divorces when one spouse proved that the other committed some wrong believed to ruin the marriage. Such wrongs often included adultery, physical cruelty, or desertion. The spouse charged with fault could try to prove his or her innocence. In addition, that spouse could try to show that the other spouse was also guilty of marital misconduct. As a result, divorces could be very bitter, prolonged legal actions.

Gradually courts moved away from the narrow-minded idea of fault, allowing a divorce for *constructive desertion.* This meant that one spouse made the other so unhappy that leaving home was the only choice. Courts also allowed divorcing spouses to show mental, rather than physical, cruelty.

Q. May a couple get a divorce without lawyers?

A. Most states permit do-it-yourself divorces. The law calls them *pro se* divorces, a Latin term meaning "for oneself." In these divorces the spouses manage the entire process without lawyers. Spouses usually can find the forms and procedures at office supply stores and the courthouse. Most people can understand them without difficulty. However, some complex points in a divorce, such as tax ramifications (consequences) and discovering and valuing property, may require expert guidance. That is why most people should seek legal and financial advice during a divorce.

Q. Are most divorces contested?

A. No, at least not by a trial. Only about ten percent of divorcing spouses go to trial. Instead, the parties usually agree on certain terms, often after long negotiation. These include division of property and debt, spousal and child support, custody, and other terms. These agreements, often called *separation agreements, property settlement agreements,* or *stipulations,* are postmarital contracts. The spouses present them to the court for its approval.

No-Fault Divorces

All states today have laws permitting *no-fault divorce.* These laws require only a showing that a marriage has failed. The most common no-fault grounds are *irretrievable breakdown, irreconcilable differences,* or living apart for a certain period of time. No-fault grounds make it nearly impossible for someone who does not want a divorce to prevent the other spouse from getting one. Some states have only a no-fault ground. Other states simply added a no-fault ground to their fault grounds. Courts now grant almost all divorces on no-fault grounds. In about half the states, however, fault may still help decide financial settlements in no-fault divorces.

Grounds for Divorce

	Irreconcilable differences or irretrievable breakdown as sole ground	Irreconcilable differences or irretrievable breakdown added to traditional grounds	Incompatibility as ground	Living separate and apart as ground	Judicial separation or maintenance as grounds	Mutual consent divorces
Alabama		X	X	2 years		
Alaska			X			
Arizona	X					X
Arkansas				3 years		
California	X					X
Colorado	X					X
Connecticut		X		18 months[1]	X	X
Delaware		X	X			
District of Columbia				6 months[5]		
Florida		X				
Georgia		X				
Hawaii	X			2 years	any period	X
Idaho		X		5 years		
Illinois		X[2]		X[2]		X[2]
Indiana		X				
Iowa	X					
Kansas			X			
Kentucky	X					
Louisiana				6 months		
Maine		X				
Maryland				1 year[3]		
Massachusetts		X[4]				
Michigan	X					
Minnesota	X			180 days		
Mississippi		X				
Missouri		X				
Montana	X			180 days		
Nebraska	X					
Nevada			X	1 year		
New Hampshire		X				
New Jersey				18 months		
New Mexico			X			
New York					1 year	
North Carolina				1 year		
North Dakota		X				
Ohio				1 year		X
Oklahoma			X			
Oregon	X					X
Pennsylvania		X		2 years		
Puerto Rico				2 years		
Rhode Island		X		3 years		
South Carolina				1 year		
South Dakota		X				
Tennessee		X		3 years		
Texas				3 years		
Utah		X		3 years	3 years	
Vermont				6 months		
Virginia				1 year		
Virgin Islands	X					
Washington	X					X
West Virginia		X		1 year		
Wisconsin	X					X
Wyoming		X				

1. Eighteen months living separate and apart *and* incompatibility.
2. Irretrievable breakdown *and* two years living separate and apart required; if both parties consent the period becomes six months.
3. Voluntary 12 consecutive months or two-year uninterrupted separation.
4. Separation agreement also required.
5. Six months by voluntary separation, one year living separate and apart.

Source: Reprinted with permission from T. Walker & D. Jonas Freed, "Family Law in the Fifty States: An Overview," *Family Law Quarterly* (Winter 1990)

Q. Does the court have to accept an agreement made by divorcing spouses?

A. In some states, spouses present agreements to the court as proposals. The court may then modify them. In other states, courts must go along with agreements on property and spousal support if the agreement is not unconscionable and was fairly made. "Not unconscionable" means the contract is fair and reasonable and not one-sided. (A previous section in this chapter talks about conscionable premarital agreements.) It does not matter whether spouses use do-it-yourself negotiating, lawyer negotiation, or mediation. In any case, the court will review and approve the settlement according to the same standards. Some states do not treat premarital, marital, and postmarital contracts as binding. Even in these states, however, courts almost always approve postmarital agreements and include them in divorce judgments.

Q. May a couple use a premarital agreement (or an agreement they made while still married) in a divorce proceeding?

A. They may be able to use it. Enforceable terms from these contracts may control who gets the property after a divorce. These terms also may decide how much spousal support the court grants. (An earlier part of this chapter discusses this topic under "Premarital Contracts.")

Q. Is mediation always a good option?

A. Some critics argue that mediation is never proper when one spouse has abused the other. Mediation also is not for everyone. Some people prefer to resolve the dispute by lawyers representing them in negotiation or in the courtroom. Other people "need" to vent frustrations and to convince a judge that they are right.

Q. How much does mediation cost?

A. It usually costs less than negotiation by lawyers. As with a divorce, the exact cost depends on how complex the couple's finances are and whether they have children. The spouses normally share the cost of mediation.

Q. How does someone find a mediator?

A. There are mediators in every state, especially in metropolitan areas. The back of this chapter lists the address of the

MEDIATION AND DIVORCES

More and more people use mediation to settle their disputes in a separation or divorce. In mediation, the spouses sit down with a trained person called a *mediator*. Lawyers representing the parties usually are not present. The spouses discuss the issues until they solve them. The mediator does not make decisions for them (that is what an arbitrator or judge does). Rules of evidence or prior judicial decisions also do not control the process. The mediator teaches skills for resolving conflicts to the spouses. This allows them to work out their own agreement.
Couples may use mediation to settle any or all terms of a separation and divorce. In some states, mediation is mandatory for child custody issues. In many states, spouses may file the agreement without help from lawyers. However, spouses usually have lawyers review the mediation agreements.

Academy of Family Mediators. However, there are few standards established for mediators. People seeking mediation should carefully select a fully qualified and experienced professional. Find out if the mediator has been trained in mediation by an organization recognized by the state or by a national group.

Property

Although few divorce cases go to court, what the spouses could expect if they chose to contest (rather than agree) affects negotiation. The following questions and answers look at how courts resolve many issues.

Q. Have changing attitudes about property affected family law?

A. Yes. Years ago, courts in common-law property states lacked the power to redistribute property during a divorce. Their primary role concerning property was to identify who owned it. The courts could only divide jointly held property, such as a joint bank account or property with a title held in both names. Now, however, courts in both common-law and community-property states are normally free to divide marital property no matter which party owned it during the marriage or whose name is on the title.

Q. How does a court divide property when a couple divorces?

A. States handle this in various ways. About half the states divide only *marital* or *community property,* which is property acquired during the marriage. (*Separate* property is that which one spouse owned before the marriage or inherited or received as a gift during the marriage.) The other states allow courts to divide all property. In most of these states, however, courts consider the separate property when deciding who will get what.

Many states presume that marital property will be evenly divided after a long marriage. Other states reject that concept but often do distribute property evenly. Most states have detailed standards for the court to consider when distributing property. These may include some or all of the following:

- The length of the marriage;
- The ages, health, and positions in life of the spouses;
- The spouses' occupations;
- The amount and sources of income;

- The spouses' vocational skills;
- The spouses' abilities to find new jobs;
- The needs of each spouse;
- The standard of living during the marriage;
- The amount each spouse contributed to the getting, preserving, improving, or wasting of marital property;
- The contributions of a homemaker, including child care and additions to the career potential of the main money-maker;
- The need of the parent with custody of the children to own or live in the marital residence;
- Whether one party will receive spousal maintenance payments;
- The loss of inheritance or pension rights; and/or
- The income tax effects of the property division.

Q. Do courts consider fault when dividing property?

A. Some states forbid courts to consider fault. In other states, economic fault may play a role in dividing property. In those states, courts may consider that one spouse wasted the marital assets. This will affect how the property is divided.

Q. Is the transfer of property between divorcing spouses taxed?

A. Divorces often transfer property that has increased in value from one spouse to the other. The Internal Revenue Service (IRS) does not tax this property as a capital gain. The recipient takes the property at the same cost basis as the spouse who first owned it, not at fair market value.

Q. How do divorcing couples handle debts?

A. Few divorcing couples have a lot of property to divide. Most have debts, which must be divided. Courts usually give separate debts to the spouse who incurred them. However, courts normally divide debts from items that benefit both of them between both spouses. If the divorce decree orders one spouse to pay a specific debt, the other spouse may still have an obligation to the creditor.

Q. How do divorces affect pensions?

A. Pension or retirement benefits may be the only major assets a couple has accumulated. Courts must consider them during a

(continued)

WHO GETS THE HOUSE?

When there are minor children, the home usually goes to the custodial parent. If the house is the only major property asset, it may be impossible to compensate for that award by giving different property to the other parent. In those cases, courts often award the home to the custodial parent until the children reach majority. When they reach that age, the custodial parent must sell the home and divide the money.

Property Division

	Community property states		Equitable distribution common law states		
	1 Equal or presumption of equal	2 Equitable	1 All property considered	2 Only marital property considered	3 Gifts, inheritances excluded
Alabama				X[1]	yes[1]
Alaska			X		
Arizona		X			
Arkansas				X[2]	
California	X[3]				
Colorado				X[4]	yes[4]
Connecticut			X		no
Delaware				X	no
District of Columbia				X	yes
Florida			X		
Georgia				X	no
Hawaii			X		no
Idaho	X				
Illinois				X	yes
Indiana			X		no
Iowa			X		yes
Kansas			X		no
Kentucky				X	yes
Louisiana	X				
Maine				X	yes
Maryland				X	yes
Massachusetts			X		
Michigan			X		no
Minnesota				X	yes
Mississippi				X[5]	
Missouri				X	yes
Montana			X		no
Nebraska				X	no
Nevada		X			
New Hampshire			X		no
New Jersey				X	yes
New Mexico	X				
New York				X	yes
North Carolina				X	yes
North Dakota			X		no
Ohio			X		no
Oklahoma				X	yes
Oregon			X		no
Pennsylvania				X	yes
Puerto Rico		X		X	yes
Rhode Island				X	yes
South Carolina				X[4]	yes
South Dakota			X		unclear
Tennessee				X[4]	yes
Texas	X[6]				
Utah			X		
Vermont			X		
Virginia				X	yes
Virgin Islands				X[7]	yes
Washington	X				
West Virginia				X	yes
Wisconsin	X				yes
Wyoming			X		

1. Unless property is used for the common benefit of both parties.
2. Equal unless such division is inequitable.
3. Unless one party has misappropriated community property deliberately.
4. Except as to increase in value.
5. Jointly acquired assets considered.
6. Unless the court finds equal division would be inequitable.
7. Personal property only.

Source: Reprinted with permission from T. Walker & D. Jonas Freed, "Family Law in the Fifty States: An Overview," *Family Law Quarterly* (Winter 1990).

divorce. Both community property states and common-law states tend to treat retirement benefits as property to be split up during a divorce. During a divorce, the spouses may divide the current value of the part of the pension that was earned during the marriage. Another option is to assign part of the future benefits to each spouse. These portions will be awarded when the pension pays the benefits.

Alimony or Spousal Support

Q. When do courts award alimony or spousal support?

A. At one time, courts could order husbands to pay *alimony* to their former wives. This lasted until the ex-wives married again or died. The courts felt this continued the husband's duty to support his wife. Courts were very likely to award alimony in cases where the husband was guilty of marital fault and the wife was innocent.

Modern courts often refer to alimony as *spousal support* or *maintenance*. Courts award these payments not by gender or to punish for fault, but rather on the basis of need and ability to pay. Maintenance is awarded less often today because there are more two-income couples and fewer couples in which one is financially dependent on the other.

Q. What are the tax consequences of spousal support?

A. Payers may deduct spousal support from their taxable income. Recipients must include spousal support as taxable income. There are some complex tax consequences if the amount of support exceeds certain dollar limitations.

Q. What is rehabilitative support?

A. The most popular spousal support today is *rehabilitative support*. It is based on the idea that a spouse who was financially dependent or disadvantaged during marriage should become self-supporting. The intent is that this support will provide a chance for education, training, or job experience. It should help make up for opportunities lost by a spouse who left a job to help the other spouse's career or to assume family duties.

Rehabilitative support may be proper for a period of change after even a brief marriage. In any event, courts award it for a limited period. Some states end this support

(continued)

Alimony

	Marital fault not considered	Barred by marital misconduct	Ended or modified by cohabitation	Marital fault is factor
Alabama		X	X	
Alaska	X			
Arizona	X			
Arkansas	X			
California	X		X	
Colorado	X			
Connecticut				X
Delaware	X			
District of Columbia				X
Florida				X
Georgia		X	X	
Hawaii	X			
Idaho		X		
Illinois	X		X[1]	
Indiana	X			
Iowa	X			
Kansas	X			
Kentucky				X
Louisiana		X	X	
Maine	X			
Maryland	X		X[1]	
Massachusetts	X			
Michigan				X
Minnesota	X			
Mississippi	X			
Missouri				X
Montana	X			
Nebraska	X			
Nevada	X			X[2]
New Hampshire				X
New Jersey	X			
New Mexico	X			
New York	X		X	
North Carolina		X		
North Dakota				X
Ohio	X		X[3]	
Oklahoma	X			
Oregon	X			
Pennsylvania			X	X
Puerto Rico		X	X	
Rhode Island				X
South Carolina		X		
South Dakota				X
Tennessee			X	X
Texas				
Utah			X	
Vermont	X			
Virginia		X		
Virgin Islands	X			
Washington	X			
West Virginia		X		
Wisconsin	X			
Wyoming				X

1. To the extent it changes economic status.
2. Recent decisions indicate that fault may be considered.
3. Permissive.

Source: Reprinted with permission from T. Walker & D. Jonas Freed, "Family Law in the Fifty States: An Overview," *Family Law Quarterly* (Winter 1990).

when the rehabilitative efforts succeed. If the recipient stops making an effort during the specified period, some states end the support. Certain states extend the period if the spouse did not succeed in these efforts. Many states stop this support if the recipient marries again. Of course, support ends upon the death of the recipient.

Q. What is permanent support?

A. Courts award *permanent spousal support* to provide money for a spouse who cannot be rehabilitated. They also award it to a spouse who can become somewhat self-supporting but whose earning capacity and resources differ greatly from those of the financially stronger spouse. When deciding the amount of permanent support, courts often use the same criteria as for dividing property. About half the states still consider fault in these decisions. Fault may be a reason for adding to or reducing the amount of permanent support. In a few states, a court will not award support to a spouse against whom it granted a divorce on fault grounds.

Q. Does the law help newly divorced spouses who must now get their own health insurance?

A. Yes. Getting low-cost health insurance is often a problem when a spouse's employer-sponsored group plan had covered the divorced person who does not have a job that offers health insurance. A new federal law has eased that problem a bit. The law now requires employer-sponsored group health plans to offer divorced spouses of covered workers continued coverage at group rates for up to three years.

Q. Suppose one spouse supports the other through graduate school. Does the supporting spouse have a right to share in the other spouse's future earnings?

A. In some states, the supporting spouse may get a share of the other spouse's earnings. Some courts offer a new kind of compensation when neither property distribution nor spousal support is appropriate. For example, one spouse may have supported the other through graduate or professional school. The supporting spouse may have expected that both would benefit from the educated spouse's enhanced earning capacity. However, the marriage ends before any material benefits were earned. The supporting spouse does not need rehabilitation because that spouse has worked during the entire marriage, and there is no major property to be distributed because marital resources went to the educational effort. Then the courts may award this new compensation.

HOW LONG DOES PERMANENT SUPPORT LAST?

Courts usually do not state how long permanent support should last. They may change this support if the ability of the payer or the needs of the recipient change greatly. Permanent support will end after the recipient remarries. It also may end if the recipient decides to live with someone. Sometimes courts award both rehabilitative and permanent support.

GUIDELINES FOR AWARDING CUSTODY

Most states have set up guidelines for courts to follow. These may involve:

- **The age and sex of the child;**
- **The wishes of the child;**
- **The child's relationship with the parents, brothers and sisters, or anyone else who may greatly affect the child's interest;**
- **The emotional ties between the child and the parents;**
- **The capacity and willingness of the parents to provide for the child's needs and education;**
- **The permanence and continuity of proposed custodial environments;**
- **The extent the parents cooperate in allowing the noncustodial parent to foster a continuing relationship with the child;**
- **The child's adjustment to home, school, and community;**
- **The mental and physical health of all people involved.**

In such situations, some states now award periodic payments to the supporting spouse. These aim to compensate for donations to the educational expenses and general support of the spouse who leaves the marriage with an advanced degree and greater earning capacity. The courts may change or end such payments if the expected earnings do not occur.

Custody

Q. What is child custody?

A. *Child custody* is the right and duty to care for a child on a day-to-day basis and to make major decisions about the child. The law assumes that the person with sole custody of a child will have the child live with him or her most of the time and will make major decisions about the child. These include where the child goes to school, where the child lives, whether the child will get braces, and so on.

Q. How have attitudes toward custody changed?

A. Until the middle of the nineteenth century, fathers had a nearly absolute right to retain custody of their children. Then, well into the twentieth century, courts almost always awarded custody of "children of tender years" to their mothers. In most states now, courts decide custody based on the best interest of the children, without preferring either mothers or fathers. Unwed parents also have a right to claim custody. In practice, courts normally award custody to mothers. However, when fathers contest custody, they often succeed.

Q. Do some factors outweigh others in awarding custody?

A. In most states, stability and the fitness of the custodial parents weigh more heavily. However, some experts believe there can be problems when guidelines do not place weight on other specific factors. It makes custody decisions between two fit parents unpredictable and encourages legal action. It also places the parent less able to risk the uncertainty of legal action at a disadvantage. Other experts endorse using nonweighted factors. They believe that trial judges must be free to decide what is best for the child in each particular case.

(continued)

Custody

	States with statutory custody guidelines	States that consider the children's wishes	States with joint custody laws
Alabama	X	X	
Alaska	X	X	X
Arizona	X	X	
Arkansas			
California	X	X	X
Colorado	X	X	X
Connecticut		X	X
Delaware	X	X	X
District of Columbia	X	X	
Florida	X	X	X
Georgia		X	
Hawaii	X	X	X
Idaho	X	X	X
Illinois	X	X	X
Indiana	X	X	X
Iowa	X	X	X
Kansas	X	X	X
Kentucky	X	X	X
Louisiana	X	X	X
Maine	X	X	X
Maryland			X[1]
Massachusetts			X
Michigan	X	X	X
Minnesota	X	X	X
Mississippi	X		X
Missouri	X	X	X
Montana	X	X	X
Nebraska	X	X	
Nevada	X	X	X
New Hampshire		X	X
New Jersey		X	X[1]
New Mexico	X	X	X
New York			
North Carolina			X
North Dakota	X	X	
Ohio		X	X
Oklahoma		X	X
Oregon	X		X
Pennsylvania			X
Puerto Rico		X	
Rhode Island			
South Carolina			
South Dakota		X	
Tennessee		X	X
Texas		X	X
Utah	X	X	X
Vermont	X		X
Virginia	X	X	
Virgin Islands			
Washington	X	X	
West Virginia		X	
Wisconsin	X	X	X
Wyoming		X	

1. Case law only.

Source: Reprinted with permission from T. Walker & D. Jonas Freed, "Family Law in the Fifty States: An Overview," *Family Law Quarterly* (Winter 1990).

Joint Legal Custody

Joint legal custody refers to both parents making major decisions about the child together. It involves *shared parenting,* sometimes referred to as *co-parenting*. When parents agree to joint legal custody, or when a court orders it, they must share major decisions about their children. Most states require parents to specify the decisions they will share. These states also order parents to indicate what process they will use if they disagree. Many parents agree to mediate or use private arbitration. Supporters of joint legal custody point out that this is a guarantee that children continue to receive the benefit of both parents' points of view. If parents agreed about the raising of the children, they probably will be good candidates for joint legal custody. This is true even if they fought tooth and nail about everything else.

Q. What other points are there to consider?

A. There are two recent alternatives to giving the above factors equal weight. One favors the parent who has done the most to take care of the child during the marriage. Supporters of this view argue that caretaking creates strong psychological bonds. Critics argue that this is just a disguised "tender years doctrine" that favors mothers, who are more likely than fathers to have been primary caretakers.

Q. What about joint custody?

A. The other alternative is to award *joint custody*. It can mean joint legal custody, joint physical custody, or both. This sometimes involves dividing physical custody evenly or nearly evenly between the parents. It often involves their sharing legal custody, so that they make important decisions for the child together. Supporters of joint custody stress that "parents are forever." Although a couple's marriage may have failed, they remain parents. It is important to protect and improve the child's relationship with each parent. Critics worry about instability and potential conflict for the child. There is also the cost of keeping two homes for the child.

Some states now prefer joint legal custody. They may or may not also favor joint physical custody. In these states, the law requires judges to arrange some form of joint custody unless it is not in the best interest of the child. These laws vary widely. Any parent facing a divorce should read and understand these laws.

Q. What is joint physical custody?

A. *Joint physical custody* is a legal arrangement in which a child lives in the homes of both parents. This does not always mean equal time. It does mean that both parents will maintain a "real" home for the children. This usually includes room(s) for the children and their toys and clothing. Often the children spend some school nights at each home. They go to school or day care directly from each home. The child may spend part of each week with each parent, or spend alternating weeks. If the parents live in different areas, one often has the child during the school year, and the other has the child during vacations.

Q. How does joint physical custody affect child support?

A. In most states, the amount of time spent with each parent and the parents' incomes help determine the allocation of child support between the parents.

Q. What are the pros and cons of joint physical custody?

A. Supporters of shared custody believe it is the only way to make sure that the children do not "lose" a parent because of the divorce. Critics fear that shared-time parenting is unworkable. Because it requires keeping two homes for the child, shared custody costs more than sole custody.

Like joint legal custody, the best forecast of success usually is whether the parents shared most of the child care when their marriage was working. It is usually easiest on the children to make the custodial arrangement just after the divorce similar to the parental pattern right before the separation. However, children's needs for each parent change as they grow. Parents probably should avoid locking in any parenting plan forever. Rather, they should plan to review the custody arrangement as the children grow and the children's needs change.

Q. Are child custody decisions final?

A. No. A court may always change child custody arrangements to meet the changing needs of the growing child and to respond to changes in the parents' lives. The court may do this because it keeps its jurisdiction over the case while the child is under the age of majority. A parent looking for a change in custody through the court usually must show (at the least) that the conditions have changed greatly since the last order. The parent also must show that changing the custody arrangement would be better for the child.

Visitation

Q. If the court awards sole physical custody to one parent, may the other parent visit the child?

A. The noncustodial parent has a right to visit the child unless it would be contrary to the child's best interest, as in cases involving abuse. An important point in awarding sole physical custody often is whether the custodial parent is willing to help continue the child's relationship with the other parent by allowing visitation privileges.

Q. Under what circumstances may the custodial parent deny the other visitation?

A. The parent with custody must have a good reason to deny the other parent visitation rights. An example would be when the

Child Snatching

Child snatching is a form of kidnapping. It occurs when a parent or someone working with the parent disobeys a court's custody order by taking or keeping a child away from the other parent. In the past, it was difficult to get help from legal authorities if the person moved a child across state lines because other states did not have to honor the custody award of the first state. Sometimes, the noncustodial parent could convince the second state to give him or her legal custody under that state's laws.

State and federal laws now require all states to uphold lawful custody decrees made in other states, as long as the court had proper jurisdiction under the Uniform Child Custody Jurisdiction Act. These laws make it harder to change a custody decree

(continued)

(continued)

without going back to court in the state that granted the decree. This makes it easier to return the child to the parent who originally had custody. These laws also provide for the return of the child to its home state for the holding of custody proceedings. (The "home state" is where the child lived at least six months before the child snatching.) There does not even have to be a court order for the child's return.

The United States and 13 other countries are members of the Hague Child Abduction Convention. This requires the return of a child whom someone wrongfully removed from or kept in another country. The child must be returned to the country where the child had formerly lived. After the child's return, a court holds custody proceedings. However, this procedure requires that both countries be members of the Convention.

custodial parent suspects the other of heavy drug or alcohol use or of molesting the child. Or the custodial parent may believe the other plans to kidnap the child or behave in a way that may harm the child. In these cases, the custodial parent may ask the court to end or restrict visitation rights. A law enforcement officer may be ordered to escort the child on visits.

Child Support

Q. Who is liable for child support?

A. Courts once placed the duty to support children in a marriage almost entirely on the father. Today, state law places the duty of child support on both parents. When parents divorce, the noncustodial parent usually must pay money to the custodial parent each month. If the mother has custody, the father ordinarily pays child support. If both parents share custody, the parent with the higher income will pay child support. Children of unwed parents are entitled to as much support as children of married parents.

Federal law requires parents liable for child support to name their minor children as beneficiaries on any group or employee health and dental insurance plans. The only exception to this is if the parents can get similar or better coverage for the children at a lower cost.

All states have child support guidelines to determine ranges of support. Many of these are percentage formulas normally based on either the noncustodial parent's income or both parents' income. A recent federal law requires that the guidelines act as *rebuttable presumptions*. This means that judges must award the amount set by the guidelines unless they explain why it would be unfair. Courts usually order the level of support set in the state law, though they may consider other factors as well to avoid unfairness in a particular case. Typical guidelines include:

- The financial resources and needs of the child;
- The financial resources and needs of both parents;
- The standard of living the child would have enjoyed had the marriage not ended;
- The value of the services given by the custodial parent;
- The physical and emotional condition of the child; and
- The child's educational needs.

Q. How do courts collect support?

A. Courts collect child support in several ways. Sometimes the court orders that an amount be withheld from the wages of the noncustodial parent. In some states, the money goes directly to the court, which passes it along to the custodial parent.

Q. What happens when parents disobey child support orders?

A. Courts have the same remedies as they have for unwed fathers who do not pay support. One remedy assigns part of the parent's wages to the child. Another garnishes the parent's wages (automatically transfers the owed amount from the parent's pay). Courts also may seize the parent's property or bank account. In addition, they may jail the parent for contempt of court.

Though courts have these powers, the history of disobeying child support orders has been a national disgrace. Recently, there have been hopeful efforts to reduce those problems. Federal and state parent-locator services help find parents who tried to avoid their duties. Under the federal Child Support Enforcement Amendments of 1984, computer networks track child-support offenders across state lines. This law requires states to withhold income from wages of parents who are behind in child support payments.

Income may be withheld from other assets to meet support duties. A 1988 federal law requires income to be withheld from wages in certain situations, even when parents are not behind in child support payments. For example, starting in 1990, employers will withhold income from wages of absent parents of children receiving Aid to Families with Dependent Children. Income withholding will become required in 1994 for *all* noncustodial parents. The only exception to automatic withholding will be if the custodial parent says not to do this. Federal and state tax refunds may be withheld when parents are behind in child support payments. Civil contempt actions in court also may enforce child support. In addition, courts may not reduce past-due child support after the fact. Bankruptcy also does not enable a parent to avoid paying overdue child support.

Asking for Lower Child Support Payments

Noncustodial parents may ask the court to reduce the amount of child support they must pay. Courts have the power to change the amount of child support if there has been a change in circumstances or in the needs or resources of the parents. The custodial parent may seek an increase in support because of higher expenses of caring for the child.

Grandparents and Stepparents

Q. What are grandparents' rights?

A. Though their son or daughter obtained a divorce, grandparents still have the right to a continuing relationship with their grandchildren. If their son or daughter does not have custody and the custodial parent denies the grandparents access to the grandchildren, the grandparents may ask the court to grant them visitation. If they had a close relationship with the grandchildren before the divorce, the court may set specific times and places for visitation.

Q. May courts award grandparents custody of their grandchildren?

A. Yes, if neither parent wants the children, or if the parents are unfit. Courts examine such factors as the grandparents' age and general health. The courts also consider where they live and their ability to care for the children. Courts will not deny grandparents custody because of their age, as long as they are healthy.

Q. If a couple divorces, does the stepparent have a right to visit the ex-spouse's child?

A. It depends on a few factors. If the stepparent had adopted the child, the stepparent would have the same rights as the biological parent. If the stepparent did not adopt the child, however, the divorcing spouses may reach an agreement. If they cannot agree, the court may order some visitation rights for the stepparent if the stepparent can prove a close relationship to the stepchild.

A Stepparent's Duties

The responsibilities of a stepparent depend on state law. A stepparent usually is not liable for a spouse's children from another marriage. An exception is if the stepparent adopts them or accepts financial obligation for their support. Until then, the children's biological parents are liable for their support. Some states, however, make stepparents who take children into their home liable for their support in certain cases.

If a stepparent adopts a spouse's children, the stepparent becomes their legal parent. Then the stepparent has the same rights and duties as the biological parent. The adoptive parent is liable for their care and support even if the couple divorces later or the biological parent dies.

(continued)

WHEN A SPOUSE DIES

This complex topic affects most families. For a discussion of its terms and ideas, see the "Wills, Trusts, and Estate Planning" chapter.

Wills and Other Devices

Q. Does the surviving spouse get anything if the other spouse dies?

A. In general, the surviving spouse must get the share specified by state law (usually one third or one half). The spouse can give up this right in writing (as in a premarital agreement). Sometimes the state disqualifies the survivor due to prior desertion or marital misconduct.

Q. How does the surviving spouse inherit property?

A. If the deceased left a valid will, the surviving spouse may "take" (assume ownership) under that will. The will disposes of *probate property*. This can mean property solely in the name of the deceased. It also can be property that the deceased held as a tenant in common with other people.

In community property states, each spouse has a right to one half of the property acquired during the marriage. This does not include property inherited or received as a gift. A will may give the deceased's one-half interest to others, including the surviving spouse.

Q. Must a spouse wait to obtain the deceased's property?

A. Not if the deceased used sound planning. Then most of a married couple's property will go to the surviving spouse as nonprobate property. If the deceased does not own probate property, there is no need to probate the estate.

Q. How may I avoid probate?

A. Many legal devices, created while a person is still alive, transfer real and personal property to the survivor right after the person dies. For example, the home is usually in the name of the husband and wife as tenants by the entirety or joint tenants with the right of survivorship. When one spouse dies, the property passes to the surviving spouse. It does not go through probate. The same is true for life insurance policies when the surviving spouse is named as the beneficiary. Other legal devices include joint checking and savings accounts. They pass the money to the surviving spouse without probate.

Q. What if the deceased wrote a will before the marriage?

A. Some states may revoke the entire will if the will does not mention the surviving spouse, and if the deceased did not otherwise provide for the survivor. Other states may give the surviving spouse the share required by law if the deceased had died without a will *(intestate)*.

If There Is No Will

Q. What if a spouse dies without a will?

A. Then the courts will distribute property under the state's *intestate succession law*. These laws vary from one state to

(continued)

A stepparent who does not adopt a spouse's children normally may not claim custody of them if the marriage ends in divorce. Stepchildren usually do not share in the estate of a stepparent. An exception is if the stepparent has provided for the stepchildren in a will. However, unmarried stepchildren under 18 may receive supplemental retirement benefits from Social Security. If their stepparent dies, they may receive survivor's benefits under Social Security.

LIVING TRUSTS

A major device for transferring property without probate when a spouse dies is the *living trust*. In a trust, one person—a *trustee*—agrees to hold legal title to real or personal property and manage it for the beneficiaries. For example, a husband may set up a trust naming himself as trustee and beneficiary for life. After he dies, the property could go to his wife as the other beneficiary. His property could go directly to her or continue in the trust. The latter requires the selection of a successor trustee, who might be the wife. The terms of the trust dictate how the trustee manages and invests the property and also decide when and how much the surviving spouse receives. People often use living trusts to support the surviving spouse and other family members. The trust may treat each family member differently. The trust may provide for more or less financial support depending on various conditions.

another. However, all states guarantee that the surviving spouse will share in the deceased's probate estate. The amount depends on whether other close relatives, such as children and parents, survive. If the deceased has no living close relatives, the surviving spouse usually gets the entire probate estate.

Other Laws

Q. What other laws protect a surviving spouse?

A. Besides giving a spouse probate and nonprobate property, states have other laws to protect a surviving spouse. These may include the elective share, the homestead, exempt property, or family allowance.

Q. What is the elective share?

A. The *elective share* allows the surviving spouse to take a share of the deceased's property. Some people call this the *statutory* or *forced share*. The share is elective because the surviving spouse may elect to take this share instead of taking under the will or under the state's intestate succession law. (However, the surviving spouse may do this only if he or she did not sign the deceased's will.) Various factors may, in effect, disinherit the surviving spouse. Perhaps a will gave the survivor little or nothing. Maybe there was little or no probate property to be distributed under the intestate succession law. The elective share protects the disinherited surviving spouse.

States vary on what surviving spouses may claim as their share. In some states, the share may be a *fee simple* interest in a specified fraction of the deceased spouse's land. (That is, an interest in the property that the surviving spouse may dispose of in any desired way.) Or it may be a fraction (often one third or one half) of the probate estate. The elective share also may be the share owed to the disinherited surviving spouse under the state's intestate law if there was no will.

In other states, the surviving spouse may elect to take one third of the *augmented estate*. This estate combines three elements. The first is the net probate estate. The second is the value of specified property that the deceased gave during the marriage to other people without the surviving spouse's consent. The third is the value of the property that the deceased gave to the surviving spouse and that the survivor keeps after the deceased dies.

These states entitle the surviving spouse to one third of the augmented estate. They reduce this amount first by what the surviving spouse receives or has received under the first and third elements described above. Then other people who received property from the deceased might have their gift reduced to make up any amount unpaid to the disinherited surviving spouse. These people received the property either by will, intestate succession, or by a gift specified in the second element described above.

Q. What are exempt property laws?

A. When one spouse dies, state laws entitle the surviving spouse, the surviving children, or all these survivors to exempt property allowances. State laws vary in the amount and type of property they may claim. Sometimes they may take money instead of property. These allowances protect the property from creditors. The allowances also may protect the surviving spouse against disinheritance.

Q. What are family allowance laws?

A. Besides homestead and exempt property allowances, the law entitles the surviving spouse and children to a family allowance. State laws allow a court or the estate's personal representative to pay support to the surviving spouse and children while the proper authority administers the estate. Some states limit the amount of cash and the time period for receiving that money. Other states do not set any limits, allowing the court to decide these questions. Family allowances also may protect the surviving spouse and children from creditors.

In addition to the family protection benefits (homestead, property exemptions, and family allowance), the law usually entitles the surviving spouse and children to the intestate share (what the spouse and children receive when there is no will), the elective share, or what the surviving spouse and children receive under the will. However, the law or a will might not offer all these family protection benefits to the surviving spouse and children.

Children as Heirs

Q. What does the law entitle children to when their parents die?

A. The law allows children to take any property given to them by a trust, joint account, or other legal devices created for them. The law also entitles children to take probate property given by a valid will. Parents often make a will before they bear or

Homestead Laws

Homestead laws are designed to give a family a place to live. These laws allow property owners to set aside a specific amount of property or their entire dwelling that their creditors may not take. This usually includes residences and certain personal property items. The amount of money or property they may set aside varies among the states.

Here is how one claims a homestead exemption. Property owners themselves may file the homestead claim with the appropriate court or the appropriate property records office. In most states, if the owner did not make a claim, the owner's surviving spouse and minor children may do so. The homestead exemption continues while the surviving

(continued)

adopt children. Thus, the will does not mention the children. If the parent fails to provide otherwise for the children, they usually get what they would have received had the parent died without a will. The law refers to these children as *pretermitted heirs*. However, almost all states allow parents to disinherit their children if the will shows a clear intent to do so.

Disinherited children are not permitted to take an elective share. However, the laws governing homestead, exempt property allowances, and family allowances may protect the children. Homestead laws generally benefit children only while they are minors. Some family allowance laws cover only minor children. Exempt property laws are not always available to children, especially if a spouse survives.

Q. What if a parent dies without a will?

A. Then the children will share in that parent's probate estate under the state's intestate succession law. Their share depends on who survives the parent and on the division of the property in the state's law. Children usually share their deceased parent's estate with their surviving parent. Most states have laws for when no spouse survives the deceased. Then the children (and the children of their deceased siblings—that is, their nieces and nephews) will receive the entire estate.

(continued)

spouse is alive or while the couple's children are minors. Some states give complete title of the homestead to the surviving spouse and minor children. This protects it forever against the deceased's creditors. The heirs may dispose of the homestead as they wish.

However, homestead laws do not necessarily protect against all creditors. If a spouse has died, the surviving spouse could lose the property if he or she signed the mortgage. Mechanic's liens and real-estate taxes also may be valid against the survivor, despite the homestead laws.

WHERE TO GET MORE INFORMATION

Adoption

Every state has a state adoption officer. These officials usually have offices in the state capital. The state government information operator can help you locate the officer for your state. For information about agency adoptions, contact the Child Welfare League of America, 440 1st Street N.W., Suite 310, Washington, D.C. 20001. Its telephone number is (202) 638-2952. You also may wish to contact the National Committee for Adoption, 1930 17th Street N.W., Washington, D.C. 20009. Its telephone number is (202) 328-1200. For information on independent adoption, check with your state bar association. Ask if independent adoptions are legal in your state. Also ask if the bar association will refer you to lawyers who handle independent adoption.

Battered Spouses

Many communities offer shelters for battered spouses and their children. Details on these shelters are available from the police, churches, family or conciliation courts, local newspapers, or women's organizations. Johnson & Johnson sponsors the National Domestic Violence Hot Line. Its toll-free telephone number is (800) 333-SAFE. This hot line can refer you to shelters and safe homes for domestic violence victims in locations across the country. You also can use this toll-free number for details and support. Another resource is the National Coalition Against Domestic Violence, P.O. Box 34103, Washington, D.C. 20043. Its telephone number is (202) 638-6388 or (202) 638-6389. The local or state chapter of the National Organization for Women (N.O.W.) also should be able to provide information to help battered spouses.

Child Support

You can obtain details about how current state law upholds child support from state and county enforcement agencies. The state government switchboard can direct parents to a suitable officer. Another resource is the Office of Child Support Enforcement Reference Center, Washington, D.C. 20201. (This office is part of the U.S. Department of Health and Human Services.) This office can help parents find their state's enforcement officers. The Office of Child Support Enforcement will provide a free fact sheet and booklet (Publication 505W) entitled *Handbook on Child Support Enforcement*. To order, write to: Consumer Information Center-N, P.O. Box 100, Pueblo, Colorado 81002.

Also available from the Consumer Information Center-N, at the above address, is *Wage Withholding for Child Support—An Employer's Guide for Small Business*. Beginning in November 1990, employers will have legal responsibilities for enforcing child support. This pamphlet provides an overview of how this law will work. It contains useful information as well for both absent (noncustodial) and custodial parents. This guide also lists the telephone numbers of the State Child Support Agency Wage Withholding Offices. Two pages. (1989) Publication 502W. Free.

Credit and Bankruptcy

Two chapters in this publication discuss these topics. The "Consumer Credit" chapter also lists many free publications.

Whom You Can and Cannot Disinherit

You cannot disinherit your spouse, unless it is a case of marital misconduct, desertion, or a premarital agreement. However, in almost every state, you can disinherit your children—and your relatives, too. (For further information on this topic, see the "Wills, Trusts, and Estate Planning" chapter.)

Divorce

Most local public libraries offer books written about divorce. Ask both the general circulation and the reference librarians for help.

Mediation

The best source is the Academy of Family Mediators, P.O. Box 10501, Eugene, Oregon 97440. Its telephone number is (503) 345-1205. The academy has lists of family mediators in every state by training and experience.

Missing Children

Various agencies can offer help in finding children who are missing. They include:

Missing Children Help Center
410 Ware Boulevard, Suite 400
Tampa, Florida 33619
Telephone: (813) 623-KIDS
or (800) USA-KIDS (toll-free)

or

National Center for Missing and Exploited Children
2101 Wilson Boulevard, Suite 550
Arlington, Virginia 22201
Telephone: (800) 843-5678 (toll-free)

Pensions

One resource on pensions is the U.S. Department of Labor. The proper office is Pension and Welfare Benefits Administration, U.S. Department of Labor, Division of Technical Assistance and Inquiries, Room N5658, 200 Constitution Avenue, N.W., Washington, D.C. 20210.

The Pension Rights Center informs employees of their rights involving pensions. This private organization also offers booklets that explain related topics. Write to: Pension Rights Center, 918 16th Street, N.W., Suite 704, Washington, D.C. 20006. Or call (202) 296-3776.

Social Security

Your local Social Security Administration office can provide information and literature on benefits. You can find its address and telephone number in your local telephone directory.

Taxes

The basic resource on federal income taxes is the Internal Revenue Service (IRS). You can find your regional office in the phone book under "U.S. Government." You also may wish to contact an accountant or a tax lawyer.

Free publications on family taxes available from the IRS include *Community Property and the Federal Income Tax* (Publication 555), *Tax Information for Divorced or Separated Individuals* (Publication 504), and *Tax Rules for Children and Dependents* (Publication 929).

Wills and Estate Planning

The "Wills, Trusts, and Estate Planning" chapter near the back of this publication discusses these topics and lists related resources.

Women's Issues

The Legal Defense and Education Fund of the National Organization for Women (N.O.W.) sells a very handy guide. *State by State Guide to Women's Legal Rights* covers many aspects of family law. It is available for $12.95 (plus $2 postage) from NOW LDEF, 99 Hudson Street, New York, New York 10013. You also can write to this address for a free list of other publications from N.O.W.

BUYING AND SELLING A HOME

INTRODUCTION

A home is the biggest investment most Americans will ever make. Yet many people plunge into buying or selling a home with less care than they give to buying or selling a car.

If you are one of the millions of Americans about to buy or sell a home, you should understand the many factors that affect your decision. These factors include state and federal law, the economy, your personal preferences, your financial situation, the real-estate market, mortgage rates, and real-estate taxes. You also will need to work with a variety of people, including the buyer or seller, real-estate agents, attorneys, home inspectors, appraisers, lenders, and insurance agents, to name a few. In short, buying and selling a home is not a simple matter.

Whether you are buying your first home or selling your tenth, you will want to make sure that you understand how the law affects your decisions. This chapter begins with questions related to buying a home. Then it continues with financing the home purchase. (This topic also is discussed near the end of this chapter.) If you are selling your home, you may want to move directly to the next part of this chapter ("Selling a Home"). However, it is a good idea to become familiar with the legal aspects from the buyer's side as well. This is particularly true if it has been a while since you bought a home. Practices and laws do change, and you will want to be aware of the buyer's considerations and responsibilities besides your own. Remember, someone must be willing to buy a home before you can sell it, and vice versa. The sale will involve negotiations and legal consequences. Like any other contract negotiations, it is a good idea to understand the goals of both parties in the transaction. (Note that "home" as used in this chapter refers to a single-family dwelling built on land. Many of the topics covered also will apply to townhomes, condominiums, co-operatives, or mobile homes, but each of these has some different characteristics. The end of this chapter discusses some of these.)

BUYING A HOME

Q. Why isn't buying a home as simple as buying some item of personal property, such as a car?

A. There is no easy answer to this question. The law treats personal property (non-real estate) and real property (real estate) differently because they have distinct characteristics. Generally, personal property is easily moved, like an automobile or stocks and bonds. You often own it for a short period of time. Ownership may be shown by possession. In contrast, real estate is not transportable. That is, you cannot move it. While a building may not be permanent, the land is permanent. Also, real estate is not in someone's "possession" all the time. The large size of some real estate makes it hard for one person to show "possession" physically. Showing possession is often difficult even with smaller parcels (portions) of real estate. Another characteristic of real estate is that many different people may own various interests in real estate at the same time.

Q. Why should I buy a home?

A. There are many different joys and benefits of homeownership. They range from privacy and security to tax benefits and the prospect of owning your home without a mortgage. For most people, buying a home represents the largest purchase of their lifetime. With proper planning, that home also will provide one of the greatest satisfactions of a lifetime.

Q. What is a "buyer's market"?

A. A *buyer's market* occurs during periods when home sales slow down. There are various ways to recognize a buyer's market. Is it taking longer to sell homes in your area? Are foreclosures increasing? Are there large reductions in home prices? Is unemployment increasing? Is there a decline in the number of building permits issued? All these factors—or even some of them—indicate a "soft" market. People call this a buyer's market, because the buyer can deal from a stronger position than the seller. The buyer has many choices of homes and can ask sellers for special consideration.

Q. What is a "seller's market"?

A. A *seller's market* is the best time to sell your home. You can recognize a seller's market when prices are increasing, there

REAL ESTATE—WHAT IS IT REALLY?

Real estate consists of:

- **The land;**
- **The minerals beneath the land;**
- **Crops growing on the land;**
- **Improvements or fixtures on the land; and**
- **Airspace above the land.**

Different people may own each of these five components of real estate. Each of these ownerships may be subject to legal claims and liens. Also, each of them may be leased. An entire body of real-estate law exists to protect the rights of people claiming interests in real estate. The laws designed to protect those interests apply equally to complex commercial deals and the sale of a home or condominium.

are few homes on the market, and the local economy is in good health. In those periods, sellers can and do demand high prices for their homes. They can often dictate the terms of the contract. In such a "hot" seller's market, people often sell their homes within days. Many sellers receive competing bids during such periods.

If you can choose the time to sell your home, there is no question that it is a lot easier in a seller's market. If you can choose the time to buy a home, you will save money by avoiding buying in a seller's market.

CAN YOU AFFORD A HOME?

What you can afford depends on many factors: How much money have you saved for a down payment? What is your current income and what are your current expenses? Do you have a good credit history? What are the current interest rates on mortgages? What are your priorities and life-style? All these must be considered in order to determine whether you can afford to purchase a home.

Q. How expensive a home can I afford?

A. This is one of the first things to consider when buying a home. What you can afford will narrow your range, so you will not waste time by looking at homes that cost too much. This will make it easier to shop for a home. First-time buyers often become disappointed when they find the home of their dreams but discover they cannot afford it.

A down payment is very important. Unless you are looking for a special government loan, you will need ten to 20 percent of the purchase price. Thus, a $100,000 home would require a $10,000 to $20,000 down payment. Most homebuyers and lenders prefer a down payment of 20 percent. With less than a 20-percent down payment, you probably will have to pay a monthly charge for Private Mortgage Insurance (PMI). This insures the lender against nonpayment of the difference between the full down payment and the amount actually paid. Suppose you purchased a $100,000 home but paid a down payment of ten percent ($10,000), rather than the customary 20 percent ($20,000). If you fail to make payments and the lender has to foreclose, PMI guarantees that the lender will receive the $10,000 that you did not pay as a down payment. The charge for PMI can be expensive—sometimes an extra 50 to 60 dollars per month. Most homebuyers put 20 percent down to avoid paying for PMI.

In addition, you will need between four to six percent of the mortgage amount to pay for *closing costs*. These include appraisal, title insurance, attorney, title search, tax fees, and other expenses such as recording fees and homeowners' insurance.

Getting a Mortgage

Q. How much money will a lender give me for a mortgage?

A. The amount a lender will provide for a mortgage directly depends on your income and expenses. As a homeowner, you will be paying a monthly mortgage charge, along with costs for insurance, property taxes, utilities, and maintenance. A lender looks for a solid history of income, employment, and credit. The lender also will review your expenses, including car payments, credit-card debt, child support, alimony, and so on. If you are borrowing money for your down payment, the lender also will look at any future interest payments as expenses.

Q. What about interest rates?

A. Along with the type of mortgage you choose (see "Financing a Home Purchase" later in this chapter), interest rates will affect the cost and amount of your mortgage. For example, a one-percent increase in the interest rate on a $100,000 mortgage adds approximately $75 each month on a 30-year mortgage. Mortgage rates can change quickly. They usually are the last rates to decline when rates are falling. They also are the first to rise when rates are climbing. Thus it is important to estimate your potential mortgage payment based on current rates. If you select a variable-rate mortgage, be sure you will be able to pay it during times of high interest rates. (A later section in this chapter discusses variable-rate mortgages.)

Q. Is there a formula for figuring out what I can afford?

A. The traditional "affordability" rule says that a home should cost no more than 2.5 times your annual income. Thus, if your income is $50,000, your limit might be $50,000 multiplied by 2.5, which equals $125,000. You also need to consider your life-style and priorities. Suppose costly vacations, dining out, and entertainment are important in your life. Or perhaps you have significant medical or educational expenses. Then you probably will want to buy a home that costs less than the traditional rule says you can afford. Many people, however, are willing to give up some luxuries to obtain the home they want. Others decide they are willing to stretch their budget for the home they want, exceeding the affordability rule.

Q. I want to buy a home, but my credit history is poor. What may I do?

A. There are several responses to this situation. First, if you have a poor credit history—paying bills late or not paying at all—you will want to improve your credit record. Begin immediately to pay all bills on time, pay off any overdue bills,

(continued)

Payment Tables*
15-Year Mortgage

Amount Financed	8%	9%	10%	11%	12%	13%	14%	15%
$50,000	$477.83	$507.13	$537.30	$568.30	$600.09	$632.63	$665.88	$699.80
$80,000	$764.52	$811.41	$859.68	$909.28	$960.14	$1,012.20	$1,065.40	$1,119.67
$100,000	$955.65	$1,014.27	$1,074.61	$1,136.60	$1,200.17	$1,265.25	$1,331.75	$1,399.59

*Table gives the amount of monthly payments (principal and interest) to repay loans that fully pay off the debt over the term of the lease.

Payment Tables*
30-Year Mortgage

Amount Financed	8%	9%	10%	11%	12%	13%	14%	15%
$50,000	$366.88	$402.31	$438.79	$476.16	$514.31	$553.10	$592.44	$632.23
$80,000	$587.01	$643.70	$702.06	$761.86	$822.90	$884.96	$947.90	$1,011.56
$100,000	$733.76	$804.62	$877.57	$952.32	$1,028.62	$1,106.20	$1,184.88	$1,264.45

*Table gives the amount of monthly payments (principal and interest) to repay loans that fully pay off the debt over the term of the lease.

and establish a positive credit record. While doing this, you may have to delay your home purchase.

Second, credit-reporting agencies can and do make mistakes. If you believe your credit report is in error, you may challenge the report. You have a right to inspect the report. A summary of the report must be made available free of charge. However, the law allows the credit-reporting agency to charge a fee for the full report. In any case, you may obtain the complete report. If you prove there are inaccuracies, you can demand that the agency correct them. If necessary, you may want to consult your lawyer if you are unable to get the credit bureau to change the report. (See the "Consumer Credit" chapter for more details.)

Using a Realtor and/or Lawyer

Q. Who should be involved in the purchase of a home?

A. The answer depends on many factors. Sometimes a buyer purchases a home directly from a homeowner, with very few other people involved. However, most transactions today are not so simple. Usually, in buying a single-family home, you will want the services of a lawyer, a real-estate agent, and a home inspector. In addition, you may want to consult a financial planner or accountant about financing the home.

Besides the people with whom you will directly consult, there may be others involved in the purchase. These may include the seller's lawyer, the seller's real-estate agent, and the seller. You may not ever meet these people until the closing, but they will be behind the scenes. (The *closing* occurs when the seller and buyer close the sale and transfer the property title to you.) In addition, you probably will work with several people in getting your loan. You also may deal with a title company or a title insurance company during the transfer of the title.

If you are buying a home from a builder, you may or may not work through a real-estate agent. However, you may want to consult a lawyer to avoid any legal problems. Typically, purchase contracts are drafted by the builder's attorney and are in a form that favors the builder's interests. When buying from a builder, you may avoid home inspections. Regardless, some buyers prefer an independent inspection despite the newness of the structure.

Q. When should I see an attorney about buying a home?

A. You do not have to consult a lawyer before you begin your search for a home. However, you will want to protect your interests once you start to consider making an offer. You should consult with an attorney before signing any paper concerning a real-estate purchase. It is a good idea, for example, to see a lawyer before you sign an "Offer to Purchase," a "Preliminary Binder," a "Deposit Receipt," or any purchase agreement. Once signed by the seller and buyer, it may be a legally binding contract. The time to ask for and receive legal advice is before signing that document.

Q. How do I choose an attorney?

A. There are several methods of selecting a lawyer. First, many state and local bar associations will give you the names of attorneys practicing real-estate law. The phone number for a local lawyer referral service usually appears in the yellow pages of your phone book under listings for "Attorneys" or "Lawyers."

Another way to choose an attorney is to talk to friends who have used the services of local attorneys in real-estate transactions. They should be able to give you the name of a lawyer whose services they found satisfactory.

Bar-related title insurance companies have lists of attorneys who work on many real-estate transactions. Lawyers affiliated with bar-related title insurance companies are able to issue title insurance policies. They also can provide other legal services concerning the transaction.

The real-estate agency may have a list of local attorneys who often work with their clients. You might find this a helpful way to select an attorney. The real-estate agent is not permitted to recommend a particular attorney. However, you may choose a lawyer from a list offered to you.

In some states, attorneys who practice in the real-estate field are designated by the state bar. You can find them listed in the yellow pages of your local telephone directory under "Attorneys, Real-Estate" or "Lawyers, Real-Estate."

Finally, make sure the attorney that you select satisfies you. Buying a home can sometimes involve difficult and even intense negotiations. You want to be able to trust your lawyer to represent your interests and make you feel comfortable with the transaction. Your attorney can give you advice and the assurance that your interests are protected.

Q. What will I have to pay for the lawyer's services?

A. The price for an attorney varies from city to city and state to state. Fees for services normally are competitive. The major factor will be the time required to complete your transaction. In a simple transaction, the fee should be under $500. Be warned, however, that the fee can increase if there are complications in the negotiations and in closing the sale.

The estimated fee the lawyer discusses on your first visit usually is just that—an estimated fee. The fee should be only one factor to consider. The quality of service is equally important. A good attorney can help you save many times the amount of the fee in reduced taxes and contract terms. (For more information, see the "When and How to Use a Lawyer" chapter.)

Q. What is the real-estate agent's role?

A. The seller's agent lists the home and helps determine its price. Also, the seller's agent suggests how to market the home more attractively. In addition, the seller's agent shows it to prospective buyers, and otherwise assists in its sale.

The buyer's agent can help you locate the kind of home you prefer in the kind of neighborhood you want. Some agents specialize in helping you get financing. Most professional agents will be able to answer your questions throughout the home-buying process. In addition, the agent can:

- Provide you with recent selling prices of similar homes;
- Contact the listing agent (who put the home on the market) to ask questions you may have about the home;
- Monitor the entire deal to avoid any problems or delays;
- Help you negotiate a purchase price.

Remember, however, that the commission of both the seller's agent and the buyer's agent not only depends on the sale, but is paid by the seller. This means that the buyer's agent actually works for and acts on behalf of the seller.

Q. What if I'm not comfortable with that situation?

A. Most buyers feel comfortable having their agent's fee paid by the seller and prefer avoiding any extra costs. However, you may enlist the help of a buyer's broker to represent you personally. This would avoid any potential conflict of interest. A buyer's broker may require a nonrefundable fee. The fee may vary with the length of your search and extent of the broker's services. If you choose this option, you will want to have a specific contract with the broker. It should specify the services to be provided and the fees you will pay. If possible, avoid having the fee connected to the purchase price of the home. You do not want to provide an incentive for the agent to encourage *any* sale (even one that is unfair to you) or a more expensive sale than necessary.

Q. How do I, the buyer, choose a real-estate agent?

A. The professional qualifications of a real-estate agent are just as important as those of a lawyer. You will want to look for

Discuss Attorney's Fees in Advance

Do not hesitate to discuss fees on your first visit with an attorney. Most lawyers will be happy to discuss fees with you in advance. If a particular attorney shows no interest in discussing fees, you should consider seeking the services of another lawyer. Depending on the attorney and local circumstances, a lawyer might charge by the hour. Or an attorney might have a set fee for a specific type of real-estate transaction.

an experienced agent familiar with the area that interests you. Choosing an agent requires that you do your homework on both the agent and the real-estate broker for whom the agent works.

Your best approach is to interview several agents from different offices. Ask about the agent's sales for the last six months or a year. How do they compare with the sales of other agents in the firm? Also ask the agent for the names of recent buyers who used the agent's services, and talk to them. Inquire about the sales by the real-estate office, including the names of recent clients. How do the sales of that office compare with the sales of other firms? Ask to see the Multiple Listing Book, and check the listings of the broker's office and the agent. The Multiple Listing Book includes all listings of properties for sale by members of the Multiple Listing Service (MLS). Compare the listings of your broker to those of other brokers in your area.

You will want to make sure that your agent has experience. Two years experience as a broker is a good rule of thumb. In addition to the number of years, the number of closings that a broker has participated in is also important in determining experience. Obviously, if an agent has had two years experience and closed only two real-estate transactions during that time, that agent probably is not as experienced as one would like. On the other hand, if the agent has handled a substantial number of closings in that period of time, the agent may very well be experienced enough to handle a real-estate transaction.

Also make sure that your agent and broker have a good record in helping buyers locate and purchase the types of homes that interest you. For example, an agent who customarily has clients seeking $200,000 homes may not spend much time working for a client seeking a $100,000 home. Remember, the agent's commission depends on the selling price of the home. Thus, an agent may spend more time with a client looking for a more expensive home.

Most importantly, before you start working with an agent, try to make decisions about the type of home you want, the amount you are willing to pay, and all the other important aspects of home buying. Agents quickly become frustrated when a couple or any two people buying a home together seem to have different things in mind.

Some Advance Work Before You Buy

Before you, as a buyer, contract with an agent, you may want to stop at "open houses" to get a feeling for various neighborhoods and the style of home you are seeking. You also may want to be *prequalified* by a lender for a loan. You become prequalified by working with a lending institution *before* you have a specific home in mind. That means filling out financial statements, making the necessary financial disclosures, and having your credit record checked. This will give you a rough idea of how much money the lender will loan you, and thus pinpoint your price range.

Determining Property Taxes

Q. How may I determine the property taxes on a home?

A. The seller should be willing to reveal the property taxes paid on the home. You or your agent can obtain the current assessment and tax information from the local tax assessor's office. This information is a matter of public record. You also will want to investigate the potential increase in taxes *after* the sale. For example, in some states, property tax increases occur only when a home changes ownership. Then the tax assessor reassesses the home, and taxes may skyrocket. In addition, many states reassess property every three or four years. If you are buying the home at the end of that cycle, you may see a large increase in property taxes. While the amount of taxes may not be the deciding factor, you will want to consider the taxes, at least when determining your potential monthly payment.

Q. What is the difference between "assessed value" and "appraised value"?

A. The *assessed value* of a home, determined by the tax assessor, is the basis for property taxes. It may or may not reflect the *market value,* which is the price for which the home would sell. If you know the assessed value of a home, you can then determine the taxes to be paid on it. You can determine the taxes by contacting the assessor's office of the city or county in which the home is located and asking for the total tax rate of the jurisdiction (including local governments, schools, community colleges, parks, and so on). The tax rate usually is applied to each $1,000 of assessed valuation. For example, a tax rate of ten on a home assessed at $100,000 would be $1,000.

The *appraised value* is an appraiser's estimate of the property's market value. A lender normally will require an appraisal to determine that the selling price does not exceed the property's market value or the lender's mortgage.

The Fair Housing Act

Q. May a homeowner refuse to sell me a home?

A. A homeowner may not discriminate against you because of race, religion, or several other specific factors. The Fair Housing Act, Title VIII of the Civil Rights Act of 1968, covers housing discrimination. This law prohibits housing discrimination by real-estate firms and homeowners. This means that homeowners may not refuse to lease or sell property to you based on your race, religion, gender, color, or national origin. In some localities, housing discrimination also covers sexual orientation and whether you have a handicap. This does not mean, however, that sellers *must* sell you their home. It means that you could take legal action if the seller refused to sell you the home and you felt it was due to discrimination.

However, a homeowner may discriminate on economic grounds. Suppose your poor credit rating or your ability to obtain a mortgage worried a homeowner. Then the homeowner could accept another bid or even refuse your bid without too much fear of legal action. On the other hand, homeowners may not refuse to sell the home because they do not want to offend their neighbors.

The law prohibits real-estate agents from *steering*. This is the practice of showing homes, for instance, to black persons in black neighborhoods.

You may suspect discrimination if:

- Somebody tells you that a listed home is no longer for sale;
- An agent avoids showing you homes in areas you have requested; or
- A seller refuses a full-price bid on a home.

If you suspect that someone has discriminated against you, call the federal Department of Housing and Urban Development (HUD) at (202) 755-6420. Its job is to investigate such complaints. You also may consult a lawyer about possible legal action.

WHAT EXACTLY IS EARNEST MONEY?

When the buyer signs the offer to purchase, the buyer usually must deposit some money with the seller or the seller's real-estate broker. Some people call that deposit a *good faith* or *earnest money* deposit. It is different from the down payment. (The buyer must pay the down payment when the buyer and seller sign the purchase contract.) The listing agent or the seller's attorney usually holds the earnest money. It often draws interest for the buyer during this phase of the process.

Making an Offer

Q. How do I begin negotiations to buy a home?

A. Your real-estate agent or attorney will provide an "offer to purchase" form. This is a formal, written offer (sometimes called a *preliminary binder*) that will include the price you are willing to pay. It may have different names in different parts of the country. It also may list other items, such as the possession date (when you may occupy the home) and financing conditions. The seller may not accept your first offer. Often this is the start of negotiations. Then the offer to purchase may be passed back and forth between the buyer and seller. A date after which the offer is no longer valid should appear in the offer to purchase. This may be as little as 24 hours from the time the seller or the seller's agent receives it. The offer to purchase also is usually valid only if both the buyer and seller sign a purchase contract within a certain time period. Usually, an *earnest money* deposit (to show good faith) accompanies the offer to purchase.

Q. What is the purchase contract?

A. The contract for the sale of a home is the blueprint for the entire transaction. In some areas, the buyers prepare the purchase contract. In other areas, the sellers prepare it. When completed, the purchase contract will govern the entire transaction. Some people refer to this document as an agreement of sale, sales contract, purchase agreement, sales agreement, or contract of purchase. The name varies from one locality to another. However, under any name, it is a legal document that requires careful review. Once it is fully executed and the buyer makes a deposit, it becomes a binding contract on the parties.

Purchase contracts may follow standard forms. Like leases, you can often pick them up at stationery stores. However, you may negotiate each clause. Besides the purchase price, the time when it must be paid is negotiable. The buyer will want the contract to be dependent upon getting financing. The seller will want a specific time limit during which the buyer will obtain that financing. If the buyer is to assume an existing mortgage—and not all are assumable—that also should be noted, depending on the lender's approval. (A section near the end of this chapter discusses assumable mortgages.)

Q. What are the key provisions or clauses in the purchase contract?

A. The purchase contract will include many provisions, reflecting all terms of the sale. At the very least, the contract should contain:

(1) The purchase price and how it is to be paid. This should include the amount of cash required, any planned financing, its cost, interest charges, and the length of the mortgage.
(2) A legal description of the property (a street address is not adequate). Sometimes it requires a survey of the property.
(3) A good title furnished by the seller, as shown by an abstract of title, certificate of title, or a policy of title insurance. *Good title* is also called *marketable title* by attorneys. It indicates that there are no claims or liens against the property, such as mechanic's liens, or an encumbrance, such as a right-of-way. Good title indicates that the seller really owns the home, often as shown by title that is without any breaks in the chain of title back to the original owner.
(4) Warranties of title, including title restrictions and any other rights and limitations that may affect the title.
(5) The date of transfer of possession.
(6) Provisions for paying utility bills, property taxes, and similar expenses up to the date of the closing.
(7) The name of the party responsible for risk of fire or other hazard, until the closing or transfer of possession occurs.

(8) An itemized list of all furnishings, appliances, shrubbery, fixtures, air conditioners, and other personal property included in the sale.
(9) The basic terms of any escrow agreement.
(10) A provision for returning the down payment if the buyer and seller do not complete the sale or if financing is denied. This is a very important clause that you should not overlook. Buyers can and have lost their down payments, which often involved a large amount of money.
(11) Signatures of the parties and the date of the contract.

Q. What other clauses should be in the contract?

A. As noted above, if the buyer must get financing, the contract should include a financing contingency clause with a specific time limit. The buyer also will usually want to have the contract dependent on a complete and satisfactory inspection of the premises. The inspector should check for: termites; the condition of the roof; the electrical, plumbing, heating, and air-conditioning systems; and the like. The seller may want to limit the warranties for the furnace, roof, or major appliances by adding an "as is" clause to the contract. In any event, the seller should specify a date by which the buyer must complete the inspection. If either party signs without using a lawyer, it is a good idea to include a contingency clause making the contract subject to attorney approval.

Q. Is that all there is to consider?

A. No, there is more. The seller and buyer should establish a firm date for possession. The buyer should request a provision requiring the seller to pay a specific amount as rent if the seller does not leave the home by the agreed date. If the buyer wants to take possession before closing, the seller should have the buyer pay a specific amount as rent for that period of time. (Some experts advise against allowing the buyer to take possession before the closing. Serious difficulties might arise later if the buyer and seller do not complete the sale.)

As noted above, the contract should have a clause stating who will be responsible if a fire or other hazard damages or destroys the property before the closing. In some states, the Uniform Vendor-Purchaser Risk of Loss Act will apply. It provides that the seller has the risk of loss until the transfer of either the title or possession. After the transfer of either one, the risk of loss goes to the buyer.

Both parties also will want a clause that binds the successors, heirs, or representatives of the other party if the buyer or seller dies or becomes disabled. Finally, in some states, the buyer and seller must sign other forms. These may include disclosures about the condition of the roof, appliances, and fixtures. Other disclosure clauses deal with hazardous materials and floodplain zoning. In some states, for example, homes must be free of lead paint or that fact must be disclosed to the buyer. Or the hazardous materials clause could involve an inspection by a professional engineer, who makes a report. If certain levels of hazardous materials were found, the purchaser could void the contract. Floodplain zoning involves the location of the home on the federal floodplain map. Again, it would provide an opportunity for the purchaser to terminate the contract in the event that the property were in a flood-prone area.

Most states, however, do not require disclosure clauses. The phrase "caveat emptor" ("buyer beware") implies that the responsibility of knowledge about the purchase is imposed on the buyer, not the seller.

Earning Interest on Your Down Payment

You may and should earn interest on this money. However, you will have to specify that in the purchase contract. Do not assume that someone will automatically invest your money. It is best to state that you want your money placed in an FDIC-insured bank account and that you should be paid or credited with the interest at the closing.

Q. What happens to my down payment if we do not complete the sale?

A. Generally, contract provisions allow the buyer to get back the money and interest, unless the buyer is at fault. Suppose you are the buyer, and you consider backing out of the deal. Then the seller may challenge your right to get back the down payment.

Q. Why does the contract include contingency clauses?

A. In some parts of the country, the seller and buyer normally sign a contract that includes contingency clauses (or *riders*). These may allow for home inspections and approvals by attorneys. They also may make the transaction contingent on getting a mortgage at a certain rate of interest. A contingency clause allows the buyer to be certain everything is satisfactory before the sales contract becomes binding. Contingency clauses also can work to the benefit of the seller, particularly an attorney's rider. Both parties may benefit from the same contingency clause. Suppose there are some unknown matters in connection with the property that the seller is not aware of. If the seller closes on a transaction with those problems existing, the seller might be subjected to substantial liabilities. And the buyer would have bought a home with serious flaws.

Q. What is an attorney-approval rider?

A. One common rider makes the purchase contract subject to approval by the buyer's and seller's respective attorneys within a short period of time. This usually is five to ten days after acceptance of the offer. In such cases, the standard contract form should include the phrase, "SUBJECT TO THE APPROVAL OF THE ATTORNEYS FOR THE PARTIES WITHIN ____ DAYS," with the number of days specified. Without such a condition in the contract, both the seller and the buyer will be bound by the terms of the contract, which may be unclear or may not be as the parties intended.

Q. Does an attorney-approval rider give a buyer an "out" from the contract?

A. Yes, it does allow a buyer to get out of a contract. In fact, some sellers will not accept such clauses for that reason. An attorney-approval rider could avoid this pitfall by limiting the attorney's approval to legal matters, such as the state of the title. In addition, the rider could specify that a lawyer must state such disapproval in writing, with the other party able to change the contract accordingly.

This type of rider ensures that the contract need not bind the parties if their lawyers find an unfair statement in the small print. Meanwhile, the buyer and seller can sign the contract knowing that the other party may not easily back out of the contract because of a minor defect or objection.

Q. What is a mortgage contingency?

A. This common provision allows the buyer a certain time to get a commitment for financing at a specified interest rate for a certain amount of money. It usually lasts for 30 to 60 days, depending on the usual time needed to obtain a mortgage in your area. The clause might read, for example, that the contract is contingent on the buyer obtaining approval for a loan of $100,000 at 9.5-percent interest within 45 days. This clause also may protect a buyer from sudden jumps in interest rates. However, experts usually advise buyers to lock in the rate at the time of the loan application.

The seller may refuse to agree to a mortgage contingency. This can and does happen in a very hot seller's market. Then there is not much the buyer can do. Some real-estate agents suggest that buyers obtain "prequalification" from a lender (this was discussed earlier in this chapter). This means that the seller can be reasonably assured that the buyer will use the mortgage contingency only in very special circumstances.

Q. What is an inspection rider?

A. Another very important safeguard for the buyer is an *inspection rider*. Two types are commonly used. The first gives the buyer the right to have the property inspected by a professional home inspector of the buyer's choice. If the inspector finds fault, the buyer has the right to cancel the contract within a specified time. This type of rider raises some of the same issues as the unrestricted attorney-approval rider, since inspectors can often easily find problems in homes. Thus, it can give buyers a few extra days to decide whether they want to buy the home.

Q. What is the second type of inspection rider that is commonly in use?

A. It is a more complex inspection rider that often describes when the inspection must be made. It also gives the seller time to either repair any problems uncovered or agree to reduce the price by the cost of repairing such problems. If a seller decides not to make the repairs or reduce the price, the seller must inform the buyer. The seller then must give the buyer a chance to withdraw the inspection disapproval and accept the home "as is." If not taking the home "as is," the buyer must notify the seller that the buyer wants to cancel the contract and get back the down payment.

Q. Which type of inspection rider is better?

A. Some prefer the simpler inspection rider described earlier. Although it is open to occasional abuse by fickle buyers, it is simpler. It also requires fewer back-and-forth discussions between the buyer and seller. If there is a serious problem and the seller really wants to sell, the parties usually can make a new deal.

Still, the choice is yours. Just remember that a real-estate purchase contract is no different in principle than any other contract. That is, its terms are negotiable. By using properly drafted riders, you may quickly turn a brokers' form contract into one that deals with your personal concerns.

Q. Should I allow the seller to remain in the home after closing?

A. Most buyers want immediate possession, because they will be paying the mortgage after closing and will not want to pay for two residences. Sometimes, however, you may allow the seller to remain. For example, the seller may be moving to another state one month after the closing. Or perhaps the seller is waiting for a builder to finish a new home. If you find yourself in this situation, do not rely on oral promises or simply a statement about the date on which the seller promises to vacate the premises. Make sure your contract states how long

What to Expect from the Home Inspection

The buyer normally hires a contractor or home inspector to check out the home. The inspector does not care about cosmetic problems that the buyer could easily see, such as peeling wallpaper, torn carpet, or flaking paint. The inspector shows an interest only in the structural and mechanical aspects of the home. A professional inspector will examine the home for problems that a buyer is unlikely to notice. These include foundation and structural problems and the age and condition of the roof. The inspector also will examine the condition of the chimney, storm windows, gutters, electrical wiring, and plumbing.

If possible, you will want to accompany the inspector and take notes. Some inspectors charge a smaller fee if the potential buyer does not require a written report. An inspection usually will cost between $100 and $200.

the seller may occupy the home after closing and specifies the rent owed to you for that period. The contract also should specify any penalties if the seller does not move or pay you rent. In addition, the contract should state the penalties for any damage to the property during the seller's occupancy. Sometimes your attorney will prepare a separate lease agreement to cover these and other contingencies, including eviction and liability insurance.

Paying Taxes

Q. What taxes does owning a home involve?

A. First is the property tax. This is a yearly tax based on the assessed value of your property. You pay the tax to your local community. You may deduct the property tax you pay from your federal income tax return. Depending on your state's laws, it also may be deductible on your state income tax return.

In addition, you may deduct from your federal tax return interest paid on the mortgage loan you obtained for your home. Interest paid on a home-equity loan or a second mortgage of up to $100,000 also is deductible. You can use this money for any purpose. If the home-equity loan or second mortgage is for more than $100,000, you can deduct the interest if you use the money for home improvements. If you want to use a loan of more than $100,000 for other purposes, you must be able to prove that your home equity plus improvements at least equals the cost of the loan. (A later section in this chapter discusses home-equity loans.) Other mortgage loan interest you pay (such as on a second home) also may be deductible. Consult your tax adviser.

Depending on the laws of your state, there may be a transfer tax on the amount paid to purchase the home. If the home is financed, there may be a documentary tax on the note and an intangible tax on the mortgage. Generally, the seller pays the cost of the transfer tax, but in most cases it is negotiable. The buyer generally pays the cost of the documentary tax on the note and taxes on the mortgage.

Does Owning a Home Affect Your Will?

Yes, owning a home will affect federal estate taxes and state inheritance taxes. If you are a first-time home-buyer, you now own real estate, so you should review your will to see if changes are required. If you do not have a will and have bought real estate, you should review your entire estate plan and draft a will. (For more details, see the "Wills, Trusts, and Estate Planning" chapter.)

The Title

Q. How do you obtain title to a property?

A. In most areas of the country, there is no single piece of paper that constitutes the title to a parcel of real estate. The exceptions to this rule are those areas that have a Torrens or title registration system. As stated earlier, real estate consists of the land, improvements, minerals, crops, fixtures, and air space. Each of these various components of real estate may be owned, leased, or subject to other claims or liens, all at the same time. As a result, the "title" to real estate consists of the ownership of, the interests in, and the right to use the real estate.

When you are buying a home, you want to make sure that you receive as many of these rights as possible. Government regulations, in the form of zoning laws or use and occupancy laws, may limit your use of the real estate. There also may be subdivision covenants prohibiting you from making certain uses of your property. *Subdivision covenants* are quasi-zoning restrictions. They could, for example, restrict you from using your property to store liquor, prevent you from renting the home, or place architectural controls on your property. Subdivision covenants written long ago contain all kinds of restrictions that today are unenforceable, such as prohibiting you from selling your home to a person who is not white-skinned. These can be ignored, but covenants that could be enforceable should be understood. Ask for a copy of these restrictions before you sign your contract to purchase. Your attorney can help you decide if a covenant is legal and binding.

In addition, people or institutions may have some interest or claim on your title. Examples would be mineral rights held by prior owners, unpaid mortgages (which give lenders a claim on the property), judgments or tax liens against former owners, or power-line easements or road rights-of-way that could limit your use of the property. Another example is a gap in the chain of title, so that it is impossible to prove that the person whose name appears right after the gap was the lawful owner. Because of these title defects, title insurance has become popular in some parts of the country.

Q. What is title insurance?

A. It is an insurance policy that a title insurance company issues to the purchaser. It provides that the company will reimburse the purchaser (the insured) for any loss the purchaser might suffer because of defects in title. Lenders often will insist that buyers get title insurance. If the title insurance company discovers any defects, it will exclude them from the coverage. By discovering these defects, title insurance companies aid buyers. They provide buyers with information that enables them to make an informed decision on whether or not they wish to close on the transaction. The defects should be remedied prior to closing, or the buyer does not have to close on the purchase. Typically the responsibility for remedying title defects is on the seller. For these reasons, even in areas of the country where the buyer receives a title insurance policy, buyers and sellers may want the advice of a lawyer. Buyers and sellers should check to see what types of title insurance policies are available, their costs, reliability, and so forth.

Q. Are there other title services?

A. Yes. Depending on which area you live in, title searches may be conducted by title companies or by attorneys. A title search may take the form of an abstract. This provides a summary of the property's history of ownership.

The Closing

Q. What happens at the closing?

A. The real-estate closing is a meeting at which the buyer and seller (and their agents and lawyers, if any) formally complete the sale. During the closing, they do whatever is necessary to fulfill the terms of the contract. At this meeting, the buyer usually makes all the required payments. The seller produces all documents necessary for the transfer of title and delivers a deed that transfers the title to the buyer. At that time, the actual title to the home passes to the buyer, and the seller will deliver the keys to the home.

Before the closing, the parties and their lawyers will review all documents to see that everyone is fulfilling all conditions and promises of the contract. They also will prepare a closing statement or *settlement sheet*. It fully lists the financial aspects of the closing. If the real-estate transaction involves a "federally related mortgage loan," then the Real Estate Settlement Procedures Act (RESPA) applies. That means a settlement sheet developed by the Department of Housing and Urban Development (HUD) will be used. In other closings, another form of settlement sheet may be prepared.

Q. What are some financial aspects of the closing?

A. At the time of closing, the seller and buyer will total up various credits in order to determine how much money the buyer must pay. The seller will receive credits for such items as fuel on hand, unused insurance premiums, prepaid interest, and escrow deposits for insurance and taxes. These credits also will include any other items prepaid by the seller that will benefit the buyer. The buyer normally will receive credits for such items as taxes or special assessments that the seller has not paid. The settlement sheet also will state who is responsible for the payment of various expenses. These will include broker's fees or commissions and the costs of the title

The Walk-Through

Many buyers like to inspect the property 24 hours before the closing. They do this to be sure it is in the same condition as it was when they signed the offer to purchase. Another reason is to make sure that all property to be included in the sale remains on the property. If somebody has removed anything (such as a chandelier or appliance), the buyer should quickly notify the agent and the attorney to see if the item will be returned to the home before the closing. If agreeable to both parties, the buyer and seller may decide to reach a financial compromise instead.

search, inspections, recording fees, transaction taxes, and the like. The allocation of such expenses will depend on your locality, so obtain estimates at the time of your loan application. These expenses must be paid in cash at the time of the closing. The buyer should be certain to have enough money to pay these expenses plus the purchase price.

The chart on the following page by no means exhausts the list of fees that might be charged at closing. Other common fees include: loan origination fee (to cover the lender's administrative costs in processing the loan); credit report fee; mortgage insurance application fee; mortgage insurance premium; and hazard insurance premium. Buyers also may have to put money into escrow to assure future payment of such recurring items as real-estate taxes. Also, there often are separate document fees that cover the preparation of final legal papers, such as a mortgage or deed of trust.

Choosing the Best Form of Ownership

Q. What form of ownership is best for a home?

A. There are various types of ownership. To "take title" to the home, ownership must be declared in one of various ways. This may be as a single owner, joint tenancy with or without a survivorship right, tenancy in common, or tenancy by the entirety.

Q. What is the most common form?

A. *Joint tenancy with right of survivorship* is probably the most common form of ownership. Each person owns an undivided interest in the real estate. This interest can be disposed of by each individual during that person's lifetime. When one of the joint tenants dies, however, that person's interest immediately vests and goes to the survivor. In other words, the surviving joint tenant becomes the sole owner of the property. In a joint tenancy with right of survivorship, people named in the will of the deceased joint tenant would not have a claim to the property. This also avoids the problem of the home becoming involved in probate. Under the federal tax law, the estate of the first spouse to die includes half of the value of all property owned by joint tenants who were married.

Tenancy by the entirety is similar to joint tenancy with right of survivorship, but it requires that the tenants be husband and wife. Some states do not recognize this form of ownership.

(continued)

CLOSING COSTS

Closing costs usually include all or most of the following:

Appraisal fee	This is the fee paid for an appraisal of the property. It is required by the mortgage lender and often is paid for by the buyer. The Federal Housing Administration (FHA) and Veterans Administration (VA) establish the appraisal fees for FHA and VA mortgages.
Attorney's fee	The buyer and seller pay the fee for their own lawyers. In some states, buyers are required to pay for the lender's attorney. This fee usually is a certain percentage of the mortgage.
Survey fee	If the lender requires a registered survey, the buyer probably will pay the fee. You may be able to avoid this fee if the lender agrees to accept a recent survey done for the seller. However, the seller must sign a document assuring that the property lines have not changed since the completion of the survey. Even then, a title insurance company will require a new survey unless the survey is current or has been recertified recently.
Loan discount fee (points)	This is the lender's charge to the buyer to obtain the mortgage. The buyer may have paid some of this fee in advance to secure the loan.
Inspection fees	Charges for general inspections or inspections required by local laws. The buyer or seller may be responsible for fees paid for inspections, depending on the contract and local laws.
Title fees	Cost of title search or title insurance.

A Sample Settlement (Closing) Worksheet

This is a sample worksheet for a family purchasing a $100,000 house and getting a new $80,000 loan. Line 103 assumes that their total settlement charges are $4,000. This figure is merely illustrative. The amount may be higher in some areas and for some types of transactions, and lower for others.

J. Summary of Borrower's Transaction	
100. Gross Amount Due From Borrower	
101. Contract sales price	100,000.00
102. Personal property	
103. Settlement charges to borrower	4,000.00
104.	
105.	
Adjustments for items paid by seller in advance	
106. City/town taxes to	
107. County taxes to	
108. Assessments **6/30 to 7/31 (owners assn)**	40.00
109. **Fuel Oil 25 gal. $1.00/gal.**	25.00
110.	
111.	
112.	
120. Gross Amount Due From Borrower	104,065.00
200. Amounts Paid By Or In Behalf Of Borrower	
201. Deposit or earnest money	2,000.00
202. Principal amount of new loan(s)	80,000.00
203. Existing loan(s) taken subject to	
204.	
205.	
206.	
207.	
208.	
209.	
Adjustments for items unpaid by seller	
210. City/town taxes to	
211. County taxes **1/1 to 6/30 $1,200/year**	600.00
212. Assessments **1/1 to 6/30 $200/year**	100.00
213.	
214.	
215.	
216.	
217.	
218.	
219.	
220. Total Paid By/For Borrower	82,700.00
300. Cash At Settlement From/To Borrower	
301. Gross Amount due from borrower (line 120)	104,065.00
302. Less amounts paid by/for borrower (line 220)	(82,700.00)
303. Cash ☒ From ☐ To Borrower	21,365.00

Source: Department of Housing and Urban Development.

Options for Owning Property

Most couples probably own property in joint tenancy with a right of survivorship, or as tenants by the entirety. There are other options.

A *partnership* may purchase property. However, it is the partnership itself that owns the property, not the people.

***One spouse* also may own a home. Sometimes a spouse does this for estate-tax purposes. However, it may present a problem if the couple divorces.**

In any event, you will want to learn about the advantages and disadvantages of the various types of ownership. Then you can make a decision about the best form of ownership for your particular situation.

Q. What is a tenancy in common?

A. *Tenancy in common* gives each owner a separate legal title to an undivided interest in the property. This allows the owners the right to sell, mortgage, or give away their own interests in the property. When the owner dies, the interest in the property does not go to the survivor. Instead, it transfers to the owner's heirs.

Q. What if I live in a community property state?

A. If you live in a community property state, the state generally holds that the property you bought while married belongs to each member of the couple equally. (Community property states include Arizona, California, Idaho, Louisiana, Nevada, New Mexico, Texas, Washington, and Wisconsin.) Check your state law for details.

Buying Foreclosed Property

Q. How may I buy a foreclosed property?

A. Lending institutions or government institutions that guarantee mortgages usually own foreclosed properties. (Some people refer to foreclosed properties as REOs, for Real Estate Owned by the lender.) For one reason or another, owners failed to make payments and the lenders foreclosed on these properties. This means lenders have taken title to the properties and will be the sellers.

Foreclosed properties include both homes and condominiums. The institutions sell them both individually and through auctions. Some institutions advertise their lists of foreclosed properties, while others deal strictly through real-estate agents. Local real-estate agents usually have a current list of the foreclosed properties in their area, and can provide information on the homes. *Fannie Mae,* the Federal National Mortgage Association, is a large government holder of mortgages. It offers a toll-free telephone number that buyers can call to get a list of foreclosed properties in their area. The telephone number is (800) 553-4636; (800) 221-4636 in Maryland.

The Federal Housing Administration (FHA) usually sells its foreclosed properties through an auction. The classified sections of local newspapers announce the auction. Potential buyers submit bids on the day of the auction. Along with the bid, a potential buyer presents a certified check for a percentage of the bid price. The highest bidder usually gets the home.

SELLING A HOME

Q. How can a real-estate agent help me sell my home?

A. Experienced, reputable agents can be an invaluable asset to the seller of a home. Real-estate agents can offer advice to the seller on the suggested listing price. The agents also can advise the seller on how to best show the home and how long it may take to sell it.

The broker with whom you sign a listing agreement is known as the *listing agent*. Most brokers (real-estate firms) are members of the *Multiple Listing Service* (MLS). Usually within 24 hours of signing an agreement with an MLS broker, all MLS-broker offices in your area will get a notice that your home is for sale. Because most homebuyers work with agents, this immediately makes information about your home available to a wide range of potential buyers.

Your listing agent should be responsive to you, keeping you informed of the progress. The agent should tell you who has expressed interest in the home. Also, your agent should follow up on the visits of potential buyers.

Q. How do I choose a real-estate broker and agent to sell my home?

A. Choosing an agent requires that you do your homework both on the qualifications of the agent and the broker. You may want to interview several agents from various local firms. Ask them about their sales for the last six months or one year. Inquire about such items as how long their clients' homes are on the market, how much the broker advertised them, and how close they sold to the list price. Additionally, you will want to know how familiar the agents are with your area—how well they know its schools, facilities, and public transportation. The better an agent is able to answer questions from potential buyers, the better chance the agent has of selling your home. You also will want to know about the sales of the brokerage office. Lastly, make sure you are comfortable with the agent you choose. You should have confidence in your agent's ability.

Q. What is the broker's typical commission?

A. Usually the commission is between five to seven percent of the sales price of the home. The seller pays the commission. The office that lists the home (the *listing agent*) and the office that sells the home (the *selling agent*) split the commission. Brokers' commissions are negotiable. Though in many localities agents customarily fix them at a certain rate, sometimes it may be possible to negotiate a lower commission.

Q. How do I establish the price of my home?

A. There are several methods. An agent should be able to give you a price range for homes recently sold in your neighborhood that are similar to your home. If this is hard to do, you may want to have an appraisal from a professional appraiser. An appraisal is the fair market value of the home, so it should be close to the probable selling price. Lenders usually order their own appraisals, often paid for by the buyers, before they approve mortgages. They do this to ensure that each home is worth the selling price. If you intend to sell your home on your own, without an agent, an appraisal can provide valuable market information. You will have to pay a fee for such an appraisal. Remember, however, that determining market value is not an exact science. A home is worth what someone will pay for it.

Q. What is the listing agreement?

A. One of the first decisions a seller considers is the listing agreement with a broker. If the seller chooses to use a real-estate broker, the seller and the broker will enter into an agreement known as a listing agreement. The listing agreement is standard only in the sense that brokers may use the same form. Generally, however, the law does not require that particular form. The listing agreement is a binding contract when signed by both parties. Thus, before signing, make sure you know exactly what the terms are.

Q. What terms are negotiable?

A. In theory, they all are. At the very least, the broker should be willing to negotiate provisions on:

- The length of the contract. Many of the standard forms provide that the contract renews automatically;
- When the broker earns the commission. For example, this might occur only when the seller and buyer actually complete the sale, not when they sign the purchase agreement; and
- Who will be responsible for the advertising expenses—the seller or the broker.

Read the listing agreement carefully. Do not hesitate to discuss any provisions you would like to change.

Q. Is the broker's fee really negotiable?

DIFFERENT TYPES OF LISTING AGREEMENTS

Various kinds of listing agreements exist. *Open listings* give sellers the right to list the property with other brokers or to sell it themselves. When the property is sold, only the broker who procures (obtains) the ready, willing, and able buyer will receive a commission. *Exclusive agency listings* guarantee fees to one broker, even if another broker sells the property. However, in some states, these listings also reserve the seller's right to sell the home personally without paying the broker a fee. *Exclusive right to sell listings* require the seller to pay a commission to the broker no matter who sells the property, even if it is the seller.

(continued)

A. Yes, it is open to negotiation. A broker may calculate it in one of several ways:
- The *flat-fee method* means that the broker charges a set price to sell the home, regardless of the selling price.
- The *percentage method* is the most common commission. It means that the broker will receive an agreed percentage of the sales price. For residential real estate, the percentage is usually somewhere between five and seven percent. Often the broker applies one amount, say six percent, to the first $100,000 of the selling price, with a lower percent applied to amounts beyond $100,000.
- The *net method* means that the broker will keep any amount of the selling price that is more than an agreed amount. Net commission listings are not favored, and they are illegal in some states.

Q. What legal protection do I have after signing a listing agreement?

A. Once you sign a listing agreement, the real-estate broker becomes the agent acting for a *principal* (in this case, the seller). The entire body of principal-agent law comes into play. The real-estate broker is a *fiduciary*. This means that the agent must be absolutely loyal to the principal. The broker owes the duties of care, obedience, accounting, loyalty, and notice to the principal. In return, the principal owes the broker the duty of payment according to the terms of the agreement. The fiduciary responsibility owed to the principal means that the broker may not represent two parties in the same transaction without each party's approval.

Q. Is the real-estate agent liable if a potential buyer steals something from my home?

A. Unless the agent was negligent, it is unlikely that the agent is responsible for thefts. Sellers should take the precaution of storing away small, valuable items.

Selling Your Home Yourself

Q. What are the advantages of selling my home myself?

A. The main advantage is the savings of the real-estate commission. While this may seem like a large savings, you must prepare yourself to assume all the responsibilities. This includes advertising your home, working with potential buyers, and negotiating the sale. Sellers with some familiarity

(continued)

In an area where real-estate brokers are members of a Multiple Listing Service (MLS), they will combine their exclusive right to sell listings. They will do this in order to make the home available to as many prospective buyers as possible. When a sale occurs, a predetermined arrangement defines how the brokers will divide the fee paid to the listing broker. The multiple listing agreement that the brokers have signed contains this arrangement.

with local sales procedures and the real-estate market may choose to sell their homes themselves. There are various books available that will help you sell your home without using a real-estate broker. Experts generally recommend that the seller hire both a lawyer and appraiser at the beginning to help in the process. An appraiser can help you establish a price for your home. The attorney can help you with the legal issues and papers.

Q. What are the disadvantages of selling my home myself?

A. There are three distinct disadvantages. First, you will lack the many resources that a real-estate broker has to attract buyers. Second, you will have to arrange your time to show your home and talk to potential buyers. Third, you will be directly involved in negotiating the sales price and other contract provisions. At first glance, this last duty may seem desirable. However, many sales fall through without the mediating influence of a third party (the agent) who brings the buyer and seller together on a variety of issues.

What You Must Tell a Potential Buyer

Q. What does the seller have to reveal to the buyer?

A. Various state laws cover this. These range from requiring the seller to reveal almost no details to ordering notice of any known defect. Generally, the seller should reveal to the buyer any known material defects, zoning problems, and other aspects that could seriously affect the home's value. Some states require the seller to tell the buyer about defective items that appear to be functioning, such as a furnace, hot-water heater, and the like. In other states, the seller must fill out a form that asks about any problems with several items, ranging from the roof to the plumbing.

As a seller, you will want to avoid any future legal problems involved with the sale of your home. If the buyer or the buyer's agent asks questions, respond honestly. Make sure you know about all disclosure laws in your state and your duties under them.

Q. What about the real-estate agent's obligations in this area?

A. Generally, the Code of Ethics of the National Association of Realtors governs real-estate brokers and agents. This code requires the agent to disclose all known facts that are relevant. A professional agent also will try to get all the buyer's questions answered. For example, if the buyer has spotted water damage in the basement, the agent should ask about it, and tell the buyer about the cause of the problem.

Paying Taxes on Your Profits

Q. Do I have to pay federal taxes on the sale of my home?

A. If you are selling a home, the profit realized on the sale is generally taxable. However, there are ways to defer (delay) or avoid the taxes if your home is your primary residence. Suppose you buy a new primary residence within 24 months of the sale of your former home. Then you may defer taxes on profits from the home you sell if the new home costs more than the selling price of your old home. Certain people, including some military service employees and people who have lived outside the United States, may be eligible for a longer time period. Check with your tax adviser for details.

Q. How do I determine my profits?

A. You can calculate your profits by subtracting the *adjusted cost basis* of your home from its *adjusted sales price*. You can compute the adjusted cost basis by subtracting certain items—such as the broker's commission, lawyer's fees, and fix-up expenses—from the price of your home when you bought it.

To calculate the adjusted sales price, start with the selling price. Then subtract the cost of capital improvements made while you owned the home and closing costs not deducted when you bought it. Note that you may not subtract the cost of repairs. The Internal Revenue Service (IRS) is very strict about what it considers improvements. For example, repairing a water heater is not an improvement, but adding a dishwasher is. Also, you may deduct the labor costs paid to a tradesperson (such as a carpenter), but not any costs for your own labor. The IRS requires home sellers to complete a form in the year of the sale that includes these calculations. You also will want to keep all receipts for any costs you are deducting from the sale. Without such written proof, the IRS is not likely to allow your deductions.

Q. Now I have figured my profits. What about figuring my taxes?

A. First, remember that if there is no profit, you do not have to worry about paying taxes. However, the IRS does not allow you to deduct any loss either. If you do not buy a new primary residence within 24 months, if your new primary residence does not cost more than your old home, or if you choose to pay the taxes, you owe taxes on the profits. The amount of your taxes will depend on your tax bracket.

Q. What about the home exemption I have heard about?

A. Taxpayers aged 55 and older are eligible for an exclusion of up to $125,000 of capital gains on the sale of their main residence. This means they do not have to pay taxes on up to $125,000 in profits on the sale of their homes. This is a *once-in-a-lifetime* exclusion. You should use it only after careful consideration. For example, the IRS views a married couple as one person for purposes of this exclusion. If one spouse has already used the exclusion, the other spouse may not use it on the sale of another jointly owned home. The IRS requires other criteria to use this exclusion. You must live in the home as your primary residence for a minimum of three of the last five years before the sale. Also, you may not rent out your home or fail to live there for more than six months at least three of the five years before the sale. If you fail to meet these guidelines, the IRS will not allow the exclusion. If you are considering using this exclusion, first consult a qualified professional, such as a financial planner, accountant, or tax attorney.

Q. Will I also owe state and local taxes on my profits?

A. It depends. You may live in a state or city that will require you to pay state or local taxes on the profits of a home. Some local communities also charge a "transfer tax" on the sale of property.

Inspection Riders

Q. May the seller refuse an inspection rider or a mortgage contingency clause?

A. Unless they are selling their homes in a very hot market, sellers usually accept the mortgage contingency. You will want to check that the proposed interest rate is reasonable, based on current rates. You also should confirm that the mortgage commitment date is not too far into the future. You may refuse inspection riders, but you also might lose a potential buyer at the same time.

Beware of Contingencies

If an offer to purchase your home contains any contingency, you should arrange a time period for compliance, after which the offer shall expire. Otherwise, your home could be off the market for months, with no assurance that the sale will go through.

If a buyer extends an offer that is contingent on VA (Veterans Administration) financing, note that your acceptance of the offer could obligate you to pay points (percentages of the loan amount). In this case, you would want to place a limit on the points to be paid.

Q. What may I do if I disagree with an inspection report?

A. Your response as a seller to a negative inspection report will depend on the buyer. Sometimes, such a report may scare away the buyer. Then there probably is nothing you can do that will overcome the buyer's doubts. If you strongly disagree with the inspection, you may want to obtain your own inspection, with a written copy, for other buyers. Another option is to negotiate any problems that the inspector discovers. Suppose the inspector discovers that your home has inadequate or outdated electrical wiring. Then you may offer to have the wiring updated or to reduce the price by an agreed-upon sum to cover the buyer's costs of updating the wiring.

As a seller, you should be aware that some homebuyers will take any problems and turn them into major roadblocks. They usually do this with the hope of forcing an anxious seller to reduce the selling price. If you find yourself dealing with such a buyer, you may be better off by simply returning the buyer's deposit and placing the home back on the market.

When Things Go Awry

Q. What may I do if the state tries to take my property under condemnation proceedings?

A. State and local governments—and the federal government—have the right of *eminent domain*. This allows them to force the sale of property under condemnation proceedings. Governmental bodies use their power of eminent domain when they decide that they need your property for public purposes. An example is when the government needs your property for a road right-of-way. The governmental body takes possession of your property through a legal proceeding called a *condemnation proceeding*. Under the Constitution, the government must pay you "just compensation" (payment that is fair both to the owner and the public) when it takes your property.

This means you will lose your property but get paid. It does not mean that you should roll over and play dead. Many homeowners have prevailed in court against the government, or at least dragged out the process for years. You have various options available. Discuss your legal rights with a lawyer. If you do agree to sell, remember that the government must repay you for your property. You may want to have an attorney handle these negotiations. You may wish to contact your local bar association for a referral. If you cannot afford a lawyer, talk to a legal-aid office to see if you can qualify for help.

Q. What may I do if I am behind on my mortgage payments, and the lender threatens to foreclose?

A. First, call your lender (usually its mortgage servicing department), and try to negotiate a payment schedule. Explain why your payments are overdue, and try to work out some way to pay what you owe. If you have been trying to sell your home, have unexpected medical payments, or have some other crisis, the lender probably will understand your problems and try to help you.

If you do not respond to the lender's letters or phone calls, most lenders will begin some formal legal proceeding, because they cannot ignore lack of payments. Communication is very important.

If you have an FHA or VA mortgage, you can call the FHA or VA to see what help you can obtain. Or you can check with the mortgage loan servicing company, which is a private lender that contracts with the FHA or VA to manage such mortgages. In addition, various housing counseling agencies may be able to help you. The local office of the federal Department of Housing and Urban Development (HUD) may be able to refer you to such an agency. If necessary, seek help from a lawyer.

The worst thing you can do in this situation is to do nothing. If the lender forecloses, you may face losing all the equity in your home.

When the Lender Forecloses

Lenders do not like to foreclose on property, because they usually will not get the full amount of their money back. A lender may recover all its money only if it is foreclosing on a home that has much more equity than the money owed on the mortgage. *Equity* is the value of your unencumbered interest in your home. You figure it by subtracting the unpaid mortgage balance, and other debts, from the home's fair market value.

ALTERNATIVES TO SELLING YOUR HOME

Q. What is a home-equity loan?

A. It is a loan for which the equity you have built up in your home acts as collateral.

Q. Why are these loans advantageous?

A. Because of changes in the tax law, home-equity loans are becoming more attractive. The Tax Reform Act of 1986 is phasing out consumer interest deductions. In 1991, they will be completely eliminated. Examples of consumer interest deductions include interest paid on car loans and credit-card bills. Beginning in 1991, you may not deduct any of this interest from your taxable income. Interest paid on mortgage loans, however, still is 100-percent deductible on first and second homes. In addition, there is a home-equity deduction of up to $100,000. In other words, if a lender will lend you up to $100,000 on your home equity, you can use the money for any purpose and deduct the interest.

Q. What is the difference between a home-equity loan and a traditional second mortgage loan?

A. Many home-equity "loans" are actually "lines of credit." By using the equity in your home, you may qualify for a sizable amount of credit, to use how and when you please, at a relatively low rate of interest.

If you are thinking about a home-equity line of credit, you also might want to consider a more traditional second mortgage loan. This type of loan provides you with a fixed amount of money repayable over a specific period of time. Usually the payment schedule calls for equal payments that will pay off the entire loan within that time. You might consider a traditional second mortgage loan instead of a home-equity line if, for example, you need a set amount for a specific purpose, such as an addition to your home.

In deciding which type of loan best suits your needs, consider the costs under the two alternatives. Look at the APR (annual percentage rate, discussed later in this chapter and in the "Consumer Credit" chapter) and other charges. You cannot, however, simply compare the APR for a traditional mortgage loan with the APR for a home-equity line of credit because the APRs are figured differently. The APR for a traditional mortgage takes into account the interest rate charges plus points and other finance charges. On the other hand, the APR for a home-equity line of credit is based on the periodic interest rate alone. It does not include points or other charges.

Q. Are there other alternatives to a home-equity loan?

A. If you need to borrow using equity from your home, there are several alternatives to a home-equity loan. The most popular are reverse mortgages, gift annuities, and sale-leasebacks.

Q. What is a reverse mortgage?

A. Generally, a *reverse mortgage* allows a homeowner to borrow against the equity, receive a monthly income, and not have to move. At the same time, the lender shares in the home's increase in market value, if there is any. A reverse mortgage can be helpful in situations when the homeowner cannot qualify for a home-equity loan. This is particularly true for senior citizens living on a fixed income. Often most of their assets are in their home, but they do not want to move. A

GETTING A REVERSE MORTGAGE

Few lenders have shown an interest in offering reverse mortgages. However, this may change now that the Federal Housing Administration (FHA) has started to insure reverse mortgages. Under the FHA rules, the homeowner must be 62 years old or older and own a home that has a very small mortgage or no mortgage at all. The FHA limits borrowing to between $67,500 and $101,250. The lender may share a maximum of 25 percent of the home's appreciation in market value. Under the FHA rules, the borrower may receive the borrowed money as a monthly income or a line of credit. This lets the borrower use the money for emergencies, such as medical care. For more information, the toll-free number is (800) 245-2691.

However, you always should get professional advice about the terms and conditions of a reverse mortgage before signing on the dotted line.

reverse mortgage can help them obtain money from their home while remaining in the home.

The most familiar reverse mortgage is the Individual Reverse Mortgage Account (IRMA). The lender offers a fixed monthly sum in return for part or all of a homeowner's value in the home. This will include its appreciation (increase in the home's value) until the homeowner repays the loan. The lender grants the homeowner the right to remain in the home until the homeowner moves or dies. Reverse mortgages such as this depend on the home's value and the life expectancy of the owner. When the owner dies, the estate pays off the loan.

Another type of reverse mortgage, a *term reverse mortgage,* exists only for a certain period of time, such as ten years. This type of mortgage requires homeowners to sell the home or get the money by another method to pay off the loan at the end of its term. Most retirees should avoid term reverse mortgages because of this requirement.

Q. What is a gift annuity?

A. A *gift annuity* works somewhat like a reverse mortgage. The owner donates the home to a charitable institution in return for a lifetime annuity (money paid at regular intervals). Also, the donor may receive a tax deduction for the gift. With a gift annuity, the donor receives a life estate in the home. This allows the donor to remain in the home for life. The donor continues to pay for the home's insurance, taxes, and maintenance. When the donor dies, the home becomes the property of the charitable institution. If you are considering making such a donation, it is a good idea to consult a lawyer beforehand.

Q. What is a sale-leaseback?

A. A *sale-leaseback* occurs when you agree to sell your home to a buyer who agrees to rent the home to you for a certain period of time. Usually the seller receives a large down payment. The seller then acts as a lender for the remainder of the term of the contract by granting the buyer a mortgage. In return, the buyer receives rent from the seller. The seller remains in the home, and can use the down payment to provide additional income. The seller also may use the periodic (usually monthly) loan payment as extra income. The buyer may use the tax deduction of paying interest. In addition, the buyer will benefit from any increased value in the home.

Families usually set up sale-leasebacks among themselves. Often a son or daughter uses this transaction to provide parents with income during retirement. Be aware, however, that the IRS requires both a fair market value and an equitable rental payment in such a deal. If the IRS determines that the rental payments are too high or too low, it will assign a new value. In other words, the IRS will not permit you to structure a sale-leaseback to lower your estate taxes. A sale-leaseback often provides the most advantages to retirees in low tax brackets with children in high tax brackets. The family can structure it so that the children carry the burden of paying interest and take the benefit of deducting the interest from their taxes. The parents benefit by receiving income.

FINANCING A HOME PURCHASE

Q. How do I finance the purchase of a home?

A. Buying a home normally is the largest financial transaction in a person's lifetime. Very few people have enough cash to buy a home. Almost everyone buys a home with borrowed money. Many different types of lenders have money available for residential home purchases. Or you may be able to have the seller finance your purchase.

Banks, savings and loan associations, insurance companies, and mortgage bankers all provide money needed to finance the purchase of a new home. Some loans may be insured by the Federal Housing Administration (FHA) or the Veterans Administration (VA). Such loans provide the borrower with reduced interest rates, extended terms of repayment, or some combination of the two. The FHA and VA usually require sellers and buyers to pay additional fees for these types of loans. This reduces the advantages gained by a lower interest rate.

Q. What is a fixed-rate mortgage?

A. A *fixed-rate mortgage* is one having an interest rate that does not change. Until recently, the typical financing arrangement involved a standard fixed-rate mortgage. Usually the purchaser borrowed approximately 80 percent of the purchase price of the home. The loan carried a fixed interest rate that remained the same throughout the term of the loan, usually 25 to 30 years. Each monthly payment made by the borrower was the same; it never changed. In the early years of repayment, the lender applied most of the payment to the interest on the loan. The lender applied very little of the

(continued)

HIGHLIGHTING THE ESSENTIALS

Type	Description
Fixed-rate mortgage	Fixed interest rate, usually long-term; equal monthly payments (applied unequally toward principal and interest) until debt is paid in full.
15-year mortgage	Fixed interest rate. Requires down payment or monthly payments higher than 30-year loan. Loan is fully repaid over 15-year term.
Adjustable mortgage	Interest rate changes over the life of the loan, resulting in possible changes in your monthly payments, loan term, and/or principal. Some plans have rate or payment caps.
Balloon mortgage	Monthly payments based on fixed interest rate; usually short-term; payments may cover interest only with principal due in full at term end.
Graduated payment mortgage	Lower monthly payments rise gradually (usually over five to ten years), then level off for duration of term.
Assumable mortgage	Buyer takes over seller's original, below-market mortgage.
Land contract	Seller retains original mortgage. No transfer of title until loan is fully paid.
Reverse mortgage	Lender makes monthly payments to borrower, using owner's equity in property as collateral.

Source: Federal Trade Commision.

payment to the principal (the money borrowed). As time progressed and the amount owed became increasingly smaller, the lender applied more of each payment to the principal, and less to the interest.

Today, fixed-rate mortgages normally come in two varieties—the 30-year fixed mortgage and the 15-year fixed mortgage. The borrower pays off both of these loans over the life of the mortgage (30 years or 15 years) in equal monthly installments. These payments cover both the interest on the loan and the principal. The monthly payment on a 15-year mortgage is higher than the payment for a comparable 30-year mortgage. However, the major advantage is that you pay much more principal each month. Thus, the interest costs over the life of the loan are much lower. The 30-year fixed-rate mortgage also remains popular. However, older homebuyers with considerable equity often find that they can cover the higher monthly costs of the 15-year fixed-rate mortgage. This allows them to achieve more quickly their goal of owning their home without a mortgage to pay.

Q. What is an adjustable mortgage?

A. An *adjustable mortgage* is one having essential terms that may change. Because of changes in our nation's economy, in the 1970s financial institutions found themselves holding large numbers of fixed-rate low-interest loans at a time when they had to pay much higher rates to acquire new money to lend to customers. To protect themselves, many lenders began encouraging borrowers to enter into different types of loan transactions. These loans called for changes in the rate of interest, amount of payment, or length of time for repayment.

These arrangements vary widely. The rate of interest changes during the life of the mortgage in the *variable-rate mortgage* (VRM), *adjustable-rate mortgage* (ARM), *rollover mortgage* (ROM), and *renegotiable-rate mortgage* (RRM). Sometimes the monthly payment remains the same even though the interest rate increases. In these mortgages, if the monthly payment cannot cover the extra interest caused by the interest rate increases, the lender may lengthen the time period for repayment. In other cases, the monthly payment will change over the course of the mortgage because of increases or decreases in the interest rate.

Q. What is a balloon mortgage?

A. A *balloon mortgage* is usually a mortgage established for a short period of time (three to five years). The lender sets up either fixed or variable payments for the term of the mortgage. The unpaid balance is due at the end of the mortgage. Builders often use balloon mortgages to attract buyers in periods of high interest rates. Usually they offer rates lower than the current rates. Some lenders will guarantee refinancing when the final payment is due, but it is unlikely that they will guarantee an interest rate. Borrowers who take a balloon mortgage hope that interest rates will decline by the time the payment is due or that they can refinance the mortgage before the payment is due.

Q. What other options are available?

A. When interest rates rose rapidly, and fewer people found they could afford to borrow money to buy a home, lenders developed other new mortgages. These called for lower payments in the early years of the mortgage and higher payments in later years. They include the *graduated-payment mortgage* (GPM) and the *growth-equity mortgage* (GEM). A GPM is particularly useful for younger couples who expect to increase their earnings substantially. A GPM can be dangerous for people who are unlikely to see their income increase. Sometimes a borrower might wish to have part of the monthly payment come from a savings account that the borrower pledges to the lender. The name of this type of program is the *flexible loan insurance program* (FLIP) or *pledged-account mortgage* (PAM).

Getting Mortgage Information

No matter what kind of loan, federal law requires that the lender provide you with details about it. Prepare yourself for a lot of reading material. If you want to understand it thoroughly before you apply for the loan, do your homework in advance. Also, be sure you understand exactly how, when, and why the lender may adjust your interest rate.

Q. How do lenders determine the interest rate?

A. Generally, lenders link adjustable-rate mortgages (ARMs) to an index, such as the one-year Treasury bill (T-bill) rate. Lenders usually may change the rate only once a year. Most ARMs have a two-percent annual cap (limit) on increases or decreases in the interest rate and a six-percent lifetime cap. In other words, suppose an ARM begins with a nine-percent interest rate. That rate may never exceed 15 percent, no matter what the index does. An even better ARM has a three-percent lifetime cap.

Q. Are there combination adjustable/fixed-rate mortgages?

A. Yes. Lenders call them *convertible ARMs*. These offer some type of conversion (way to change) to a fixed-rate mortgage, usually on the anniversary of when the loan began. These loans normally have a fee (ranging from $250 to one percent of the loan) for making the conversion. Most convertible ARMs offer the conversion for a limited period of time. It usually is from three to five years from the date the loan began. Convertible ARMs usually begin with an interest rate that is slightly higher than regular ARMs.

Q. What is negative amortization?

A. *Negative amortization* means that instead of paying off the principal of a loan, the principal increases with each payment. This means you are falling farther behind with each payment. When a lender sets up a mortgage with negative amortization, the monthly payment is not enough to cover the amount of interest you owe each month. The lender adds the amount you owe for the unpaid interest to your debt. This means that the size of your debt increases.

The worst problem with negative amortization occurs in a market in which home values decrease. Then the size of your debt could increase to the point where it would exceed the equity in your home. Sadly, you could sell your home and not be able to repay what you owe. Most professionals advise buyers to avoid a negatively amortized mortgage. If you cannot determine whether a loan includes negative amortization, ask the lender. The law requires the lender to tell you about a mortgage with negative amortization.

Q. How do I apply for a loan?

A. Regardless of the type of loan arrangement, the process of obtaining a loan is similar. The prospective borrower must first fill out a loan application. This provides information that the lender will use to decide whether to grant the loan. The information requested by the lender varies. Usually you will have to show proof of employment, credit history, and all outstanding assets and debts, among other items.

Also, the lender should reveal all costs of the loan. This includes service charges, appraisal fees, survey fees, title insurance or escrow fees, any lender's attorney's fee, and most importantly, the interest rate on the loan. The lender must state the interest rate as an annual percentage rate (APR). This may be somewhat higher than the rate of interest stated in the mortgage note. The lender will calculate the APR by including not only the stated interest, but certain other fees that the lender requires the borrower to pay.

If the lender approves the loan, the lender will then prepare a *loan commitment,* agreeing to lend a certain amount of money on specific terms. If your purchase contract has a mortgage contingency clause, inform the lender when you apply for the loan that you need the commitment by the deadline specified.

Q. What documents must I sign to secure the loan?

A. The borrower will sign two separate documents to complete the loan transaction. One is a *promissory note* agreeing to repay the lender the money borrowed plus interest. This

BUYING AND SELLING A HOME

SHOPPING FOR INTEREST RATES

You can and should shop for rates. As noted earlier, a one-percent change on a $100,000 30-year mortgage could mean a $75 difference in each monthly loan payment. The mortgage market is competitive. Lending institutions often will offer lower-than-market rates to attract borrowers.

There are several ways to shop for mortgages. Many metropolitan newspapers carry a weekly listing or sampling of mortgage rates offered in their areas. Remember that mortgage rates can change very rapidly, so these may not always be accurate. However, they can give you a good idea of the market. In addition, several reporting services offer details on a wide variety of available mortgages from area institutions. Prices of these services range from ten to 30 dollars. Therefore, you may want to use a reporting service only when you are ready to apply for a loan. You also can call a real-estate broker for information.

promissory note is a legally enforceable contract. The borrower may be responsible for repaying the note even if he or she later sells the home to a buyer who assumes the mortgage. The second document is the *mortgage* or *deed of trust*. This document gives the lender a security interest in the real estate. That means the lender may enforce repayment of the loan by selling the property. If you do not pay, you could lose your home.

Q. What is an assumable mortgage?

A. An *assumable mortgage* allows you to transfer your existing mortgage debt to the buyer of your home. The new owner would "assume" (take over) your mortgage and pay you the difference between the amount you still owe and the agreed-upon sale price. Most lenders no longer allow buyers to assume mortgages. They prefer a "due-on-sale" clause (see below) in which the new owner must get a new mortgage. Some assumable mortgages remain on the market, however. If the interest rate is attractive, you should explore them. Some lenders will allow a mortgage to be assumed by charging a fee or adjusting the interest rate that they will charge on the assumed mortgage.

Before agreeing to assume a mortgage, however, the homebuyer should obtain a written statement from the lender stating:

- The amount still owed on the loan;
- The rate of interest for the remainder of the loan;
- The length of the repayment period remaining; and
- When the lender has the right to call in the loan (order payment of the entire amount) or change any of the existing terms.

Before the buyer assumes the loan, the lender may require the buyer to go through the lender's normal application procedure. This allows the lender to be sure that the buyer is creditworthy. The particular form of assumption agreement will vary depending upon your location.

Q. What is a due-on-sale clause?

A. A *due-on-sale clause* permits the lender to demand the entire amount owed when the property transfers from the seller to the buyer. Most mortgages now have such a clause. This means that if you sell your home, the lender does not have to accept payments from the new buyer. The due-on-sale clause thus permits lenders to retire loans that may carry a low rate of interest. It is another way for lenders to protect themselves from rapidly rising costs of funds. Federal law generally permits enforcement of due-on-sale clauses. It has replaced state laws in this area.

Q. What is a late-payment charge?

A. Most mortgages include a *late-payment charge*. The lender charges it to the borrower if the monthly mortgage payment is late. These charges can be large. Be aware of any such charge, and avoid late payments.

Q. What is a prepayment penalty?

A. Many mortgages include a *prepayment penalty*. It imposes a charge if the borrower pays off the loan ahead of schedule. This penalty usually is one or two percent of the mortgage. It is not unusual for mortgage contracts to include a prepayment penalty for the first few years of the mortgage. However, you should avoid mortgages that include a prepayment penalty beyond the third year.

Q. What are FHA and VA loans?

A. The Federal Housing Administration (FHA) offers insured lower-interest loans made by the federal government and approved lending institutions. There is a cost for this insurance, which the FHA charges at the closing. FHA loans are not available through all lenders. However, in some areas, they are very popular.

The Veterans Administration (VA) offers government-insured loans to qualified veterans. Information about these loans is available at local VA offices.

Q. What is a land contract?

A. When it is hard or expensive to borrow money from a lending institution to finance the purchase of a home, sellers often use an installment *land contract*. Under this contract, the seller provides the financing for the purchaser. The buyer usually makes a down payment. The purchaser also agrees to make periodic payments (monthly, quarterly, or annually) to the seller over an agreed number of years. Usually, the buyer moves into the home when the buyer and seller sign the contract. If the buyer fails to make the required payments, the contract normally allows the seller to keep all amounts paid. The seller also may sue to recover all rights to the home, including possession of it. Depending on the state, the buyer may have certain protections.

A land contract usually entitles the buyer to possession of the home. However, legal title does not transfer from the seller to the buyer until the buyer has made all payments at the end of the contract period. In other words, the seller keeps the title to the home to ensure that the buyer will make all the payments. Installment land contracts should contain most of the provisions in the traditional real-estate contract. Remember that such contracts involve a continuing relationship between the seller and the buyer over an extended number of years. Be sure you are comfortable with the other party. Both sellers and buyers should enter into installment contracts cautiously. Each should get advice from lawyers and other real-estate and financial professionals.

Q. What is a bridge loan?

A. Many lenders offer a *bridge loan* to allow buyers to buy another home while they await the sale of their existing home. Usually you can get a bridge loan if you have a contract to sell your old home, and you need the loan for a specific, short period of time. It is much harder to get a bridge loan if you have no contract to sell your home and you need to carry mortgages on two properties. Suppose your present home has considerable equity and you can show that you can carry two mortgages for a reasonable period of time. Then you could obtain a bridge loan, although the loan would be expensive.

MORTGAGE INSURANCE

Several types of insurance contracts pay your mortgage if you die or become disabled. Mortgage life insurance, for example, establishes an annual premium cost for the life of the mortgage. Because your mortgage declines as you pay down the principal (main amount of the loan), the amount of insurance coverage decreases each year, though the cost stays the same. You may want to compare the price for mortgage life insurance with the price for term life insurance. The latter will pay you the same amount of money—not less—each year in the future. Mortgage disability insurance pays a specified benefit in the event that you become disabled. These contracts are very specific. You will want a financial professional, or an attorney, to check these types of insurance before committing yourself to them.

OWNERSHIP IN A MULTIUNIT DWELLING

Q. What does ownership in a condominium mean?

A. The *condominium* form of ownership permits you to own an apartment or unit in the condominium. You may sell, lease, or mortgage the individual condominium unit much like a traditional single-family house, but the condominium association often has the right to approve or disapprove the transfer of title and the type of financing. The law treats condominium owners as homeowners for the purposes of estate and gift tax laws, income tax laws, and the rules about title. The difference is that the unit owners as a group own or manage the common areas, such as hallways, stairs, elevators, and recreation areas.

Q. How does the law determine ownership in a co-op?

A. A *co-op,* or *co-operative,* is very different from a condominium. In a co-op, a corporation usually holds title to the real estate. The people who occupy apartments in the building own shares of stock in the corporation. A person generally must be a shareholder of the corporation even to lease a particular apartment. Even though the "owners" of the co-operative are tenants, they receive some favorable tax treatment because of their ownership interest in the co-op corporation.

Q. Are there differences between multiunit homeownership and single-family homeownership?

A. In single-family homeownership, the control, decisions, and expenses are all the responsibility of a single person or couple. In contrast, there are many rules and regulations governing what you may and may not do with your condominium, co-op, or other multiunit dwelling. Be sure to obtain all the information on the terms of sale and such regulations. Ask to see the bylaws, operating budget, management agreement, and regulating agreement of the multiunit dwelling.

For example, the cost of the unit is not the limit of your financial obligation in multiunit real estate. There will be monthly assessments to cover maintenance and related expenses in operating the common areas. These assessments will be in proportion to the percentage of the total complex you own. If all the apartments in a ten-unit building are the same size, each owner will own ten percent of the building. This means that each owner will pay ten percent of its assessments (expenses).

These costs may well increase over time. You should determine the amount of the monthly assessment and the potential increase *before* signing any binding contract. You also should be sure that there is enough liability insurance coverage for the entire development project. The liability insurance policy should name as the insured the board of directors and each unit owner individually as a co-owner of the common areas.

Q. What is the role of the board of directors in managing a multiunit dwelling?

A. The board has an important role, having broad powers under state law. The board may raise or lower assessments and make special assessments to cover specific repairs. It also may insist that unit owners obey the multiunit association's policies.

There may be major restrictions on the purchaser's right to lease, finance, or resell his or her unit. Many multiunit associations grant the board of directors a right to buy a unit. The way this generally works in practice is that the owner must offer to sell the unit to the board before offering it for sale to any other person.

Q. May I obtain a mortgage for a co-op?

A. The law defines owning a condominium as owning a piece of real estate. Owning a co-op, however, means that you own shares of stock in a building. Formerly, it was not easy to get a mortgage to buy a co-op. That was why prices on co-ops usually were much lower than condominium prices. When the federal government amended the law, the Federal National Mortgage Association (Fannie Mae) began buying co-op loans. This has made it much easier for prospective co-op owners to get mortgages. It is now not much harder to obtain a mortgage for a co-op than for a condominium.

WHERE TO GET MORE INFORMATION

Nearly every state has federal information centers. These centers can help consumers get information on federal services, programs, and regulations. Check the yellow pages of your local telephone directory for the office nearest to you.

Your local library can be a good source of helpful, free information that can point you in the right direction.

Various nonprofit agencies, such as the Better Business Bureau (BBB) offices, can help you get more information on your legal rights and obligations in buying and selling a home. Look in your local telephone directory for the BBB office nearest to you.

The federal government publishes a listing of many available pamphlets. This listing can be obtained from the Consumer Information Center-N, P.O. Box 100, Pueblo, Colorado 81002. Some of the low cost pamphlets available from the center include:

A Consumer's Guide to Mortgage Lock-ins. It describes how you can lock-in interest rates and points when applying for a mortgage. 13 pages. (1988) Publication 427W. 50 cents.

A Consumer's Guide to Mortgage Refinancing. This pamphlet tells what the costs are and how to tell if the time is right to refinance your home. Seven pages. (1988) Publication 428W. 50 cents.

Home Buyer's Vocabulary. For the first-time homebuyer, it defines common words and terms used in the real-estate world. 13 pages. (1987) Publication 137W. One dollar.

Homeowner's Glossary of Building Terms. This pamphlet briefly defines basic construction, repair, and maintenance terms used by builders. 13 pages. (1987) Publication 138W. One dollar.

How to Buy a Manufactured (Mobile) Home. It includes things to consider when buying a manufactured home, such as selection, placement, warranties, installation, and inspection. 23 pages. (1985) Publication 429W. 50 cents.

The Mortgage Money Guide. This handy guide discusses different types of mortgages and loan financing options. It includes a table of monthly mortgage costs at various rates. 16 pages. (1986) Publication 139W. One dollar.

Settlement Costs. This is a comprehensive guide on the settlement (closing) process. It defines various charges, lists homebuyers' legal rights and obligations, and includes worksheets to help calculate and compare costs. 45 pages. (1989) Publication 140W. $1.50.

When Your Home Is on the Line. Your home serves as collateral for one form of revolving credit. This pamphlet has questions, features, and a checklist to use to find the best deal. It includes a glossary of common terms and where to go for help. 16 pages. (1989) Publication 430W. 50 cents.

Wise Home Buying. This guide discusses how to find the right home, when to use a broker, having the home inspected, and shopping for a mortgage. 24 pages. (1987) Publication 141W. One dollar.

Since offerings and prices change regularly, contact the Consumer Information Center to verify the costs and pamphlet availability before ordering.

For information on HUD programs, contact the federal Department of Housing and Urban Development (HUD), Library and Information Services, 451 Seventh Street, S.W., Room 8141 Washington, D.C. 20410. Telephone: (202) 755-6420. This information also may be available at some local HUD offices.

Home-Made Money: A Consumer's Guide to Home Equity Conversion is another handy guide. It is available from The American Association of Retired Persons (AARP), AARP Fulfillment, Home-Made Money, Department BHG, 1909 K Street, N.W., Washington D.C. 20049.

The Internal Revenue Service (IRS) is an excellent source of information on tax questions relating to owning a home. Its tele-tax service has recorded tax information on 140 topics. You can find the toll-free phone number for your state by calling the IRS office in your area. Topics include the sale of a home, reporting gains from home sales, installment plans, and exclusion of gain for people aged 55 or older.

The IRS also publishes several free pamphlets dealing with common tax questions. These include: *Real Estate Taxes* (Publication 530), *Interest Expense* (Publication 545), *Limits on Home Mortgage Interest Deductions* (Publication 936), and *Tax Information on Selling Your Home* (Publication 523).

RENTING RESIDENTIAL PROPERTY

LEASES

THE LANDLORD AND TENANT GET TOGETHER

Usually the first and most revealing encounter a tenant and landlord have involves discussing the terms of the tenancy. This discussion normally will begin with an oral agreement. It may go on to include a lease. Either way, the landlord and tenant will agree on when the tenant will move in and how much the rent will be.

Q. What is a lease?

A. A *lease* is an agreement between the landlord and the tenant that defines their rights and duties. It is legally binding and enforceable through the courts. The lease will specify the parties, the rental property's address, the tenancy's time period, and the amount and due date of rental payments. Beyond these basic terms, the parties may include anything that they can agree to. Of course, illegal provisions should not be included. Even if they are, the courts will invalidate them (strike them down).

Signatures on the lease agreement usually are proof that the people who signed have read the lease and agreed to its terms. Most leases have an *integration clause*. This provides that the written lease is the entire agreement between the parties. It also provides that no other promises will be enforced. So, the moral of the story is: *Read the entire lease carefully before you sign.*

Q. Is an oral rental agreement binding?

A. Yes, almost all jurisdictions accept oral rental agreements for periods of less than one year as valid contracts. The necessary terms of oral agreements—parties, premises, and rent—are the same as with a written lease. However, there is one major difference. All state laws assume that an oral agreement in which rent is payable monthly creates a month-to-month tenancy. (This is always true of an initial agreement to rent, but it may not be true of an oral agreement that follows a written lease, since some states say that such agreements might extend the lease for another year.) Month-to-month tenancy allows either party to end the tenancy with 30 days written notice. It also allows the landlord to raise the rent each month, if the tenant receives proper notice. A written lease, however, usually fixes the rent for the entire period of the tenancy.

The main problem with oral rental agreements is proving what they contain. It is one person's word against another's. That is why courts are skeptical of oral agreements. Specific promises, therefore, should be made in writing. Or at the very least, a witness should be present. Examples of such promises include decorating the unit or not having pets.

Q. What are the advantages of a long-term lease?

A. It usually fixes the monthly rent at a given amount for the entire period of the tenancy. The long-term lease also reduces common sources of landlord aggravation. These include interruptions in rent flow, turnover of apartments, and costs of rerenting a unit. Tenants, however, should beware of *escalation clauses*. These allow the landlord to raise the monthly rent during the period of the tenancy. If taxes or maintenance or other operating costs increase, the landlord passes on the costs to the tenant.

Some observers believe that standard form leases also benefit landlords, since they routinely require tenants to sign away rights that they have under common law. An example would be the tenant's right to privacy, which is superceded by the provision in most leases that gives the landlord the right to enter the premises.

Q. Should tenants avoid any lease clauses?

A. Yes, tenants should look for several clauses in leases. Common lease provisions that the tenant should avoid include:

(1) Waiver of the right to privacy. This clause usually allows the landlord to enter a unit without the tenant's approval for inspecting, repairing, or displaying the unit. Except for emergency repairs, the tenant should negotiate for a reasonable advance notice of entry.

(2) Waiver of the right to jury trial. This clause seeks to deny tenants the right to trial by jury in eviction proceedings. The law guarantees this right in many states and municipalities.

(3) Waiver of the right to notice. This clause allows the landlord to do such things as raise the rent or evict a tenant without giving the written notice required by state law.

(4) Waiver of the right to a day in court. This permits the landlord to evict the tenant in a court proceeding

(continued)

Advantages of a Month-to-Month Tenancy

A month-to-month tenancy exchanges the stability of the long-term lease for flexibility. Both parties may end the tenancy on 30 days written notice. In addition, the landlord may raise the rent after proper notice. If the landlord repeatedly raises the rent, however, the tenant may have a case for retaliatory eviction (see the "Retaliatory Actions" section that appears later in this chapter). As noted in the answer to the nearby question "What are the advantages of a long-term lease?" tenants may preserve their common-law rights better in the absence of a written lease.

NOTICE OF RENT INCREASE
(Month-to-Month Tenancy)

TO: TENANT *(name[s] as it [they] appear[s] on the rental agreement or on checks, receipts, notices, etc.)*

RE: The rental premises located at: *(street name and number, unit number, city, and state)*

This is to notify you that on *(date at least thirty days from receipt of this notice)*, the monthly rental for your unit will be increased to $ *(amount)* .

____

(Signature of landlord or agent)

Source: Reprinted, with permission, from Blumberg and Grow, *The Rights of Tenants,* an ACLU handbook.

without the tenant's presence. Most areas have outlawed this practice. Others will accept legal arguments against it.

(5) Waiver of other legal rights. These clauses seek to remove the benefit of recently achieved tenant rights. They either have the tenant abandon the rights entirely or have the tenant agree to limitations.

(6) Limitations on landlord liability. Usually called *exculpatory clauses,* these try to limit the landlord's liability for acts that cause damage to the tenant or the tenant's guests. This may include hazardous conditions of the property. Many states will not enforce such clauses.

(7) Prohibition of subletting or assigning. These clauses prevent a tenant who wishes to move from substituting another tenant for the rest of the lease without the landlord's written consent.

(8) Attorney's fees. The tenant agrees to pay the landlord's attorney fees and legal costs if there is a dispute over the lease.

(9) Late fees. The tenant agrees to pay fees or penalties for late rent payments. The courts will usually refuse to enforce the collection of such fees that do not reasonably relate to the landlord's damages.
(10) Maintenance. The tenant agrees to assume the landlord's responsibility for maintenance and repair. Because the legality of these clauses varies among the states, it is important to check local law.
(11) Rent escalators. The tenant agrees to pay a rent increase during the term of the lease if certain expenses of the landlord increase. Commonly called an *escalator clause,* this provision allows the landlord to pass on increases in operating expenses. These may include taxes, utilities, maintenance, and capital improvements. Courts almost always enforce such provisions if the rent increase reflects the actual increase in costs.

As noted in the descriptions of several of these clauses, courts in many jurisdictions will not uphold a number of the provisions on the list.

Q. Is a lease binding if it includes illegal clauses?

A. Yes, in almost all cases. The court will strike (cancel) illegal clauses in any legal battle. However, the court usually will enforce the rest of the lease.

Q. May a tenant negotiate the provisions of a standard form lease?

A. Yes. However, success in doing so will depend on the tenant's bargaining power.

Q. Is a tenant permitted to alter the rental property after moving in?

A. The tenant may be able to make changes. It depends mainly on the terms of the lease. Most leases contain a clause forbidding the tenant from making any alterations or additions without the landlord's prior written approval. Any violation *(breach)* of such a clause may allow the landlord to evict the tenant on short-term notice. The tenant may even be liable for the destruction of property. Without a lease term covering alterations and additions, the common-law doctrines of "fixtures and waste" define tenants' rights. These doctrines permit tenants to make alterations or additions so long as they do not significantly reduce the value of the property to the landlord.

(continued)

Other Lease Clauses Tenants Should Avoid

The list of lease clauses in the answer to the question "Should tenants avoid any lease clauses?" is not complete. Some less common, but equally controversial, lease provisions include:

- **The shortening of legal-notice periods;**
- **Broad prohibitions against any "illegal conduct" on the premises;**
- **Broad limits on the number of occupants of a unit (which may limit the tenant's right to have guests); and**
- **Subordination provisions, which say that the lease is subordinate to (less important than) all mortgages. The effect of this clause often is that if the landlord defaults on the mortgage payments, the mortgage holder can void the lease, evict the tenant, and even keep the tenant's security deposit.**

LEASE FORM

Office supply stores sell standard lease forms. These vary from state to state. They also vary in how favorably they treat landlords and tenants. No one form, then, is typical of the whole country. Here is one prepared by the National Housing Law Project and used in California. It is quite pro-tenant.

1. Parties
The parties to this agreement are ______________________________ ,
____
hereinafter called "Landlord," and ____________________________ ,
____
hereinafter called "Tenant." If Landlord is the agent of the owner of said property, the owner's name and address is ___________
____

2. Property
Landlord hereby lets the following property to Tenant for the term of this Agreement: (a) the property located at ________________
____
and (b) the following furniture and appliances on said property:
____
____

3. Term
The term of this Agreement shall be for ______________ beginning on ______________ and ending on ______________.

4. Rent
The monthly rental for said property shall be $ ______________ due and payable on the first day of each month to the Landlord at
____ .
If rent is paid in cash, Tenant shall be given a written rent receipt.

5. Utilities
Utilities shall be paid by the party indicated on the following chart:

	Landlord	Tenant
Electricity	__________	__________
Gas	__________	__________
Water	__________	__________
Garbage	__________	__________
Trash removal	__________	__________
Other ______________	__________	__________

(Where the tenant is indicated as the responsible party, there shall be a separate utility meter for that unit.)

6. Use of property
Tenant shall use the property only for residential purposes, except for incidental use in trade or business (such as telephone solicitation of sales orders or arts and crafts created for profit), so long as such incidental use does not violate local zoning laws or affect Landlord's ability to obtain fire or liability insurance.

7. Tenant's duty to maintain premises
Tenant shall keep the dwelling unit in a clean and sanitary condition and shall otherwise comply with all state and local laws requiring tenants to maintain rented premises. If damage to the dwelling unit (other than normal wear and tear) is caused by acts or neglect of Tenant or others occupying the premises under his/her control, Tenant may repair such damage at his/her own expense. Upon Tenant's failure to make such repairs and after reasonable written notice by Landlord, Landlord may cause such repairs to be made and Tenant shall be liable to Landlord for any reasonable expense thereby incurred by Landlord.

8. Alterations
No substantial alteration, addition, or improvement shall be made by Tenant in or to the dwelling unit without the prior consent of Landlord in writing. Such consent shall not be unreasonably withheld, but may be conditioned upon Tenant's agreeing to restore the dwelling unit to its prior condition upon moving out.

9. Noise
Tenant agrees not to allow on the premises any excessive noise or other activity which disturbs the peace and quiet of other tenants in the building. Landlord agrees to prevent other tenants and other persons in the building or common areas from similarly disturbing Tenant's peace and quiet.

10. Inspection by landlord
Landlord or his agent may enter the dwelling unit upon 48 hours' written notice and with Tenant's consent only for the following purposes: to make repairs, and to exhibit the unit to prospective purchasers, mortgagees, and tenants. Such entries shall not be so frequent as to seriously disturb Tenant's peaceful enjoyment of the premises. Such entries shall take place only with the consent of Tenant, which consent shall not be unreasonably withheld. If, however, Landlord or his agent reasonably believes that an emergency (such as a fire) exists which requires an immediate entry, such entry may be made without Tenant's consent. If such emergency entry occurs, Landlord shall, within two days thereafter, notify Tenant of the date, time and purpose of such entry.

11. Security deposit
a) Tenant shall pay Landlord, upon execution of this Agreement, a security deposit of $________, which in any case does not exceed one month's rent. Said deposit may be applied by Landlord toward reimbursement for any reasonable cost of repair or cleaning necessitated by Tenant's acts or omissions in violation of this Agreement (normal wear and tear excluded) and for rent which is due, unpaid, and owing.

b) Landlord shall place this security deposit in a bank savings account or savings-and-loan institution account bearing the prevailing rate of interest and shall credit such interest to the Tenant's security deposit. Within fourteen days of the date of this Agreement, Landlord shall notify Tenant in writing of the location of such account and the account number.

c) Within two weeks after Tenant vacates the premises, Landlord shall return to Tenant the security deposit, with accrued interest, less any deductions Landlord is entitled to make under section (a) of this paragraph. If any deductions are made, Landlord shall also give Tenant a written itemized statement of such deductions and explanations thereof.

d) If the Landlord fails to comply with sections (a), (b), or (c) of this paragraph, then the Landlord waives the right to make deductions from the security deposit and will be responsible for returning the entire deposit to Tenant when Tenant vacates the premises.

12. Landlord's obligation to repair and maintain premises
a) Landlord shall provide and maintain the building and grounds appurtenant to the dwelling unit in a decent, safe, and sanitary condition, and shall comply with all state and local laws, regulations, and ordinances concerning the condition of dwelling units, which at a minimum must be maintained in decent, safe, and sanitary condition.

b) Landlord shall take reasonable measures to provide and maintain security on the premises and the building and grounds appurtenant thereto to protect Tenant and other occupants and guests on the premises from burglary, robbery, and other crimes. Tenant agrees to use reasonable care in utilizing such security measures.

c) As repairs are now needed to comply with this paragraph, Landlord specifically agrees to complete the following repairs on or before the following dates:

Repair	Date

This list is not intended to be exhaustive, nor is it to be construed as a waiver as to any other defective conditions which may exist.

d) If Landlord fails to substantially comply with any duty imposed by this paragraph, Tenant's duty to pay rent shall abate until such failure is remedied. Upon Landlord's failure to make necessary repairs, Tenant may make or cause to be made said repairs and deduct the reasonable cost of said repairs from the next month's rent. This section (d) shall apply to defects within Tenant's dwelling unit only, and then only if Tenant has notified Landlord or his agent of such defects and has given Landlord a reasonable time to make repairs. The remedies provided by this section (d) shall not be exclusive of any other remedies provided by law to Tenant for Landlord's violation of this Agreement.

13. Subleasing

Tenant shall not assign this Agreement or sublet the dwelling unit without consent of Landlord. Such consent shall not be withheld without good reason relating to the prospective tenant's ability to comply with the provisions of this Agreement. This paragraph shall not prevent Tenant from accommodating guests for reasonable periods.

14. Retaliation

If Tenant reasonably and peacefully exercises any right granted under this Lease Agreement or any state, local, or federal law, or if Tenant joins or organizes a tenants' union, Landlord agrees not to retaliate against or harass Tenant in any way, specifically including but not limited to eviction or threat of eviction, rent increase or services decrease, refusal to renew a term tenancy, or substantial alteration of lease terms.

Landlord shall bear the burden of proving a good motive or good cause for any act which Tenant alleges to be retaliatory and which takes place within six (6) months of Tenant's exercise of a legal right pursuant to this Lease Agreement or state, local, or federal law.

15. Destruction of premises

If the premises become partially or totally destroyed during the term of this Agreement, either party may thereupon terminate this Agreement upon reasonable notice.

16. Tenant's termination for good cause

Upon 30 days' written notice, for good cause, Tenant may terminate this Agreement and vacate the premises. Said notice shall state good cause for termination. Good cause shall include, but not be limited to, entry into active duty with U.S. military services, employment in another community, and loss of the main source of income used to pay the rent.

17. Termination

Upon termination of this Agreement, Tenant shall vacate the premises, remove all personal property belonging to him/her, and leave the premises as clean as he/she found them (normal wear and tear excepted).

18. Lawsuits

If either party commences a lawsuit against the other to enforce any provision of this Agreement, the successful party may be awarded reasonable attorney fees and court costs from the other. Landlord specifically waives any right to recover treble or other punitive damages.

19. Notices

All notices provided by this Agreement shall be in writing and shall be given to the other party as follows:

To the Tenant: at the premises.
To the Landlord: at ______________________

20. Holdovers

If the Tenant holds over upon termination of this Agreement and Landlord accepts Tenant's tender of the monthly rent provided by this Agreement, this Agreement shall continue to be binding on the parties as a month-to-month agreement.

WHEREFORE We, the undersigned, do hereby execute and agree to this Lease Agreement.

LANDLORDS:	**TENANTS:**
Signature	*Signature*
Signature	*Signature*
Date of Signature	*Date of Signature*

Source: Reprinted, with permission, from Blumberg and Grow, *The Rights of Tenants,* an ACLU handbook.

The doctrine of fixtures also determines who owns additions to the premises made by the tenant. For example, if a tenant builds bookshelves into the wall, and no lease provision applies, who owns them when the tenant leaves? If the tenant and landlord cannot agree, the courts may decide. The courts will seek guidance from previous court cases in that jurisdiction that have looked at the facts of specific disputes and decided who owns what.

Q. Is a tenant permitted to sublease the rental unit to someone else?

A. The tenant may have the right. It depends on whether there is a lease and what it says about subleasing (subletting).

Usually, a lease provision will prohibit subletting without the landlord's written approval. If the lease does not mention it, the tenant probably may sublet the premises for the term of the tenancy. A tenant may not, however, transfer more than the lease allows. So, if five months remain on a year tenancy, the tenant may sublet for only five months or less.

If there is no written lease, the tenant may not, and normally need not, sublet.

Subletting and the Tenant's Liability

Subleasing does not end the tenant's liability to the landlord. In a sublease arrangement, the lease remains in full effect. The tenant still is liable for performing all provisions. This includes paying the rent on time. Any violation of the lease agreement—by the tenant or the subtenant—may allow the landlord to sue for damages and eviction. A subleasing arrangement puts the original tenant in the middle. To the landlord, the original tenant still is liable as a tenant. However, the subtenant views the original tenant as the landlord.

Q. May a tenant move out before the lease ends?

A. Yes, but the tenant has signed a binding legal contract for a set period of time. Therefore, the tenant may be liable for the rent for that period. However, the situation is different in an oral or written month-to-month tenancy. Then a tenant may move out without being liable for future rent. The tenant only has to give the landlord proper written notice. The minimum time for such notice usually is 30 days.

Q. Must the landlord look for a new tenant if the old one moves out early?

A. The answer depends on the state where the unit is located. Sometimes it is the landlord who must look for a new tenant. If the landlord refuses to release the tenant from the rental agreement, there may be a limit to the tenant's liability for damages. This is so because the law recognizes the duty of landlords to take reasonable steps to reduce their losses. This requires a landlord to make reasonable efforts to rerent the unit for the same amount of rent and the same period of time. If this is impossible and the landlord rerents for less money or a shorter time period, the original tenant may have to pay the difference. This also is true if there is a delay in getting a new tenant. If the security deposit is too small to cover this debt, the landlord may sue the tenant for the rest of the debt.

THIRTY-DAY NOTICE OF TERMINATION OF TENANCY (Termination of Month-to-Month Tenancy by Tenant without Stating Cause)

_____________*(date)*______________

Dear ___*(landlord or agent)*___:

Please regard this as notice of my intention to terminate the month-to-month tenancy under which I have occupied the residential premises located at ___*(street name and number, unit number, city, and state)*___.

I intend to vacate the premises on ___*(date at least thirty days from receipt of this notice)*___.

____
(tenant)

Source: Reprinted, with permission, from Blumberg and Grow, *The Rights of Tenants,* an ACLU handbook.

Q. How does the tenant know that the landlord has made a reasonable effort to rerent the premises?

A. A tenant may ensure that the landlord's efforts to cut the losses are reasonable by taking certain steps. The tenant should send a letter to the landlord as soon as possible. This letter should state the tenant's plan to leave. The tenant should keep a copy. This will give the landlord plenty of time to find a new tenant. Also, the tenant may want to help look for new tenants by advertising that the place is available. The tenant should send a list of interested, responsible tenants to the landlord (and keep a copy). Evidence of the tenant's efforts will be useful if the landlord takes the tenant to court to collect unpaid rent.

Another Way of Moving out Early

Constructive eviction means that if the unit is unlivable for any reason—and, after notice, the landlord has not corrected the problem—the tenant may move out immediately without liability for future rent. Examples of such reasons may include serious code violations or significant fire damage to the premises. Constructive eviction is another method of moving out before a lease ends, without liability for rent or damages. Before using this doctrine, tenants should consult a lawyer to make certain it applies. The "Tenants' Remedies for Substandard Housing" section that appears later in this chapter discusses this doctrine in greater detail.

Q. Must the tenant move out when the lease expires?

A. Leases almost always require that the tenant move out when the lease expires. Typical lease provisions require the tenant to return possession of the premises to the landlord when the term ends. Other leases might provide for automatic renewal of the lease. This requires the tenant to tell the landlord in advance to stop the tenancy at the end of the term. Otherwise, the law considers the tenant to be agreeing to renew the tenancy on the same terms, usually for the same period of time. In some leases, if the tenant keeps the unit after the term ends and the landlord accepts rent, the lease's original term binds both parties again.

If the lease does not mention renewal, and the tenant stays in the unit after the ending date, state law determines the tenant's rights. These laws generally are of two types. The first type requires the tenant to leave without any advance notice from the landlord. The theory is that the contract was for a set period of time and the tenant knows when it ends.

The second type of law allows the tenant to remain in possession if the landlord accepts rent after the lease ends. Some laws consider the tenant to be a month-to-month tenant under the provisions of the original lease. Other laws specify that the lease is renewed for an additional year if the rent amount remains the same. The explanation for the law permitting month-to-month renewal is that landlords and tenants may need extra time to form new agreements or to find new tenants or new housing. The landlord may end the tenancy by giving proper notice under the relevant law. If so, the tenant has no legal right to renew.

Q. Do tenants have the right to keep pets?

A. It depends on the lease. Usually leases prohibit pets, but a landlord may permit pets if stated in the lease or the building rules and regulations.

Q. May a landlord evict tenants for having a pet in restricted housing?

A. Yes, having a pet in housing where pets are not permitted would be a major violation of the lease or the building rules and regulations. It would allow the landlord to evict the tenant. Most states require the landlord to notify the tenant in writing before the eviction. This would give the tenant the chance to get rid of the pet and avoid the eviction.

Suppose other tenants in the building have similar pets, and the landlord threatens only one tenant with eviction because of having a pet. That tenant may be the victim of *selective* enforcement of landlord rules. Perhaps the landlord has some hidden motive for enforcing the rules against only that tenant. Some states or municipalities identify selective enforcement as retaliatory eviction and prohibit it. (See the "Retaliatory Actions" section that appears later in this chapter.)

EVICTIONS

Q. For what reasons may a landlord evict a tenant?

A. A landlord may evict a tenant (1) for nonpayment of rent, (2) upon the ending of the tenancy by lease expiration or proper notice, or (3) "for cause." The reasons may have different names in each state. However, they all fall into one of these three categories.

Q. What is the most common reason?

A. By far the most common cause for eviction is nonpayment of rent. If a tenant does not pay the rent, or if the tenant pays it late or pays less than is due, the landlord may evict the tenant. The same is true if the tenant pays the rent to the wrong person or at the wrong place. The eviction process often starts upon short notice (usually three days, though it varies among the states).

Q. May landlords evict tenants for failing to pay rent increases?

A. Yes, that is an adequate reason. If the tenants fail to pay a valid rent increase, the landlord may evict them. It does not matter whether the increase is by an escalator clause in the lease or by receiving proper notice. (Usually 30 days is enough for a proper notice in a month-to-month tenancy.) If the tenants feel that the rent increase was invalid, they may pay it under protest. Then they may challenge the increase in court. Or they may pay only the old amount and defend against the likely eviction on the premise that the increase is invalid.

Q. What about not paying other fees?

A. The lease may classify other fees—such as parking, laundry, and gardening—as rent. Landlords also may evict tenants for failing to pay these.

The Kinds of Pets that the Law Permits

Tenants must use reasonable discretion in selecting a pet. Obviously, a tenant may not keep a horse in a fifth-floor apartment. The state and local housing codes provide detailed regulations of the type of animals allowed within specified city limits. However, the landlord also must recognize reasonable discretion. This means that the landlord probably could not prohibit a tenant from keeping a goldfish.

THIRTY-DAY NOTICE TO QUIT
(Termination of Month-to-Month Tenancy by Landlord without Stating Cause)

(date)

TO: Tenant *(name[s] as it [they] appear[s] on the rental agreement or on checks, receipts, notices, etc.)*

RE: The rental premises located at: *(street name and number, unit number, city, and state)*

You are hereby notified that your month-to-month tenancy at the residential premises described above will terminate on *(a date at least thirty days from receipt of this notice)*.

You must peaceably vacate the premises and remove all of your personal property on or before the date specified above. You are responsible for leaving the premises in as good condition as they were when you moved in.

If you fail to comply with the terms of this notice, suit for eviction and damages may be filed against you pursuant to applicable state law.

Signature of landlord or agent

Source: Reprinted, with permission, from Blumberg and Grow, *The Rights of Tenants*, an ACLU handbook.

Q. What if the tenant will not leave when the tenancy has ended?

A. A landlord also may evict a tenant for remaining in possession *(holding over)* after the tenancy legally ends. The tenancy may validly end in two ways. The term of the tenancy may expire, as agreed upon in the lease. Or, in a month-to-month arrangement, the landlord may give proper notice as the law requires.

When the tenancy ends, some tenants try to keep possession of the premises by offering the next month's rent. If the landlord accepts this money, the landlord loses the right to end the tenancy. This usually creates a new month-to-month tenancy. (The landlord could end this new tenancy by giving 30 days notice.) In some states, if the rent stays the same, accepting the money, in effect, renews the existing lease. If the landlord refuses the money, the landlord may evict the holdover tenant.

The tenant also may face double or triple damages for holding over. However, courts are reluctant to award more than actual damages. Courts usually reserve double or triple damages for only the most extreme cases involving very unreasonable tenants.

Q. What is eviction "for cause"?

A. All other reasons for eviction may be part of the broad category of *for cause*. This includes violating major terms of the lease, violating the law, and breaking any house rules or regulations. It also involves the destruction of property and disturbing the neighbors' "quiet enjoyment" of the premises. A landlord seeking to evict a tenant for any of these reasons usually must take the tenant to court. The landlord must prove the truth of the facts claimed and show that they are a cause for eviction. The tenant has the right to contest the landlord's version of the facts. The court will decide whose story to believe.

If the court believes the landlord, it must determine whether the tenants' conduct forms an adequate cause for eviction. Courts may decide these matters in practically any manner they choose. That is why it is worth the tenants' time and effort to appear and explain the situation. A sympathetic judge may be reluctant to evict tenants for a minor violation such as a having one noisy party.

Q. Must the landlord give tenants advance notice before eviction?

A. Yes, the tenant usually must receive notice of the landlord's plan to start a legal eviction *before* the landlord files a complaint with the court. This notice normally must be in writing. The period of the notice varies with the reason for the eviction. (Remember, when the lease term expires, there may be no need for notice.)

Despite variations among the states, there are certain generalizations about notice requirements. A notice must specify the parties' names, the property's address, the nature of the violation or amount of rent overdue, and the date of the notice. Many states have very strict rules about how the notice must be served. Tenants often must be served with notice personally (by hand) or by registered or certified mail. Other states permit the notice to be delivered by regular mail or simply left at the unit.

Landlords Who Refuse the Rent and Evict the Tenant

Suppose a tenant offers *(tenders)* the proper amount of rent on time and the landlord wrongly refuses it. Then it still may appear that the tenant failed to pay the rent. If the landlord tries to evict the tenant in court for nonpayment, the tenant must prove that the rent was offered properly and refused wrongfully. It helps to keep a copy of a letter sent to the landlord after the refusal. This letter should again try to have the landlord accept the rent. Witnesses to the refusal also can help.

If the landlord is seeking eviction because of unpaid rent, the tenant often may avoid the eviction by paying the rent during the notice period. If the eviction is for violating any other lease provision, the tenant may be able to avoid eviction by curing the violation.

Q. Must a landlord go to court to evict a tenant?

A. Yes, in almost all states, only the courts may evict a tenant. Every state has laws covering eviction. The state might call these laws *unlawful detainer, holdover, forcible entry and detainer* (FED), or *summary eviction process*. Most require at least minimal involvement of the courts. However, the degree of involvement varies widely among the states. Where the issue has appeared in the courts or legislatures, most states have outlawed *self-help evictions*. These occur when the landlord evicts the tenant by force. Many states and municipalities allow the tenant to sue the landlord for damages if the landlord uses such methods.

NOTICE TO PAY RENT OR QUIT
(Short-Term Notice for Nonpayment of Rent)

______________ *(date)*

______________ *(name)* ______________, Landlord, hereby notifies ______________ *(name)* ______________, Tenant, to pay rent currently due in the amount of $______________ or quit the premises located at ______ *(street name and number, unit number, city, and state)* ______, within __________ days from the date of this notice. If you fail to either pay the rent due or quit the premises within __________ days of the date of this notice, suit for eviction and damages may be commenced against you under applicable state law.

____

Signature of landlord or agent

Source: Reprinted, with permission, from Blumberg and Grow, *The Rights of Tenants*, an ACLU handbook.

Q. How long might an eviction take?

A. From the day the tenant receives the landlord's notice of eviction to the day the officer of the court (often a sheriff) arrives to put the tenant on the street may take as little as three weeks. Often, however, eviction takes two or three months, or more.

Q. What happens if the tenants do not show up in court?

A. Then they lose. If the tenants do not show up to contest or defend the eviction, the court has no choice. It must enter a default judgment against them. If the tenants want their side of the story heard, they must exercise their right to a day in court.

Q. Do tenants have the right to a trial by jury in eviction proceedings?

A. That is a possibility. State laws, court rules, or the state constitution determine the right to a jury trial in an eviction proceeding. Several state laws provide for a jury trial in eviction proceedings. However, many state laws are silent on the matter. The easiest way to find out about the right to a jury trial is to call the clerk of the local court and ask which rule or statute provides the right. Callers should double-check the information to be certain that the right has no restrictions. The most common restriction is that tenants must pay the expenses that the government incurs for a jury trial, always before the trial.

If the tenants do not request a jury, the law will consider that they gave up their right to a jury trial. The same is true if the tenants do not pay the required fee on time or do not get a waiver of the fee. It is also possible that the tenants have waived their right to a jury trial by a lease provision, though courts will not enforce the anti-jury provisions in some states. If the tenants have given up this right, a judge will hear their case.

Q. How may tenants defend themselves from eviction?

A. Defenses will depend on the grounds for eviction stated in the complaint. If the eviction is for nonpayment of rent, the tenants may try to prove that they paid the rent, that the unpaid rent was not actually owed, or that the eviction notice or its service (delivery to the tenants) was inadequate procedurally. Additional defenses, available in many jurisdictions, include claiming that someone or something has violated:

Eviction Proceedings

An eviction proceeding often is a *summary* action to determine whether the landlord or tenant has the immediate right to the possession of rental housing. In evictions, "summary" simply means that the court will act quickly to resolve the dispute. To do this, courts usually narrow the range of issues they will decide. They also reduce the amount of procedures that would have been available in a conventional trial.

- The tenants' right to quiet enjoyment of the premises;
- The implied warranty of habitability; and
- The tenants' statutory right to repair the premises and deduct the cost (discussed later in this chapter).

Suppose the eviction is for nonpayment of a rent increase or holding over after the receipt and expiration of a 30-day notice. Then the tenants may defend by:

- Attacking the procedural adequacy of the notice or its service (if any). That is, the tenant may claim that the notice or the serving of the notice to the tenant did not give the tenant the required information in a timely fashion; or
- Showing that the landlord's motive for eviction or rent increase was illegal, not allowed by the lease or law, or retaliatory (if it was).

If the eviction is "for cause," the tenants may defend *on the merits* by telling their side of the story, as with any civil suit. (The beginning of this section discusses evictions for cause.) Or the tenants may defend on the grounds that the landlord accepted rent after knowing about the violation, thus surrendering the right to evict.

Lawyers and Eviction Proceedings

Tenants are not required to have a lawyer in an eviction proceeding. However, they should have one. The landlord almost certainly will, and the tenants may be at a considerable disadvantage without legal help. The law does not *entitle* tenants to a lawyer. However, if tenants cannot afford a lawyer, it never hurts for them to ask the court to provide a lawyer free of charge.

If tenants do represent themselves, the law permits them to do anything a lawyer could do, and the court expects them to be competent.

Q. What kind of judgment may the court enter in an eviction case?

A. The judge may award the possession of the rental property to either party. The judge might also order the payment of the rent.

Q. Suppose the court enters a judgment for rent against a tenant. Then may the court take the tenant's money or possessions?

A. Yes, if the tenant does not make arrangements to pay the judgment voluntarily, the court may order an officer of the court to collect the debt. (This is true of any civil money judgment.) The officer, who is often the sheriff, may take most of the tenant's valuable assets to satisfy the judgment. The court will estimate the tenant's ability to pay by determining the value of his or her assets. These assets include bank accounts, most home appliances and furnishings, jewelry, clothing, cars, and future income. Depending on the state laws, the sheriff will take enough of the tenant's assets to pay the debt.

Q. May a landlord seize the tenant's property on his or her own?

A. Executing a judgment usually requires the courts to participate in or supervise part of the process. In a few states, though, the law permits a landlord to enter a rented property and seize the tenant's property legally.

Q. May all the tenant's property be seized under court order?

A. The laws in many states protect certain types of tenant possessions. These usually are items that the tenant either uses to earn a living or that are essential to daily life. Federal law exempts welfare or social-service payments. This includes Social Security, veterans' benefits, and public aid.

Q. What does it mean when tenants are "judgment-proof"?

A. If all the tenants' possessions are exempt and the law protects their wages from being garnished (see sidebar) the tenants are *judgment-proof.* A court order will give the landlord nothing. The landlord will be unable to collect the debt until the tenants' financial position improves.

However, practically speaking, many poor tenants are, in effect, judgment-proof. That is because most landlords are reluctant to undergo the involved process of judicial seizure and sale of the tenants' goods. Because of this, landlords often are satisfied simply to regain possession of the premises without pursuing their claim for rent.

Q. May a sheriff physically throw tenants out of their home if the landlord wins a judgment for possession?

A. Yes, this may happen after the court enters the final judgment, the tenant has lost any appeals, and all requests for a stay of execution have been denied. Then the court will order a sheriff or constable to evict the tenants. The sheriff or constable might give a few days advance notice before doing so, depending on the local custom. If the tenants refuse to leave, the officers may use all necessary and reasonable force to remove them. The officers may deposit the tenants and the contents of their apartment on the street.

HOUSING CODES

Q. What are housing codes?

A. *Housing codes* are state or local laws that determine the minimum standards of health and safety for residential

Garnishing Wages to Pay a Judgment for Rent

If the tenant does not have enough money or assets to satisfy a judgment for rent, the court may order the tenant's employer to set aside part of the tenant's future wages. The court will use this money to pay the judgment. The legal term for this is *wage garnishment*. State and federal laws will determine how much of a worker's pay can be taken. If the paycheck falls below the minimum set by law, none of the pay can be garnished.

HARDSHIPS THAT DELAY EVICTIONS

In many states, after the court has decided against a tenant, it may *stay* (stop) or postpone the eviction. The basis for this stay usually is the hardship caused to the tenant by immediate eviction. There often are some conditions for such a *stay of eviction*. These may require the tenant to have searched unsuccessfully for another place to live and to maintain good conduct. These also may require the tenant to pay all back rent, court costs, and future rent as it comes due. Sometimes local laws or customs require sheriffs to delay evictions in cold winter weather.

Even without a stay of eviction from a court, state law often allows a short period between the time the court orders the eviction and the time the tenant must leave.

housing. The codes establish the landlord's basic duty to maintain rental property that meets those minimum standards. These codes represent the first public regulation of the private landlord-tenant relationship.

Q. Do housing codes cover most conditions that probably will arise in a rental unit?

A. Yes, housing codes often contain detailed regulations of minimum housing standards. There are various reasons for this detail. One is to protect some landlords' property from the economic effects of other landlords' failure to maintain their property. Another reason is to stop the spread of contagious diseases.

All codes cover room temperature, water temperature and pressure, electrical and fire safety, plumbing, rodent and insect infestation, and building structure. More detailed codes regulate the number of garbage cans and require dead-bolt locks on outside doors. They also may order a full-time superintendent to be on the premises.

Q. May tenants use code violations as evidence?

A. Yes, they may do so if they go to court against their landlord to charge that their unit violates the implied warranty of habitability (discussed in the next section). Then a copy of a code violation report is the tenants' best evidence to prove the condition of their home.

Q. How do tenants report a possible code violation?

A. To report a possible code violation, tenants should:

(1) Call the municipal building inspection department (or similar name). It usually is in the city hall. Tell them the nature of the complaint, and request an inspection of the home.

(2) Find out the day and time the inspector will arrive. If possible, tenants should be there to show the conditions needing repair. Tenants should help the inspector notice these conditions and include them in the report.

(3) Urge the inspector to check the rest of the rental unit and the common areas of the building for other violations.

(4) When the inspector files a report (usually within a few days), get a copy. Go to the department and make a copy, or pay them to send one. These reports are public records available upon request. If there are errors or missing items, call the department. Ask for either changes or a new inspection.

Q. What happens if the code inspector finds violations?

A. Then the landlord receives a copy of the report. The landlord also receives an order to repair the violations. These repairs must take place within a certain amount of time (usually 30 to 60 days).

The department and the courts then have the responsibility for enforcement. Concerned tenants should find out if either one holds a hearing. The tenants may attend to be certain that their side of the story comes out at the hearing.

IMPLIED WARRANTY OF HABITABILITY

Q. What is the implied warranty of habitability?

A. It exists in the vast majority of states. In these states, each rental agreement carries an implied *warranty of habitability*. This warranty gives tenants a legal tool. They can use it in an effort to assure that they will not have to pay for essential services or decent housing that they do not receive.

The warranty of habitability is a contractual guarantee. The law implies it in every residential rent agreement, oral or written, where it exists. It guarantees that the landlord will provide the tenant with decent, safe, sanitary, and habitable housing. Most jurisdictions that recognize the warranty of habitability define it by housing codes.

Q. What is the reasoning behind this warranty?

A. The philosophy behind this warranty seems obvious. After all, why pay for what you do not receive? However, beginning with court decisions in the early 1970s, it marked a tremendous change in the rental law. This philosophy is in direct contrast with the traditional property-law view of the landlord-tenant relationship, which required the landlord to give possession of the land to the tenant for a certain period of time. The law required the tenant to pay the full rent for the land. The land's condition did not matter. The landlord's promise to provide the land was independent of the tenant's promise to pay rent.

The modern view considers the landlord's promise to provide habitable housing and the tenant's promise to pay rent to be interdependent. That is, if the landlord fails to provide the tenant with a habitable dwelling, the tenant does not have to pay the full rent.

The Enforcement of Housing Codes

In the past, city officials often viewed codes as regulations affecting only the city and the landlord. In this view, tenants were unimportant parties who might benefit from the codes but took little part in enforcing them.

Many tenants today are actively using the codes to upgrade their units. The law gives tenants the right to complain about violations. However, it leaves inspection and further enforcement up to local officials. A tenant may get a code inspector to make an inspection. The inspector has the power to cite (charge) the landlord with violations and order the landlord to repair them within a set period of time. There is a threat of a fine if the landlord does not obey the order.

Q. Does the warranty apply even if the lease denies it or fails to mention it?

A. Yes, the law implies the warranty of habitability in all residential rental agreements, written or oral. A private agreement may not waive (cancel) the warranty. In states recognizing the warranty, if a lease does not mention the warranty or even if it specifically rejects it, courts will treat the lease as if it included the warranty.

Q. How do tenants know when a landlord has violated the warranty of habitability?

A. It depends. If a home has no heat in the dead of winter, it is legally uninhabitable. However, a few ants in the cupboard or some mold in the bathroom is not a violation of the warranty.

Q. What will the court consider in determining a violation?

A. The court will consider many factors in deciding whether the landlord has violated the warranty. The tenant also should consider these points in deciding whether to use the warranty. These factors include:
(1) Has there been a violation of any housing code or building or sanitary regulation?
(2) Does the defect affect an important facility?
(3) What is its effect on safety and sanitation?
(4) How long has the violation continued?
(5) Was the tenant responsible for the defective condition?
Landlords sometimes argue that the age of the building and the amount of the rent also ought to be considered. However, courts are not usually receptive to these arguments.

TENANTS' REMEDIES FOR SUBSTANDARD HOUSING

Constructive Eviction

Q. May tenants move out if their home is uninhabitable?

A. Yes, the common-law doctrine of *constructive eviction* allows tenants to move out of uninhabitable homes, often without giving notice and always without liability for future rent, if their "enjoyment" or use of the premises is impaired substantially. This doctrine applies to any condition that

PROBLEMS WITH CODE ENFORCEMENT

Even if the enforcement procedure works properly, tenants should consider certain problems. If the violations are very serious and not easily repaired, tenants risk the condemnation and demolition of their homes. Then a code violation complaint may lead to "eviction by bulldozer." The city may turn the homes into vacant lots.

The most common problem with code enforcement is that if tenants have a month-to-month tenancy, the landlord may increase their rent. The landlord might do this to recover the cost of repairs or simply because the unit is worth more. Laws against retaliation may limit the landlord's ability to raise rents to punish the tenant.

makes the premises basically useless to the tenant. It generally does not matter what the cause is (fire, storm, flood, or landlord's failure to maintain), except that the tenant may not move out because of conditions caused by the tenant. When the doctrine was new, the courts thought that the presence of such a condition was a form of eviction by the landlord. That is why it got the name "constructive eviction."

Q. Does this apply in every state?

A. It might apply in all states. Courts, not legislatures, created this doctrine. The coverage of this doctrine and the requirements for its use differ among the states.

Q. May I assume that courts will rule in the tenants' favor if they use this doctrine?

A. No, that is not a safe assumption. If the tenants move out and the landlord takes them to court, the court may decide that the condition was not a constructive eviction. Then the tenants will be liable for future rent payments.

The more likely problem that the tenants will face, even if they use constructive eviction properly, is the lack of other affordable housing. Recognizing this, courts and legislatures have provided other remedies. These allow for repairing the defect while keeping tenants in their home.

Repair-and-Deduct

Q. May a tenant repair the unit and charge the landlord for the repair?

A. Yes, in many jurisdictions this is legal. In a growing minority of states, tenants may repair certain defective conditions in their homes and then deduct the cost of repairs from their next rent payment. Several state restrictions, which vary, affect this remedy, known as *repair-and-deduct*. This tenant self-help remedy does not require court supervision. However, because the tenants are submitting a repair bill instead of all or part of the rent, the landlord may try to evict them for nonpayment of rent.

Then the tenants must prove in court that their use of the remedy was proper. If their use of this remedy meets the requirements of the local law, tenants should have little or no problem defending the eviction. The facts should speak for themselves. If the court finds that the tenants did not use the remedy properly, they will have to pay the entire month's

Taking Matters into Your Own Hands

This section discusses tenants' remedies against a landlord who has failed to provide decent, safe, sanitary, and habitable housing. A tenant can use these remedies by acting alone (self-help) or with other tenants. (This is unlike the remedies for code enforcement, which require administrative action.) Using these remedies often will involve court action later, as the landlord may challenge the remedy's legality. However, if the tenant carefully chooses the correct remedy and follows the proper procedures, there may be few problems if there is a trial.

Tenant remedies include acting on the doctrine of constructive eviction, repair-and-deduct, rent reduction, and injunctive relief. (This section will explain these terms as they arise.) Also discussed is the tenants' decision to sue the landlord *(affirmative action)* for violating the warranty of habitability.

rent. It will not matter that they have spent part of it on repairs.

Q. Are there any limitations on the use of repair-and-deduct?

A. Yes, each state law has its own restrictions. Generally, these restrictions require:
(1) That the tenant give reasonable notice to the landlord requesting repairs. The tenant must give the landlord a chance to complete those repairs before using the remedy;
(2) That the tenant may deduct only a certain amount for repairs, usually no more than one month's rent; and
(3) That only certain types of defective conditions justify the use of this remedy. At least one state limits the number of times a tenant may use this remedy per year.

Q. How do tenants use repair-and-deduct?

A. Repair-and-deduct is easy to use if the tenant has a basic, working knowledge of the local law. A tenant should employ the following general steps in using this remedy:
(1) *Determine the nature of the defective condition.* The tenant first will have to decide whether the local repair-and-deduct law covers the defect. Does the condition substantially affect a "vital facility" essential to habitability (health or safety)? Or is it the lack of a mere "amenity" (convenience) that, although unpleasant, does not interfere with basic living requirements?
(2) *Give the landlord notice and a chance to repair the defect.* Tenants must tell the landlord of the defective condition, preferably in writing (often required by law). They should state their intent to use the remedy unless the landlord makes the repairs within a reasonable time. Local law may specify that amount of time. If not, the courts have interpreted "reasonable time" to mean the amount of time it should take to complete the repair, assuming the landlord acts in good faith. One month's notice normally is more than enough. Emergency situations (for instance, no water) require far less notice.
(3) *Make the repair.* If the landlord does not respond to the notice by setting up a work schedule or completing the repairs, the law entitles tenants to make the repair themselves or hire someone to do it. Some states require two or more written estimates. The only requirement for the quality of the repair is that the repairperson works in a skilled and competent manner. If tenants do the work themselves, they may charge for materials. Tenants should save the receipts for anything they buy to make the repair. If they hire someone, the tenants should get an itemized bill.

Use Repair-and-Deduct Cautiously

Repair-and-deduct favors the tenant. After all, it allows tenants to make repairs without losing possession of their homes. However, local restrictions on the use of the remedy may make it ineffective. Suppose a restriction says that a tenant may deduct only $50 or less. Then the tenant can repair only minor defects. If a tenant may use repair-and-deduct only once a year, fixing a leak in March may prevent repairing a broken toilet in August. Therefore, before you use repair-and-deduct, contact your local housing department to see if any such restrictions exist in your area.

(4) *Deduct the cost of the repairs from the next rent payment.* Tenants should submit the receipts and bills along with the difference in rent. They should keep copies of everything they submit.

NOTICE OF DEFECTIVE CONDITIONS (To Be Used by Tenant to Satisfy Prerequisite of Written Notice to Landlord of Defects on the Premises)

______________ *(date)* ______________

To ______________ *(name)* ______________, landlord of premises located at *(street name and number, unit number, city, and state)*.

Certain defective conditions and/or code violations exist at the premises mentioned above. They are:

____

____

____

____

____

I would appreciate your repair of these conditions within a reasonable time. Should these conditions remain unremedied, I intend to exercise my rights under existing law, including code enforcement, affirmative actions, rent withholding, repair-and-deduct, or quitting the premises.

Thank you for your cooperation.

____

(tenant)

Source: Reprinted, with permission, from Blumberg and Grow, *The Rights of Tenants*, an ACLU handbook.

Rent Reduction

Q. Are tenants required to pay the full rent if the rental unit is uninhabitable?

A. Not if they live in a state that recognizes the warranty of habitability. In all such states, tenants need not pay for services they do not receive. A legal name for this reduction in rent is *rent abatement*. It is the primary enforcement method when landlords violate the warranty. However, rent reduction is unavailable in states without the warranty of habitability.

Rent reduction has two purposes. It compensates the tenant for a violation of the warranty. In so doing, it reduces the rent flow. This gives the landlord an economic reason to make the repairs.

Unless the state law says otherwise, the tenant usually will decide when to withhold all or part of the rent. However, courts ultimately will determine the amount of rent reduction. As with other tenant remedies, the courts will review the defects that supposedly violate the warranty to decide whether the remedy was proper. Courts generally will apply the same standards for review here as with repair-and-deduct. Courts will ask whether the defect substantially affects habitability (vital facility, health, or safety). The courts also will ask whether the tenant gave the landlord proper notice to repair the defect.

Using Repair-and-Deduct as a Group

The law *might* allow a group of tenants to collectively use repair-and-deduct to make major repairs. It limits individual tenants using this remedy to repairing minor defects, mainly because of the limit on the dollar amount of the deductions. However, repair-and-deduct can be invaluable to tenants who use it collectively to repair major defects that affect many or all of the building's tenants. Repair-and-deduct cases and laws neither authorize nor prohibit the collective use of this remedy.

Q. Are rent withholding and rent strike the same as rent reduction?

A. They are nearly identical. These remedies achieve basically the same result. They keep the rent money away from a landlord who violates the warranty of habitability. However, they do so in slightly different ways. In a few states, the law creates rent withholding as a remedy. It requires the tenant to deposit withheld rent money into a special court escrow account. The deposit shows that tenants are acting in good faith.

People have referred to the collective use of legal rent withholding or reduction as *rent strike*. Others also have used this term for the illegal withholding of rent by a group of tenants. Therefore, it suggests something more militant. Legal or illegal rent strikes, because of their collective nature, have been effective in achieving limited tenant goals.

Q. How may tenants use the remedy of rent reduction?

A. A tenant must first determine whether the defective conditions violate the warranty of habitability. If a tenant thinks a violation exists, the tenant must give the landlord adequate notice of the defect, preferably written, and a reasonable chance to make the repair. If the landlord does not make the repairs, the tenant may withhold all or part of the next monthly rent payment.

Unlike repair-and-deduct, the tenant will not know the amount of rent reduction that is due. Only the court may make the final decision. (The court will get involved if the landlord tries to evict the tenant or force the tenant to pay the back rent.) However, the tenant must make a guess immediately. Since there is no penalty for withholding all the rent if a tenant acts in good faith (and obeys the applicable state law), the tenant usually should do so. Then the tenant should let the court determine the proper amount of the reduction.

If the court rules in the tenant's favor and reduces the rent, the tenant still must pay the remaining portion.

Q. Does a tenant have to wait to be sued by the landlord to use rent reduction?

A. No. It is true that tenants often use rent reduction in defending against a suit by the landlord. With the warranty of habitability, it is a defense to an eviction for nonpayment of rent or a defense to a suit for back rent. However, in most states, tenants also may use them as the basis for a lawsuit filed by the tenants against the landlord. This simply means that tenants do not have to wait to be sued by the landlord to use rent reduction as a remedy.

Q. Are there any other kinds of suits that the tenants are permitted to file?

A. Besides seeking damages against the landlord, tenants also may sue for "declaratory and injunctive relief." When asking for *declaratory relief,* tenants are asking the court to review the landlord-tenant relationship and to "declare" the parties' respective rights and remedies. A request for *injunctive relief* asks the court to order the landlord to either do a specific act (for example, to fix the boiler) or not do a particular act (for instance, to no longer use poisonous lead paint).

Q. How will courts usually rule on these suits?

A. Courts usually will grant declaratory relief. However, they are very reluctant to award injunctive relief. It requires the court's continued participation to ensure that the landlord obeys the order.

Beware of Eviction for Nonpayment of Rent

Because rent reduction, withholding, and rent strike are part of the warranty of habitability, they are legal only in those jurisdictions that recognize the warranty. Unless the law changes, using these remedies in any other jurisdiction is illegal. It may result in an eviction for nonpayment of rent because the tenant may not use violation of the warranty as a defense.

RENTING RESIDENTIAL PROPERTY

SHOULD TENANTS SUE LANDLORDS?

There are a few reasons why tenants would prefer to file suits, rather than have the landlord sue them. Being a plaintiff instead of a defendant is a strategic advantage. Many observers think that courts are likely to be sympathetic to a tenant who takes the time and trouble to sue. Courts may reason that the problem must be pretty bad to force the tenant to seek a legal remedy. And the worst that can happen to a tenant who sues is that the court decides in favor of the landlord, and conditions stay as they are. If the landlord sues the tenant and wins, the tenant might be evicted and forced to pay back rent. There also are a few other advantages. A regular civil court, not an eviction court, hears lawsuits by the tenant. The restrictions of summary procedures do not limit the regular courts. This allows tenants to seek a much wider range of damages.

Q. What method will a court use to calculate a rent reduction?

A. Courts use one of two methods to compute the amount of a rent reduction:

(1) Fair market value. This approach requires the court to determine the fair rental value of the premises in their substandard condition during the time of the tenancy. The court then subtracts this estimated rental value from the rent that the tenant originally agreed to pay.

(2) Percentage loss of use. Courts using this method will consider the defective condition of the premises. Then the courts will try to determine the extent that the tenant's use of those premises has decreased. The decrease in use, reflected as a percentage, will determine the amount of the rent reduction.

These calculation methods try to translate defects into an estimate of monetary damages. In reality, no method is capable of precisely measuring actual damages. An educated guess is the best tenants can expect.

Q. If the unit is substandard and tenants move in anyway, have they given up their remedy of rent reduction?

A. No, the tenants still may use rent reduction. Suppose the unit were substandard when the tenants moved in and they did not know about the defective conditions. Then no court will say they have given up their right to use rent reduction as a remedy. But what if the tenants knew or should have known about the defects? Some people have argued that when tenants rent an apartment knowing of the defects, they take the place "as is." Thus, these people feel that tenants are giving up their right to use rent reduction later. However, all courts agree that, except in cases where the tenants act deceptively, the tenants do not give up the remedy by moving in while knowing about the defects.

Q. May tenants seek a rent reduction for past months when the unit was uninhabitable but they paid the rent?

A. Yes, but not every jurisdiction permits this remedy.

Q. Must tenants use rent reduction money to repair the premises?

A. No, rent reduction money belongs to the tenants. There are no strings attached. Rent reductions compensate tenants for their "loss of the bargain" caused by the landlord's violation of habitability. Rent reductions do not give the tenants a profit. They simply pay less because they received less. Tenants may not use rent reduction and repair-and-deduct simultaneously for the same defect.

Retaliatory Actions

Q. What is retaliatory-action protection?

A. It protects tenants against an eviction caused by the landlord's desire to retaliate against them for exercising their rights or engaging in legal activities.

This chapter previously discussed various tenant remedies for violations of the warranty of habitability or for violations of housing codes. These remedies aim to provide tenants with decent housing. What good are these remedies if a landlord may evict tenants for exercising their legal rights? Many jurisdictions specifically prohibit retaliatory action by landlords.

Q. May a landlord evict a tenant for joining or organizing a tenant's union?

A. No, at least not in most of the jurisdictions that provide some form of retaliatory protection. However, most of the 50 states do not specifically protect tenants from retaliation for participating in organizing activities. Some federal courts have provided judicial protection against retaliation where no state laws exist.

Q. Do courts ever consider a landlord's acts other than eviction as being retaliatory?

A. Yes, courts do treat other acts as being retaliatory. Although eviction or threat of eviction is the most common form of retaliation, it is not the only one. Some landlords will increase the rent of a month-to-month tenant. Others will be more subtle. They may decrease services normally provided or change the rules of the tenancy.

All the state laws that protect tenants from retaliation specifically prohibit eviction or threat of eviction. Most of these states also prohibit retaliatory rent increases and decreases in services.

Tenants with long-term written leases normally are free from retaliation by eviction or rent increases during the term of their tenancy. However, even long-term tenants may be affected by decreases in services or by their landlord's refusal to renew their lease.

Protection for Tenants Who Complain

A landlord usually may not evict a tenant for complaining about housing conditions. Many jurisdictions protect tenants who report code violations to the proper authorities. Most states also protect tenants reporting code violations or substantial defects to the landlord. The public policy of decent housing cannot be achieved without protection from retaliation. Tenants will not complain about substandard conditions if they fear eviction, increase in rent, or decrease in services.

Claiming Retaliation While Not Paying the Rent

If the landlord is evicting the tenants for nonpayment of rent, the landlord has a presumably legitimate motive for eviction. However, it is different if the tenants feel the rent is not due to the landlord and has been withheld in good faith. Then the tenants defend on the merits of this issue; the question of retaliation is not involved.

The question of retaliation is involved only where the retaliation takes the forms of a rent increase. If the tenants refuse to pay that increase and the landlord seeks to evict for nonpayment, the tenants may defend against the eviction by claiming retaliation.

Q. Is it hard for tenants to prove that their landlord's acts are retaliatory?

A. Yes, it is very hard. One of the most difficult problems anyone can face in a courtroom is proving a person's motive. This requires you to read the mind of that person at the time the offensive act took place. However, even if you do that to your satisfaction, you still must convince the judge or jury. This is very hard if the witness will not admit to retaliating.

Tenants almost always will need to hire a competent lawyer. Outside evidence will be very important. This may include a damning note from a landlord or a statement made in the presence of a reliable witness.

In response to this problem, many states provide a *presumption of retaliation* in their laws. This is a belief that shifts the burden to the landlord to prove the absence of a retaliatory motive. Usually there must have been some specific action by the tenant to trigger the presumption. An example would be complaining to the housing authorities. Once the presumption is triggered, the tenant does not have to prove the landlord's retaliatory motive. Suppose that, at the trial, the landlord does not successfully prove a nonretaliatory motive for the eviction. (An example would be nonpayment of the rent or a substantial violation of the lease.) Then the tenants should win the case, and defeat the eviction. They will thereby keep possession of the premises.

Q. Will protection against retaliation keep the tenants in the unit indefinitely?

A. No, this will not allow tenants to stay forever. The defense of retaliation theoretically is available each time the landlord acts in a prohibited manner. However, practically speaking, a landlord may eventually succeed in retaliating against a disliked tenant. In states without a presumption of retaliation, the tenant must prove the landlord's improper motive. This is hard to do, and repeated success in using this defense is highly unlikely. Even in states with a presumption of retaliation, the law usually limits the protection to a specified period of time. This normally is six months from when the protected activity occurred, though the Uniform Residential Landlord-Tenant Act (discussed later in this chapter) specifies 12 months protection. Versions of the Act have been adopted in some jurisdictions, giving certain tenants from six months to 12 months worth of protection.

All this means that in states providing protection, if a month-to-month tenant reports code violations and gets on the landlord's blacklist, the landlord may simply wait for the presumption period to expire. Then the landlord may give notice one day later to evict the tenant in 30 days. This would force the tenant to prove the landlord's retaliatory motive. Or the landlord may try to evict the tenant on short-term notice for a major violation of the lease agreement.

However, the picture is not quite this bleak. If the eviction is retaliatory, the tenant might convince the court to throw out the eviction.

If there is a written long-term lease, it generally protects the tenant against retaliation, regardless of the state law. This is because ordinary lease terms forbid an increase in rent, decrease in services, or undeserved ending of the tenancy during the term of the lease. The problem of retaliation arises here when the lease expires and the tenant wants to renew it.

Lockout/Seizure of Tenant's Possessions

Q. May landlords legally lock tenants out of their homes without a court order?

A. No, the vast majority of states outlaw this remedy and require a landlord to use the eviction process set up by law. This guarantees the tenant both notice and a day in court. The idea behind the judicial eviction procedure is that a court should decide landlord-tenant disputes, rather than permitting landlords to be, in effect, judges in their own disputes.

Q. What is the effect of a lockout on a tenant?

A. There are two effects of a lockout. It denies the tenant occupancy of the unit *(distress)*. A lockout also usually denies the tenant access to personal possessions left in the apartment *(distraint)*. The tenant is locked out, and the tenant's goods are locked in.

Most states have abolished the landlord's common-law right to seize the tenant's personal property to satisfy a claim for unpaid rent. A few states still allow landlords to take tenants' personal property under laws known as *landlord lien statutes*. These states may not provide the tenant with a prior hearing on the merits of the landlord's claims. In addition, the court may not have to supervise the landlord's seizure of tenant property. Courts in several states have held these laws unconstitutional. Thus, the modern trend is moving toward abolishing distress and distraint.

Q. Is the use of a lockout or seizure of tenant property common?

A. Yes. Despite being illegal in most areas, these practices still occur. Self-help measures involve much less cost and effort

LANDLORD OR TRESPASSER?

In jurisdictions that have declared it illegal, a lockout is the same as trespassing in the tenants' home, violating their quiet enjoyment, and wrongfully taking ("converting") their property. If a stranger performed these acts, tenants would have no problem calling the police or suing for damages. A landlord has no greater right to seize or lock up the tenants' property than does a stranger. However, because it is the landlord who is entering the home, tenants have been reluctant to act. Usually, they are not sure of the legality of the landlord's entry.

for the landlord than going to court. The best way to end these self-help measures is for tenants to be willing to exercise their legal rights.

Q. What, if anything, should tenants do about an illegal lockout?

A. A tenant may do a few things. The first and most obvious is to call the police, and complain of an illegal criminal trespass. In a few cities, police will advise the landlord of the illegal nature of the lockout and potential criminal penalties. The police also have the power to remove the lock from the door if the landlord fails to do so immediately. However, the police usually will respond that "this is a civil matter that you must settle with your landlord in court." In most places, the police will do nothing to help the tenants.

If the police are not helpful, tenants still have other avenues open to them. If the landlord does not physically possess the unit, tenants could simply reenter the premises, either by going in through a window or by taking the lock off the door. This gives them an important tactical advantage—they have taken back what the landlord tried to take from them. However, tenants should check the local law on this approach before using it. They could be liable for the property they damage in getting back in.

Tenants have other options as well. A lawyer should be able to get a court order putting tenants back into their home on short notice. If tenants cannot get free legal aid, they may recover certain expenses from the landlord in a civil damage action. These may include the cost of court and attorney's fees, and any other damages tenants suffer (the cost of hotel, food, transportation, and the like). By using the civil damage action itself, often authorized by law, tenants might discourage illegal lockouts.

The Law and Security Deposits

Generally, the law does cover security deposits, which have recently received widespread legislative attention. Nearly every state has enacted protective laws regulating the collection and return of security deposits. Tenants often get their money back in small claims courts and without legal representation.

SECURITY DEPOSITS

Q. What is a security deposit?

A. A *security deposit* is money paid by the tenant to the landlord. It ensures that the tenant performs all the duties of the tenancy as required by the lease or applicable law. It is the landlord's insurance policy against any future debts that the tenant might owe. Since the landlord already holds the tenant's money, the landlord will not have to go to court to prove and collect a debt. Rather, the tenant must file a lawsuit and prove that the landlord is not owed the debt claimed.

Q. What does a security deposit cover?

A. It varies, but a security deposit may cover a great deal. A security deposit is a negotiable lease item, and the landlord will almost always have the advantage in lease negotiations. As a result, security deposits may cover more than paying rent on time and keeping the premises in good condition.

Q. Does the security deposit include other advance payments such as the last month's rent or cleaning fees?

A. It may include such things. Paying an advance fee for a specific item or service does not technically qualify as a security deposit. However, in reality, landlords often combine advance fees with security deposits, which tenants pay in a single sum at the beginning of the tenancy.

The two most commonly required prepayments are the first and/or last month's rent in advance and a cleaning fee. The latter covers cleaning expenses before tenants move in, when they move out, or both. These payments are not deposits. The landlord does not intend to return this money to the tenant, and the tenant should not expect to get it back.

Some exceptions to this rule arise in the following cases. Suppose the tenants have paid the last month's rent in advance. Then they give notice ending their tenancy in the middle of the month (assuming the lease entitles them to do so). They should be entitled to get back half of the advance rent payment. Likewise, if the landlord asks for a "cleaning deposit" rather than a "cleaning fee," the tenants might be able to get a refund if they leave the place in a clean condition.

In general, deposits are refundable if the tenants meet all conditions, and fees or payments are nonrefundable. To avoid unnecessary confusion, tenants should make clear the nature of their payments and deposits. They also should define the conditions for either their return or loss. Tenants may do this in the lease or on the deposit receipt.

Q. Is there any such thing as a nonrefundable security deposit?

A. No, it does not exist. All security deposits are refundable if the tenant obeys all the conditions specified in the security clause of the lease agreement.

The lease may have a provision allowing the landlord to deduct a specific sum of money from the security deposit for certain tenant acts. These might include paying the rent late, moving out within a certain period of time, or losing the keys. The landlord is not permitted to make any deductions if these acts do not occur. This follows the reasoning behind

Limiting the Amount of Security Deposits

Most states have enacted broad protections for tenants in the collection and return of security deposits. Nearly all these states limit the amount of security a landlord may require. They usually limit the security deposits to one month's rent. Tenants and landlords should consult their state's law for the current limitation.

DEDUCTIONS FROM THE SECURITY DEPOSIT

In all states with security-deposit protection, landlords must notify their tenants in writing of all deductions from the deposit. The landlords must do so within a specified number of days.

In most states requiring notice, the landlord must give the tenant a written list of itemized deductions from the deposit. This list should specify the nature and amount of the expense. When the tenant receives the list, the tenant also should receive a check from the landlord. The amount of the check should equal the entire security deposit minus the deductions. The law requires the landlord to send the list and check to the tenant within a set period of time after the tenancy ends. This time varies from two weeks to one month.

security deposits. By paying the rent late, for example, tenants have failed to obey the lease agreement, which the security deposit insures.

The legal problem arises with the amount of these deductions. The courts usually are suspicious of clauses specifying the amount of damages before the event occurs *(liquidated damages)*. If the tenant goes to court to challenge such a deduction from the security deposit, the court will examine the reasonableness of the amount deducted. The court will award the landlord only the amount of damages actually suffered.

Q. Are there any restrictions on where the landlord holds the deposit and how the landlord uses it?

A. There usually are no such limitations. In the states without security-deposit protection, there are no restrictions. In nearly all the states with protection, there are no limitations on the landlord's use of or manner of holding a security deposit. In a few states, the landlord must hold the deposit in a bank account.

Some people argue that when the landlord accepts a security deposit from a tenant, a special *fiduciary* relationship is formed. This would require an accounting to the tenant of the use of, deductions from, and profits from the deposit. Not many courts have accepted this argument. However, a few states have enacted legislation that seems to employ the basic idea of a fiduciary relationship.

Q. Does the law entitle tenants to receive interest on their security deposits?

A. Not in most states. However, a minority of states have laws that guarantee tenants some interest on their security deposits. Many of the states differ about the amount payable.

Q. May a tenant challenge a landlord who keeps part of a security deposit?

A. Yes, the tenant has this right. Because the landlord already has the tenant's money, it is the tenant's responsibility to challenge the landlord's act of keeping some or all of the deposit. The tenant may do this by filing suit in small claims courts. These courts are well suited to this type of claim, since the dispute usually involves small amounts of money, almost always under $2,500.

The tenant may challenge both the landlord's failure to return any of the deposit and any deduction made from it. The tenant may question whether there was a need for the deduction and, if so, whether the amount was reasonable. Suppose the landlord fails to provide an itemized list of deductions from the deposit and refuses to return any of the deposit. The tenant would then file a complaint in small claims court for return of the full security deposit. The tenant would explain to the judge that the landlord failed to return the security deposit or to explain the reasons for the deduction. The court would ask the landlord the reasons for this failure to return or to explain. Suppose the landlord says the apartment needed a paint job that cost the total amount of the security deposit. Then the tenant and the court may ask about the need for and reasonable cost of the paint job. If the tenant did not unusually harm the paint during the tenancy, there is no reason for the tenant to pay for repainting. On the other hand, if the tenant did damage the paint, the tenant may attack the cost of the paint job as being unreasonable.

As previously mentioned, all states allow the tenant to sue for return of the security deposit in small claims courts. This basically is a contract action. Many of those states that have enacted security-deposit protection have included special damages to penalize landlords who withhold security deposits in bad faith.

Q. Is the tenant responsible for normal wear and tear to the rental unit?

A. No, both court cases and laws agree that the landlord should bear the cost of normal wear and tear. Everybody knows that nothing lasts forever. Paint fades, linoleum cracks, carpets wear out, wood warps, and even plaster deteriorates with time. There is no reason for the tenant to bear the direct cost of repair or replacement of the landlord's property that has outlived its usefulness.

The big problem arises in trying to determine what "normal wear and tear" means. The hole in the wall caused by a picture hook might seem normal to a tenant. However, the landlord might argue that the hole has damaged the property. (The landlord might have the better of the argument on this point.) Nobody can provide a formula or even guidelines to determine whether normal wear and tear caused the condition.

Sometimes leases provide guidance. For example, a lease might say that tenants must bear the cost of repainting for normal wear and tear. If the lease is silent on this point, tenants would not normally be liable for repainting. (An exception would be if their children scribbled on the walls with crayons.)

Municipal or state laws also might clarify a dispute. Some laws, for example, prohibit the landlord from requiring cleaning beyond normal wear and tear.

Inspecting the Premises Together

In many localities, it is the custom that the tenant and landlord make a joint inspection of the unit when the tenant moves in. The tenant and landlord write down the condition of various elements of the unit. They make a similar inspection when the tenant moves out, noting the damage (if any) that the tenant has caused. This provides a written record of damages that will help avoid (or resolve) disputes about getting the deposit back.

If the tenants seem to be responsible for a specific repair, they probably would be better off making the repair themselves or having it done for them. If they let the landlord do it and deduct the cost from the security deposit, they might end up paying more.

If there is no guidance from the lease or specific laws, it is almost impossible to predict the outcome of court cases on these matters. Tenants may benefit from the doctrine of normal wear and tear when it comes time to decide who is responsible for the premises' condition when the tenancy ends. Certain variables will help define what was a normal use of the premises. These variables include the condition of the premises when the tenant moved in and the degree of maintenance provided by the landlord during the tenancy. They also include the landlord's knowledge of the use the tenants were to make of the premises. (Examples include having pets or many children and making home crafts.)

UTILITY SHUTOFFS

Q. May the landlord evict a tenant by shutting off the utilities?

A. No, shutting off the utilities is just another form of self-help eviction, which almost all states (and many municipalities) prohibit. As stated earlier, generally only the courts may evict a tenant. Eviction by utility shutoff therefore is an illegal act for which the landlord may be criminally and civilly liable.

Some states, such as New York and Connecticut, consider eviction by utility shutoff to be very serious. These states have passed laws that provide criminal penalties for offending landlords. Other states give the tenant a civil remedy for damages. California allows the tenant to collect up to $100 for each day the tenant is without utility service. Massachusetts provides for the landlord to pay three months' rent or actual damages.

Tenants should check their state and local laws to find out if the laws protect them against utility shutoff. If so, tenants should check to see what damages the laws entitle them to seek. Utility shutoff also might be a violation of the right to quiet enjoyment or possibly a trespass under the common law. At the very least, it violates the warranty of habitability.

Q. What may a tenant do to have utility service restored if the landlord shut it off wrongfully?

A. The criminal and civil remedies discussed above will provide penalties against the landlord. However, these remedies will not get the lights, heat, or water turned back on. To do that, a tenant may seek *injunctive relief*. This is an order from the court requiring the landlord to restore utility services immediately. The legal papers that must be filed with the court are highly technical. Therefore, the help of a lawyer usually will be necessary to get an injunction. Landlords almost always will obey a court-ordered injunction because penalties for not doing so are very harsh. The landlord may have to go to jail, pay a fine, or both.

Even if tenants get both an injunction and their utilities restored, the law may entitle them to damages. These damages would compensate the tenants for the time they had to live without utility service. The law also may entitle the tenants to damages if they had to move out because their utilities remained off. This is true even if a state does not have laws granting damages for utility shutoffs, because a utility shutoff almost always violates the warranty of habitability.

Q. May the utility company end its service because it did not receive payment for the bill?

A. Yes, but the time and notice requirements for ending service may vary depending on whether the utility company is public or private. These requirements also may depend on who holds the account, the landlord or the tenant.

The Constitution requires government-owned utility companies to meet the constitutional standards of due process of law. This includes adequate notice and a hearing before ending its service. Privately owned companies are not covered by the Constitution. They do not have to meet the constitutional standards, but very strict laws in some states regulate all utilities, including privately owned ones. These laws protect almost all tenants. In Illinois, for example, state laws governing utility shutoffs cover all buildings with three or more units.

The next question is whether the utility company provides service individually to each tenant or for the entire building under the landlord's name. If service is individual and the tenants fail to pay the bill, the utility company will end their service. Due process requirements for publicly owned companies, or protections in state or local laws, may give the tenants a little extra time. However, if the bill remains unpaid, the shutoff is unavoidable. If the utility service is under the landlord's name and the rental agreement provides for utilities, the landlord's failure to pay the bill also will end in shutoff, unless the tenants make other arrangements directly with the utility company. Laws in many states and localities require that the utility gives notice to *tenants* that service will be shut off. The law will often specify what information the notice must contain. Sometimes the law will give tenants the option of paying for the service and deducting the money from their rent. Tenants may try to negotiate payment of any unpaid bills or deposits. Some states, however, require the utility company to offer service directly to the tenant without a deposit or payment of back bills.

Paying the Bill Out of Future Rent

If the landlord must provide utility services as a part of the rental agreement, the tenants may be able to pay the utility bill out of future rent. The tenants may do this by calling the utility company and making suitable arrangements. Or the tenants may seek a reduction in or return of rent to compensate for the loss of habitability.

DISCRIMINATION IN PRIVATE HOUSING

Q. May a landlord refuse to rent to a prospective tenant who is able to pay the rent?

A. The landlord may have that right. It depends on the reason for the refusal. Some reasons are legitimate, while others are illegal. Suppose a family of five seeks to rent a two-bedroom apartment. Then the landlord may reasonably refuse to rent to them because of overcrowding. Similarly, if someone who has a large dog applies for the vacant unit, the landlord may reject that person's application in favor of others. There are many such legitimate reasons for a landlord's refusal to rent to someone.

The major question is whether the law prohibits the landlord's reason for choosing one tenant over another. The law of discrimination comes from three major sources: the federal, state, and local governments. The federal law uniformly protects most tenants nationwide. State and local laws vary greatly in the amount of additional protection they provide.

Federal Laws

Q. What federal laws protect against discrimination?

A. The Civil Rights Act of 1866 prohibits discrimination because of race in the rental or purchase of privately owned real estate. This old, but still valid, law applies to all tenants no matter what state they live in or how many units their landlord owns. Racial discrimination probably is still the most common form of discrimination in the rental housing market. If people can prove that a landlord has discriminated against them because of their race, this law allows them to sue for money damages. They also may try to get a court order requiring the landlord to rent to them.

The Fair Housing Act of 1968 extends tenants' protection to skin color, religion, and national origin. Other amendments to the Act have prohibitions against discrimination against the handicapped and tenants with children, as well as discrimination based on sex. However, the Act does not cover a large group of small-scale landlords. It does not apply to:

(1) Landlords who live on premises that have four or fewer rental units;

(2) Landlords who own or have an interest in three or fewer single-family houses and who do not sell more than one house in a two-year period. The law excludes personal residences; and

(3) Landlords who are religious or other private organizations (clubs and the like) who are renting to their own members on a noncommercial basis.

The technical legal language of the laws that apply to these three exclusions is extremely confusing, even to the experts. What it seems to mean is that small-scale property owners are permitted to discriminate under federal law on grounds other than race.

Q. Besides the Civil Rights Act and the Fair Housing Act (and its amendments), is there any other federal protection against housing discrimination?

A. Yes, at least one other federal protection exists. A 1962 Executive Order prohibits the discrimination described above in all federally owned, operated, or assisted housing. This includes all public, Federal Housing Administration (FHA), Veterans Administration (VA), and Farmers Home Administration (FmHA) housing. The agency managing the program enforces the Executive Order. It limits the enforcement to an ending of federal funds to the offending landlord.

State Laws

Q. Are there any state laws that provide protection against housing discrimination?

A. Yes, there are numerous state laws that prohibit housing discrimination. State fair housing and civil rights acts seek to extend coverage provided by federal law. Nearly every state and the District of Columbia provide tenants with some form of extra protection against discrimination. The range of protection varies greatly. One Georgia act simply forbids discrimination against blind people. A comprehensive act protects tenants in the District of Columbia (D.C.) against discrimination because of many reasons. These reasons include race, religion, color, national origin, sex, marital status, physical disability, age, personal appearance, sexual orientation, family responsibility, student status, political affiliation, source of income, place of residence, and place of business. Tenants in the very few states without extensive fair housing laws lack much protection against discrimination beyond that afforded by federal law.

Enforcing the Fair Housing Act

People may enforce it by filing a complaint with the Department of Housing and Urban Development (HUD). Or they may file a complaint with the state or local agencies charged with enforcing similar state laws. Tenants also may sue privately under the Act for money damages. Fortunately, none of these enforcement methods require the tenant to understand the complexities of the law. The various agencies or lawyers will do that for them when investigating their complaint. If the investigation shows an established "pattern and practice" of illegal discrimination by a landlord, the U.S. Attorney General has the power to prosecute.

Local Laws

Q. Do any local laws protect against housing discrimination?

A. Many cities and towns also have local ordinances prohibiting certain kinds of discrimination. For example, San Francisco and Berkeley (in California) have laws that prohibit landlords from refusing to rent to families with children.

To find out about your community's laws, call the town council office, city attorney, or city clerk. Ask for details on housing-discrimination laws. The local ordinance will specify the enforcement methods. These usually involve criminal complaints to the local district attorney or private suits for damages.

Proving Discrimination

Q. May tenants prove that a landlord has illegally discriminated against them?

A. Yes, but it is difficult. Tenants may "know" that their landlord is discriminating against them. However, proving it in a court of law is a different matter.

Q. What can individuals do against a landlord who illegally discriminates?

A. Prospective tenants who feel a landlord has discriminated against them may either pursue an administrative course of action through a state or federal agency, or they may choose a private course of action by hiring a lawyer and filing a lawsuit. Both approaches may require the offending landlord to pay damages either as compensation for the tenant's suffering or as a penalty for the landlord's illegal conduct. The tenant's choice of which course to take will depend on the situation.

Q. How do tenants pursue an administrative complaint for discrimination?

A. The federal government and all the state agencies have their own systems for filing and enforcing discrimination complaints. HUD's procedure for the enforcement of Title VIII of the Civil Rights Act of 1968 is typical. Tenants may report discriminatory acts covered by the Fair Housing Act by calling the toll-free HUD discrimination hot line at (800) 424-8590, or by mailing complaints to:

Administrative vs. Private Action

The main difference between administrative and private action is the cost. The administrative action costs the tenant nothing but time and effort. A private suit, however, may be very costly. Unless the tenant qualifies for free legal services, the tenant will have to hire a private lawyer and pay other costs. Both courses are capable of requiring the landlord to rent the desired unit to the prospective tenant. The administrative remedy, because it costs no money to the tenant and involves government investigators, appears better suited to this purpose. If the tenant is seeking large punitive damages, however, the tenant might prefer a private lawsuit, since administrative damages tend to be small.

Fair Housing
c/o the nearest HUD regional office
(Check your local telephone directory for the address.)

Tenants should get written complaints notarized if possible. They must send the complaints to HUD within 180 days of the alleged discriminatory act.

HUD will investigate the complaint. If the law covers it and HUD decides to resolve the complaint, HUD may try informal, confidential conciliation to end the discriminatory housing practice. Or it may inform the tenant of the right to seek immediate court action. Sometimes HUD may refer the complaint to the Attorney General of the United States.

HUD also may refer the complaint to a state or local agency that administers a law that is very similar to the federal law. If the state or local agency does not begin proceedings within 30 days and carry them forward with reasonable promptness, HUD may require the agency to return the case. In any event, the tenant will be notified of the type of action to be taken.

After receiving a complaint, HUD will furnish a copy to the person charged with discrimination. That person may then file an answer in writing, which also should be notarized.

Q. Are there any limits to what a tenant may do about discrimination?

A. Yes, limits do exist. The most important limitation is the time restriction for filing a complaint. Tenants must file federal actions under Title VIII of the Civil Rights Act of 1968 within 180 days from the occurrence. State laws usually require filing within 30 to 60 days.

Some states present another limitation. If tenants file a complaint with a state agency, they must surrender their right to pursue the complaint with a private lawsuit.

UNIFORM RESIDENTIAL LANDLORD–TENANT ACT (URLTA)

Q. What is the URLTA?

A. It is model legislation that includes many of the basic tenants' rights recently adopted around the country. The URLTA includes most of the tenants' rights described in the preceding sections. The National Conference of Commissioners on Uniform State Laws drafted URLTA. (This group monitors trends in the development of state law.) It did so with an eye toward creating a uniform package of law to be adopted by as many states as possible.

Q. What does the URLTA do?

A. It allows a state to replace its laws with a single, more modern law governing the landlord-tenant relationship. The URLTA contains moderate versions of most of the recent reforms in tenants' rights. It covers unconscionability (gross unfairness) of certain lease clauses, rental agreement terms, security deposits, and the warranty of habitability. The URLTA also includes the reasonableness of landlord rules and regulations, repair-and-deduct, rent reduction, and retaliatory protection. In addition, the URLTA abolishes distress and distraint and other forms of self-help eviction.

The URLTA also protects landlords. It includes the tenant's duty to use and maintain the premises properly and the landlord's right to evict the tenant for failure to pay rent or obey the rental agreement. In addition, the URLTA includes the landlord's right to repair and add on for the tenant's failure to perform day-to-day upkeep. The URLTA also has remedies for the tenant's abandonment of the premises.

If a state enacts the URLTA into law, the state fully regulates the rights and duties of landlords and tenants. However, many states have not adopted the URLTA as it currently exists. Rather, these states have modified some of its terms. Since the URLTA is a product of landlord-tenant compromise, any major change may shift the balance of rights and duties.

Q. Have many states adopted the URLTA?

A. A growing minority of states have enacted it.

Q. Does the URLTA favor landlords or tenants?

A. It depends. The model itself aimed to balance the rights and duties of landlords and tenants. The legislative process may upset this delicate balance if a state legislature makes major changes to the original act.

Benefits of Organizing Tenants

Like workers who form a labor union, members of tenant organizations can achieve more when they act collectively rather than separately. Also, collective action lessens the risk of retaliation against active members. Many other tenants probably confront the housing problems faced by a single tenant. An individual solution may solve a specific housing problem, but it will rarely help others in the same situation. For that matter, it probably will not stop the problem from repeating. A tenant organization might be the answer.

TENANT ORGANIZING

Q. May a tenant begin to organize other tenants?

A. Yes, the opportunities for tenant organizing are as numerous as the problems that tenants confront. The most obvious place to begin is in the tenant's own building. A tenant may simply knock on doors or post a notice of a meeting in the lobby. Common problems among tenants also may arise throughout the neighborhood, city, or state. Tenants in different buildings owned by the same landlord often face similar problems and may find that collective action is appropriate. There is no magic formula for tenant organizing. The essential element is commitment.

Q. Are some issues better than others for tenant organizing?

A. Yes, the problems confronting tenants usually will determine the type of organization to be developed. Immediate and narrow problems—such as a broken boiler—will usually require a limited organization centered on a specific short-term goal. When the organization achieves this limited purpose, breaking up the organization seems to be natural. However, tenants should avoid this short-sighted course. By its success, the organization has proven that it works. This is the time to expand the group to deal with other issues, rather than dissolve it. Other problems are certain to arise. That is why it is a good idea to have an active tenant organization prepared to deal with them. Tenants in a building may consider trying to get their landlord to recognize their group. This will help them negotiate the terms of the landlord-tenant relationship. Some tenants have been able to formalize this arrangement into a collective-bargaining agreement.

A local tenants' group might want to explore the possibility of joining with similar groups around the city or state to support broader tenant issues. Rent-control and tenants' rights legislation, such as the URLTA, are good issues for broad-based tenant organizing. These issues affect all tenants regardless of their economic class, race, or location.

Q. Are there many statewide or citywide tenant organizations?

A. Yes, during the past 20 years tenant organizations have sprung up around the country. Most are local, but a few are statewide. Membership ranges from the small local groups to the statewide New Jersey Tenants Organization.

These organizations provide basic information about tenants' rights and organizing. In addition, depending on their size, they may provide legal advice and representation. They also serve an educational function by representing tenant interests in the news media and before state and local governments. Many organizations publish handbooks explaining tenants' rights in their jurisdiction, as well as newsletters containing local developments of interest to tenants.

RENT CONTROL

Q. Has there ever been nationwide rent control in the United States?

A. Yes, during World War I, a largely voluntary program of rent and eviction controls was managed by local Fair Rent Committees. Only Washington, D.C., and New York City adopted mandatory rent controls. However, the emergency situation brought on by World War II created the need for uniform national price controls. In January of 1942, Congress enacted the Emergency Price Control Act. By July of 1942, every major city in the U.S. was subject to rent and eviction controls. Nationwide controls lasted for over ten years, until July of 1953. Thus, before the 1960s, the American rent-control experience consisted only of war-related crises that forced across-the-board rent freezes. These controls generally did not permit any increase in rent.

Q. What are today's rent-control laws?

A. In the late 1960s and early 1970s, many states and communities began to consider rent controls as a way of combating inflated rents. People refer to these controls as *second-generation* rent controls, to distinguish them from wartime emergency rent freezes. Today's rent controls depend on economic factors, such as low vacancy rates and high rates of inflation in rents.

These rent controls are not absolute rent freezes. They allow landlords to increase rents, but restrict the amount of the increase. Landlords also may pass through to tenants increases in property taxes, utilities, and capital-improvement costs. Most second-generation rent control laws guarantee landlords a cost-of-living rent increase, or as an alternative, a "fair return on investment." The law exempts from these controls certain classes of housing, including new construction, luxury housing, and owner-occupied buildings with four or fewer units.

The goal of modern rent control is to soften the harsh effect of rising rents on the tenant. Without rent control, rent increases will reflect not only the landlords' increased business costs, but also the landlords' superior bargaining position created by the critical shortage of housing. Second-generation controls seek to eliminate this windfall profit for landlords by limiting rent increases to legitimate cost increases. This means that rent increases might continue. However, thanks to modern rent control, the increases will be kept to a reasonable amount.

Rent Control and Ancient History

Most people think rent control is a recent innovation. However, the exact opposite is true. Rent control, like most price-control laws, is not simply the creation of legislators. Rather, it is born of necessity. In rent control, the necessity traditionally has been a crisis that affects the supply and price of available housing.

Ancient Rome enacted rent controls to relieve the burdens of discrimination against the Jewish community. In the 1500s, a severe housing shortage in Spain and a plague in Paris caused strict rent controls. An earthquake in Portugal in 1775 created a similar response.

During World War I, Europe, Australia, and most of Africa enacted rent and eviction controls. Rent control is anything but a new idea.

Q. Are tenants anywhere in the U.S. now covered by rent controls?

A. Yes, in the last two decades there has been a trend toward state and local rent controls. Rent-control laws tend to come and go rather rapidly. Therefore, tenants should check with local officials to find out if rent control is in effect in their area.

Q. Are there different ways of enacting rent controls?

A. Yes, there are three basic ways to enact rent controls:
(1) Local ordinance. Either the city council or the voters, by use of the local ballot *(initiative process),* may enact a rent-control law without any action by the state legislature;
(2) State statute. The legislature may enact a rent-control law covering the entire state; and
(3) State enabling legislation. The state legislature may authorize local governments to enact rent-control laws. The local governments may do so either at their own discretion or when a certain triggering event occurs. An example of such an event might be a drop in vacancy rates to a critically low level.

Q. Are there different methods of regulating rents?

A. Yes, there are three basic approaches:
(1) Fair return-on-investment formulas that limit profits;
(2) Annual percentage rent increases with pass-throughs; and
(3) Rent levels based on the tenants' ability to pay.

Q. What does a fair return-on-investment formula involve?

A. A fair return-on-investment formula attempts to unravel the complicated network of real-estate financing. It tries to determine the reasonable profit level of a given building. This helps eliminate rent gouging (overcharging). The complex process for determining profits boils down to a review of the landlord's actual investment and costs of operation.

Q. How do annual rent increases with pass-throughs work to regulate rents?

A. The simplest form of rent regulation permits an annual percentage rent increase, along with pass-through increases to cover higher taxes and other increases in costs.

As in the return-on-investment system, the landlord first sets rents as of a given date. The landlord may then raise rents annually by a percentage established by law. This

How to Get Rent-Control Laws Passed

People interested in getting rent-control laws passed may go to their state legislature, city council, or sometimes to the people. (For the latter, the initiative process allows voters to put measures on the ballot by petition.)

Usually states will adopt a combination of a state statute and an enabling act. This allows states to impose either rent-control standards or guidelines for local communities that choose to enact rent controls.

increase would not require any action by the local rent-control board. In addition, with the approval of the rent-control board, landlords may pass through certain cost increases in the form of rent hikes. These *pass-throughs* usually include tax increases, boosts in utility rates, and capital-improvement costs.

Under either of the two rent-control systems just discussed, rents may increase or decrease based on existing housing-code violations. In other words, if a unit is seriously substandard, the local rent-control board may deny a landlord's request for a rent increase. In fact, it may grant a rent decrease. (In some localities, mayors appoint the members of rent-control boards. In others, the voters elect members of the boards. Elected members tend to be more pro-tenant.) Rent-control systems often permit larger rent increases when the unit changes tenants.

RENT CONTROL AND EVICTIONS

Rent-control systems also regulate evictions. Otherwise, landlords might evade rent-control restrictions by evicting tenants and renting to a fresh group of tenants. These regulations restrict the landlord's traditional right to evict a tenant in retaliation for exercising tenant's rights under the rent-control law. Such laws also often do away with all evictions except just-cause evictions.

Q. How does the approach of tenants' ability-to-pay work?

A. Tenants' ability to pay now affects only setting rents for public housing. The federal government, through the Department of Housing and Urban Development, pays the difference between the tenants' rent payment and the unit's actual rental cost. Private housing has never adopted tenants' ability to pay.

Q. Will landlords try to raise rents in anticipation of rent control?

A. Yes, but to eliminate this problem, most rent-control laws include a *roll-back provision*. This specifies that rent levels existing at a prior date act as the base rent for the purposes of regulation. Preferably, this date will be set at a time just before rent control became a major public issue.

Q. Are there any arguments against rent control?

A. Yes, many such arguments exist. Most arguments concern the economic effects of rent control on the local tax base, the supply of rental housing, and the quality of that housing. Opponents of rent control argue that because rent control keeps rents down, it also keeps down the assessed value of rental property. Since cities tax property on its assessed value, the argument says that the city will collect less tax revenue under rent control than it normally would. The argument says that other property-taxpayers must make up this lost tax revenue. It points to homeowners as the logical source for lost tax revenue. Opponents also argue that regulation will reduce the supply and quality of rental housing.

WHERE TO GET MORE INFORMATION

The Department of Housing and Urban Development (HUD) is a nationwide resource. Nearly every major city has an office. It can answer questions about public and other types of housing. The office also can accept discrimination complaints.

The National Housing Institute provides general information and provides a referral service to local tenant organizations. The National Housing Institute may be contacted by calling (201) 678-3110 or by writing to 439 Main Street, Orange, New Jersey 07050.

Many states have a state department of housing, which also should be a good resource. Cities generally have housing offices, too. In some cities, the housing department has an office dealing with rental units. Housing departments can provide copies of the city building codes. They also can answer questions and respond to complaints. Check the government listings in your local telephone directory.

In addition, some states and many cities have organized tenant groups. The names of these groups usually begin with "Tenant" or the name of the city or state. Thus you can find them easily in the white pages of your local phone book. These groups can answer your questions and refer you to legal help. They often can provide you with pamphlets and newsletters about local housing issues.

Landlords can get information from a local organization of real-estate brokers. In several areas around the country, landlord organizations provide services and information to other landlords.

Bar associations are also a source of information. Many publish pamphlets on the rights and duties of landlords and tenants. Some also offer recorded telephone information on such topics as leases and evictions. Some have lawyer hot lines to answer questions.

Many states and cities have groups that fight housing discrimination. Check the yellow pages of the telephone directory under "Housing," or the white pages under "Fair Housing."

The IRS (Internal Revenue Service) publishes free pamphlets dealing with common tax questions of landlords. These include *Residential Rental Property (Including Rental of Vacation Houses)* (Publication 527), *Passive Activity and At-Risk Rules* (Publication 925), *General Business Credit* (Publication 572), and *Depreciation* (Publication 534).

CONSUMER CREDIT

INTRODUCTION

The use of credit is a way of life in the United States. It is almost as American as apple pie. At any one time, about three fifths of American families have installment debts outstanding. They owe money for cars, appliances, clothing, and other purchases. For these families, payments on their installment debts absorb about ten percent of the family income.

Many families have mortgages, which are another form of debt. Another chapter in this publication covers mortgages. This chapter, however, deals with *consumer* credit—credit-card purchases, cars bought on installment, and so on.

The use of consumer credit has become a major part of our lives. For this reason, this chapter can be very important. It can help you better understand how to use credit. This chapter also can help you determine if you are reaching or have reached your credit-debt limit. In addition, it can tell you what to do if you have exceeded that limit.

This chapter also will help you better understand the federal rules, regulations, and laws about consumer installment credit. The federal government designed them to protect you, the consumer. In addition, this chapter will help you decide when you may need a lawyer to handle your credit problems. (If you are married, see the "Family Law" chapter for topics regarding credit and marriage. "The Rights of Older Americans" chapter also contains credit-related discussions.)

Credit: What Is It and What Does It Cost?

Q. What exactly is credit?

A. Credit allows you to buy and use goods and services *now,* and pay for them later. For example, credit lets you have a car or a washing machine before you have fully paid for them. You may pay for them while you use them. Of course, you could save to buy the car in the future. However, you may want or need the car now, not three years from now. Similarly, you may buy a pair of shoes or a dinner on your credit card now and pay for them later.

Q. What does credit cost?

A. To buy now and pay later, you usually must pay a finance charge. The reason for this is that you have the benefit of using another person's money to pay a supplier. The supplier may be the car dealer, appliance dealer, shoe store, or restaurant. Only you can decide whether it is worth the cost of the finance charge to have a car or other goods and services now, rather than later.

Q. I keep seeing references to the Truth in Lending Act. What is it?

A. The Truth in Lending Act (TILA) requires that all creditors provide information that will help you decide whether to buy on credit, and if so, which interest rate is the best for you. Creditors (or credit grantors) include banks, department stores, credit-card issuers, finance companies, and so on. For example, you may want to borrow $4,000 from your bank to buy a used car now. It may cost you the $4,000 plus a finance charge at an annual percentage rate (APR) of 11 percent for three years. Is a "now car" worth the finance charge? If the term of your loan is three years (36 months), your monthly payment may be $131. Can you afford that? If you decide that the car is worth it and you can afford it, you should shop around for the best terms. For example, do other credit grantors offer a lower annual percentage rate?

The key consumer information provided by the TILA is the *annual percentage rate* (APR). The APR is an annual rate that relates the total finance charge to (1) the amount of credit that you receive and (2) the length of time you have to repay it. Think of the APR as a price per pound, like 20 cents per pound for potatoes. You may buy five pounds for one dollar or ten pounds for two dollars. In either case the *rate* is 20 cents per pound. However, the total cost in dollars (finance charge) depends on the amount of potatoes you buy.

Q. How does the APR relate to a purchase of, for example, a car?

A. This discussion illustrates the use of the APR in shopping for *closed-end credit.* This is credit that has a fixed number and amount of monthly payments. Suppose that you're buying a $5,000 used car. You might put $1,000 down and plan to borrow $4,000. How could you use the credit terms disclosed to select the best credit contract? Before you sign a loan, the credit grantor must show you several points to consider. These include the amount to be financed ($4,000), length of time to repay the loan, monthly payment, total finance charge, and the APR.

Compare these four possible credit arrangements*:

	APR	Length of Loan	Monthly Payment	Total Finance Charge
Creditor A	11%	3 years	$131	$714
Creditor B	11%	4 years	$103	$962
Creditor C	12%	4 years	$105	$1,056
Creditor D	12%	2 years	$188	$512

*Please note that these figures are correct even though the arithmetic sometimes appears to work out slightly different. Creditors often round off monthly payments to the nearest dollar, and adjust the final payment to make up the difference.

Notice that the four-year loan of Creditor B is a better deal than the four-year loan of Creditor C. If their lengths are equal, an 11-percent loan is better than a 12-percent loan for the same amount of money.

However, look what happens when the lengths of the loans vary: The total finance charge of an 11-percent loan from Creditors A and B is greater than that of a 12-percent loan from Creditor D. On the other hand, Creditors A and B offer a longer period of credit service and lower monthly payments.

CAREFULLY EVALUATE YOUR OPTIONS

The examples on these pages illustrate the importance of checking all financing options—and determining your final payment—before making a decision. The loan or credit arrangement that appears at first to be most reasonable is not always the best deal.

Fortunately, the law allows you to access the information you need to comparison shop. However, your own circumstances and needs will determine which loan or credit arrangement is best for you.

Q. Does this mean that I should look only at the APRs when shopping for credit?

A. No, when buying on credit, you will not be shopping wisely if you merely compare APRs. For example, your car dealer may be pushing "incentive financing" by offering a 4.9-percent rate. Your credit union may be charging 12 percent on new car loans. Then you need to find how much the dealer would charge for the car if you paid cash. Now you are ready to see which arrangement would yield the lowest monthly payment. You can do this if you do not change the down payment and the length of the loan from the dealer or credit union. In essence, you make all the terms of the two credit arrangements the same, except the monthly payment. Then take the deal that gives you the lowest monthly payment to buy the car.

For example, a major car maker recently offered a choice of a $1,500 cash rebate or 5.8-percent financing for four years on certain models. Assume that the car you would like to buy costs $16,000. If you have $2,000 for a down payment, you have the following choices:

(1) Finance through the dealer. A $2,000 down payment, if required, would leave $14,000 to be financed over four years at 5.8 percent. Monthly payments would be $327.51.

(2) Finance through a bank, credit union, or another credit grantor. With the $1,500 cash rebate and your $2,000, you have $3,500 to apply to the purchase price of $16,000. This leaves $12,500 to borrow ($16,000 −$3,500 = $12,500). If you borrow $12,500 for four years at 11.17 percent, you will find that your monthly payments are $324.10.

Q. Are there any other points to consider when using installment credit?

A. Yes, consider whether the interest you pay is deductible when calculating your federal income taxes. Almost all homeowners may still deduct their entire mortgage interest for tax purposes. However, the interest that you pay on credit-card debt, student loans, auto loans, and other debts is no longer entirely deductible. During 1988, only 40 percent was deductible, and the deductible portion declined to 20 percent in 1989. In addition, it falls to ten percent in 1990. In 1991, the new tax laws totally eliminate it. When you use your home to secure a line of credit on a credit card, the interest may be deductible.

The new tax laws have eliminated or limited previously deductible items, such as sales taxes. Therefore, most consumers will find that even the allowable interest and other deductions are unlikely to be as high as the standard deduction. Hence, interest on consumer installment credit (not including mortgage interest) usually will not help you cut your tax bill.

CHOOSING A CREDIT CARD

Q. What is revolving credit?

A. *Revolving credit* includes credit cards and overdraft checking accounts that allow you to write checks for more than your bank account's actual cash balance. Revolving credit is becoming increasingly popular in this country, as more people have credit cards than ever before. American Express Optima, Discover, Visa, and MasterCard are but a few of the many credit cards available. American Express and Diners Club cards offer neither revolving credit nor *installment* or *closed-end credit* (which has a fixed number and amount of monthly payments), since they usually require payment in full within 30 days. Rather, these cards offer open-end credit.

Q. How may I choose a credit card that is right for me?

A. The law helps you make comparisons between credit-card options. It requires credit grantors to tell you how they figure the finance charge you pay. The law also forces credit grantors to tell you the APR. You can always determine the finance charge by applying the APR to the amount you owe (your *balance*). However, credit grantors use many different methods to compute that balance. This means that credit grantors who apply an identical APR may charge you very different finance charges. It depends on how you use the account and how they calculate the balance.

How Credit Operates

TYPE OF CREDIT	BASIC OPERATION
Open-end credit	Balances owed on such cards usually require payment in full within 30 days. Such arrangements are not considered installment credit. Travel and entertainment cards, such as American Express and Diners Club, operate this way, as do most charge accounts with local businesses.
Installment Credit	Consumer agrees to repay a fixed amount in equal installments over a definite period of time. Automobile loans are usually of this type, as are personal loans.
Revolving Credit	In this more flexible method, the consumer has options of paying off the entire outstanding balance, only a specified minimum, or something in between. Bank credit cards, and those issued by major retail establishments and gasoline companies, usually work this way.

Source: Based on data from the Federal Trade Commission.

Ways of Figuring the Balance

Q. How do credit grantors figure an account's balance?

A. Some card issuers apply the APR to the *average daily balance* in your account over the billing period. This period is usually about 30 days. Other credit grantors compute the balance by subtracting payments made or credits given during the billing period from the total amount you owe. They refer to this as the *adjusted balance method.* Other credit grantors do not subtract from the balance any payments made during the billing period. This *previous balance method* can cost you more than the other two methods. For example:

	Average Daily Balance	Adjusted Balance	Previous Balance
Monthly Interest Rate	1.5%	1.5%	1.5%
Previous Balance	$500	$500	$500
Payment (on 15th day)	$400	$400	$400
Finance Charge	$4.50 (average balance of $300 x 1.5%)	$1.50 ($100 x 1.5%)	$7.50 ($500 x 1.5%)

As you can see from these examples, finance charges may vary greatly depending on how the credit grantor calculates them. In the first example, the average daily balance of $300 determines the amount of interest owed. The average daily balance is the average of the $500 owed for half a month and the $100 ($500 minus $400) owed for the other half. You owe the $500 and the $100 each for half a month because you paid the $400 during the middle of the month. In the adjusted balance method, you owe a finance charge only on the amount owed at the *end* of the period. Since you paid $400, and thus only owe $100, you pay a finance charge only on the $100. In the previous balance method, you owe a finance charge on the amount owed at the *beginning* of the pay period—the entire $500.

Q. Are there any other points that may affect how much finance charge I must pay?

A. Yes, the TILA requires revolving credit grantors to disclose whether you have a *free period.* They may call this a *free-ride*

CHOOSING A CREDIT CARD

Several complicated factors come into play in determining the credit card that is best for you. Many people believe that the annual percentage rate (APR) is the most important factor. Others think that a combination of the APR and the grace period (the time between the end of the billing cycle and the date you must pay the entire bill to avoid a finance charge) determines which credit card costs the least.

However, if you regularly pay the entire balance due, then you should look at other aspects of the revolving credit arrangement. Various fees, for example, can determine which card will end up costing you the least. Some cards offer extremely low APRs while charging very high annual fees. Others assess costly fees for late payments, cash advances, and extra cards for your spouse or children. In the end, the deciding factor will be the manner in which you use your credit card and how you pay the balance due.

period or *grace period*. If you do have one, they must state how long it is. The free period is the time between the end of the billing cycle and the date you must pay the entire bill to avoid a finance charge. It is usually between 20 and 25 days.

Some financial institutions do not provide a free period. They levy a finance charge from the dates that they post your purchases, or loans, to your account. They refer to this method of assessing finance charges as the *true average daily balance method*. Bank cardholders who take out cash advances almost always pay interest by this method. They very often pay a cash advance fee as well.

The credit grantor may change the free period under another method of assessing monthly charges: the *retroactive balance method*. Under this system, you will avoid a finance charge by paying your *entire* bill within the free period. However, if you do not pay your entire bill, your next monthly bill will include a finance charge. This charge will be on the portion of purchases that you did not pay for in full. The credit grantor will calculate this portion from the date it posted those purchases to your bill.

For example, assume that you bought a $500 item that the credit grantor posted to your account on March 15. Say that the credit grantor bills you on April 1, and you must pay in full by April 20 to avoid a finance charge. Assume further that you make a payment of only $200, which the credit grantor credits to your account on April 18. Then your next bill (say May 1) will include a finance charge composed of two parts. One portion of the finance charge will be for the use of $500 for the period from March 15 to April 18. The other charge will be for the $300 balance remaining to the closing date for the May bill. Suppose you do not pay your entire account within the free period in May. If so, additional purchases on the May 1 bill will gather finance charges from the date of purchase.

Other Charges

Q. Should I expect to pay a charge each year for the right to use a credit card?

A. Yes, credit cards issued by financial institutions often have an *annual fee*. It may be $15 to $25, and perhaps $35 to $60 for "premium cards" that provide a higher line of credit. If you usually pay your credit card accounts in full each month, you do not expect to pay a finance charge. Then you should shop for a credit card with no annual fee or one that is low. However, if you often don't pay the balance in full each month, then a low APR and a long free period may be better than a low annual fee.

Q. If I do not pay the minimum payment when it is due on my credit card, will I have to pay a late fee?

A. Yes, most credit-card issuers charge a *late payment fee*. It may be, say, five percent of the amount past due. However, it usually is not less than one dollar or more than ten dollars per month.

Q. What happens if I go over the limit on my credit card?

A. The credit-card issuer may charge an *over-the-line fee*. Some financial institutions charge a fee of perhaps $10 or $15 each time you exceed your credit limit. That is the maximum amount that the institution is willing to let you borrow.

Q. Does the APR on a credit card always stay the same?

A. Not if there are *variable-rate provisions*. Some credit-card issuers set APRs that vary with some interest-rate index. It may be the published market rates on three-year U.S. Treasury bills (T-bills). These issuers must show you the index and the *spread*. The latter is the percentage points added to the index to determine the rate you will pay. These issuers also must show how often they will adjust the rate.

A mortgage on the cardholder's home may secure some variable-rate credit cards provided by financial institutions. They refer to these credit-card accounts as *home equity lines of credit* (HELC). Under a new federal law, credit grantors must limit the maximum lifetime interest rate increases on these accounts. Most credit grantors today set the lifetime cap at five or six percentage points above their current starting rate. Thus, if the starting rate is 12 percent, the lifetime cap would be 18 percent. Other credit grantors set the lifetime cap at a specific figure. For example, a large bank in New York may offer an interest rate that is only 1.4 percentage points above the bank's prime lending rate. The bank may set a lifetime cap of 25 percent, which is the New York limit.

PROTECTIONS FOR THE CONSUMER

Q. How does the Truth in Lending Act affect me?

A. The federal Truth in Lending Act (TILA) helps you choose credit wisely. It requires credit grantors to give you plenty of information before you make a choice. However, the law alone cannot protect you fully. You have to cooperate by being an informed consumer.

The TILA does not set interest rates. It also does not tell you what rates are fair or unfair. Though 35 states set some upper limits on interest rates, these rates may vary widely below this limit. That still leaves 15 states in which interest rates may legally rise to 50 percent or more.

Although the TILA applies to all grantors of consumer installment credit, it requires them to state only the rate of interest—the APR—clearly. So long as this occurs, the credit grantor has obeyed that law. It does not matter if the rate is sky-high and far higher than rates you could obtain from others. So truth in lending is only a start. It makes sure that you have access to crucial information. However, you must look for it—read the credit agreement! Also compare it with rates and terms from other credit grantors.

Unsolicited Cards

It is illegal for card issuers to send you a credit card unless you ask for or agree to receive one. However, a card issuer may send, without your request, a new card to replace an expiring one. If you do receive an unsolicited card, cut it up and return it to the card issuer.

Limits on Finance Rates

Q. How can I limit the amount of finance charges that I pay for credit?

A. The shopping around you do for credit plays a key role in limiting and minimizing finance charges you must pay. It does not matter whether you are looking for closed-end credit (installment loans), revolving credit, or open-end credit. That is true even though most states impose rate ceilings on various credit grantors or types of credit. For example, state law often limits the rates that finance companies may charge. Some states also restrict the rates that retailers may charge citizens who hold their credit cards.

Q. If this is true, why does one of my credit-card companies charge a higher rate than that allowed by my state law?

A. These limits do not always apply across the board. For example, national banks may "export" their finance rates on credit cards. Thus, a national bank may issue cards from an office in South Dakota. This state has no interest rate ceiling on bank cards. So the bank may charge cardholders in Iowa any rate it chooses. Yet retailers selling to Iowa consumers may not charge interest rates on their credit cards higher than Iowa law permits. In real life, competition forces national banks to keep their rates in line with those charged by state-chartered banks, other financial institutions, and

(continued)

PROTECT YOUR CREDIT CARDS

(1) In a safe place, keep a list of your credit-card numbers, expiration dates, and the phone number of each card issuer.

(2) Credit-card issuers offer a wide variety of terms (annual percentage rate, methods of calculating the balance subject to the finance charge, minimum monthly payments, and actual membership fees). When selecting a card, compare the terms offered by several card issuers to find the card that best suits your needs.

(3) When you use your credit card, keep an eye on your card after you give it to a clerk. Take your card back promptly after the clerk is finished with it, and make sure it is yours.

(4) Tear up the carbons when you take your credit-card receipt.

(5) Never sign a blank credit-card receipt. Draw a line through any blank spaces above the total when you sign receipts.

(6) Open credit-card bills promptly, and compare them with your receipts to check for unauthorized charges and billing errors.

(7) Write the card issuer promptly to report any questionable charges. Written inquiries should not be included with your payment. Instead, check the billing statement for the correct address for billing questions. The inquiry must be in writing, and it must be sent within 60 days to guarantee your rights under the Fair Credit Billing Act.

(8) Never give your credit-card number over the telephone unless you made the call. Never put your credit-card number on a postcard or on the outside of an envelope.

(9) Sign new credit cards as soon as they arrive. Cut up and throw away expired credit cards. Cut up and return unwanted credit cards to the issuer.

(10) If any of your credit cards are missing or stolen, report the loss as soon as possible to the card issuer. Check your credit-card statement for a telephone number for reporting stolen credit cards. Follow up your phone calls with a letter to each card issuer. The letter should contain your credit-card number, the date the card was missing, and the date you called in the loss.

(11) If you report the loss before a credit card is used, the issuer cannot hold you responsible for any subsequent unauthorized charges. If a thief uses your card before you report it missing, the most you will owe for unauthorized charges on each card is $50.

Source: Federal Trade Commission.

retailers. In this example the pressures of the marketplace—the choices made by informed consumers—set the rates. The law does not set them.

There is something you may do if you believe a credit grantor has charged you a finance rate that exceeds your state's rate ceiling. You should contact the office of your state's attorney general.

Reporting TILA Violations

Q. What if a credit grantor fails to obey the TILA?

A. You should inform the proper federal enforcement agency, as listed in the back of this chapter. Report a creditor that fails to disclose information required under the Truth in Lending Act. The same applies if the creditor gives you inaccurate information or does not follow the rules about credit cards. You also may bring a lawsuit for actual damages (any money loss you suffer). In addition, you may sue for twice the finance charge. The least a court may award you is $100, and the most is $1,000. If you win the lawsuit, the law also entitles you to court costs and attorneys' fees.

Truth in lending originally applied to goods that someone sold. It did not apply to products that somebody leased. To broaden consumer protection, there is now a Consumer Leasing Act. It applies to any lease of consumer goods for more than four months. This law requires the lessor (the owner of the property) to disclose the amount of each payment and the total amount you will pay. The lessor also must state whether there is a large payment (balloon payment) due at the end of the lease. You have the same rights to sue for violations of this act as under the TILA. You should report offenses to the proper federal agency.

HOW TO APPLY FOR CREDIT

Equal Credit Opportunity Act

Q. When I apply for credit, are there factors that credit grantors must consider in a fair manner?

A. Yes, and it does not matter what credit standards credit grantors use. The law requires them to apply the standards fairly and without bias.

The *Equal Credit Opportunity Act* (ECOA) says that credit grantors may not use certain factors to discriminate against you in a credit deal. A credit grantor may not use age, race, color, national origin, sex, marital status, religion, or receipt of public aid to:

- Discourage or prevent you from applying for a loan;
- Refuse you a loan if you otherwise qualify;
- Lend you money on terms different from those granted someone with similar risk (as determined by such factors as income, expenses, credit history, and collateral); or
- Give you less money than you asked for, if someone with similar risk would have received more.

The Equal Credit Opportunity Act does not, however, guarantee that you will receive credit. You still must meet the credit grantor's standards of whether you are worthy of receiving credit.

Determining Creditworthiness

Credit grantors may use some or all of the following factors to decide whether to extend credit. However, if your credit history is bad, they usually will not give you credit or else charge you a high interest rate for the risk they will accept.

Factor	Explanation
Ability to repay	This depends on your current job or income source, and how much you earn. In addition, the length of time you have worked or will receive that income is important. Credit grantors also look at your expenses: rent or mortgage payments, credit payments, or average yearly family-related costs. The latter may consist of food, clothing, and school tuition.
Credit history	This shows how much money you owe and how often you borrow. A very important consideration is whether you pay bills on time and whether you have filed for bankruptcy or had judgments issued against you.
Stability	How long you have lived at your current or former address suggests your stability. The length of time that you have worked is also important. In addition, credit grantors consider whether you own your home or rent.
Assets	Assets such as a car, home, and so on may be useful as collateral for a loan. Credit grantors also look at what you may use, other than income, to repay the debt. This may include savings or investments.

Age Discrimination

Q. When I apply for credit, may a credit grantor ask my age?

A. Yes, but if you are old enough to sign and be liable for a contract (usually 18 to 21, depending on state law), a credit grantor may not:

- Refuse to give you credit or decrease the amount of credit just because of your age;
- Refuse to consider your retirement income in rating your credit application;
- Cancel your credit account or require you to reapply for credit just because you are a certain age or have retired;
- Refuse you credit or cancel your account because you cannot get credit life (or related) insurance due to your age.

The law does allow a credit grantor to consider certain age-related facts. These include how long your income will continue or how long it will be until you reach retirement age. Consider, for example, a loan that will take a long time to pay back. If an older applicant does not provide adequate security, he or she may not be a good credit risk.

Public Assistance

Q. May a credit grantor deny credit if I receive public aid?

A. Not if you receive Social Security or public assistance payments such as Aid to Families with Dependent Children. Then a credit grantor may not deny you credit for that reason alone. However, credit grantors may ask the age of your dependents. You may lose federal benefits when they reach a certain age. A credit grantor also may consider whether you will continue to meet residency requirements for receiving benefits.

Discrimination Against Women

Q. Does my sex or marital status affect whether I am worthy of credit?

A. No, the law protects both men and women from discrimination based on sex and marital status. Much of the Equal Credit Opportunity Act responds to charges that past discrimination made it hard for women to get credit.

Information the Creditor Cannot Use

The Equal Credit Opportunity Act does not guarantee that you will get credit. You must still pass the creditor's tests of creditworthiness. But the creditor must apply these tests fairly, impartially, and without discriminating against you on any of the following grounds: age, sex, marital status, race, color, religion, national origin. The creditor also may not discriminate against you because you receive public income such as veterans benefits, welfare, or Social Security, or because you exercise your rights

(continued)

In general, a credit grantor may not deny you credit just because of your sex. A credit grantor also may not refuse credit just because you are married, single, widowed, divorced, or separated. Other points to consider include:

- A credit grantor usually may not ask your sex when you apply for credit. One exception would be a loan to buy or build a home. This information helps the federal government look for housing discrimination. It also compares how many females and males buy houses. You may refuse to answer this question;
- You normally do not have to use a gender title (Mr., Miss, Mrs., or Ms.) when applying for credit. Sometimes credit grantors may ask whether you are married, unmarried, or separated. However, it must relate to their right to obtain repayment;
- A credit grantor may not ask women if they use birth control or whether they plan to have children; and
- You do not have to reveal child support or alimony payments to a credit grantor. If, however, you choose to do so, a credit grantor must consider it as income.

Marital Status and Separate Credit Accounts

Q. May married people open credit accounts that are not also in their spouses' names?

A. Yes, spouses may open credit accounts or take out loans in their own names. They do not have to open joint accounts or take out loans with spouses. A credit grantor may not:

- Refuse to open a credit account just because of your sex or marital status;
- Require your spouse to cosign your account, unless you live in a community property state where spouses are liable for each other's debts; or
- Ask about your spouse or ex-spouse when you apply for credit based on your own income. This does not apply when your income includes alimony, child support, or maintenance payments from your ex-spouse.

Change in Marital Status

Q. If my marital status changes, may a credit grantor force me to reapply for credit?

A. No, a credit grantor may not require you to reapply for credit just because you marry or divorce, or your spouse has died.

(continued)

under Federal credit laws, such as filing a billing error notice with a creditor. This means that a creditor may not use any of those grounds as a reason to:

- **Discourage you from applying for credit;**
- **Refuse you a loan if you qualify; or**
- **Lend you money on terms different from those granted to another person with similar income, expenses, credit history, and collateral.**

A credit grantor also may not close your account or change its terms for these reasons alone. There must be a change in how worthy of credit you are, such as a decrease in your income. For example, if your spouse dies or you get a divorce a credit grantor may have you reapply if you had used your spouse's income to get credit. The credit grantor must allow you to use the account while considering your new application

Denial of a Credit Application

Q. What happens if a credit grantor denies credit to me?

A. Under the Equal Credit Opportunity Act, a credit grantor must notify you whether it has approved or denied your credit application. The credit grantor must do this within 30 days after you apply for credit. If the credit grantor denies credit to you, the notice must be written. It also must list the reasons for denying credit or tell you how to request an explanation. The Fair Credit Reporting Act affects credit denials, as well. It requires the notice to tell you if the credit grantor used a credit report to deny you credit. If so, the credit grantor must supply the name and address of the credit bureau that provided the report. These rights also apply if a credit grantor closes an existing credit account or reduces an open line of credit.

Q. What may I do if a credit grantor will not say why it has denied credit to me?

A. First ask the credit grantor to supply a written explanation as required by law. If you think the credit grantor has discriminated against you, tell the credit grantor why you think this. Then try to resolve the issue through negotiation. If the credit grantor still refuses to extend credit to you and has not given a satisfactory explanation, you have two options. You may contact a lawyer or a federal enforcement agency (see the end of this chapter). These rights also apply if a credit grantor closes an existing credit account.

Q. Can I sue if a credit grantor has discriminated against me?

A. Under the Equal Credit Opportunity Act, you may sue for actual damages. These are the actual losses you suffered. You also may sue for punitive damages of up to $10,000 if the credit grantor should have known it was violating the law. Punitive damages penalize the credit grantor because it has violated the law.

꞉REDIT RECORDS

꞉low to Establish a Credit Record

꞉. How can I get credit if I never previously had it?

꞉. First-time borrowers soon realize that in order to get credit they must have a credit history. There are several ways to start building a good, solid credit history. For example, you may:

- Open a checking or savings account. When credit grantors see such accounts they can judge whether you have adequate money and know how to manage it;
- Apply for limited credit from a local department store. Many firms actively seek prospective customers with little or no credit history. Credit grantors look at these accounts to see if you pay your bills on time after you have used the accounts for a while;
- Deposit money in a bank, savings and loan association, or savings bank. Then borrow against it; or
- Have someone cosign the loan with you. That person must have a favorable credit record and will be liable for the debt if you cannot pay. This secures your first loan based on someone else's credit. After you pay back the loan, it will be easier to get credit on your own.

꞉. Should husbands or wives get credit in their own names?

꞉. Yes, they should do it while still married, especially if they do not earn wages. Many divorced or widowed spouses do not earn a living and do not have credit histories separate from their former spouses. In these cases, credit grantors must look at the credit history of any accounts held jointly with the former spouses or any account held only in the former spouse's name. This is true only if non-earning spouses can show it reflects how worthy they are of credit. The non-earning spouses may show this with checks, receipts, or other records. If their former spouses had poor credit records, non-earning spouses may show that the records do not reflect whether they deserve credit. Non-earning spouses may do this by producing previous explanatory letters sent to credit grantors, copies of contracts signed only by the spouse, receipts, or other evidence.

꞉. What is a credit bureau?

꞉. Many credit grantors use records kept by consumer credit reporting agencies when you apply for a loan or credit.

UNDERSTANDING YOUR CREDIT REPORT

Contrary to popular belief, a credit bureau neither tracks all aspects of your personal life nor evaluates credit applications. Credit bureaus are simply organizations that collect and transmit four principal types of information: identification and employment data; payment histories; credit-related inquiries; and public record information.

Credit bureaus also cooperate with each other, passing information to other bureaus when people move, for example. However, since they are for-profit businesses, credit bureaus also compete for subscribers (credit grantors) who judge credit bureaus on the completeness of their records and the quality of their service.

People also refer to these consumer credit reporting agencie as *credit bureaus*. Several credit bureaus may operate in your area. Each credit bureau may have nearly the same information about you as another bureau has. However, the compete against one another for the business of various credit grantors. Credit bureaus maintain computer files of financial payment histories, public record data, and persona identifying data. These bureaus provide reports to qualified firms that grant credit. This data also may play a role when you apply for insurance or employment.

Credit bureaus do not make credit decisions. They only provide data to credit grantors who use it to make credit decisions. The law permits credit bureaus to disclose data t any person or organization with a genuine business need for it. The need must concern a transaction involving the consumer.

How to Check Your Credit Record

Q. May I look at my credit record?

A. Yes, you have the right to know the content of credit files tha contain information on you. Many consumer credit experts suggest that you examine these credit files on a regular basis A periodic checkup will enable you to find out what the credi bureaus have in their files on you that they will report to those businesses looking for information about your credit record. The Fair Credit Reporting Act allows you to review your file at any time. The credit bureau is permitted to charg you a reasonable fee for providing this service. This usually costs less than $20.

As noted earlier, a credit grantor may turn you down because of a report from a credit bureau. If so, the law requires the credit grantor to give you the bureau's name an address. You are allowed to request facts about the data fron the credit bureau by phone, mail, or in person. Although federal law does not entitle you to an exact copy of your credi file, many credit bureaus will provide you with one. If you don't get a copy of your file, you will at least receive an oral summary of it.

The law also requires the credit bureau to tell you the names of the creditors who provided the data. In addition, the credit bureau must tell you who has received a report on you in the last six months. This time period is two years for employment reports. The credit bureau also must help you interpret the data. If a credit grantor has denied you credit within the past 30 days because of data supplied by a credit bureau, the bureau may not charge you for the information.

WHAT A CREDIT REPORT COVERS

Identification and employment date	Your name, birthdate, address, Social Security number, employer, and spouse's name are routinely noted. The bureau also may provide other information, such as your employment history, home ownership, income, and previous address, if a credit grantor requests it.
Payment history	Your account record with different credit grantors is listed, showing how much credit has been extended and how you have repaid it. Related events, such as referral of an overdue account to a collection agency, may be noted as well.
Inquiries	Credit bureaus are required to maintain a record of all credit grantors who have requested your credit history within the past six months. They normally include such credit grantor inquiries in your credit file for at least this long.
Public record information	Events that are a matter of public information record and are related to your creditworthiness, such as bankruptcies, foreclosures, or tax liens, may also appear in your report.

Source: Federal Trade Commission

Q. What may I do if I believe the credit bureau has incorrect information in my file?

A. If you find that information in the credit report is inaccurate, incomplete, or outdated, you may challenge the accuracy or completeness of any data. You may do this by notifying the credit bureau. Then the credit bureau must either verify its facts within a reasonable period of time or delete them from its files. This requirement does not apply if the bureau has reason to believe the dispute is petty or irrelevant. If you disagree with the credit bureau's decision, you may challenge it in court.

If the credit bureau finds that its information is incorrect, it must correct its file accordingly. Consumer credit reports are not permitted to include certain unfavorable data more than seven years old (suits, court judgments, and tax liens). Credit bureaus, however, are allowed to report bankruptcies for ten years.

If reinvestigation of disputed information by a credit bureau does not resolve the matter, you may file your version of the story in a brief statement. The credit bureau must include your statement, or a clear and accurate summary of it, in all future reports containing the disputed item. You also may ask the credit bureau to mail copies of your statement to anyone who received a report containing the disputed item during the last six months. This time period is two years for employment reports.

Q. What does the law allow me to do if the credit bureau will not cooperate?

A. Under the Fair Credit Reporting Act, you may bring a lawsuit against any credit bureau or credit grantor who violates any provisions of the Act. This includes any credit reporting agency that fails to observe the restrictions about who may access your credit file. It also applies to any credit bureau that does not properly reinvestigate and correct inaccurate data in your file that you have disputed. However, if the agency has followed reasonable procedures, it has obeyed the law. If you win the lawsuit, you deserve to receive actual damages. The law also entitles you to punitive damages if you prove the violation was intentional. If you are successful, you also will receive court costs and a reasonable amount for attorneys' fees. The law punishes unauthorized persons who lie to obtain a credit report, or credit bureau employees who knowingly and deliberately supply a credit report to unauthorized persons. These people may receive fines of up to $5,000 or prison terms for one year, or both, if they are proven guilty.

Q. What is the story behind companies that advertise their abilities to repair faulty credit histories? They sound too good to be true.

A. These "credit repair clinics" can help you review and update your credit record and report. However, their fees could be as high as $1,200. If your credit report has an error, you may correct it yourself at no or very little cost. Be very suspicious and careful if a credit repair clinic promises that it can remove accurate records of bankruptcy and bad debts from your credit record. In general, if a credit program sounds too good to be true, it probably is.

HOW TO CORRECT CREDIT MISTAKES

Billing Errors

Q. Why should I keep a sales receipt when I buy an item on credit?

A. One reason is so you may return the item. You may have accidentally purchased a defective or damaged item. Perhaps you bought a product that was the wrong size or color.

However, a more important reason to keep sales slips may be to avoid billing errors. Most companies provide a sales slip only at the time of purchase, not with the monthly statement. Under this billing procedure, the statement usually gives the date and amount of purchase. It also may identify the store and department from which you bought the item. Therefore, you should keep all sales slips. It will allow you to check them against the monthly billing statements.

Q. Will my credit rating suffer if my bill contains an obvious error?

A. No, the Fair Credit Billing Act requires credit grantors to correct errors promptly. In addition, they must do so without damaging your credit rating.

Q. What exactly is a billing error?

A. The law defines a billing error as a charge:

- For something you didn't buy, or for a purchase made by someone not authorized to use your account;
- That is not properly identified on your monthly statement, or that is for an amount different from the actual purchase price; or
- For something that you refused to accept on delivery or that the supplier did not deliver according to your agreement.

Billing errors also may include:

- Errors in arithmetic;
- Failure to reflect a payment that you made or other credit to your account;
- Failure to mail the billing statement to your current address (if the credit grantor received notice of that address at least 20 days before the end of the billing period); or
- An item for which you request further explanation.

A CARDHOLDER'S NIGHTMARE

After you have established credit, the best way to keep in good standing is to repay your debts on time. However, what happens if there is an error on your bill? What if you accidentally bought damaged or defective goods on credit? If you simply fail to pay for them, the creditor will then report it. This will hurt your credit rating. This section discusses what to do if this happens to you.

Q. What should I do if my bill seems wrong?

A. If you think your bill is incorrect, or if you simply want more details about it, take the following steps:

(1) Notify your credit grantor in writing so that it receives the notice within 60 days after it mailed the bill. You must send the letter to the address your credit grantor has supplied for this purpose. *A phone call will not preserve your rights* if your credit grantor has given you an address for such written notifications.

(2) The letter should contain your name, address, and account number. State that you believe your bill contains an error. Specify the error and why you believe it is wrong. Finally, include the date and the suspected amount of the error.

Q. What happens after I notify the credit grantor about the possible billing error?

A. The law requires the credit grantor to acknowledge your letter within 30 days. This does not apply if the credit grantor can fix the billing error in less time. The credit grantor must correct your account within two billing periods. It should never take longer than 90 days from the time the credit grantor receives notice of your dispute. If the credit grantor does not correct the error, it must tell you why it believes the bill is not wrong.

If the credit grantor does not find an error, it must promptly send you a statement showing what you owe. The credit grantor may include any finance charges that accumulated. Any minimum payments you missed while questioning the bill also may appear on the statement.

Q. Must I pay finance charges on the contested amount?

A. Not if your bill does contain an error. You also do not have to pay any minimum payments that apply to it.

Q. While I am trying to solve a billing problem, may a credit grantor threaten my credit rating?

A. Not because you fail to pay the disputed amount or related finance or other charges while you're trying to resolve a billing dispute. The law steps in if you have taken the steps described above by writing down your credit question and sending it to the credit grantor. It prohibits your credit grantor from telling other credit grantors or credit bureaus that you have failed to pay the disputed amount or related finance or other charges. Until the credit grantor answers your complaint, the law forbids it from taking any action to collect the amount in dispute.

Q. What happens after the credit grantor has explained my bill?

A. Then the credit grantor may take action to collect if you do not pay in the time allowed. The credit grantor also may report you to the credit bureau as overdue on the amount in question.

You may still disagree with the credit grantor in writing if this happens. If you do this, the credit grantor must report to the credit bureau that you have challenged the bill. The credit grantor also must give you written notice of the name and address of each person who has received information about your account.

When you settle the dispute, the credit grantor must promptly contact each person who has received information about your account. The credit grantor must do this to report the outcome.

Q. What happens if the credit grantor does not follow all the rules within the proper time limits?

A. The law does not permit the credit grantor to collect the first $50 of the amount in dispute. This is true even if it is money you truly owe.

Defective Goods or Services

Q. May the law help me if I bought a product on credit that is of poor quality?

A. Yes, if you use a store credit card to purchase shoddy or damaged goods or poor quality services, the Fair Credit Billing Act may help. It allows you to withhold payment for the disputed transaction at the time you first notify the merchant of your claim or defense. However, you may do this only if you have made a *real* attempt to solve the problem with the merchant.

If you bought the goods or services with a bank, travel, or entertainment card, you must still make a genuine attempt to solve the problem with the merchant. The same is true for any other card not issued by the store where you made your purchase. The law also limits your right to withhold the payment to purchases totaling over $50 that took place in your home state or within 100 miles of your home address.

If you refuse to pay because the goods or services were defective, the credit grantor might sue you for payment. Then the court will consider the defective nature of the goods or services. If the court finds the goods or services to be truly defective, it is a defense to that suit.

Lost or Stolen Credit Cards

Q. Am I liable for all the bills that may arise if I lose my credit card or someone steals it?

A. No, the Truth in Lending Act (TILA) limits your liability on lost or stolen credit cards. However, it is very important that you notify the credit-card company as soon as you notice the loss or theft of your card or cards. You do not have to pay any unauthorized charge made after you notify the company. The most you will have to pay, however, for any unauthorized charges is $50 on each card.

Under the Truth in Lending Act, a credit-card company also may not collect any loss from you—even the first $50—unless it can prove:

(1) That the company issued you the card at your request or as a renewal or substitute for an accepted card. If this was not the case, the credit-card company must prove that you used the card at least once before it left your possession;

(2) That the company provided some means on the card, such as a signature line, to identify you as the person authorized to use it;

(3) That the company notified you of your potential $50 liability; and

(4) That the company notified you that you may give oral or written notification of having lost the card or that someone stole it. The company also must prove that it described a way for you to notify the company.

Q. How may I prepare for the possibility of losing a credit card or having it stolen?

A. It is a good idea to keep a list of all your credit cards. The list should include the account number on each card and how to notify the credit-card issuers if this happens. Since you are most likely to lose credit cards when traveling, always take a copy of the list with you. Keep the list separate from your credit cards. Then, if you lose your cards or someone steals them, you will be able to notify your credit grantors immediately. This procedure may help minimize your financial losses.

DEBT COLLECTION AND THE LAW

Q. Who is a debt collector?

A. Under the law, a debt collector is someone, other than a credit grantor, who regularly collects debts for others. (There are a few minor exceptions to this definition.) Federal law does not cover creditors, although your state laws probably govern them. These laws usually are similar to the federal Fair Debt Collection Practices Act.

Q. How may a debt collector contact me?

A. A debt collector may contact you by mail, in person, or by telephone or telegram during convenient hours. Unless you agree, a collector may not contact you at inconvenient or unusual times or places. Examples of poorly chosen times are before 8:00 A.M. or after 9:00 P.M. Also, a debt collector is not permitted to contact you at work if your employer disapproves.

Q. How can I stop a debt collector from contacting me?

A. You may notify a debt collector by mail not to contact you. After that, the debt collector may no longer try to contact you. There are only two exceptions to this. The debt collector may tell you that there will be no more contact. The collector also may say that some specific legal or other action may be taken. However, debt collectors may state this only if they actually plan to take such action.

Debt collectors also must stop trying to contact you if you notify them, by mail within 30 days after they first contact you, that you dispute all or part of the debt. However, debt collectors are permitted to begin collection activities again if they send you proof of the debt. Such proof may be a copy of the bill.

Q. What does the law require the debt collector to tell me about my debt?

A. Within five days of your first contact, a debt collector must send you a written notice stating:

- The amount of money you owe;
- The name of the credit grantor to whom you owe the money;
- That the collector will assume the debt is genuine unless you challenge it within 30 days; and
- What to do if you believe you do not owe the money.

Do Not Fear the Collector

If, for some reason, you cannot pay your debts, a debt collector or collection agency may approach you. The Fair Debt Collection Practices Act prohibits abusive, deceptive, and unfair practices by debt collectors. The main goal of this federal law is to see that debt collectors treat people fairly. This section discusses this topic in greater detail.

Q. Whom may a collector contact about my debt?

A. A debt collector may contact any person to locate you. However, in doing so, the collector usually may not talk to anyone more than once or refer to the debt when talking to that person. If debt collectors use the mail to contact you or another person, they may not send letters in envelopes identifying themselves as bill collectors. They also may not send a postcard. Once collectors know that you have hired a lawyer, they may communicate only with your lawyer.

Q. What types of debt collection practices does the law prohibit?

A. A debt collector may not harass, oppress, or abuse any person. For example, a debt collector may not:
- Use threats of violence to harm you, your property, or reputation;
- Use obscene or profane language;
- Repeatedly use the telephone to annoy you; or
- Make you accept collect calls or pay for telegrams.

A debt collector may not use false statements when trying to collect a debt. For example, a debt collector may not:
- Misrepresent the amount of the debt;
- Falsely imply that the debt collector is a lawyer;
- Tell you that you will be arrested or imprisoned if you do not pay the debt (unless this is legally possible, and the debt collector or the credit grantor fully intends to do so); or
- Tell you that your property or wages will be seized, garnished, attached, or sold, unless the debt collector or the credit grantor intends to do so and it is legal.

Q. What may I do if the debt collector breaks the law?

A. If debt collectors violate the Fair Debt Collection Practices Act, you may sue them in a state or federal court. However, you may do so only within one year from the date they violated the law. You may recover money for the actual damage you suffered. In addition, the court may award up to $1,000 for an individual suit and up to $500,000 in a class action suit. (The latter is a suit brought by a group of people who claim that the illegal debt collection practice injured them. In other words, it injured them as a class.) You also may recover court costs and attorneys' fees. However, consumers found acting in bad faith against a debt collector may have to pay for court costs.

You also should contact and file a complaint with the proper federal government enforcement agency. (See the "Where to Get More Information" section at the end of this chapter for more details.) Many states also have debt collection laws of their own. Check with your state attorney general's office to determine your rights under state law.

CREDIT COUNSELING

Q. Are all financial counseling services the same?

A. No, there are nonprofit and for-profit financial counseling centers. Nonprofit centers get most of their fees from credit grantors. Hence, the costs to you may be lower than those of for-profit centers, which must cover all their costs from charges to consumers who use the centers' services. However, some believe that nonprofit centers may favor arrangements that benefit creditors the most. While many for-profit financial counseling centers provide worthwhile services, some may exaggerate the benefits that they promise.

Q. What kinds of services can I get from a nonprofit credit counseling center?

A. These Consumer Credit Counseling Services (CCCS) provide two types of services. First, they can help you set up a realistic budget so that you can manage your debts better. Second, if you still have trouble paying your debts on time, the center will contact your creditors and arrange a repayment plan based on your budget. You will make a single payment each month to the CCCS, which will then distribute the payment among your creditors until it pays all your debts in full. There may be a small monthly service fee. Most creditors prefer this type of plan (since they eventually will get most of their money) rather than "straight" bankruptcy.

Under a repayment plan through a CCCS, you may still pay interest charges on your debts. However, many creditors will waive (not require payment of) interest charges and delinquency fees after you have agreed to repay your debts through a CCCS.

Q. How can I find a CCCS?

A. There are about 500 CCCS offices located in 48 states. To find one near you, check your local telephone directory. If you want, you can call toll-free 800-388-2227, or write and send a self-addressed, stamped envelope to:

National Foundation for Consumer Credit, Inc.
8701 Georgia Avenue
Silver Spring, Maryland 20910

WHERE TO GET MORE INFORMATION

If you believe a credit grantor has violated one of the laws discussed in this chapter, you may complain to the agency charged with enforcing that law. You can determine the responsible agency by the type of credit grantor involved in the apparent violation. The first part of this resource section lists the major federal laws and the agencies responsible for enforcing those laws. First, determine the federal act that applies to your complaint. Second, figure out the type of credit grantor against whom you have a complaint. Then look up the address of the agency so you can write to make your complaint. If you need more help, call your local consumer protection office. For its telephone number, look in your local telephone directory under the listings for your local or state government.

The second part of this resource section lists various low-cost federal publications that will help you obtain and use credit more effectively.

WHERE TO GET CREDIT COUNSELING

You can get credit counseling from several sources. These include credit unions, lawyers, university extension agencies, and military bases. Specialized financial counseling services are also available.

Federal Laws on Credit and Debt Collection

The *Truth in Lending Act* requires all credit grantors to provide you with the annual percentage rate (APR) of the loan. Typical credit grantors are banks, department stores, credit-card issuers, finance companies, and so on.

The *Fair Credit Reporting Act* sets up a procedure for correcting mistakes on your credit record. The Act also requires that the record be kept confidential.

The *Equal Credit Opportunity Act* prohibits discrimination against a credit applicant because of age, sex, marital status, race, color, religion, national origin, or receipt of public aid.

The *Fair Credit Billing Act* sets up a procedure for promptly correcting errors on a credit account. It also prevents damage to your credit rating while you are settling a dispute.

The *Consumer Leasing Act* requires disclosure of information that helps you compare the cost and terms of one lease with another. It also orders firms that offer leases to reveal facts that help you compare the cost and terms of leasing with those for buying on credit or with cash.

The *Fair Debt Collection Practices Act* applies to people and firms that regularly collect debts for others. It prohibits them from performing abusive collection practices. This act also allows consumers to dispute a debt and to halt unreasonable collection activities.

Where to File Your Complaint

You should file complaints about consumer credit reporting agencies or debt collection practices with the Federal Trade Commission (FTC). The same goes for complaints about credit issued by retail stores, department stores, and small loan and finance companies. This is also true for credit-related complaints about oil companies, public utility companies, state credit unions, or travel and expense credit-card companies. Mail your complaints to:

Federal Trade Commission
Bureau of Consumer Protection
6th Street and Pennsylvania Avenue, N.W.
Washington, D.C. 20580

Instead of contacting the FTC's national headquarters at the address shown above, you can send your complaint to one of the FTC Regional Offices listed below:

Atlanta
Suite 1000
1718 Peachtree Street, N.W.
Atlanta, Georgia 30367
(404) 347-4836

Boston
Suite 1184
10 Causeway Street
Boston, Massachusetts 02222
(617) 565-7240

Chicago
Suite 1437
55 East Monroe Street
Chicago, Illinois 60603
(312) 353-4423

Cleveland
668 Euclid Avenue
Cleveland, Ohio 44114
(216) 522-4210

Dallas
Suite 500
100 North Central Expressway
Dallas, Texas 75201
(214) 767-5501

Denver
Suite 2900
1405 Curtis Street
Denver, Colorado 80202
(303) 844-2271

Los Angeles
Suite 13209
11000 Wilshire Boulevard
Los Angeles, California 90024
(213) 209-7890

New York
13th Floor
150 William Street
New York, New York 10038
(212) 264-1207

San Francisco
Suite 570
901 Market Street
San Francisco, California 94103
(415) 744-7920

Seattle
Suite 2806
915 Second Avenue
Seattle, Washington 98174
(206) 442-4655

CONSUMER CREDIT

If your complaint concerns a financial institution, as a general rule you may get a satisfactory response by first contacting an officer of the credit grantor against whom you have the complaint. To compete effectively, most credit grantors wish to keep good customers by settling complaints fairly and quickly. However, if that approach does not work, you can turn to various government agencies.

If a financial institution has violated a banking law or regulation, the regulatory agency that oversees that category of institutions might be able to help you. The following information will help you decide which agency to contact.

- National bank. If the word "National" appears in the bank's name, or the initials N.A. appear after its name, write to:
  Comptroller of the Currency
  Consumers Affairs Division
  490 L'Enfant Plaza East, S.W.
  Washington, D.C. 20219
- State-chartered bank that is a member of the Federal Reserve System, FDIC insured. The bank will noticeably display two signs on the door of the bank or in the lobby. One will say "Member, Federal Reserve System." The other will state "Deposits Insured by the Federal Deposit Insurance Corporation." For violations of federal laws, write to:
  Federal Reserve System
  Division of Consumer and Community Affairs
  20th and Constitution Avenue, N.W.
  Washington, D.C. 20551

Or you can write the Federal Reserve Bank serving the area in which the state member bank has its office.

Atlanta
104 Marietta Street, N.W.
Atlanta, Georgia 30303
(404) 521-8788

Boston
600 Atlantic Avenue
Boston, Massachusetts 02106
(617) 973-3000

Chicago
P.O. Box 834
Chicago, Illinois 60690
(312) 322-5322

Cleveland
1455 East Sixth Street
P.O. Box 6387
Cleveland, Ohio 44101
(216) 579-2000

Dallas
400 South Akard Street
Station K
Dallas, Texas 75222
(214) 651-6111

Kansas City
925 Grand Avenue
Federal Reserve Station
Kansas City, Missouri 64198
(816) 881-2000

Minneapolis
250 Marquette Avenue
Minneapolis, Minnesota 55480
(612) 340-2345

New York
33 Liberty Street
New York, New York 10045
(212) 720-5914

Philadelphia
10 Independence Mall
Philadelphia, Pennsylvania 19105
(215) 574-6116

Richmond
P.O. Box 27622
Richmond, Virginia 23261
(804) 697-8000

San Francisco
101 Market Street
San Francisco, California 94105
(415) 974-2000

St. Louis
P.O. Box 442
St. Louis, Missouri 63166
(314) 444-8444

For violations of state laws, write to your state banking department. For the address and telephone number, consult the state government listings in your local telephone directory.

- State-chartered bank, insured by the Federal Deposit Insurance Corporation (FDIC), but not a member of the Federal Reserve System. The bank will display a very noticeable sign that says "Deposits Insured by Federal Deposit Insurance Corporation." However, there will not be a sign saying "Member, Federal Reserve System." Write to:
  Federal Deposit Insurance Corporation
  Office of Bank Customer Affairs
  550 17th St. N.W.
  Washington, D.C. 20429
- Federally chartered or federally insured savings and loan association. The word "Federal" usually appears in the name of the savings and loan association. Another possibility is that its name includes initials such as "FA." These show its status as a federal savings and loan association. It will prominently display a sign on the door or in the lobby that says "Deposits Insured by FSLIC." Write to:
  Federal Home Loan Bank Board
  1700 G Street, N.W.
  Washington, D.C. 20552
- Federal savings bank. The word "Federal" normally appears in the name of the savings bank. Its name also may include initials such as "FSB." These show its status as a federal savings bank. The bank will display a highly noticeable sign on the door or in the lobby that says "Deposits Insured by FSLIC" or "Deposits Insured by FDIC." Write to:
  Federal Home Loan Bank Board
  Office of Community Investment
  1700 G Street, N.W.
  Washington, D.C. 20552
- State-chartered FSLIC insured savings institution. It will prominently display a sign on the door or in the lobby that says "Deposits Insured by FSLIC." The word "Federal" does not appear in the name, nor do any initials such as "FA" or "FSB." Write to:
  Federal Home Loan Bank Board
  Office of Thrift Supervision
  1700 G Street, N.W.
  Washington, D.C. 20552

- State-chartered banks or savings institutions without Federal Deposit Insurance. This type of institution has none of the above described characteristics. For violations of federal laws write to the Federal Trade Commission (see above). For violations of state laws, write to your state banking department
- Federally chartered credit union. The term "Federal credit union" appears in the name of the credit union. Write to:
  National Credit Union Administration
  1776 G Street, Suite 800, N.W.
  Washington, D.C. 20006
- State-chartered, federally insured credit union. It will display a sign by stations or windows where it accepts deposits, indicating that the NCUA (National Credit Union Administration) insures the deposits. The term "Federal Credit Union" does not appear in the name. Write to your state agency that regulates credit unions or to the Federal Trade Commission (see the "Where to File Your Complaint" section).
- Other institutions. If your complaint involves an institution that has none of the characteristics described, contact the proper state agency for violations of state laws. Contact the Federal Trade Commission for violations of federal laws.
  The FDIC maintains a toll-free telephone hot line for consumers. It allows the public to ask questions or offer views and complaints about consumer protection or civil rights matters involving FDIC-supervised banks. These include about 8,700 state-chartered banks that are not members of the Federal Reserve System. The toll-free number is (800) 424-5488. It is in daily service, Monday through Friday, from 9:00 A.M. to 4:00 P.M. Eastern Time. In the Washington, D.C., area the consumer information number is (202) 898-3536. The toll-free number also reaches a telecommunication device for the deaf (TDD). You can reach the device in the Washington area by calling (202) 898-3537.

You should first address complaints that do not involve a violation of banking laws or regulations to the financial institution or other credit grantor. If you cannot resolve the problem directly, contact your local Better Business Bureau or consumer protection office for assistance.

Publications

You can find the addresses and telephone numbers for consumer protection offices in your local telephone directory. You also can find them in the *Consumer's Resource Handbook*, available free by writing to:

Handbook
Consumer Information Center-N
P.O. Box 100
Pueblo, Colorado 81002

Publications from the Federal Reserve

You can obtain various publications without charge from:
Board of Governors of the Federal Reserve System
Publications Services
Mail Stop 138
Washington, D.C. 20551

These publications include:

Consumer Handbook of Credit Protection Laws (This 44-page booklet explains how to use the credit laws to shop for credit. It also tells you how to apply for credit, keep up your credit ratings, and complain about an unfair deal.)
Fair Credit Billing
How to File a Consumer Complaint
A Guide to Business Credit and the Equal Credit Opportunity Act
Annual Percentage Rate Tables

Publications from the Federal Trade Commission

The Federal Trade Commission (FTC) publishes many popular consumer publications. Write to:
Federal Trade Commission
Public Reference
6th and Pennsylvania Avenue, N.W.
Washington, D.C. 20580

These publications include:

About Credit
Building a Better Credit Record
*Cosigning a Loan**
Credit and Charge Card Fraud
Credit and Older Americans
*Credit Practices Rule**
*Equal Credit Opportunity**
*Fair Credit Billing**
Fair Credit Reporting
*Fair Debt Collection**
*Fix Your Own Credit Problems**
Lost or Stolen: Credit and ATM Cards
*Solving Credit Problems**
Women and Credit Histories
Getting a Loan: Your Home as Security
Refinancing Your Home
Second Mortgage Financing
Using Ads to Shop for Home Financing
Car Ads: Low Interest Loans and Other Offers

*Available in Spanish

BANKRUPTCY

ALTERNATIVES TO BANKRUPTCY

WHEN YOU HAVE FINANCIAL PROBLEMS

Being in over your head financially is frightening. If you find yourself in this unhappy position, several kinds of help are available. You need to examine the options available to you and decide which course of action is best for you.

Some people in financial trouble can improve their situation by negotiating with credit grantors. Others get help from a financial counseling program or a consumer credit counseling service with experience in negotiating with credit grantors and in budgeting plans. For some people, a form of bankruptcy may be the only realistic alternative.

(continued)

Q. Right now, I cannot pay my debts. Besides bankruptcy, do I have any options?

A. Yes, there are alternatives that you may use to take care of debts you cannot pay. Credit grantors might be willing to settle their claim for a smaller cash payment. Or they might be willing to stretch out and reduce the size of the payments. This would allow you to pay off the debt by making smaller payments over a longer period of time.

Q. Is there anybody in particular whom I should talk with about these options?

A. Yes. If the credit grantor is a retailer, you probably should contact the credit manager. If the credit grantor is a financial institution that has issued you a credit card, you should talk with the credit-card manager. For past-due accounts with either a credit-card company or a retailer, you should contact the person in charge of collections.

Q. I owe money to several creditors. What should I do?

A. If you owe money to many credit grantors, you should contact them individually. Ask them to agree to a voluntary plan for the payment of your debts. The problem with this approach is that a credit grantor might not want to give you more time without knowing what other credit grantors are willing to do.

Q. That sounds helpful, but is there any other alternative?

A. Yes, if you are having problems paying your bills and need help, another option is a financial or consumer credit counseling program. Some universities, local courts, extension agents, military bases, credit unions, housing authorities, and banks operate such programs and charge little, if anything, for their services. For-profit counseling centers provide counseling services for a fee. It pays to choose your adviser carefully.

Some financial counseling programs set up repayment plans. These enable you to pay the program a certain amount each month. The program then distributes the money among credit grantors until it pays all your debts in full. There may be a small monthly service fee. However, credit grantors provide most of the support for financial counseling services. Most credit grantors prefer this kind of plan (since they will eventually get most of their money) rather than "straight" (Chapter 7) bankruptcy.

Under a repayment plan through a financial counseling service, you still might have to pay interest charges on your debts. However, many credit grantors will waive interest charges and delinquency fees.

(continued)

If you find yourself in financial trouble serious enough to be considering these options, you probably should seek advice from a lawyer who is familiar with the bankruptcy laws. The choice of a remedy is not easy. A lawyer or a financial expert in a credit union, bank, or similar institution can best advise you about the most fitting solution to your financial problems. (See the "Family Law" chapter for topics regarding bankruptcy and marriage. In addition, the "Consumer Credit" chapter contains bankruptcy-related discussions.)

BANKRUPTCY DEFINED

Q. What exactly is bankruptcy?

A. People and businesses sometimes cannot pay their debts when they become due. Such people and businesses may declare bankruptcy by filing a petition with the U.S. Bankruptcy Court. If they qualify as a debtor, they are in bankruptcy the day they file the petition. An *order for relief* is entered automatically upon the bankruptcy filing. Bankruptcy laws exist for the benefit and relief of both credit grantors and borrowers. On the one hand, bankruptcy laws provide an orderly process for dividing the borrower's property and repaying each credit grantor as much as possible. On the other hand, the laws aim to give borrowers a fresh start in rebuilding their economic lives.

Q. Is there more than one type of bankruptcy?

A. Yes, there are specific chapters of the federal bankruptcy law. Proceedings under Chapter 7 *(straight bankruptcy)* involve taking most of the borrower's property *(non-exempt assets,* as explained later). The court appoints a trustee to liquidate (sell off) the assets and distribute the cash among the creditors. Proceedings under Chapter 13 *(wage earner's bankruptcy)* involve the borrower proposing a plan for repaying a portion of the debt in installments from the borrower's income. Chapter 11 of the federal Bankruptcy Act generally is not for use by consumer debtors. Its proceedings are expensive and complex. Consumer debtors normally use Chapter 7 or Chapter 13.

Under any chapter, once the bankruptcy proceeding ends, the borrower is no longer liable. (The bankruptcy proceeding ends when the bankruptcy court enters a *discharge order* in a Chapter 7 case or the borrower has paid the debts due the credit grantors according to a plan in a Chapter 11 or 13 case.) In legal terms, the court has *discharged* the borrower from the debts. The borrower then starts over again with a clean financial slate—except that the record of the bankruptcy will remain on the borrower's credit record for up to ten years.

Q. What points should I consider when selecting a lawyer to represent me in a bankruptcy action?

A. Be careful in your selection. Satisfy yourself that your lawyer is familiar with bankruptcy law and procedure, and has a good reputation. Bar associations and groups operated for people with special needs, such as the elderly or handicapped, often operate referral services. They will put you in touch with lawyers practicing in a given area of law. Recommendations from a friend, relative, or associate who has had a good experience with a particular lawyer also may help. Lawyer advertisements will at least make you familiar with the names of some lawyers. Certain ads also will describe the lawyer's area of concentration. They might even state the fee or price range for a specific type of case. For more details, see the first chapter—"When and How To Use a Lawyer"—in this publication.

Remember that you can, and should, discuss your lawyer's fees in advance. This will give you as clear an idea as possible of what the bankruptcy procedure will cost. Under certain circumstances, you can pay the lawyer from the assets of your estate administered by the court in the bankruptcy procedure.

CHAPTER 13 OF THE BANKRUPTCY ACT

Q. Do people often use Chapter 13?

A. About one fifth of consumer (nonbusiness) filings under the bankruptcy code are under Chapter 13. It allows people who have steady incomes to pay all or a portion of their debts. Under Chapter 13, you file a bankruptcy petition and a proposed payment plan with the U.S. Bankruptcy Court. Under the rules for a Chapter 13 filing, your payments must represent all your *disposable income*. That is whatever you do not need for shelter, food, and other necessities. Chapter 13 is available only to certain borrowers. They must have less than $100,000 in unsecured debts (such as credit cards) and less than $350,000 in secured debts (such as mortgages and car loans). Anyone with greater debts usually must declare bankruptcy under Chapters 7 or 11 of the Bankruptcy Act. Chapter 11 covers businesses that are restructuring while continuing operations. However, a person also may file for Chapter 11 bankruptcy.

Q. What happens after I file a bankruptcy petition and a proposed payment plan with the U.S. Bankruptcy Court?

A. Under a Chapter 13 filing, the court will distribute your proposal to the credit grantors. A trustee also will verify the accuracy of your petition. The court must approve your plan for it to become effective. Your proposal is likely to be acceptable if your *unsecured credit grantors* will not receive less than they would have if you had filed a straight bankruptcy petition. (Unsecured credit grantors are those who hold no collateral for their loans, as opposed to credit grantors who make secured loans, such as mortgages.)

A repayment plan under Chapter 13 normally extends your time for paying debts. The permitted repayment period usually is up to three years or, with special permission of the court, up to five years. A Chapter 13 repayment plan also might allow you to repay less than you owe. Under this plan, you usually give the same amount of money every month to the trustee, who then pays your credit grantors.

Q. Compared with straight bankruptcy, are there any advantages to filing for Chapter 13?

A. Yes, there are several advantages. The first advantage occurs if you had people cosign any of your loans or other credit. Your credit grantors cannot collect from your cosigners until it is clear that the Chapter 13 plan will not pay the entire amount owed to the credit grantors. In contrast, if you file a straight bankruptcy petition, your credit grantors have the right to immediately demand payment from your cosigners.

The second advantage is that the discharge of debts under Chapter 13 is broader than it is under Chapter 7. Suppose you successfully complete a repayment plan under Chapter 13. Then individual credit grantors cannot require you to pay them in full if you gave them false financial information when you applied for the credit, or if you used some other fraudulent means to get credit. (However, if you partially complete a plan and the court discharges you anyway, you can be held liable for the full amount of fraudulent debts, even under Chapter 13.) The story is different if you file for straight bankruptcy. Then any credit grantor to whom you gave false or fraudulent information may object to discharging you from repaying the debt you owe the credit grantor.

The third advantage is that you may file under Chapter 13 more often than under Chapter 7. The law forbids you from filing under Chapter 7 more than once every six years. However, Chapter 13 allows you to file repeatedly.

There may be one other advantage to using Chapter 13. It occurs when you want to reapply for credit after the end of your bankruptcy proceeding. Then potential credit grantors might prefer to see a Chapter 13 filing in your credit record instead of a straight Chapter 7 bankruptcy. Chapter 13 often results in the eventual repayment of your debts. At least they will know you are paying a greater percentage of your debt than you might in straight bankruptcy. Credit grantors have no legal duty, however, to give you any special consideration on this basis. You would have to discuss it with them when the time comes.

USE BANKRUPTCY WITH CAUTION

Bankruptcy may be the best, or only, solution for extreme financial hardship. However, it should be utilized exclusively as a last resort, since it always has long-lasting consequences. The record of a bankruptcy remains in your credit files in credit bureaus for as long as ten years, which is a long time in today's economic system that is so dependent on having good credit. Be sure to consult a financial expert before resorting to bankruptcy as means of solving your economic troubles.

Q. Do Chapter 13 bankruptcies normally succeed?

A. No, they have a high failure rate. It is especially important to choose a reputable lawyer or financial adviser to set up your repayment plan. The plan must be realistic. If you are unable to make your payments under a Chapter 13 plan, you may still file for Chapter 7. To do this, however, you must not have filed for Chapter 7 for six years.

STRAIGHT BANKRUPTCY: CHAPTER 7

Q. What does Chapter 7 bankruptcy involve?

A. Straight bankruptcy under Chapter 7 is available if less drastic methods will not solve your financial problems. It allows you to *discharge* (extinguish) most debts. A section below describes the types of debts that you cannot avoid in any form of bankruptcy.

Q. How does a Chapter 7 bankruptcy proceeding begin?

A. It starts when you file a petition with the U.S. Bankruptcy Court asking it to relieve you (or you and your spouse) from your debts. As of the date you file the petition, your assets will be under the protection of the court. In addition, most collection efforts against you must stop. You must sign the petition under oath.

When you file the petition, you also must file a Statement of Financial Affairs. This describes your personal background and financial history.

However, under Chapter 7, you might have to turn over many of your assets. When you have borrowed to buy a car, boat, or other durable item, the seller may have a *lien* (legal claim) on that property. If so, you may be able to keep your car, boat, or other durable item by reaffirming your debt (as explained later in this chapter). If you do not reaffirm the debt, you may have to give the property to the credit grantor who financed its purchase.

The bankruptcy court will demand that you give all your *non-exempt assets* to the trustee for the bankruptcy court. The trustee will then liquidate (sell off) these non-exempt assets for the benefit of your credit grantors. Non-exempt assets are those that are not necessary (in the eyes of the state or federal legislature) for you to have a "fresh start." These non-exempt assets include most real property with equity of more than $7,500 ($15,000 if jointly owned by a husband and wife).

The trustee also may have a right to take personal property, such as jewelry, art objects, stocks, bonds, and other valuable luxury items if the property falls outside of exempt property guidelines. (States may differ slightly as to these guidelines.) In practice, however, most borrowers filing under Chapter 7 have little if any of this kind of property.

Meanwhile, you also must file schedules that detail your assets and liabilities. Under liabilities, you must include:

- Your priority debts (such as taxes);
- Your secured credit grantors (auto dealers, home mortgages, and so on); and
- Your unsecured credit grantors (department store credit cards and the like).

Under assets, you must include:

- All your real property (real estate and so forth);
- All your personal property (such as household goods, clothing, cash, retirement funds, accrued net wages);
- All other assets that you did not list on other schedules.

You also must list all the exemptions you are claiming. The court will sell your non-exempt assets to obtain money to help pay off your debts. These assets include everything except those that either state or federal law allow you to keep after your bankruptcy. If you lie or fail to reveal something important, you are liable for perjury. This may cause the court to deny or cancel your discharge from debts. If you make a mistake in claiming your exemptions, the court may allow you to make amendments later to reflect the required changes.

Q. What happens after I submit all the above information to the court?

A. The bankruptcy court clerk will notify your credit grantors that you have filed a petition. The court, or, in most areas, a U.S. Trustee, will appoint a trustee, usually a private lawyer who does this kind of work in the normal course of practicing law. After the clerk has notified your credit grantors of your petition, they must stop any efforts to collect the debts you owe.

In what is called the *first* meeting of creditors, the trustee will examine your petition, Statement of Financial Affairs, and schedules. Then the trustee will determine whether to challenge any of your claimed exemptions. If you disagree with the trustee's decision, you may protest to the court. Then the court will make the final decision.

After the trustee determines your exemptions, the trustee will assemble and liquidate your non-exempt assets (if there are any). Then the trustee will first pay the entire amount of any priority claims, such as certain taxes or money owed to secured credit grantors. Next, the trustee will pay your general unsecured credit grantors on a pro rata (proportionate) basis. Say, for example, that the profits from the sale by the trustee of your non-exempt assets equal 30 percent of your remaining debts. Then the trustee will pay each unsecured credit grantor 30 percent of what you owe. After this, the court will discharge you from paying any remaining balances on your general unsecured debts.

Q. What is the difference between exempt and non-exempt property?

A. Debtors' *exempt property* includes some equity in their homes (usually), personal items and clothing, the tools of their trade (carpenter's tools, for example), and household furnishings of nominal (modest) value. The debtors are permitted by law to keep this exempt property in Chapter 7 bankruptcy.

Q. How may I keep certain possessions that I do not want the court to sell?

A. You may *reaffirm* some debts, if the court approves and the credit grantors are willing. By reaffirming these debts, you promise to pay them in full. Then the court will allow you to keep the property involved. So if you do not wish to lose property secured by a valid lien, such as a financed car or mortgaged house, you must continue paying off such debts. You may do so according to the pre-existing or renegotiated terms.

GENERAL COMPARISON OF CHAPTER 13 AND CHAPTER 7 BANKRUPTCY

Feature	Chapter 13 Payment Plan for People with Regular Income	Chapter 7 Straight Bankruptcy Liquidation
Basic operation	File bankruptcy petition and proposed payment plan with court. Payment plan makes payments over a maximum of three to five years. Payments are made from disposable income (i.e., whatever is left over after necessities [food, shelter, etc.] have been allowed for), while debtor retains assets.	File bankruptcy petition with court. Trustee appointed to administer bankruptcy. All non-exempt assets sold. Debtor retains only exempt assets. Money is split among creditors, according to priority established by the Bankruptcy Code.
Limitations on availability	For less than $100,000 in unsecured debt and less than $350,000 in secured debt.	No monetary limitations. Not available if debtor was discharged in bankruptcy within past six years.
Percentage of consumer filings under Bankruptcy Code	About 20 percent.	About 80 percent.
Availability	Can be used repeatedly.	Can be used only if not used during previous six years.
Effect on debts	All or a portion of debts paid off over a period of time under a specific plan. With exceptions noted in text, debts are discharged. Liability to creditors ends when plan successfully carried out.	With exceptions noted in text, most debts are discharged (extinguished) upon bankruptcy. Liability to creditors ends with discharge order from court.
Effect on home	Home will be preserved if plan successfully carried out. If not, home may be preserved under homestead exemption or marital ownership law.	Home may be preserved under homestead exemption or marital ownership law.
Effect on automobile	Auto will be preserved if plan successfully carried out. If not, it might be taken by creditors (unless arrangements are made to pay off lien).	Auto might be taken by creditors (unless necessary for work and arrangements are made to pay off lien).
Effect on non-exempt assets	No effect if plan carried out successfully. If not, non-exempt assets can be sold to pay creditors, as in Chapter 7 bankruptcy.	All non-exempt assets will be sold.
Time to repay	Usually up to three years, sometimes up to five years.	Not applicable.
Payments	All "disposable income" is available for payments; that is, whatever remains after necessities (food, shelter, etc.) are taken care of.	Most forms of debt discharged; however, other debts, such as taxes and child support, will have to be paid.
Portion of debt repaid	May allow payments for less than actual debts.	Will depend on the value of non-exempt assets sold to pay off debts.
Result at conclusion of bankruptcy proceedings	Borrower is no longer liable for most debts if plan successfully carried out.	Bankruptcy court enters a discharge order, ending enforceability of all debts that can be discharged in bankruptcy.
Requirement for bankruptcy proceedings to end	Borrower must have made all payments in accordance with court-approved plan.	Court must have entered a discharge order.
Effect on credit	Record of bankruptcy may remain on credit record for up to ten years. Creditors may prefer to see this form of bankruptcy, since successful completion of plan may pay more debts that will be paid under Chapter 7 filing.	Record of bankruptcy may remain on credit record for up to ten years.

DEBTS BANKRUPTCY WILL NOT DISCHARGE

Q. May I use bankruptcy to get rid of all my debts?

A. No, bankruptcy does not discharge all types of debt. These include some tax claims, alimony, child support, and most student loans. Bankruptcy also will not release you from claims for punitive damages for "malicious or wanton" acts such as drunk driving. You will still owe and are still liable for these debts, even after you declare bankruptcy.

Luxury Purchases Immediately Prior to Bankruptcy

There are numerous exceptions to the general rule concerning the discharge of debts through bankruptcy. One exception involves a last-minute spending binge for luxury goods or services. This type of debt is not discharged through bankruptcy if: (1) it totals more than $500; (2) it was payable to a single credit grantor; (3) it was spent on luxury goods or services; and (4) it was incurred by the debtor within 40 days before the bankruptcy order was entered.

AN ALTERNATIVE FOR FARMERS: CHAPTER 12

Q. Does the law offer farmers a special type of bankruptcy?

A. Yes, farmers have the option of a special type of bankruptcy under Chapter 12 of the bankruptcy code. It is one of a series of special farm-aid provisions enacted to help farmers survive periodic economic slumps. Chapter 12 allows farmers with a lot of real-estate debts to avoid foreclosure. They could pledge part of the profits from their future crop to pay off the debts. Meanwhile, the farmers temporarily pay credit grantors an amount similar to a fair-market rent. Only farmers acting in good faith have the right to file a Chapter 12 petition. In order for a petition to proceed quickly, as in other chapter filings, the debtor must submit several items to the U.S. Bankruptcy Court. These include a list of credit grantors, a list of assets and liabilities, and a Statement of Financial Affairs.

The farmer-debtor usually will require legal help. Any lawyer representing the farmer-debtor must file a statement with the court declaring how much the farmer is paying the lawyer.

IN CONCLUSION

Q. What results from bankruptcy?

A. Neglecting your bills, getting in debt over your head, or bankruptcy may hurt your credit history for many years.

Fortunately, there are no longer debtors prisons. In addition, federal law protects your right to file for bankruptcy. For example, you cannot be fired from your job merely because you filed for bankruptcy. However, credit grantors may deny you credit in the future. Remember, most unfavorable information in your credit file stays there for seven years. Credit reporting agencies may report bankruptcy on your credit record for ten years. So long as your credit record has unfavorable information, you may have credit problems. You may have trouble getting a loan to buy a car or a mortgage for a house. You also may find it difficult to get a credit card or to rent an apartment.

Nonetheless, declaring bankruptcy is sometimes your only reasonable choice. People who file bankruptcies are doing so because of financial difficulties. These may have resulted from the loss of a job or from a serious illness or accident. Whatever the reason, you have a legal right to file for bankruptcy. A lawyer or other professional who specializes in bankruptcy can help you decide what is best for you.

WHERE TO GET MORE INFORMATION

The resources for bankruptcy and credit are quite similar, since both topics deal with consumer economics. For this reason, if you need further details or assistance, see the "Where to Get More Information" section at the end of the "Consumer Credit" chapter, which precedes this chapter.

CONTRACTS AND CONSUMER ISSUES

INTRODUCTION

Knowing what constitutes a contract is the key to understanding many legal questions. Very often a dispute c not on whether someone has violated a contract, but whe there was a contract in the first place. Other disputes cen whether a change in circumstances has made the contrac unenforceable.

This chapter contains five sections. The first section, "A Contract Defined," outlines the basics of what contracts a how people form them. The second section, "What a Con Not," looks at specific examples of how the necessary par contract may be missing. It also discusses your defenses t other people's claims that they have a contract with you. third section, "Practical Contracts," focuses on contracts i life. It highlights issues of interest to consumers. The four section, "Special Types of Contracts," discusses leases, warr advertising, door-to-door sales, and other special types of contracts. The fifth section, "Breaches and Remedies," dis different ways to deal with disputes arising out of contrac alleged contracts.

A CONTRACT DEFINED

Q. What is a contract?

A. A *contract* is a voluntary promise between competent parties to do (or not to do) something. It is a promise that the law will enforce; it is a binding promise. Depending on the situation, a contract could obligate you even if you want to call it off before receiving anything from the other side.

In order for such a promise to qualify as a contract, it has to be supported by the exchange of something of value between the parties. This *consideration* is most often money, but can be some other bargained-for benefit or drawback. The final qualification for a contract is that the subject of the promise may not be illegal.

Suppose that a friend agrees to buy your car for $1,000. That is the promise. You benefit by getting the cash. Your friend benefits by getting the car. Assuming it is your car, the sale is legal. You and your friend have a contract.

Q. May anyone enter into a contract?

A. No, in order to make a valid contract, people have to be able to understand what they are doing. That requires both *maturity* and *mental health*. Without either of these, it could result in one person being at a disadvantage in the bargaining process. That could cancel a contract.

Q. What determines enough maturity to make a contract?

A. State contract law defines maturity as the age of majority. That usually is 18 years old.

Q. Does that mean minors may not make a contract?

A. No, minors may make a contract. However, they may ask a court *not* to enforce it. That means the minors could receive benefits and not have to pay for them. However, the minors would have to return goods still in their possession. The court may require the minors or their parents to pay the fair market value for "necessaries." The fair market value is not necessarily the contract price. The definition of a "necessary" depends entirely on the person and the situation. It probably will always include food and probably will never include records and tapes. If the minor reaches full age and does not disavow the contract, the minor may then have to comply with all its terms.

Q. When does mental illness prohibit a valid contract?

A. While the age test for maturity is easy to determine, the standards for determining mental illness are remarkably complex. They differ widely from one state to another. One very common test is whether people had the capacity to *understand* what they were doing and to appreciate its effects when they made the deal. Another approach is evaluating whether people can *control* themselves, regardless of their understanding.

Q. May an intoxicated person get out of a contract?

A. Very often such a person may get out of a contract. The courts do not like to let a voluntarily intoxicated person revoke a contract with innocent parties this way. However, if someone acts like a drunk, the other person probably was not so innocent. On the other hand, if someone does not appear to be intoxicated, that person probably will have to follow the contract. The key in this area may be a person's medical history. If someone can show alcohol abuse, blackouts, and the like, that person may avoid the contract, regardless of how that person appears.

Q. Do I need a lawyer to make a contract?

A. If you satisfy the maturity and mental health requirements for competence, you do not need a lawyer. However, it probably is a good idea to get a lawyer before you sign complex contracts. This includes contracts about business deals or those involving large amounts of money.

Q. Must contracts be in writing?

A. Many types of contracts do not have to be written to be enforceable. An example is purchasing an item in a retail store. You pay money in exchange for an item that the store implies and warrants will perform a certain function. Your receipt, even if not signed, is proof of the contract.

Although most states recognize and enforce oral contracts, *the safest practice is to put any agreement in writing.* If someone can prove the existence of an oral contract, however, the courts will enforce it. (Proving that an oral contract exists most often occurs by showing that outside circumstances would lead a reasonable person to conclude that a contract most likely existed.) There always is the problem as to what the oral contract contained. The courts can only look to nonrefuted (uncontested) testimony to help them "fill in the blanks." On the other hand, in all areas of the law, courts are hesitant to *add* words or terms to any writing. At best the courts might delete any provisions that are confusing to the parties.

Get any promise from a salesperson or an agent in writing. Do this especially if there already is a written contract covering any part of the same deal. A written contract may be an order form or receipt that you sign. Otherwise the courts will assume that the final, signed form represents the entire agreement.

Writing down the terms of a good-faith agreement is the best way to ensure that everybody is aware of their rights and duties. This is true even if neither party intends to lie about the provisions of the agreement.

Q. Which contracts have to be in writing?

A. Under laws in most states, the courts will fully enforce certain contracts only under two conditions. First, they must be in writing. Second the people who are going to be obligated to fulfill the contracts must sign them. These contracts include:

- Any promise to be responsible for someone else's debts—people normally call this being a *cosigner* of a *surety* contract;
- Any promise, made with consideration, to marry;
- Any promise that the parties cannot possibly fulfill within one year from when they made the promise;
- Any promise involving the change in ownership of land or interests in land (for example, leases and broker agreements when you sell your home);
- Any promise for the sale of goods worth more than $500;
- Any promise to bequeath property (give it after death)—people often call this a *will*; and
- Any promise to sell stocks and bonds.

Some states have additional requirements for written contracts. These statutes are designed to prevent fraudulent claims.

Give and Take

A contract may only come about through the bargaining process, which may take many forms. This section discusses the definitions of offer and acceptance and of consideration. A later section will look at contracts that involve less give and take. However, all the principles discussed here will have to be present in some form in any contract.

Making a Contract

Q. What is an offer?

A. Offer and acceptance are the most fundamental parts of a contract. An *offer* is a communication by an offeror of a present intention to enter a contract. (The *offeror* is the person making the offer.) It does not simply mean to bargain, such as at an auction or in preliminary negotiations. For the communication to be effective, the *offeree* (the one who is receiving the offer) must receive it. To be valid, an offer usually must answer these questions:

- Who is the offeree?
- What is the subject matter of the offer?
- How many of the subject matter does the offer involve (quantity)?
- How much (price)?

Let us say you told your friend, "I'll sell you my mauve Edsel for $1,000." Your friend is the offeree, and the car is the object. Also, describing the car as a mauve Edsel makes your friend reasonably sure that both of you are talking about the same car (and only one of them). Finally, the price is $1,000. It is a perfectly good offer.

Q. Is an advertisement an offer?

A. No, courts usually consider advertisements as something short of an offer. They are an "expression of intent to sell" or an invitation to bargain. The later section on consumer law will discuss this subject further.

Q. Does an offer stay open indefinitely?

A. Not unless the offeree has an *option*. That is an irreversible offer for which the offeree bargains. Otherwise, an offer ends when:

- The time to accept is up—either a "reasonable" amount of time or the deadline stated in the offer;
- The offeror cancels the offer;
- The offeree rejects the offer; or
- The offeree dies or something incapacitates the offeree.

Even an option-holder loses an option if:

- A change in the law makes the contract illegal; or
- Something (or somebody) destroys the subject matter of the contract (see below).

Q. What makes up the acceptance of an offer?

A. *Acceptance* is the offeree's voluntary, communicated assent to the terms and conditions of the offer. Assent means some act or promise of agreement. Continuing our earlier example, an assent might be your friend saying, "I agree to buy your mauve Edsel for $1,000."

Generally, every term agreed to must be the same as in the offer. Thus, if the offer requires acceptance by mail, you must accept by mail for the offer to be effective. If there is no such requirement, you just have to communicate your acceptance by some reasonable means.

The Reasonable Person

Throughout this publication, and any law book, the term "reasonable" will appear many times. Very often, you will see references to the "reasonable man" or the "reasonable person." Why is the law so preoccupied with this mythical being? The reason is that no contract can possibly predict all the hundreds, if not thousands, of disputes that might arise under it. Similarly, no set of laws regulating liability for personal injury can possibly foresee the countless ways human beings can manage to hurt each other.

(continued)

Q. May silence make up an acceptance?

A. In most cases, the answer is no. It is not as a general rule fair for the law to allow someone to impose a contract on someone else. In some circumstances, however, failure to respond may result in a contract. For example, suppose an insurance company, according to past practice, sends you a renewal policy and bills you for the premium. If you keep the policy and months later refuse to pay the premium, you probably will be liable for the premium. You will be liable at least until the date you positively canceled the policy. This is not necessarily a bad result. For instance, what if your house burned down after the original insurance policy had expired but before you had paid the renewal premium? You obviously would want to claim that the policy was still effective.

Q. May acts make up an acceptance?

A. Yes, someone does not have to accept an offer in words, either orally or in writing. Any conduct that would lead a reasonable observer to believe that the offeree had accepted the offer qualifies as an acceptance. Suppose you say, "John, I will pay you $50 to clean my house on Saturday at 9 A.M." Then John only has to show up at 9 A.M. on Saturday and begin cleaning to show acceptance.

To take another example, you do not normally have to pay for goods shipped to you that you did not order. (A later section will discuss this in more detail.) However, if you are a retailer and you put them on display in your store and sell them, you have accepted the offer to buy them. This obligates you to pay the price. Sometimes people call this an *implied* (as opposed to an *express*) contract. However, it is a genuine contract.

Q. When is the acceptance effective?

A. The contract usually is in effect as soon as the offeree transmits the acceptance. However, this is not the case when the offeror has specified that the acceptance must be received before it is effective or before an option takes effect (discussed previously). In these situation, there is no contract until the offeror receives the answer.

Q. What is the "meeting of the minds"?

A. This term describes an offer that the offeree accepts in all its critical *(material)* terms. This term also implies that both parties understand (or reasonably should understand) these terms in the same way. It is a useful phrase to help determine

(continued)

Since the law cannot provide for every possibility, it has evolved the standard of the "reasonable" person to furnish some uniform standards and to guide the courts. Through the "reasonable person," the law creates a standard that the judge or jury may apply to each set of circumstances. It is a standard that reflects community values, rather than the (good or bad) judgment of the people involved in the case. Thus a court might decide whether an oral contract existed by asking whether a "reasonable person" would conclude that one did exist. The court might decide a personal injury case by asking what a "reasonable person" might do in a particular situation.

in your own mind whether you ever got past the bargaining stage of the negotiations.

Q. Is an "agreement to agree" a contract?

A. Generally not, because it suggests that important terms are still missing. Rarely will a court "supply" those terms itself. An agreement to agree is another way of saying that there has not yet been a meeting of the minds. However, if the formal contract is merely a written version of what the parties have otherwise agreed to, then a court probably will enforce the agreement. This is true even if the parties never sign the formal agreement.

Q. What is a condition?

A. Lawyers often use the word "condition" to mean one of the terms of a contract. However, a more specific meaning is that a *condition* is an event that has to occur if the contract is to be performed. In our earlier example, your friend might have said, "I'll buy your mauve Edsel for $1,000 only if you paint it blue." If you go ahead and paint it blue, your friend will have to perform the contract by buying the Edsel.

Conditions may be after the fact, too. You may make the payment for a renovation of your house conditional on your complete satisfaction. If the contract did not state that, it would only guarantee you normally acceptable work.

The other party does not have to agree to a condition. Also, you may have to pay extra for it. You must decide whether it is worth it to you.

Q. How much consideration, or payment, must there be for a contract to be valid?

A. There is no minimum amount. A price is only how people choose to value something. Hence, there is no absolute standard of whether a price is "fair" or "reasonable." The courts presume that people will only make deals that they consider worthwhile. So if you want to sell your car to your friend for one dollar instead of $1,000, you may do it. The exception is something that would "shock the conscience of the court." A later section in this chapter will consider this when it discusses the idea of unconscionability.

Q. Does consideration have to be money?

A. No, it is any *promise, act, or transfer of value that induces a party to enter a contract*. Consideration is a bargained-for benefit or advantage, or a bargained-for detriment or disadvantage. A benefit might be receiving a dollar. First dibs (rights) to Super Bowl tickets might be an advantage. A disadvantage may involve promising not to perform some act (for example, suing the other person). For these purposes, even quitting smoking is a detriment, even though it is good for your health. It is a detriment because it took effort that you would not otherwise have made.

In our first example, you could agree to give your car to your friend in exchange for his promise that he will stop letting his dog out late at night. Your friend is giving up what is presumably his right to let his dog out any time he wants. In return, you are giving up your car. Other types of valid considerations include a promise to compromise an existing dispute.

Q. Do both sides have to give consideration?

A. Yes, there is a principle in contract law called *mutuality of obligations*. It means that both sides have to be giving up something. If either party reserves an unqualified right to bail out, that person's promise is merely *illusory*. In other words, it is no promise at all.

Q. Does the consideration have to be a new obligation?

A. Yes, because someone who already must do something has not suffered any "detriment" by promising it again. Suppose you agree to have a contractor paint your house this Thursday for $500. Before starting, though, the contractor's workers strike. This causes the contractor to increase their wages. The contractor tells you on Wednesday night that the job now costs $650. You need the house painted by next weekend, and there is no time to hire another contractor, so you agree. Regardless, the new agreement is not enforceable. The contractor already had to paint your house for $500. The contractor should have figured the costs of possible increases into the original price. You did not get anything of benefit from the modified contract, since you already had the contractor's promise to paint the house. Therefore, you only owe $500.

Q. Does that mean I may not renegotiate a contract?

A. No, it only means that someone may not *force* you to renegotiate by taking advantage of an existing agreement. In the previous example, you might have decided that the painter deserved more money than you had bargained for. More realistically, you may have agreed that the contractor should do some work not included in the original contract or you could want to use the contractor later. Or, you might feel that the contractor does the best job at any price. (Considerations like these allow many sports stars to renegotiate their contracts.)

Whenever you get involved in a deal, you are taking a risk that it might be less beneficial for you than you planned at the beginning. The other party does not have to ensure your profit. However, sometimes the other party might want to.

Q. Is a promise to make a gift a contract?

A. Not if it truly is only a promise to make a gift. That is because a gift lacks the two-sided obligation discussed above. However, if the person promising the gift is asking for anything in return, even by implication, a contract may be formed. The key, again, is consideration.

Q. What if someone makes a promise without consideration, but I rely on it?

A. Remember that consideration may be a disadvantage to one party. From that idea, the law has developed the idea of *reliance*. This means that a contract may be formed if one party reasonably relies on the other's promise, and that reliance causes some loss.

Suppose that rich Uncle Harry loves your kids with all his heart. On previous occasions he had asked you to buy them expensive presents and has reimbursed you for them. This past Christmas, Uncle Harry told you he would like you to build a swimming pool for them behind the house, and send him the bill. You did so, but moody Uncle Harry changed his mind. He claims you may not enforce a promise to make a gift. However, the pool is no longer a gift under contract law. You acted to your detriment in reasonable reliance on his promise. You did this by taking on the duty to pay for a swimming pool you would not normally have built. Under contract law, Uncle Harry must pay if you prove that he instructed you to build the pool and that this conduct was consistent with many previous "gifts." Remember, however, especially in the area of gifts, that you still have to live with your Uncle Harry.

Q. May someone else make a contract on my behalf?

A. Yes, but that person may do so only with your permission. The law refers to such an arrangement as *agency*. We could not do business without it. For example, when you buy a car, you bargain and finally make a contract with a salesperson. However, he does not own the car he is selling you. He might not even have a car. How can that be? He is an *agent,* someone with the authority to bind someone else by contract. The law refers to that someone else (the car dealer) as a *principal.*

To take another common example, real-estate brokers act as your agent when you buy or sell a home. As the principal, you generally establish the conditions of the deal. (For example, "I'll buy if he will come down to $100,000 and agree to repair the garage.") Then your agent goes into negotiations on your behalf.

As long as the agents do not exceed the authority granted them by the principals, contracts they make bind the principals as if the principals had made the contracts themselves. If something goes wrong with the contract, you would sue the principal if you could not resolve the dispute in a friendly manner. A principal's agent normally does *not* have any personal obligation. While acting on behalf of the principal, the agents are required to put their own interests after those of the principal whom they represent. Agents also are not permitted to personally profit beyond what the principal and agent have agreed to in their employment contract.

Q. What happens when the agents do exceed the authority granted them by the principals?

A. That depends on the circumstances. Suppose the agent exceeds her authority, but circumstances are such that the person she's dealing with does not understand that she is exceeding it. Also suppose that the principal knows that the agent in similar circumstances has exceeded her authority, but the principal has done nothing about it. Then a court might say that the principal is bound by the contract negotiated by the agent.

Q. May I transfer my duties under a contract?

A. Yes, unless the contract prohibits such a transfer. The law refers to a transfer of duties or responsibilities as a *delegation.* Also, if someone contracts with you because of a special skill or talent only you have, you may not be able to transfer your duty. Such cases are quite narrow. There are no car mechanics who are so good at tuning an engine that they may not delegate someone else to do it for them. However, they may not delegate it if they specifically promise to do it themselves. On the other hand, if you hire well-known entertainers to perform at your wedding, they may not send even highly competent entertainers as substitutes without your permission.

Agents Who Exceed Their Authority

On occasion, while making a contract, an agent might exceed the authority granted by the principal. An example might involve an automobile salesperson who signed a contract on behalf of a car dealer without the dealer's authority. Suppose the contract's terms gave the customer a warranty for 40,000 extra miles. In that case, the dealer might be bound by the contract if the buyer did not know that the salesperson did not have authority and the dealer knew that the agent had exceeded his or her authority in the past and had done nothing about it.

Q. May I delegate my rights?

A. A transfer of rights, called an *assignment,* is more flexible than a transfer of duties. (For example, you may wish to transfer the right to receive money from a buyer for something you have sold.) Generally, a contract right is yours. You usually may do as you wish with it as long as you did not agree in the contract not to assign the right. You may sell it or give it away. Most states, though, require you to put an assignment in writing, especially if it is a gift.

However, as is often the case with the law, there are exceptions. If an assignment would substantially increase the risk, or materially (significantly) change the duty, of the other party to the contract, it may not be assignable. This may be true even if there is no agreement to the contrary in the contract.

WHAT A CONTRACT IS NOT

Bars to a Contract

Q. May someone make a contract to do or sell something illegal?

A. No, the courts will not help someone collect an illegal gambling debt, or payment for illegal narcotics or prostitution. The law treats these "contracts" as if they never existed. It refers to this as the defense of *illegality.*

Q. What if the contract became illegal after the people made it?

A. Then the contract becomes unenforceable on the ground of impossibility of performance, which a later section will discuss. The difference between a contract that *becomes* illegal and one that *started* that way is important. If someone already made a payment but the contract becomes illegal before the parties complete it, the person who received the payment must return it.

Q. Does the same hold true for a contract to do something immoral?

A. No, the courts will only enforce a moral code that the law already reflects. Examples are laws against prostitution or

Is It or Isn't It a Contract?

The principles discussed will go a long way toward determining if people have formed a contract. You now know that a contract has to be made between willing, competent parties. Also, the contract must concern a legal subject matter. The preceding section also discussed many aspects of consideration.

Applying these principles is not always easy. Sometimes special protections in the law complicate matters. If one of these special factors is present, it could provide a complete defense against someone claiming you owe them money or something else you supposedly promised.

(continued)

stealing. You may feel that X-rated movies or fur coats are immoral. However, as long as they are legal, they may be the subject of a fully enforceable contract.

Q. May a contract made against my will be enforced against me?

A. No, a contract that one person agrees to *under duress* is void. Duress is threats or acts sufficient to overcome your free will. The classic case of duress is a contract someone signs "with a gun to his head."

Duress goes beyond persuasion or hard selling. Persuasion in bargaining is perfectly legal. It also is not duress to say that "I would never pay that much for an Edsel if I had a choice." Duress involves actual coercion, such as a threat of violence or imprisonment.

Q. Are there other kinds of duress besides physical threats?

A. Duress requires suspending your free will. This may be done by other threats than physical violence. It may be duress to threaten to abuse the court systems to coerce someone's agreement.

There is also *economic duress*. That was discussed earlier when the contractor demanded more money after his workers went on strike and you needed your house painted before the weekend. This is not the same as "driving a hard bargain." Rather, the contractor had already made a deal. Then the contractor threatened to withhold the deal, leaving you with no practical choice but to agree. A court will set aside a contract made under economic duress.

Q. What should I do if someone forces me to sign a contract under duress?

A. First, get out of danger, especially if that person threatened you with physical harm. Next, see a lawyer, who can tell you how to protect yourself. The lawyer can decide whether you have assumed any obligation, and what legal rights you might have besides disavowing the contract. It is important to act quickly. The courts may doubt a claim of duress made long after the danger has ceased.

Q. Are there other uses of unfair pressure, less severe than duress, that void a contract?

A. There is a contract defense called *undue influence,* which does not involve a threat. It is the unfair use of a relationship

(continued)

Some of these *contract defenses*—such as illegality or duress (intimidation)—could show that there never was a valid contract. Since the contract was *void* (unenforceable), either party may safely ignore it. Other contracts are *voidable,* not void. A contract produced by fraud is not void in itself. The person who was victimized by fraud may declare that contract void. Until that person does so, however, it is a valid contract. The difference between void and voidable contracts also is important to third parties (other people or companies) affected by a contract. A checklist of contract defenses appears in this section.

of trust to pressure someone into an unbalanced contract. Undue influence cases usually involve someone who starts out at a disadvantage, perhaps by illness, age, or emotional pain. The other person often has some duty to look out for the weaker one's interests.

An example would be a court-appointed guardian who "persuades" his 12-year-old charge to lend him $25,000 free of interest. The loan contract would be void because of undue influence. It does not matter whether the minor has the capacity to make a contract.

Q. What is fraud?

A. A contract is voidable because of fraud when one person knowingly made a *material misrepresentation* that the other person reasonably relied on and that disadvantaged the other person. A material misrepresentation is an important untruth. It does not have to be made on purpose to make the contract voidable.

Consider our earlier example involving a car sale. You offered to sell your Edsel to a friend. Suppose you knew it had no transmission, and you knew your friend wanted it for the usual purpose of driving it. You told your friend it was working fine, and your friend relied on your statement. Then the contract you made may be set aside on the grounds of fraud.

Here, there is no matter of the seller's opinion, or *puffing,* as the law calls it. You did not merely say it was a great car when really it was a lousy car. Saying it is great is merely an opinion. No fraud normally would be involved there. Remember that fraud requires a knowing, outright lie about an important part of the contract. For that reason—and because corrupt people often know the fine line between fraud and puffing very well—actual fraud that will make a contract voidable is a lot less common than people think.

When Someone Forces You to Sign

Between the defenses of duress and undue influence, you should never have to fear a court holding you liable for a contract that someone forced you to sign. However, both ideas are puzzling; people often use them interchangeably. Also, their limits vary from one state to another. If you think either might apply to an agreement you want to get out of, see a lawyer.

Q. If I entered into the contract under a mistaken impression, does that affect the contract's validity?

A. Probably not, assuming the other party did not know about your mistake. This defense, a defense of *unilateral mistake,* is almost impossible to prove. That is true even if it is about the most important terms of the contract. If allowed, it probably would lead to a lot of abuse. Many people would claim they made a mistake in order to get out of a contract they did not like, even though they had no valid legal defense. Therefore, courts hardly ever permit such a defense, and even then, only in specialized business cases.

Q. Is unilateral mistake ever a defense?

A. Sometimes you may void a contract because of mistake when the other party knows about your false impression and does not correct it, or takes advantage of it. This is true only in some states.

The case would be clearer if you specifically state your mistaken idea. At that point, the other party has a duty to correct you. The issue is no longer one of mistake but of fraud. In our car-sale example, suppose the car's transmission worked, but was faulty, and you knew that. Under contract law, if you and your friend had not discussed it, you would not have to tell your friend about it. However, suppose your friend told you, "The best thing about this car is that it's so hard to find an Edsel with a perfect transmission." Then, according to contract law, you would have to tell your friend that the transmission was faulty. If you did not, many states would permit your friend to set aside the contract, or they would allow your friend to collect damages for repairs required on the transmission.

Q. What if both sides make a mistake?

A. Then you do not have the "meeting of the minds" discussed earlier. Or perhaps more accurately, the minds are not meeting with the facts. Then, in order to avoid injustice, the court will often set aside the contract, under the theory of *mutual mistake*.

A classic case of mutual mistake occurred when someone sold a supposedly barren (infertile) cow for $80. It turned out soon afterward that the cow was pregnant, which made the animal worth $800. The court ruled that since both parties thought they were dealing with a barren cow, the contract could be set aside.

Q. Does that mean that contracts always have a built-in guarantee against mistakes?

A. No, as you can imagine, this is a very tricky and unpredictable area. After all, many people make purchases on the understanding that the object is worth more to one person than to the other. You wouldn't pay $80 for a cow if she were not worth at least $80.01 to you. Also, the seller would not sell her if she were worth more than $79.99 to the seller. Both people have to be getting some benefit to agree to the sale. The difference in a mutual mistake case is that neither the buyer nor the seller had any idea whatsoever that the cow was worth $800.

However, various courts draw the line between $80.01 and $800 at different places, if at all. Competent legal advice about the law in your state is crucial if you are considering voiding a contract because of mistake.

THE POWER OF BARGAINING

Throughout this section and others, remember that the terms of a contract may deal with many types of unforeseen circumstances and risks. You may include any possibility in a contract. You may make one party or the other, or both, liable for the parties' happiness or the cost of ensuring it. Keep in mind when you sign a preprinted contract that the other party may already have done just that—possibly at your expense.

Will state law assign some of these risks? It may. In many consumer deals, state laws will assign certain risks to the seller. As in many areas of law, state laws will apply to any circumstance that a contract or agreement does not cover. If, however, both parties have agreed on and included terms to cover possible future events, then these terms will overrule state laws.

Changing Situations

Q. What if it becomes physically impossible to perform a contract?

A. Suppose that you hire a contractor to paint your house on Thursday, and it burns down Wednesday night. Then the contract will be set aside. There is no way to perform the contract. You will not have to pay the painter, under the doctrine of *impossibility of performance*. Both of you are out of luck. The same is true if the contract covers a specific kind of product, and it becomes unavailable because of an act of God. Courts usually will not enforce such a contract. For example, suppose you contract to deliver 100 barrels of Arabian oil by a certain date. Then an earthquake devastates the Arabian oil field, making delivery of the oil impossible. You probably are off the hook under these circumstances.

Q. However, what if changing circumstances make it much more costly to fulfill the contract, but it still is possible to do what the contract promised?

A. The courts probably would enforce the contract. They would do so on the grounds that the new circumstances were foreseeable, and the possibility of increased costs could have been built into the contract. For instance, suppose that you contract to deliver 100 barrels of Arabian oil. This time, fighting breaks out in the Persian Gulf, interrupting shipping and greatly increasing the cost of the oil. When a court considers these facts, it is likely to say that you should have foreseen the possibility of fighting and built that risk into the price. The contract will stand. (The section on remedies that appears later in this chapter will discuss what to do about it.)

Q. What if the contract can be performed, but to do so would be pointless?

A. Sometimes a change in conditions does not make performance impossible, but it does make performance meaningless. The legal term for this is *frustration of purpose*. Suppose you rented a banquet room in London to allow many people to view the June wedding parade of a royal couple. However, because of an unforeseen blizzard, the couple canceled the parade. Courts would likely excuse you from paying for the room. After all, through no fault of your own, the whole purpose of renting it disappeared.

There are three important rules to have a contract set aside under frustration of purpose. First, the frustration must be substantial—nearly total, and with almost no chance at improved benefit. Second, the change in circumstances must not be reasonably foreseeable. Third, the frustration must not have been your fault.

Q. May someone set aside a contract because it simply is not fair?

A. It is possible, but not likely. Courts have a powerful weapon called *unconscionability* (from the word "conscience") at their disposal. Unconscionability means that the bargaining process or the contract's provisions "shock the conscience of the court." For example, a contract for several thousand dollars of dancing lessons sold to an 85-year-old widow whose sole income was Social Security would likely be held unconscionable. An unconscionable contract is grossly unfair. Its terms suggest that one party had some unfair advantage over the other one when they negotiated it. The courts are reluctant to use this weapon. However, consumers—especially in installment contracts—have a better chance with it than anyone else.

The example given above is an instance of *substantive unconscionability*. The very substance of the agreement is so outrageous that nobody in his or her right mind would agree to such an arrangement. There is another kind of unconscionability—*procedural unconscionability*. Here one party is unfairly surprised by what the contract means. The contract's legal language or fine print deceived that person. This type of unconscionability might not "shock" the courts, but they still might, in certain circumstances, set the contract aside.

The important thing to remember is that you should not rely on unconscionability in making a contract. Though courts sometimes will void contracts on these grounds, especially if they are consumer contracts, the application of unconscionability is uncommon and uneven. You should not depend on a court giving it to you as a possible "out" when agreeing to a contract containing terms you do not fully understand. It also is unconscionable to let someone take advantage of you.

PRACTICAL CONTRACTS

Q. Are form contracts worth reading?

A. Believe it or not, it pays to read them. Failure to read a contract is not a valid legal defense. Most states have cases

GETTING OUT OF A CONTRACT

A contract may be set aside if competent parties had not made it voluntarily. It also may be set aside if there was not sufficient consideration. In addition, certain contracts must be in writing, or they are also unenforceable. Here is a list of other contract defenses:

- **Illegality;**
- **Duress;**
- **Undue influence;**
- **Fraud;**
- **Mistake;**
- **Unconscionability;**
- **Impossibility of performance; and**
- **Frustration of purpose.**

If you can prove any of these, they probably will make a contract void or voidable. It is as if there never were a contract. If either party paid money, it has to be given back.

Later, the section on remedies also will discuss the defense of the *statute of limitations*. That takes effect when the time to sue someone on a contractual obligation has run out.

holding that a person is bound by all the terms in a contract, even if one party did not read the contract before signing it. However, this does not apply if the other party engaged in fraud or unconscionable conduct. Do not trust the other party to tell you what it means. Also, be extra suspicious if the salesperson urges you to "never mind, it's not important." (Ask the salesperson, "If it is not important, is it okay to cross out the whole page?") As long as a substantial amount of money is at stake, take the time to sit down with it, and underline parts you do not understand. Then find out what they mean from someone you trust. (See "Where to Get More Information" at the end of this chapter.)

At the same time, you have to be realistic about exercising your right to read a form contract. At the rent-a-car counter at the airport, you probably do not have time to read the contract and get an explanation of the terms you do not understand. Even if you did take the time, who would you negotiate with? The sales clerk almost certainly does not have the authority to change the contract.

Read the Fine Print

Perhaps the most unpleasant part of making contracts comes after negotiating your best deal. It occurs when a salesperson presents you with a *form contract*. It often is one or two pages of tiny print that you could not understand even if you could read it. Even many law school graduates do not know what these pages mean. Unfortunately, the law assumes that you read and, to a reasonable extent, understand any contract you sign.

Q. What if all the time I take to assert my legal rights results in my losing a great bargain?

A. Rarely will a truly great bargain not be there tomorrow. It is a cliché, but remember: If it sounds too good to be true, it probably is. For all the great deals that work out fine, the one you will remember is the one that went sour. It will be the one when they socked you with the fine print you did not bother to read. You are unlikely to have a great bargain fall into your lap anyway. That requires a lot of footwork, research, and comparison.

Q. What can be so dangerous in fine print?

A. Very often the fine print contains more terms that could greatly affect your personal finances than the actual deal would lead you to believe. It often may contain details about credit terms and your right to sue if there is a problem.

Q. What may I do about the fine print?

A. First, try to read it. Often if you sit down with it, sentence by sentence, you will find that you can understand a lot more than you expect. This is especially true in states that have passed "plain English" laws. They require that consumer contracts use clear, easy-to-understand words. The trick is not to be intimidated by the salesperson, your spouse's eagerness to complete the transaction, or the fine print in the contract.

Q. If I understand it but do not like it, must I follow the contract?

A. No, every part of a contract is open for negotiation, at least in theory. Just because the salesperson gave you a form contract does not mean that you must stick to the form. You may cross out parts you do not like. You also may write in terms that the contract does not include, such as oral promises by a salesperson. (Make sure that all changes to the form appear on all copies that will have your signature.) That does not mean the other side has to agree to your changes. You have no more right to dictate terms than they do. However, if you get a lot of resistance, take a hard look at who you are dealing with. This is especially true if they resist your request to get oral promises in writing.

Q. What if I come across "legalese" that I just cannot figure out?

A. Until you understand every important term in a contract, do not sign it. Legalese most often occurs in contracts that include some type of credit terms. An example occurs when you buy something on installment payments. The chapters on consumer credit and automobiles explain many of these terms. If you still have questions, ask someone you trust (not the salespeople) to explain the terms to you. That could be someone experienced with the kind of contract you are considering. It also might be a state or local consumer agency. (See "Where to Get More Information" at the end of this chapter.) Or, if the deal is big enough, ask a lawyer.

Q. Are there any laws that protect consumers against the use of confusing language?

A. Yes, several such laws exist. Many states now require plain English consumer contracts. Also, many of the most confusing contract clauses (sections) now must be written in a specific, standard way—with precise, standard terms. In certain states, the law requires some of this language. Federal law requires other language throughout the U.S. An example is the Truth in Lending Act (TILA). It requires that credit grantors provide certain information. Finally, the rule dealing with *contracts of adhesion* protects you.

Q. What are contracts of adhesion?

A. These are contracts that give you little or no bargaining power. This often is the case in many of the form contracts discussed above. The law protects you, the consumer, from

Get It in Writing

When dealing with a written contract, a court will almost always treat the contract's terms as the final, complete contract. The court will not even consider oral promises that are not in the contract. This protects both parties, since they know that once they sign the contract, it sets the terms.

Do not be swayed if the salesperson orally promises you an extended warranty, or a full refund if not completely satisfied. Get it in writing.

confusing or misleading language in contracts of adhesion. It protects you by interpreting such language in the most favorable possible way for you. This does not mean that you also will get the benefit of the doubt in the plain language in a contract of adhesion. It only applies to confusing or unclear clauses.

Like the doctrines of unconscionability and fraud discussed earlier, this rule is not something to depend on prior to signing a contract. Rather it is a possible strategy that you and your lawyer may choose if a problem arises.

SPECIAL TYPES OF CONTRACTS

Leases

Q. Is a lease a contract?

A. Yes, it has all the elements of a contract explained earlier. It is a contract involving something someone lends you for a specified time, for a specified fee. There are two main kinds of leases. The first involves real-estate leases, such as for an apartment (discussed more fully in the "Renting Residential Property" chapter). The second includes all other kinds, such as leases for office equipment, vehicles, and so forth.

Q. What should I look for in a lease?

A. These leases, usually on preprinted forms with very few blanks, often offer little room for bargaining. Hence, it is very important that you understand the terms and are sure you will be able to meet them. That holds true especially for the terms of an *option to buy*. Make sure that the lease states the price at which you will be able to buy the item. The lease may specify the price as a dollar figure or as a percentage of some amount that you should be able to figure out easily. Also be sure that it is a price worth paying.

Q. Why would I lease something instead of buying it?

A. Leases do not require you to invest as much of your money as buying something. Also, equipment often has a short usable life. Once you buy it, you own it forever. However, it could be obsolete after a few years. A lease protects you somewhat

(continued)

READ BEFORE YOU SIGN!

Leases vary widely. Below are explanations of clauses found in a typical pro-landlord lease and in a lease that is more balanced between the rights of landlord and tenant. Leases similar to these are available in many stationery stores. The pro-landlord lease has few rights for the tenant and many tenant obligations; the balanced lease has obligations for both landlord and tenant and rights for both. Whether you are a landlord or a tenant, make sure you read and understand any lease before you sign it.

CLAUSE	PRO-LANDLORD LEASE	BALANCED LEASE
Interest on security deposit	No interest unless required by state law.	Interest at 5% per year.
Return of security deposit	Will return after deducting for tenant's failure to comply with terms of lease.	Landlord required to provide a written statement of repairs done to premises, with receipts.
Condition of premises/repairs	By signing lease, tenant acknowledges that premises are in good repair, except as noted in lease. No specific space provided on lease to write in repairs that are needed.	Landlord expressly warrants that premises are fit and comply with all applicable codes. Space provided for repairs needed and date repairs will be completed.
Limitation of liability/ regulations	Restricts or eliminates landlord's liability for failure to keep premises in repair (e.g., damage caused by plumbing failures or leaks in roof). Landlord not responsible for damage caused by his or her actions or by neglect of his or her duties to keep premises in repair.	No clause waiving landlord's liability.
Default	If tenant fails to pay any part of rent, or breaks any other part of lease, landlord is authorized: to terminate lease without notice; to enter premises without process of law to remove tenant; to possess and sell tenant's property to recover rent owed; and to have a first lien on all personal property of tenant as security.	No comparable clause.
Fire and casualty	Landlord has 30 days to repair damage that makes dwelling unfit for use, or landlord can simply terminate lease.	Tenant has right to terminate lease in case fire or other casualty makes unit uninhabitable.
Confession of judgment	In the event that landlord sues tenant, tenant appoints landlord's attorney to represent tenant in court; tenant waives right to be served and to notice of the suit; tenant confesses judgment (admits to the complaint filed against him by the landlord); agrees to pay landlord's court costs and attorney fees; waives all errors that might be made at trial; waives all rights to appeal; consents to immediate eviction.	No comparable clause.
Option to renew lease	None.	Tenant has option to lease for another period of time, at a stated rent. Landlord cannot arbitrarily refuse to renew lease.
Duty to maintain/ warranty	None (no part of lease says that landlord will make repairs if something breaks during the tenancy).	By warranting that premises are fit and meet code requirements, landlord is promising to keep them that way.
Entry by landlord	Landlord has free access without notice.	Only with 24-hour advance notice, and only for specified purposes.
Additional landlord obligations	None.	Spelled out in detail (e.g., adequate exterminator services for unit, adequate locks, screens, secure mail boxes).
Tenant remedies if landlord does not maintain premises	None.	Tenant has right to hire repairpersons and buy materials, and deduct costs from rent, after giving landlord adequate notice of the need for repairs.
Tenant's right to terminate	None.	Tenant has right to end lease in event of job loss or transfer.

from that. Leases also normally come with service contracts of some sort. A later section will discuss this more fully. The flip side of a lease is that after any number of years of payments, you do not own anything more than you did when you started.

Q. Are there laws designed to protect renters?

A. Yes, most states have laws that protect people who lease real estate. The chapter on rental property discusses them fully. Many states also have laws that require special disclosures (revealing of information) and other protection for people who enter into other types of consumer leases. For now, it is important to know that many states and localities have laws that set certain terms of leases. These laws may even cancel out what the contract states.

Warranties

Q. What is the difference, if any, between a guarantee and a warranty?

A. In law, there is a very fine difference. However, it is one that will rarely mean anything to consumers. The two terms basically mean the same thing. Both words have the same root meaning, "to protect." Each represents obligations on the part of the provider (or imposed on the provider by law). Some warranties deal with the quality of the goods: Will they do a specific job or meet certain specifications? Are they reasonably fit for their intended purpose? Other warranties might deal with the ownership of the goods: Does the seller have good title that he or she may transfer to the buyer?

Federal law (the Magnuson-Moss Act) covers written warranties for merchandise costing more than $15. It does not *require* that merchants make written warranties. However, if they do make such warranties, the law requires that the written warranties meet certain standards. The warranty has to be available for you to read before you buy. It must be written in plain language, and must include the following:

- The name and address of the company making the warranty;
- The product or parts covered;
- Whether the warranty promises replacement, repair, or refund, and if there are any expenses (such as shipping or labor) you would have to pay;
- How long the warranty lasts;
- The damages that the warranty does *not* cover;
- The action you should take if something goes wrong;

- Whether the company providing the warranty intends to use any specific informal (out-of-court) methods to settle a dispute; and
- A brief description of your legal rights.

Consider all these warranty terms when you shop. The terms of a warranty are seldom negotiable. This is especially true for terms about the length of the warranty, whether it covers only parts or certain problems, and what you must do to use your rights. However, the price or other aspects of the warranty may be negotiable.

Some states have warranty laws that provide consumers with greater protection than does the federal warranty law.

Q. What is the difference between a full warranty and a limited warranty?

A. A full warranty is a promise that the product will be repaired or replaced free during the warranty period. State and federal laws require that if the *warrantor* (the company making the warranty) repairs it, the company must fix it within a reasonable time. It also must be reasonably convenient to get the product to and from the repair site. Many stores will offer a short (30 to 90 days) full warranty of their own, above what the manufacturer offers. A limited warranty covers less. It usually covers only parts, and almost never the cost of the labor to replace the parts.

Q. What are express and implied warranties?

A. *Express warranties* are any promises to back up the product that a warrantor expresses either in writing or orally. Suppose your friend bought your Edsel and you said, "I guarantee you'll get another 10,000 miles out of this transmission." That is an express warranty. This type of warranty is not an opinion about quality or value, such as, "This Edsel is the best used car on sale in town." Rather, it is a specific fact or promise.

A warrantor does not express *implied warranties* at all—they are automatic. There are two main types of implied warranties: The implied warranty of *merchantability* and the implied warranty of *fitness for a particular purpose.*

Q. What is the implied warranty of merchantability?

A. When someone is in the business of selling a specific kind of product, that item must be good for the purpose for which it was intended. This would not apply to someone buying your used car, unless you were a used-car salesman. Then, under normal circumstances, you would have a duty to sell only cars that run.

WARRANTY SENSE

The best-made products usually have the best warranties. That is because they're less likely to need them. Therefore, the manufacturer can guarantee a long period with little risk. The warranty is a statement about the maker's confidence in its products. Because it involves the manufacturer's pocketbook, it is a statement you should take seriously. Figure the value of a warranty into the price you are paying. Make it part of your formula for buying.

Q. What is the implied warranty of fitness for a particular purpose?

A. It means that any seller—even a nonprofessional —guarantees by implication that an item will be fit for the purpose for which you are buying it. However, in order for this to apply, you must let the seller know the special purpose you have in mind. Even when you sell your used Edsel to your friend you make this warranty. Suppose your friend told you he needed a car that could be driven, fully loaded, up steep hills in the snow. When you sell the Edsel to your friend knowing this, you have made a warranty that it will do that. On the other hand, if your friend tells you he is buying your car only because he needs spare Edsel parts, you may sell your Edsel to him whether it runs or not.

Q. How long do implied warranties last?

A. It depends on the type of product involved and your state law concerning statutes of limitations. In some states, implied warranties may last for up to six years. In other states, the period may be much less. The terms of the contract sometimes will determine the length of the warranty. An example is a new-car warranty that runs for four years or 40,000 miles, whichever occurs first.

Q. May a merchant disclaim a warranty?

A. Not after you have made the purchase. However, before you buy, both unwritten express and (in most states) implied warranties may be disclaimed *if* the disclaimer is in writing. If it is part of a contract, the disclaimer has to be obvious. Also, the word "merchantability" often must appear in any disclaimer of the implied warranty of merchantability. However, the implied warranty of fitness for an intended purpose may be disclaimed merely by a written statement that the seller is selling the product "as is." Many states forbid this and other types of warranty disclaimers. A person may not disclaim an express warranty that is in writing.

Q. Is disclaiming a warranty common?

A. No, it is unusual. More often, a seller will offer a warranty, but the contract that the seller has you sign will provide the remedy. This avoids having to disclaim warranties while still protecting the seller, at least to some extent. For example, the contract may provide that the seller will repair or replace the merchandise, if necessary, but that the customer has no right to get back any money. This protects the seller against the worst-case scenario (having to give back money) while still protecting the buyer.

Q. Do guarantees provided in the law ever overrule the guarantees contained in a warranty?

A. Yes, they do, and *lemon laws* provide a good example. These laws exist in many states to provide extra guarantees to people who have been unlucky enough to buy cars so bad that they fit the definition of a "lemon." (See the "Automobiles" chapter for details on lemon laws.)

Q. Most warranty limitations exclude consequential damages. What are consequential damages?

A. *Consequential damages* are damages that the product's defect causes. They also are your time and expense in getting the product fixed. A later section on remedies will discuss this more fully. So if your new home computer breaks and destroys weeks of work, you may get a new computer. However, because of the wording in the warranty that came with the computer, the warrantor usually will not reimburse you for the lost work or software programs.

Q. What about extended warranties or service contracts?

A. Both of these will cost you extra. You must take a hard look at the cost and ask if the benefits are worth what the company providing the warranty or service contract is asking. Consider what you are getting compared with what your regular warranty offers. Find out where you will have to take or send the product for repairs. Also look, especially in service contracts, at whether there is a deductible amount. For example, the contract might not cover repairs costing less than $50. The deductible amount, or a per-repair flat fee, can add up to erase all the expected savings. Sometimes it pays to wait until after the warranty has expired before deciding to buy a service contract. Then you have a sense of a product's reliability.

Finally, take a good look at who is backing up the contract or warranty. Is it a well-known manufacturer? The store that sold it? Or a company you have never heard of with only a post-office box for an address?

Q. How may I protect my warranty rights?

A. First, keep your receipts through the warranty period. They are your proof of when the warranty period starts and ends.

Read Warranties Before You Buy

Do not wait until a product needs repair to find out what is covered in the warranty. Compare the terms and conditions of the warranty *before* you buy. Look for the warranty that best meets your needs.

There are several points to consider. How long is the warranty, and when does it start and end? Will the warranty pay 100 percent of repair costs? Does it cover parts but not labor? What kinds of problems are covered? What do you have to do? And when? Are regular inspections or maintenance required? Do you have to ship the product to the repair center? If so, who pays for shipping? What about a loaner? Who offers the warranty—the manufacturer or retailer? How reliable are they?

The receipts are more important than the warranty return card. (That card often is just a marketing device to learn more about you.) Also remember that any violation of the manufacturer's operating instructions probably will void the warranty.

If a problem arises, try the store where you bought the item. It may be able to go around the warranty process, especially if it is very soon after your purchase. If you end up contacting the manufacturer, do so only as instructed in the warranty. Keep a list of whom you have spoken or written to and when. It is a good idea to contact the manufacturer in writing, keeping copies of all correspondence, at the address specified in the warranty. That is especially true if you are not getting quick responses. It will protect your warranty rights near the end of the coverage period. For more details, see the section on contract remedies later in this chapter.

Advertising

Q. An earlier section said that store advertisements are not usually offers. Are there any exceptions to this?

A. Yes, exceptions do exist. Suppose a store advertises that it will give a free gift or a special discount to "the first 100 customers" or something like that. It may be anything that requires special effort on your part. If so, the store has made an offer, which you may accept by being among the first 100 customers.

Q. What is false advertising?

A. *False advertising* is an unfair method of competition forbidden under federal law and in most states. The advertiser's intent is not important. The overall impression conveyed is what counts.

False advertising misleads about a product's *place of origin, nature* or *quality,* or *maker*. An example of misleading about a product's place of origin is putting French labels on sweaters made in Texas. Promising first-quality socks and delivering irregulars or seconds is misleading about an item's nature or quality. Claiming an Edsel is a Mercedes is misleading about a product's maker. As for services, false advertising would mislead you into thinking that someone has qualifications (such as being a master carpenter) that the person actually does not have.

Q. How exact do advertisements have to be?

A. They must be accurate about material (substantial) parts of the product or service in the offer. It is no crime to sell a dress that looks better on a fashion model in an ad than on a normal person. It also is legal to prepare a food product specially to make it look more tempting on television than at home. If an advertisement led you to expect green file cabinets and you got gray ones, the ad almost certainly did not materially harm you.

Q. What about contests and investment schemes?

A. The rule is this: Any contest or get-rich-quick scheme that requires you to part with money probably is a losing proposition. Often these are "pyramid schemes." Someone may notify you either by mail or over the phone. The promoter will promise you some crazy return on your money, telling you of real people who made a bundle in the scheme. It is true, they did get a lot of money. However, they did it in violation of postal regulations. That is a federal crime. The only way you could do the same is to con a large number of people to make the same mistake you did. The courts have held these scams—and any promotion that promises an unrealistic return—to be false advertising and postal violations.

Q. What is "bait and switch"?

A. The bait is a newspaper ad luring you with the promise of an unbeatable deal on an appliance. The switch occurs when you walk into the store (or invite the salesperson to your home or to a meeting at another place, such as a restaurant). The salesperson tells you that the advertised model is not available, but a much more expensive model is. The salesperson has "switched" you from the one you wanted to buy. This practice is illegal in most states if the advertised model was never available. You have a right to see the model that appeared in the newspaper ad. If the store is "fresh out of them," it also may be guilty of false advertising. Do not let someone talk you into buying a model you cannot afford.

Door-to-Door Sales

Q. What are the problems in door-to-door sales?

A. Most people feel secure in their homes. Ironically, that feeling makes them especially vulnerable to door-to-door salespeople. That is especially true of homebound people, such as the elderly or invalids. You have few facts by which to judge a door-to-door salesperson. There is no manager, no showroom, and no immediate way to assess the company that the salesperson represents.

Q. Do any laws protect purchases made as a result of door-to-door sales?

A. Most states now require a "cooling-off period." It usually lasts for three days. During that time, you may cancel purchases you make from someone who both solicits and closes the sale at your home. (Sometimes this applies only to credit purchases.) You do not have to give any reason for changing your mind. Also, the three days do not start until you receive formal notice of your right to cancel. Federal law allows you to cancel almost any sale not made at a fixed place of business. Examples are sales made at your home, someone else's home, or a motel. Federal law extends this cooling-off period to both credit and noncredit sales. It also forbids the company from charging you any cancellation fee. (Some state laws allow such fees.) The more protective federal law will apply to most sales.

Q. What if you do buy from a door-to-door salesperson?

A. Federal and state laws require such salespeople to provide you with the following details on your receipt:

- The seller's name and place of business;
- A description of the goods and services sold;
- The amount of money you paid, or the value of any goods delivered to you; and
- Your cooling-off period rights (see above).

Also, if the salesperson makes the sale in Spanish or another language, you may have the right to all the above details in that language.

Q. What happens if I cancel my order during the cooling-off period?

A. State laws usually will require the salesperson to refund your money, return any trade-in you made, and cancel and return the contract. The salesperson has ten business days to do this under federal law. You must make the goods available to be picked up during that period. Under federal law, if the salesperson waits longer than 20 calendar days, you may be allowed to keep the goods.

Q. What about a door-to-door home repair sale?

A. Do not believe anyone who supposedly has some leftover asphalt, shingles, or other material from a nearby job. That person will offer you a sweet deal to fix your driveway, roof, or whatever. Make your home repairs when you are ready. Also, do so only with contractors you know how to reach if there is a future problem. (See the section below on home repairs.)

Buying by Mail

Q. How long does a mail-order company have to deliver goods that I ordered?

A. According to federal law, the goods must be in the mail within 30 days of your order. If they are not, you must at least have received a letter informing you of the delay and of when to expect delivery. The seller also has to offer you a refund within one week if you do not want to wait any longer. The exception is goods that you understand not to be available until a certain time, such as magazines or flower seeds. Many states have laws that protect you even more.

Q. May the company send substitute goods to me?

A. Yes, but you do not have to accept them. You may send them back and ask for a refund. If you keep them, you have to pay the usual price, unless the company offers them for less.

Q. What about unordered merchandise I receive in the mail?

A. Federal law requires the sender of an unordered item sent through the mail to mark the package "Free Sample." (The law permits charities to send you Easter Seals, greeting cards, and the like, and ask for a contribution.) Consumers who receive unordered merchandise in the mail should consider it a gift. They have no obligation to pay for the merchandise, and they may keep it. Sending you a bill for such merchandise may be mail fraud. That is a federal crime. Report such practices, or any harassment to force you to pay the bill, to the Postal Service and your state consumer protection bureau. However, make sure you, or a family member, did *not* order the item in question.

Q. Does the same rule apply to merchants?

A. No, this rule does not cover them. A merchant who receives unordered merchandise from a supplier does not have to pay

Catalog Purchases

Shopping through catalogs has grown tremendously in the last few years. It has been a blessing for consumers with little time to browse in stores. However, there occasionally are some drawbacks, including delays in receiving orders, uneven customer service, and inconvenience if repair or replacement is necessary. In addition, the possibility of fraud exists, since it is hard to assess the company without seeing a showroom or salespeople. Try to find established merchants that have been in business for at least a few years. Placing an order for an inexpensive item is a good way to check a company's performance before investing in more costly merchandise. Payment by credit card also is highly recommended—it usually makes it easier to resolve disputes.

for the merchandise. However, if the merchant does something, like selling the merchandise, showing that the merchant is willing to buy it, then the merchant must pay for it.

Pets

Q. What may I ask about a pet before I buy it?

A. You have a right to ask about the pet's health, family history, training, and medical care, both normal and unusual.

Q. Do states have pet laws that cover an owner's rights?

A. Many states do have such laws. If your state does not, then general warranty laws apply.

Q. It seems as though I do have protection when buying a pet, like when buying a defective product. Is that correct?

A. Generally, that is true. If you unknowingly buy a sick or injured pet, you probably have a right to a replacement or a refund. Suppose a seller advertises that a pet is purebred or specially trained. If you buy that pet, you have a right to rely on that information.

Q. What should I do if my pet purchase does not satisfy me?

A. Immediately notify the seller *in writing, keeping copies for yourself.* Keep all contracts, papers, and even the original advertisement, if there was one. If you have not received a replacement or refund within 30 days, consider filing a small claims lawsuit. Do not worry about becoming an expert on pet law. The judge will likely base a decision on the fairness of the case, not on technicalities.

Home and Home Appliance Repairs and Improvements

Q. Does the law protect consumers who need home repairs or improvements?

A. Yes, many laws apply to this area. The Federal Trade Commission concerns itself with this area. Federal

Buying Sick or Injured Pets

Suppose you buy a pet, and it turns out that this pet is sick or injured. Legally, what may you do? The answer may depend on whether you bought the pet from a pet shop or a private owner. It also may depend on whether you had a written contract, and what express and implied warranties exist under your state's laws. It also might depend on whether you bought this pet for a specific purpose, like breeding it for competition. In general, it is best for you and the seller to sign a written agreement about your pet. This will clarify most of a new owner's questions.

Another way of avoiding problems is to ask the seller for the name of the pet's veterinarian. Ask the vet for an opinion on the pet's health. This may alert you to potential problems before you complete the purchase.

truth-in-lending laws also come into play. To a certain extent, the states regulate this area, too. Thus, your protection partially depends on where you live. Generally, home repair contractors may not mislead you in any way to get the job. (This is the same as in any other contract.) Be aware of these tricks:

- Promising a lower price for allowing your home to be used as a model or to advertise their work;
- Promising better quality materials than they will use (beware of "bait and switch" as well);
- Providing "free gifts"—find out when you receive them, or try to get a price reduction instead;
- Not including delivery and installation costs in the price;
- Starting work before you sign a contract, to intimidate you;
- Falsely claiming that your house is dangerous and needs repair;
- Falsely claiming that the contractor works for a government agency; or
- Offering you a rebate or referral fee if any of your friends agree to use the same contractor.

Q. How may I protect myself?

A. Get several written estimates. Check into a contractor's track record with other customers before you sign a contract. Do not pay the full price in advance, and certainly not in cash. Do not sign a completion certificate or receipt until the contractor finishes the work to your satisfaction—including cleanup. Once you sign, you may have signed away many rights.

Q. Are there special things to look for in a home-improvement contract?

A. Yes, be sure the contract has all the details in writing. Too often a contract of this type will read "work as per agreement." Instead it should include who will do the work, a description of the work and materials to be used, and the dates of starting and completion. It also should contain all charges, including any finance charges if you are paying over a period of time. In addition, the contract should include the hourly rate on which the total cost is to be based. Be sure the contract has any guarantee in writing. Beware of any mortgage or security interest the contractor takes in your home. A security interest means that you may forfeit your home if you do not pay for the work. (If the contractor takes a security interest, federal law gives you three days to change your mind and cancel.) Consider having a lawyer look at the contract. If problems do arise that threaten your rights to own your home, see a lawyer immediately.

CONTRACTS AND CONSUMER ISSUES

THE TOP TEN CONSUMER PROBLEMS

The state of New Jersey's Office of Consumer Protection has published a list of the ten most troublesome consumer problems in that state. The list also includes basic advice for each problem, which surely exists in every state.

(1) Fly-by-night home repair contractors (as discussed previously in this chapter).

(2) Telephone solicitations. Always ask the caller to send written information. Also, determine your total obligation before agreeing to anything. Do not give your credit-card information to strangers over the telephone.

(3) Furniture delivery delays. Do not take "ASAP" (as soon as possible) as a delivery date in a sales contract. Get an exact date. If the

(continued)

Q. What about appliance repairs?

A. Much of what the "Automobiles" chapter discusses about car repairs applies to home appliance repairs. You can best protect your rights by getting a written estimate. At least make sure you get an oral estimate before work begins. Ask how the repair shop will figure the total charge, including parts and labor. Also, tell the repair shop to get your approval before beginning work. It will then be able to give you a better idea of how much the repair will cost.

Q. How can I determine whether is it no longer worth fixing a major appliance?

A. When deciding whether to repair or replace, consider these points:

- The appliance's age and likely life span after this repair, compared with that of a new appliance;
- How the repaired appliance will compare with a new appliance in operating costs and efficiency;
- The length of the warranty on the repair, compared with the warranty on a new appliance; and
- The price of a new appliance compared with the cost of the repairs.

Buying Clubs

Q. What is a buying club?

A. There are several different types of buying clubs. One of the more popular kinds is a record or music club. It offers five or ten records, tapes, or compact discs (CDs) to you for an initial nominal price. You might pay only a nickel or a dollar, plus postage and handling. In return, you agree to buy a certain number of records, tapes, or CDs at the regular club price over a period of time. Note that the "regular club price" is much higher than the initial price. It also often is higher than normal retail store prices. However, the average price usually works out to your benefit. The problem with these clubs is that they automatically send you a record, tape, or CD every month or so. Before shipping the item, the club sends you a special notice warning of the upcoming shipment. The only way to prevent the automatic shipment is by returning the notice before the date on the notice.

Q. If you do not send back the cancellation notice, isn't that a case of considering silence an acceptance of an offer?

A. No, because you already agreed to that arrangement when you joined the club. You are not making a new contract each month.

Q. So should I avoid these clubs?

A. You may not necessarily want to avoid them. You may want to meet your additional-records (or tapes or CDs) obligation quickly and then quit the club. Also, the clubs do offer many incentives to try to keep you as a member. These may be worthwhile to you. However, suppose you forget to promptly return the monthly notice that stops the shipment of the latest selection. Then you will receive unwanted records, tapes, or CDs, and you will be obligated to pay for them.

Q. What about merchandise clubs?

A. The idea behind these is that you pay a fee in order to qualify for discounts. The club presumably obtains these discounts because of its volume buying power. Before joining one of these, take a good look at what it promises. Will it limit you to certain manufacturers? Are catalogs easily accessible? Buying clubs often appear on lists put out by state attorney generals' offices and consumer protection agencies. Check with them first.

Funeral Homes

Q. What is the Funeral Rule?

A. This federal law requires mortuaries or funeral homes to give you prices and other information you request over the telephone. This helps prevent corrupt funeral home operators from requiring you to come to their showrooms, where they can prey on your weak emotional state.

Q. Does the Funeral Rule require anything else?

A. If you visit a funeral home, it must give you a written list with all the prices and services offered—including the least expensive. You can keep this list. You have the right to choose any service offered, as long as it does not violate state law. If it does, the funeral home must give you a copy of that state

(continued)

(continued)

merchandise does not show up by that date, you have the right to cancel.

(4) Free vacation offers. An example is the postcard telling you about a "free vacation" you have won. Just call a toll-free number and "confirm" your credit-card number. Later the vacation is not as free as you thought. Play it safe—book your travel arrangements through a reliable agent or directly with travel carriers.

(5) "Bait and switch" tactics (see the above "Advertising" section).

(6) Mail-order rip-offs. When shopping by mail, you are always taking a risk. When the offer sounds too good to be true, it probably is.

(7) Work-at-home schemes. Usually aimed at young mothers and the

(continued)

SAMPLE COMPLAINT LETTER

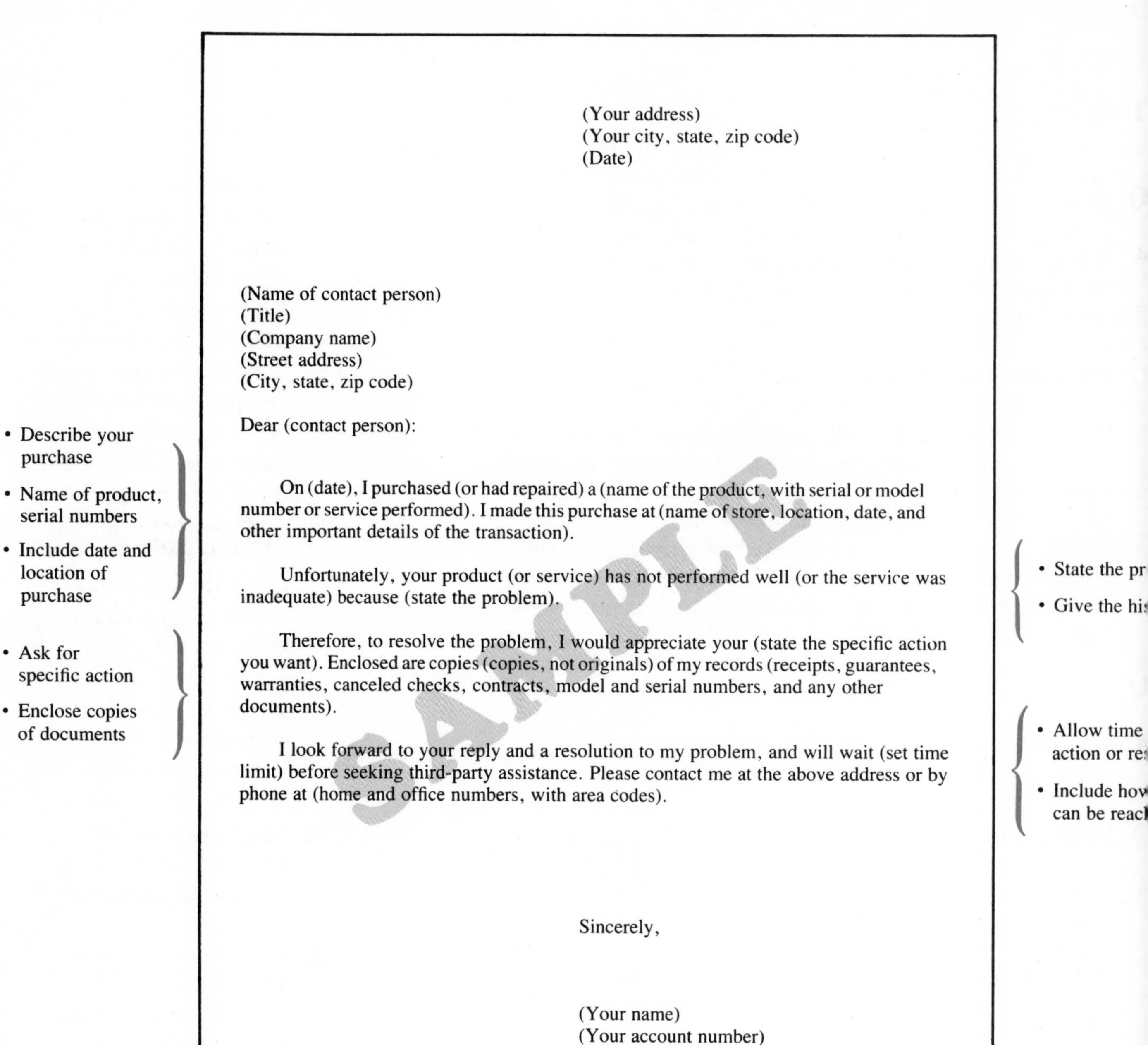

(Your address)
(Your city, state, zip code)
(Date)

(Name of contact person)
(Title)
(Company name)
(Street address)
(City, state, zip code)

Dear (contact person):

On (date), I purchased (or had repaired) a (name of the product, with serial or model number or service performed). I made this purchase at (name of store, location, date, and other important details of the transaction).

Unfortunately, your product (or service) has not performed well (or the service was inadequate) because (state the problem).

Therefore, to resolve the problem, I would appreciate your (state the specific action you want). Enclosed are copies (copies, not originals) of my records (receipts, guarantees, warranties, canceled checks, contracts, model and serial numbers, and any other documents).

I look forward to your reply and a resolution to my problem, and will wait (set time limit) before seeking third-party assistance. Please contact me at the above address or by phone at (home and office numbers, with area codes).

Sincerely,

(Your name)
(Your account number)

• Keep copies of your letter and all related documents

Source: U.S. Office of Consumer Affairs

law. The funeral home must reveal any fees charged for outside items, such as flowers. The Funeral Rule also entitles you to an itemized list of all charges you incur. The general idea of the Funeral Rule is that the funeral home must inform you of your options every step of the way. (For more details, see "Where to Get More Information" at the end of this chapter.)

Travel

Q. Is overbooking by hotels a violation of my contract?

A. It is if you have paid in advance. Otherwise, the reservation is just a "courtesy." Therefore, it is often worth it to pay for a hotel reservation by credit card when you make it. If you cancel within a couple of days of the reservation, you probably will get a complete credit. Also, many premium credit cards guarantee their patrons' hotel rooms to a certain time if you use their card to reserve it. Contact the credit-card company if the hotel does not honor your reservation. If your room is still unavailable then, speak to the manager. You could have a contract claim. However, it probably will not be worthwhile to pursue it legally because of the cost. Perhaps the best advice is to request that the hotel arrange suitable alternate accommodations for you.

Q. What about an airline bumping me off my flight?

A. Generally, even if you have prepaid, you do not have a contract to go at a certain time. You only have a contract for a ticket to go to a certain city. However, that does not mean that you have no rights. Federal regulations require that if you get bumped against your wishes, the airline must give you a written statement. This must describe your rights and explain how the airline decides who gets on an oversold flight and who does not. Travelers who do not get on the flight often are entitled to an on-the-spot payment as compensation. The amount depends on the price of their ticket and the length of the delay. However, there is no compensation if the airline can arrange to get you on another flight that is scheduled to arrive at your destination within one hour of your originally scheduled arrival time. If the substitute transportation is scheduled to arrive more than one hour after your original time of arrival (but less than two hours from it), the airline must pay you an amount equal to the one-way fare to your final destination (with a $200 maximum). You are entitled to more money if your arrival is further delayed.

These rules have exceptions and conditions. "Fly-Rights" is a pamphlet published by the U.S. Department of

(continued)

disabled, these schemes promise to help you "Earn money in your spare time." They will ask you for $20 in "start-up" costs. What you will get is information about how to rip off someone else the way they just cheated you.

(8) Absence of contract cooling-off periods (see the above "Door-to-Door Sales" section). Federal law only protects you if you sign the contract in your home or somewhere other than the normal place of business. Do not depend on this—think before you sign.

(9) Health spa memberships. Most complaints center on high-pressure sales tactics. A year's membership can cost quite a bundle. Make sure you will use it. Also, get all promises in writing.

(continued)

(continued)

(10) Time-share lures. People often buy time-sharing vacations on impulse. Be sure you are ready to go to the same place during the same period of time for years to come. If the time-sharing resort (or condominium or whatever) is not fully built, make sure all occupancy dates are in the contract. Review these contracts with a lawyer. High-pressure time-share sales pitches have led to a federal law giving consumers some protections. The federal Interstate Land Sales Full Disclosure Act gives you the right, in some circumstances, to get out of a time-share contract.

Transportation. It contains a full discussion of this and other areas of airline law. It is available from the Superintendent of Documents, U.S. Government Printing Office, Washington, D.C. 20402. The pamphlet costs one dollar. The order number is 050-000-00513-5.

If you are just delayed, not bumped, ask the airline staff to find out what services they will provide. Ask about meals, telephone calls, and overnight accommodations.

You can complain to the Federal Aviation Administration if you think an airline has abused you. However, write to the airline first. Airlines often are responsive to consumer complaints.

Q. How may I protect myself when paying for charter tours?

A. Your money often takes a twisting route to the tour operator. This leaves you vulnerable to many different stops that exist in-between. The tour operator's brochure usually will specify the name of an escrow bank account where all payments eventually go. Make out your check to that account. Also put the destination, dates, and other details on the face of the check. This should guarantee that the payment goes where it should go. It gets you your money back if the tour is canceled or if the tour operator or travel agent goes out of business. Your contract is with the tour operator.

Often, the travel agent will insist that the check be made out to the travel agency. This is because the policy of some agents is to write a single check to the tour operator themselves. In that situation, get a written guarantee from the tour operator and the agency. Reputable agents and operators should be willing to stand behind the tour.

You also can protect yourself by getting trip insurance. This guards you if you have to cancel the trip because of your illness or an illness in the immediate family.

BREACHES AND REMEDIES

Breach of Contract

Q. What is a breach of contract?

A. A breach of contract is one party's failure, without a legal excuse, to live up to any of his or her responsibilities under a contract. A breach can occur by:

- Failure to perform as promised;
- Making it impossible for the other party to perform; or

- *Repudiation* of the contract (announcing your intent not to perform).

Q. What qualifies as a failure to perform?

A. One party must not have performed a *material* (important) part of the contract by a reasonable (or stated) deadline. A breach is important depending on the intent of the parties. Suppose your friend made a quick handwritten contract. He promised to buy your Edsel for $1,000, and to pay you "some time early next week." It would be a material breach for your friend never to pay you. However, if your friend paid you on Thursday of the next week, it probably would not be a breach. Neither of you made time an *essential* part of the contract.

Q. How is a contract breached by making performance impossible?

A. Suppose a woman hires a cleaning service to clean her house on Saturday at a rate of $90 for the day. She goes out for the day, neglecting to make arrangements to let the cleaning people into her house to clean. The homeowner has breached by making performance impossible. She would owe the money since the cleaning service could not clean and because the service probably turned down requests to clean for other clients.

Q. What if something or someone partially breaches a contract?

A. That happens when a nonmaterial (unimportant) part of the contract gets breached. It may happen if the contract has several *divisible* parts, each of which you may treat as a separate contract. Then you could sue for damages even though there is not a total breach. An example of this would be agreeing to perform a duty once every three months for one year, and then not performing for the final three months.

Q. What is a breach by repudiation?

A. Repudiation is a clear statement by one party *before* performance is due that the party cannot or will not perform a material part of that party's contract obligations. Suppose that the day before your friend was to pick up the Edsel that you promised to sell to him, you sent your friend a message that you decided to sell the car to someone else. That would be repudiation. It also would be repudiation if your friend

WHAT IF SOMETHING HAPPENS?

Now you know how contracts should work, and how to avoid the more troublesome kinds of contracts. However, what happens when something goes wrong?

A significant violation of a contract is a *breach*. A *remedy* is how you can go about repairing a breach, or getting paid back for the loss it causes. This section discusses breaches and remedies.

heard from another reliable source that you sold the car to someone else. (There would be no reason to believe that you would get it back to sell to your friend tomorrow.)

It is not repudiation if one party will not perform because of an honest disagreement over the contract's terms.

Remedies for Breach of Contract

Q. What are the main types of remedies for a breach?

A. When someone breaches a contract, the other party is no longer obligated to keep its end of the bargain. From there, that party may proceed in several ways:

- The other party may urge the breaching party to reconsider the breach;
- If it is a contract with a merchant, the other party may get help from local, state, or federal consumer agencies;
- The other party may bring the breaching party to an agency for alternative dispute resolution;
- The other party may sue for damages; or
- The other party may sue for other remedies.

Q. What is the point of getting the breaching party to reconsider?

A. One advantage is that it is cheap. Often the only cost is the price of a phone call and a little pride. The breaching party may have breached the contract because of a misunderstood communication from you. Perhaps the breaching party just needs a little more time. Or maybe you could renegotiate. That could still leave both of you better off than if you went to court. If you do hire a lawyer, the first thing that lawyer is likely to do is try to convince the breaching party to perform.

Q. Should I keep records of my communications with a breaching party?

A. Yes, once you see you are in for a struggle, make a file. Keep copies of any letters you send. Move all receipts, serial numbers, warranty cards, and the like to this file.

Q. Assuming the breaching party does not budge, what else can I do?

A. If the dispute is between you and a merchant, you might want to contact the manufacturer of the product. If it involves a large chain of stores, contact the management of the chain. This goes for services, too.

If that does not help, contact a consumer protection agency, either in your city or state. The Federal Trade Commission (FTC) is less likely to get involved in small disputes. However, if the FTC believes that what happened to you has occurred to many people nationwide, the FTC's involvement carries a lot of weight. Another federal resource is your local post office. There you may report any shady business practices that took place through the mail.

Q. What about private agencies and groups?

A. Chambers of commerce may be able to help. Other business groups often have industry grievance panels in which the merchant may participate. You also might try consumer groups, such as the Better Business Bureau. You might try broadcast and print media "action lines."

Q. If these methods do not work, what else can I do short of filing a lawsuit?

A. The first and second chapters discuss many different types of alternative dispute resolution systems, such as arbitration.

Take a look at the contract. Very often it will include a specific type of alternative dispute resolution that you must use. The contract might forbid you (or the other party) from going to court.

Stopping Payment

Q. What if I want to cancel a contract or void a purchase that I made, but I already paid with a check?

A. First, you should call the seller and ask for a cancellation of your contract and the return of your check. If the seller will not do this, you may call your bank and "stop payment" on that check. Remember, you still are liable for the check. You may be sued by the seller for its amount. The suit may succeed unless you have a legal defense.

Q. Isn't stopping payment on a check a criminal act?

A. No, it is not the same as having insufficient funds to cover the check. (That may have criminal penalties attached.) Stopping payment on a check is your legal right.

GETTING OUT OF A CONTRACT

This chapter has tried to emphasize that it is more important to recognize when people have actually made a contract than to plan for a breach of contract. Sometimes, though, someone will breach a contract with you. Or, you will find yourself in a position where you have to breach a contract. It is not always a "bad" thing to do, as long as you are ready to take your lumps. Sometimes the price you pay, through any of the remedies for breach, is less damaging than performing a contract that has just become a big mistake.

Remember, though, that a contract does represent your pledge. If you want to be known for keeping your word, you will take your contract commitments seriously. You may wish to do so even if you do not profit each time.

Q. How do I stop payment on a check?

A. You need only call your bank. A bank representative will take the information about the check that they require, and then send you a form to confirm your wishes in writing. You must return this form within a certain number of days. If you fail to do this, the bank may not honor your original request. And if you do not provide all the information your bank requires, your stop payment order might not be good. The bank also will charge you for this service, usually $10 to $20. Do not try to avoid this by reducing your bank balance so the check will not clear. Other checks you have written may not be paid. The bank might even pay the check you do not want to be paid as an overdraft in the belief that the bank is accommodating you.

Q. Is there anything else that I should do after I place the order to stop payment?

A. You could inform the seller of your action. However, the law does not require you to notify the seller.

Q. What if the seller has already deposited the check in a bank account?

A. If the check has not cleared your account, your bank may still put through the stop payment order. If your bank has paid the check, your options probably will involve trying to avoid the contract in other ways already discussed.

Q. What if I am dissatisfied with goods or services that I have paid for with a credit card?

A. Then the Fair Credit Billing Act may provide some important protections. Under the Act, products that you refused to accept on delivery or that were not delivered according to an agreement qualify as billing errors. The same is true of shoddy or damaged goods or poor-quality service. The Act may allow you to withhold payment or to get back your money, if you have already paid. See the "Consumer Credit" chapter for more details.

Suing for a Breach of Contract

Q. What is the most common remedy for a breach of contract?

A. The usual remedy for breach of contract is a suit for damages. The main kind of damages awarded in a contract suit are *compensatory damages*. This is the amount of money it would take to put you in as good a position as if there had not been a breach of contract. The idea is to give you "the benefit of the bargain."

Q. What is an example of compensatory damages?

A. Suppose you hired a contractor to paint your house for $500. It is really a $650 job, but you are a good bargainer. Now the contractor regrets agreeing to the $500 price and breaches. If you can prove all the facts just stated, you can recover $150 (or whatever the difference is between $500 and what it cost you to have your house painted).

Q. What other kinds of damages are there?

A. The most common ones include:

- *Nominal damages,* awarded when you win your case but you have not proved much of a loss. The court may award you a small amount as a matter of course.
- *Punitive damages,* available if the breaching party's behavior was offensive to the court. In most states, punitive damages may not be recovered in a breach of contract action. However, it may be possible to get punitive damages under a special law or if the suit is for fraud.
- *Liquidated damages,* the amount of which both parties built into the contract. Although one or both parties have effectively breached the contract, this term will stand, as long as it fairly estimates the damages. The courts will not enforce a *penalty clause*. That is an amount of liquidated damages that is way out of line with the actual loss.

Q. Are there other remedies in a contract suit besides damages?

A. Yes, the main one is *specific performance*. That is a court order requiring the breaching party to perform as promised in the contract. Courts are very reluctant to award this because it is very awkward to enforce. Courts usually will impose specific performance only if there is no other remedy available because of the contract's unique subject matter. The most common examples involve the sale of real estate or a unique piece of personal property (such as a "one-of-a-kind" item or an antique). After all, you cannot merely "substitute" one piece of land for another. Although personal services are unique, courts will rarely force someone to work for someone else against his or her will.

LAWSUITS AS REMEDIES

This section will discuss the different kinds of relief you can ask a court for, considering what you have already learned about contract defenses.

Remember: ***Any time one side can prove one of the contract defenses discussed in the second section, there is no breach of contract because there is no contract.*** **Then the party that does not or cannot perform merely has to pay back any money or return any goods transferred in the agreement.**

Q. What else can a court do?

A. A court may *rescind* (cancel) a contract that one party has breached. The court may then order the breaching party to pay the other side any expenses incurred. Or, the court could *reform* the contract. That involves rewriting the contract according to what the court believes the parties actually intended.

Q. If I have a contract for services or goods with a company that goes out of business, what may I do?

A. Suppose another firm bought the company, as in a corporate merger. Then you should ask if the new company is taking responsibility for the contract obligations of the old company. If the new company is responsible, your worries are over.

If the company truly is in critical financial condition, your chances of recovering anything of value are small. If you have a contract that still is in force with a troubled company, you may have to go elsewhere to get what you need. If the cost of replacing the goods or services you have lost under the contract is high, you have a right to sue the old company, its representatives, or both, if you still can find them.

Q. I realize that I may have to get goods from another company. What about any money the first company may owe me under the contract?

A. If the company is in bankruptcy, you may file a claim against it through the bankruptcy court. You will have to "stand in line" with the other creditors, and you may get only a small percentage of what the company owes you, if you recover anything at all. Suppose the business is a corporation that is dissolving legally, through the proper state agencies (usually the secretary of state). Then you may file a claim against the corporation through the state agency for any losses you have accumulated. Whatever assets remain will be divided according to the number of claims filed.

Q. If the financially troubled company is holding goods for me on layaway, may I still get my goods?

A. Most companies that go out of business will notify people that they are closing. Such companies will want you to come and finish the purchase because they will need the cash flow. If they have tried to contact you and you have not responded, they may sell those goods, and you will have no way to recover the merchandise. However, the law still entitles you to any money you may have paid toward the purchase.

Q. If the merchandise is gone and I have paid money, how may I recover that money?

A. If the store still is open, it probably will pay you when you present your receipt for payments made toward the purchase price. If the store has closed, you might need to file a claim in the bankruptcy court or with the proper state agency, as described above.

Q. What do I do about merchandise that was under warranty? Who will cover it now that the company has gone out of business?

A. If you have purchased a national brand of goods, there probably will be a service center or a licensed warranty center in your area. However, it may not be as convenient for you as the seller's store. Almost all manufacturers will stand behind their products regardless of where you purchased them. The only drawback is that you may need to present an original receipt to show that the manufacturer's warranty still covers the product. Such warranties usually cover a product for only a very limited time.

Q. I also purchased an additional retailer's warranty when I bought my goods. It extended the manufacturer's warranty. What will this extra retailer's warranty cover?

A. Retailers usually offer this warranty to extend parts and labor for a much longer period of time than the manufacturer offers. Unfortunately, the retailer's warranty is useless since the place that made the promise is now out of business, unless the obligations of the company have been taken over by another company.

CONCLUSION

This chapter has discussed how to make a contract and how to find out if you have unknowingly made a contract. It also covered some special consumer contract issues, how to identify a breach of contract, and what to do about a breach. Yet this has merely scratched the surface of this highly complex area of law. It has not even dealt in detail with the millions of contracts made every day between merchants and other businesses. While many common contracts do not require the services of a lawyer, be aware of when legal assistance may help avoid serious problems in the future.

WHERE TO GET MORE INFORMATION

You can use many sources to find out about consumer rights. In most states, a state agency, often the attorney general, has an office of consumer affairs and protection. In some states, the secretary of state has such an office. These offices are good starting points. This is true both for filing complaints and for free literature on consumer protection. These offices appear in your telephone directory under the state government listings. You also might call any state governmental information number.

Don't forget federal agencies as well. An example is the Federal Trade Commission if you have been subjected to a deceptive practice.

State and local bar associations often publish free pamphlets and handbooks on legal problems. They also can provide lists of lawyers who handle consumer cases.

The local Better Business Bureau (BBB) can be very helpful. It can help settle claims against a merchant.

Many larger television stations or newspapers have "action lines." These services follow up on complaints. They often get results in exchange for being able to use your complaint on the air or in the paper.

The federal government publishes helpful handbooks for consumers. They are available for little or no charge from the Consumer Information Center-N, P.O. Box 100, Pueblo, Colorado 81002. These handbooks include:

Consumer's Resource Handbook. This publication lists many contacts to help with consumer problems. Phone numbers, addresses, and specific contact people are given for corporate consumer offices, private dispute resolution programs, Better Business Bureaus, trade associations, and car manufacturers. It also lists federal, state, county, and city government agencies that help consumers. The handbook tells how to avoid purchasing problems and how to write effective complaint letters. 100 pages. (1990) Publication 569W. Free.

Lista de Publicaciones Federales en Español para el Consumidor. It lists over 100 free federal consumer publications printed in Spanish. Eight pages. (1989) Publication 572W. Free.

Consumer Guide to the FTC Funeral Rule. This pamphlet discusses your legal right to facts about the prices and options of funeral services. Six pages. (1984) Publication 457W. 50 cents.

Telemarketing Travel Fraud. This handbook tells how to check out those "free" trips and bargain vacations. It also discusses how to protect yourself from common scams marketed by telephone. Three pages. (1987) Publication 449W. 50 cents.

AUTOMOBILES

BUYING A NEW CAR

Advertising/Sales Practices

Q. What information should an automobile ad include?

A. It varies from one state to another. In some places, the ad must include the number available of that type of vehicle. Other items to look for include price, dealer and factory-installed options, and warranty terms. In addition, if the vehicle is "on sale," the ad should state the date the sale ends.

Q. What if the dealer fails to disclose defects?

A. Suppose the dealer knows of important facts, but fails to reveal them. The law may consider that as a deceptive act. It may enable you to cancel the deal and even recover damages in court. Clearing up the missing facts later does not erase the dealer's deceitful act. (For more information, see the "Lemon Laws and Other Consumer Protection Statutes" section that appears later in this chapter.)

The New Car Contract

Q. Must a car contract be in writing?

A. Yes, according to the Statute of Frauds of the Uniform Commercial Code (UCC). It says any sale of goods of $500 or more must be in writing and signed by the party against whom enforcement is sought. The courts are not permitted to enforce an oral contract in this instance, if the contract is challenged.

Q. Who signs the sales contract?

A. Besides you, either an authorized salesperson or a supervisor or manager signs it. *Before* you sign, make sure you

"BAIT AND SWITCH" ADS

"Bait and switch" is advertising a vehicle that the dealer does not intend to sell. The dealer does this to lure the unsuspecting customer toward buying an unadvertised, often higher-priced vehicle. The ad draws the customer into the showroom. However, the car is not available at that time or stated price. If you suspect that you have been the victim of such advertising, contact the consumer protection division of your state attorney general's office.

TERMS THAT THE CONTRACT SHOULD INCLUDE

The sales contract should describe the car and include the vehicle identification number (VIN). You can find it on the driver's side of the dashboard near the windshield. The contract also should state whether the car is new, used, or has had a previous life as a demonstrator, rental car, or taxicab. In addition, the contract should include price terms consistent with your oral agreement, and details on any trade-in that you will supply, including mileage and the dollar amount credited. Insist on a cancellation provision that also enables you to get your deposit back. The contract should state the warranty terms very clearly. (See the "Warranties" section of this chapter.) The contract's financing terms should state price, deposit, trade-in allowance, annual percentage rate (APR), and length of term.

understand and accept all the contract terms. Usually, you just abide by a contract you have signed, even if you have not read it. Read the contract carefully. Ask questions. Cross out blank spaces to avoid any additions after you sign. Make sure that all the dealer's promises appear in the contract. Do *not* sign until the contract satisfies *you*. The contract you sign binds you, and escape from the contract is both difficult and expensive.

Q. May I change a seller's preprinted contract?

A. Yes, if the seller agrees. If you do change terms, cross out the unwanted language. Then write or type the substitute terms. Both you and an authorized dealer representative should initial the changes. Handwritten or typed changes to a printed contract overrule printed terms.

Q. May I cancel the contract even after I sign it?

A. It depends. Suppose you were a minor when you signed it (under 18 in most places) and you contracted with an adult. Then you are permitted to cancel the agreement at any time for any reason while still a minor. You also have the right to do so within a reasonable time after reaching the age of majority. You may do this as long as the car is not a "necessary" item (food or clothing are necessary items). The law protects inexperienced young people from being bound by bad deals with tricky adults. Most car dealers know this rule, however, so they will avoid contracting with a minor. These dealers will insist that the car be bought by, or in the name of, a financially responsible adult.

Q. How else may I get out of the contract?

A. If, for example, the car you buy is not what the dealer promised, the dealer may have breached its warranty. (See the "Warranties" section in this chapter.) If so, then you might attempt to cancel the contract because of the breach. Or you might try canceling for no reason. However, you risk losing your deposit. The dealer also might file a lawsuit to recover lost profits, for time spent with you and on your car, and other damages.

Q. If we wind up in court in a contract dispute, may I offer other information?

A. The court, under the *parol evidence rule,* probably will ignore any terms that are not in your document. (Courts might consider additional terms that explain or supplement, but do not change the contract's meaning.) Generally, though, the court confines itself to the "four corners" of the document that you present. The court assumes that both parties read and understood the contract before signing it. Also, the court disallows prior terms that vary from or contradict the contract. You may be able to present evidence of an oral agreement made after the written agreement. In addition, you are permitted to present outside facts to prove that there actually was no contract or to prove that fraud caused you to sign.

Q. What if I want to add something after I sign the contract?

A. Ask the dealer to write a contract addendum (a supplement), or write it yourself. Both parties should sign it. Make sure that whoever signs for the seller has the legal power to do so. Mention the original contract in the addendum, and attach the two documents together. In the addendum, state that everyone should consider it an inseparable part of the original contract and that the addendum overrides any inconsistent terms in the two documents. This will help you avoid the parol evidence rule discussed above.

What Happens to Your Deposit if You Cancel the Contract

If you cancel the sales contract, what happens to your deposit depends on the stage of the transaction and on the contract terms you signed. The earlier in the deal, the more likely the dealer will refund your deposit and the less likely you will be sued. Some states entitle you to a refund if, for example, you decide to cancel before the dealer representative signs the contract. Some states also allow you to get a refund if you cannot get financing, despite your best efforts, provided the contract is subject to getting financing.

Bank Loan Versus Dealer Financing

Q. What if I do not have enough cash to buy my new car, even after my trade-in?

A. Then you need financing. Banks, credit unions, loan companies, and car dealers are all potential funding sources. Interest rates will vary among these options. Shop around for the best deal. Do this by comparing the various loan terms and annual percentage rates (APRs). For further information on comparing terms and APRs, see the "Consumer Credit" chapter.

Q. What must the creditor tell me?

A. The creditor must inform consumers of:
(1) The annual percentage rate (this must be obvious, for example, printed in red or in much larger type than the rest of the document);
(2) How the creditor sets the finance charge;
(3) The balance on which the creditor computes the finance charge;
(4) The finance charge amount (this also must be obvious);

(5) The amount to be financed;
(6) The total dollar amount that will be paid; and
(7) The number, amount, and due dates of payments.

Q. What if the creditor does not follow the rules?

A. Creditors who disobey the rules may have to pay you any actual damages that you have sustained. They also may have to pay a fine based on the finance charge, and court costs and lawyers' fees. If someone files a class-action lawsuit, the penalty could be much larger.

Q. What is the maximum APR that I have to pay?

A. That depends on the laws of the state in which you live or where the deal occurs. The states allow different maximum APRs, depending on their "usury" laws. Remember, an APR is negotiable, though a creditor may not exceed an upper limit.

Title

Q. When do I get title to my car?

A. In most states, in any sale of a car—new or used—title passes when the previous owner endorses the certificate of title or ownership over to the new owner. Check with your local Department of Motor Vehicles for the law in your state.

Q. Suppose I sign the contract, but do not yet have title. What if something happens to the car?

A. The answer depends on who has the risk of loss. Usually, the party who possesses the vehicle bears the risk and is more likely to have insurance against the loss. Under the UCC, if the seller is a merchant (for example, a car dealer), the risk of loss passes to buyers when they receive the car. If the seller is not a merchant, as in a private sale of a used car, the risk passes to the buyer on *tender of delivery*.

Q. What is "tender of delivery"?

A. Tender of delivery occurs when the seller actually tries to deliver the car, or makes the vehicle available for a pick-up arranged by a contract.

Making Sure a Creditor Treats You Right

The Truth in Lending Act (TILA) protects consumers. Congress passed it in 1969. TILA ensures that consumers get enough facts to enable them to make an informed decision about financing. It applies to consumers who seek credit for money, property, or services for personal, family, or household purposes. (TILA does not cover business, commercial, and agricultural credit. It also does not apply to financing that exceeds $25,000.) Creditors, either people or organizations, who regularly extend consumer credit that is payable in more than four installments are subject to the Act. The same is true when a creditor requires (or may require) a finance charge.

Q. What if I have title but the dealer still has the car?

A. A merchant seller who keeps physical possession may bear the risk of loss long after the title has passed and after the dealer has received payment.

Q. May the risk of loss move from the seller to me?

A. Yes, the UCC provision governing risk of loss allows this. A sales contract that specifies when the risk of loss passes will override the UCC provision.

Q. How may I lose title?

A. You may lose title if you fail to make your payments as they become due. The creditor is then permitted to repossess your car.

Q. So if I do not pay, may the secured party take my car?

A. Yes, the secured party is permitted to take the car. The only limitation is that the repossessor does it without breaching the peace (the creditor can come and get the car if its agents do not cause property damage like breaking the garage door). In many states, the creditor does not have to sue the debtor. In these states, the creditor does not even have to notify the debtor of the default before reclaiming the vehicle.

Q. What is a breach of the peace?

A. A breach of the peace generally is any act likely to produce disorder or violence, such as an unauthorized entry into your home. If you protest strongly enough when a repossessor appears, it may create a breach of the peace, and any repossession may be invalid.

Q. What happens after the repossession?

A. Eventually, the creditor has the right to resell. However, before that happens, the debtor has the right to buy back, or redeem, the collateral.

Q. How does redemption work?

A. The debtor must pay the entire balance due, plus any repossession costs and other reasonable charges. Watch out

The Right to Repossession

By agreement, the debtor may give the creditor rights in the debtor's property that overrule other creditors' rights. This agreement gives the creditor a lien on some of the debtor's property. Then if the debtor fails to pay, the creditor may try to take the property and apply it to the payment of the debt. In car-loan jargon, the consumer purchaser becomes the *debtor*. The creditor (for example, the bank) becomes the *secured party,* and the new car is the *collateral*. The bank has a security interest in the car. The security agreement signed by the parties creates this security interest.

for consumer credit contracts containing acceleration clauses. These force the debtor to pay the entire outstanding debt, not just the overdue payments. Because a default and repossession have already occurred, it is unlikely that the debtor will have enough money to pay the entire balance.

Q. What if I do not redeem the car?

A. The UCC gives the creditor two choices. First, it may sell the car to satisfy the debt. If the profits from the sale are not enough to pay expenses and satisfy the debt, you would be liable for the difference. The only limitation placed on the creditor by the UCC is that the sale be "commercially reasonable." In some states, that means first getting court permission to hold a sale. The sale may be public or private. However, the creditor must give you reasonable notice of the time, place, and manner of the sale. If it is a public sale, you have the right to take part. If the sale produces too much money, the creditor must pass that along to you.

Q. What is the second choice?

A. The creditor may keep the car to satisfy the debt fully. The law refers to this as *strict foreclosure*. There is no duty to return excess money in a strict foreclosure. Creditors seldom use it, because car dealers want to sell, not keep, cars.

Used Vehicles

Buying and selling a used car has some unique features, but it is similar to buying a new car. The advertising rules are largely the same. So you must still beware of "bait and switch" ads that look too good to be true.

Basically, the law about forming and executing the contract for purchase or sale is the same for new and used cars. The car's title transfers via the same mechanism. Lenders may examine the purchase a little more closely to ensure they receive adequate collateral for their money. However, the procedure for getting the money does not change. Also, if you fail to pay, you lose.

BUYING OR SELLING A USED CAR

Q. What is a used vehicle?

A. It is a vehicle that was driven farther than the distance necessary to deliver a new car to the dealer or to test drive it.

Dealer Versus Private Sale

Q. Should I buy from a dealer or a private seller?

A. Go with whoever gives you the best deal and with whom you are most comfortable. Some experts believe you may be better off buying from a private seller. They think a private seller may give a more accurate description of the car's faults based on personal knowledge. You may get a lower price from a private seller. Private sellers, however, seldom give warranties, which dealers sometimes offer. (See the "Warranties" section in this chapter.) Also, some states have regulations governing used car sales that may apply only to dealers.

Q. Do I need a written contract if I buy from a private seller?

A. If you are paying more than $500, you should have a written contract. Courts cannot enforce an oral contract to sell a car for over $500 under the Statute of Frauds. Even under $500, it is always best to put the contract in writing if you are not going to conclude the deal immediately with a Bill of Sale (see next question).

Q. Do I need to get anything else in writing?

A. You should have a Bill of Sale. Many states require you to present a Bill of Sale to register your car. A Bill of Sale also may serve as a receipt. The Bill of Sale should state the amount paid and in what form (cash, check, and the like). It also should give the car's make, model, year, and vehicle identification number (VIN). The seller should sign and date the Bill of Sale.

Q. What is the Buyers Guide, and what must it say?

A. The Federal Trade Commission requires dealers to post a *Buyers Guide* on the side window of each used car. The Buyer's Guide includes a warning that spoken promises are hard to enforce, and it suggests that the buyer get all promises in writing. The Guide defines the term "as is," which is a commercial term denoting an agreement that the buyer shall accept delivery of the goods (the car) in the condition in which they are found on inspection before the purchase, even if they are damaged or defective. The Guide also lists the terms of any warranties provided. In addition, it supplies details about service contracts. The Guide suggests that the buyer have an independent mechanic inspect the car. Finally, it identifies major mechanical and safety systems, along with their recurrent (reappearing) problems in used cars.

Q. Are there other facts that a seller must tell the buyer?

A. The seller, whether a dealer or a private individual, should be truthful about the car. Suppose the car disappoints the buyer because it is not as described or does not perform as it should. Then a breach of warranty action may arise against

Special Rules for Used Car Dealers

The Federal Trade Commission has issued a Used Car Rule for dealers. Under the rule, "dealers" are those who sell six or more used cars in a 12-month period. The rule forbids used car dealers from misrepresenting the mechanical condition of a used car or any warranty terms. It prohibits them from representing that a car comes with a warranty when none exists. They must make available the terms of any written warranty they provide. Also, they must post a "Buyers Guide" on the side window of the car.

the deceitful seller. If possible, the seller should provide the buyer with the car's complete service records.

Q. Does the seller have to tell the buyer the car's mileage?

A. Yes, federal law entitles the buyer of a used car to receive a mileage disclosure statement from the seller, even if the seller is not a dealer. On request, the seller must give a signed written statement to the buyer stating the odometer reading at the time of transfer. The statement also should certify its accuracy, to the seller's knowledge. If the seller knows it is incorrect, the seller must admit it. Refusal to provide such a statement, or illegally tampering with the odometer, exposes the seller to stiff penalties.

Inspection Before the Sale

Not only are you *allowed* to take the car to your own mechanic for inspection before the sale is final, but you *should.* The Buyers Guide sticker, which applies to used car dealers, urges you to do so. Suppose the seller, whether a dealer or a private party, will not allow your mechanic to inspect the car. Then do not buy the car unless it is such a good deal that you will not mind paying for car repairs later.

Seller Withdrawing from the Deal

Q. May I get out of a contract to sell my used car?

A. The same contract laws that govern a new car purchase also cover a used car purchase. Again, it depends on the stage of the contracting process and on the contract's language.

Q. May a court force me to sell my car to a buyer after I have decided I do not want to sell?

A. Probably not. A court usually will not force a buyer to make a purchase or a seller to sell an item. If the car is an antique or unique in some way, however, the court may order the seller to perform the contract. Because the buyer cannot reasonably find a substitute for *this* car, the seller will have to take the money, and the buyer will get the car.

LEMON LAWS AND OTHER CONSUMER PROTECTION STATUTES

Q. What must I do to make lemon laws work for me?

A. First, you must notify the dealer of the defect. Second, you should keep a copy of *every* repair or service receipt you are

(continued)

States with Major-Defect Legislation (Lemon Laws)

Currently, 45 states and the District of Columbia have some form of "lemon law."

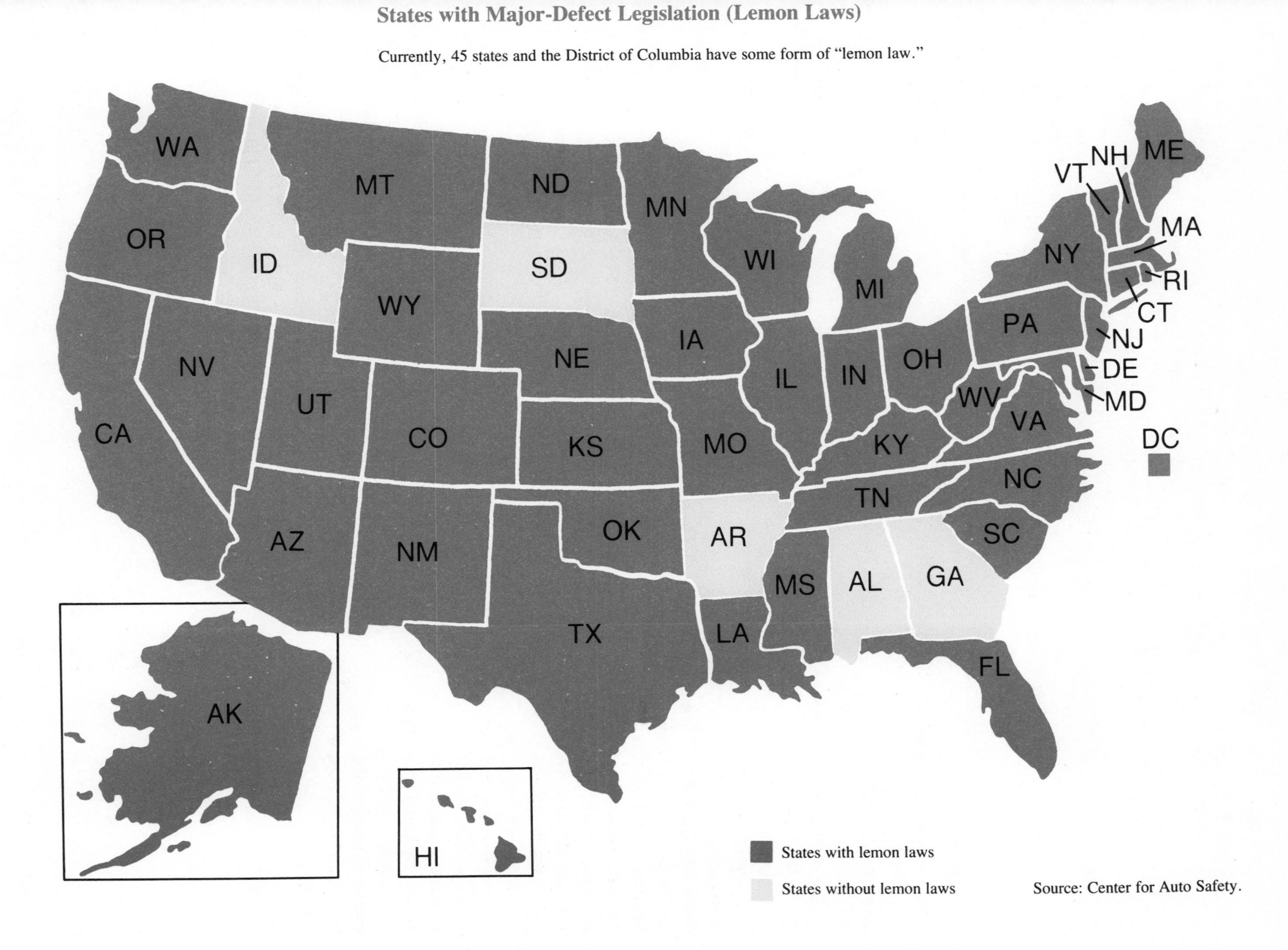

Source: Center for Auto Safety.

Lemon Laws

What can you do if the car you just bought is a real "dog"? Or what if the car you purchased is in the repair shop almost as much as in your garage? To protect consumers from such situations, most states have passed some form of "lemon laws." They usually apply to new cars purchased for personal, family, or household use. These laws entitle you to a replacement car or a refund if your new car is so defective that it is beyond satisfactory repair by the dealer. You must, however, give the dealer a reasonable opportunity to repair the car.

(continued)

given. This is especially important if your car's defect must be repaired at another garage or in another city because it was physically impossible to drive the car back to the seller's repair location.

Most states require that you go through an arbitration procedure before you can get a replacement or refund. Some states sponsor arbitration programs. Most manufacturers also run these programs. Arbitration is usually free, and results often are binding only on the manufacturer. Some states require arbitration only if the manufacturer refuses to give you a satisfactory replacement or a refund. You also may have the option of bypassing arbitration and going directly to court.

Q. Do lemon laws cover used cars?

A. Yes, they cover used cars in a growing number of states. In some places, the law applies both to dealer and private seller purchases. The laws may have a connection with the safety inspection sticker requirement. (See the "Inspections" section later in this chapter.) These sticker laws usually protect you if two conditions occur. First, the car must fail inspection within a certain period from the date of sale. Second, the repair costs must exceed a stated percentage of the purchase price. Then you are permitted to cancel the deal within a certain period. You probably will have to notify the seller in writing of your intention to cancel, including your reasons. You must return the car to the place of sale even if it requires towing. If the seller offers to make repairs, you can decide whether to accept the seller's offer or get your money back.

Q. What if the used car passes the safety inspection but still turns out to be a lemon (by requiring costly repairs or repeated repair attempts for the same problem)? Is it still considered a lemon?

A. It might pass the safety inspection and still be a lemon. Some state laws define "lemon" for used cars the same way they do for new cars—by using a formula of repair attempts/time-spent-in-the-shop. These laws protect buyers of used lemons in much the same way as buyers of new lemons. (See the previous questions and answers for details.)

Q. What if I drive the car during this period?

A. The law usually allows the seller to deduct a certain amount as a use allowance per mile driven from the money refunded to you. This applies to both new and used car sales.

Other Consumer Protection Laws

Q. What is an unfair or deceptive practice?

A. The Federal Trade Commission (FTC) defines *unfair conduct* as that which, although not necessarily illegal, offends public policy as established by statute, common law, or other means. The FTC further defines it as behavior that is immoral, unethical, troublesome, or corrupt. In addition, the FTC defines unfair conduct as that which substantially injures consumers (or competitors or other businesspeople). *Deceptive conduct* is behavior that could have caused people to act differently from the way they otherwise would have acted. It does not have to involve the product's qualities themselves. However, it may include any aspect that could be an important factor in deciding whether to buy the goods. An example would be stating that the engine has six cylinders when it really has four cylinders. The quality may be fine, but the buyer may have been seeking a car with a six-cylinder engine. The FTC regulations are the basis of many states' laws.

Q. Must the unfair or deceptive act be intentional?

A. No, in most states, the seller does not even have to know about the deception. Rather, the court considers the effect that the seller's conduct might possibly have on the general public or on the people to whom the seller advertised the product.

Q. What must I do in order to use an unfair and deceptive practices statute?

A. In many states, you must make a written demand for relief before you sue. The law allows the seller one last chance to make good. Many states require proof of "injury" before you may recover. Loss of money or property is enough to prove this. You should be able to show that the seller's actions actually caused the injury. Remember to begin the procedure before the statute of limitations expires. This time limit varies by state.

Q. What happens if I win?

A. Many states permit you to recover double or triple damages, and lawyers' fees. The purpose of these harsh penalties is to discourage sellers from committing unfair or deceptive acts in the future.

(continued)

How do you know if the law considers your car a lemon? State laws vary in their specifics. However, a *lemon* normally is a car that continues to have a defect that substantially restricts its use, safety, or value, even after reasonable efforts to repair it. This often means four repair attempts on the same problem or a directly related problem within six months or one year (the time period varies by state). Or, it might mean the car is out of commission for more than 30 nonconsecutive days during either:

(1) The year after the dealer sold it; or

(2) The duration of any express warranty, whichever is shorter.

ADDITIONAL PROTECTION FOR CAR BUYERS

Other statutes protect car buyers besides lemon laws. They include:

- **The federal Anti-Tampering Odometer Law. It prohibits acts that falsify odometer mileage readings.**
- **The Used Car Law requires that dealers post Buyers Guides on used cars.**
- **The Automobile Information Disclosure Act requires manufacturers and importers of new cars to reveal, certain details about the car. These details must appear on a label affixed to the windshield or side window.**

By far, the statutes providing the strongest protection are those prohibiting unfair and deceptive acts and practices. Every state has enacted such a law. Car buyers may recover from the seller (the dealer and/or the manufacturer), regardless of who might have done the deceiving.

WARRANTIES

Uniform Commercial Code

Q. How does a seller create an express warranty?

A. Whenever a seller makes any declaration of fact, description, or promise on which the buyer relies in deciding to make the purchase, the seller creates an express warranty. A seller may create an express warranty orally, in writing, or through an advertisement.

Q. What about the seller's opinion of the car?

A. An opinion or recommendation does not form an express warranty. Sales talk, called *puffing,* will not create an express warranty. An example is, "This car runs like a dream." Statements such as, "This car needs no repairs" or "This car has a V-8 engine," however, will create an express warranty.

Q. When does the implied warranty of merchantability arise?

A. It occurs automatically if the seller is a merchant, such as a car dealer. It requires that the car be of a quality that would pass without objection in the trade. This type of warranty also requires that the car be fit for the ordinary purposes for which the buyer will use it. This warranty essentially provides for the overall quality of the car. Most people agree that this warranty is part of a new car purchase.

Q. How does someone create the implied warranty of fitness for a particular purpose?

A. Suppose you tell the seller that you need the vehicle for a special purpose, such as towing a trailer. Then the seller recommends a specific vehicle that you accept, relying on the seller's skill or judgment. This creates an implied warranty that the vehicle can do what you told the dealer you needed it to do.

Q. What if I bought my car "as is"?

A. Then you accepted the car with all its faults. Any post-sale defects are your problem. A car may be sold "as is" through a dealer or a private person. The implied warranty of merchantability does not automatically arise in "as is" purchases.

Q. Do I get these warranties every time I buy a car?

A. Not necessarily. A seller may disclaim or change warranties. Obvious language that mentions merchantability may exclude or modify the implied warranty of merchantability. An obvious disclaimer in writing may exclude the implied warranty of fitness for a particular purpose. Language such as "sold as is" cancels implied warranties. However, if the seller has given you an express warranty, courts will not uphold any attempted disclaimer that is inconsistent with or cancels the express warranty.

Q. What if the seller gives me express and implied warranties that are inconsistent?

A. According to the Uniform Commercial Code, the parties' "mutual intention" decides which warranty takes priority. If there is no way to decide this, the following rules determine priority:
(1) Specific or technical language usually wins over descriptive language that is inconsistent and general.
(2) Express warranties override inconsistent implied warranties of merchantability.
(3) Implied warranties of fitness for a particular purpose survive other inconsistent warranties.

Remedies for Breach of Warranty

Q. What are my options if the seller will not honor its warranties?

A. If you have not already accepted the car, reject it. You may reject only within a reasonable time after delivery of the car. You also must give the seller details about what is wrong. You only have to show that the car does not, *in some way*, follow the contract. The defect need not be major. You have the option of allowing the dealer to attempt to remedy ("cure") the defects within a reasonable time. Once you reject the car, behave as if you are no longer the owner—do not drive it. You may hold the car for the seller to reclaim, or you may return it yourself.

These steps should enable you to reject the car. However, to take the next step and force the seller to live up to its warranties, you may need to consult a lawyer.

Violations of Unfair and Deceptive Practices Laws

Each statute differs about what actions could violate unfair and deceptive practices statutes. The most common violations include:

- **Hiding dangerous defects;**
- **Failing to state that service is not readily available;**
- **Not revealing that the dealer advertised the car at a lower price;**
- **Odometer tampering;**
- **Failure to reveal that the dealer is charging excessive preparation costs; and**
- **Withholding facts about the car's previous use as, for example, a racing car.**

Generally, a dealer's failure to disclose any important facts about the car, or an attempt to make such facts too hard to see, is illegal.

Secret Warranties

Strictly speaking, a "secret warranty" is not a warranty at all. Rather, it is more in the nature of a deceptive practice. A secret warranty develops when a manufacturer knows that many cars have the same problem, and it tells dealers to charge customers for the repairs unless they complain. The manufacturer hides details about the defect and makes a lot of money from unsuspecting consumers. It is secret because it is an unpublicized policy. If you suspect that a warranty should have covered your car repair or that the defect is widespread, complain to the dealer. Perhaps the dealer will fix your car without charging you. Follow up with a complaint to the consumer protection division of your state attorney general's office.

Q. How do I know if I have already accepted?

A. Unfortunately, sometimes the law considers just driving the car off the dealer's lot as acceptance. This is true as long as you had a chance to inspect the car, even if you do not discover the defect for some time. At most, you have a week or two to reject the car. Acceptance also may occur if you take possession of the car despite knowing about its defects.

Q. What may I do if I have accepted a car that proves to be defective?

A. First, once you have accepted, you must continue to make your car payments. However, you may be able to get your money back later. You may not reject a car already accepted unless you accepted it based on the assumption that the seller would repair the defect within a reasonable period. Your option now is to *revoke* your acceptance. You must give the seller notice of the defect, and show that it *substantially* impairs the value of the car to you. Revocation involves a higher standard than rejection. Different states have various standards. Generally, the defect will have to be major to allow revocation. After revoking acceptance, you must act as if you had originally rejected the car. Leave the car in your driveway until the seller reclaims it, or return it yourself.

Q. May I get my money back if I reject or revoke acceptance?

A. You should be able to recover your money. However, the seller has the right to deduct an amount per mile driven from your refund. If your rejection or revocation is unlawful, the seller may recover damages against you.

Q. May I simply use lemon laws and consumer protection statutes instead of warranties?

A. You may use them all. If you can prove seller fraud or deception, the unfair and deceptive practices statute in your state will help. You could invoke the lemon laws by showing that you tried to get the defect fixed the required number of times. You also could involve the lemon laws if you could show that your car was in the shop longer than the legal minimum before you rejected or revoked acceptance. This may require you to keep your records and receipts.

Q. What is the difference between "limited" and "full" warranties?

A. If a dealer offers a full warranty, it is promising:
- To replace a defective car or part for free, within a reasonable time;
- That the owner will not have to do anything unreasonable to get the repairs done;
- That the warranty applies to anyone who owns the car during the warranty period;
- A refund or free replacement part, including installation, if the dealer cannot fix a car or part after a reasonable number of attempts.

A limited warranty is anything else. At least one of the above promises is missing. Most car dealers do *not* give full warranties on the entire car. However, they may do so on a specific part, such as the battery.

Q. How may I use the Magnuson-Moss Act?

A. First, use all out-of-court remedies, such as arbitration, according to the warranty. If this fails, file a lawsuit. If you can prove that the dealer violated the Act, you may recover damages and court expenses, including lawyers' fees. Remember, you also may try other remedies. These include lemon laws, unfair and deceptive practices acts, and breach of warranty actions.

The Magnuson-Moss Act

The federal government also protects consumers. Congress passed the Magnuson-Moss Act in 1975. It applies to all cars manufactured after 1975 that dealers sell and warrant in writing. It does not cover "as is" sales or cars bought from private sellers. The Act mandates that if the seller gives you written warranties, the seller must conspicuously label them as either "limited" or "full."

RECALLS

Q. What is the recall system?

A. The recall system uncovers defective automobiles that are already on the road. It notifies car owners about how to get them fixed.

Q. What defects does the recall process include?

A. Generally, it includes defects that affect the car's safety or cause it to fall below federal safety standards. The defect can be in performance, construction, components, or materials found in the car or in related equipment, such as child safety seats.

Q. How does the recall process begin?

A. Many recalls result from the manufacturer's response to owner complaints. However, the National Highway Traffic

Safety Administration (NHTSA) influences and orders many of the recalls. The NHTSA receives safety-related complaints through letters and its telephone toll-free hot line. When the NHTSA registers enough complaints, NHTSA engineers perform an engineering analysis. Then the NHTSA engineers contact the automobile's manufacturer, which must show that it launched a formal defect investigation when the engineers found a defect that the manufacturer will not voluntarily remedy.

Q. How is a defect investigation conducted by the automobile's manufacturer?

A. It begins with a press release, and opening a public file to receive comments and information. If this confirms the defect and the manufacturer still will not voluntarily recall the vehicle, agency engineers recommend an initial determination of a safety defect to the NHTSA administrator. If approved, this results in a public hearing and notification to the manufacturer of the basis for the finding. After the hearing, the NHTSA decides if a final defect determination and recall is proper. Occasionally, the NHTSA administrator first seeks the transportation secretary's approval.

What Happens if the NHTSA Orders a Recall?

If the manufacturer refuses to obey voluntarily and challenges the recall in court, it faces a huge fine unless the court overturns the NHTSA order. Once the recall campaign begins, the NHTSA assigns a campaign number and file. During the campaign's first six quarters (year and a half), the manufacturer must report its completion rate based on the number of vehicles actually repaired. The NHTSA may verify these figures.

Q. How effective are recall campaigns?

A. Usually about 60 percent of the vehicles targeted by the recall receive repairs.

Q. Who pays for the recall – the automobile's manufacturer or the owners?

A. The manufacturer must remedy the defect for free. This does not apply when the first buyer bought the car more than eight years earlier. In comparison, the standard for tires is three years.

Q. What must the manufacturer do?

A. The manufacturer has the option of repairing the defect, replacing the car, or refunding the purchase price. If it refunds the money, the manufacturer may deduct a certain amount for depreciation (loss in value). The manufacturer reimburses the dealer who makes the repairs. If the manufacturer chooses to repair the defect, it must do so within a reasonable time. Otherwise the manufacturer must replace the vehicle or refund the purchase price.

AUTOMOBILE LEASING AND RENTING

Requirements

Q. What must I have or do if I want to rent or lease a car?

A. First, you must have a valid driver's license. Some of the major rental and leasing companies set a rental age minimum of 18 and require a major credit card. Other companies rent only to credit-card holders aged 25 or older. The company may waive the age requirement if you have a discount number in your name through a motor club or other association. The same is true if you have a rental account through your business. You must sign a contract when you rent or lease a car.

Q. How does leasing differ from renting?

A. A lease is essentially a long-term rental. Leases usually have a one-year minimum. Rentals may last one day.

Car Lease Contracts

Q. Are there different kinds of leases?

A. Yes, several forms exist. Under the *closed-end* lease contract, the car's value when you return it does not matter unless you have put extreme wear on the car. Payments are higher than under an open-end lease, because the lessor (the leasing company) takes the risk on the car's future worth. An *open-end* lease involves lower payments. However, you gamble that the car will be worth a stated price, the "estimated residual value," at the end of the lease. If its appraised value at the end of the term equals or exceeds the specified residual value, you owe nothing and may be refunded the difference. However, if it is worth less, you pay some or all of the difference.

Q. What will a lease cost me?

A. You probably will have to pay a security deposit and lease fee for the first month and possibly the last. You may pay an initial "capitalized cost reduction." This, in effect, could reduce your monthly payments. Other expenses may include sales tax, title, and license fee, though the lessor may pay them. A lease may include insurance. If not, you must provide your own. You might have to pay for repairs and maintenance after any warranty period expires, unless the lessor agrees to pay in your contract. At the end of the lease term, you may have to pay an excess mileage cost if you have a closed-end lease. (Under an open-end lease, the final appraised value of the car will reflect any excess mileage.) Excessive wear and tear also may cost you.

LEASE OR BUY?

Whether it is better to lease or buy a car depends on many factors. A car lease means lower monthly payments. After all, your installment payment depends on the purchase price minus the car's estimated value at the *end* of the lease term. Thus, your installment payment does not depend on the full value of the car. Leasing usually avoids a down payment and sales tax. There may be tax advantages if you lease mainly for business use. On the other hand, a leased car does not gather any equity (cash value). Buying a car on credit does. Also, you must return a leased car.

Q. May I renew or extend my lease at the end of the term?

A. Yes, if your lease contained this option or you negotiated for it. Such an option may reduce your initial costs.

Q. May I escape my lease early?

A. You have signed a binding contract. That obligates you to make payments for a stated term. Your contract may contain an early termination clause. This usually requires a minimum number of monthly payments. It also may assess a penalty.

Q. What is a purchase option?

A. It allows you to buy the car when your lease term ends. The lessor must state the purchase price or the basis for setting this price in the initial lease contract. Purchase options are more common in open-end leases than in closed-end leases.

Car Rental Contracts

Q. What should my car rental contract include?

A. It should list the base rate for the rental car and any extra fees. The length of the rental period also should appear.

Q. What extra fees could there be?

A. The rental company might offer you the Collision Damage Waiver (CDW) option. The rental company covers damage to your rented car if you accept CDW. However, coverage does not include personal injuries or personal property damage. Before accepting this expensive option, make sure your own automobile, medical, and homeowner's insurance policies do not already protect you in an accident involving a rented car. If traveling on business, your company's insurance policy might cover you. Sometimes, charging rentals on certain credit cards automatically covers you.

INSPECTIONS

States have an interest in your car beyond collecting taxes. They care equally about vehicles meeting minimum safety standards. As a result, many states have an inspection sticker requirement. The number of inspections required in a year vary from state to state.

Q. What exactly does the state inspect?

A. It varies. Most states check the car's lights, brakes, windshield wipers, and horn. Some inspect the tires, windows, body, and seat belts. Many states also test the emission levels, taking into account the automobile's make, model, and age.

Q. What if I am buying a car?

A. A new car should pass inspection easily. Someone other than the seller should inspect a used car. In many states, a used car sale is not final until the car passes inspection. In other states, failing inspection cancels the sale at the buyer's option. Contact your state Department of Motor Vehicles for further information.

Q. Where do I get my car inspected?

A. States often authorize certain private repair shops and car dealers to make inspections. A few states have government-operated inspection stations.

Q. What will happen if my car does not pass the state's safety inspection?

A. Procedures vary, but you may get a "failed" sticker attached to your windshield. You have a grace period either to make repairs or get your car off the road. If you do neither, you could be subject to fines and other penalties.

REPAIRS

Dealer or Mechanic?

Q. Where should I take my car for repairs?

A. You can bring it to a car dealer, which warranty terms may require. Other choices include an independent garage, a franchise operation specializing in specific repairs, or repairing it yourself. Each option has its advantages and disadvantages.

Q. What if I choose a dealer?

A. Dealers may charge more. However, they are more familiar with your make of car than other repair shops. Dealerships may have new and better equipment to service your car. Manufacturers want to ensure that dealerships run quality repair operations, so they invest in training mechanics.

Q. What if I bring my car to a service station?

A. This is a good option for nonwarranty work if the mechanic have adequate training and test equipment. Parts might cost more, but labor might be less expensive than dealer repairs. If you often use the service station, the mechanics get to know your car. Then they may spot potential problems early

Q. What about the highly advertised repair chains?

A. Specialty shops may repair one part of a car, such as brakes or mufflers. Or, they may advertise complete car-care services. Sheer size and volume means lower costs than dealers and independent mechanics. If you know what repairs your car needs, franchise shops can be a good deal.

MECHANIC QUALIFICATIONS

To help determine whether a mechanic is qualified, ask if the National Institute of Automotive Service Excellence (NIASE) has certified the mechanic. A certified mechanic has taken one or more written tests in areas such as engine repair and electrical systems. The NIASE certifies a mechanic who passes *all* the tested areas as a General Automobile Mechanic. Certification is not the final determination. Often, you can discover the best mechanics from friends' recommendations and word of mouth.

The Repair Contract

People often refer to the contract for repairs as a *repair order*. It is essential in getting a satisfactory repair job done on your car. The repair order describes the work that the mechanic will do on your car. Signing it creates a contract authorizing the mechanic to make the described repairs. In many states, if you do not sign the repair order, you do not have to pay for any services done by the mechanic. It also serves as your file record of service and maintenance.

Q. What should appear in a repair order?

A. It should include a description of the problem, along with your name, address, and telephone number. Your phone number is critical should unexpected problems arise. If the mechanic cannot reach you, the mechanic has to decide whether to proceed. Also, the repair order should contain the make, model, car year, mileage, and repair date. The mileage and repair date are important. They verify warranty terms and simplify keeping service records.

Q. Must I receive a cost estimate for the repairs before work actually begins?

A. It is a good idea, and a required practice in some states. In those states, the final cost must not exceed a certain percentage or dollar value of the original estimate without the customer's consent. Repair shops generally have the right to charge for making estimates, but you must receive advance notice.

False and Deceptive Repair Practices

Q. How does the unfair and deceptive practices statute protect me from a repair shop rip-off?

A. As discussed earlier, it requires price estimates and repair orders. Also, many states give you the right to keep or examine replaced parts. Many states require repair shops to prepare a detailed invoice. The invoice must state the labor and parts supplied, warranty work done, guarantees, and installation of any used or rebuilt parts. You may have the right to same-day repairs. This does not apply if you agree to a longer period or the delay is beyond the shop's control. The repair shop must correct shoddy repair work at no charge. This is especially true when the implied warranty of merchantability extends to repair work. Finally, many states require repair shops to post price lists conspicuously. If you think a repair shop has intentionally cheated you, you should notify your state attorney general's office and call your lawyer to discuss possible legal action.

Repair Warranties

The law may entitle you to some repair warranties. If a manufacturer's warranty covers the car or part, you should not have to pay if you satisfy warranty conditions. Beware of "unconditional" guarantees offered by many franchise repair shops. There are always *some* limitations on written guarantees. However, the law protects you if the repair shop makes an express warranty. Some state courts have held that the implied warranty of merchantability covers car repairs.

How a Service Contract Differs from a Warranty

Unlike a warranty, a service contract may not come from the manufacturer. Service contracts are optional and expensive. Often, coverage overlaps warranty protection. A service contract often contains more limitations and exclusions than a warranty. Service contracts may require you to pay a deductible fee. They also might not cover all parts and labor or routine maintenance. The availability of service contracts for used cars must appear on the Buyers Guide sticker. Finally, service contracts, like warranties, are covered by the Magnuson-Moss Warranty Act.

Q. What can I do if the automobile mechanic makes unauthorized repairs?

A. You may wish to sue if, for example, the shop made unneeded repairs or reinstalled the original part rather than a replacement. If the shop tried its best to correct the fault by fixing something that *was* broken, though *not* the problem's ultimate cause, you should pay the shop. After all, the repair shop *did* fix one of your car's problems.

The Mechanic's Lien

Q. What if I do not pay for the repairs?

A. In most states, if you refuse to pay for completed repairs, the shop may keep your car. The car's value and the cost of the repairs do not matter. The so-called *mechanic's lien* favors the repair shop for labor and parts as long as the car remains in its possession. If you do pay for repairs, the repair shop must return your car.

Usually, a repair shop attaches a lien after the owner has authorized extensive work, but decides the car is not worth that much after the shop completes the work. So the owner abandons the car. Then the shop obtains a mechanic's lien so it can recover as much of the cost of repairs as possible. It often does this by selling the car. In states that require written estimates and repair authorization, the mechanic's lien does not attach if the repair shop has not obeyed these formal requirements.

SERVICE CONTRACTS

Q. What is a service contract?

A. A service contract specifically covers car repairs and maintenance for a set period of time. Manufacturers, contract companies, insurance companies, and car dealers offer service contracts.

Q. Should I purchase a service contract on my automobile right away?

A. If you buy one at all, you should consider waiting until your warranty period expires.

POLICE, DRIVING, AND THE LAW

Automobile law changes constantly and the protection for people charged with violations varies by state. However, there are some basic points to remember if the police stop you.

The Stop

Q. What should I do once I realize that the police want me to stop?

A. Pull over to the side of the road as quickly and safely as possible. Get ready to produce your driver's license and car registration because the police may ask to see them.

Q. The police officer is standing by my window. Now what?

A. Stay calm, and politely ask why the police stopped you. Sometimes you may wonder if a real police officer has stopped you. This may be the case if, for example, an unmarked vehicle pulled your car over. Then politely ask to see the officer's photo identification, not just the badge.

Q. May the officer make me get out of my vehicle?

A. Whenever a legitimate stop occurs, the police have the right to ask the driver and passengers to step out of the vehicle.

Q. What will the officer look for on my license?

A. The officer will check to see that the license is still valid. The officer also may question you about your identity if the picture or physical description on your license does not seem to match your current appearance.

The Search

Q. Suppose the officer wants to search my car?

A. Ask why the officer wants to conduct a search. If you have absolutely nothing to hide, it might be best if you let the

SEARCHING YOUR VEHICLE WITHOUT A WARRANT

Whether the police are permitted to legally search your vehicle without a warrant depends on the situation. The U.S. Supreme Court recognizes an automobile exception to the Fourth Amendment's protection against warrantless searches. The Court has held that a person expects less privacy in an automobile than at home. (No one ever said, "A man's Chevy is his castle.") The logic is that the mobility of vehicles would allow drivers to escape with incriminating evidence in the time it would take police to get a search warrant. Therefore, the U.S. Supreme Court allows car searches without warrants. For a warrantless search to be valid, however, the officer *must* have probable cause.

search proceed. Generally, however, the officer is not permitted to conduct the search unless you consent to it or if the officer has probable cause. Ask courteously whether the officer has a search warrant or if you are under arrest. If the officer replies that you are under arrest, ask for an explanation.

Q. What if the officer insists on searching my car?

A. Then do not interfere. You can always challenge the legitimacy of the search later in court.

Q. What is probable cause?

A. *Probable cause,* in this context, is a reasonable basis for the officer to believe that the vehicle contains incriminating evidence and that the police should search it. (See the "Criminal Justice" chapter for more details on this topic.)

Q. What may the police search?

A. The law is always changing. Sometimes state constitutions offer greater protection against searches than the U.S. Constitution. Therefore, it is best to consult a lawyer in you[r] state. Generally, the police officer may search the immediate area at the driver's command. That is the area under and around the front seat. If the officer has arrested the driver, the officer does not need a warrant to pat down the driver's body while looking for weapons.

Q. May the officer look in my glove compartment?

A. Yes, the Supreme Court has held that such a warrantless search is permissible. The reason is that the glove compartment is within the arrested driver's reach.

Q. May the officer search a closed box inside my car?

A. Police are permitted to search containers or packages found during a *legitimate* warrantless search of a vehicle. The container must be one that might reasonably contain evidence of a crime for which the officer had probable cause to search the vehicle in the first place. In 1982 the Supreme Court ruled that the police do not need a warrant to search closed containers found in the passenger compartment of an automobile whose occupant is under arrest.

Illegal Drugs That Are in Plain View

What happens if a police officer sees a packet of marijuana on the back seat of a car? When the police can see evidence readily from a place they have a right to be in, the law does not consider it a search. It is a *plain view seizure*. As long as the officer has a legitimate reason to be standing by the car and easily sees what the officer has probable cause to believe is evidence of a crime, the officer can make the seizure. Then the officer probably could conduct a warrantless search of the rest of the passenger compartment of the vehicle and possibly the trunk (if there is probable cause to believe the trunk may contain evidence).

Q. May the police search my car without a warrant after they have impounded it?

A. The police do not need a warrant to undertake a routine inventory of an impounded vehicle. The reason is that such an inventory protects the driver's possessions against theft, and it protects the police from claims of lost or stolen property. Such an inventory also protects the holding facility from dangerous materials that may be in the impounded vehicle, and it may aid in the identification of the arrested person.

Q. What if the police find evidence or contraband during an inventory search?

A. As long as the search was proper, they can use it against you even though it is totally unrelated to the reason for impounding the vehicle.

Q. May the police pull me over in a roadblock and demand to check my license and registration?

A. The U.S. Supreme Court has said that such roadblocks are not unreasonable searches as long as the police do one of two things. Either the police stop all the cars passing through the roadblock or they follow some neutral policy, such as stopping every fourth car. The police normally may not single out your car. They may do so, however, if they suspect you do not have your driver's license or you did not register your vehicle. The police also may single out your car if you or your car may be subject to seizure for violating the law. (See the "Driving Under the Influence" section in this chapter for more information about roadblocks.)

As with other types of searches, the U.S. Supreme Court is the ultimate judge of what is constitutional. New laws might also change standards for roadblock searches.

Speeding Violations

Q. I got caught in a speed trap. What may I do about it?

A. If the speed limit was plainly visible and you were exceeding it, you must pay the fine. If you think the police have prosecuted you unfairly, you might report the trap to your auto club or state authorities. This might help to spare other drivers the same expense.

Radar Guns

Courts today regularly accept the ability of radar to measure vehicular speeds accurately. Nevertheless, you may try to prove that the operator maintained the radar gun poorly. You also may attempt to show that its operator misread the results or received inadequate training. However, it is an uphill fight to prove one of these points.

Q. May I use a radar detector to avoid speed traps and radar guns?

A. It depends where you drive. Some states have declared them illegal, issuing fines to drivers who use them. In Canada, the police can confiscate the device on the spot.

The Arrest

Q. What do I tell my lawyer if he or she calls while I am in custody?

A. Be ready to tell your attorney where the police have taken you, where the arrest occurred, and if uniformed or plainclothes police made the arrest. Also tell your lawyer the charges against you and the amount of bail you can afford.

What You Should Not Do if the Police Arrest You

Instead of concerning yourself with what you should do if the police arrest you, it is better to discuss what you should *not* do. You should *not:*

- **Speak to anyone about your case except a member of your family or a lawyer;**
- **Answer police questions or sign waivers without a lawyer's advice;**
- **Submit to a lineup or any kind of tests without your lawyer (see the "Driving Under the Influence" section);**
- **Avoid news photographers by covering your face (you will only look guilty); or**
- **Be impolite to the police.**

Driving Under the Influence

Q. How come police never say, "You are under arrest for drunk driving"?

A. Different states call the offense different names. These include driving under the influence (DUI), operating under the influence (OUI), and driving while intoxicated (DWI).

Q. Does the language really matter?

A. Yes, "operating" jurisdictions (those charging OUI), for example, do not require that the vehicle be in motion. Simply turning the ignition switch or being in a position to do so could be enough.

Q. What does "drunk driving" mean?

A. The elements of the offense vary from one state to another. However, the Uniform Vehicle Code says proof is necessary that the person is under the influence of alcohol. It also states that the person must be driving or in actual physical control of a vehicle. If a particular state's law includes language such as "on a public highway" or "intoxicating liquor," the state also must prove that point. Some states treat "driving while impaired by alcohol" as a lesser offense of DWI.

Q. How does the state prove its DWI case?

A. The prosecution relies heavily, sometimes solely, on the arresting officer's testimony about the offending vehicle's operation, the defendant's behavior, and results of field sobriety tests and breathalyzer tests. The officer might say, "The car was weaving over the center line of the highway." In another example, the police might say, "The driver had slurred speech, heavy odor of alcohol, glassy eyes, and could not walk straight."

Q. May the police force me to give a sample of my blood or my breath?

A. No, but there may be unpleasant consequences if you do not let them take such samples. In fact, you may refuse to take the test. But should you? There is no hard and fast answer to that question.

On the one hand, unless you are positive that you have had only one or two drinks, common wisdom holds that it is a good idea to refuse the tests. It generally is harder to convict a driver of drunk driving if no field sobriety or breathalyzer tests are taken.

On the other hand, if you refuse to take a breathalyzer test, your driving license probably will be suspended automatically for a long period of time. In Illinois, for example, it will be suspended for six months.

Every state has "implied consent" laws for chemical testing of intoxication. The law views people who have a driver's license as automatically agreeing to submit to blood, breath, or urine tests to determine whether they are sober.

Q. Suppose I fail the tests?

A. It is not like school. You cannot promise to study harder next time. A skilled lawyer, however, may challenge whether the police administered the tests properly. A lawyer also may dispute whether the tests effectively measure what they intend to. In addition, a lawyer may present qualifying evidence. For instance, a chronic knee injury may prevent you from supporting your weight on one foot.

Q. Do I have a right to have a breathalyzer test if I want one?

A. You probably do not have this right. Several states do give a defendant the right to an independent blood test for alcohol. Massachusetts' highest court, for instance, has held that the right to a blood test cancels any duty to allow the defendant to challenge the accuracy of a breathalyzer reading.

Q. If the breathalyzer hits .10, am I in serious trouble?

A. Not necessarily. A lawyer may show that the machine's operator received inadequate training. An attorney also may prove that the operator's certification has lapsed. In addition, a lawyer may prove that the operator did not maintain the machine well. There also could be other points to consider. Diabetics, for example, have high levels of ketones (a naturally occurring chemical). This could yield false results when people with diabetes are tested.

Q. May I change my mind after declining to take a blood or breath test?

A. The law still considers a change of heart as a refusal so far as it concerns a license suspension. Some states allow drivers up to 90 minutes to decide whether to take the test. It is a good idea to call a lawyer while you are thinking over a decision. However, unless you have a statutory right to a lawyer in your state, you will have to decide whether to take the test fairly soon after being asked to do so.

FIELD SOBRIETY TESTS

Every police department has its own preferred tests. The police may ask you to do several things after you have gotten out of the vehicle. Examples are to stand on one foot for a specified time or walk a straight line. The police also may ask you to touch your nose with your index finger with your eyes closed and head back. In addition, the police may ask you to stare at a flashlight or a pen so that the officer can see how your eyes respond.

Q. Is it legal to design a roadblock to catch drunk drivers?

A. Yes, it is legal if the selection of vehicles to be stopped is not arbitrary and it minimizes the inconvenience to drivers. Courts have upheld such roadblocks as constitutional. States disagree, however, about whether the prosecution needs to show that a roadblock is the least disturbing way to enforce drunk driving laws. Also, some states require that the ranking police officer who supervised a roadblock testify at the offender's trial.

License Suspension/Revocation

Q. What is the difference if the state suspends, cancels, or revokes my license?

A. *Suspension* involves the temporary withdrawal of your privilege to drive. The state may reinstate that privilege after a designated time period and payment of a fee. You also may get back this privilege by remedying the underlying cause of the suspension, such as buying automobile insurance. *Cancellation* involves voluntarily giving up your driving privilege without a penalty. It allows you to reapply for a

(continued)

IMPRISONMENT FOR DRUNK DRIVING

In 42 states imprisonment is mandatory for driving while intoxicated

State	Is imprisonment mandatory?	Mandatory imprisonment after which offense?	Length of imprisonment
Alabama	Yes	second	2 days
Alaska	Yes	first	3 days
Arizona	Yes	first	1 day
Arkansas	No		
California	Yes	second	2 days
Colorado	Yes	second	7 days
Connecticut	Yes	first	2 days
Delaware	Yes	second	60 days
District of Columbia	No		
Florida	Yes	second	10 days
Georgia	Yes	second	2 days
Hawaii	Yes	first	2 days
Idaho	Yes	second	10 days
Illinois	Yes	second	2 days
Indiana	Yes	second	5 days
Iowa	Yes	second	7 days
Kansas	Yes	first	2 days
Kentucky	Yes	second	7 days
Louisiana	Yes	first	2 days
Maine	Yes	first	2 days
Maryland	Yes	second	2 days
Massachusetts	Yes	second	14 days
Michigan	No		
Minnesota	No		
Mississippi	No		
Missouri	Yes	second	2 days
Montana	Yes	first	1 day
Nebraska	Yes	second	2 days
Nevada	Yes	first	2 days
New Hampshire	Yes	second	10 days
New Jersey	Yes	second	2 days
New Mexico	Yes	second	2 days
New York	No		
North Carolina	Yes	second	7 days
North Dakota	Yes	second	4 days
Ohio	Yes	second	10 days
Oklahoma	No		
Oregon	Yes	second	2 days
Pennsylvania	Yes	second	30 days
Rhode Island	Yes	second	2 days
South Carolina	Yes	first	2 days
South Dakota	No		
Tennessee	Yes	first	2 days
Texas	Yes	second	3 days
Utah	Yes	first	2 days
Vermont	Yes	second	2 days
Virginia	Yes	second	2 days
Washington	Yes	first	1 day
West Virginia	Yes	first	1 day
Wisconsin	No		
Wyoming	Yes	second	7 days

Source: *A Digest of State Alcohol-Highway Safety Related Legislation,* sixth edition, National Highway Traffic Safety Administration, U.S. Department of Transportation

HOW A BREATHALYZER WORKS

The person blows into the machine. It measures the percentage of alcohol in the person's body. The law considers a standard measure as legally intoxicated. This measure might be .10 (one tenth of one percent blood-alcohol concentration), depending on the state. The rules vary from one state to another. However, the law often entitles the defendant to two breathalyzer tests that must measure within .02 (or some other percentage) of each other.

Driving with a Suspended or Revoked License

The police probably will arrest you for driving with a suspended or revoked license. This usually is a serious misdemeanor. However, it may be a felony carrying a state prison sentence or extended periods of community service.

If you are stopped while driving with either a revoked or suspended license, you can expect to be arrested and taken to the police station to post bond. If you cannot raise the required amount of bond money, you will be taken to court for a bond hearing (usually within 24 hours) where a judge will set bond.

(continued)

license immediately. *Revocation* aims both to discipline the driver and protect the public. It involves involuntarily ending your driving privilege. Revocation generally is permanent until you apply for a new license and the state conducts a hearing. You may have to retake a driver's license examination.

Q. If State A has suspended/revoked my license, but I have a valid license in State B, may I drive in State A?

A. No, a valid driver's license from another jurisdiction does not enable you to drive on the highways of a state that has canceled, suspended, or revoked your license.

Q. What are the grounds for license suspension?

A. They vary by state. A local lawyer will be able to give you details about your state's laws. Generally, however, a state might provide that three moving violations within one year warrant a three-month suspension. Refusal to submit to a field sobriety or breathalyzer test also will result in suspension.

Q. What are the grounds for license revocation?

A. They are based on violating specific laws, such as drunken driving, using a motor vehicle to commit a felony, or fleeing from or eluding the police. Again, they vary by state.

Q. Does the law entitle me to notice and a hearing before the state revokes my license?

A. Barring an emergency, due process under the Fourteenth Amendment requires notice and a chance to be heard before the state ends a person's license privileges.

Q. What if the state charges me with an offense that requires a license suspension?

A. Unless another law says otherwise, no notice is necessary before a state may suspend your license under the mandatory provisions of a law.

Q. If the state does notify me, what should the notice say?

A. The time, place, and purpose of the hearing should appear on the notice of a hearing to suspend or revoke your license

Q. Does the law entitle me to a jury?

A. No, a suspension/revocation hearing is an administrative proceeding. It is not a judicial proceeding. The law does entitle you, however, to confront and cross-examine witnesses against you at such a hearing.

Q. What must the state prove before a court can convict me of driving on a suspended or revoked license?

A. The law varies from one state to another. However, the state usually has to show that the offender previously had a valid license before the state suspended or revoked it. The state also usually must prove that the accused had an already suspended or revoked license on the occasion in question. In addition, the state usually must show that the accused was driving a motor vehicle on a public highway at the time of the offense.

License Renewal

Q. Must I take another examination to renew my license?

A. Check your state's law. Laws in most states provide for some type of reexamination. However, only about half of those states require it. (Three states require an eye examination and a test on traffic laws every four years.)

Q. May a physical or mental affliction prevent me from driving legally?

A. Yes. A few states require doctors to report physical and mental disorders of patients that could affect driver safety.

Seat Belt Laws

Q. Do I have to wear a seat belt?

A. Consult your state motor vehicle laws to find out what your state requires. New York became the first state to enact a mandatory seat belt law for adults in 1984. Over 25 other states have passed similar laws.

(continued)

(continued)

You will then remain in jail until the bond is posted. The bond you will need to post depends on the crime you are alleged to have committed and on your previous driving record. A monetary bond might be set, or you might be released on a personal recognizance bond, requiring only your signature and your promise to return to court as ordered and to avoid violating any other laws.

You should find an attorney to represent you as soon as possible. Give your lawyer the facts surrounding your arrest and your previous driving history. Your attorney will explain the possible outcomes and consequences of your case.

Child Restraint Laws, by State

State	Law	Fine for non-compliance	Applies to out-of-state drivers?
Alabama	mandatory for under 4 years old	$10	yes
Alaska	mandatory for under 7 years old	$300 maximum	yes
Arizona	mandatory for under 5 years old or 40 lbs. or less	$50	no
Arkansas	mandatory for under 6 years old	$25	yes
California	mandatory for under 5 years old or less than 40 lbs.	may require court hearing	yes
Colorado	mandatory for under 4 years old or less than 40 lbs.	$100 maximum	no
Connecticut	mandatory for under 4 years old	may require court hearing	yes
Delaware	mandatory for under 5 years old and under 40 lbs.	may require court hearing and $25 fine	not available
District of Columbia	safety seat required for under 4 years old; safety seat or safety belt for 3 to 6 years old	$25	no
Florida	mandatory for under 6 years old	may require court hearing	yes
Georgia	mandatory for under 4 years old; child seat required for under 3 years old; seat belts okay for over 3 years old	$25	no
Hawaii	mandatory for under 4 years old	$100	yes
Idaho	mandatory for under 4 years old	$100 maximum	no
Illinois	mandatory for under 4 years old; those 4 and 5 years old may be in child restraint or seat belt	$25	no
Indiana	mandatory for under 5 years old	may require court hearing	no
Iowa	mandatory for under 6 years old	$10	no
Kansas	mandatory for under 4 years old	not available	no
Kentucky	mandatory for 40 inches in height or less	$50	if home state has like law
Louisiana	mandatory for under 5 years old	$25-$50	not available
Maine	mandatory for under 5 years old	$25-$50	no
Maryland	safety seat for under 3 years old; safety seat or belt for 3 to 5 years old	$25	no
Massachusetts	mandatory for under 5 years old	$25	yes
Michigan	mandatory for under 4 years old	may result in $10 fine and court hearing	yes
Minnesota	mandatory for under 4 years old	$25	yes
Mississippi	mandatory for under 2 years old	$10 fine and may require court hearing	yes
Missouri	mandatory for under 4 years old	$25	yes
Montana	mandatory for under 4 years old or weighing less than 40 lbs.	$10-$25	no
Nebraska	mandatory for under 4 years old	$25	no
Nevada	mandatory for under 5 years old	$35-$100	no
New Hampshire	mandatory for under 5 years old	$30	yes
New Jersey	mandatory for under 5 years old	$10-$25	yes
New Mexico	mandatory for under 11 years old	$50	yes
New York	mandatory for under 4 years old	$50 maximum	yes
North Carolina	mandatory for under 7 years old	$25	no
North Dakota	safety seat for under 3 years old; safety seat or belt for 3 to 5 years old	$20	yes
Ohio	mandatory for under 4 years old or weighing under 40 lbs.	$35 (but may be dismissed if child restraint is obtained)	nonresidents must comply if operating Ohio-registered vehicle
Oklahoma	mandatory for under under 5 years old	not available	no
Oregon	mandatory for under 16 years old; under 1 year old must be in approved child safety system	$20	if home state has like law
Pennsylvania	mandatory for under 4 years old	$25	yes
Rhode Island	mandatory for under 13 years old	$10	yes
South Carolina	mandatory for under 4 years old	$25	no
South Dakota	mandatory for under 5 years old	not available	no
Tennessee	mandatory for under 4 years old	noncompliance may require court hearing	yes
Texas	mandatory for under 2 years old; restraint or safety belt required for 2 to 3 years old	not available	no
Utah	mandatory for under 5 years old	$20	no
Vermont	mandatory for under 5 years old	$25	yes
Virginia	mandatory for under 5 years old	$25	no
Washington	mandatory for under 5 years old	$30	yes
West Virginia	mandatory for under 9 years old (3 to 8 years old may use seat belt)	$20	no
Wisconsin	mandatory for under 4 years old	$10-$200	no
Wyoming	mandatory for 2 years old and under	$25	yes

Source: American Automobile Association

States with Laws Requiring the Use of Front-Seat Safety Belts

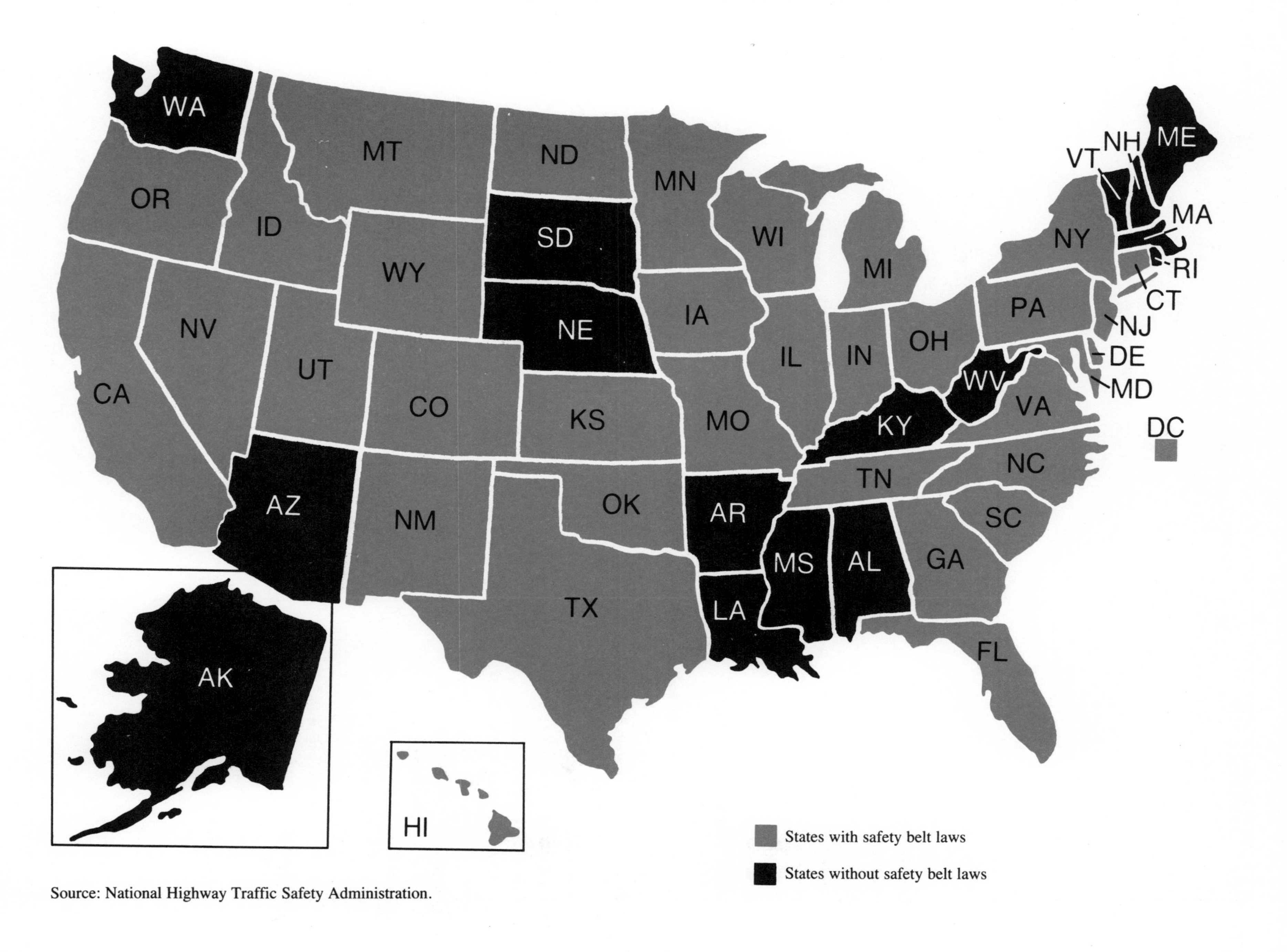

Source: National Highway Traffic Safety Administration.

Q. May I still recover payment for my injuries if I am in an accident and not wearing my seat belt?

A. Yes, most states reject the so-called "seat-belt defense." Most states will not permit evidence that plaintiffs did not buckle up as proof that they were negligent in a way that contributed to the injuries. In some jurisdictions, however, evidence of the plaintiff's failure to use a seat belt may reduce the amount of damages awarded to the plaintiff.

Children, Seat Belts, and Car Seats

All 50 states and the District of Columbia require the restraining of children riding in motor vehicles. Check your state law, however. States often make exemptions based on a child's age, the child's relationship to the driver, or the type of vehicle in which the child is riding. Seat belts and car seats are a good idea when you consider that roughly 700 children under the age of five die in passenger vehicles each year. Also, car accidents cause 45 percent of the deaths of children between the ages one and 14. Therefore, even though your children may hate wearing seat belts or riding in car seats, you might want to insist that they use them, regardless of the law.

Speeding and Other Offenses

This chapter cannot possibly discuss the many traffic offenses and statutory variations that exist among the 50 states. In general, minor traffic violations are those in which a first offense is likely to yield a fine and no jail time. Examples include parking offenses, speeding, failure to keep to the right of the center line, driving an unregistered car, and driving a vehicle with defective equipment. There also are more serious offenses that carry stiffer fines and the possibility of a jail sentence. These include reckless driving, leaving the scene of an accident, driving without insurance, and driving after a license revocation.

Q. How could I have received a speeding ticket when I was being careful?

A. A lack of due care is not an element of the charge of speeding. Simply because you were not in an accident does not prove that you were driving at a reasonable speed.

Q. What are the elements of a speeding charge?

A. It depends on whether your state bases its speeding laws on *absolute/fixed maximum limits* or *prima facie limits*. It is a violation to exceed a fixed maximum limit regardless of the circumstances at any time. On the other hand, prima facie limits allow drivers to justify the speed at which they were driving considering the traffic and road conditions and visibility.

Q. Does the type of speed limit change the nature of the complaint against me?

A. Yes, it matters a great deal. The complaint and notice or summons to appear for a fixed maximum violation will specify both your alleged speed and the maximum speed allowable within the area. On the other hand, in prima facie jurisdictions, driving above the posted speed limit is not the offense. The police must charge you with driving above a speed that was reasonable and proper given the existing conditions. One example might be driving 50 miles per hour in a school zone. Speeding laws vary greatly from one state to another. Hence, it is a good idea, for legal and safety reasons, to get into the habit of reducing your driving speed under certain conditions. Examples include approaching a railway crossing or intersection, driving around a curve, or facing special hazards, such as severe weather.

Q. What kind of details are on a traffic ticket?

A. It probably will contain the color, model, and registration of your vehicle and the date, time, and place of the alleged offense. The ticket usually will have the specific violation charged and, if it is a parking meter offense, the meter number as well. The officer's name and badge number, the fine schedule, and a notice of your ability to have a hearing to contest the ticket probably will be on a ticket. However, each jurisdiction has its own form.

Q. What does "leaving the scene of an accident" mean?

A. Ask a lawyer about your state's law. Generally, drivers of vehicles involved in an accident in which personal injury or property damage occurs must stop and identify themselves and their vehicles. They also must notify police and help any injured people. Neither the driver's intent nor the ownership of either vehicle involved in the collision are elements of the offense. (See the "Accidents" section that appears below.)

Q. What are the defenses to such a charge?

A. It is a complete defense if no personal injury or property damage resulted from the accident. The same is true if you had no knowledge that an accident had occurred. On the other hand, claiming that you drove directly to the police station to report the accident probably would not be a good defense.

Q. What is "reckless driving"?

A. The language varies from one jurisdiction to another. However, increasingly, states are following the Uniform

How to Avoid Getting a Speeding Ticket

People often ask, "Are there any standard excuses that will protect me from getting a speeding ticket?" The answer is that some reasons may succeed, but only if they are reasonable and truthful. Taking a pregnant or sick person to the hospital is one example. (You might even get a police escort.) Another is a court emergency. (You must show the court papers to the officer.) A broken speedometer also may work. (Be ready to give the officer a test ride.)

Vehicle Code. It defines reckless driving as "willful or wanton disregard for the safety of persons or property." Basically, the prosecution must show that reckless drivers did not care about the probable harmful results of their driving and that a reckless driver *should have realized* that such driving posed a hazard.

Accidents

Q. According to the law, how safely must I drive?

A. You have to use reasonable care under the circumstances. Negligence—the failure to exercise such care—is the most common basis for liability.

Q. Do I owe a higher standard of care toward pedestrians?

A. No, the same standard applies. Local ordinances give pedestrians certain rights of way, for example, while crossing streets. Motorists must exercise reasonable care under the circumstances toward pedestrians. In practical terms, this means keeping a careful lookout for them. It also means maintaining control over your vehicle to avoid injuring them. You also must sound your horn to warn of your approach when you believe that the pedestrian is unaware of the danger. The law does not, however, expect you to anticipate a pedestrian darting out into the roadway.

Q. Do I owe the same duty of care toward my passengers?

A. Generally, yes, although it may change based on your passengers' relationship to you. However, you will not be liable if a passenger gets injured through no fault of your own.

Q. What if I am a passenger in my own car?

A. The law in some states will assume you still have "control" over the vehicle. Other states require the owner to interfere with negligent driving as soon as the owner becomes aware of it.

Q. Am I responsible if I am not even in the car?

A. It depends. You still might be liable for property damage, injuries, and even death if you permit someone else to operate your defective vehicle. The same is true if you allow an inexperienced, constantly intoxicated, or otherwise incapable person to drive your car. The law refers to this as *negligent entrustment*.

Q. If I have an accident, must I identify myself to other involved parties?

A. In the past, common law did not require you to give your name before leaving an accident scene. Modern laws that require you to identify yourself after an accident in which someone gets hurt or killed have survived court challenges. You should identify yourself to a police officer. If asked, you also should show your license and proof of insurance coverage. Otherwise, you do not have to, and probably should not, say anything. Specifically, do not reveal how much insurance coverage you have.

Q. If I collide with a parked car, must I do anything?

A. The law requires you to find the owner. As an alternative, you are permitted to attach a written note to the parked car identifying yourself and your vehicle. You also should notify the police.

Q. Must I tell the police if I am in an accident?

A. Alert the police immediately if someone is hurt or killed. Under many circumstances, you must notify the police and file a written accident report within five to ten days. Often, you are required to file the report, not with the police, but with the bureau of motor vehicles or some other state agency. Written reports are essential if someone suffers a personal injury or if property damage of more than $50 to $300 occurs. (The dollar amount varies from one state to another, but there generally does not have to be a significant amount of damage.)

Q. What happens if I do not fill out a written accident report?

A. Failure to file a written report is a misdemeanor in most states. It may cause some states to suspend your driver's license until you file the report. Remember, by completing an accident report, you are verifying that the report contains all important facts known to you. Providing false information in a written report is illegal.

(continued)

What You Should Do if You Have an Accident

If possible, park on the shoulder of the road and do not obstruct traffic. If asked, give your name, address, license, vehicle registration certificate, and proof of insurance to the other driver for examination. Get the same information from the other driver. Write down the names and addresses of all passengers and possible witnesses. Also get the names and badge numbers of any police officers who respond to the scene. If you have a camera handy, photograph the damaged cars and skid marks. Most important, help any persons who have injuries.

Do not make any statements about who you think was at fault. Also, do not admit blame to the other parties or witnesses.

As soon as possible after the accident, notify your insurance company.

Accident Report Filing Requirements

All states require the filing of a report if an accident results in personal injury or death.

State	Property Damage in Excess of	Days to File Report
Alabama	$250	10
Alaska	$500	10
Arizona	$500	5
Arkansas	$250	30
California	$500	10
Colorado	$1,000[1]	10
Connecticut	$1,000	5
Delaware	$500[2]	Immediately
District of Columbia	$250	5
Florida	$500[3]	5
Georgia	$250	10
Hawaii	$300	1
Idaho	$250	Immediately
Illinois	$250	15
Indiana	$750	10
Iowa	$500	3
Kansas	$500[4]	Immediately
Kentucky	$200	10
Louisiana	$500	10
Maine	$500	5
Maryland	see note [5]	15
Massachusetts	$1,000	5
Michigan	$200[6]	Immediately
Minnesota	$500	10
Mississippi	$250	10
Missouri	$500	30
Montana	$400	10
Nebraska	$500	10
Nevada	$350	10
New Hampshire	$500	5
New Jersey	$500[7]	10
New Mexico	$250	5
New York	$600	10
North Carolina	$500	Immediately
North Dakota	$600	Immediately
Ohio	$400	30
Oklahoma	$300	10
Oregon	$400	3
Pennsylvania	$200[8]	5
Rhode Island	$500	10
South Carolina	$400	15
South Dakota	$500 per person or $1,000 per accident	Immediately
Tennessee	$400	10
Texas	$500[9]	10
Utah	$400	5
Vermont	$500	3
Virginia	$750	5
Washington	$500	1
West Virginia	$250	5
Wisconsin	$500	10
Wyoming	$500	10

Notes:

[1]State law also requires a police officer to submit an accident report (regardless of the amount of property damage) if one of the participants cannot show proof of insurance.
[2]The filing of an accident report is required if it appears that an alcohol-impaired driver was involved in the accident.
[3]State law stipulates that a driver need not submit an accident report if a police officer submits the report.
[4]State law requires that drivers shall report accidents to a police officer, who then shall submit the accident report. It also stipulates that the Division of Vehicles may require drivers to submit a written report to satisfy certain provisions of the law.
[5]No accident reports are required if: (1) the accident results in property damage only; (2) a police officer files a report; or (3) a person is physically unable to make a report.
[6]Accident reports are to be submitted to the investigating police officer who then shall forward the report to the Director of the State Police.
[7]State law requires the filing of proof of financial responsibility if a driver is involved in an accident resulting in injury, death, or property damage greater than $200 to one person.
[8]Pennsylvania law is a combination of financial responsibility, compulsory liability, and no-fault insurance reparation systems.
[9]The law requires the filing of proof of financial responsibility if a driver is involved in an accident resulting in injury, death, or property damage greater than $1,000 to one person.

Source: National Association of Independent Insurers

Q. Should I contact a lawyer after the accident? What should I tell the lawyer?

A. If you are filing a lawsuit against the other driver, you will hire your own lawyer. If the other driver is suing you, your insurance company will provide a lawyer for you. Either way, at the first meeting, supply details about your family status and employment situation. Also provide facts about the accident, including witnesses' names and addresses, and a detailed description of your injuries. If you are filing a lawsuit, tell the lawyer about all your out-of-pocket expenses. These expenses might include your doctor's bills, ambulance and hospital costs, automobile repairs, rental car costs, and any lost income.

Q. What might happen if I believe the collision is at least partly my fault?

A. You may not be in the best position to decide how the accident happened. Defective equipment in your vehicle, a nonworking traffic signal, or the other driver's intoxication are among the many possible causes of the accident. The other side may use your acceptance of blame and apology to the other driver as evidence against you at trial. Leave it to the judge or jury to decide who is at fault.

Q. If the accident is partly my fault, may I still receive payment for my injuries?

A. It depends on whether you live in a contributory negligence, comparative negligence, or no-fault jurisdiction. (No-fault insurance is discussed in the "Insurance" section that appears below.)

Q. What is contributory negligence?

A. Essentially, *contributory negligence* bars you from receiving money for your injuries if your own negligence in any way contributed to the accident. The other driver must prove that you were negligent.

Q. What is the logic behind this?

A. The reasons behind contributory negligence range from punishing you for your own misconduct to discouraging you from acting negligently again. Only a handful of states still accept the idea of contributory negligence, which once was popular.

Q. What does comparative negligence mean?

A. *Comparative negligence* divides the damages among the drivers involved in an accident based on their degree of fault. This idea is very popular, as many states follow it. In "pure" comparative negligence states, you can receive payment for your injuries regardless of how much of the blame you carry for the accident. However, the other driver also must be at fault to some degree. In "modified" comparative fault states, you may recover payment only if your own fault is below a certain point. Usually, if you and the other driver are equally at fault, you cannot recover.

Q. How exactly does comparative negligence work?

A. Suppose you get in an accident when you are driving ten miles over the limit on an icy road. However, in your opinion, the accident was largely caused by the other driver, who went through a red light.

In a comparative negligence state, the first order of business for a judge or jury presented with your suit against the other driver is to calculate the degree of fault for each of you. This is done on a percentage basis. The jury might decide that your speeding on an icy road was responsible for 20 percent of your injuries. It might decide that the other driver's running the red light contributed the remaining 80 percent.

If the jury later finds that your damages consisted of $100,000 in medical expenses, you would be responsible for $20,000 and the other driver for $80,000.

Paying a Fee to Get Back Your Impounded Car

If the police impounded your car and you had to pay a fee to get it back, that is not a violation of your constitutional rights. Courts have upheld laws allowing for impoundment of cars that people have parked illegally or left on public streets. Courts also have upheld laws requiring payment of a fee to reclaim the vehicle. These are valid exercises of local/state police power. That the police did not impound other illegally parked cars when they impounded yours is no defense. That is because such laws give the police permission to act. They do not require the police to take action.

INSURANCE

Q. How much car insurance must I buy?

A. Each state has its own insurance regulations. Not every state has mandatory insurance. Some states have *financial responsibility laws*. These require you to either have insurance or post a bond or have a sum of money in cash. People usually take out insurance to satisfy these laws. Some states have basic levels of coverage that they require their citizens to carry. Many states might require coverage for *bodily injury to others* and *damage to someone else's property*. Both types of coverage pay people for injuries that you cause. States also might require *personal injury protection*. It pays for lost wages, medical expenses, and replacement services (such as household maintenance), depending on the circumstances, caused by injuries that you and guests in your car suffer.

Q. Does my bank have a say in the amount of car insurance I buy?

A. It is possibly within your bank's right. Many states allow lenders from whom you borrowed to buy a car to require you to purchase insurance options such as collision and comprehensive. (Collision pays for damage to your car regardless of fault. Comprehensive pays for damage to your car caused by theft, fire, and vandalism.)

Q. What is a deductible?

A. A *deductible* is the amount of each claim that you agree to pay for by yourself. The higher the deductible you choose, the lower your insurance premium. However, you need more cash on hand to pay for damages when you select a high deductible. Typical deductibles are $50, $100, or $250.

Q. May my insurance agent force me to pay my premium in a lump sum?

A. Check your state's law. Some states limit the amount an agent may demand before renewing your insurance. This limit is up to a certain percentage of the premium. If you have not paid premium payments in the recent past, however, an insurance agent may legally ask you to pay your entire premium before renewal.

Q. May my insurance agent charge me a service fee for issuing or renewing a policy?

A. It depends on your state's law. Some states forbid agents from charging fees for issuing or renewing auto insurance policies. These states do not require you to pay for services your agent performs without your consent.

Q. How do insurance companies determine their rates?

A. They classify covered people based on impartial criteria. These include your age, sex, marital status, driving record, geographic location, the car's age, and its primary use. These standards help set the varying rates that drivers pay. In some states, the rates are set by the state's insurance commission, which regulates insurance companies.

PARENTS' LIABILITY FOR THEIR CHILDREN'S DRIVING

In most states, you probably are not liable if your child has an accident while driving your car. Fewer than 20 states recognize the *family purpose doctrine*. Under this doctrine, the family "head" who maintains a car for general family use may be liable for the negligent driving of a family member. The family head must have authorized that family member to use the vehicle. These states treat the family member as an agent of the vehicle owner. They assume that the vehicle owner is better able to satisfy property damage and injury claims.

Q. My teenage son's insurance premium is much higher than mine. Is it unconstitutional to discriminate based on age?

A. No, it is not. Research shows that drivers under age 21, especially males, have the highest rate of car accidents. This explains the difference in rates between adults and minors.

Q. Do I have to buy uninsured motorist coverage?

A. It depends where you live. Seventeen states now require drivers to purchase such coverage. It enables you to collect from your insurer if you get injured in an accident caused by an uninsured driver. The insurance carrier, in turn, receives *subrogation rights* against the uninsured wrongdoer. That is, the carrier takes your place (and your rights) as the legal claimant against the uninsured driver.

Q. How do I collect on my uninsured motorist coverage?

A. Generally, you must prove both that the other driver was at fault and without liability insurance to repay you. An uninsured driver actually may have no coverage. A driver also may be "uninsured" if underage, unlicensed, or otherwise ineligible for protection under the policy covering the vehicle that caused the accident. This also is the case if the driver-at-fault used the vehicle without the owner's permission. Practically speaking, if the insurance carrier of the driver-at-fault denies coverage, you are dealing with an uninsured motorist.

Q. How does underinsured motorist coverage work?

A. The injured person's insurer compensates that person for a certain amount of money. That sum is equal to or greater than what the injured insured person could have received had the driver-at-fault carried the legally established liability insurance minimum. Underinsured motorist coverage exists in most states.

Q. Do underinsured motorist policies differ?

A. Yes, a few of those states that recognize this insurance option weigh the insured accident victim's damages against the liability coverage of the driver-at-fault. Then the injured person receives compensation only if the driver-at-fault's

(continued)

Negligence, No-Fault, and Add-on Benefit States

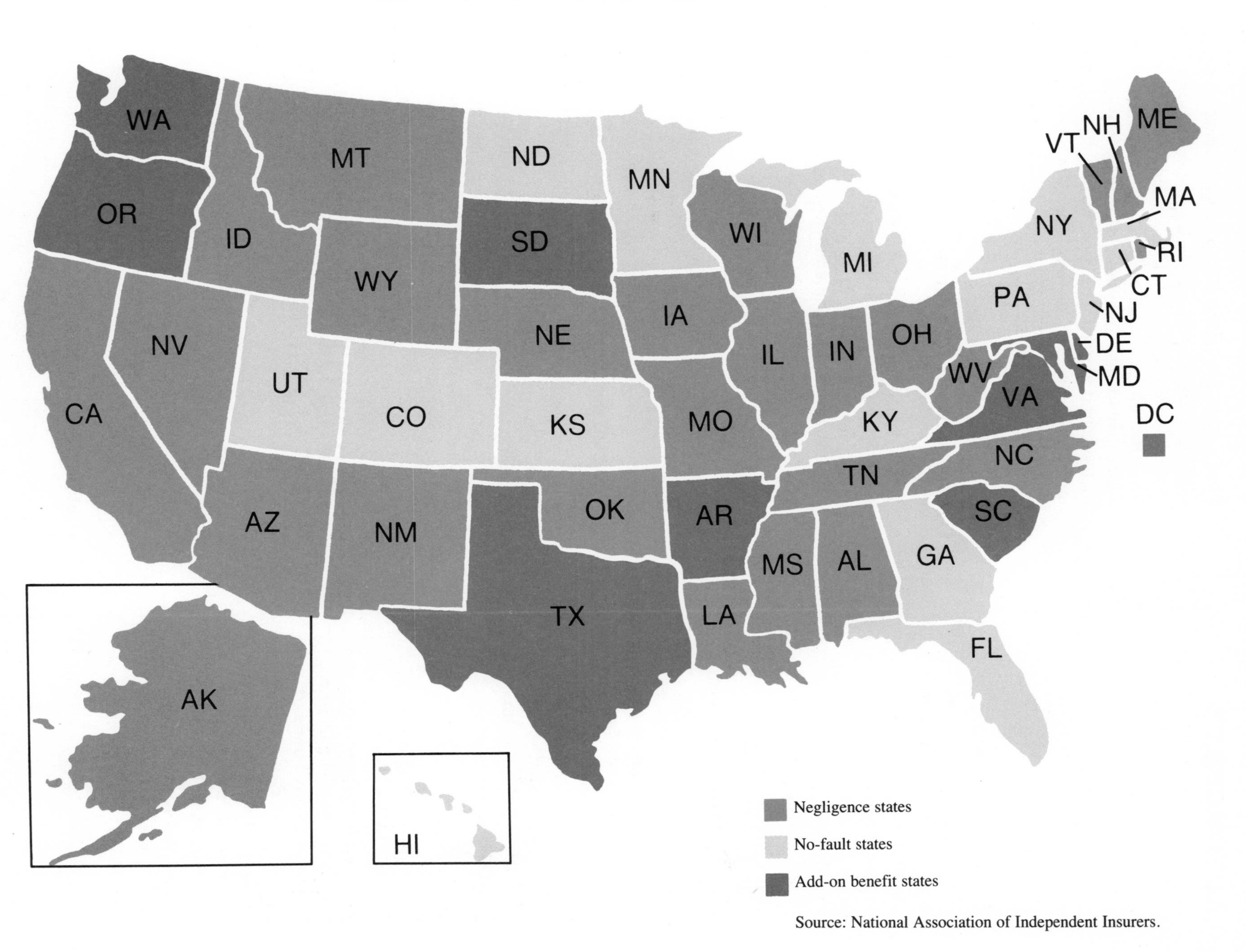

Source: National Association of Independent Insurers.

No-Fault Insurance

***No-fault automobile insurance* protects you, any passengers in your car, and any pedestrian you may strike, regardless of who is at fault for the accident. (Some states protect only the owner or operator of the insured vehicle.) If someone gets injured in an accident, the *driver's* insurance carrier will compensate the injured person for economic losses up to a specified level. Twenty-four states plus the District of Columbia have one form of no-fault insurance or another.**

Some no-fault states prohibit some injured persons from bringing lawsuits against persons believed to have caused the accident. Other states provide either mandatory or optional "add-on" no-fault benefits. In these states, persons with no-fault insurance can still sue negligent drivers.

liability coverage is less than the damages the victim suffered. Other states examine the injured person's uninsured motorist coverage and the driver-at-fault's liability insurance. Then the insurance carrier pays only when the driver-at-fault's liability insurance limit is less than the victim's underinsured motorist coverage. Most policies enable the insurer to deduct the amount the victim receives from the driver-at-fault from the sum it pays to the victim carrying the underinsured motorist protection.

Q. How much may I recover on an uninsured motorist claim?

A. This is complicated and varies by state. Check your state's law. For example, some states prohibit adding together the liability limits for two policies to determine how much coverage is available to injured persons.

Q. What does no-fault insurance cover?

A. Most no-fault laws apply only to bodily injury claims and lost wages. They do not usually cover property damage claims.

Q. What are the advantages and disadvantages of no-fault insurance?

A. On the plus side, injured people get reimbursed relatively promptly by their insurance companies. This may save the injured party from having to go to court. On the other hand, some no-fault laws restrict the injured person's right to sue the other driver for general damages.

WHERE TO GET MORE INFORMATION

The following list is a starting point for getting more details or registering various types of complaints.

Manufacturer/Dealer Associations

The Motor Vehicle Manufacturer's Association (MVMA) publishes *Motor Vehicle Facts and Figures* annually. It also publishes a complete *Directory of Motor Vehicle Related Associations.* For details on how to obtain these publications, call (313) 872-4311 or write to:

Motor Vehicle Manufacturer's Association
7430 Second Avenue, Suite 300
Detroit, Michigan 48202

The Automobile Importers of America is the foreign-car counterpart of the MVMA. For details, call (703) 979-5550 or write to:

Automobile Importers of America
1725 Jefferson Davis Highway
Arlington, Virginia 22202

The National Automobile Dealers Association is a major trade association of U.S. automobile dealers. For details, call (703) 821-7000 or (800) 252-6232 or write to:

National Automobile Dealers Association
8400 Westpark Drive
McLean, Virginia 22102

The Recreational Vehicle Industry Association is a national trade association representing manufacturers of motor homes, travel trailers, truck campers, multi-use vehicles, and component part suppliers. For details, call (703) 620-6003 or write to:

Recreational Vehicle Industry Association
1896 Preston White Drive
Reston, Virginia 22090

The Rubber Manufacturers Association offers information on tires and other rubber products. For details, call (202) 682-4800 or write to:

Rubber Manufacturers Association
1400 K Street, N.W.
Washington, D.C. 20005

Other major automobile associations include:

Automotive Service Industry Association
444 North Michigan Avenue
Chicago, Illinois 60611
(312) 836-1300

Automotive Service Excellence
13505 Dulles Technology Drive
Herndon, Virginia 22071
(703) 742-3800

You also can call the car manufacturers' headquarters or their regional offices directly. Ask your local dealer for details.

Consumer and Government Groups

Almost every state has a Better Business Bureau (BBB). Every local BBB has a hot line for automobile-related complaints, particularly regarding warranties. The BBB arranges arbitration hearings for participating manufacturers. Check your local telephone directory or write to:

Council of Better Business Bureaus, Inc.
4200 Wilson Boulevard, 8th Floor
Arlington, Virginia 22203
(703) 276-0100

The Federal Trade Commission (FTC) has many regional offices, which are listed in the "Where to Get More Information" section of the "Consumer Credit" chapter. You also can call the FTC's Bureau of Consumer Protection at (202) 326-2222 or write to:

Federal Trade Commission
Bureau of Consumer Protection
6th and Pennsylvania Avenue, N.W.
Washington, D.C. 20580

The National Highway Traffic Safety Administration (NHTSA) provides information on car recalls and defect investigations. You also can report safety-related defects. The NHTSA offers a toll-free auto safety hot line. In the D.C. area, you can call this hot line at (202) 426-0123. In the continental U.S., call the hot line at (800) 424-9393. Or write to:

National Highway Traffic Safety Administration
400 7th Street, S.W.
Washington, D.C. 20590

Ralph Nader's consumer protection organization is the Center for Auto Safety. Call (202) 328-7700 or write to:

Center for Auto Safety
2001 S Street, N.W.
Washington, D.C. 20009

The United States Consumer Product Safety Commission is a federal agency that offers safety-related information on most, but not all, products available to the consumer market. In Maryland, call (301) 492-6580 and ask for "Public Affairs." In the rest of the continental United States, call (800) 638-2772. Or you can write to:

U.S. Consumer Product Safety Commission
Washington, D.C. 20207

Other automobile-related organizations include:

Consumer Federation of America
1424 16th Street, N.W., Suite 604
Washington, D.C. 20036
(202) 387-6121

National Safety Council
444 North Michigan Avenue
Chicago, Illinois 60611
(312) 527-4800

National Transportation Safety Board
800 Independence Avenue, S.W.
Washington, D.C. 20594
(202) 382-6600

For additional assistance with automobile-related problems or questions, you also can contact your state Attorney General's offices or your state Department of Consumer Affairs. Some states have separate bureaus that handle only motor vehicle problems. Your state or local Department of Motor Vehicles also may be helpful. Check your local telephone directory.

ısurance

For information on state laws and insurance, contact:

Insurance Information Institute
110 William Street
New York, New York 10038
(212) 669-9200

The Insurance Information Institute not only has many useful pamphlets, but it also has state and regional counterparts.

Publications

The American Automobile Association (AAA) annually publishes an updated edition of the *Digest of Motor Laws.* It is a summary of laws and regulations governing passenger cars in each state. It also covers each U.S. territory and each Canadian province. Copies are available for $6.00 each from your local AAA club or from:

Traffic Safety
American Automobile Association
1000 AAA Drive
Heathrow, Florida 32746
(407) 444-7963

The Consumer Information Center has various booklets that might be of interest to you. Send the payment for the booklet(s) plus an additional $1.00 for postage (if ordering two or more free booklets) to: Consumer Information Center-N, P.O. Box 100, Pueblo, Colorado 81002. These booklets include:

Car Rental Guide. This brief booklet tells you how to get the best deal when renting a car. It includes terms used by rental agencies, a checklist for renting, and a comparison worksheet. Three pages. (1989) Publication 404W. 50 cents.

Facts for Consumers: Vehicle Repossession. What happens when the creditor seizes and resells a vehicle is discussed in this booklet. Learn your rights and how to avoid repossession. Four pages. (1989) Publication 405W. 50 cents.

What You Should Know About Your Auto Emissions Warranty. This booklet discusses what parts and repairs are covered, how long the warranty applies, and how to make claims. Eight pages. (1988) Publication 406W. 50 cents.

LAW AND THE WORKPLACE

INTRODUCTION

The law affects just about every aspect of work. Years ago the workplace was, for the most part, unregulated. Today, state and federal laws regulate the worker and boss alike.

The law helps shape the relationship between employer and employee. This does not mean the law should decide every question. A costly lawsuit is not the best way to solve problems. Employers and employees should first try to talk out their differences. Compromise can work wonders. Many employers try to anticipate problems before they occur. In addition, employers often try to solve problems so the employee has no bad feelings about the company.

This chapter may help both employees and employers avoid problems. It explains the laws and suggests places to turn for further details. Each section in this chapter briefly explains a specific area of law and then answers commonly asked questions.

LAW AND THE WORKPLACE

Q. Is there a single law of the workplace?

A. No, there is no single "law of the workplace." Today's workplace law combines federal and state laws defined by the governments and courts, civil service rules, collective bargaining agreements, contracts, company personnel handbooks, and employer practices.

Q. Will this chapter answer specific questions for the employee or employer?

A. No, you should view it as a basic road map. This chapter cannot cover every situation or offer advice on your specific problem. It will, however, tell you where to find more information.

Q. Does it matter if a person works for a government instead of a private employer?

A. Yes, it makes a big difference. Generally, labor contracts and, to an extent, federal and state laws control the relationship between a private employee and employer. However, the private employer generally has more latitude (freedom) than the public employer. This is because the federal (and sometimes the state) Constitution governs a public employer. In addition, various laws also strictly govern the relationship between a public employee and employer. These include civil service rules and local laws, as well as state and federal statutes.

Q. What is the legal significance of a union contract?

A. If there is a collective bargaining agreement, the union is the employee's bargaining representative. This means that a union contract controls an employee's salary and working conditions. If there is no collective bargaining agreement, the employee deals directly with the employer. The employee can negotiate the conditions of his or her own employment.

State laws oversee state or local government employees and unions. However, federal labor laws cover private unions and employers in all states.

Q. Does this chapter cover independent contractors?

A. No, it deals only with employers and employees. This chapter does not address self-employed people. These *independent contractors* agree to do a job for a sum of money. The law does not consider them as employees.

Suppose ABC Company hires Jill as an independent contractor to put up a fence for $1,000. ABC does not supervise Jill's work. The company cares only about getting the fence built. Jill wants profits, not wages and benefits. Her relationship with ABC ends after she finishes the job. This chapter covers the relationship between ABC and its employees or between Jill and her employees. It does not apply to the relationship between ABC and Jill.

BUSINESS ORGANIZATIONS AND THE LAW

Q. What type of business structure might I choose if I begin my own company?

A. There are three basic types: sole proprietorships, partnerships, and corporations. Because of the constantly changing tax laws, it is a good idea to check with a tax expert before picking the type of business you will form.

Q. What is a sole proprietorship?

A. It is the simplest form of business ownership. The *sole proprietor* has complete control over the business and makes all decisions. These concern hiring, firing, buying inventory, salaries—every aspect of running the business. It is easy to start this type of business. There are very few government regulations and no minimum financial requirements. You may need to buy a local license to run the business. Also, you may need to fill out and file a form if you do business under a name other than your own.

One disadvantage is that your own personal credit will limit your ability to raise funds. Also, you are personally liable for all debts or injuries caused by you or your employees. You could lose your house and car if a major problem arises.

As a sole proprietor, business profits and losses will be combined with your personal income for tax purposes. This can be an advantage when there are business write-offs and losses, which can be used to reduce your personal taxes.

Q. What is a partnership?

A. In a *partnership,* there is at least one other person with whom you will do business. Partners share the profits, losses, and management decisions. The primary way that the business raises money is by getting new partners.

S CORPORATIONS

The old term for an S corporation was a Subchapter S corporation. It is not another business type. Instead, it is an IRS tax advantage given to small corporations. Being an S corporation is an advantage for tax reasons because the shareholders are taxed on their share of the corporation's income (or losses) at the shareholder's tax rate. In a C corporation, on the other hand, the corporation has to pay a tax on the profits as a corporation. (Also known as a close corporation, a C corporation is another popular form of incorporation of a small business.) When the C corporation distributes the after-tax income as dividends to the shareholders, the shareholders must pay a second tax on this income.

(continued)

The law assumes that all the partners are in a partnership voluntarily. That means there was no duress (pressure) involved in getting the partners, their funds, or their property for the business.

Partnerships should always have an agreement defining each partner's obligations to the others, including:

- Who has the power to run the business;
- How much the business will pay partners and employees; and
- Who is responsible for debts, and to what percentage.

States have their own partnership laws. They cover all issues that a partnership agreement does not address. Like a sole proprietor, each partner is personally liable for debts and other obligations. You could lose your personal property if the business goes bad. Although the partnership's property is sold first to pay debts, if the partnership is liquidated and there still are debts, you are responsible.

There are two types of partnerships: general partnerships and limited partnerships. In a *general partnership,* each of the partners is personally liable for all the debts and other obligations incurred (acquired) by the business. On the other hand, in a *limited partnership,* the limited partners basically are treated the same as partners in a general partnership except that the limited partners are *not* personally liable for debts or losses incurred by the partnership beyond the amount of money or other property they agree to contribute to the partnership.

(continued)

Not all corporations can qualify as S corporations. The principal requirements are that the corporation has no more than 35 shareholders, all of whom are individuals or qualified trusts, and that the corporation does not have more than one class of stock.

Publication 589 of the IRS describes S corporations in more detail. The election of taxes as an S corporation is made on an IRS 2553 form, which can be obtained from any IRS office.

Q. What is a corporation?

A. A *corporation* is a separate, formal legal entity. The law treats a corporation like a person. Corporations may borrow money, sign contracts, buy property, and so forth. They offer advantages over the other two types of business organizations. These advantages include the ability to raise capital (funds) by selling shares and generally favorable tax laws. They also include protection of investors' personal property if the business fails. (Investors can give up this protection, and they often have to when they seek start-up capital from a bank.)

A corporation sells shares of stock to investors. The resulting funds provide capital for the business. Shareholders are the owners of the business. The shareholders of a small, new business should know that this investment does not guarantee success. If the business fails, shareholders may lose their entire investment. However, that is all they may lose. Their other assets usually are safe. Shareholders and directors of the corporation normally are not personally liable for the corporation's debt. That is not true, however, if they knowingly commit a fraud, act in bad faith, or guarantee payment of the debt.

The corporation may pay its profits to shareholders. These distributions are called dividends. Or it may put the profits back into the business. This is a good practice when the business is young and growing.

Q. What is a franchise?

A. A *franchise* is a contract that puts you in a business developed by someone else. A franchise is a way of being in business for yourself while receiving the benefits of marketing and management help from franchisers who have already run the same business in other locations successfully. Fast-food chains, doughnut shops, and 24-hour convenience stores are examples of franchises. Recently, many more people have used franchising as a way to go into business for themselves.

Q. Franchising sounds great. However, I would worry about depending so much on other people's services and support. What may I do to make sure franchising will work for me?

A. The Federal Trade Commission recommends that you take five basic precautions when entering a franchise agreement:
(1) Study the contracts and other documents carefully before signing them;
(2) Consult a lawyer before making a binding commitment;
(3) Be sure that all promises made by the seller or its salespersons appear in writing in the contracts you must sign;
(4) Talk with others who have already invested in the business. Find out their experiences and advice; and
(5) If you rely on earning claims of other franchise owners, study the statement giving the basis for the claims. Find out how many past investors have done equally well.

Q. What legal protection exists for people thinking about investing in a franchise?

A. In 1979, the Federal Trade Commission (FTC) enacted the Franchise Disclosure Rule. It tries to shield investors from franchisers using misleading practices to sell franchises. The Rule orders that a franchiser must present a disclosure document to any potential investor at least ten days before the signing of a contract. This document must include details on 20 subjects, including:
- The business, legal contests, and bankruptcy histories of the franchiser and its directors and key executives;
- Details of the franchise's operating expenses;

LAW AND THE WORKPLACE

The Franchiser's Sales Pitch—Fact or Fiction?

The Franchise Disclosure Rule prohibits reporting on the actual or potential sales, income, or profits of existing or prospective franchises unless the franchiser meets certain conditions. First, there must be a reasonable basis for the report. Second, the franchiser must have prepared the report using generally accepted accounting principles. Third, the franchiser must have evidence to confirm the figures. That evidence must be available to the prospective franchisee.

Be extremely wary of business "opportunities" that sound like franchises but are called "distributorships" or "dealerships." Frequently, unscrupulous entrepreneurs choose these terms as a way of getting around the Franchise Disclosure Rule. By doing so, they hope to avoid making the disclosures required by that rule.

- The required personal involvement by the franchisee;
- The franchiser's right to select or approve a site for the franchise;
- Statistics on the number of franchises and their failure rate; and
- Details of how to end, cancel, and renew the franchise contract.

Q. When do I need a lawyer in starting a business?

A. You should use a lawyer from the beginning. The lawyer can help you choose the form of ownership for your business. Your lawyer can explain and prepare any forms that you must file with any municipal or state agencies, including the Secretary of State. The lawyer also may advise you on credit, financing, insurance, and business contracts and leases. A good lawyer will help set up your corporate record book, if you incorporate. (Your lawyer can show you how to keep the records yourself. Then you will not have to rely on a lawyer to do so.) If you have employees, labor law becomes involved. A lawyer can make you aware of the laws that apply to sales, warranties, and liabilities from the beginning of your business operation.

You will not need a lawyer as often after the company is up and running. As you continue in your venture, you will become much wiser about how the law works. You will need your lawyer as new contracts or legal problems arise in the life of your business. An example would be complying with antipollution laws if you are engaged in a business using materials that raise environmental concerns. It also is advisable to have your lawyer review your business operation for potential legal problems at least annually even if you have not been sued or had a major transaction requiring legal assistance during the year. A yearly legal checkup could uncover one or more serious problems that, if dealt with immediately, could save you several thousand dollars of expenses and attorney's fees.

RECRUITING AND HIRING

Laws against discrimination greatly affect the hiring process. Federal law and many states forbid discrimination based on race, color, national origin, sex, pregnancy, religion, or age. Federal laws also ban discrimination against veterans. In addition, federal law protects the handicapped against discrimination by federal agencies and by organizations receiving federal funds such as grants or contracts. Some state and local governments forbid discrimination because of marital status, sexual preference, and handicaps.

The law affects hiring in other ways. Governments often use *merit selection* for federal, state, and local jobs. They use tests and impartial standards for hiring to avoid political favoritism. The law also governs hiring by private employers. Various laws now govern the hiring of young people. There is a federal law on the use of lie detectors in the hiring process. Many governments have adopted or are considering laws about referrals, background checks, and drug testing.

Q. A company needs to hire more salespeople. What rules apply to job ads?

A. The main idea is to avoid discrimination. Ads should attract all capable applicants and avoid words suggesting a preferred race, sex, or age. To stress this, ads always should use "salesperson" instead of "salesman." The phrase "An Equal Opportunity Employer" in an ad means the employer will judge all applicants equally.

Q. Suppose a company thinks it truly needs a young male employee?

A. First, the company probably is wrong in thinking that only a young male can do the job. Second, if it puts this in an ad, the company must be able to prove that the job demands it. This is very difficult to do. Courts do not like stereotyped job requirements. The employer will have to defend the wording in such an ad. Courts usually hold that an employer must judge each applicant individually to see if he or she meets the requirements.

A rare exception occurs when a specific age, sex, religion, or national origin is a *bona fide occupational qualification* (BFOQ). For example, a filmmaker may hire only women for female roles. Court decisions now vary on BFOQs. Some courts rule against age limits once treated as BFOQs for safety reasons (such as a mandatory retirement age for airline pilots and police). Other courts allow such limits. Race is never a BFOQ.

Q. Some employers find applicants by talking to employees. Is anything wrong with this?

A. That depends on who makes up the work force. If the workers (and referrals) are mainly whites, common sense suggests that this may be discriminatory in effect. This is also true of employers who usually recruit relatives of employees who are mostly white males.

LAW AND THE WORKPLACE

How Employers Can Hire Without Discrimination

It helps to use a standard application form that avoids useless questions. Avoid asking about age, height, weight, marital status, education, arrest record, or handicaps unless they relate to the job. For example, questions about height and weight may reject women or members of some ethnic groups who are usually smaller. Asking about marital status may suggest sex discrimination.

Employers and prospective employees both benefit when job openings are clearly defined. Employers should prepare a detailed job description for each position, specifying what the work is and what qualifications the employer requires. If both sides come to the interview with a clear idea of what the job involves, the interview is more likely to focus on the qualifications essential for doing the job or that have predicted successful job performance.

An employer can avoid problems by placing ads widely to reach all types of people. An employer should try to reach as many qualified persons as possible. The employer also should see that an applicant knows that he or she will be judged equally.

Q. Are formal recruiting methods helpful to employers?

A. Yes, using employment agencies or visiting schools will help employers reach a variety of persons, including minorities. Make sure the employment agency knows you are an equal opportunity employer. Also be sure that the agency does not discriminate. If you visit schools, choose ones that train minority students for your kind of work.

Q. Can employment interviews avoid being subjective (based on opinion)?

A. By their very nature, job interviews are subjective experiences. Prospective employers cannot help but form an assortment of impressions in judging an applicant's ambition, motivation, creativity, dependability, and responsibility.

However, by largely forbidding discriminatory questions, the law presses employers to make the job interview as objective (fact-based) as possible. This also prods employers to hire workers on the basis of their individual merit and employment records.

None of the antidiscrimination statutes specify what an employer may or may not ask in a job interview. However, the employer should not ask and the applicant should not answer certain types of questions that may imply discrimination.

Q. What are some inappropriate questions for female job candidates?

A. Many questions are based on gender (sex) stereotypes. Questions about family planning and marital status are a large area of concern because they often discriminate against women. For instance, an employer trying to determine whether a female applicant is going to stay with the company for the next few years should not ask, "Do you plan to get married?" or "Do you plan to have children?" or "What kind of birth control do you use?"

Those questions are not only inappropriate, they also are an inefficient way of getting the desired information. More direct, job-related questions might be:

- We are looking for employees who will make a commitment to the company. Is there any reason you might not stay with us for the next few years?

- What are your career objectives?
- Where do you see yourself in five years?

In the same way, suppose an employer is trying to determine a female job candidate's commitment to living in a particular area of the country. Then it is better to ask, "Do you intend to stay in the area?" rather than "Is your husband's employer likely to transfer him?"

If attendance is the issue, questions like, "Does your husband expect you to be home to cook dinner?" or "What will you do if your children get sick?" are indirect and inefficient. It would be more direct to ask, "How was your attendance record with your prior employer?"

Even questions carefully phrased in gender-neutral terms, however, can be considered discriminatory if asked only of female applicants. Therefore, employers should be sure that the questions they ask of women are the same they ask of men.

Q. What is "need-to-know," and how does it apply to job interviews?

A. Whether a question will be viewed as inappropriate often depends on whether there is an objective, job-related reason why the employer wants its applicants to answer it. Questions touching on a candidate's financial status, for instance, are seldom going to be relevant.

Sometimes employers clearly must have certain information. For example, employers do need to make their job offers dependent on candidates' production of proper documentation of their citizenship or work authorization. However, asking about national origin may be viewed as discriminatory.

Similarly, whether an applicant has ever been convicted of a crime may substantially affect the applicant's fitness for a specific job. However, questions concerning the applicant's arrest record may be inappropriate, since everyone is entitled to a presumption of innocence until proven guilty.

Q. What should an applicant do if the interviewer does ask questions that seem inappropriate or discriminatory?

A. The tactful applicant might answer by providing the information the interviewer "really wants to know." For example, "Oh—you're wondering whether I'll be able to work long hours. I can assure you that I will. My current boss can confirm that."

Q. What about the hiring decision?

A. If the interview process was as uniform and impartial as possible, and if only job-related questions were asked, the

Lie Detectors in the Workplace

The Employee Polygraph Protection Act, which became law in late 1988, governs the use of lie detectors at work. This federal law applies to almost all workers and job applicants across the country. It covers a wide variety of types of lie detectors.

Under the law, employers must show an economic loss to justify using lie detectors to test workers who have already been hired. Even then, workers cannot be penalized for refusing to take a test or for filing a complaint under the law. Employers who violate the law can be fined $10,000. They also are subject to private lawsuits by employees.

The law specifically does *not* preempt (overrule) more strict state laws or collective bargaining agreements that prohibit lie detector tests. Many states do limit the use of lie detectors and other "truth testing" methods. Check with your state civil rights agency or labor department for details.

employer should be able to follow a checklist. This should allow the employer to rate applicants in an organized and consistent manner.

Q. May an employer use a lie detector to find out if a job applicant or an employee is honest?

A. No, only in a very few cases—generally those related to government work, company security, or national security—may an employer use a lie detector to test job applicants. Even then, there are many strict controls on how the employer may use the tests.

Q. Is a bad referral from an old boss a good reason for not hiring somebody?

A. A truthful report in a bad reference may be a reason to reject an applicant. However, employers and applicants should not take referrals at face value.

Certain states require that employees have access to their personnel files and written notice of any referral given to others. Some employees have claimed that references slandered them. This has made it harder to get an honest and complete referral. Most employers now refuse to give references. Instead, they will only reveal dates of employment and positions held.

Q. May an employer run a background check on an applicant?

A. Background checks may be necessary for certain jobs. These include jobs involving security or trade secrets. Checks should be made fairly and without bias. They also should concern only issues relating to performance of the specific job.

Q. May an employer use a test to screen applicants?

A. Yes, but it should be job-related. A test or job qualification may have an illegal *adverse impact* on minorities, even if it seems fair. This may cause an employer to deny jobs to an unusually high number of minorities. For example, a test of English language skills might disqualify an unusual amount of Hispanics or others of bilingual ethnic backgrounds. If the test forms the basis for hiring, it might omit them from the work force. Unless the job requires English, the test may be illegal.

Many federal rules cover this area. They say a test has a bad impact if the pass rate for minorities (including women) is less than 80 percent of the pass rate for white men. If 50 percent of the white males pass the test, then 40 percent or more of the minorities must pass. If not, the government is permitted to question the test.

Although a test or job qualification adversely impacts women or minorities, an employer still can require it if the employer can demonstrate that the needs of the business justify the test or job qualification.

Q. With all these limits, does an employer have the right to set basic job requirements and work standards?

A. Yes, as long as they do not discriminate. If the requirements relate to the job, they will be legal even if unintended discrimination results. The employer must be able to show that the job demands the requirements. Thus, requirements for experience, specific skills, and "proper" dress (applied to men and women equally) are usually valid.

Q. What is an example of a requirement that discriminates because of its impact?

A. One that requires a high school education when the job doesn't need it. This may unfairly disqualify minorities. Not hiring single parents with young children may discriminate against women. There may be discrimination if an employer requires applicants to speak English for a job involving only physical labor.

Q. If a company has a government contract, will it affect hiring policies?

A. If the contract is for $10,000 or more, Executive Order 11246 forbids discrimination because of race, color, religion, sex, or national origin. If it is for more than $50,000 and the company has at least 50 workers, the employer must have a written affirmative action plan. It must set goals for hiring minorities and women in jobs for which they are not usually hired. Also, the federal Rehabilitation Act requires federal contractors to set goals for hiring qualified handicapped persons.

Unless someone in the company knows this area, an employer should get help in forming an affirmative action plan. A later section in this chapter discusses these plans.

Q. What laws apply to hiring a 16-year-old?

A. Every state, like the federal government, limits the type of work available to workers under 18. The laws ban factory

Drug Tests and Medical Exams for Job Applicants

Federal law allows an employer to require job applicants to take medical exams or drug tests if the employer keeps the results secret and does not use them to discriminate against minorities. Many state laws regulate when and how an employer may do drug testing. A school system, government agency, or other public employer also will have to consider the Constitution's protections of privacy and laws guarding the privacy of applicants for government jobs.

work for youths under 16 years old, limit work to 40 hours a week, and restrict the amount of work to be done at night.

A 14-year-old may work outside school hours in specific jobs under certain conditions. The youth may work only between 7 A.M. and 7 P.M. He or she also must work no more than three hours a day, 18 hours a week when school is in session. The 14-year-old must work no more than eight hours a day, 40 hours a week when school is not in session. For "hazardous" jobs, a worker must be at least 18 years old, with exceptions for some under-age apprentices.

Federal law does not govern certain jobs, so youths of any age may engage in the work. Farm work outside school hours is an example.

Many states have their own rules for youth employment. An employer must follow them if they are more strict than federal law. For example, many states require all minors to get work permits from school authorities.

Under certain conditions, employers can pay employees under the age of 20 a "training wage." This wage rate must be at least 85 percent of the minimum wage, but not less than $3.35 per hour. These wages can be paid for up to 90 days, which can be extended 90 more days if the employee is in a job training program. On April 1, 1991, the minimum training wage goes to $3.61 per hour. The training wage provision expires March 31, 1993.

You Need a License for These Jobs

State and federal rules limit some jobs to people who have state licenses. These include cosmetologists, barbers, electricians, heating/air conditioning technicians, engineers, nurses, builders, lawyers, accountants, dental hygienists, and physicians. When considering such a career, contact your state licensing authorities to see what requirements apply.

EMPLOYEES' RIGHTS AND DUTIES

Wages and Hours

Q. What is the minimum wage?

A. The federal minimum wage is $3.80 per hour. It will become $4.25 an hour on April 1, 1991. Some states set a higher minimum wage. This overrides the federal law. Employers must pay the minimum wage or higher (except for the training wage for workers under age 20, as discussed earlier). The minimum wage is an hourly rate. However, employers can use any basis as long as it meets the legal minimum. That is $3.80 multiplied by hours worked. For example, an employee may work 30 hours and earn $120. Hence, the employee earns four dollars per hour. That is more than the current minimum wage. A salesperson who works 30 hours

(continued

SELECTED STATE CHILD LABOR STANDARDS AFFECTING MINORS UNDER 18
(As of January 1988)
(Occupational coverage, exemptions, and deviations usually omitted)

State or other jurisdiction	Maximum daily and weekly hours and days per week of minors under age 16 unless other age indicated (a)	Night work prohibited for minors under age 16 unless other age indicated (a)
California	8-48-6, under age 18. School day/week: 4-28 (c) under age 18, except 8 before non-school day, ages 16 and 17.	10 P.M. (12:30 A.M. before non-school day) to 5 A.M. under age 18.
Florida	10-30-6, during school year, under age 18. School day: 4 when followed by school day, except if enrolled in vocational program.	9 P.M. to 6:30 A.M., before school day. Midnight to 5 A.M., before school day, ages 16 and 17.
Illinois	8-48-6.	7 P.M. (9 P.M. June 1 through Labor Day) to 7 A.M..
Michigan	10-48-6, under age 18. School week: 48 (b), under age 18.	9 P.M. to 7 A.M.. 10:30 P.M. to 6 A.M., ages 16 and 17 if attending school. 11:30 P.M. to 6 A.M. ages 16 and 17 if not attending school.
New York	8-40-6. 8-48-6, ages 16 and 17. School day/week: 3-23, under age 16. 4-28, age 16 if attending school.	7 P.M. to 7 A.M. Midnight to 6 A.M., ages 16 and 17.
Ohio	8-40. School day/week: 3-18.	7 P.M. (9 P.M. June 1 through September 1 or during school holidays of 5 days or more) to 7 A.M..
Pennsylvania	8-44-6, under age 18. School day/week: 4/26 (c), under age 16. 28 in school week, ages 16 and 17 if enrolled in regular day school.	7 P.M. (10 P.M. during vacation from June to Labor Day) to 7 A.M.. 11 P.M. (midnight before non-school day) to 6 A.M., ages 16 and 17 if enrolled in regular day school.
Texas	8-48.	10 P.M. (midnight before non-school day or in summer if not enrolled in summer school) to 5 A.M.

Source: Division of State Employment Standards Programs, Office of State Liaison and Legislative Analysis, Employment Standards Administration, U.S. Department of Labor.

(a) State hours limitations on a school day and in a school week usually apply only to those enrolled in school. Several states exempt high school graduates from the hours and/or night work or other provisions, or have less restrictive provisions for minors participating in various school-work programs. Separate night work standards in messenger service and street trades are common, but are not displayed in table.

(b) Combined hours of work and school.

(c) More hours are permitted when school is in session less than five days.

Minimum Wages and Overtime Pay

The federal Fair Labor Standards Act (FLSA) sets a minimum hourly wage. It applies to the entire nation. It also requires overtime pay for employees paid by the hour who work over 40 hours in a workweek. The FLSA is one of the oldest federal labor laws. Congress passed it in 1938. The FLSA applies to any business in interstate commerce. It also covers most state and local governments. The FLSA partially exempts a few industries. These include very small retail, construction, and service businesses and interstate trucking lines. Family-owned businesses that employ only members of the immediate family are also exempt. In addition, the FLSA exempts seasonal amusement or recreational firms and sailors employed on foreign vessels. However, the FLSA covers nearly all employers and workers.

and earns $120 in commissions also makes more than the minimum wage. The law cares only about the amount earned per hour. It does not matter how the employer figures it.

Q. I know that minimum wage is for each hour worked. What does the law consider as "hours worked"?

A. It is the time a worker must be on duty or at work. Employees usually do not have to be paid for certain short periods of time. Examples include time for changing clothes or washing up after work. However, employers must pay for this if the job requires special preparation or cleanup. Rest periods of 20 minutes or less count as hours worked. Meal breaks during which employees have no duties are not hours worked. This is true even if workers must stay on the plant premises. However, if a worker has duties during this time, such as watching a machine or awaiting a phone call, then the employer must count the time as hours worked.

The following situations constitute working time, when the employer orders or benefits from the time:

- Waiting time (on or off duty). However, either it must be important to the job or there is a possibility that the employer may call the employee to active duty;
- "On call" time, if workers cannot use it as they wish;
- Sleep periods at the job site, if the employer may call the worker to active duty;
- Lectures, meetings, and training programs. This does not include those that are outside the employee's regular hours or are not job-related. It also does not include those that are voluntary and require no work.
- Travel time other than between home and the job site before and after normal workdays. Special rules apply for travel away from home.
- Time spent solving complaints during normal work time.

Q. Who keeps track of time worked?

A. The employer must keep reliable time records. However, the law does not require time clocks. Employers need only pay for hours worked even if a worker punches in early or punches out late. An employer may round off time clock hours to the nearest quarter hour or less. However, this must work both ways.

Q. How can I compute overtime pay?

A. First, figure the "regular rate" of pay. This must equal or exceed minimum wage. Pay includes all wages made on any basis. The basis may be hourly rate, commission, piece rate, incentive pay bonus, or salary. It also may consist of goods or facilities. An employer must convert pay to an hourly rate for figuring overtime.

To find the regular hourly rate, total all pay for work done in the workweek. Divide this by the number of hours worked in the workweek. Assume that you earn five dollars per hour plus a production bonus of $20. If you work 45 hours in a workweek, you can compute the regular rate as follows:

Compensation	
Hourly wages	$225.00 (45 hrs. × $5/hr.)
Bonus	+$20.00
Total compensation	$245.00

Regular Hourly Rate	
Total compensation	$245.00
Hours worked	÷ 45
Regular rate	= $5.44 per hour

Your employer would pay five dollars per hour for all hours up to 40. You also would receive $8.16 (1½ times the regular rate of $5.44) for each of the five hours worked over 40.

Q. I receive a salary, not hourly pay. How can I compute overtime?

A. In your case, the regular rate equals the salary divided by the number of hours in the workweek. Employers pay workers the regular rate for each hour up to 40. An employer pays 1½ times the regular rate for all hours over 40. If your salary covers more than one week, you can convert it to a weekly basis. The regular rate is usually the same each week.

Q. May an employer pay a waitress less than minimum wage because of tips she receives?

A. Probably. Assume that a waitress usually gets more than $20 a month in tips. Then her employer can take up to 45 percent of minimum wage as a credit. Using the 45-percent figure, the waitress would get $2.09 per hour as a minimum wage. That equals $3.80 minus $1.71 (45 percent of $3.80). (The tip credit will go up to 50 percent on April 1, 1991.) However, the credit *cannot exceed* the worker's tips. Some state laws may further limit the credit. Under the FLSA, a payment is a "tip" only when the customer pays it freely for waiting services given. A service fee that the employer adds to a bill is not a tip. This is true even if the employee gets it. Gifts other than cash or check are not tips. For example, concert tickets are not tips.

Employers may not take the tip credit unless workers know of it. Employers also must prove that the tips make up for lost

When an Employer Owes Overtime Pay

Employees paid by the hour can work up to 40 hours in a week without earning overtime. If required to work more, they must receive overtime for all time over 40 hours. The overtime rate is at least "time-and-a-half." That is 1½ times the regular pay rate.

Employers must base overtime only on hours worked in one workweek. A workweek is any constant period of seven days in a row. It usually is the calendar week. Some workers might base their overtime on a period longer than a week. They include hospital workers, police officers, and fire fighters. The FLSA usually does not require daily overtime pay for work over eight hours in a day, unless there are more than 40 hours in a workweek. Some employers normally pay daily overtime. That may reduce weekly overtime pay. Some states require daily overtime pay for more than eight hours.

wages. The credit currently must not exceed 45 percent of the minimum wage. This is true even if the tips exceed 45 percent. If the worker's tips are less than 45 percent of the minimum wage, the credit may not exceed the tips received. Waiters, waitresses, and other workers may split the tips without changing these rules.

It is easy to figure overtime pay for tipped employees. First, compute the total amount of pay during the workweek. Do not include tips that exceed the credit taken by the employer. Then divide this amount by the hours worked. Most serving people earn less than the minimum wage. Thus, employers will usually pay hours worked over 40 at 1½ times the minimum wage.

Q. Do states also control such matters?

A. Many states have no wage laws. However, some states do. Employers and workers should check their state laws. They may consult the state department of labor.

Q. Must employers pay minimum wage when they give meals to workers?

A. Some employers furnish meals, lodging, and other facilities to workers. Sometimes employers may credit the cost of such "benefits" as part of the minimum wage. The employer must supply these items to benefit the employee. It must not be mainly for the employer's benefit or convenience. The true cost of such items can be deducted from the minimum wage. The employer may not deduct the cost it would charge the public. However, state laws may limit the amount of the credit. An employer usually cannot take credit for supplying uniforms, tools, or safety gear. A collective bargaining contract also may prevent such deductions.

Q. Are employee discounts on purchases part of the minimum wage?

A. No, the FLSA treats them as fringe benefits. They are not wages.

Q. What is an employer permitted to deduct from a worker's pay?

A. An employer usually cannot make deductions that reduce the hourly rate below $3.80 ($4.25 after April 1, 1991). However,

(continued)

WHO ENFORCES THE FLSA?

The Wage and Hour Division of the U.S. Department of Labor manages the FLSA. It has offices in many major cities and some smaller cities. Employees can file a complaint or request an investigation. The Wage and Hour Division will keep this filing or request confidential. Investigators act on specific complaints. They also make periodic "audits" of company practices. If it finds a violation, the Wage and Hour Division will seek payment of owed minimum wages or overtime. It may take the employer to federal court to regain owed pay. Workers can bring their own suit to recover back pay. An employer may not punish workers who use their FLSA rights.

Employment Information Form

U.S. Department of Labor
Employment Standards Administration
Wage and Hour Division

This report is authorized by Section 11 of the Fair Labor Standards Act. While you are not required to respond, submission of this information is necessary for the Division to schedule any compliance action. Your identity will be kept confidential to the maximum extent possible under existing law.

OMB No. 1215-0001
Expires: 09-30-92

1. Person Submitting Information

A. Name (Print first name, middle initial, and last name)
Mr.
Miss
Mrs.
Ms.

B. Date

C. Telephone number:
(Or No. where you can be reached)

D. Address: (Number, Street, Apt. No.)

(City, County, State, ZIP Code)

E. Check one of these boxes

☐ Present employee of establishment ☐ Former employee of establishment ☐ Other ________ (Specify: relative, union, etc)

2. Establishment Information

A. Name of establishment

B. Telephone Number

C. Address of establishment: (Number, Street)

(City, County, State, ZIP Code)

D. Estimate number of employees

E. Does the firm have branches? ☐ Yes ☐ No ☐ Don't know

If "Yes", name one or two locations: ________

F. Nature of establishment's business: (For example; school, farm, hospital, hotel, restaurant, shoe store, wholesale drugs, manufactures stoves, coal mine, construction, trucking, etc.)

G. If the establishment has a Federal Government or federally assisted contract, check the appropriate box(es).

☐ Furnishes goods ☐ Furnishes services ☐ Performs construction

H. Does establishment ship goods to or receive goods from other States?

☐ Yes ☐ No ☐ Don't know

3. Employment Information (Complete A, B, C, D, E, & F if present or former employee of establishment; otherwise complete F only)

A. Period employed (month, year)

From: ________

To: ________ (If still there, state present)

B. Date of birth if under 19

Month ________ Day ________ Year ________

C. Give your job title and describe briefly the kind of work you do

(Continue on other side)

Form WH-3
Rev. 10/89

Fair Labor Standards Act complaint form.

D. Method of payment

$ ________ per ________________
(Rate) (Hour, week, month, etc.)

E. Enter in the boxes below the hours you usually work each day and each week (less time off for meals)

M	T	W	T	F	S	S	Total

F. **Check the appropriate box(es) and explain briefly in the space below** the employment practices which you believe violate the Wage and Hour laws. (If you need more space use an additional sheet of paper and attach it to this form.)

- ☐ Does not pay the minimum wage
- ☐ Does not pay proper overtime
- ☐ Does not pay prevailing wage determination for Federal Government or federally assisted contract

  Approximate date of alleged discrimination

  ____

- ☐ Discharged employee because of wage garnishment (explain below)
- ☐ Excessive deduction from wages because of wage garnishment (explain below)
- ☐ Employs minors under minimum age for job
- ☐ Other (explain below)

(Note: If you think it would be difficult for us to locate the establishment or where you live, give directions or attach map.)

Complaint Taken By:

Public Burden Statement

We estimate that it will take an average of 20 minutes to complete this collection of information, including time for reviewing instructions, searching existing data sources, gathering and maintaining the data needed, and completing and reviewing the collection of information. Send comments regarding this burden estimate or any other aspect of this collection of information, including suggestions for reducing this burden, to the Office of Information Management, U.S. Department of Labor, Room N1301, 200 Constitution Avenue, N.W., Washington, D.C. 20210; and to the Office of Management and Budget, Paperwork Reduction Project (1215-0001), Washington, D.C. 20503.

the law does permit deductions for taxes and union dues. It does not matter if they lower the minimum rate.

In some states, employers usually may not deduct *any* amount other than normal tax withholding.

Q. What about garnished wages?

A. Employers must deduct money if a court garnished a worker's wages. The worker's creditor then receives that money. Federal law limits the amount of wages courts may garnish. It must be the lesser of 25 percent of take-home pay or the part of take-home pay exceeding 30 times the federal minimum wage. However, courts sometimes order employers to take more for support payments, in bankruptcy proceedings, or for unpaid state or federal taxes.

Q. Must employers provide fringe benefits?

A. No, the FLSA does not require this.

Job Safety

Q. What is an occupational injury?

A. An *occupational injury* is any injury caused by an accident or exposure at work. Examples include a cut, fracture, sprain, or amputation. An *occupational illness* is any abnormal condition resulting from exposure to conditions at work. It includes illness due to toxic or harmful materials.

Q. How does the Occupational Safety and Health Administration (OSHA) work?

A. It sets safety standards for employers to follow. These standards appear in the Code of Federal Regulations, which is available in the law libraries of law schools and most county courthouses.

Q. May employers or workers alter the safety standards?

A. OSHA prints proposed standards in the Federal Register. It then invites public comment. Employers may obtain temporary or permanent exceptions from the standards. To do this, employers must show that conditions beyond their control prevent them from meeting the standards. Or

Exempt from Minimum Wage and Overtime

The law exempts several types of employees from minimum wage and overtime. It does this even if they work in covered industries. The most important exemptions are:

- **"White collar" employees, including executives, administrators, and professionals who earn ample salaries. The same is true for outside salespeople. The exemptions depend on the worker's duties.**
- **Commission-paid employees. The law exempts from overtime pay employees who earn at least half of their income from commissions. However, such workers must receive a minimum level of income.**
- **Full-time students. Employers may apply for a certificate allowing them to hire full-time students for less than minimum wage. The pay rate must be at least 85 percent of minimum wage.**

OSHA AND THE OSH ACT

The Occupational Safety & Health Act (OSH Act) founded the Occupational Safety and Health Administration (OSHA). Congress passed the OSH Act in 1970 to create safe working conditions.

The OSH Act covers employers and workers in all 50 states. It also applies to the District of Columbia, Puerto Rico, and all other federal territories. The OSH Act does not protect self-employed persons. Nor does it cover farms where only immediate members of the farmer's family work. It also does not cover working conditions that other federal laws protect. The OSH Act does cover federal agencies. However, it does not protect state and local government employees. Many states have similar laws. They may be stricter; if so, the state laws would provide additional protections.

employers may prove that working conditions are as safe as OSHA's proposed standards. Workers have the right to a hearing on an employer's requested exceptions.

Standards concern how clean the workplace is and the care of equipment. They also deal with safety gear and methods for handling dangerous machines or materials. If workers have contact with toxic compounds, OSHA lets them review medical and other employer records.

Q. May OSHA inspect a workplace to see if an employer is obeying its rules?

A. Yes, OSHA has this power. Workers have the right to have a union official or other agent attend the inspection. If no employee agent exists, the inspector must talk to a reasonable number of workers about safety.

Q. Does OSHA require a safe workplace?

A. Yes, the employer must maintain a safe and healthful workplace. An employer should identify hazards. It also should make sure workers use safe equipment. An employer should know about OSHA standards.

OSHA requires employers of 11 or more workers to record job-related injuries and illnesses. Employers also must supply medical examinations when required by OSHA standards.

Employers should let workers obtain copies of OSHA standards. The employers also should post OSHA notices of citations and hang up posters detailing employee rights.

Q. May an employee try to get a safe workplace without employer retaliation?

A. Yes, employees have that right. Sometimes employees believe their employer has discriminated against them for using OSHA rights. If so, they should contact the nearest OSHA office. Workers must do this within 30 days of the discrimination. OSHA keeps worker complaints confidential. It investigates after receiving a complaint.

Q. What are an employee's duties under the OSH Act?

A. Workers should use their rights under the OSH Act in a responsible way. They should:

- Read OSHA posters at the job site;
- Obey OSHA safety standards;

(continued)

Form Approved
OMB No. 0920-0102
Exp. Date Aug. 31, 1992

U.S. DEPARTMENT OF HEALTH AND HUMAN SERVICES
CENTERS FOR DISEASE CONTROL
NATIONAL INSTITUTE FOR OCCUPATIONAL SAFETY AND HEALTH

REQUEST FOR HEALTH HAZARD EVALUATION

This form is provided to assist in registering a request for a health hazard evaluation with the U.S. Department of Health and Human Services. Public reporting burden for this collection of information is estimated to average 12 minutes per response. Send comments regarding this burden estimate or any other aspect of this collection of information, including suggestions for reducing this burden to PHS Reports Clearance Officer; ATTN: PRA, Hubert H. Humphrey Bg, Rm 721-H; 200 Independence Ave., SW: Washington, DC 20201, and to the Office of Management and Budget; Paperwork Reduction Project (0920-0102); Washington, DC 20503. (See Statement of Authority on Reverse Side)

Establishment Where Possible Hazard Exists ____________
Company Address Street ____________ Telephone ____________
City ____________ State ____________ Zip Code ____________

1. Specify the particular building or worksite where the possible hazard/problem is located.

2. Specify the name, title, and phone number of the employer's agent(s) in charge.

3. What Product or Service does the Establishment Produce?

4. Describe briefly the possible hazard/problem which exists by completing the following:

   Identification of Hazardous Physical Agent(s) ____________

   Identification of Toxic Substance(s) ____________

   Trade Name(s) (If Applicable) ____________ Chemical Name(s) ____________

Manufacturer(s) ____________
Physical Form of Substance(s): ____Dust ____Gas ____Liquid ____Mist ____Other
How are you exposed? _____Breathing ____Swallowing ____Skin Contact
Number of People Exposed ______Length of Exposure (Hours/Day) ____________
Occupations of Exposed Employees ____________

Form to request an inspection of a workplace.

5. Using the space below describe further the circumstances which prompted this request. ____
____
____

6. To your knowledge has NIOSH, OSHA or any other government agency previously evaluated this workplace? ____yes ____no

7. (a) Is a similar request currently being filed with or under investigation by any other Government (State or Federal) agency? ________________
(b) If so, give the name and address of each___________________________
____

8. Requester's Signature_______________________________ Date________
Typed or Printed Name____________________________Phone: Home-__________
Street____Business-__________
Address
City______________________State__________________Zip Code_______

9. Check only One of the Following:
_____ I am an Employer Representative
_____ I am an Authorized Representative of, or an officer of the organization representing the employees for purposes of collective bargaining. State the name and address of your organization.
____
____
_____ I am a current employee of the employer and an Authorized Representative of two or more current employees in the workplace where the substance is normally found. Signatures of authorizing employees are below:

Name_____________________________________ Phone_________________
Name_____________________________________ Phone_________________

_____ I am one of three or less employees in the workplace where the substance is normally found.

10. Please indicate your desire: ____ I do not want my name revealed to the employer.
____ My name may be revealed to the employer.

Authority:
Sections 20(a)(3-6) of the Occupational Safety and Health Act, (29 U.S.C. 669(a)(6)) and Section 501(a)(11) of the Federal Mine Safety and Health Act, (30 U.S.C. 951(a)(11)). Confidentiality of the respondent requester will be maintained in accordance with the provisions of the Privacy Act (5 U.S.C. 552a). The voluntary cooperation of the respondent requester is necessary to conduct the Health Hazard Evaluation.

For Further Information:
Telephone: AC 513/841-4382

Send the completed form to:
National Institute for Occupational Safety and Health
Hazard Evaluations and Technical Assistance Branch
4676 Columbia Parkway, Mail Stop R-9
Cincinnati, Ohio 45226

- Follow the employer's safety rules;
- Use protective equipment (this is very important);
- Report dangerous conditions and job-related illnesses or injuries to the employer; and
- Cooperate with OSHA inspectors when asked about health and safety conditions at work.

Employee Privacy

Q. What federal laws affect employees' privacy rights?

A. There are two important federal laws. The Freedom of Information Act (FOIA) gives the public access to a wide range of federal records. Congress passed the Act in 1966. Many court rulings broadly interpreted the FOIA. In 1974, Congress passed the federal Privacy Act. This helped ensure the privacy of public workers.

The Privacy Act requires federal agencies to allow workers access to their work records. The Act also allows employees to challenge "facts" in their file. In addition, it limits outsider access to the file. Federal agencies may not reveal employees' records without their written consent. The Privacy Act restricts the worker information that a federal agency can gather. The facts must be necessary and relevant to fulfill a purpose of the agency.

Q. What privacy protections do nongovernment workers have?

A. Employer policy may ensure that private workers can see their records. So might a collective bargaining agreement. Also, OSHA entitles employees to see certain medical records and records of exposure to toxic materials at work.

Private workers in certain states have the right to see their personnel files. These states include New York, Pennsylvania, Connecticut, New Hampshire, Illinois, Michigan, Wisconsin, and California, among others. State laws differ.

Q. What about other state laws on privacy?

A. Various state laws concern workers' privacy rights. Some protect a worker more than federal law.

Q. May employers listen to employee phone calls?

A. A 1968 federal law forbids this. (However, an employer may listen in through operators of switchboards monitoring the

Searching Workers

Some employers search employees and their belongings to detect stolen items, drugs, and the like. Contrary to popular belief, within limits, such searches are legal. A private employer has more latitude (freedom) than a public employer. However, even for private employers, a collective bargaining agreement might restrict such searches. Also, an employer must be careful about how it conducts searches. It should give notice that such searches might be done and make such searches in the least disturbing manner possible. An employer might conduct the searches out of sight of other workers. Making searches in the plant

(continued)

quality of the phone services provided by the employees. The law calls this the *extension phone exception.*) Many states have similar laws. Some protect the worker more than the federal law.

Q. May employers use video cameras to monitor workers?

A. Employers seem to have this right. It is not against federal law. In addition, state laws usually permit it.

Q. May an employer require a physical exam to get or keep a job?

A. Yes, employers have the right to require medical examinations. They may do this to judge a worker's ability to do job-related tasks. However, employers must keep the results confidential. Many states require employers to pay for required physical exams.

Q. May a private employer reveal personnel files to people inside or outside the company?

A. A private employer usually may do this. Private workers have little control over personnel files. There are few limits on private employers who choose to reveal worker files. However, government employers have greater limits on releasing worker information. Some state laws ensure workers access to their files at reasonable times.

Q. May a former employer tell a potential employer information about a worker?

A. Many states allow this. However, the potential employer must have a genuine need to know. The material should be truthful and relevant. Employers should not supply false information or hearsay that could be slander or libel. Many state laws forbid blacklisting of workers. A former employer who improperly discloses private facts may be liable for invasion of privacy. Such facts may include medical details from a worker's file. In many states, a former employer must provide certain facts to a potential employer at the worker's request.

Q. May a union get information from a worker's file?

A. A union can usually obtain facts from an employer about workers represented by the union. However, these facts

(continued)

might be better than doing so in the parking lot. An employer may step out of bounds during searches. If so, it may be liable for assault, battery, or false arrest charges.

Since public employers are restricted by the Constitution, they may need to have more than a hunch to search workers. Public employers may need reasonable grounds to conduct searches of workers employed in *nonsensitive* jobs. (In recent cases, courts have held that *sensitive* jobs include train and engine crews involved in accidents and customs workers who conduct drug searches.)

normally must concern employment conditions such as raises, promotions, seniority, punishment, a collective bargaining agreement, or contract negotiations. However, some facts may be restricted. For example, an employer does not have to reveal an employee's test scores to the union without the worker's consent. A collective bargaining agreement may cover this situation.

Q. May an employer ask a credit bureau for an investigative report on an employee?

A. Yes, but the Fair Credit Reporting Act applies. The employer must tell the worker that an investigative report is being prepared. If asked, the employer must explain about the inquiry. Upon request, it also must supply a copy of the report to the worker.

Sometimes a report harms a worker. For example, an employer might not hire or promote an employee because of a report. If so, the law entitles the worker to several things. The employee has the right to receive the name and address of the investigating agency. A worker also has the right to have the disputed facts re-examined. The law entitles employees to have their version of the facts included in later reports. Many state laws imitate this federal law. You should check your state's law.

Q. Does any federal law offer further protection for employees in this subject area?

A. Yes, the federal bankruptcy laws prohibit retaliation by an employer against an employee because he or she has filed for bankruptcy.

Q. May an employer force a long-haired, bearded worker to get a haircut and shave?

A. Private employers usually are permitted to have a grooming or dress code. Public employers have less authority to limit a worker's freedom of individual expression. Even so, the employer must show only that the limitation is fair. Discrimination laws might protect employees when the limitations affect a certain ethnic group or class of workers more than others. For example, the law looks closely at rules requiring stricter weight limits for female workers. The same is true for policies requiring black employees to shave even if they are apt to aggravate a skin condition by shaving. Such rules might be illegal because they are more likely to affect protected persons.

Employer Questions About an Employee's Life-Style

Within limits, a private employer is permitted to ask about a worker's life-style. However, these questions must adhere to the bans against discrimination on the basis of sex, race, ethnic group, or religion. There also are certain limits on asking about criminal records. Some state and local laws forbid discrimination based on marital status or sexual preference, so questions in these areas also could be out of bounds.

Public employers have more limits on what they can ask. They must show a reasonable basis for making most personal inquiries. They might require a compelling need in order to ask about political actions.

LOOKING OUT FOR THE WORKER

Unions enable workers to bargain with an employer as a group rather than alone. They might negotiate wages, hours, and other terms. This is called *collective bargaining*. When a union wins an election, it becomes the *exclusive representative* of the group of employees. This also is true when an employer voluntarily recognizes the union. This group of workers makes up the *bargaining unit*. The employer is not permitted to negotiate with any other organization or person about wages and employment terms for such workers. If there is no union, an employer is allowed to set wages and other terms without negotiating or consulting others.

(continued)

Unions and Collective Bargaining

Q. What is the National Labor Relations Act?

A. The National Labor Relations Act (NLRA) gives private workers the right to bargain collectively. However, this is only true if the Act covers their employer.

Q. When does the NLRA cover an employer?

A. Many factors decide this point. The National Labor Relations Board (NLRB) administers the Act. It has power over private companies whose actions "affect" interstate commerce. The Act covers many types of companies. It applies to firms doing business in more than one state. The Act also covers those shipping or receiving out-of-state goods. In addition, it covers businesses that do a certain gross volume of business, as well as certain types of enterprises (for example, public utilities). The NLRA might not apply to very small firms doing little interstate business. When the NLRA does not apply, workers lose the right to bargain collectively. They also lose other NLRA protections. However, an individual employment contract can contain similar rights and securities. Individual employees can have a contract even without a collective bargaining agreement.

Q. Are there state laws regarding unions?

A. Some states have laws similar to the NLRA. These state laws apply to public and private employers not covered by the NLRA. Most states permit some form of public employee collective bargaining.

Q. Are there any transportation workers who are covered by the NLRA?

A. No. However, the Railway Labor Act (RLA) of 1926 allows collective bargaining by employees of railway and air carriers. The RLA sets up procedures and committees to settle labor disputes in interstate travel promptly. The RLA takes the place of the NLRA for air and railway workers.

Q. Does the NLRA cover public workers?

A. No, it does not apply to public employees. However, other federal or state laws may allow public workers to bargain collectively. The law permits federal employees to do so. The Federal Labor Relations Authority oversees this process.

Q. Where can I find out more about the NLRB?

A. For help, call the closest NLRB regional office. You also should seek legal help. The NLRB's rules can be complex.

Q. If the NLRA covers an employer, how does this affect the employees?

A. In the words of Section 7 of the NLRA, workers have the right:

> [T]o self organization, to form, join, or assist labor organizations, to bargain collectively through representatives of their own choosing, and to engage in other concerted activities for the purpose of collective bargaining or other mutual aid or protection...or to refrain from engaging in these activities.

Workers generally are free to engage in union activities on their own time. In fact, the NLRA assumes that soliciting members in nonwork areas during nonwork time is legal.

Q. How does a union come to represent a group of employees?

A. The union must show that a majority of workers want the union to represent them. First, the union gathers support among a group of employees. The workers must have enough in common so one union can represent them. They share a "community of interest." Unions usually ask workers to sign a card showing their interest. It often is called an *authorization card*.

If at least 30 percent of the workers sign the cards or show their interest in another way, the union can ask the NLRB to hold an election. The secret-ballot election will decide if a majority of employees want a union.

If a majority of employees sign the cards, the employer might voluntarily recognize the union. However, an employer has *no obligation* to do so. An employer has the right to have the issue decided by a secret vote of the bargaining unit.

Before the vote, both the union and employer may present their views to the workers. If a majority of the voting employees select the union, then the NLRB certifies the union as the sole agent of the bargaining unit. If the union does not receive a majority of the votes, things will proceed as before. Workers will represent their own individual interests. Employees have a right to decide what they want to do.

(continued)

Union supporters believe collective bargaining balances the negotiating power between employers and employees. Then workers can help set and uphold their employment terms. This protects their job security, seniority, and work safety. Critics argue that unions are costly, unnecessary, and upsetting. They say that unions promote group interests at the expense of the single worker. Most union elections raise these points. Then, by secret-ballot vote, the employees in each bargaining unit decide whether to have a union.

The NLRA and Collective Bargaining

The NLRA does not give all employees the right to bargain collectively. It excludes certain workers—farm workers, domestic employees of a family, and managers. The same is true for persons employed by a parent or spouse, independent contractors, and supervisors. The last exception—supervisors—is especially important. Under the Act, supervisors have no *right* to bargain collectively. However, the Act does not forbid them from doing so. That means supervisors can organize without NLRA protections. It also means that an employer can fire supervisors for supporting collective bargaining.

Q. What employee activities are "unprotected"?

A. Slow-downs, "quicky" intermittent strikes, violence, sabotage, or destroying company property are forbidden. So are strikes when a contract has a "no-strike" clause. Some other acts may or may not be protected, depending on the specific facts of the case. These acts include unannounced job actions and refusal to do valid and safe work.

The difference between "protected" and "unprotected" actions can decide whether workers might legally lose their jobs. Whether the law protects an activity depends on the situation. Actions aimed at job safety and security are likely to be protected. However, the law does not protect violent actions.

Q. Do workers have the right to reject a union?

A. Yes, employees may vote against the union. Their NLRA rights include the choice *not* to have a collective bargaining representative. However, it is the majority of employees who decide. Single workers cannot choose to reject a union if their bargaining unit chooses one. Once a majority votes for it, the union becomes the *sole representative* of all workers in the bargaining unit.

Q. Once workers choose a union, must an employee finance it?

A. Workers generally have to support the union, at least indirectly. Some "union security" devices allow the law to enforce an employee's duties to the union. These devices also limit "free riders." The law approves union security devices because these devices supply some financial security to the union. This enables the union to carry out its duties. These duties include collective bargaining and handling grievance and arbitration cases.

Usually the collective bargaining agreement sets up the union security plans. An *agency shop* provision is an example of union security. It requires workers in the bargaining unit to finance the union. This may be through union dues or through a fee similar to an initiation fee and dues. When using the fee option, the union does not require union membership. There also is no duty to follow internal union rules. However, the union may decide that any worker who is not a member cannot take part in union affairs.

A similar provision is the *union shop*. It requires all new workers to join the union. They may do so after a grace period of at least 30 days. However, workers in a union shop do not actually lose their jobs if they do not join so long as they pay dues or fees. This results from the NLRA. Hence, union shop and agency shop provisions have similar effects. They require only economic support.

The old *closed shop* provision is now illegal. It forced workers to join the union in order to get hired. Some states have "right-to-work" laws. These make other union security devices illegal. Most of these states are in the South and West.

Q. What is a labor union's legal duty?

A. A labor union's legal duty has two parts. The first is to bargain collectively with the employer for the workers. The second is to fairly represent all the workers in the bargaining unit. The employer and union must bargain in good faith. If they cannot agree, a strike may occur. Union negotiations often result in contracts. Most collective bargaining contracts cover the basic terms and conditions of employment. These include wage scales, work hours, fringe benefits, work rules, seniority, and job and shift assignments. They also include order of lay-off and recall, promotions, and transfers. Nearly all contracts have a system to resolve complaints affecting all employees. They also offer ways to handle specific disciplinary problems of single workers. Unions call this a *grievance procedure*.

Q. How does a grievance procedure work?

A. Usually, the union represents a worker if there is a problem about how the contract applies to a particular situation. (In some situations, one or more workers may complain to the employer without involving the union.) A grievance procedure normally contains several steps. There are many chances to resolve the problem at each step. If there is no solution, many contracts order a hearing before a neutral person. This person is an *arbitrator*. At the hearing, the union presents the worker's side of the issue. Meanwhile, the employer presents its side. Each side offers witnesses and arguments. The arbitrator then makes a decision. This ruling may uphold or deny the complaint. The decision binds the employer and worker to its terms. Courts can uphold these decisions, sometimes called *awards*.

Q. What if the union refuses to represent workers or improperly represents them?

A. A union has a duty to adequately and fairly negotiate for its members. The union does not have to raise each worker's issues during contract negotiations. The union may obtain a contract that is less favorable for a specific job or group of employees.

WORKER ACTIVITIES PROTECTED BY THE NLRA

Workers have the right to engage in *concerted activity*. The NLRA forbids employers from punishing or firing employees for engaging in protected activities. The NLRA protects *group* activities, such as union meetings, solicitation of support, and other actions related to union organizing. Thus, actions by groups of employees to improve their position at work are protected concerted activities. It does not matter whether the workers have a connection with a union nor if a union represents them. For example, group protests over dangerous working conditions are protected activities.

So is an organized strike and picketing to advertise the dispute. (An organized strike involves withholding services to enforce collective bargaining demands.)

HIRING HALLS

A *hiring hall* is an agreement between a union and employer. It permits the union to recruit and refer workers to employers for hiring.

Despite what some people think, hiring halls are legal. Hiring halls help keep track of workers. They also help provide security and seniority systems in certain industries, such as construction. In these industries, employees usually work temporarily for one employer. Under some contracts, the union is the sole job referral agency. Hiring halls enhance the union's power. They also offer a useful way for employers to get workers.

Unions must run hiring halls within certain rules to avoid illegal abuses. For example, the union cannot refuse to refer nonunion workers. Workers having problems should consult a union official, the employer, the NLRB, or a lawyer.

If workers have a valid complaint, the union has a duty to fairly represent them. The union has to explore worker complaints in good faith. It does not have to pursue every grievance. However, the union must treat similar employee problems the same. It must do so without bias or bad faith. However, a worker does not have a right to make the union pursue a complaint to arbitration.

Representing worker grievances is important. Most unions take it very seriously. Sometimes the union's failure to represent employees fairly harms them. Then the workers may file charges with the NLRB or take the union to court. However, mere negligence by the union in its effort to represent a worker does not violate its duty of fair representation.

The duty of fair representation is important as it regards discrimination. That is, the union cannot discriminate against its members because of race, sex, or other offending and arbitrary groupings. The NLRA entitles employees to be free from unfair treatment by their union. A union that discriminates may be guilty of unfair labor practices. This also opens the union to lawsuits for damages.

Q. How do state collective bargaining laws and the NLRA differ?

A. Public workers usually lack the right to strike. If they have it, state law highly controls that right. Civil service systems coexist with collective bargaining agreements. Both civil service systems and collective bargaining agreements cover many rights. These include job review, job criteria, testing, and seniority. Other rights involve firing, discipline, overtime, and layoffs.

Q. Are the laws affecting public workers different from those for private employees?

A. Yes, they are quite different. Besides state collective bargaining laws, other laws apply to public workers. Civil service laws or teacher tenure rights interact with collectively bargained rights and constitutional guarantees. Hence, union workers with questions about reviews, promotions, transfers, and the like should talk to union officials. They usually can answer these questions. Nonunion workers may consult a civil service advisor, personnel officer, labor relations expert, or lawyer.

Q. What other related questions concern unions and collective bargaining?

A. Many questions are beyond the scope of this chapter. These include replacing strikers, picketing, and firing workers for valid reasons versus for union activity. There are also questions about grievances and how much workers may engage in union activities on company premises. In addition, there are questions about organizing health care workers and other problems unique to unions and collective bargaining. Workers and employers should seek the advice of an expert in labor law.

Discrimination

Q. What do job discrimination laws cover?

A. The laws protect all aspects of work, including hiring, wages, benefits, and reviews. They also cover promotions, duties, firing, and so on. These laws ban intentional discrimination. They also forbid unintentional discrimination unless it is legally justified. (Further information on this topic appears later in this chapter.)

In general, there are more and more laws against discrimination. Some of these protect such groups as the handicapped and aliens. Some state laws and municipal ordinances extend coverage to marital status and sexual orientation.

Q. What are the main laws?

A. Two main federal laws apply. The first is Title VII of the Civil Rights Act of 1964. The second is the Age Discrimination in Employment Act (ADEA). Together, they ban discrimination because of race, sex, color, national origin, religion, or age (if over 40). These laws forbid employers, unions, and employment agencies from engaging in discrimination based on these characteristics. In some cases, the Fifth and Fourteenth Amendments to the U.S. Constitution forbid discrimination by government employers. Some state laws may be even stricter. These laws try to ensure that all job-related actions and decisions treat everyone equally.

Q. What points should I consider if I claim discrimination?

A. There are many factors. First, job discrimination laws often have strict time limits for making a claim. Thus, you should get expert advice and act without delay. Second, if fired or not hired for discriminatory reasons, you should *seek another*

Everyone Has a Chance

Americans believe that democracy should ensure equal opportunity, but not necessarily equal results. This means every citizen should have the same chance to succeed. It also means that fairness at work is important to success. Many laws forbid job discrimination based on race, sex, color, national origin, religion, marital status, age, and handicap. These are federal, state, municipal, and local laws. They also include agency rules and executive orders. However, many issues arise. Can the law ensure an equal opportunity for disadvantaged groups without being unfair to others? Can the law be race conscious without fostering racism? Are quotas allowable? If so, when and in what cases? This section confronts some of these issues.

job. Do so even if it seems that the law entitles you to the former job. If you do not find other work, it looks like you would not or could not work. This can weaken your claim. It also can limit any award of back pay. It is important to show that you want to work.

Racial Discrimination

Q. Whom does Title VII cover? What does it do?

A. It forbids almost any employer from discriminating because of race, color, religion, sex, or national origin in job-related matters. It does not cover employers with less than 15 employees. Title VII applies when discrimination by an employer, union, or employment agency affects some job-related aspect. For example, Title VII would not apply to race discrimination in social functions. Still, the idea of employment is quite broad. It includes earnings, terms, conditions, and privileges of employment. To violate Title VII, an employer does not have to fire or refuse to promote a worker. If an employer allows the workplace to become a hostile (racist) climate, a worker might take action under Title VII. This might force the employer to solve the problem. Title VII requires an employer to prevent any known racial intimidation and harassment.

Q. What discrimination does Title VII prohibit?

A. It forbids all intentional discrimination. One example is an unwritten "whites only" hiring policy. Another is using race to set wages, assign shifts, and the like. Intentional discrimination is usually proven by showing that the employer treats a minority worker less favorably than a white person in the same job. The reason for this must appear to be race. People sometimes call this *disparate treatment*. For example, an employer might fire a black worker who often is late for work. At the same time, the employer merely scolds or suspends white employees in similar jobs who arrive late. Intentional discrimination exists if the employer knew or should have known of the unequal treatment and failed to correct it. The employer usually is liable for the acts of a supervisor.

Title VII also bans job-related tests or requirements with a racially discriminatory impact. It does not matter if the impact is unintentional. People sometimes call this *disparate impact*. It usually becomes obvious only when a study shows that the test or requirement disqualifies more minorities than whites. Thus, a minimum educational level might

Discrimination Based on Race

Federal law forbids job discrimination because of race. This applies to private and public employers. Executive Order 11246 also commands that employers doing large amounts of business with the federal government not discriminate because of race. It requires such employers to hire and promote racial minorities. Nearly every state and many local governments have laws to eliminate racial discrimination by employers. These laws protect all races and national origins, including blacks, Hispanics, Asians, Native Americans, and whites.

screen out a greater ratio of minorities than whites. (This chapter's previous "Recruiting and Hiring" section discusses hiring tests.) Discriminatory impact is illegal unless the employer is able to show that the job requirement is business related.

Q. What agency enforces Title VII?

A. The Equal Employment Opportunity Commission (EEOC) upholds it. The EEOC looks into charges filed by workers. It then tries to see if the parties can solve their problems by negotiating. As a last resort, the EEOC takes the employer to court.

Q. How should workers pursue claims of illegal discrimination?

A. First, they should talk to their employer. The employer may not know about the discriminatory act or the attitudes of a supervisor. If this does not solve the matter, the worker may file a claim with the EEOC. In many states, an employment discrimination agency or a human rights commission accepts such filings. The EEOC will often allow the state agency to handle the initial processing.

There are very strict time limits for filing claims. If workers do not meet them, the court or agency will not uphold their claims. An employee should file a claim within 180 days from the date the discrimination occurred. This time limit differs when a state agency has the authority to handle such claims. Then the workers must file the charge with the EEOC within 300 days from the date the discrimination occurred or within 30 days after the state proceeding ends, whichever happens first.

The state agency time rules vary. To find out the situation in their state, workers should talk to the EEOC or state civil rights agency. They should be sure about the time limits. Employers may not punish workers for filing claims.

The process for filing a charge is:

- A worker files a charge with the EEOC. The employee may do this either initially or after a state agency declines to proceed.
- The EEOC informs the employer.
- The EEOC begins to investigate. It usually reviews employer records. The EEOC may have an informal "fact-finding" meeting with the employer and worker. This allows everyone to be heard.
- The EEOC tries to reach a voluntary settlement. If the parties do not agree, the EEOC will decide if there is "reasonable cause" to believe there was discrimination.
- The EEOC informs both parties of the decision.

AFFIRMATIVE ACTION

Affirmative Action usually is a special plan or program that an employer adopts. It places job-related requirements on the employer. These plans aim to avoid or correct illegal discrimination in the work force and against job applicants. Such plans or programs are *Affirmative Action Plans*.

An Affirmative Action Plan (AAP) can have many goals. An employer usually tailors a plan to its specific situation. One goal might be to ensure that the employer does not discriminate against workers and job applicants. Another might try to remedy past discrimination or eliminate improper practices. An employer also might create an AAP to use the skills of minorities and women to a greater degree than in the past. This would allow the employer's work force to represent minorities or women more fairly.

- If the EEOC finds reasonable cause, it may take the employer to court. Or it will give the worker a "right to sue" letter. Then the matter of whether to continue is up to the employee.
- If the EEOC does not find reasonable cause, it still will issue the worker a "right to sue" letter.
- If the EEOC holds a claim for 180 days after a worker files it, an employee may request a "right to sue" letter. It will not matter whether the EEOC has finished with the case.
- Workers can file lawsuits in federal court within 90 days after receiving the "right to sue" letter.
- If the employee does not act within this time limit, the employee loses the right to sue.

Once a worker files a suit in court, the employee must prove that the employer violated the law. However, a state civil rights agency might retain the case. After its investigation (following procedures similar to EEOC), the agency will make a ruling. Various state agencies act differently.

Q. Will an employer's Affirmative Action Plan (AAP) affect nonminority employees?

A. It is hard to say. That depends on a specific plan. However, AAPs (explained in the nearby "Affirmative Action" article) involve recruitment, hiring, promotion, transfer, and, sometimes, seniority or layoff, as well as other terms and conditions of employment. Since AAPs deal so broadly with the workplace, nonminority employees probably will be affected to some degree. In most cases, however, an AAP probably would not threaten job security or seniority. An AAP is more likely to affect job applicants or, to a lesser degree, promotions.

Q. Does the law require AAPs?

A. It depends on many points. Title VII does not require all covered employers to adopt an AAP. However, Title VII does permit AAPs. If an employer is a major government contractor, Executive Order 11246 may require the employer to have an AAP. Thus, the government may impose an AAP as a contractual duty. The Office of Federal Contract Compliance Programs (OFCCP) manages Executive Order 11246. The OFCCP regulates in considerable detail the "Affirmative Action" requirement and related plans. Employers should seek expert advice about this area.

Another point is whether state laws require AAPs of employers with state or local government contracts. Moreover, governors or mayors and other public bodies may require public employers to adopt AAPs. Finally, a court may order an employer to adopt an AAP to remedy illegal discrimination.

Q. Are there other reasons to create AAPs?

A. Yes, some AAPs result from lawsuit settlements. The parties may resolve the dispute by agreeing to negotiate an AAP. Thus, the AAP may be the result of a court-authorized *consent decree*.

Sometimes an AAP results from a voluntary agreement between an employer and labor union. Thus, a collective bargaining agreement may contain an AAP. An employer, on its own, also may adopt an AAP.

Q. Why do employers adopt AAPs when they have no legal duty?

A. It might protect them from discrimination claims or lawsuits. Hence, the employers could avoid very costly legal fees. For self interest or political reasons, an employer may comply with the national policy of a discrimination-free workplace. Thus, customer or community pressure might make it "good business" to adopt a voluntary AAP. Good labor/management relations also might require collectively bargaining an AAP. In addition, an employer might want more federal or state contracts. Hence, the employer uses a voluntary AAP to prepare for future AAP requirements imposed on government contractors.

Q. Suppose an AAP gives special treatment to members of groups not adequately represented. Doesn't this violate Title VII, which forbids job discrimination? After all, it amounts to reverse discrimination.

A. No, this is not the case. Authorities interpret Title VII to permit voluntary AAPs to remedy an obvious imbalance in typically segregated job categories. However, this becomes a very difficult problem when it harms nonminority workers.

The courts are now setting some guidelines on when employers are permitted to give special treatment to members of disadvantaged groups. There are still serious disputes on this matter. The law is in a state of change.

Q. What do courts consider when ruling on AAPs that treat disadvantaged groups better than others?

A. Courts stress many points in examining a "voluntary" AAP that gives special treatment to minorities or women. First,

Reverse Discrimination

You may have read that most AAPs (Affirmative Action Plans) result in *reverse discrimination*. This means that they give special treatment to minorities and women at the expense of others. You also may have heard that AAPs have rigid hiring quotas based on race, sex, or national origin. Is this true? In general, the answer is no. AAPs do not themselves create reverse discrimination. AAPs also do not authorize rigid quotas. However, some employers use AAPs to represent minorities and women fairly in the work force. Employers often decide whether they employ minorities and women fairly by using studies. They might examine the ratio of minorities and women in the qualified labor force from which they are hiring. The studies then compare this ratio to ratios of minorities and women in the work force.

(continued)

(continued)

After this, employers decide how much their work force does not fully include qualified minorities. Suppose, in one job class, that the employer does not hire qualified women. However, the area's labor market shows that 45 percent of qualified women work in that job class. The employer sets a goal (not necessarily 45 percent) to recruit women. The employer may use internal promotions or hire new workers to more fairly represent women.

Employers tailor goals to their needs. Their goals usually consider several factors. These involve turnover rates, number of qualified minorities and women, and amount of job openings. They also include required degree of training and experience. Their goals consider the number of in-house candidates as well.

the voluntary plan's purpose should be to eliminate obvious racial or sex-based imbalances in the work force. Such imbalances should clearly affect the disadvantaged groups that Title VII protects (that is, groups identified by race or sex).

Second, the plan cannot "unnecessarily trammel [confine] the interests" of nonminority (white or male) workers. It should not automatically exclude nonminority employees from, say, promotions. These employees have genuine, firmly rooted expectations about their jobs. The courts care deeply about this. The employer should design the AAP to reduce the effect on current workers. The AAP also should lessen any interference with genuine employee expectations.

Third, the minority person favored by the plan must be qualified. Employers should avoid AAPs favoring unqualified minorities.

Fourth, the AAP should not adopt strict quotas. It should strive toward realistic goals. Such goals should account for turnover, layoffs, lateral transfers, new job openings, and retirements. These goals also should take into account the number of qualified minorities in the area's work force. Thus, strict quotas are not acceptable.

Fifth, courts probably prefer plans that focus on recruiting and hiring new employees. Courts seem to favor these plans more than those that deal with promotion, seniority, or layoffs.

Finally, an AAP should be temporary. It should not be a long-term or permanent condition. Thus, an employer may design a plan to *attain* a balanced work force. However, it should not necessarily use an AAP to *maintain* a balanced work force.

Remember that many points concern the courts. One is upholding the national policy against job-related discrimination. Another is balancing the interests of protected minorities against those of the majority in a given work force. Courts also care about expanding voluntary adoption of plans by employers.

Sex Discrimination

Q. What laws ban sex discrimination?

A. Title VII forbids job-related sex discrimination. The federal Equal Pay Act requires employers to pay men and women equally for essentially equal work. The Fourteenth Amendment to the U.S. Constitution guarantees "equal protection of the laws." Courts have used this to forbid sex discrimination in certain cases. The NLRA bans such discrimination by unions. Executive Order 11246 bans sex discrimination by employers who do business with the federal government. Most states have laws against job-related sex discrimination.

Q. Do these laws protect only women?

A. No, they also protect men. This has opened jobs formerly reserved for one sex or the other.

Q. Are there exceptions to sex discrimination laws?

A. Yes, exceptions do exist. One exists when an employer can prove that the sex of an applicant for a certain job is a Bona Fide Occupational Qualification (BFOQ, which was discussed earlier in this chapter's "Recruiting and Hiring" section). However, the law limits this exception greatly. The EEOC has rules for setting up a BFOQ. They require the employer to prove three points:
(1) There must be a logical tie between the gender (sex) required and the performance of a specific job.
(2) The gender requirement must be necessary for proper job performance.
(3) The job must touch the "essence" of an employer's operation.

Courts have been very reluctant to treat sex as a BFOQ. They usually uphold it only in obvious cases. These include fashion models and actors and actresses.

Another very limited exception exists when a requirement is a "business necessity." It allows an employer to use an employment standard that has an *unintentional* discriminatory impact so long as the standard is related to the ability to do the specific job. For example, an employer can defend a height standard for pilots for safety purposes. It does not matter that the standard has a negative impact on women.

Q. Assume that a garage owner believes women mechanics are less competent. The owner also thinks that women "get in the way" and that male mechanics prefer not to work with them. If so, may the employer hire only males?

A. No, an employer's biases do not justify this action. Neither does the preference of coworkers or customers for members of a certain sex.

Q. Suppose a small woman (five feet tall and 100 pounds) applies for a warehouse job. However, the employer

TYPES OF SEX DISCRIMINATION PROHIBITED BY LAW

The laws discussed in this section apply to every work-related aspect, from hiring to firing. They forbid intentional discrimination *(disparate treatment)*. An example is an employer that treats one sex differently from the other. These laws also prohibit unintentional discrimination *(disparate impact)*. This occurs when employment practices have a discriminatory impact on working conditions or when job openings favor one sex over another.

Suppose an employer supplies insurance coverage for males only. Then female workers are victims of disparate treatment. Assume a police department hires only people weighing over 160 pounds. Then female applicants are victims of disparate impact. This is due to the negative impact such a physical standard has on women.

Passing Over Women to Promote Less-Qualified Men

May an employer pass over a female employee and promote a less-qualified man because he has more seniority? The employer probably can do this legally. Bona fide seniority systems are immune from Title VII. This is true even if they unintentionally discriminate. However, employers are not permitted to use seniority systems to hide intentional discrimination. AAPs to eliminate sex discrimination sometimes conflict with seniority systems. (A discussion of seniority systems as they affect workers over 40 appears later in this chapter.)

thinks she is too small for the job. May the employer reject her on this basis?

A. No, the U.S. Supreme Court has held that height and weight restrictions generally violate Title VII. (However, this is not true if the employer can show a BFOQ or business necessity.) Such restrictions are illegal because they affect women more harshly. Another reason is that the restrictions come from stereotyping abilities. The law entitles all workers to be judged on whether they, as individuals, can do the job. An employer may refuse to hire people who cannot do the job. For example, if a job requires lifting heavy objects, the employer may require that an applicant be able to do this. However, an employer may not assume from somebody's sex that the person cannot do it. All job applicants must have a chance to prove their ability.

Q. May employers provide dependent health care coverage to married male workers, but deny it to married women? Also, may employers give women fewer benefits than they do men?

A. No, employers must offer all benefits equally to both sexes. Thus, employers must provide health insurance benefits to the spouses of male and female workers equally. Benefits for husbands of female employees must be available on an equal basis to wives of male workers. This includes pregnancy-related benefits. The U.S. Supreme Court held that not doing so gives married male employees more benefits than married female workers.

Q. May employers have different retirement and pension plans for each sex?

A. No, the U.S. Supreme Court has ruled that contributions made to pension plans must be equal. The same is true for benefits received from such plans. Tables showing that women live longer than men do not justify requiring women to contribute more or paying women lower benefits.

Q. May employer-sponsored life or disability insurance plans discriminate?

A. No, these also should apply equally to both sexes. If an employer contributes to a plan, it must do so equally. It does not matter whether the insurance company charges different premiums based on sex. At least one state—Montana—prohibits insurers from using sex or marital status to compute premiums and policy benefits.

Q. May employers fire female workers because they plan to marry?

A. Doing so would violate laws in most states. It also probably would violate Title VII. The only possible defense would be that the employer also fired male employees who marry.

Title VII does not protect workers based on their marital status. However, employment policies about marriage may lead to sex discrimination claims. Many states have laws forbidding discrimination based on marital status. This means employers are not permitted to fire or unfavorably treat workers simply because the workers marry, divorce, or are single.

Q. What should I do if my employer discriminates against me because of my sex?

A. First, talk to your employer. If this doesn't work, contact the EEOC, the state human rights agency, or a lawyer. Filing a sex discrimination claim under Title VII is the same as for other types of discrimination. (See the previous discussion.) State sex discrimination laws might offer other remedies or procedures. You should consult the state employment rights agency.

Sexual Harassment

Q. Is sexual harassment illegal?

A. Yes, under Title VII and some state laws, it is a form of illegal sex discrimination. Some state laws treat sexual harassment as a separate offense.

Q. What is sexual harassment?

A. EEOC rules about job-related *sexual harassment* define it as:

> Unwelcome sexual advances, requests for sexual favors, and other verbal or physical conduct of a sexual nature.

State laws prohibiting sexual harassment usually define it the same way. EEOC rules say that sexual harassment occurs:

(1) When employees believe they will lose their jobs if they do not submit to sexual proposals;
(2) When employees will lose a promotion or good work assignments if they don't submit to sexual proposals; or
(3) When such conduct interferes with the employee's job or creates a hostile working environment.

EXAMPLES OF SEXUAL HARASSMENT

Sexual harassment consists of physical conduct of a sexual nature. It also includes verbal advances such as requests for sexual favors. More casual advances like occasional touching, off-color jokes, or repeated sexual references could become sexual harassment. It depends on the situation. Courts could find a combination of these acts to be sexual harassment. Sexual harassment can take many forms. It can be vulgar or lewd comments, or forcing workers to wear sexually revealing uniforms. Also it can involve unwanted physical touching or fondling, or invitations to engage in sexual conduct. Even embarrassing cartoons posted on a bulletin board can be sexual harassment.

(continued)

Q. Does sexual harassment have to result in discrimination about the terms and conditions of employment before legal action is proper?

A. Yes, most authorities believe this to be true.

Q. What does discrimination about the "terms and conditions of employment" mean?

A. It suggests two things. First, it means sexual harassment that links job benefits to sexual favors. This includes hiring, firing, promotion, review, assignments, transfer, or other economic benefits. Second, the U.S. Supreme Court recently ruled on discrimination about the terms and conditions of employment. The Court ruled that it includes sexual harassment that unreasonably interferes with an employee's performance, or *creates an intimidating, hostile, or offensive working environment.* This second type does not have to involve economic benefits. Creating a hostile environment is enough for a sexual harassment case.

(continued)

The EEOC considers all circumstances to decide if sexual harassment has occurred. This includes the nature and frequency of the advances. It also involves the conditions under which the offender made them. A court might rule that certain evidence is relevant in a given case. Such evidence can be the worker's provocative behavior or dress. It also can be the employee's promiscuity or publicly expressed sexual fantasies.

Q. If a sexually harassed worker "voluntarily" has sex with a supervisor, will it prevent a finding of sexual harassment against the employer?

A. Not necessarily. The U.S. Supreme Court ruled that the employee only must show that the sexual advances or actions are "unwelcome." The Court ruled that it only matters whether the employee's conduct showed that the sexual advances were unwelcome. It does not matter whether the worker had sex voluntarily.

Q. Is an employer liable for sexual harassment against an employee by a coworker?

A. In a Title VII claim, an employer is liable only if it knew or should have known about the sexual harassment between coworkers. Even then, the employer may not be liable if it can show that it corrected the problem as soon as it came to its attention.

Q. What should an employer do to avoid sexual harassment claims?

A. Prevention is the best practice. Here are the steps an employer should take:

(1) Develop a written policy dealing with sexual harassment. It should show the employer's disapproval. The employer

should contact the EEOC in Washington, D.C. (2401 E Street, N.W.), for its guidelines on sexual harassment. These will help the employer formulate its own policies.

(2) Develop an effective complaint procedure for workers who are being sexually harassed. It should allow them to go beyond their supervisor when that supervisor took part in the sexual harassment or did not take proper action. The grievance procedure should encourage a prompt solution to the problem.

(3) The employer should *promptly* and effectively respond to sexual harassment complaints.

(4) An employer should act to prevent sexual harassment before it occurs. The employer can circulate or post its antiharassment policy. An employer also should talk about the subject openly. It should not wait for workers to complain. The employer should show strong disapproval of such conduct. The employer should tell employees of their right to be free from harassment. The employer also should properly discipline supervisors or coworkers for sexual harassment.

(5) The employer should post the EEOC rules on sexual harassment.

Q. If an employer develops a sexual harassment policy with a prompt and effective complaint procedure, will this protect the employer from liability?

A. This will not guarantee it. However, an effective policy can strongly influence certain issues. These may include coworker harassment, employer liability for supervisory acts, and the employer's general integrity. The key is not only whether harassment policies exist. It also is whether they work promptly and effectively.

Q. Besides federal laws, are there other bans on sexual harassment?

A. Yes, several states have their own laws. At least eight states prohibit sexual harassment of workers. They are California, Connecticut, Illinois, Michigan, Minnesota, New York, North Dakota, and Wisconsin. Almost every other state prohibits sex discrimination against employees without referring to sexual harassment. State laws and policies tend to follow the federal rules. Also, it is becoming more common for collective bargaining agreements to forbid sex discrimination. This is true for both the public and private sectors. Such agreements usually have a grievance procedure that ends in binding arbitration. Thus, workers might file sexual harassment complaints as violations of the collective bargaining agreement.

Employer Liability for Sexual Harassment by Supervisors

In general, an employer is liable if a supervisor sexually harasses an employee by giving job benefits for sexual favors. Courts usually say that supervisors who link real job benefits to sexual favors are acting for the employer. Thus, the employer is liable for its agents' actions.

However, this is not quite true for the hostile environment type of sexual harassment. The U.S. Supreme Court recently ruled on this. It held that employer liability for supervisors' actions in cases involving hostile environments depends on the situation. A basic question is whether the supervisor was acting as the employer's agent.

Q. Suppose a worker gives in to a supervisor's sexual advances. If that worker gets a promotion that should have gone to another employee, what can the denied employee do?

A. That employee should talk to the supervisor's superior. The EEOC believes an employer may be liable to a denied employee when another worker gains unfair advantage through sexual favors. The denied employee has been the victim of a different form of sexual harassment. The supervisor used the authority of a supervisory position to reward one worker for sexual favors at the expense of another.

What Should Victims of Sexual Harassment Do?

They should *immediately* notify their supervisor. If the supervisor is the harasser, the worker should go to the supervisor's superior. Employers cannot solve the problem if they do not know about it. If there is a grievance procedure for sexual harassment claims, the employee should use it. An employee also can file a claim with the EEOC. The process is the same as with other types of discrimination. This includes the right to sue in federal court. If the state in which the employee lives prohibits sexual harassment, the worker should contact the proper state agency.

Pregnancy and Maternity/Paternity Leave

Q. May an employer fire a worker because she is pregnant?

A. No. In 1978, Congress made it illegal for an employer to discriminate because of pregnancy, childbirth, or related conditions. An employer may not refuse to hire a pregnant woman. An employer also may not fire her because of her pregnancy. In addition, an employer may not force her to take maternity leave. The law requires employers to treat pregnancy and childbirth like other temporary disabilities. Health insurance plans must cover these conditions if they handle other temporary disabilities. The law protects the rights of pregnant workers to the same extent as for disabled employees. These rights include giving back their jobs and accumulating seniority for them after they give birth. Some states have laws protecting the maternity/pregnancy benefits of employees.

Q. After having a baby, may an employee choose to stay home for a couple of months?

A. That would be considered *extended* maternity leave. Women usually are considered medically disabled for a period of weeks, not months, after childbirth. Unless complications arise from childbirth, or unless the employer's policy permits such leaves, the employer does not have to provide extended maternity leave.

However, the law requires employers who grant leaves of absence for other personal nondisability reasons to grant maternity leave on the same terms. Most employers limit the time of such leave. It usually is without pay.

If there is a medical reason for staying off the job, the employer must treat it as any other medical or disability leave. Workers who wish to take extended maternity leave should check their employer's policy. Employees also should see if health insurance benefits can be continued during maternity or other leave.

Q. How do employers handle giving jobs back to women who have had babies? What about accumulating seniority during maternity leave?

A. An employer must restore women to their jobs and accumulate seniority for them while they are on medical leave, just as the employer would for workers on other types of disability leave.

Q. Does the law require employers' insurance carriers to pay for abortions?

A. No, employers' insurance carriers do not have to pay for abortions that are not medically necessary.

However, employers cannot discriminate against women about leave policy or medical leave for complications from an abortion. The law considers this a "pregnancy-related" condition.

Wage Discrimination and Comparable Worth

Q. What is the difference between comparable worth and equal pay for equal work?

A. People often confuse these two ideas. However, they are quite different.

In *comparable worth,* if one job has the same worth to an employer as another job, both jobs have comparable worth. Therefore, people in these jobs should be paid the same. For example, a secretary might have the same worth to a specific employer as a truck driver. Comparable worth supporters argue that pay for the two jobs should be similar. Lawsuits have claimed that an employer's failure to pay equally for jobs of comparable worth is sex discrimination. It supposedly violates Title VII. So far, most courts have rejected this legal theory, though some have accepted it.

Equal pay comes from the Equal Pay Act of 1963. It requires employers to pay the same rate to all workers doing jobs that are identical or almost the same. The Equal Pay Act orders employers to pay males and females the same in jobs of equal skill, effort, responsibility, and similar working conditions. However, the Act permits employers to pay

Paternity Leave

It is not settled whether the law entitles expectant fathers to paternity leave on the same terms as maternity leave. If an employer provides nondisabled women with maternity leave, the employer may have to do the same for fathers to avoid sex discrimination. The employer usually limits the time of such leave. It normally is without pay.

workers differently for one of four reasons. Employers may do this because of seniority systems, merit systems, systems based on production quantity or quality, or any factor other than sex. Several states also have equal pay laws.

Pay equity refers to the idea of fairness in setting wages. Supporters of comparable worth often use it interchangeably with comparable worth, but it is not the same. Comparable worth deals with equalizing pay for *different* jobs. Equal pay seeks to equalize pay for the *same* job. Federal laws require equal pay for equal work. However, it generally is legal to pay unequal wages for jobs of comparable work. A few state laws order equal pay for comparable work.

What to Do About Violations of the Equal Pay Act

Suppose an employer pays an employee less than an employee of the opposite sex who does the same work. What can the first employee do? That employee should talk with the employer. If that fails, the first employee can contact the EEOC. It enforces the Equal Pay Act. A violation may entitle the victim to receive double back pay.

Disabled Workers

Q. Can any federal law help disabled people find work?

A. Perhaps the federal Rehabilitation Act of 1973 can help. It forbids discrimination against handicapped persons. The Act applies to the federal government, federal contractors with over $2,500 in contracts, and programs receiving federal aid. Such programs include public agencies, universities, and health care facilities.

Q. Whom does the Act cover?

A. It covers people who have a physical or mental impairment that greatly limits one or more "major life activities." This includes nearly all physical disabilities. It also applies to many mental or emotional handicaps.

Q. What about the state laws for the disabled?

A. Nearly all states have laws banning discrimination because of a handicap. Some are broader than the federal law and apply to private businesses. Other state laws affect only the state government. States define "handicap" differently. Some definitions are broader than the federal idea. Others are narrower. Contact your local/state human rights or labor department. The federal law often influences state law.

Q. What should someone do about discrimination against the disabled?

A. Federal government workers should turn first to the agency for which they work. They *must* file a complaint with the agency's EEO office—not the EEOC—within 30 days from the discriminatory act. That office normally has 21 days to review the complaint and issue a decision. The employee then has 15 days to file a "formal" complaint with the agency, if the worker desires. If not, the employee may appeal to the EEOC within 20 days of the final decision. The worker also has a third choice. If the EEO office takes no action or if its decision does not satisfy the employee, the worker may file a civil lawsuit. This filing must occur within 180 days from the date of the original complaint. However, the worker may not appeal to the EEOC *and* file a civil lawsuit. The employee must do one or the other.

Workers employed by federal contractors can complain to the Department of Labor. It can see that guilty employers do not receive future federal contracts. Normally, such workers have no right to sue.

For programs receiving federal support, individual federal agencies administer the handicapped rules. For instance, the U.S. Department of Education oversees whether schools receiving aid obey the Rehabilitation Act.

A few statements apply generally. It is enough that a program simply receives federal funds. The program does not have to specify the funds for handicapped people. If necessary, an individual suit may be brought. Also, state law may apply to the situation.

Q. Is there Affirmative Action for the handicapped?

A. There is for federal workers and those who work for organizations receiving federal money. Federal contractors and agencies must take Affirmative Action to hire qualified handicapped persons. Employers must review their procedures to make sure they do not discriminate against handicapped persons.

There is no violation if the handicapped person simply cannot do the job. However, the Rehabilitation Act and many state laws require employers to make "reasonable accommodations" for the disabled. This may require altering the workplace or a specific job to allow the person to work. However, employers do not have to suffer "undue hardships" when doing so. Courts decide what is an undue hardship on an individual basis.

Q. Must an employer hire handicapped applicants who do not qualify for the job?

A. No, under the Rehabilitation Act, an employer does not have to hire them. Even after making reasonable accommodations, employers do not have to hire handicapped people who still cannot perform a specific job's duties. Handicapped persons must prove that they qualify for the job. These rules may be slightly different under some state laws. However, an employer almost always does not have to hire handicapped workers whose conditions obviously disqualify them from performing a job.

Q. Do any laws provide disabled veterans with special rights and protections?

A. Yes, although some issues are still unclear. The Agent Orange controversy and the emerging problems of Vietnam Vets Syndrome or Post Traumatic Stress Syndrome may give greater benefits to disabled veterans. Veterans should contact the Veterans Administration, U.S. (or state) Department of Labor, or a veterans' support group for details.

Q. Do disabled Vietnam veterans receive specific protection under the law?

A. Yes, the Vietnam Era Veterans Readjustment Assistance Act offers some help. It requires firms having federal contracts of $10,000 or more to hire and promote handicapped Vietnam veterans.

Age Discrimination

Q. May employers force older workers out of their jobs in favor of younger ones because the employer wants "young blood"?

A. No, the federal Age Discrimination in Employment Act of 1967 (ADEA) prohibits job discrimination against people over 40 years old. Before January 1, 1987, the ADEA applied only to persons between the ages of 40 and 70. The Age Discrimination in Employment Amendments of 1986 (ADE Amendments) eliminated the age 70 limit. Like Title VII, the ADEA forbids job-related discrimination because of age. This includes hiring, firing, and the terms and conditions of employment (including health benefits). It also prohibits discriminatory advertising for jobs. Examples include "under 45" and "recent college graduate." The law protects workers from retaliation for filing ADEA claims.

The Act applies equally to all persons in the protected age group. Thus, it is illegal for an employer to discriminate because of age against a 50-year-old in favor of a 60-year-old. The same is true if it were the other way around. Both workers are over 40, and the Act protects both of them.

Q. How do the states treat age discrimination?

A. Many states have laws that apply. These often are more complete than the ADEA. Some ban discrimination no matter what the person's age—even if that person is under 40. If the state law is narrower than the ADEA, the federal law still protects workers. Federal laws overrule narrower state laws.

Q. What can a worker do about age discrimination?

A. First, the employee can meet with the employer. If this fails, the worker can contact the EEOC, and—if it handles such problems—a state employment agency or human rights commission. A worker must file a charge with the EEOC within 180 days after the discriminatory act occurred. This time limit differs when a state agency handles such claims. Then the worker may file the charge with the EEOC within 300 days after the violation or within 30 days after the state proceeding ends, whichever is earlier. A worker may file a lawsuit 60 days after notifying the EEOC of the claim. The suit must be brought within two years of the violation. The EEOC tries to settle the dispute out of court.

Q. What employers are covered by the ADEA?

A. It applies to employers, employment agencies, and labor organizations. The ADEA defines a covered employer as an organization having 20 or more employees that does business in interstate commerce. The ADEA also applies to state and local governments. State laws may cover more employers.

Q. Are there exceptions to the ADEA?

A. Very few exist. As with Title VII, employers can defend age discrimination if they show that age is a Bona Fide Occupational Qualification (BFOQ). (A previous section in this chapter—"Recruiting and Hiring"—discussed BFOQs.) As with other BFOQs, the job criteria must be necessary to the "essence" of the employer's business. Age is a BFOQ when an employer can show that all or almost all people older than a given age cannot do a specific job. There also must be no practical way to decide who qualifies among those older than that age. Some recent court decisions have limited the use of forced retirement ages. They did so because employers could not show that age was the only practical way to separate physically fit employees from those who are unfit. Other recent cases have allowed more liberal use of the BFOQ exception in jobs involving public safety. Examples include fire fighters, police officers, and pilots.

MUST WORKERS RETIRE AT AGE 65?

No, the ADEA usually forbids mandatory retirement. Employers also cannot use pension plans or seniority systems to force retirement. That means employers cannot retire an older worker with less seniority than a younger worker. Nor can employers withhold a pension to force an employee to retire. An employer may try to *induce* an employee to retire by providing extra benefits if the employee retires by a certain age. However, the decision to retire still is the employee's. The employer cannot force the employee to retire.

Federal employees face no required retirement age. Some state laws protect workers of all ages. This makes any mandatory retirement age illegal in those states.

An exception to the ADEA rule against mandatory retirement applies to executives or other policymakers. An

(continued)

LAW AND THE WORKPLACE

(continued)

employer may force them to retire at age 65 or older. However, their jobs must entitle them to retirement benefits of at least $44,000 per year. This figure does not count Social Security. Fire fighters, police officers, and prison guards employed by state and local governments also may be forced to retire at age 65 or older. Another exception is for tenured professors. It expires in 1993.

Age discrimination laws protect employees from actions taken because of age. When illness or disability prevents workers from working satisfactorily, an employer may force them to retire. Similarly, antidiscrimination laws only protect employees from actions taken because of age, not on the basis of unsatisfactory job performance. If the employee is habitually late, has poor work habits, or violates company policies that apply to all workers, regardless of age, the ADEA does not protect that employee.

If a job requirement unintentionally affects older workers, it is legal only if a "business necessity" justifies it. Showing a business necessity for age discrimination is similar to doing so for sex or race discrimination. The requirement must concern the ability to do the job. For example, a hearing test for a school bus driver probably is legal, even if it disqualifies more older workers than younger ones.

Q. How does this affect seniority plans?

A. Like Title VII, the ADEA allows age discrimination if an employer follows a bona fide seniority plan. This is true even if the plan unfavorably affects older workers. Consider an employer who has recently started hiring older workers. Suppose that employer has to lay off employees and a union contract requires it to lay off the least senior employees first. This would not violate the ADEA, even though older workers had to be laid off first. The Act also allows age to change the funding or benefit levels of employee benefit plans. These may include retirement, pension, or health insurance plans. Finally, the Act permits discrimination for any "reasonable factor" other than age. (For further information, see "The Rights of Older Americans" chapter.)

AIDS in the Workplace

Q. What is AIDS?

A. *Acquired immune deficiency syndrome* (AIDS) is a disease complex characterized by a collapse of the body's immune system. This makes AIDS patients vulnerable to one or more unusual infections or cancers. These infections or cancers are not a threat to anyone whose immune system works normally. The cause of AIDS appears to be a specific virus.

Q. How contagious is AIDS?

A. AIDS is unlike most communicable diseases, such as colds and the flu. Sneezing, coughing, or eating or drinking from common utensils cannot spread AIDS. Merely being around infected people for a long time also cannot transmit AIDS. The vast majority of scientific evidence appears to indicate that AIDS can be spread *only* by sexual contact or any exchange of infected blood, semen, or vaginal fluids.

Medical experts have studied AIDS for roughly ten years. It is evident that casual contact with AIDS patients does not threaten others. Scientists have not found any AIDS cases due to casual (nonsexual) contact with a household member, relative, coworker, or friend. Health workers and others who care for AIDS patients have caught AIDS only when they have pricked themselves with contaminated needles or in other ways been directly contaminated by the patient's blood, semen, or vaginal fluids. No health worker has ever contacted AIDS from casual contact with an AIDS patient.

Q. May employers fire workers because they have AIDS?

A. This probably is illegal. Developments in New York, California, and Florida suggest that, under state law, employers must treat AIDS as a handicap. Thus, the states with the most AIDS cases suggest a trend to protect AIDS victims from losing their jobs.

The District of Columbia and 47 states have laws that forbid work-related discrimination based on a handicap.

In 1987, the U.S. Supreme Court ruled that a contagious disease (tuberculosis) is a protected handicap under the federal Rehabilitation Act. (A general discussion of the Rehabilitation Act appeared earlier in the "Disabled Workers" section.) This implies that the Act probably would protect an AIDS victim from discrimination on the theory that AIDS is a handicap. It is not clear now whether this applies to someone who merely tests positive for the presence of the AIDS virus. The courts may settle this issue soon.

Q. What will it mean if courts consider AIDS as a handicap?

A. It means that employers may not discriminate against AIDS victims. Employers also may not discriminate against people that others perceive to have AIDS. This does not apply if the employer proves "a reasonable probability of substantial harm" to coworkers or others. This exception must consider current medical opinions about AIDS.

Some laws target the AIDS problem directly. For example, laws in California, Wisconsin, and Florida prohibit using the results of certain blood tests to make employment decisions. Public health laws that encourage AIDS testing centers usually require that they keep test results secret.

Q. Will health insurance cover a worker with AIDS?

A. Check with the insurance carrier and employer. Some states have laws limiting an insurance carrier's ability to exclude

AIDS ON THE JOB

New York, California, and Florida now have the most cases of AIDS (acquired immune deficiency syndrome). AIDS laws are changing quickly. Therefore, read this section knowing that major changes might happen soon. Employers and employees should seek updated facts from their state health department. The medical information in this section comes from a report by the New York State Department of Health entitled *100 Questions and Answers, AIDS.* The U.S. Centers for Disease Control (CDC) in Atlanta, Georgia, also has information for employers and employees. Guidelines for the workplace are of particular value. They are available by calling (404) 639-3534 or by writing to the Centers for Disease Control, Public Inquiries Office, Building 1, Room B46, 1600 Clifton Road N.E. Atlanta, Georgia 30333.

AIDS victims. The high medical costs related to AIDS greatly concern the insurance industry.

Q. What can an employer do about AIDS?

A. First, the employer should make someone responsible for informing management about current events. The Center for Employment Relations and Law (CERL) offers an employer guide, *AIDS and the Workplace.* You can order it from CERL, College of Law, Florida State University, Tallahassee, Florida 32306.

Second, consider hiring a medical consultant familiar with AIDS. As an alternative, get advice from the state or local health officer in charge of AIDS.

Third, consider developing company policies about AIDS. The U.S. Centers for Disease Control (CDC), your state health authority, or other companies or organizations may already have established guidelines. It might help to write to the proper health authorities in New York, California, or Florida.

Fourth, educate your employees. Public health officials and the CDC have materials that you can distribute to your employees.

Fifth, do not overreact if an employee of your company develops an AIDS problem. Seek expert legal and medical advice about the proper action that you should take. Tell your supervisors and middle-level managers to refer the matter to a higher authority.

Other Types of Discrimination

Q. Does an employer have to let Seventh-Day Adventists take off work to observe the Sabbath on Saturday?

A. That depends on the situation. An employer only has to accommodate religious beliefs to a certain extent. If this causes an employer to endure a major cost or hardship, the employer need not oblige the worker. It does not matter whether it directly or indirectly affects the employer. Finding a replacement worker for Saturday, probably at overtime wages, might cost too much for an employer to bear.

Q. What actions can a worker take when confronted with religious discrimination?

A. First, try to talk to the employer. If that does not work, contact the EEOC.

Religious Discrimination

Employers may not fire workers because of their religion. The First Amendment protects government employees from religious discrimination. Similarly, Title VII protects private employees.

These laws apply to all beliefs that people sincerely hold, not just the main religions. In addition, they need not be organized religions. However, social ideology (such as white supremacy) and economic theory (such as communism) are not religious beliefs.

Q. Do any state or local laws protect homosexuals?

A. A few states and counties, and many cities, have laws protecting gays in public employment. Some also cover employees of private businesses contracting with the government.

Q. Do private businesses protect gay rights?

A. Some firms have policies against discrimination based on sexual preference. Also, some unions, such as the Screen Actors Guild, have such protections in their collective bargaining agreement. Other than that, employment law rarely protects gays.

Q. May an employer hire an illegal alien?

A. Not since Congress passed the Immigration Reform and Control Act of 1986 (IRCA). This makes it illegal for an employer to hire "undocumented" aliens. IRCA applies to even very small employers.

Q. How can an employer know if a worker is an illegal alien?

A. IRCA has a documentation procedure that the employer must follow for *all employees*. This is *not just for workers who appear to be Asian, Hispanic, or another nationality*. The employer must fill out an eligibility form (Form I-9) for each new employee. It has a checklist of documents that the employer may accept as evidence of a job applicant's legal status. The documents include a U.S. passport or an INS-issued certificate of U.S. citizenship or naturalization. (INS is the Immigration and Naturalization Service.) Employers also can ask to see a resident alien card with photographs or an unexpired foreign passport with valid work authorization. Or the employer may use a combination of other documents. These may include a birth certificate, driver's license, and Social Security card. The employer must sign an oath on Form I-9. This oath states that the employer believes, under penalty of perjury, that the documents provided by the applicant or new worker are valid. The employer does not have to keep copies of the documents.

Q. What can happen to employers who hire illegal aliens?

A. Before May 31, 1988, the first time employers knowingly hired an illegal alien they received a warning. After May 31, 1988, first-time offenders do not receive a warning. For the

GAY RIGHTS

Title VII does not protect the employment rights of homosexuals. It applies only to discrimination based on race, color, religion, national origin, or sex. Note that sex discrimination does not include discrimination on the basis of sexual orientation.

In addition, no federal laws specifically protect gay rights. However, the Constitution requires the government to treat all public workers equally. Thus, government employers may violate the Constitution by firing a gay worker without job-related grounds.

Laws Governing the Employment of Noncitizens

The Federal Immigration and Naturalization Act (INA) and the Federal Immigration and Control Act of 1986 cover this area. This topic is very complex. Seek expert help if a question arises.

There are various categories of aliens. *Nonimmigrant* aliens remain in the U.S. temporarily. *Immigrant* aliens are those staying in the country who may eventually become citizens. The law treats each type differently. To qualify for employment, nonimmigrant aliens need a visa authorizing specific employment. Several types of visas allow temporary employment. Each has specific limitations.

The U.S. admits immigrant aliens for one of two reasons. One reason is that they are in one of four family relationship categories. The other reason is that they are in one of two work-related categories.

first offense, the government may fine the employers $250 to $2,000 *per worker*. The second offense brings a fine of $2,000 to $5,000 per worker. A fine of $3,000 to $10,000 for each worker applies to the third offense. Repeat offenders may receive more fines and imprisonment.

Q. Must an employer fire or document an alien who has been working for several years?

A. No, IRCA applies only to those hired after November 6, 1986. That is the date when President Reagan signed the bill into law. An employer was liable for workers hired after that date and who remained in employment through June 1, 1987.

Q. May an employer fire a worker suspected of being an illegal alien?

A. No, not if the employer merely suspects the worker because he or she has an accent or looks "foreign." IRCA forbids employment practices based on national origin or noncitizenship status. Title VII also may prohibit such action. IRCA's provisions are much broader than Title VII, covering even very small employers. IRCA also *covers all employees,* not just those who work 20 calendar weeks.

Suppose, however, the employer had more than just a suspicion. Say the employer had reason to believe that a worker hired before IRCA took effect had lacked the proper documentation and was an illegal alien. Then the employer would face penalties if the employer did not fire the worker.

Q. Do any other laws affect the employment of aliens?

A. The National Labor Relations Act also protects aliens. They have the right to organize and join unions. Their immigration status does not play a role.

Unique Rights of Government Employees

Q. Do government employees have constitutional rights on the job?

A. Yes, federal, state, or local government workers have some unique protections. These exist because the U.S. Constitution restricts their employer—the government.

State constitutions also limit state and local governments. Local charters or constitutions restrict local governments.

Civil service laws and collective bargaining agreements also offer protections.

Nobody has a right to be hired by the government. You may not demand a job. However, once you apply for a government job, the government may not treat you arbitrarily or discriminatorily when making employment decisions. A government employer must have a reason for its action. This reason must concern a legitimate purpose of the government.

An inadequate reason in one case might be sufficient in another. Suppose that the Commerce Department fires a records clerk because a supervisor does not like the clerk's hairstyle. That probably would be unconstitutional and "arbitrary." However, a police department may have a grooming code because it legitimately wants to maintain discipline and a neat appearance among its personnel.

These constitutional limitations also mean that public employers need a legitimate reason for imposing upon a worker's private life and relationships. Government employers usually cannot interfere with employees' freedom of speech or religion. Government employers also cannot interfere with the workers' right to associate with people or groups. In addition, government workers have a right to be secure from unreasonable searches. (However, if national security might be affected, then a search could be reasonable.)

Q. How do collective bargaining agreements protect public employees?

A. First, an agreement must exist. Most states have laws allowing some or all state and local government employees to bargain collectively. (An earlier section in this chapter discussed this topic.) An existing union contract may offer rights and benefits protecting employees, besides those mentioned above.

Performance Reviews and Discipline

Q. Assume that an employer uses performance reviews to determine raises and promotions. What guidelines should the employer follow for these reviews?

A. The Equal Employment Opportunity Commission (EEOC) treats these reviews as "tests." The EEOC believes that these reviews are subject to the same standards as pre-employment testing. This means that the reviews must be job-related. They also must not discriminate against any protected class, such as minorities or older workers. In addition, the supervisor must have adequate knowledge both of the job

Civil Service Laws

All levels of government have employment systems. They generally use some form of civil service or merit system that rewards employees' qualifications rather than political affiliation. However, most merit systems allow elected officials to fill some high-level positions with people whose views are compatible with their own. Each level of government normally adopts its own civil service or merit system. Under a civil service system, government employees may have much greater job security than the average worker. Besides forbidding the same discrimination as Title VII, civil service systems sometimes prohibit other forms of discrimination, such as those based on marital status. Nearly all civil service laws forbid employers from firing workers except for good cause. This can be very hard for an employer to prove. The employer also must follow specific procedures to punish or fire employees.

and the person under review. Reviews relying on subjective (opinion-based) conclusions alone are suspect. The supervisor could easily use them to hide discrimination. It is better if the reviewer uses objective (impartial) facts.

Q. Are employee reviews confidential?

A. Generally, they are not confidential. No federal law says that private firms must keep these files confidential. Nor does federal law require state and local governments to keep them confidential. Some state laws require employers to notify an employee or obtain an employee's consent before giving out details about the employee. The Privacy Act of 1974 may protect federal workers if they do not agree to a review of the records by another person.

Q. To what extent may employers punish workers?

A. It depends. Government employees or union members fall under civil service laws or collective bargaining agreements. Then discipline normally must be for "just cause" related to job performance. The amount of discipline also must relate to the misconduct's seriousness. In addition, discipline often becomes more severe with repeated cases of misconduct or poor performance.

If civil service rules or union contracts do not apply, the issue is less clear. If a written company policy regarding discipline exists, an employer may have to follow it. The discipline should not affect minorities or women less favorably. Finally, discipline ordinarily may not be retaliatory. For example, many laws forbid employers from taking action against workers for union activity. These laws also may prohibit employers from punishing workers for informing government agencies of illegal behavior or for engaging in other such "protected" acts.

Employers have a good deal of freedom in this area. There is not a lot that workers can do even if the discipline seems unfair. As before, employers and workers should try to solve their problems through negotiations.

Are Workers Permitted to See Their Job Reviews?

That depends on the employer. No federal law requires employers to show reviews to employees. However, some state laws give workers the right to check their personnel records, including reviews. Most companies have employees read and sign their reviews. This protects the companies against charges of arbitrary reviews. If you want to see your review, check your company's policy. Also examine any state laws.

DAY-CARE SERVICES

Q. May the state license private homes to provide day care?

A. Yes, but the regulations vary from state to state. There is a distinction between "family" day care and "group" or "center-based" day care. "Family" day care usually describes day care in someone's home, typically for no more than five children. In some states, this is not licensed at all. The day-care provider may only have to fill out a form that enables the business to be registered by the state. In other states, such businesses are licensed but regulated less closely than larger centers. These larger centers, often called "group" or "center-based" day-care centers, usually must meet higher standards to be licensed, and they face more stringent evaluations by the state.

Q. If the day-care business is carefully regulated, what would someone have to do to become licensed?

A. Generally, if the day-care provider meets state guidelines, fills out applications, and submits references, the state will license the day-care provider. The licensing can take time because there is a lot for the state day-care agency to do. Most agencies will thoroughly check references and visit the facility. They will take all precautions to assure that the day-care provider meets all requirements before the state will grant certification.

Q. What are the typical requirements for licensing a day-care center?

A. State day-care agencies might require, among other things, that:

(1) The day-care service submits menus for each day in advance. The menus must represent the four major food groups;
(2) Each child has a separate cot for naps. The day-care service must clean these cots daily and wash the sheets weekly; and
(3) The provider reports any obvious abuse or neglect to the agency immediately.

These are just examples. The specific regulations may be different in your state. Remember, licensing requirements may not be so stringent for day care provided in someone's home. Your state's licensing agency will have booklets that explain the provider's duties in greater detail.

Q. Do day-care centers have to follow state guidelines for disciplining of children?

A. Yes, when guidelines exist, whether in law or regulation, they apply to *all* day-care providers, from the largest to the smallest. More and more state legislatures are passing laws prohibiting the use of corporal (bodily) punishment in

Evaluating Day-Care Providers

Most state day-care agencies will visit the facility in order to observe and evaluate. They will watch the children interact at play and during meals. The agencies will ask questions of the children if they are old enough to talk. They will even oversee food preparation and serving techniques. The state may suspend or revoke licenses if the provider fails to meet the guidelines. A day-care provider also can expect a building department inspection in most states for any type of day-care business. This inspection may find violations that the provider will have to fix in order to open the day-care center and keep it open.

providing day care to children. In states where the lawmakers have not done this, the state day-care licensing agencies are setting their own rules to cover this problem. These laws and rules are available to anyone on request.

OUT OF WORK

HELP FOR THE UNEMPLOYED

Unemployment is never welcome. Fortunately, the law can provide some comfort. It protects some workers against losing their job. For workers who do lose their jobs, the law provides various services. The form of help available depends on how the worker lost his or her job.

You can lose your job for many reasons. You can be laid off, fired, disabled, or you can quit. (You also can retire. That is discussed later in this chapter and in "The Rights of Older Americans" chapter.) Each raises different legal points.

Job Security

Q. I have heard that many workers are employees "at-will." What does this mean?

A. They may lose their job without notice and for any reason or no reason at all. Similarly, the worker may quit a job without notice and for any reason or no reason at all. An employee at-will usually works in the private sector.

Q. Are workers covered by a collective bargaining agreement in the "at-will" category?

A. No, their contracts cover when and how they can be legally terminated (fired).

Q. Does the at-will rule always apply to other workers?

A. No. Federal, state, and local government employees are covered by civil service laws. These laws normally require that such employees be fired only for "just cause."

In addition, courts in 30 to 40 states have created one or more exceptions to the at-will rule for private employees. There are two main exceptions. The first is that employees who are fired because they refuse to perform an act that violates public policy can sue to recover damages. The second exception deals with contract violations. In these cases, employees usually allege that firing them violated an oral assurance of job security or failed to comply with a policy statement in a personnel file that nobody would be discharged except for just cause.

Under these theories of *wrongful discharge,* an employer may be sued for firing a worker for specific reasons or in certain situations.

Q. What is an example of wrongful discharge because a worker refused to violate public policy?

A. One example is that the worker may have refused to commit a crime. Some state laws also protect "whistle blowers." A *whistle blower* is a worker who discloses ("blows the whistle on") employer actions that are illegal or violate other regulatory guidelines.

Q. What is an example of wrongful discharge in a situation where an implied contract may have been violated?

A. Assume an employer's personnel manual promises to fire employees only for just cause. Or suppose the employer made the promise orally. If the employer then fires a worker without just cause, the worker may be able to sue.

To take another example, courts may recognize implied contracts when an employee has a long and favorable work record with the employer, and when the employee pledges something valuable to the employer. For instance, in one case, an employee signed an agreement not to compete with the employer within one year of his termination and to disclose all computer-related information to his employer as long as he was employed. A court held that such promises of loyalty can create legally enforceable promises on the part of employers to surrender their authority to terminate employees at will.

Wrongful discharge is not available in all states or situations. Fired workers should seek legal advice.

Q. Are there any other limitations on an employer's ability to fire at will?

A. Yes, the NLRA, the OSH Act, and other federal statutes protect the rights of employees who complain to the government about working conditions or engage in lawful activities such as union organizing.

In addition, Title VII, the ADEA, and other antidiscrimination laws limit an employer's ability to fire workers for discriminatory reasons.

Q. Must employers always notify workers before firing them?

A. Employers do not always have to do this. If a worker is under contract or belongs to a union, a notice requirement probably exits. If formal discharge and disciplinary procedures exist, the employee will already know that discipline is underway. The relevant rules usually do not entitle employees at-will to notice. However, some company policies provide notice before firing a worker. If so, an employee might have a legal right to notice.

Severance Pay

An employer must give severance pay if there are contracts or collective bargaining agreements that provide severance benefits. These will cover some workers. Employees at-will usually must rely on their employer's generosity. However, some state laws require severance pay under certain conditions.

Becoming Eligible for Unemployment Insurance Benefits

Assuming they have coverage, various factors determine when unemployed workers become eligible for Unemployment Insurance (UI) benefits. Employees must be out of work through no fault of their own. This usually means that the workers did not quit their jobs. Their employer also must not have fired them for misconduct. Examples of misconduct include disobeying an order or violating a company policy. In many states, unemployed workers may get UI benefits if they quit for "good cause." The meaning of "good cause" varies greatly among the states. Some states allow the unemployed to receive UI benefits if they are out of work for personal reasons.

(continued)

Q. What is the difference between laying off and firing a worker?

A. This can be very important. Firing a worker ends the employee/employer relationship, usually because the employer judges the worker to be inadequate. The employee may be eligible for certain benefits. One such benefit is severance pay. However, the worker may lose eligibility for others, such as insurance.

When laid off, an employee can be considered satisfactory, but the layoff may occur because of a work shortage or economic problem. A layoff may be temporary. It also may be for an indefinite period. If it is quite long, it can effectively end the working relationship. The amount of benefits received depends on company policy or the union contract. Layoffs imply that the employees will be back at work if the company expands the work force again. However, layoff policies contain a cutoff point. After that point, a worker loses any seniority or re-employment rights.

If told by their employer not to come in, employees should find out whether the employer has laid them off or fired them. They also should ask about their rights.

Q. May a company fire or lay off workers based on their race or sex?

A. Federal laws prohibit discharge based on race, color, religion, sex, or national origin. This is also true for age, citizenship, and, under certain conditions, a handicap or veteran status. Firings or layoffs that unfavorably affect these groups without proof of being legitimate are discriminatory. It does not matter whether the discrimination is intentional or not.

Q. Is a bona fide seniority system discriminatory?

A. Not as long as it does not intend to harm the classes mentioned above. Also, seniority systems that are impartial and nondiscriminatory are valid even if a layoff effectively "freezes-in" (continues) past discrimination.

Unemployment Benefits

Q. What is the purpose of unemployment insurance?

A. Unemployment insurance (UI) provides workers and their families with weekly income. This aims to help them through unemployment that is not their fault. When unemployed by plant closures, layoffs, or natural disasters, employees may receive UI. This also is true when unemployed by other acts or circumstances that are not the workers' fault.

Q. Who manages the UI program?

A. Both the federal and state governments control the UI program. All states follow federal regulations in providing unemployment benefits. The states have rules as well, however, and UI programs differ widely among the states.

Each state's employment security agency pays benefits to workers. Federal unemployment taxes on employers pay for these benefits. In addition, many states provide benefits supported by state taxes on employers.

Q. Are there other UI programs besides this federal/state effort?

A. Yes, and one is the Disaster Unemployment Assistance Program. In addition, many collective bargaining agreements offer extra unemployment benefits. An example is in the automobile industry. The employer pays for these extra benefits. Unemployed workers receive these extra payments besides government UI benefits.

Q. How do workers know if they have UI coverage?

A. They should check with the state employment security agency. In most states, to be eligible for benefits, a person must work for someone else. Self-employed persons usually do not qualify. An employee must work a certain minimum amount of time to get benefits. The states decide how long an employee must work. Certain workers usually do not qualify for UI. They include casual (temporary) laborers, minors working for their parents, and student interns.

Q. Are striking workers entitled to UI benefits?

A. The law usually does not entitle them to UI benefits. Even a union member who does not support a strike normally will not receive benefits. However, if permanently replaced during a strike, a worker may become eligible. Some states deny benefits for a fixed period of time. These states then provide benefits if the strike continues and the striker is available for work. A few states provide complete benefits to strikers available for other work. A "strike" may be treated differently than a "lockout." The local unemployment office can supply details about your state's UI law.

(continued)

Examples include having to care for a sick relative or following a spouse who has found work in another state. Most states, however, require that "good cause" be due to the employer's action. This might include working conditions so bad that they would cause any reasonable person to quit. The "reasonable person" standard is very important. It is not enough that a situation is intolerable to a specific worker. The conditions must make a reasonable person, in the same position as the employee, also feel compelled to quit.

Q. May a worker refuse a job offer and still get UI benefits?

A. A worker may reject a job if it is not "suitable work." Generally, a job is unsuitable if the worker has no experience in it. If the job is more hazardous than the old job, the new job also is unsuitable. The same is true if age or physical condition prevents the worker from accepting it. The state also may consider travel costs and time, bad working hours, community wage levels, and compelling personal problems in determining if a job may be rejected. Finally, workers usually cannot lose benefits for refusing a job that is available because of a strike. In some states, employees cannot lose benefits for rejecting a job that would force them to join or quit a union against their will.

If the wages and conditions of a new job are below those of the old job, the worker might not have to take it. This depends on how the state defines "ready, willing, and able" to work. For example, a skilled craftsman is permitted to refuse a job as a janitor. However, after a certain period of time, most states require the worker to accept even a lesser job. You should check your state law for the time limit, if any, in your state.

Moving Out of State and Collecting Unemployment

If workers move to another state to look for work, they still are permitted to collect UI benefits. They may do so because all states belong to the Interstate Reciprocal Benefit Payment Plan. This plan allows workers to register for work and file for UI benefits in a different state. However, the law of the state in which the employee worked applies here. The worker must satisfy that state's requirements in order to get UI benefits in the new state.

Q. If I get laid off, how do I apply for UI benefits?

A. Apply at the state unemployment office as soon as possible. Bring your Social Security card and pay slips. Also take other documents proving that you are out of work and eligible for benefits. You should register to get a job through the state employment office. Most states require a waiting period before you can collect benefits. It normally is for one week. After filing, report to the employment office regularly (usually every week). Also report when notified of job openings. Failure to report without good cause could result in a loss of benefits.

Q. How long do UI benefits last? How much do they pay?

A. The usual maximum is 26 weeks. Sometimes it is longer. It depends on the state. The amount of benefits also varies by state. It depends on the worker's earnings. UI benefits are usually quite low. Ask your state unemployment office for details.

Q. May an unemployed worker receive other benefits or earn extra money while collecting UI benefits?

A. Some states ignore small amounts of money earned while a worker receives UI benefits. However, they usually deduct income above a certain very low level from UI benefits. Most states reduce or stop UI benefits for weeks in which an unemployed worker receives disability benefits, severance pay, and other types of income.

Social Security Disability

Q. May a worker who becomes disabled receive Social Security benefits?

A. Yes, if the employee is in a job covered by Social Security. To receive full coverage, the worker also must have worked the required number of quarters. A later section on Social Security retirement benefits discusses this topic more fully.

Q. May a disabled worker's spouse and children receive benefits because of the disability?

A. If the spouse and children meet the requirements for Social Security retirement benefits, they should qualify for disability benefits.

Q. What if workers do not suffer from the medical equivalent of a listed impairment (see the article at right)?

A. Then the employees have to prove that they have a disability in another way. They must show that their condition or disease is so severe that it prevented them from doing their former job or other similar work. It is not easy to prove this.

Q. Where can I apply for Social Security disability benefits?

A. Go to the local SSA office. You should submit a medical history along with a detailed statement from a doctor about why you have a disability. You also should offer details about your work history, education, and so forth. This will help the SSA decide whether your condition is disabling. You also may submit statements from family and friends.

Q. What happens if the SSA rejects an application for benefits?

A. There is an appeals process for rejected applications. It appears in a later section on Social Security retirement benefits.

Social Security's Definition of Disability

The types of ailments that Social Security considers "disabling" depends on the disability. Some handicaps and diseases are so serious that Social Security automatically treats them as disabilities. Examples are severe epilepsy and loss of vision or hearing. These appear in a list of impairments written by the Social Security Administration (SSA). If workers do not have a listed impairment, they can still prove that they have a disability. They must show that their condition or disease is the medical equivalent of a listed impairment. Their condition or disease must be equal in severity and duration to a listed one.

Workers' Compensation

Q. What is workers' compensation?

A. This term describes various state and federal laws. Their goal is to provide benefits to workers and their families as compensation for work-related injuries, diseases, and deaths. All states have some type of workers' compensation. These laws vary in the amount of benefits provided, but they are similar to each other. (See the chart on page 438.) Early in this century, injured workers had a hard time winning lawsuits against their employers. In response to the public outcry that ensued, the states passed these laws.

Q. Are all workers covered?

A. These laws apply to most employees. Some states exempt certain classes of workers, such as farm employees. Others make coverage optional for the employer. Check with the state department of labor (or its equivalent) to see if these laws cover you.

Q. If I injure myself on vacation, will workers' compensation cover me?

A. No, because it covers only injuries received on the job. These range from being injured by a defective machine to being hit by a truck entering the loading dock.

Q. How does workers' compensation operate?

A. It entitles workers to receive benefits for all job-related injuries. This is true even if the employee is at fault. Families will get benefits if the worker dies because of an injury.

Workers or their dependents get a fixed weekly benefit. The size of the benefit depends on the worker's regular salary. This assures the injured worker or the worker's dependents of some income. Only the employer pays for the cost of providing workers' compensation. It cannot be deducted from wages. Employers are required to buy workers' compensation insurance or they must provide self-insurance.

In return, the employer benefits by limiting its responsibility. If workers' compensation covers the employees, they are not permitted to sue the employer. In many states, though, the worker can still sue other negligent parties who may have played a role. Such parties may include coworkers, producers of defective machinery, and so on.

Chemicals and Workers' Compensation

The laws vary among the states about whether workers' compensation covers employees who work with chemicals that cause cancer or another illness. Workers should ask a lawyer to find out if workers' compensation covers them. State laws not only cover injuries that occur on the job, but they also cover "occupational diseases" resulting from on-the-job exposure, such as asbestosis, silicosis, and black lung disease. However, they do so only if the job presents a greater risk of getting the disease than other jobs.

Q. What kind of benefits does workers' compensation provide?

A. It depends on the extent of the injury. An employee usually recovers such costs as hospitalization and other medical care resulting from the injury. The injured worker also may be entitled to necessary medical or vocational rehabilitation. The law sets the maximum amount that a worker can recover. Also, an employee may receive weekly disability benefits. The amount of such benefits depends on whether the disability is temporary or permanent, total or partial. Benefits are calculated on preinjury wages. The benefits usually amount to one half to two thirds of the weekly wages. Besides this, an employee may receive "scheduled," or fixed, benefits for losing an organ, limb, or other body part.

Q. I hear about huge amounts awarded in lawsuits for "pain and suffering." Will workers' compensation pay for this?

A. Generally, workers will not get paid for this. Disability benefits usually are all an employee gets. This is true even if the pain and discomfort are very severe. The law provides the worker enough to pay bills. However, it is not intended to pay for damages or punish the employer.

Q. Must a worker file a claim within a certain amount of time?

A. Yes, each state has a time limit for filing claims. Workers should file claims promptly to avoid losing rights.

Q. What happens to an employee whose employer fails to be covered by workers' compensation?

A. If the employer is not covered by a plan, the worker is permitted to sue the employer. However, the worker must show that the employer's negligence caused the injury.

Special Disability Plans

Q. If workers' compensation or Social Security do not cover a worker who is not a veteran, do other programs apply?

A. Some programs might cover the worker. Many state and federal programs compensate for work-related injury, disease,

(continued)

What to Do After Getting Injured at Work

The worker should notify the employer as soon as possible after an injury occurs and request or obtain treatment. Then the employee should file a claim with the state agency managing the workers' compensation plan. If an employer contests a claim, a hearing will give everyone a chance to be heard. The worker or employer may appeal an undesirable decision within the agency or to the court. If this does not satisfy the appealing party, that party may pursue the matter in appellate courts.

MAXIMUM BENEFITS FOR TEMPORARY TOTAL DISABILITY PROVIDED BY WORKERS' COMPENSATION STATUTES (as of January 1988)

State or other jurisdiction	Maximum percentage of wages	Maximum payment per week amount
Federal (FECA) (a)	66⅔% (b)	$1,029.48
(LHWCA) (a)	66⅔%	616.96
Alabama	66⅔%	331.00
Alaska	80% of worker's spendable earnings	1,094.00 (c)
Arizona	66⅔%	253.19 (d)
Arkansas	66⅔%	189.00
California	66⅔%	224.00
Colorado	66⅔%	357.63 (e)
Connecticut	66⅔%	643.00 (f)
Delaware	66⅔%	250.53
District of Columbia	66⅔% or 80% of worker's spendable earnings	481.92
Florida	66⅔%	344.00 (c)
Georgia	66⅔%	175.00
Hawaii	66⅔%	334.00
Idaho	69% to 90%	282.60 to 392.50 (g)
Illinois	66⅔%	554.27
Indiana	66⅔%	190.00
Iowa	80% of worker's spendable earnings	632.00
Kansas	66⅔%	256.00
Kentucky	66⅔%	330.53
Louisiana	66⅔%	262.00 (h)
Maine	66⅔%	447.92 (h)(i)
Maryland	66⅔%	382.00
Massachusetts	66⅔%	411.00 (j)
Michigan	80% of worker's spendable earnings	397.00 (k)
Minnesota	66⅔%	$376.00
Mississippi	66⅔%	140.00
Missouri	66⅔%	269.81
Montana	66⅔%	299.00 (e)(l)
Nebraska	66⅔%	235.00 (m)
Nevada	66⅔% (n)	353.01
New Hampshire	66⅔%	525.00 (n)
New Jersey	70%	320.00
New Mexico	66⅔%	270.97
New York	66⅔%	300.00
North Carolina	66⅔%	356.00
North Dakota	66⅔%	299.00 (o)(p)
Ohio	72% for first 12 weeks; 66⅔% thereafter	385.00 (q)
Oklahoma	66⅔%	231.00 (r)
Oregon	66⅔%	355.04
Pennsylvania	66⅔%	377.00
Puerto Rico	66⅔%	45.00
Rhode Island	66⅔%	337.00 (s)
South Carolina	66⅔%	319.20
South Dakota	66⅔%	272.00
Tennessee	66⅔%	210.00
Texas	66⅔%	231.00 (t)
Utah	66⅔%	335.00 (u)
Vermont	66⅔%	486.00 (v)
Virginia	66⅔%	344.00
U.S. Virgin Islands	66⅔%	193.00
Washington	60% to 75%	288.70 (e)
West Virginia	70%	350.83
Wisconsin	66⅔%	348.00 (e)
Wyoming	66⅔%	352.70

Source: Reprinted with permission of *The Book of the States 1988-89,* copyright © by The Council of State Governments, based on Division of State Workers' Compensation Programs, Office of State Liaison and Legislative Analysis, Employment Standards Administration, U.S. Department of Labor.

Notes:

(a) Federal Employees' Compensation Act (FECA) and the Longshoremen's and Harbor Workers' Compensation Act (LHWCA). LHWCA benefits are for private-sector maritime employees (not seamen) who work on navigable waters of the U.S., including dry docks.
(b) Benefits under FECA are computed at a maximum of 75 percent of the pay of a specific grade level in the federal civil service.
(c) Payments subject to Social Security and Unemployment Insurance benefits offsets.
(d) Additional $10 monthly added to benefits of dependents residing in the U.S.
(e) Payments subject to Social Security benefit offsets.
(f) Additional $10 weekly for each dependent child under 18 years of age, up to 50 percent of basic benefit, not to exceed 75 percent of worker's wage.
(g) Additional seven percent ($20.23) of state's average weekly wage is payable for each dependent child up to five children.
(h) Payments subject to Unemployment Insurance benefit offsets.
(i) Benefit payments are frozen at $447.92 until August 1, 1988.
(j) Additional $6 will be added per dependent if weekly benefits are below $150.00.
(k) Payments subject to reduction by Unemployment Insurance and Social Security benefits, in addition to benefits paid by an employer disability, retirement, or pension plan.
(l) Benefit payments are frozen at $299 for injuries occurring on or after 7/1/87 until 7/1/89.
(m) Effective July 1, 1988, maximum weekly benefit will be $245.
(n) If the employee's average weekly wage exceeds 40 percent of the state's average weekly wage, compensation will increase to 66⅔ of the employee's average weekly wage (not to exceed 150 percent of the state's average weekly wage).
(o) Additional $5 per week for each dependent child, not to exceed worker's net wage.
(p) Payments are reduced by 50 percent of Social Security benefits.
(q) Payments are subject to offset if concurrent and/or duplicate with those under employer nonoccupational benefits plan.
(r) Benefit payments are frozen at $231 from November 1, 1987 until November 1, 1990.
(s) Additional $9 for each dependent, including a nonworking wife; aggregate not to exceed 80 percent of worker's average weekly wage.
(t) Each cumulative $10 increase in the average weekly wage for manufacturing production workers will increase the maximum weekly benefit by $7 per week.
(u) Additional $5 for dependent spouse and each dependent child up to four, but not to exceed 100 percent of state's average weekly wage.
(v) Additional $10 will be paid for each dependent under age 21.

and death in certain cases. The U.S. Department of Labor and the state labor agency can provide details.

PLANNING FOR RETIREMENT

Social Security

Q. There is some debate about changing Social Security. Is it likely that the present requirements will stay the same?

A. No, Social Security is likely to change. It will remain a hot topic as more Americans reach retirement age. The facts discussed below may change. For current details, contact the local Social Security Administration (SSA) office.

Q. Whom does Social Security cover?

A. Social Security applies to nearly all U.S. workers. It does not cover federal government workers and certain state and local government employees. It also does not apply to railroad workers. (The Railroad Retirement Program covers them.) Social Security applies to workers that other federal programs do not ordinarily cover. They include self-employed persons and domestic and farm workers.

BENEFITS OFFERED BY SOCIAL SECURITY

Social Security offers three basic types of benefits. The first includes retirement and disability benefits payable to workers. Then there are benefits for spouses and children of retired or disabled workers. The third type consists of survivor benefits for the surviving spouse and children of deceased workers.

Q. Do people in a covered class automatically get benefits?

A. No, workers must meet certain standards before they may receive Social Security. First, a worker must work a minimum number of calendar quarters. The employee must earn a certain amount of money during this time. The number of quarters depends on the type of benefit. Survivor benefits normally require the least number of quarters. Retirement benefits usually require the most. Now, a person who turns 62 in 1991 or later must work 40 calendar quarters to receive retirement benefits. That equals ten full years. Social Security covers employees only if their employer pays Social Security taxes. This includes amounts deducted from the worker's pay and the employer's required contributions.

Q. When may a worker start drawing benefits?

A. Currently, an employee who retires at age 62 can start receiving reduced benefits. The longer a worker delays retirement, the larger the monthly benefit received. The age at which you can retire and receive full Social Security benefits is age 65. However, for workers reaching age 62 in the year 2005, the retirement age for receiving full benefits will be raised to age 66; for workers reaching age 62 in 2022 and later, it will be age 67.

Q. Will Social Security benefits maintain a worker's standard of living after retirement?

A. They probably will not be enough. Social Security benefits aim to provide a basic level for qualified workers and their families. This level is not very high. Extra income may be necessary. Examples include an Individual Retirement Account (IRA), pensions, and investments. A part-time job after the worker "retires" also may help.

Earning Money and Collecting Social Security

As a retiree, you are permitted to earn money and keep Social Security benefits, but only up to a certain amount. If you earn more than that amount, Social Security will reduce your benefits by one dollar for every two dollars you earn above the limit. Certain types of income do not count when figuring whether you have earned above the limit. These include stock dividends, pensions, and interest from savings accounts. Your local SSA office has details about the current limit.

Q. May I collect Social Security benefits based on how long my spouse worked?

A. Husbands or wives sometimes may receive retirement benefits based on their spouse's work record. It depends on the situation. These benefits may or may not be besides those received based on their own work record. The benefits usually will be one half of the benefits that Social Security entitles their spouse to receive. If a wife will get $300 a month, her husband deserves $150. A husband no longer has to prove that he depends on his wife to draw retirement benefits based on her record.

Q. Suppose someone divorces a spouse after 20 years of marriage. May that person receive Social Security retirement benefits based on the ex-spouse's work record?

A. A person may do this under certain conditions. The spouse must be age 62 or older. The marriage must have lasted for ten years or more. In addition, the spouse must be unmarried when the person applies for benefits.

Q. Do children in high school qualify for the benefits of their parents?

A. Yes, they are eligible if they are dependent, unmarried, and under age 18. (They can be 19 if they are full-time high school students.) As with a spouse, their benefits will be one half that of the worker's benefits. This also covers stepchildren, adopted children, and, under certain cases of dependency, grandchildren.

Q. How does a claimant receive Social Security benefits?

A. A claimant must apply with the SSA. The local SSA office has application forms and details about the process. It also can supply facts about documents and details the applicant will need to supply. The SSA will process the application, and either approve or reject it.

Q. What happens when the SSA rejects an application, or if it incorrectly figures the benefit level?

A. The applicant may appeal. The appeals process has many steps. The SSA first "reconsiders" the application. If the SSA still rejects the application, the applicant may request a formal hearing. An administrative law judge will hold the hearing. If the judge rules against the applicant, the applicant may request a review by the Social Security Appeals Council. Its office is in Washington, D.C. If the council decides against the applicant, the applicant may sue in federal court. (For further information on Social Security, see "The Rights of Older Americans," "Wills, Trusts, and Estate Planning," and "Family Law" chapters.)

Pension Plans–ERISA

Q. Does the law require employers to provide pensions?

A. No, they do not have to do this. If an employer does offer a pension plan, the federal Employee Retirement Income Security Act (ERISA) probably covers it. An employer may set up a plan on its own. The employer also may do so jointly with a union. A plan covered by ERISA must meet certain standards. ERISA applies to plans that are "qualified" under the federal tax laws and/or affect interstate commerce. The tax laws provide important advantages, so most pension plans fall under ERISA. (For further information on pensions, see "The Rights of Older Americans," "Wills, Trusts, and Estate Planning," and "Family Law" chapters.)

Q. What are the participation provisions of pension plans?

A. Before ERISA, many pension plans excluded large groups of workers for various reasons. Perhaps it was because they worked part-time. Maybe they had not served long enough with the company. Possibly they were not old enough. Now, under ERISA, workers usually must be allowed to participate in a pension plan. However, they must be at least 18 years old

Survivor Benefits

When a worker entitled to Social Security benefits dies, the surviving spouse and dependent children qualify for survivor benefits. To qualify for full benefits, a surviving spouse must be age 65 or older. Their marriage must have lasted for nine months or more (exceptions exist). Social Security also must have fully covered the deceased at the time of death. The surviving spouse also must be unmarried or must not have remarried until over 60. Partial benefits may be available at age 60. If the surviving spouse has a disability, partial benefits may be available between ages 50 and 60. A younger surviving spouse can receive benefits for caring for the deceased worker's surviving dependent children. The benefits for surviving children are three-quarters of a worker's payment.

THE PURPOSE OF ERISA

ERISA protects workers who take part in pension plans. It also covers the beneficiaries of such workers. Since 1975, ERISA has overruled almost all state laws covering pension and other benefit plans.

ERISA deals with the following aspects of pension plans:
(1) Participation;
(2) Vesting, benefit accrual, and breaks-in-service;
(3) Funding;
(4) Administration of funds;
(5) Reporting and disclosure;
(6) Joint and survivor provisions; and
(7) Plan termination insurance.

ERISA sets legal minimums. An employer's pension plan may provide more liberal terms. However, it must provide at least the terms set forth in ERISA.

and have completed one year of service. ERISA defines "one year of service" as a 12-month period during which an employee has worked 1,000 hours or more. A plan usually may not exclude workers because the employer considers them too old.

Q. What are the vesting, benefit accrual, and break-in-service provisions?

A. *Benefit accrual* is the process of building up benefits once an employee qualifies for the pension plan. *Vesting* refers to the point after which employees' accrued benefits cannot be denied. Suppose employees retire or have a break-in-service before benefits "vest." Those workers will not be able to receive benefits. They may access only their contributions.

Normally employees start accumulating benefits as soon as they join a pension plan. An employer must give participating employees at least partial pension credit if they work 1,000 hours in a year.

ERISA allows different plans for vesting. One basic plan requires five years of service before the employee's pension vests. However, the benefits must become 100-percent vested at this time. Another provision allows a plan to require seven years before benefits become 100-percent vested. In this plan, partial vesting must begin after three years of service, and the vesting also must be at the rate of 20 percent a year until the pension is 100-percent vested after seven years of service. (These are the legal requirements; employers can be more generous.)

If a break-in-service occurs before benefits become vested, the worker loses them. If an employee works less than 500 hours in a year, the employer can say a break-in-service has occurred. The results of this depend on the extent that the worker's benefits have vested. They also depend on the type of pension plan and the length of the break-in-service.

Q. What are ERISA's funding provisions?

A. Generally, these require that the employer and employee contribute enough money to cover pension withdrawals when they become due. Funding provisions aim to strengthen pension funds and prevent abuses. The employer and the fund's administrator must meet these requirements.

Q. How does ERISA prevent misuse of pension funds?

A. Those who manage pension funds under ERISA must use "care, skill, prudence, and diligence." ERISA prohibits a plan administrator from borrowing money from the fund for personal use. ERISA also greatly strengthens the right of a worker to sue administrators for breach of their duty and for violating ERISA.

ERISA's reporting and disclosure provisions require an employer to furnish workers with various facts. These include substantial details about the plan. You may request a copy of a summary plan description from your employer or plan administrator. You also may ask for more details.

Q. If a plan participant dies before a spouse, may the spouse still collect a pension?

A. The spouse usually may collect. Under ERISA, a "joint-and-survivor" annuity automatically takes effect. It provides a periodic payment to the spouse if the plan participant dies. The joint-and-survivor annuity means lower pension payments while the participant is alive. However, it ensures that a surviving spouse will receive a monthly payment after the participant's death, though it will be a reduced amount. Unless a participant and spouse reject the joint-and-survivor annuity in writing, they will receive this type of payment.

Q. If a participant gets divorced, does the ex-spouse get part of the pension?

A. This depends on state law. Some states consider a pension to belong partly to a participant's spouse. Check your state law or talk to your lawyer about this.

Q. What happens if my employer decides to end the pension fund? Is this legal?

A. Yes, it is legal. Nothing in ERISA requires an employer to continue a pension fund. Unless the pension is part of a collective bargaining agreement, the employer may eliminate it. ERISA does afford some protection, however. It established the Pension Benefit Guaranty Corporation (PBGC). This protects certain benefits in specific types of funds. ERISA requires defined-benefit pension plans to pay insurance premiums to the PBGC. In return, the PBGC guarantees vested benefits in the fund. The law sets a limit on these benefits. The PBGC does not guarantee other benefits provided by some pension funds. Examples include medical and disability benefits. Under ERISA, therefore, the PBGC may not fully protect you if you do not participate in a defined-benefit plan, if your benefits in the plan have not yet vested, or if your plan provides medical and disability benefits.

Firing Workers to Avoid Paying Pensions

Employers may *not* fire employees to avoid paying benefits or prevent benefits from vesting. Employers also may not force workers to quit for these purposes. ERISA makes this illegal. However, a worker can lose nonvested benefits if fired for other reasons.

Q. Where can I get more facts about ERISA?

A. The Department of Labor can supply details. Your employer also must provide you with a summary plan description. That will answer many questions. (For more information on pensions, see "The Rights of Older Americans" chapter.)

How Changing Jobs Before Retirement Affects Pensions

If you change jobs before retiring, ERISA entitles you to all your *vested* benefits. You usually forfeit any benefits not vested at the time of the job change. You may put the vested funds in an IRA (see article on facing page) to avoid taxation. You also may transfer the funds to the new employer's pension plan. Although you can do as you wish, you may want to "roll them over" (quickly transfer them) into an IRA or another qualified plan. If you do not roll them over, the funds probably will be subject to income tax.

WHERE TO GET MORE INFORMATION

This chapter is a basic road map to make you aware of the laws governing employment. If you have questions about your rights and duties, or if you want more details, the resources in this section will be helpful. To find a federal agency, look in your local telephone directory under "United States." It will often list the nearest local office.

Discrimination

For more information about workplace discrimination and equal employment, contact your local office of the federal Equal Employment Opportunity Commission (EEOC). The address of the EEOC national office is:

Equal Employment Opportunity Commission
2401 E Street, N.W.
Washington, D.C. 20506
(202) 663-4000

Your state also may have its own civil rights agency that handles employment discrimination. The EEOC has details on state agencies.

If you work for a federal contractor, you can receive more details about additional requirements and Affirmative Action Programs (AAPs) from:

Employment Standards Administration
Office of Federal Contract Compliance Programs
200 Constitution Avenue, N.W., Room C3310
Washington, D.C. 20210
(202) 523-9475

The American Civil Liberties Union (ACLU) and the National Association for the Advancement of Colored People (NAACP) are both very active in discrimination issues. Their local chapters can answer many questions.

Employers who wish to avoid discrimination in their hiring process can find several helpful publications. One is *Law for Personnel Managers: How to Hire the People You Need Without Discriminating.* This easy-to-read booklet details some of the pitfalls that employers can avoid. The publisher is:

Bureau of Law & Businesses, Inc.
64 Wall Street
Madison, Connecticut 06443
(203) 245-7448

Another useful publication for employers who wish to avoid discrimination is *A Professional and Legal Analysis of the Uniform Guidelines on Employee Selection Procedures.* The same is true of *Personnel Director's Legal Guide* and *Sex and Salary: A Legal and Professional Analysis of Comparable Worth.* The publisher of these handy guides is:

Society for Human Resource Management
606 North Washington Street
Alexandria, Virginia 22314
(703) 548-3440

OSHA

Direct your questions about job-related safety to your regional Occupational Safety and Health Administration (OSHA) office. They can answer your questions and send literature about the Act. The regional offices are:

Region I (CT, ME, MA, NH, RI, VT):
133 Portland Street
Boston, Massachusetts 02114
(617) 565-7164

Region II (NY, NJ, PR, VI):
Room 670
201 Varick Street
New York, New York 10014
(212) 337-2378

Region III (DE, MD, PA, VA, WV):
2100 Gateway Building
3535 Market Street
Philadelphia, Pennsylvania 19104
(215) 596-1201

INDIVIDUAL RETIREMENT ACCOUNTS

An Individual Retirement Account (IRA) can be set up by workers or employers. Like ERISA-qualified pension plans, IRAs permit you to defer income to retirement without paying taxes now. The Tax Reform Act of 1986 greatly restricts who may make tax-deductible contributions to an IRA. It also limits how much tax-deductible money you may contribute. (Anyone has the right to contribute to an IRA. However, their contributions might not be tax-*deductible*. In any case, all contributions are tax-*deferred*.) These restrictions have made IRAs less attractive to many workers. Thus, ask a financial institution that handles IRAs to decide if an IRA is suitable. You also may want to ask an accountant or tax lawyer.

Region IV (AL, FL, GA, KY, MS, NC, SC, TN):
Suite 587
1375 Peachtree Street, N.E.
Atlanta, Georgia 30367
(404) 347-3573

Region V (IL, IN, MI, MN, OH, WI):
32nd Floor, Room 3244
230 South Dearborn Street
Chicago, Illinois 60604
(312) 353-2220

Region VI (AR, LA, NM, OK, TX):
Room 602
525 Griffin Square
Dallas, Texas 75202
(214) 767-4731

Region VII (IA, KS, MO, NE):
Room 406
911 Walnut Street
Kansas City, Missouri 64106
(816) 426-5861

Region VIII (CO, MT, ND, SD, UT, WY):
Room 1576
1961 Stout Street
Denver, Colorado 80294
(303) 844-3061

Region IX (CA, AZ, NV, HI, Guam, American Samoa, Trust Territory of the Pacific Islands):
Suite 415
71 Stevenson Street
San Francisco, California 94105
(415) 744-6670

Region X (AK, ID, OR, WA):
U.S. Department of Labor—OSHA
Room 715
1111 Third Avenue
Seattle, Washington 98101
(206) 442-5930

The national office for the Occupational Safety and Health Administration (OSHA) is located at:

U.S. Department of Labor—OSHA
Francis Perkins Building
200 Constitution Avenue, N.W.
Washington, D.C. 20210
(202) 523-7198

Job Safety Fundamentals advises employers on how to create a safe working environment. This booklet is available from the Society for Human Resource Management, at the address listed previously.

Unions

For information on forming a union, contact:

National Labor Relations Board
1717 Pennsylvania Avenue, N.W.
Washington, D.C. 20570
(202) 254-8064

You can get details about the rules governing a union's election of officers and its financial affairs from:

Labor-Management Services Standards
U.S. Department of Labor
Washington, D.C. 20216
(202) 523-7377

The AFL-CIO is a source of information on unions and a wide variety of other matters about law in the workplace. You can obtain a listing of their publications from:

AFL-CIO
Pamphlet Division
Room 208
815 16th Street, N.W.
Washington, D.C. 20006
(202) 637-5000

Unemployment Compensation

Contact the local office of your state's employment security or unemployment department or the state job service.

Social Security, Medicare, and Medicaid

Your local Social Security Administration can provide details and literature on your benefits. Your state and county health and welfare offices also should have information.

Workers' Compensation

Since the individual states manage these programs, write to your state department of labor.

Analysis of Workers' Compensation Laws shows provisions of these laws in all 50 states. This publication is revised annually. You can order it from:

U.S. Chamber of Commerce
Publications Fulfillment
1615 H Street, N.W.
Washington, D.C. 20062
(301) 468-5128

Pensions

For information about ERISA and your rights under a pension plan, write to:

Pension and Welfare Benefits Administration
U.S. Department of Labor
Room 5658
200 Constitution Avenue, N.W.
Washington, D.C. 20210
(202) 523-8233

The Pension Rights Center is an organization designed to inform employees of their rights about pensions. It also publishes booklets that explain ERISA and other pension-related topics. You can reach them at:

Pension Rights Center
Suite 704
918 16th Street, N.W.
Washington, D.C. 20006
(202) 296-3776

Wages and Hours

Contact the local Wage and Hour Division of your local U.S. Department of Labor office for details on laws affecting wages and working conditions. They offer many publications. The Bureau of National Affairs, Incorporated, also has a summary of federal wage and hour laws. Write for this summary at:

Bureau of National Affairs, Incorporated
Attention: Customer Service
1231 25th Street, N.W.
Washington, D.C. 20037
(202) 452-4200

Government Publications

The federal government publishes hundreds of pamphlets about employment. These range from "how to" books for teenagers looking for jobs to statistics on the number of OSHA claims in a specific year. To find out if there is a pamphlet about your specific problem, check the government bibliographies. They cover subjects such as employment and occupations, retirement, and civil rights, listing all the government publications available under that heading.

The following is a list of the bibliographies about employment issues:

Handicapped—SB-37
Employment and Occupations—SB-44
Labor-Management Relations—SB-64
Women—SB-111
Workers' Compensation—SB-108
Veterans Affairs & Benefits—SB-80
Personnel Management, Guidance, and Counseling—SB-202
Civil Rights and Equal Opportunity—SB-207
Occupational Safety and Health—SB-213

The bibliographies listed above are available without charge from the Superintendent of Documents, U.S. Government Printing Office, Washington, D.C. 20402. The telephone number is (202) 783-3238.

The federal government's Consumer Information Center also distributes free or inexpensive booklets on the law of the workplace. They are available from Consumer Information Center-N, P.O. Box 100, Pueblo, Colorado 81002. Two of these booklets dealing with employment are:

Handy Reference Guide to the Fair Labor Standards Act. This booklet is for both employees and employers. It contains information about federal laws on the minimum wage, overtime pay, child labor, and more. 13 pages. (1987) Publication 401W. 50 cents.

A Working Woman's Guide to Her Job Rights. Among the rights discussed in this comprehensive booklet are the freedom from discrimination and harassment, maternity leave, minimum wage, and pension and retirement benefits. 64 pages. (1988) Publication 109W. $2.00.

Information on Small Businesses

The Consumer Information Center distributes booklets on starting and running a small business. Some are:

Directory of Business Development Publications. This guide lists more than 55 booklets available for a small charge from the Small Business Administration (SBA) on financing, planning, marketing, staffing, and more. This directory is useful for both new and established small business owners. Two pages. (1988) Publication 501W. Free.

Doing Business with the Federal Government. This guide discusses how to bid on government contracts, market products to federal agencies, and other useful guidelines for efficient trading with Uncle Sam. 48 pages. (1989) Publication 110W. $2.75.

Financial Management: How to Make a Go of Your Business. Eight out of ten new businesses fail because of poor financial planning. This booklet provides an overview of financial and management essentials for a better chance at success. 73 pages. (1986) Publication 111W. $2.50.

Guide to Business Credit and the Equal Credit Opportunity Act. This booklet discusses what you can expect when applying for a business loan and how the law protects you from discrimination. 12 pages. (1986) Publication 402W. 50 cents.

Starting and Managing a Business from Your Home. For the would-be home business entrepreneur, this booklet covers: assessing your skills, experience, and life goals; evaluating your product and market; setting a price; and tips on structure, financial planning, zoning, insurance, and more. 48 pages. (1986) Publication 113W. $2.00.

Wage Withholding for Child Support—An Employer's Guide for Small Business. Beginning in November 1990, employers will have legal responsibilities for enforcing child support. This booklet contains an overview of how this law will work. It also offers useful information as well for both absent and custodial parents. In addition, this guide lists the telephone numbers of the State Child Support Agency Wage Withholding Offices. Two pages. (1989) Publication 502W. Free.

The Internal Revenue Service (IRS) is an excellent source of information on tax questions. The IRS offers a tele-tax service featuring recorded tax information about 140 topics. You can find the toll-free number by looking on your federal income tax return or by calling your local IRS office.

IRS representatives also are available to help you with your tax questions. Consult your local IRS office to find out about help by phone, mail, or in person.

In addition, the IRS publishes several free pamphlets dealing with common tax questions for people who operate a small business. These include:

Tax Information on S Corporations (Publication 589)
Business Expenses (Publication 535)
General Business Credit (Publication 572)

To order any IRS publication, call (800) 424-3676 to receive an order form. You may be able to obtain the desired publication(s) more quickly by contacting your local IRS office.

Other Publications

For a more detailed discussion of employee rights, see *The Rights of Employees* and *The Rights of Government Employees.* The American Civil Liberties Union (ACLU) publishes both of them. They are available for under five dollars from your local ACLU chapter. The ACLU also publishes *The Rights of Union Members.* This handbook discusses your rights you belong to a union. For a list of available publications, contact your local ACLU chapter or call (212) 944-9800 and ask or the literature department.

Another short, easy-to-read book covering a wide range of mployment issues is *The Law of the Workplace: Rights of Employers and Employees,* by James W. Hunt. The book is available from the Bureau of National Affairs, Incorporated, 1231 5th Street, N.W., Washington, D.C. 20037.

Still Have Questions?

The law of the workplace is complex. Your decisions and ctions may have far-reaching results. It is often worthwhile to consult with a lawyer trained to deal with these matters. Government agencies often advise people with questions to retain lawyer to represent their unique interests. Contact your state or local bar association for details on lawyers in your area. Many of these organizations have a lawyer referral service. The first chapter n this publication ("When and How to Use a Lawyer") can help ou find a lawyer.

PERSONAL INJURY

INTRODUCTION

Personal injury law protects your interests if someone wrongfully hurts or kills you or damages your property. Lawyers call this area *tort law*.

Personal injury law protects you when the person who injures you or your property acts intentionally or negligently. Car accidents provide a good example of how personal injury law works. (Note, though, that the system may work very differently in states that have passed no-fault laws.) When you receive an injury in an accident, you may have a claim against the other driver if that person did not drive with reasonable care. As explained later in this chapter, the claim may be resolved by a settlement or by a lawsuit. The term for driving without reasonable care is *negligence*. Personal injury law allows you to recover damages wrongfully inflicted by such drivers.

Also, in certain cases, people could be liable to you even if there is no intentional act or negligence on their part. You may have a case if a defective product hurts you, or if a store detective stops you for suspected shoplifting, or under certain limited circumstances, if you are injured at work. If someone damages your reputation, you may be able to sue for *defamation*. If someone hits you, even as a practical joke, you may be able to sue for *battery*.

Q. Battery is a crime. Do torts fall under criminal law?

A. No, criminal law does not apply to torts. Criminal assaults and batteries do exist (see the "Criminal Justice" chapter), but the government brings those charges because it considers them to be injuries to the public. Personal injury suits for assault and battery are civil cases, as are all tort actions. The law considers them to be wrongs against an individual, and the individual can sue for money damages.

Q. How do I know if I have a personal injury case?

A. Talk to a lawyer who handles personal injury cases. Tell the attorney everything you can about your accident or injury. After considering all the facts you provide, your lawyer probably will be able to say whether you have a case. Your attorney also will tell you what facts might prevent you from having a good case. For instance, in some states your own negligence might prevent a recovery of damages. In other states, your recovery may be reduced based on a comparison of your negligence against the negligence of the person who injured you.

Q. How do I find a personal injury lawyer?

A. Talk with lawyers you know. If they do not practice in the personal injury field, they often will be able to refer you to someone who does. If you do not know any lawyers, talk to your friends and neighbors. They may be able to recommend a personal injury lawyer they have used or heard about. Local bar associations, whose telephone numbers you can find in your telephone directory, also offer referral services. In general, you probably should try to obtain the services of a lawyer who concentrates on personal injury. The law has become increasingly specialized over the years. As a result, you will probably be most satisfied with someone who has had extensive experience. (For more information, see the "When and How to Use a Lawyer" chapter.)

Q. I have seen advertisements for personal injury lawyers on television. Should I call one of them?

A. Because recent court decisions have reduced the restrictions on where and how attorneys may advertise, some personal injury lawyers are using newspapers, radio, and television advertisements. However, many qualified lawyers refuse to advertise. You are free to call any attorney whose ad you have seen or read. Keep in mind, the important thing is to feel comfortable with a competent lawyer. You should feel

Types of Injuries Required for Lawsuits

It is not always necessary to have a physical injury to bring a personal injury lawsuit. While most personal injury lawsuits are based on some physical injury inflicted by another person, they also may be based on a variety of nonphysical losses and harms. Assault, for example, is your expectation that some harm will come to you. It too is a personal injury. (Assault is described in more detail later in this chapter.) You may have an action if someone has attacked your reputation, for example. Also, you may have an action for intentionally inflicted severe emotional distress and for other psychological and psychiatric injuries.

Time Limits for Filing Lawsuits

Every state has certain time limits governing the period during which you may bring personal injury cases. The law refers to these time limits as *statutes of limitations*. For example, in some states, you may have as little as one year to file a lawsuit based on an assault or battery you have suffered. The amount of time depends on the state in which you live. The same kind of limitations cover negligence actions for injuries suffered in car accidents. Defamation actions carry other time limits. As explained later in this chapter, limitations in medical malpractice cases are often calculated in a different way. That is why it is important to talk with a lawyer who will be familiar with the statutes, as soon as you receive or discover an injury.

confident about your attorney's ability to handle your case. That may mean talking to several lawyers before making a decision, and making sure that the one you choose has had extensive experience in the area of law that governs your case.

Q. What kind of legal fees should I expect?

A. Personal injury lawyers generally charge their clients on a contingent fee basis. That means you have to pay your lawyer a fee only if you win your case. (However, if you lose the case, you still may have to pay your lawyer's expenses incurred in the investigation and litigation of your case.) If you win, your lawyer would then take an agreed-upon percentage—usually one third—of the total amount recovered. Always negotiate a written retainer agreement with your lawyer. Writing it down should clarify the agreement and lessen problems down the line.

Q. Should I provide my lawyer with any documents?

A. Yes, if they might be relevant to your case. Police reports are available in such situations as auto accidents, fires, and assaults. These reports may contain eyewitness accounts and details about the conditions surrounding the incident. Copies of medical reports from doctors and hospitals will describe your injuries. You should supply all available documents to your lawyer. The more facts you give your lawyer, the easier it will be for your lawyer to determine whether you are likely to win your lawsuit.

Q. How will my case be resolved?

A. Your lawyer and the lawyer from the opposing side often *settle* personal injury cases, with your consent, out of court. It is important that you receive advance notice of any settlement in writing. It is up to you to decide whether you agree to the settlement.

Some personal injury cases do *go to trial.* A jury decides nearly all the cases that proceed to trial.

Q. What will I get if I win my case?

A. If you win, the court or the jury will award you money, known as *damages,* as compensation for your injuries. That amount will include such expenses as your medical bills and the wages you lost when you were out of work because of your injury. The damages also might include your future wage loss and future medical expenses, and possibly money for your

Million-Dollar Verdicts Reported by Liability

The total number of verdicts and rank (order) are cited for 18 nonvehicular and five vehicular liabilities from 1962 to 1989.*

Nonvehicular	Total	Rank
Accidental	25	14
Aircraft	77	9
Dram shop	32	13
False arrest	22	16
Freak accidents	10	18
Government	270	5
Intentional assaults	132	7
Libel and slander	38	11
Medical malpractice	833	2
Negligent supervision	35	12
Premises and occupier	261	6
Products liability	843	1
Professional negligence	402	4
Railroad	109	8
Shipping	24	15
Sports	20	17
Utility companies	67	10
Work-related	467	3

Vehicular	Total	Rank
Bicycle	23	5
Common carriers	39	4
Motorcycle	61	3
Pedestrian	107	2
Other vehicular	458	1

Source: Jury Verdict Research, Inc.

*1989 data is incomplete

physical pain and suffering. In addition, you may receive damages for any physical disfigurement or disability that resulted from your injury.

Q. Will the person who caused my injury get punished?

A. Defendants in civil cases do not receive jail terms or stiff fines as punishment. However, courts sometimes will order people whose intentional acts injure you to pay what the law calls *punitive damages*. Courts use these payments to punish people (and more often large corporations) who behaved recklessly or against the public's interest. The courts also hope that ordering the payment of punitive damages will discourage such defendants from engaging in the same kind of harmful behavior in the future. In recent years, however, courts have become more and more reluctant to award punitive damages in civil cases.

Million-Dollar Verdicts Reported by Injury

The total number of verdicts and rank (order) are cited for 31 injury categories from 1962 to 1989.*

Injury	Total	Rank	Injury	Total	Rank
Abdomen	28	18	Facial scarring	15	22
AIDS	7	27	Genitalia	41	14
Amputation	331	3	Gunshot	14	23
Arm	30	17	Kidney and bladder	20	21
Arthritis	9	26	Leg	201	7
Asbestosis	40	15	Loss of services	20	21
Back	53	12	Lung	22	20
Brain damage	718	2	Multiple injuries	143	9
Burns	144	8	Paraplegia	275	4
Cancer	30	17	Pelvis and hip	41	14
Death	968	1	Quadriplegia	257	5
Disc	92	10	Rape	30	17
Ear	12	25	Spinal nerve	31	16
Emotional distress	222	6	Throat and mouth	13	24
Eye	85	11	Vertebra fracture	48	13
Facial nerve	24	19			

Source: Jury Verdict Research, Inc.

*1989 data is incomplete

Q. What if I lose my personal injury case?

A. You will not have to pay for your lawyer's time. However, you probably will have to pay certain fees and expenses your attorney incurred before and during the trial. These include such things as court filing fees, payments to investigators and court reporters, and the like. It is important that you and your lawyer spell out these fees, and who will be responsible for them, in a written retainer that you both agree to at the beginning of the case.

Q. What if more than one person caused my injury?

A. You are permitted to bring an action against every person who caused your injury. If a jury establishes two or more wrongdoers, the law refers to them as *joint tortfeasors*. Under established law, each of them is 100-percent liable for your injury. By recent legislation, however, some states have limited or abolished such joint liability. Therefore, a jury may determine how much a certain defendant was at fault, and order that defendant to pay accordingly. This is called the *rule of comparative negligence*. It exists in most states.

PRINCIPLES OF NEGLIGENCE

Q. If someone else causes an accident and I am hurt, on what basis will that person be responsible (liable)?

A. That person will be liable if he or she was negligent in causing the accident. Negligence is the basis for liability in a majority of personal injury lawsuits.

Persons who act negligently never set out (intend) to cause results such as your injuries. Rather, their liability is based on careless or thoughtless action or on a failure to act when they should. Their conduct is called "negligent" when it falls below a legal standard that has been established to protect you against unreasonable risks of harm.

Q. Negligence law seems so confusing. It uses words such as duty and causation. What do they mean?

A. Negligence law can be complex and confusing even for people who are familiar with it. To understand it better, forget all the legal terms you have heard, and think about the car accident example. Drivers have a duty to use a reasonable amount of care to protect anyone they meet on the road. If drivers fail to use reasonable care and they injure you, they will be responsible *(liable)* to you for those injuries.

Q. How will a court determine whether they acted reasonably?

A. A court will look at what an "ordinary person" or a "reasonable person" would have done in similar circumstances. This will help the court (or jury) determine whether the driver who injured you acted negligently. If the driver's conduct departed from that standard, it was unreasonable in view of the risks to you and others. Then a court probably will find the driver negligent.

Q. What about malpractice actions against professionals such as lawyers? I recently hired one who seemed inexperienced.

HEIRS AND LAWSUITS

If the person who received an injury in the accident dies, that person's heirs may recover money through a lawsuit. Every state has some law permitting an action when someone causes the wrongful death of another. In a few states, the amounts recoverable are subject to minimums and maximums set by state law. And if a person with a claim dies from unrelated causes, the claim may survive and be brought by the executor or personal representative of the deceased person's estate.

I was unhappy with the way this lawyer handled the case, and I did not like its outcome.

A. Lawyer *malpractice* is a developing area. Most malpractice actions probably occur in the medical field. In general, however, lawyers and other professionals must follow a standard of practice equal to those in their same or similar communities. Not only must they exercise reasonable care in handling your case, they also must have a minimum of special knowledge and ability. That means that they will be liable to you if their own skills fall short and the result injures you. You may have a malpractice case against the attorney for handling your case negligently. However, dissatisfaction with the outcome of the case alone will not be the basis for a malpractice case against your lawyer.

MEDICAL MALPRACTICE

You bring a *medical malpractice* case against a physician who has failed to use reasonable care in treating you, and who injures or harms you as a result. If your doctor was careless, for example, or lacked proper skills, or disregarded established rules, a jury may find that the physician was negligent. The doctor will be liable to you for your injuries.

Q. How do I begin a medical malpractice case?

A. Talk to a lawyer who specializes in such work. Tell the attorney exactly what happened to you, from the first time you visited your doctor through your last contact with him or her. What were the circumstances surrounding your illness or injury? How did your doctor treat it? What did your doctor tell you about your treatment? Did you follow your doctor's instructions? What happened to you? Answers to these and other relevant questions become important if you think your doctor may have committed malpractice.

Q. My aunt discovered that a sponge left in her during an operation years ago was the source of her stomach trouble. May she still sue?

A. Like other personal injury cases, medical malpractice lawsuits are subject to specific statutes of limitations (discussed earlier in this chapter). Until recently, your aunt may have been out of luck. In many statutes, time limits on filing began when the injury occurred—on the day of the operation. To alleviate such a harsh—and final—result, many states today have altered their laws. Some of these new laws do not start the statute of limitations' clock until people discover that they have suffered an injury, or should have discovered it. In Illinois, for example, the statute permits suits within four years of such discovery.

Q. My father's job exposed him to asbestos. Now he has contracted a lung disease. Is it too late to file a claim?

A. It may not be too late. Many people who suffered injuries from such toxic substances as asbestos did not know at the time of exposure that the compounds were harmful. As a result, some states have enacted laws allowing people to file lawsuits for a certain amount of time from the date when the lung impairment or cancer begins, rather than from the date of discovery or exposure. A lawyer can tell you whether your father still has time within the statute of limitations.

In general, the area of workplace illnesses is covered by workers' compensation (discussed later in this chapter and in the "Law and the Workplace" chapter). Normally, workers are not permitted to recover from their employer. If they have a claim against their employer, their state's workers' compensation law will apply.

Q. What is likely to happen in a medical malpractice case?

A. The lawyers for each side typically gather facts through written questions (interrogatories) or from depositions (questions that are asked in person and answered under oath). This process is called *discovery*. After discovery, some medical malpractice cases get settled out of court. On the other hand, some cases do go to trial. In most of them, a jury will consider testimony by experts—usually other doctors. They will testify about whether your physician's actions followed good medical practice or fell below the accepted standard of care. It is likely that there will be doctors testifying for each side.

In some states, your case will be subject to arbitration. Typically, if you are not satisfied with the arbitration result, you may then file suit in court.

Q. How do jurors know if your doctor's actions fall within the standards of good medical practice?

A. Courts once asked jurors to look at whether a doctor's treatment was similar to what other doctors in the same community would have done. However, physicians increasingly have become subject to a national practice standard. So a jury asked to consider whether your heart surgeon was negligent probably will be told to consider what competent heart surgeons across the country would have done.

Q. If a court finds that the consent form I signed is valid, is it still possible to recover damages in a malpractice action against my doctor?

A. Yes, you still may be able to recover damages. A consent form does not release from liability a physician who did not perform the operation following established procedures or who was otherwise negligent. You could base a malpractice

Signing Consent Forms Before Surgery

Before an operation, you probably will sign a form that gives the doctor your consent (approval) to the surgery and possibly to other procedures. Hospitals today commonly use such forms. Before you sign it, your doctor must give you a full description of the surgery, its risks, the alternatives to surgery, and the results of not getting such treatment. If you can prove that your physician did not adequately inform you of the risks and benefits before surgery, your consent may be invalid. The only time the law excuses doctors from providing such information is in emergencies or when it would be harmful to a patient. But even if your doctor should have secured your consent and did not do so, you still have to show damages.

case, for example, on surgery the physician performed that went beyond the consent you gave. Then the doctor might even be liable for battery.

Q. What if I'm just not satisfied with the results of my surgery? Do I have a good malpractice case?

A. In general, there are no guarantees. You would have to show damages that resulted from the doctor's deviation from the appropriate standard of care for your condition.

Q. My religion prohibits blood transfusions, yet the hospital that treated me following a recent accident gave one to me anyway. Can I recover damages against the hospital and the doctor who administered the transfusion?

A. This is an extremely rare set of circumstances, and courts have not often ruled on cases in this area. A few courts have said that it was all right for a hospital to give blood transfusions, even when the patient's religious views would prohibit them. However, a patient generally has the right to refuse transfusions. A court might say otherwise if you were near death and not competent to make the decision at the time.

Q. I got pregnant even though my husband had a vasectomy. Can we recover damages?

A. Yes, you may be able to win a case. Courts increasingly are allowing a new type of case for so-called *wrongful conception* or *wrongful pregnancy* when a doctor has failed to prevent the birth of a healthy, but unwanted, child. A number of the cases are filed against physicians for performing unsuccessful vasectomies or other methods of sterilization that resulted in unwanted children.

Q. We think our son, who is suffering from muscle spasms, should see a specialist. Our family practitioner says he does not need one. What should we do?

A. This is not primarily a legal question. Common sense suggests that you probably should go see a specialist. Your family physician may be right, but a second opinion from a specialist will not hurt. The law expects family doctors to know the limits of their abilities. They must refer their patients, as appropriate, to medical specialists. If they do not—and this is where the law comes in—the courts could, under some circumstances, find the family doctors negligent in their treatment.

Q. My doctor prescribed a drug for treatment but failed to tell me it was part of an experimental program. What may I do?

A. Your physician had a duty to tell you that the drug was part of an experimental program. You had the right to refuse to participate in it. You now may have grounds for an action against your doctor.

Q. My adult daughter set up a doctor's appointment, but she refuses to tell me anything about it. Don't I have a right to know?

A. There are certain decisions that your daughter and doctor may make with which you may not interfere. In some states, if she discusses or receives treatment for drug or alcohol abuse or mental health problems, it is between her and her physician. The same is true if she seeks help in birth control or family planning from her doctor.

Q. May I recover medical and hospital bills from someone who caused an injury to me, even though my insurance company has paid the bill?

A. Yes. However, if you do recover payment from the person who injured you for those bills, some states require you to refund your insurance company. In those states, the law does not allow you to get a double recovery. Often the insurance policy contains a subrogation clause that does not permit double recovery.

Q. I was staying at a motel when there was a fire. Shouldn't the management have helped us escape?

A. The motel management probably should have exercised reasonable prudence about the fire alarms and fire escapes. And they should have helped you escape. When there is a special relationship, a duty often arises to aid those in trouble. Innkeepers usually have such a duty to aid their guests, particularly in cases of fire.

Q. What about airlines? Do they have a duty to aid passengers in an emergency?

A. Yes. Common carriers that transport people for a fee—bus lines, airlines, and railroads—also have a special relationship with their passengers. The carriers must do everything they can to help their riders in an emergency.

Medical Records—Confidential or Not?

After a recent hospital stay, you may wish to see your medical records. Does the hospital have the right to refuse to turn them over to you? Most states have laws that cover access to medical information and records, which the laws consider to be confidential. Whether the hospital turns them over to you depends on the law in your state. Some states allow patients full access to such records. Others allow patients to see them with certain restrictions.

Although your medical records normally are confidential, there are a few exceptions. Suppose a physician was treating you for a communicable disease or gunshot wound, or a doctor suspected abuse in a child under treatment. Under those circumstances, the doctor must tell the proper authorities.

SHOULD YOU STOP AND HELP SOMEONE IN AN EMERGENCY?

Most states have passed so-called *Good Samaritan laws*. They excuse doctors from liability for negligence for coming to the aid of someone in an emergency. The laws in some states include protection for people who are not doctors and who give emergency treatment.

Do you have an obligation to help someone in danger? Generally, you do not have such a duty. You might be an expert swimmer but you have no legal responsibility to rescue someone whom you see drowning. In fact,

(continued)

Q. Suppose I injure someone while driving. Do I have to help that person?

A. It depends on the state in which the accident occurs. In some states, you must help a person injured by your car, regardless of who was at fault.

Q. I received an injury when the bus I ride to work got in an accident. May I recover compensation from the bus company?

A. As noted above, the law says that common carriers have a special responsibility to their passengers. That means they must be extra cautious in protecting their riders and do everything they can to keep them safe. Whether you win your case will depend on the circumstances of the accident. Did the driver pull out in front of a car and have to slam on the brakes? What were the road conditions? A jury will have to consider those kinds of things to determine if your driver acted negligently. However, as an employee of the common carrier, the driver must provide you with a high degree of care.

Q. Someone attacked my daughter on the campus of the college she attends. May I hold the school responsible for this attack?

A. Your daughter *and* you might have a cause of action against the college. Some courts have found universities and colleges liable for attacks on their students because the schools did not exercise reasonable care in protecting the students. Courts increasingly are finding that other entities—like governments and innkeepers—also have a duty to prevent harm inflicted by a third person. In a case that drew headlines in the 1970s, for example, a court awarded $2.5 million to singer Connie Francis for an attack at a Howard Johnson's Motor Lodge. The court found that the motel did not take proper and reasonable steps to prevent the attack. In your daughter's case, a court would look at the facts and ask whether similar attacks had occurred previously in the same area. If so, the court would ask what security precautions the college had taken.

Q. Is there anything else victims may do?

A. Yes. Most states have laws compensating victims of violent crimes for lost wages, counseling, and medical expenses. There also are several victim assistance programs. Check with your local prosecutor's office (possibly called the office of the state's attorney or district attorney).

Q. A furniture deliveryman was injured when he tripped over an electrical extension cord in my living room. Can he recover damages from me?

A. He could sue, though it is not certain that he would win. Under the law, whether you are liable to someone injured in your home depends on the reason for the person's visit. You have a special duty to people who come to your home to do work for you, as the deliveryman did. Just as a store owner must make the store premises safe for customers, you must make your home reasonably safe for such visitors. Was the cord visible—and dangerous—to anyone who came into your living room? Or was it only obvious if someone moved your furniture? Did you warn the deliveryman to watch out for the cord? Courts would need the answers to such questions to decide if you should be liable to the deliveryman. By the way, homeowner's insurance policies generally protect homeowners in cases such as these.

Q. What if I get injured while at the home of my neighbor, who invited me there for a party?

A. As a social guest, you might be able to recover from your neighbor, depending on how your injuries happened. Homeowners must tell their guests about—or make safe—any dangerous conditions that the guests are unlikely to recognize. Suppose, for example, that while at your neighbor's party, you tripped on a throw rug and got injured. You may be able to recover if you can prove that your neighbor knew that other people had tripped over it and you were unlikely to realize its danger. Your neighbor probably should have warned you about it or even removed it during the party.

Q. A door-to-door salesman tripped on our front steps, injuring himself. May he hold me responsible?

A. Yes. Like the social guest, a door-to-door salesman may expect that you will warn him about dangerous conditions on your property that may not be obvious. If your steps were in perfect condition and the salesman merely tripped, a court will not hold you responsible. However, if he tripped because one of the stairs was wobbly and you knew about it, you should have repaired it or posted a warning sign.

Q. Would I be liable if a trespasser gets injured on my property?

A. You generally are not liable for injuries trespassers receive on your property. However, suppose you know that some people

(continued)

you may sit on the shore and watch that person drown. The law says that if you did not cause the problem and if you and the victim have no special relationship, you need not try to rescue that person. Some courts, however, have begun to look at the circumstances of the rescue. They say that if you know someone is in extreme danger, that could be avoided with little inconvenience on your part, you must provide reasonable care to the victim. You also are free to go voluntarily to the aid of someone in trouble. However, if you abandon your rescue efforts after starting them, you may be liable if you leave the victim in worse condition than you found him or her.

PERSONAL INJURY

If You Get Injured in a Store

Suppose you tripped and fell on a spilled can of paint in a hardware store where you were shopping, injuring your head. Can you recover damages from the store? It depends on the facts of the case. Store owners must keep their premises reasonably safe for customers. If they do not, they may be liable. Store owners must inspect and discover dangerous conditions. They also must keep all aisles clear and properly maintained. If there are dangerous conditions, such as slippery floors, store owners are responsible for them. Was the owner aware that the paint can was in the aisle? How long had it been there? These are questions a court will consider when deciding whether you may recover damages from the store owner. However, a court also might find that you discovered the spilled paint and proceeded to walk right through it. Then the court might deny you damages.

are continually trespassing on your property, perhaps using it as a shortcut. Then a court might find that you should have notified them about any hidden artificial conditions of which you were aware that could seriously injure them.

Q. A group of eight-year-old children has been playing in a vacant lot that I own. Could I be liable if one of them gets injured?

A. Yes, the law places a greater burden on landowners when injuries involve children. The reason is that children are too young to understand or appreciate danger in certain situations. Something called the *attractive nuisance doctrine* protects children. Under this doctrine, if you know or should know about potentially dangerous conditions on your lot, you must warn the children who are playing there. Or you must take reasonable precautions to protect them. If, for example, there is machinery or other equipment on your vacant lot that could present an unreasonable risk to children, you should remove it. You could very well be liable to them for any injuries they suffer.

Q. Our children's friends often come to swim in our backyard pool, even though we are not always able to be there. What if one of them gets hurt?

A. You are liable. You should make sure an adult is present when children are swimming there, though this will not necessarily avoid liability. And warning the children that they should not swim without an adult present may not be enough to avoid liability if one of them gets injured. Also check with your city or town to find out the requirements for residential swimming pools.

Q. My son and his boyfriends went snowmobiling on a nearby farm. When the vehicle ran into a fence, one of them got hurt. The farmer now says he is not liable. Is that true?

A. If landowners know that others are using their land for snowmobiling, most states say they must warn snowmobilers about hidden dangerous conditions or remove them. Was the fence visible? Did the farmer recently build it? A few states, such as Michigan, have laws specifically dealing with liability when someone uses property for recreational purposes without permission. In those states, the farmer, unless he acted recklessly, probably would not be liable if he did not authorize the boys to be on his land. You might want to ask a lawyer about your state's law.

Q. May a parent sue if a day-care center hurts a child?

A. Yes, but someone other than the parent should first evaluate the extent and nature of the injury to establish that the suit has merit. (This is true of any personal injury suit.) Accusations made without proof and evaluation may only lead to problems for the parents. It is particularly difficult to prove mental and emotional injury, although it is less difficult to show that a center is responsible for a child's broken arm.

Q. What is the difference between child abuse and hurting a child while giving discipline?

A. The difference is a thin line that is very hard to draw. In states that prohibit day-care providers from using corporal punishment, any corporal punishment may qualify as child abuse. If there is no such law or regulation, the inappropriate use of corporal punishment might be the basis of a personal injury suit against the day-care provider.

Because it is difficult to distinguish between child abuse and less serious but still inappropriate corporal punishment, many state laws are prohibiting *all* forms of corporal punishment. The American Bar Association, in the 1985 House of Delegates Report, declares that no state should allow any corporal punishment in any day-care setting.

Q. What should I do if I suspect that some adult in a day-care center is abusing the children?

A. First, you should talk to the director of the facility if that seems logical and the director seems open-minded. If this is not an option, talk to a lawyer for advice on how to proceed. If it is the policy of the center to use corporal punishment, complain to the state licensing authority. If the abuse is obvious and severe, notifying the police also may be appropriate. As an alternative, you might want to consult with other parents whom you trust whose children attend the day-care center. Perhaps together you can determine a course of action.

Q. My son received an injury during basic training in the U.S. Army. May he recover damages from the federal government?

A. No. People in the armed services who receive injuries during the course of their duties are not permitted to recover for their injuries. However, a statute known as the Federal Tort Claims Act permits, under certain conditions, recovery in

You Are Not Allowed to Sue Certain Persons or Entities

The law considers some people and entities to be immune from—or protected against—having others file lawsuits against them. Under the so-called *sovereign immunity doctrine,* for example, the law has prohibited suits against governments unless a statute permits such actions. While many jurisdictions have done away with sovereign immunity, you may not be able to sue the federal government, states, and municipalities. Some states also prohibit personal injury lawsuits between spouses and between parents and children. However, many states have abandoned those limitations.

personal injury lawsuits against the United States government for torts committed by its employees. These actions are brought in the U.S. Claims Court (see the "How the Legal System Works" chapter). Some states have their own courts of claim. In other states, claims actions can be brought through other courts.

Q. I fell on a broken piece of a city sidewalk and injured my ankle. Do I have a case against the city?

A. In many states, municipal immunity prohibits recovery in many kinds of cases against a city or town. However, municipalities have a duty to keep streets and sidewalks in repair. You might have a successful case against the city if it failed to maintain the sidewalk properly.

LIABILITY FOR PUBLIC SIDEWALKS

When would a homeowner be liable for injuries you receive on a public sidewalk in front of the owner's house? In some places, ordinances say that landowners whose property is next to the public sidewalk are responsible for keeping it in repair and clear of ice and snow. However, in certain towns in some states, owners have no duty to remove ice and snow that has collected on their premises or on adjacent public sidewalks. In fact, they may be liable for negligence if they undertake such a job and do not make the sidewalks safe.

Q. I was walking on a public sidewalk next to a construction site when I tripped and fell on a brick from the site, spraining my ankle. May I recover damages from the construction company?

A. Yes, you may recover damages. The company must take reasonable steps to keep sidewalks nearby its construction sites free from bricks and other debris. If it fails to remove such obstructions and you trip and fall, the company may be liable for your injuries. Construction companies should tell pedestrians that they could get injured if they stray from the sidewalk. If the companies have failed to place barriers or warning lamps by a building pit, for example, they will be responsible if anyone falls into it and gets injured.

Q. A drunk in a bar hit me for no reason. What may I do about it?

A. If you live in a state that has a *Dram Shop Act,* you may be able to recover from the tavern owner. Such acts usually come into play when intoxicated people served by the bar later injure somebody while driving. Some of those laws also make tavern owners liable when drunk customers injure others on or off the premises.

Q. My wife received an injury in a car accident. Some kids who had been drinking at the home of our neighbor, who supplied the liquor, caused the accident. May I take any action against the neighbor, who has done this in the past?

A. Possibly. Courts have imposed liability against such hosts when they have served liquor to minors.

Q. I was in a car accident during my pregnancy and my baby was born with a deformity. Does my child have a legal recourse?

A. Many states today will permit an action by the child for the consequences of such prenatal (before birth) injuries. (In states with no-fault automobile insurance, your right to sue often is limited.) Most courts also will allow a wrongful death action if the baby dies of the injuries after birth.

Q. Someone recently stole my car. The thief then got into an accident, injuring passengers in the other car. Now they are trying to sue me. Can they recover?

A. Probably not, though a lot would depend on the statutes in the state involved. Suppose you negligently left your car unlocked with the keys in it, making it easy for the thief to steal. Even then, most courts generally will not hold you liable if the thief later injures someone by negligent driving. That is because courts say you could not foresee that your actions ultimately would result in such injuries. In a few cases, though, courts have looked at whether your actions caused an unreasonable risk to someone else. Let us say you left your car parked with the engine running in a rundown neighborhood where there was a likelihood that it would get stolen. In this example, you might be liable if the car thief then injures children who were playing nearby. In a no-fault state, it might be difficult—if not impossible—for them to sue you. Lawsuits also would be less likely in no-fault states in the situations described below.

Q. I received an injury when my automobile collided with a truck driven by a deliveryman. Can I recover damages from the deliveryman or the employer?

A. You may be able to recover from the deliveryman's employer. Under the law, employers may be held liable for acts committed by an employee acting within the extent of the job. Although the employer was not negligent, the employer is indirectly liable for the negligence of its employee. This indirect liability is called *vicarious liability*. Was the employee making a delivery when the accident occurred? If so, courts easily could find the employer liable, since deliveries clearly were part of the driver's job. Courts in some states might also impose liability on the company if the accident took place while the employee was going to or from work, if the employment created special dangers. However, if the employee had first stopped at a restaurant for drinks and dinner with friends, the employer probably would be free from any liability.

LIABILITY AT SPORTING EVENTS

Suppose you went to a baseball game, and a ball that a player hit into the stands injured you. What may you do? If you file a lawsuit, you may not win. Spectators at a baseball game know they may be injured by a flying ball. That is why courts generally say that spectators assume the risk of being hurt by a ball. The same usually holds true if a golf ball hits you while you are watching a golf match. Likewise, if a wheel from a car in an automobile race flies into the stands, you assume the risk of getting hurt. The legal term for this doctrine is *assumption of the risk*. It means that you agreed to face a known danger.

Q. Someone sued me for negligence after we were involved in a car accident. However, I think the other man driving the other car also was negligent. What may I do?

A. In the past, the rule was that if you could prove that the other driver contributed to the accident, courts would bar him or her from recovering anything from you. Now, however, most states have rejected such harsh results. Instead, they look at the comparative (relative) fault of the drivers. Sometimes you may recover even if you were more negligent than the defendant. Courts will calculate the damages, and then reduce them by the proportion of your fault. (See the "Automobiles" chapter for more on standards of negligence for car accidents.)

Q. A neighbor who rides with me to work received an injury when I got into a car accident. Do I have to pay her medical bills?

A. In many states today, your no-fault insurance would cover the bills. Previously, many states had what they called *automobile guest statutes*. These laws made you liable for injuries to a nonpaying—or guest—passenger only if you were "grossly negligent" because you failed to use even slight care in your driving. In many states, courts have found automobile guest statutes to be unconstitutional, or legislatures have abolished them. In those states that still have such laws, you will not be liable to your neighbor unless you were grossly negligent. However, suppose she can prove that she was not a guest passenger—that both of you agreed to share expenses, for example. Then she could recover from you under ordinary negligence principles.

Q. We recently got a call from the hospital where someone had taken my mother. The hospital told us that she had died of a heart attack. However, it was not true. The hospital's false report devastated us. What may we do?

A. The circumstances you describe are rare. Nonetheless, you may be able to recover from the hospital for the negligent infliction of emotional distress. That is, you may be able to sue the hospital successfully for negligently causing you to endure emotional pain. Courts generally used to say that a person had to have physical injuries to recover in such cases. However, courts in some states have allowed recovery when there are no physical injuries. Other successful emotional distress suits have involved bystanders. For example, a court allowed a mother who saw her child fatally hit by a car to recover money damages.

1988 RECOVERY PROBABILITIES
VEHICULAR LIABILITY

Liability	Recovery	Liability	Recovery
Backing collisions	39%	No vehicular contact	40%
Bicycle and vehicle	39%	Parked vehicle	63%
Collision with object	42%	Parking lot	42%
Disabled vehicle	46%	Passenger suit	68%
Head-on collision	72%	Pedestrian suit	63%
Intersection collision	66%	Railroad-related	60%
Lane change	47%	Rear-end collision	61%
Merging vehicle	48%	Snowmobile	50%
Motorcycle and vehicle	58%	Stopped vehicle	42%
Multiple vehicles	80%	Turning collision	56%

"Recovery probability" refers to the likelihood that plaintiffs will recover damages or monetary compensation from a personal injury lawsuit. On average, the plaintiff recovery probability is greatest for vehicular accidents involving multiple vehicles and for head-on collisions.

The plaintiff recovery probability for backing collisions and bicycle and vehicle collisions (the first two items on the chart) is 24 percentage points below the national norm. (The national norm equals 63 percent, which means that 63 out of 100 plaintiffs recover damages in *all* liability situations, not just vehicular.)

Plaintiff recovery probabilities are below the national norm in 14 vehicular liability categories.

Recovery probabilities for specific liabilities within each category may vary significantly from the overall category statistic.

Source: Jury Verdict Research, Inc.

Q. The store where I bought my wedding gown failed to deliver it in time for the ceremony. What may I do?

A. You, too, no doubt suffered some distress at not having your wedding gown by the time of your wedding. However, it is unlikely that you have a personal injury case. The store was merely negligent in failing to deliver your dress by the time of your wedding. Although it may have been traumatic for you, generally you would have to show physical consequences or injury. You may, however, have a case for breach of contract.

(continued)

1988 RECOVERY PROBABILITIES
NONVEHICULAR LIABILITY

Liability	Recovery	Liability	Recovery
Aircraft	65%	Premises liability	51%
Animal-related	68%	Products liability	56%
Bad faith	53%	Professional negligence	56%
Dram shop	57%	Re-trial of cases	67%
False arrest	52%	Sports-related	55%
Intentional assaults	71%	Unusual and freak accidents	64%
Libel and slander	73%	Work-related	73%
Medical malpractice	50%	Wrongful termination	58%
Negligent supervision	60%		

On average, plaintiffs recover most often for personal injury claims involving intentional assaults, libel and slander, and work-related accidents.

The plaintiff recovery probability continues to be lowest for claims alleging medical malpractice and premises liability.

Plaintiff recovery in cases involving bad faith by an insurance company continues to average below the national norm. However, the study by Jury Verdict Research, Inc., indicates that both the number of verdicts and the plaintiff recovery probability are consistently increasing.

The three most frequent allegations of bad faith involve denial of coverage, delay in payment of a claim, and inadequate settlement offers.

A second emerging liability issue is that of claims involving wrongful termination. Not only is the recovery probability improving for plaintiffs, but the size of the plaintiff verdicts has also increased significantly in the last two years.

Recovery probabilities for specific liabilities within each category may vary significantly from the overall category statistic.

Source: Jury Verdict Research, Inc.

Q. We got behind on our bills, and a bill collector has been stopping by and calling us day and night. The bill collector intimidates us, calls us names, and threatens to destroy our credit record. We are nervous wrecks. What may we do?

A. You may be able to make a case that the collector's conduct is causing you mental distress. Courts recently have begun to recognize such actions as extreme and outrageous conduct that someone else intentionally inflicts on you. For you to recover damages, a court would take a close look at the collector's tactics. To recover on an emotional distress claim, you usually must show more than that your feelings were hurt. Without aggravating (intensifying) circumstances, most courts have not allowed recovery if the collector was merely profane, obscene, or abusive. Courts also have not permitted recovery if the collector threatened and insulted you. The collector would need to have used outrageous and extreme high-pressure methods for a period of time. What did the collector do and say? If the collector touched you offensively without your consent, you might even want to consider adding claims for two other intentional torts—assault and battery. You also might want to consider a case against the collector's employer. Just as employers are vicariously (indirectly) liable for the negligent acts of an employee, employers can be liable for the intentional acts of an employee. (See the "Consumer Credit" chapter for other legal protection against debt collectors.)

INTENTIONAL WRONGS

Q. Is a lawsuit based on liability for an intentional tort (a civil wrong) different from a lawsuit based on negligence?

A. Yes. A person who is found liable for an intentional tort does more than just act carelessly, which might make him or her liable for negligence. That person is said to intend the consequences of his or her action. If you pick up a stick and point it at another person, for example, you are going to scare that person. Under the law of intentional torts, you may be liable for an assault.

You do not have to intend to harm someone else to be liable for an intentional tort, either; you even may be attempting to help that person. In one reported case, for example, a defendant was found liable for an intentional tort when, despite her protests, he proceeded to set the broken arm of a woman who had fallen.

Q. I got a black eye in a fistfight with a man whose car accidentally bumped into mine while we sat at a red light. I would love to get even with him. Can I recover if I sue him?

A. Normally you could recover in a civil battery case against someone who hits you. However, a court might hold that two people who get into a fistfight, in effect, agree to being hit by one another. If so, a battery case probably would fail. A lot

BATTERY

A *battery* is a harmful or offensive touching of one person by another. Anyone who touches you or comes into contact with some part of you—even your purse—when you do not agree to it may be liable to you for battery. The law does not require any harm or actual damage. You do not even have to know a battery is occurring at the time in order to bring a battery case. The person committing the battery may have meant no hatred or ill will in the contact. In one case, for example, a plaintiff successfully recovered damages for an unwanted kiss. In another case, a court found a defendant liable for spitting at someone's face. Finally, a court found a battery when a person forcibly removed someone's hat.

would depend on the facts of the case. Who started the fight? Were there witnesses? What would their testimony be?

Q. My neighbor fired his shotgun to scare a solicitor whom he did not want coming to his door. The bullet grazed a passerby. Will my neighbor be liable?

A. Under a legal doctrine known as *transferred intent,* your neighbor probably will be liable for a battery to the passerby. This is true even though the passerby was an unexpected victim whom your neighbor did not intend to harm. The solicitor also is likely to win an assault case against your neighbor. The firing of the gun placed the solicitor in reasonable apprehension of a battery.

Q. A security guard in a store suspected me of shoplifting and detained me. I have heard about something called false imprisonment. Can I recover damages?

A. If the security guard was acting in good faith, most courts will allow the guard to detain you briefly on the store premises. A number of states by law have given shopkeepers a limited privilege to stop suspected shoplifters for a reasonable amount of time to investigate. However, you may, nonetheless, recover damages for false imprisonment. Suppose the security guard genuinely restrained you against your will, intending to confine you. Then you should talk to a lawyer about a false imprisonment action. If a court finds that the guard held you against your will, you may receive compensation for your loss of time and any inconvenience, physical discomfort, or injuries. If the guard acted maliciously, you also may be able to receive punitive damages.

ASSAULT

An *assault* is a reasonable apprehension (expectation) of some harm that may come to you. Unlike a battery, you must know that an assault is occurring at the time it takes place. A court will look at what happened. A great deal will depend on the reasonableness of your own feelings when threatened. The court will consider whether the closeness of the physical threat should have subjectively upset, frightened, or humiliated you. Words alone usually are not enough to bring a case for assault.

Q. Someone broke into my house in the middle of the night and attacked me. It was dark and I could not see the intruder well. I chased and knocked down a teenager running down the street because I thought he had committed the crime. However, he had not done so. Will I be liable to him?

A. Mistake sometimes may be a defense. A lot depends on the specific facts of the case. If you reasonably believe someone broke into your house and attacked you, you have the right to defend yourself by injuring him, even though it turns out that you were wrong. If you believe someone is about to inflict bodily harm, you may use nondeadly force to defend yourself. Courts allow deadly force only if you think someone is about to inflict death or serious bodily harm. Courts also consider whether the force you used was reasonably necessary.

In this particular case, if the teenager already was running down the street, courts may say that there no longer was danger to you or your property. Then you might well be liable.

STRICT LIABILITY

Q. Is there any other basis for liability besides negligence and wrongful intent?

A. Courts sometimes hold persons or companies *strictly liable* for certain activities that harm others, even when they have not acted negligently or with wrongful intent. (Lawyers and judges sometimes use the phrase "absolutely liable" to describe this type of liability.) Persons or companies engaged in blasting, storing dangerous substances, or keeping dangerous animals, for example, can be strictly liable for injuries caused to others.

The theory behind imposing such liability—which has been called *liability without fault*—is that those activities and certain other ones pose an undue risk of harm to members of the community. When something goes wrong—even innocently—and someone is harmed, the person who posed the risk is in the best position to pay for it. Workers' compensation laws, in which employers pay for employees' injuries even when no one is at fault, are a good example of how strict liability works.

Q. We live near a site where a gasoline company stores its flammable liquids. We worry about the possibility that an accident may occur. Will we be able to recover damages if one occurs?

A. Quite possibly. Courts have found such storage to be an inherently dangerous activity. This means that the act is hazardous by its very nature, whether it is done well or badly. Courts normally are likely to impose strict liability against the company for injuries that an accident may cause. Courts still might look at the location of the storage, however. If storage in the middle of a large city poses unusual and unacceptable risks, then courts might impose strict liability. The same holds true when a factory emits smoke, dust, or noxious gases in the middle of a town. However, a court might decide there is no strict liability if the companies conducted such activities in a remote rural area. In those situations, courts would impose strict liability only if the company conducted the activity in an unusual way. Then a great deal would depend on the facts of the case.

Q. What legal responsibility does a person who keeps wild animals have?

A. Most states impose strict liability against keepers of animals such as bears, lions, wolves, and monkeys. Merely keeping them exposes others to abnormal risks. If an injury occurs on the owner's premises and is caused by a confined or restrained animal, however, courts tend to deny strict liability. The courts reason that you assumed a risk by going there.

Q. Am I automatically liable if my dog, normally a friendly and playful pet, turns on my neighbor and bites her?

A. It may depend on where you live. In some states, courts hold that owners of dogs and other pets generally are not liable for injuries caused by their pets unless they know or have reason to know that their pet has a dangerous trait that is uncharacteristic (not typical) of that type of animal. The old saying in the law that describes this is that every previously well-behaved dog has one free bite. By legislation and case law in most states, however, courts have held dog owners strictly liable for their pets' first unprovoked attack. This is the trend in the law today, and it may be bad news for dog owners. Also, your neighbor may be able to recover on a negligence claim if she can show that you did not exercise due care in controlling the pet.

Visiting a Zoo

Zoos go to great extremes to protect visitors from the risks posed by their animals. Generally they restrain or confine them. For that reason, courts usually do not impose strict liability when a visitor to the zoo gets injured. Instead, the visitor must show that the zoo was somehow negligent in how it kept the animal.

Q. Our neighbor has a vicious watchdog. We are scared to death that the dog will bite one of our children, who often wander into the neighbor's yard. What may we do?

A. Your neighbor might take special pains to control the dog if he were made aware of the ways in which the law deals with vicious dogs. Unless your neighbor posts adequate warnings, he may be strictly liable for injuries caused by a vicious watchdog. (And there is a question of whether written warnings could be effective to a child.) Even if it never has bitten before, the mere fact that the dog is known to be vicious—or has certain dangerous traits—is the basis for imposing such liability. The situation you describe is a common one. Precisely for that reason, cities and towns often regulate it by passing an ordinance. A great deal would depend on the ordinance where you live.

Q. A car ran over my dog. Can I recover from the driver?

A. Yes, you might win a lawsuit. A dog is property, and you have suffered property damage. You will have to show that there was negligence in the person's driving.

Q. Our brand-new power mower backfired and injured me. From whom may I recover damages?

A. This is a typical *product liability* case. You may be able to prove that the manufacturer of the lawn mower made a defective product. Product liability can be based on intentional acts, negligence, or breach of warranty. However, most courts today hold companies responsible for a defective product strictly liable to consumers and users for injuries caused by the defect. The product may have had a flaw or the manufacturer may have designed it defectively. Another possibility may be that the producer or assembler failed to provide adequate warning of a risk or hazard.

Q. A disclaimer that came with the lawn mower said the manufacturer did not warrant it in any way. Will that defeat our claim?

A. Probably not, since courts do not look favorably at such clauses. Most courts find them invalid, either because you, as the consumer, were not in an equal bargaining position or because such clauses are unconscionable (grossly unfair) and contrary to public policy.

Q. I suffered a severe allergic reaction from some cosmetics I used. It required medical treatment. May I recover from the manufacturer?

A. Possibly. Did the manufacturer warn you that the cosmetic could cause such a reaction? Some courts normally will not hold the manufacturer liable for failing to warn you of the risk of an adverse reaction unless you can prove that an ingredient in the product would give a number of people an adverse reaction. You also must prove that the manufacturer knew or should have known this and that your reaction was because you were in that group of sensitive people. In addition, courts will determine whether you used the product according to the directions provided with it. Misuse is one of the defenses recognized in strict liability. If the court does not find strict liability, you still might recover on negligence claim.

Q. I was opening a soft-drink bottle when it exploded in my face, and flying glass cut me. Was somebody at fault?

A. Yes, someone was at fault, since bottles ordinarily do not explode in a person's face. Some courts decide such cases under the principles of negligence. If the bottler sealed it and the bottle was handled carefully between the time it left the bottler's possession and the time of the explosion, some

If You Get Injured at Work

Workers' compensation laws cover most workers injured on the job. Under these laws, employers compensate you for your injuries, including medical expenses and permanent or temporary disability, regardless of who was at fault. Legislatures created the laws because they thought that liability for workplace accidents should be placed on the one who was most able to bear the loss—the employer. In most states, if a workers' compensation law covers you, it prohibits

(continued)

courts presume—or consider it circumstantial evidence—that the bottler was negligent. Judges give such an instruction to juries in cases where something has gone wrong with a normally safe and commonplace activity. The jury still is free to find for the bottler, however.

Other courts decide such cases under the principles of strict liability. Then you would not have to prove negligence. You would just have to prove that the bottle exploded and that you were injured by it.

Q. I got injured on a ski lift. May I recover against the ski resort?

A. Possibly. Can you prove that the resort was negligent? Remember that some states have laws limiting the liability of resorts, saying there are certain risks that a person assumes in skiing.

Q. I got hepatitis from a blood transfusion. Is someone liable?

A. In many states, laws protect suppliers against strict liability when people who receive blood transfusions contract an illness from contaminated blood. However, you may recover if you can show negligence by the supplier.

Q. I was injured because of a brake defect in a used car that I bought. May I recover from the dealer?

A. A used car dealer has been subject to a negligence action for failing to inspect or discover such defects. However, courts remain split on whether dealers in used goods should be subject to strict liability.

DEFAMATION

Q. What is the difference between slander and libel?

A. A defamation action for *slander* rests on an oral communication made to another that is understood to lower your reputation or keep others from associating with you. *Libel* generally is considered written or printed defamation that does the same thing. Radio and television broadcasts of defamatory material today are nearly universally considered libel.

(continued)

you from filing other actions against your employer for conditions covered by the law. If such a law does not cover you, you may be able to recover from your employer on a negligence claim. To do so, you must show that your employer failed to exercise reasonable care in providing you with safe working conditions. You also must prove that your employer failed to warn you of unsafe conditions that you were unlikely to discover. Other possible suits against your employer might allege intentional injury. Or your spouse might sue for *loss of consortium* (see the "Family Law" chapter for more details).

Q. My late grandfather, who owned a textile factory, was called "unfair to labor" in a recent book about the industry. Is that libelous?

A. While it can be libelous to write that someone is unfair to labor—or is a crook, a drunk, or an anarchist—no defamation action can be brought for someone who is dead.

If your family still owns the factory and the same accusation made against your grandfather was made against some of you, a defamatory action could be brought.

Q. I have a tax-return preparation business, and a neighbor recently told a potential client that I did not know a thing about tax law. Isn't that slander?

A. You might have a case. If someone says something that affects you in your business, trade, or profession, you can recover in a slander action even without showing actual harm to your reputation or other damages. You can do the same in three other situations—if someone says that you committed a crime, that you have a loathsome disease, or that a specific female is unchaste (impure).

Of course, you can recover in other slander cases, but in those you must show that you were actually damaged.

Q. Are there defenses to defamation?

A. There are several defenses that will defeat a defamation claim. Consent is one; truth is another. And certain persons and proceedings (such as a judge in his or her courtroom, witnesses testifying about a relevant issue in a case, and certain communications by legislators) are said to be privileged. They are protected from defamation claims.

WHERE TO GET MORE INFORMATION

The Consumer Product Safety Commission, the Food and Drug Administration (FDA), and the Federal Trade Commission (FTC) have a duty to help consumers. There are also consumer protection agencies in virtually every state. State attorney generals' offices offer information and accept complaints. You also can contact state boards that regulate the conduct of lawyers, doctors, veterinarians, and even barbers. Check the government listings in your local telephone directory for the phone numbers of these agencies.

TWO FORMS OF DEFAMATION

Defamation **involves your reputation. If something that someone says or writes to another is understood to lower your reputation, or keep others from associating with you, you may have a defamation claim. *Libel* and *slander* are two types of defamation. To recover for defamation, you have to prove that the information is false. Defamation generally is easier to prove if you are a private person. Courts treat public officials and figures differently from private persons in deciding whether someone has defamed them. Public figures must show that the speaker or publisher either knew the words were false or was negligent in saying them. Courts have established certain constitutional protections for statements about public officials. That is why they must show that the speaker or publisher made the statement knowing it was false or seriously doubting its truth.**

CRIMINAL JUSTICE

INTRODUCTION

For many people, the criminal justice system may seem intimidating. Most people have never even seen the inside of a jail. Their only experience with police officers may have been a quick stop on the highway for a speeding ticket. For people who have never been charged with a crime, facing criminal charges can be disturbing. However, our system of justice aims to prevent people from being unfairly convicted. It guarantees many legal rights to anyone charged with a crime. This chapter will discuss those rights and give you a basic understanding of the steps in the criminal justice system. Finally, it will suggest where you can look for more help.

It is important to be informed about the criminal law in your state. Most crimes are punishable under state, not federal, laws. Though all states must comply with certain federal constitutional minimums, there are considerable variations from one state to another. Therefore, the information in this chapter will be true in most states, but it will not be true in all.

THE BASICS OF CRIMINAL LAW

Q. How do civil and criminal law differ?

A. Both criminal and civil cases involve a dispute over the rights of the people involved (the *parties*). However, the punishments *(penalties)* are different. In civil matters, one of the parties files suit. The party who loses the dispute or whom the court finds at fault might be ordered to pay money *(damages)* to the other party. Or the court might order that party to fulfill an obligation (such as performing that party's portion of a contract). In a criminal case, the government starts the legal action. A person whom the court finds guilty of a crime (the *defendant*) might be ordered to pay a fine. The defendant also might have to serve time in jail or prison or be put on probation. It is the possibility of losing one's freedom (being *incarcerated*) that distinguishes criminal from civil penalties.

Our society places a very high value on personal liberty. That is why it considers incarceration as a more severe penalty than a monetary fine. Therefore, our criminal justice system has built-in safeguards to ensure that it does not unfairly deprive people of their liberty. Those safeguards begin with the *presumption of innocence*. This means that anyone tried for a crime is innocent until proven guilty. A defendant does not have to prove his or her innocence. Rather, the prosecutor (generally a district attorney, or D.A.) must prove the defendant's guilt *beyond a reasonable doubt*. This is a much higher burden of proof than the law requires in a civil case. A *preponderance of the evidence* (in other words, "more likely than not" or more than a 50-percent likelihood) is enough to prove most civil cases.

Criminal defendants have many other rights that the law does not give to those involved in civil cases. The United States Constitution guarantees many of these rights to criminal defendants. These rights include, at the very least:

- The right to an attorney (and to have one appointed if you cannot afford one);
- The right not to be forced to incriminate yourself (this means you have the right to remain silent when questioned by the police and the right not to testify at your trial);
- The right to compel witnesses to appear in your defense in court; and
- The right to confront (through cross-examination) witnesses who have testified against you.

Later sections in this chapter will discuss these and other rights of the criminally accused.

(continued)

WHAT IS A CRIME?

A *crime* is an act defined by the legislature in a statute, or law. The law considers it an offense against society as a whole rather than against the individual victim. The titles of criminal cases are "State" or "People" or "United States" v. "Defendant." Many, but not all, crimes involve acts of violence. For example, robbery is the taking of goods or money from a person through force or fear. Shoplifting involves taking goods from a store without paying for them. Both are crimes in which criminals have taken something that does not belong to them. Because of the possible danger posed to the victim in a robbery, that is a much more serious crime than shoplifting. Therefore, legislatures have included robbery in the more serious category of crimes called *felonies*. Shoplifting generally is a *misdemeanor*, depending on the value of the goods.

WHAT ARE THE CHARACTERISTICS OF SOME SERIOUS CRIMES?

Crime	Definition
Homicide	Causing the death of another person without legal justification or excuse, including crimes of murder and nonnegligent manslaughter and negligent manslaughter.
Rape	Unlawful sexual intercourse with a female by force or without legal or factual consent.
Robbery	The unlawful taking or attempted taking of property that is in the immediate possession of another, by force or threat of force.
Assault	Unlawful intentional inflicting, or attempted inflicting, of injury upon the person of another. Aggravated assault is the unlawful intentional inflicting of serious bodily injury or unlawful threat or attempt to inflict bodily injury or death by means of a deadly or dangerous weapon with or without actual infliction of injury. Simple assault is the unlawful intentional inflicting of less-than-serious bodily injury without a deadly or dangerous weapon or an attempt or threat to inflict bodily injury without a deadly or dangerous weapon.
Burglary	Unlawful entry of any fixed structure, vehicle, or vessel used for regular residence, industry, or business, with or without force, with the intent to commit a felony or larceny.
Larceny-theft	Unlawful taking or attempted taking of property other than a motor vehicle from the possession of another, by stealth, without force and without deceit, with intent to permanently deprive the owner of the property.
Motor vehicle theft	Unlawful taking or attempted taking of a self-propelled road vehicle owned by another, with the intent of depriving him or her of it, permanently or temporarily.
Arson	The intentional damaging or destruction or attempted damaging or destruction by means of fire or explosion of property without the consent of the owner, or of one's own property or that of another by fire or explosives with or without the intent to defraud.

Sources: U.S. Department of Justice, Office of Justice Programs, Bureau of Justice Statistics (BJS) *Dictionary of Criminal Justice Data Terminology,* 2nd edition, 1981. BJS *Criminal Victimization in the U.S., 1985*. Federal Bureau of Investigation *Crime in the United States 1985*.

Q. What is a citation?

A. A *citation* is the penalty for the least serious offenses. Most jurisdictions have decriminalized these offenses. They will not jail you for a *citable* offense. The normal penalty is a fine, which usually is less than $100. Police typically give citations for such offenses as minor traffic violations (for example, speeding, parking in a no parking zone, or jaywalking). If the police cite you for such an offense, they will issue a ticket to you. You have the option of not contesting the citation. This involves mailing in the ticket with the specified payment. Or if you feel the police have wrongly given you a ticket, you have the right to contest the citation at a hearing.

Not all traffic violations are citable offenses, however. The most serious traffic violations, such as driving while intoxicated, are criminal offenses. The law classifies them as misdemeanors or felonies.

Q. What distinguishes a misdemeanor from a felony?

A. Each state has a body of criminal law that categorizes certain offenses as felonies and others as misdemeanors. These offenses generally appear in the state's "penal code," the vehicle code, or the health and safety code (for drug offenses).

Felonies are more serious crimes than misdemeanors. Robbery, kidnapping, rape, and murder are examples of felonies. Public drunkenness, resisting arrest, and simple battery are misdemeanors. However, the same offense might be either a misdemeanor or a felony, depending on its degree. Petty larceny (stealing an item worth less than a certain dollar amount) is a misdemeanor. Over that amount, the offense is grand theft (a felony). Similarly, the first offense of driving while intoxicated may be a misdemeanor. After a certain number of convictions for that same offense, the state may prosecute the next violation as felony drunk driving.

Most states classify felonies as all crimes that carry a maximum sentence of more than one year. Misdemeanors are offenses punishable by a sentence of one year or less. Some states, however, draw the line based on the place of possible confinement. If incarceration is in the state prison, the offense is a felony. If the offense is punishable by a term in jail (usually a county facility), it is a misdemeanor.

Q. How do the police investigate crimes?

A. When the police receive a report of a crime in progress (such as a home burglary in progress), they send an officer to the scene as soon as they can. If the officer arrests a suspect, the officer will bring that person to the police station for *booking*. The officer will write an *arrest report*. It will detail when and why the officer went to the scene, any observations, and why the officer arrested the suspect. The officer also will fill out a *property report*, detailing what items (for example, drugs or cash) the police found on the suspect during booking. The officer also will list any items of evidence found at the scene, such as a knife that the criminal might have used in a stabbing.

If the crime is complex or serious, the police then assign an investigating officer (usually a detective) to the case. That

How to Report a Crime

Call the police and say that you wish to report a crime. If you have observed a crime or know that a crime took place, the law considers you a *witness*. If somebody has committed a crime against you, the law regards you a *victim*. In either case, the police will want to talk to you. They need to determine what you know about the incident, so they can decide whether to investigate further. If you were in any way involved in the crime, the law might consider you a *suspect*. In this instance it is a good idea to call the local public defender or a lawyer before you talk to the police. A lawyer is permitted to accompany you to the police station and be present to protect your interests during police questioning. Many people believe that what they say to the police is not admissible unless written down, recorded on tape, or said to a prosecutor or judge. That is not true. *Anything* you say to *anybody* is admissible.

officer also will visit the crime scene, look for more evidence and interview any other witnesses. If somebody reported a crime but the police have not arrested anyone, the detective will analyze the evidence and try to narrow down the list of suspects. The detective will question suspects and sometimes will obtain a confession.

Q. How do the police recommend that criminal charges be filed against someone?

A. Criminal cases go through a screening process before a defendant faces charges in court. This is a two-step process that begins with the police inquiry. The investigating officer (or another officer superior to the arresting officer) will review the arrest report. That officer will determine whether there is enough evidence to recommend filing charges against the arrested person. If the officer decides not to recommend filing charges, then the police will release the arrested person from jail.

If the officer decides to recommend that a charge be filed a prosecuting attorney (usually from the district attorney's office) will review the officer's recommendation. Based on the arrest report and any follow-up investigation, an assistant prosecutor in the complaints division of the D.A.'s office will decide whether to file charges and which criminal offenses to allege. These allegations will appear in a *complaint* filed in the court clerk's office.

Q. How are charges filed against someone?

A. As explained in the second chapter, "How the Legal System Works," charges may be brought by an indictment voted by grand jury or an information filed by a prosecutor. Briefly, each of these mechanisms is used to conduct long-term investigations of possible criminal activity. They do not determine the guilt or innocence of individuals. They do, however, determine whether there is sufficient evidence to bring a person to trial.

Q. What happens next?

A. The filing of the complaint sets the wheels in motion. The defendant will then have a first judicial appearance. This is the defendant's first appearance in court. (It has different names in various states. In Pennsylvania, for example it is called a "preliminary arraignment".) During this brief appearance, the judge will discuss the defendant's rights and the charges in the complaint.

WHO EXERCISES DISCRETION?

These criminal justice officials . . .	. . . must often decide whether or not or how to:
Police	• Enforce specific laws • Investigate specific crimes • Search people, vicinities, buildings • Arrest or detain people
Prosecutors	• File charges or petitions for adjudication • Seek indictments • Drop cases • Reduce charges
Judges or magistrates	• Set bail or conditions for release • Accept pleas • Determine delinquency • Dismiss charges • Impose sentences • Revoke probation
Correctional officials	• Assign to type of correctional facility • Award privileges • Punish for disciplinary infractions
Paroling authority	• Determine date and conditions of parole • Revoke parole

Source: *Report to the Nation on Crime and Justice,* second edition, Department of Justice, Bureau of Justice Statistics, March 1988.

This process serves some of the functions of the grand jury, in that the judge determines whether there is enough evidence to charge the defendant with committing a crime. (Remember that most defendants are not charged by a grand jury, but through some other mechanism.) Another purpose of the first judicial appearance is to ensure that the defendant is informed of the charges against him or her and is made aware of his or her legal rights.

If the judge concludes that the state does not have sufficient evidence to support the charges, the judge will order the charges dismissed. If the judge believes the evidence is sufficient, the judge usually will set the amount of the defendant's bail.

Q. If the judge finds there is enough evidence to support the charges, what is the next step?

A. The case is generally then set for arraignment (in some states called a *preliminary hearing*). When defendants appear for arraignment, the charges are read to them, their rights are explained, and they enter their plea. If the defendant pleads not guilty, the court will set a date for the next step in the process—the trial. If the defendant pleads guilty, a date will be set for sentencing, although probation, fines, or other sentences will be determined immediately for some minor crimes.

CRIMINAL COURT PROCEEDINGS

Q. What is the initial appearance in court?

A. As explained above, the first appearance usually is called the *first judicial appearance*. There the judge will advise you of your rights and the charges against you in the complaint.

This usually is a brief proceeding where the prosecutor will call only those witnesses necessary to show the judge that a crime happened and that there is a strong likelihood that you committed it. Often this is just one witness. It usually is a police officer who investigated the crime or who arrested you.

The accused person must be present at the hearing, though he or she generally does not introduce evidence in his or her defense. In most jurisdictions the accused can waive the initial appearance, but it usually is not a good idea.

If there is not enough evidence, the judge will dismiss the charges. However, the defendant usually will be *held to answer* for the crime(s) charged. The judge will set a time for arraignment.

Q. May I get out on bail until my trial?

A. *Bail* is money that you provide to ensure that you will appear in court for trial. If you do not have the money to post bail, a relative or friend can post bail on your behalf. After the trial ends, the court will refund the bail money, usually keeping a percentage for administrative costs.

The law does not guarantee you a right to bail. It is up to the judge whether to release you on bail. If the judge decides that the nature of your crime or other factors make you a danger to the public, the judge is likely to deny bail. Then you would have to remain in jail until a judge or jury decides the case.

The judge also will consider whether you pose a substantial *risk of flight*. In other words, the judge must decide whether you are likely to flee if the court releases you on bail. Points in your favor include strong family ties in the area, longtime local residence, and current local employment. The judge also will consider any negative information that appears about you on a probation report.

If the judge decides bail is proper, the issue then becomes the amount of money that you must post for your release. Your bail may not be excessive (unreasonably high). However, there are no specific guidelines about what the amount of bail should be. Your attorney is permitted to make a request to reduce the bail or possibly to set no bail. The term for that is releasing you on your *own recognizance* (O.R.). This means you will not have to post any bail money. However, you will have made a binding promise to return to court on a date specified by the judge.

If the court grants you O.R. status or releases you on bail, you must reappear in court as agreed. If you do not appear, the judge could revoke your bail or O.R. status. The judge also could issue a *bench warrant* for your arrest. The police then will find you, take you into custody, and place you in jail. And you will lose your bail money.

Q. What happens at the arraignment?

A. As explained earlier, you will enter a plea. If you plead guilty or nolo contendere, the court will set a date for sentencing. If you plead not guilty, a date will be set for trial.

The vast majority of criminal cases result in a plea of guilty or of *nolo contendere*. Under either plea, you are guilty of the crime charged. Nolo contendere means "I do not contest it." On the other hand, a guilty plea is a specific admission of guilt. The practical effect is that the nolo plea avoids automatic *civil* liability. Let us say a nursing home operator is accused of the crime of abusing patients. If the operator pleads guilty, anyone who sues him or her for civil damages will not have to prove that the abuse occurred. However, if the operator pleads nolo contendere, the civil court will have to decide whether the acts alleged took place.

WITNESSES

Q. Who are witnesses? What makes a good witness?

A. Witnesses might be victims or defendants who are voluntarily testifying on their own behalf. A witness also might be

EXPERT WITNESSES

Expert witnesses **are specialists in certain fields, such as narcotics, psychology, medicine, or other areas of expertise. The prosecution or the defense calls them to testify at a trial. Their testimony is another form of evidence that the judge or jury will consider. Experts normally will offer an opinion of what they think the evidence means. For example, a narcotics expert might testify that the quantity of drugs seized and the way the defendant packaged them suggests that the defendant intended to sell them.**

(continued)

someone testifying on behalf of a person who is a victim or a defendant. Or a witness might be someone testifying as an impartial eyewitness to a crime. In any event, the most important thing is to be honest. When you are on the witness stand, the law requires you to tell the truth. Answer the questions as completely as possible. Do not add details that are not necessary to answer the question. If you do not understand the question, politely ask the lawyer to rephrase it. Do not answer any questions if you are unsure of the answer. If you do not know the answer, your answer should be, "I don't know." If you hear a lawyer say "objection" after the other lawyer asked you a question, do not answer the question. Wait until the judge rules on the objection. The judge will then tell you whether you may answer the question.

Testifying can be tiring and frustrating. Try to remain relaxed and keep a pleasant attitude. The worst thing you can do is to appear angry, lose your temper, or argue with the lawyer who is asking the questions. If the judge or jury disapproves of your behavior or attitude, they might not believe your testimony.

(continued)

If an expert testifies against you, your attorney might challenge the expert's credentials or conclusions on cross-examination. You also are permitted to call an opposing expert to testify on your behalf. Most experts get paid by the hour or day to testify. However, if you are *indigent* (unable to afford an expert), in some circumstances you may be entitled to have the court pay a reasonable fee for an expert.

Q. May the court force me to testify?

A. If you are a defendant, no. The Fifth Amendment of the U.S Constitution gives you a right against forced self-incrimination.

If you are a witness, a subpoena compels you to testify, even if you "don't want to get involved." However, you may refuse to answer certain questions on the witness stand if you feel the answers might incriminate you. The same applies to the victim of a crime.

Sometimes crime victims "get cold feet" and change their mind about testifying. This is especially true if the victim knows the defendant personally or is afraid of revenge. Even if you reported the crime and later decide you want the charges dropped, the prosecutor might not agree. The prosecutor often considers a victim's wishes. However, technically, the injured person is only a witness. The "victims" are the people of the state where the criminal committed the crime. Therefore, it is up to the district attorney to decide whether to proceed with the case and whether to subpoena a witness to testify.

Q. Are any resources available to help witnesses?

A. Most district attorney's offices have "witness assistance" departments. These departments will give you directions to court. They will even arrange transportation for you if necessary. If you must travel a distance to testify, these departments may provide you a *per diem* (daily) money allowance for food and lodging. Witness assistance coordinators can help you with other necessary arrangements (such as child care) so you can testify.

If you are testifying in a dangerous case, witness protection programs are available. The police will escort you between your home and court if necessary. If you are a confidential informant in fear for your life, steps will be taken to hide your identity.

Q. Should I talk to the police if they want to question me about a criminal investigation?

A. If you are a witness to a crime, you should share your knowledge with the police. Without information from witnesses, police would be unable to solve crimes and prosecutors would be unable to convict guilty defendants in court. However, if you played a role in the crime or you think the police want to question you as a possible suspect, do not talk to the police. Tell them you want an attorney. Only after talking to a lawyer should you talk to the police.

Q. What should I do if I receive a subpoena?

A. If you receive a subpoena ordering you to appear in court at a certain date and time, you must obey. Otherwise you probably will be held in contempt of court. Several different things could happen as a result—perhaps a fine or jail sentence. Or it could mean that you have to pay certain court costs for time lost because the case could not proceed.

The court might direct another type of subpoena at an item you possess, not at you. This *subpoena duces tecum* (SDT) orders you to produce certain evidence. Usually this evidence involves documents. Before you obey this type of subpoena, call a lawyer. Depending on the content of the documents, you might be able to fight the subpoena as forced self-incrimination.

THE POLICE AND YOUR RIGHTS

Q. Do the police have the right to tap my phone?

A. Yes, if they can show the court that they have enough probable cause that intercepting your phone conversations is necessary to help solve certain types of crimes (such as treason, narcotics trafficking, wire fraud, and money laundering). *Probable cause* is defined as facts sufficient to

STOPPING AND FRISKING SUSPECTS

Do the police have the right to stop and frisk you? That depends on the circumstances. Suppose the police suspect that you are engaging in a criminal activity and that you may be armed and dangerous. Then they may stop you briefly to frisk you for weapons. For example, the police observe you walking back and forth in front of a store in the dark. They see you looking around nervously and apparently "casing" the place to break into it. The police are permitted to stop you to conduct an outer-clothing "pat-down" (also known as a "frisk") for weapons. If they feel a hard object in your pocket that might be a gun, for example, they are permitted to reach in and remove it.

Suppose, however, that the police feel something soft (such as a pack of cigarettes) in your pocket that could not possibly be a weapon. Then they

(continued)

(continued)

have no right to seize it. Even if the police discover that the soft item contains drugs, this would be an illegal search. The police could not use that illegally seized evidence against you in court because they did not reasonably suspect you of possession of drugs when they saw you apparently casing the store. In contrast, if they had probable cause to believe you had just purchased drugs, they could seize the soft packet.

In addition, police can stop, briefly detain, and question a suspect based on reasonable suspicion, even if no weapons are suspected. And, in these circumstances, they do not have to give Miranda warnings (these are discussed in "The Miranda Rules" article on page 499).

support a reasonable belief that criminal activity is probably taking place or knowledge of circumstances such that there is a fair probability that evidence of crime will be found. It requires more than a mere "hunch," but far less than proof beyond a reasonable doubt.

However, the law considers wiretapping to be very intrusive. Therefore, federal law closely regulates it. A court will permit wiretapping only for a limited period of time. The authorities (usually FBI agents) who listen to your phone calls must make efforts to minimize this intrusion. That is, they must attempt to limit the number of intercepted calls that do not involve the investigation. An example of this would be tapping a bookie's phone only during the hours that bets likely will be placed. After the wiretap period has ended, the authorities must inventory the calls and reveal to the court the content of the conversations they intercepted.

A less intrusive form of electronic surveillance is the *pen register*. This device records every number dialed from your phone. However, a pen register simply lists phone numbers. It does not enable anyone to listen to your conversations.

Q. May the police search me without a warrant?

A. That depends on whether you are under arrest. If the police have lawfully arrested you, they are permitted to search you. They also are allowed to search the area under your immediate control (also known as your *wingspan,* or where you can reach). In the example in the "Stopping and Frisking Suspects" article on the previous page, the police *would* have the authority to seize the cigarette pack containing drugs from your pocket if you were under arrest. They could then use that evidence against you in court.

If you are not under arrest, the police generally are not permitted to search you without a warrant. You may consent to a search if you choose, but this is not wise.

Q. Does the law permit the police to search my home or items in it?

A. You have greater rights in your home than you do in your car. (See the "Automobiles" chapter for information on car searches.) That is because the courts have decided that the law entitles people to greater "privacy rights" in their home. Therefore, the police normally cannot search your home unless they have a warrant. The warrant must specify what the police are looking for and at what location they are likely to find it. The law limits the search to areas where it is reasonable to believe the item might be. You cannot look for a bazooka in a breadbox. After all, it is not sensible to look for a large item in a container too small to hold it.

The police do not need a warrant to search your home if you agree to the search. This usually is not a good idea, however. If you do not agree, the police still are permitted to search your home without a warrant if there are sufficient *exigent circumstances*. This involves an emergency situation where the police believe someone's life is in danger, or a suspect is about to escape, or they have reason to believe you might destroy the evidence if they did not conduct the search immediately. For example, the police might believe you will flush some illegal drugs down the toilet. In cases such as these, when there is no time to get a warrant from the court, the police will search your home without permission. You have the right to challenge the legality of a warrantless search in court, however.

Q. If the police stop me for drunk driving, what tests may the police force me to take?

A. If the police observe you driving strangely or violating the rules of the road, they are permitted to stop your vehicle. If the police then smell alcohol on your breath or have other reasons to believe you are driving while intoxicated or under the influence of alcohol, they have the right to ask you to take certain tests. The law refers to these as *field sobriety tests*. Typical tests involve walking a straight line heel-to-toe or touching your finger to the tip of your nose with your eyes closed.

If you do not perform these tests satisfactorily, the police will ask you to submit to a scientific test that shows how much (if any) alcohol is in your body. Many states will offer you one of three choices. You may choose to give a blood sample. Or you may choose to supply a urine sample. You also have the choice of taking a breathalyzer test. This involves blowing into a balloon attached to a machine that measures the percentage of alcohol in your breath (breath-alcohol concentration, or BAC).

The police are not allowed to force you to take these tests. However, depending on the law in your state, they might use your refusal to do so as evidence against you in court. Also, in many states, refusal to submit to such tests will result in an automatic suspension or revocation of your driver's license.

Q. After arresting me, may the police make me provide fingerprints, a handwriting sample, or a voice example?

A. Generally, yes, the police are permitted to force you to supply these. They will take your fingerprints during the "booking" procedure at the police station. The law considers handwriting samples and voice examples evidence of physical characteristics. Therefore, you may not claim that the police

When Must Police Knock Before Entering

The police must execute a search warrant promptly after the court has ordered it. Some jurisdictions have a *knock-notice* requirement. This means that the police must knock on the door and announce their presence before entering the premises to search for the item in the warrant. If there are sufficient exigent circumstances, however, the police have a right to force entry without knocking to execute the warrant. Also, some states are beginning to pass "no knock" laws for some searches, like drug raids.

are forcing you to incriminate yourself through these identification procedures. The police may use these samples as evidence against you in court if they are appropriate to the crime. For example, your handwriting may be compared to the signature on a forged check or to the writing on a note handed to a teller in a bank robbery.

Q. What are my rights if the police put me in a lineup?

A. In a lineup, several people who look somewhat similar will be shown to victims or witnesses who observed the crime. The police will ask the witnesses if they can identify anyone in the lineup as the person who committed the crime.

If formal charges have been filed against you and the police put you in a lineup, you have a right to have an attorney present. Your lawyer will protect your rights. A lineup is not supposed to be unfairly suggestive to the victim. That is, the police are not permitted to suggest to the victim that a certain person in the lineup is their main suspect. They also are not permitted to make suggestions in photographic identifications, when the police ask a witness to pick the criminal from six similar photographs on a card. (However, you do not have a right to have a lawyer present during photographic identification.)

When you are in a lineup, the police have the right to ask you to speak if the witnesses feel they can identify you by your voice. The law permits the police to have you speak the words used during the crime. They might ask you to say, for example, "Give me your money."

Q. May the police use information from a confidential informant against me?

A. The law allows police to use such information if it is reliable. Confidential informants are people who supply information to the police without having their identities disclosed. The police often use such information to obtain search warrants. For example, an informant might tell the police where someone has hidden evidence of a crime. The police will provide this and other information (such as the informant's prior reliability, how the informant obtained the information, and evidence obtained from other sources that confirms the informant's story) to a magistrate (a type of court official). If the magistrate determines there is probable cause to believe that this evidence will be found at the location specified, the magistrate will issue a search warrant.

Q. What procedures must the police follow while making an arrest?

Where Police Are Permitted to Make Arrests

Where the police are allowed to arrest you depends on whether the police have a warrant for your arrest. The police make most arrests without a warrant. If you commit a misdemeanor in the officer's presence, that officer is permitted to arrest you without a warrant. If the officer has probable cause (the minimum level of evidence needed to make a lawful arrest) to believe that you committed a felony, the officer is allowed to arrest you without a warrant, even if he or she did not see you commit the crime. The law permits warrantless arrests in public places, such as a street or restaurant.

To arrest you in a private place, except when exigent circumstances apply, the police must have a warrant. There

(continued)

A. The police do not have to tell you the crime for which they are arresting you, though they probably will. They are not permitted to use excessive force or brutality when arresting you. If you resist arrest or act violently, however, the police are allowed to use reasonable force to make the arrest or keep you from injuring yourself.

While the police are arresting you, they might read you your "Miranda" rights (discussed later in this chapter). However, they do not have to read you these rights if they do not intend to interrogate you.

Q. When am I in custody?

A. You might be in custody even if the police do not say, "You are under arrest." Generally, the law considers you in custody when you have been arrested or otherwise deprived of your freedom in a significant way. One example of this occurs when an officer is holding you at gunpoint. Another is seen when several officers are surrounding you. Other examples are when you are in handcuffs or when the police have placed you in the back seat of a police car. Of course, you are in custody when the police do say, "You are under arrest."

Q. What makes up interrogation?

A. Interrogation might be explicit questioning, such as the police asking you, "Did you kill John Doe?" Interrogation also might be less obvious, such as comments made by the police that they know are "likely to elicit" incriminating information from you. For example, suppose the police know that a murder suspect is deeply religious. To get the suspect to reveal where the body is, they might tell the suspect a lie. The police might say, "The only way for that woman to get a decent Christian burial is if we find her body before the snowstorm tonight." The suspect is as likely to answer as if the police asked a question. The law considers this as indirect questioning or the "functional equivalent" of interrogation.

CRIMINAL CHARGES

Q. What does it mean if the police recommend charging me with an "attempt"?

A. An *attempt* means that you had the intent to commit the crime, but for some reason you did not complete the crime. Usually it means that you took a *substantial step* to commit the

(continued)

are two types of warrants: an *arrest warrant* and a *search warrant*. To arrest you in your own home, the police must have an arrest warrant. However, if they lack a warrant but have probable cause for a warrantless arrest, they are permitted to put your home under surveillance. They will then wait until you leave your home and arrest you in a public place. (If the police arrest you without a warrant, the law entitles you to a prompt hearing to determine whether there was probable cause for the arrest.)

If the police wish to arrest you in someone else's home, they must have a search warrant. The warrant must name you as the "item" for which they will search.

crime. Suppose you went into a bank and demanded money from a teller at gunpoint. Then an alarm rang, so you ran out of the bank before you could get the money. The police would recommend you be charged with attempted robbery. In many states, the punishment for an attempt is as severe as that for the completed crime.

Q. What is a conspiracy?

A. A *conspiracy* is an agreement between two or more people to commit a crime. The conspiracy itself is a separate crime. Therefore, the police are permitted to recommend that you be charged with conspiracy *and* with the crime you planned to commit. These carry separate penalties. If you are convicted of both conspiracy and a crime that you accomplished by the conspiracy (the "substantive" count), you might receive two sentences.

Q. What is complicity or accomplice liability?

A. *Complicity* is the act of being an accomplice. An *accomplice* is someone who helps in the commission of a crime. The court sometimes refers to this person as an *aider* or *abettor*. This person did not commit the crime, but this person's actions helped enable someone else to do so. Examples of complicity include supplying weapons or supplies, acting as a "lookout," or driving the getaway car. Other examples are bringing the victim to the scene of the crime or signaling the victim's approach. There are many other ways a person can serve as an accomplice.

Accomplice liability means that anyone who helps in the commission of a crime is as guilty as the person who committed the crime. If you are convicted as an accomplice, you could be punished as severely as the person who committed the crime.

Q. What are plea bargains?

A. *Plea bargains* are legal transactions in which a defendant pleads guilty to a lesser charge or pleads guilty in exchange for some other form of leniency. Generally such offers are more generous in the early stages of prosecution. The prosecution extends such offers at the time set for the arraignment. This also is the time that the defense usually accepts such offers. (In certain cases, the defense would be better off waiting to thoroughly investigate the case and await a later offer.) If you do not accept the offer when the prosecution first makes it, the prosecutor is allowed to reduce or withdraw the offer.

Types of Immunity

If you had some involvement in a crime with someone else, the prosecutor might agree to lesser charges against you (and thus a shorter stay in jail) if you agree to testify against your partner. Then the court will give you a *grant of immunity*. This means that the information you reveal while testifying in court will not be used to prosecute you for your involvement in the crime. Once you accept immunity, you must testify.

Talk to your attorney before you accept immunity. Different types of immunity give different protections. *Use immunity* means the prosecutor is not permitted to use what you say to prosecute you later. *Transactional immunity* gives far greater protection. It means the prosecution will never prosecute you for the crime, even based on evidence independent of your testimony.

You do not have a right to have the prosecutor enter *plea negotiations.* However, the district attorney usually will make such an offer in order to reduce the heavy caseload of the courts. In most jurisdictions, the court has no obligation to adhere to the bargain the prosecution offers.

For more on plea bargains, see the "How the Legal System Works" chapter.

EVIDENCE IN CRIMINAL CASES

Q. How may I recognize and preserve evidence to help me at my trial?

A. *Physical evidence*—such as a gun or a piece of clothing—can be very important in helping a judge or jury piece together what actually happened. These people were not there when the alleged crime took place. The physical evidence can provide a way to prove that your version of the facts is correct.

You should preserve any items that might be useful as evidence. In fact, it is against the law to destroy evidence. This is true whether you think the evidence will help or harm your case. In any event, let your lawyer determine whether the evidence is harmful. For example, you might believe that the prosecution will use a gun with your fingerprints as evidence against you in a shooting. However, your attorney might be able to show that the gun was too big or the trigger too hard for someone of your size to have fired it. The only logical explanation then would be that you picked up the gun after the shooting. This may persuade the jury of your innocence.

Q. What kind of evidence may the prosecution use against me at the trial?

A. It is permitted to use almost any type of legally admissible evidence that will help establish your guilt. This includes *physical evidence,* such as a murder weapon or items stolen during a burglary. *Testimonial evidence* is likely to be used as well. That involves testimony (oral statements) from a person on the witness stand. For example, the owner of a stolen car might testify that no permission was given to anyone to take the car on the day the crime occurred. The prosecution also might introduce *circumstantial evidence.* An example of circumstantial evidence is destroying physical evidence, since getting rid of something incriminating circumstantially indicates a consciousness of guilt.

FORGOTTEN EVIDENCE

Some evidence is far less obvious than a gun. At a crime scene, tiny items such as rug fibers, hair, cigarette ashes, or matches may become important evidence in your defense. Therefore, if you are at the scene of a crime before the police arrive, leave everything undisturbed. Do not vacuum, move items, or touch anything. The police will secure the area and record everything to maintain what the law calls *crime scene integrity*. Once evidence gets misplaced or damaged, you have lost a crucial link in establishing your innocence. In addition, the judge or jury might view this as an indication of your guilt.

The nature of the offense will determine the evidence to preserve. For instance, if the prosecution charges you with an economic crime such as fraud, you must preserve any important documents.

CRIME REQUIREMENTS

Most crime requires both a guilty act *(actus reus)* and a guilty mind *(mens rea)*. Even if you committed an offense, you might be able to show that you did not have the required mental state, or wrongful purpose.

If the facts in your case show that you did not have this intent, that might be a defense. Your lawyer will help you decide which defenses apply to your case.

On the other hand, sometimes you can be convicted even if you did not have any intention of committing a crime. A person who kills another by accident has committed a crime if the defendant's actions were reckless or sufficiently negligent. For example, if the accident occurred while the defendant was driving under the influence of alcohol or drugs, that is vehicular homicide, even if the driver had no intention of harming the victim.

If a lawyer asks a witness to testify about someone else's out-of-court statement, the opposing lawyer may object that the testimony is inadmissible because it involves hearsay. To decide whether the testimony would in fact be hearsay, the court must decide why the witness is being asked the question. If the witness's testimony about someone else's out-of-court statement is being introduced for the purpose of proving the truth of the out-of-court statement, it is hearsay. If it is only being introduced to prove that the out-of-court statement was made, it is not hearsay.

For example, assume Jane testifies that "John told me my husband was having an affair." If John's out-of-court statement that "Your husband is having an affair" is being introduced to prove that he was in fact having an affair, it would be hearsay. The problem with hearsay is that John, the person who made the statement, is not on the stand and is unavailable for cross-examination.

If, on the other hand, Jane is only testifying about what John said in order to explain why she slapped him in the face, her testimony would not be hearsay. Here the only issue is whether John made the statement, not whether the statement was true.

However, there are many exceptions to the rule against hearsay, so do not be surprised to hear such statements allowed during the trial.

DEFENSES AGAINST CRIMINAL CHARGES

Q. What are my possible defenses?

A. One defense is an *alibi.* That is an explanation that at the time in question, you were not at the crime scene. For instance, if you were out of town on the date the crime happened, you can raise an alibi defense.

Depending on the nature of the crime, you might be able to offer the defense of *entrapment.* This means that in order to obtain evidence of a crime, the police induced (encouraged) you to commit a crime you had not been considering. This is a common defense in offenses involving the sale of drugs to an undercover agent. Precisely because it is a good defense, police work to counteract it by making sure that they file charges as a result of more than one sale. They also rarely charge someone with an illegal purchase *from* an undercover agent. As a result of these precautions, the defense of entrapment does not often succeed in drug cases. As long as the prosecutors can show that the defendant was either predisposed to the crime, or that the inducement (lure) was not outrageous, they probably will succeed over a defense of entrapment.

If the prosecutor charges you with a violent crime, you may be able to argue that you did it in *self-defense*.

There also are many other possible defenses. These include *intoxication, mistake, insanity, defense of others, defense of property,* and many more.

Q. Should I take the stand in my own defense?

A. Listen to your lawyer's advice. However, the final decision regarding whether to testify is yours. Many defendants do not testify. The judge will instruct the jury not to hold this against you because the Fifth Amendment gives you the right not to incriminate yourself.

Many defendants feel that they should testify because they are innocent and have "nothing to hide." However, anyone who testifies is subject to tough cross-examination from the opposing lawyer. For a defendant, that means questioning by the district attorney. A skillful prosecutor may be able to put you in a very bad light. For instance, if you take the stand, the prosecutor may ask you whether you have had any prior felony convictions. You must answer truthfully. If you do not take the stand, nobody will reveal such information to the jury.

Q. What is the role of a jury in a criminal case?

A. The jury weighs the evidence and finds the defendant guilty or not guilty.

Juries are discussed more fully in chapter two, "How the Legal System Works." It is important to understand that you have certain rights. First, you have a right to a jury trial in most criminal cases. Second, you have a right to a jury that is chosen from a fair cross-section of the community and is not biased against you. Third, you have a right to a jury from which members of your particular class or group have not been systematically excluded.

SENTENCING OF CONVICTED CRIMINALS

Q. If a judge or jury convicts me, how and when will the court sentence me?

(continued)

TRIAL BY JURY OR JUDGE?

Should you exercise your right to a jury trial, or waive it in favor of a bench (judge) trial? This is a decision that you and your lawyer must make. In "nonpetty" criminal cases punishable by more than six months imprisonment, you have the right to be tried by a jury of your peers. Your chances might be better with a jury, because the prosecutor must convince each juror that you are guilty. However, juries are unpredictable. In some cases, you might stand a better chance of acquittal with a judge. Listen to your lawyer's advice.

JURY TRIALS ARE A SMALL PERCENTAGE OF FELONY CASES FILED

Jurisdiction	Percent of cases filed resulting in jury trial	Number of cases filed
Seattle, Washington	15%	3,126
New Orleans, Louisiana	10%	3,659
Washington, D.C.	9%	8,442
Des Moines, Iowa	8%	1,401
Lansing, Michigan	7%	1,358
Portland, Oregon	7%	3,892
Denver, Colorado	6%	3,772
Minneapolis, Minnesota	6%	2,364
St. Louis, Missouri	6%	3,649
Dallas, Texas	5%	14,784
Salt Lake City, Utah	5%	2,745
Brighton, Colorado	4%	1,142
Colorado Springs, Colorado	4%	1,484
Philadelphia, Pennsylvania	4%	13,796
Tallahassee, Florida	4%	2,879
Davenport, Iowa	3%	1,312
Fort Collins, Colorado	3%	776
Geneva, Illinois	3%	1,263
Manhattan, New York	3%	30,810
Rhode Island	3%	5,485
San Diego, California	3%	11,534
Chicago, Illinois	2%	35,528
Cobb County, Georgia	2%	4,427
Golden, Colorado	2%	1,838
Greeley, Colorado	2%	630
Miami, Florida	2%	21,413
Pueblo, Colorado	1%	339

Source: Barbara Boland with Ronald Sones, INSLAW, Inc. *Prosecution of Felony Arrests, 1981*. BJS 1986.

A. After a court official reads the verdict, the judge will set a time and date for sentencing. (In some states, juries set sentences.) Sentencing is a separate procedure. The court will order a presentencing report from the probation department. It will examine your past record and will make recommendations about your sentence.

In most states the judge has some discretion in choosing your sentence. For misdemeanors, the judge usually chooses between a fine, probation, suspended sentence, or a jail term (or a combination of these). For felonies, the choice is often between imprisonment and probation, depending on the crime.

(continued)

Status of death penalty as of 12/31/88 and 1988 executions

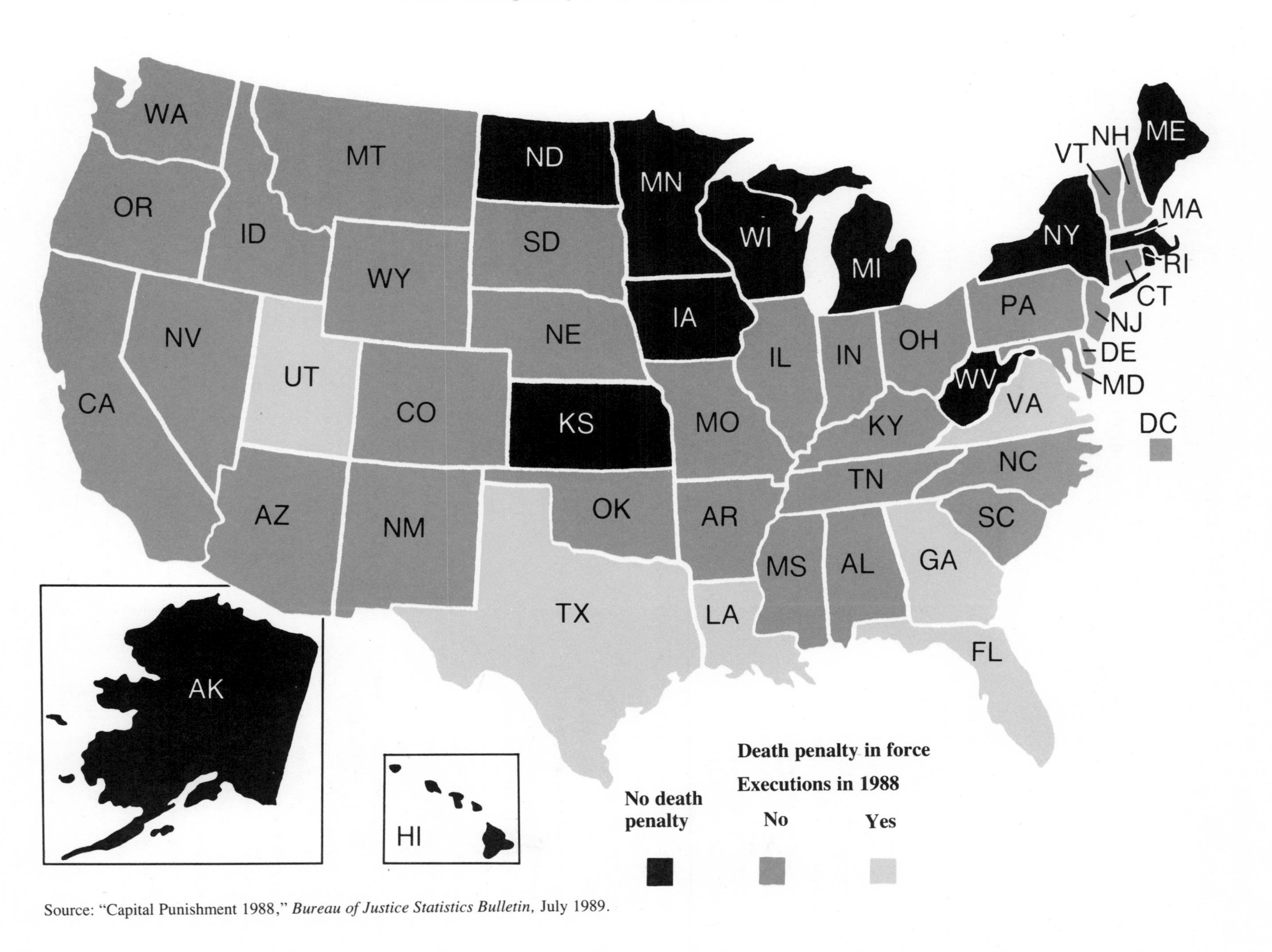

Source: "Capital Punishment 1988," *Bureau of Justice Statistics Bulletin*, July 1989.

LIGHT VS. STIFF SENTENCES

***Aggravating circumstances* include factors such as the brutal nature of your crime, the fact that you show no remorse, or having a long "rap sheet" of prior offenses. These may persuade the judge to impose the maximum sentence. On the other hand, *mitigating circumstances* include factors such as no prior offenses, strong family ties, or the fact that you were a minor participant in a crime. These might cause the judge to treat you with some leniency.**

In addition, before imposing your sentence, the judge will allow you to make a statement. You should discuss this with your lawyer in advance. Sometimes a plea for mercy or a promise to improve your behavior will be effective at this point. However, it depends on the judge and on whether the judge believes you.

For state offenses, the criminal code often specifies the minimum and maximum sentences for each specific crime. For federal offenses, the court follows the recently approved federal sentencing guidelines. (Similar guidelines have been adopted by some states, including Minnesota and Michigan.) This involves a complex formula that calculates an offense level based on several factors. It then gives a range of incarceration (prison) time. In some very limited instances, the judge might be able to sentence you to a term that varies slightly from the required guidelines.

Q. Are there any alternatives to jail or prison sentences?

A. Yes, and one option is monetary. The judge may order you to pay a fine as punishment, or to make *restitution* (repayment to a victim who lost money because of your crime). Another possibility is *probation*. When you are on probation, the court has released you in the community. However, you must obey the conditions set forth by the court. One example is submitting to periodic drug testing. If you violate these conditions, the court can revoke your probation and resentence you.

These alternatives are frequently combined. For example, a person on probation also may be required, as a term of release, to pay restitution (reimbursement) or perform community service.

A less restrictive sentence involves *community service*. The court could require you to donate a certain number of hours (usually hundreds or thousands of hours) of your service to a community center. Often this involves working at youth facilities or lecturing at schools on the evils of your particular crime.

Another possibility is *diversion,* a program whose successful completion avoids a criminal conviction. Diversion programs usually are specialized alternatives taking place *before* the defendant is tried. The prosecutor's office normally runs diversion programs. Diversion ordinarily involves your participation in a service program designed to rehabilitate you. For example, some states allow a first-time drug offender to attend a program such as Cocaine Anonymous instead of going to prison.

LAWYERS AND CRIMINAL LAW

Q. If the police arrest a friend or relative, may I send a lawyer to the jail to offer help?

A. Yes, but the right to counsel is *personal to the accused.* This means that the person who is under arrest must tell the police that he or she wants a lawyer. Suppose your friend waives the right to counsel and agrees to talk to the police. Then the police do not have to tell your friend that you are sending a lawyer. If your friend has not requested a lawyer, the police are even permitted to turn away the lawyer upon arrival at the station without telling your friend. The best thing you can do if your friend phones you is to say that a lawyer is on the way to offer help. Tell your friend to claim the right to counsel and urge your friend not to talk to the police until the lawyer arrives.

Q. When do I have a right to an attorney–before or during police interrogation?

A. You have a constitutional "right to counsel" (right to have an attorney's advice) *before and during* police interrogation. As soon as the police read your Miranda rights to you, tell them you want a lawyer. Do not answer any questions. Say nothing until your attorney arrives. If the police place you in a lineup, the law entitles you to have a lawyer present if you have been formally charged. This right continues at all your court appearances except your first appearance, where you do not have the right to have your lawyer present unless you are required to enter a plea there.

Q. How do I find a lawyer?

A. If you have one, call your family lawyer immediately. If your family lawyer does not do criminal work, he or she may be able to recommend another lawyer who does. If you cannot afford an attorney, tell the police you wish to have a lawyer appointed on your behalf. A counsel for the defense–whether private, a public defender, or assigned–will be appointed on your behalf. The first chapter in this book ("When and How to Use a Lawyer") discusses this topic in greater detail. Above all, say nothing else to the police until your lawyer arrives.

Q. What should I tell my lawyer?

A. You should tell your attorney the truth. Your lawyer has to know exactly what happened in order to defend you effectively. Tell your lawyer as many details as you can remember. Anything you tell your attorney is confidential. This means that what you tell your lawyer in confidence will be kept secret. The law refers to this as the *attorney-client*

The Miranda Rule

The Miranda rights became required because of a case called *Miranda v. Arizona*. When a person is in custody, some version of the Miranda rights, such as the following, is read to him or her before questioning: "You have the right to remain silent. If you give up the right to remain silent, anything you say can and will be used against you in a court of law. You have the right to an attorney. If you desire an attorney and cannot afford one, an attorney will be obtained for you before police questioning."

If the arrested person indicates in any manner a desire to consult with an attorney before speaking, there can be no questioning without violating that person's constitutional rights.

The best rule is to remain silent. You have the right to an attorney. Insist on it.

privilege. However, a lawyer also has an ethical obligation to the court. An attorney may not lie to the court for you or knowingly offer a false defense.

Q. May I represent myself without a lawyer?

A. You are permitted to represent yourself before trial. At trial, however, the court might allow you to act as an attorney in your own defense, or it might not permit this. The law refers to self-representation as *pro se*. If you request to proceed pro se, the judge will determine whether you are mentally and physically able to represent yourself. The judge will decide whether you are making an informed and voluntary decision to give up your constitutional right to counsel. Also, the judge will determine whether you are aware of the dangers and disadvantages of self-representation.

Those dangers are many. It is not a good idea for untrained people to try to represent themselves in criminal cases. The opponent will be a skilled prosecutor who has conducted many trials. The judge or jury will not necessarily be sympathetic toward you simply because you decided to "go it alone."

Some defendants choose to represent themselves because they feel they can do a better job than a lawyer whom the court has appointed to represent them free of charge. This simply is not true. First, any lawyer is sure to know more than you do about the legal system. Lawyers must complete a multiyear extensive program in law school and pass a rigorous bar examination. Second, do not think that the public defender is an inadequate lawyer who could not get a "real job" in a law firm. Many top law students choose public-interest work because they want to help people.

In addition, most people charged with a crime are too close emotionally to their own problems. Therefore, they cannot maintain the clear, coolheaded thinking that is necessary in court. Even lawyers charged with a crime usually hire another attorney to represent them. This follows the old saying, "A lawyer who represents himself has a fool for a client."

By representing yourself, you are giving up a very important constitutional right: the right to counsel. If you represent yourself and the court convicts you, you cannot claim that your incompetence as a lawyer denied you *effective assistance of counsel*.

For these reasons, self-representation is a risk that most criminal defendants should not take. Remember that you always have the right to dismiss your attorney should you become dissatisfied. Then you could change lawyers or reconsider representing yourself, if the court will allow it (though the court may require you to proceed immediately with the case, without extra time for you or your new lawyer

Admissible Confessions

A lot of people believe that only written, signed confessions are admissible as evidence. This is not true. Confessions that are oral, and unsigned written confessions, are also admissible.

Whether you may withdraw a confession that you made before a lawyer arrived depends on whether you gave up your right to a lawyer and your right not to talk. If you voluntarily talked to the police after they read you your Miranda rights, you might have *waived* (given up) your right to counsel. The prosecution probably could use the confession against you in court.

(continued)

to prepare). However, once you have experienced the complexities of the legal process, you probably will realize that you need a professional there at all times to protect your interests.

APPEALS OF CRIMINAL CASES

Q. May I appeal my conviction?

A. Usually a person convicted at a trial has the right to appeal the conviction at least once. (There are very few grounds for appeal if the defendant pleaded guilty.)

On appeal, the defendant can raise claims that mistakes were made in applying and interpreting the law during the trial. For example, the defendant might claim that the judge erroneously allowed hearsay testimony, gave improper jury instructions, or should not have permitted the prosecution to use evidence obtained in violation of the defendant's constitutional rights. Appeals also may claim the judge permitted the prosecution to make improper closing arguments. If the appellate court agrees that there were significant errors in the trial, the defendant will get a new trial.

Q. What if the law changes after a court convicts me?

A. If a court convicted you for something that is no longer a crime, you might be able to have your conviction overturned. This also might be possible if a trial court denied you a right that the U.S. Supreme Court later rules is guaranteed by the U.S. Constitution. However, your rights will depend on whether the new rule or law is *retroactive* (applied to past court decisions). If the U.S. Supreme Court has not yet determined whether to give retroactive effect to the new law, your lawyer may be able to argue that the new rule should apply to your case.

THE RIGHTS OF ALL INVOLVED PARTIES

Q. What are my rights as a prisoner?

A. The law entitles you to fair treatment as a human being. This means your jailers may not subject you to brutality. The law

(continued)

However, if the police continued to question you after you told them you wanted a lawyer, your confession probably would not be admissible in court. In either case, your lawyer might be able to persuade the judge to *suppress* (exclude) the confession as evidence.

Remember that you are permitted to change your mind about wanting a lawyer. If you voluntarily begin to talk to the police, then tell them that you want a lawyer present, the questioning must stop immediately. Or if you have talked to the police once, you may refuse to talk to them a second time until a lawyer arrives.

also entitles you to food, water, and medical attention. In addition, the law entitles you to access to the legal system. If your state laws provide for a right to *parole* (early release from prison), you can apply for parole when you become eligible. If the parole board denies your request for parole, you must be told why and you must be given an opportunity to be heard.

Q. What are my rights as a victim?

A. You have a right to a reasonable amount of perseverance (effort) by the police in trying to find the person who committed the crime. If they find this person, you can tell the prosecutor whether you wish to have that person prosecuted. Often the prosecutor will consider the victim's wishes, but the prosecutor does not have to.

In a serious or violent crime, the victim may be afraid to testify. If the defendant or someone on the defendant's behalf has tried to threaten you into not testifying, tell the police. The law entitles you to police protection, and the police will protect you to the extent they can.

If the court releases the defendant from custody, the law still entitles the victim to protection. The court has the authority to order the defendant to stay away from you and your family if you so request. The police will try to ensure that the defendant obeys this order.

Q. Will the court protect jurors in dangerous cases?

A. The law entitles jurors to such protection. Sometimes the court *sequesters* (houses in a hotel to isolate from outside influences) the jury throughout the trial. Police officers or court officials escort the jury to and from court. After the trial, the police will continue as best they can to ensure the safety of the jurors, at least for a time.

JUVENILE CRIMINAL CASES

Q. How do juvenile proceedings differ from adult criminal proceedings?

A. A juvenile does not have a constitutional right to a jury trial unless tried as an adult. A judge hears most juvenile cases. Juveniles also do not have a right to a public trial or to bail.

(continued)

Getting a Lawyer for Your Appeal

Because trial work and appellate (appeals) work are two different types of legal practice, the lawyer who represented you at the trial will not automatically file or handle your appeal. You must ask the attorney to do so, or find another lawyer who will. For those unable to pay, the county public defender (or private assigned counsel) usually represented them at trial. The state public defender (or another assigned counsel) generally will handle the appeal.

Trials require the skills of a lawyer who has experience in the courtroom and working before juries. Appeals involve a large amount of writing and legal research, as well as the ability to argue legal doctrines before a judge.

COMPENSATION PROGRAMS TO HELP VICTIMS OF VIOLENT CRIME

Forty-two states, the District of Columbia, and the U.S. Virgin Islands have compensation programs to help victims of violent crime.

State	Victim compensation financial award	To qualify, victim must:		
		show financial need	report to police within	file claim within
Alabama	$0-$10,000	no	3 days	12 months
Alaska	$0-$40,000	yes	5 days	24 months
Arizona	**	yes	3 days	**
California	$100-$46,000	yes	*	12 months
Colorado	$25-$10,000	no	3 days	6 months
Connecticut	$100-$10,000	no	5 days	24 months
Delaware	$25-$20,000	no	*	12 months
District of Columbia	$100-$25,000	yes	7 days	6 months
Florida	$0-$10,000	yes	3 days	12 months
Hawaii	$0-$10,000	no	*	18 months
Idaho	$0-$25,000	no	3 days	12 months
Illinois	$0-$25,000	no	3 days	12 months
Indiana	$100-$10,000	no	2 days	24 months
Iowa	$0-$20,000	no	1 day	6 months
Kansas	$100-$10,000	yes	3 days	12 months
Kentucky	$0-$25,000	yes	2 days	12 months
Louisiana	$100-$10,000	no	3 days	12 months
Maryland	$0-$45,000	yes	2 days	6 months
Massachusetts	$0-$25,000	no	2 days	12 months
Michigan	$200-$15,000	yes	2 days	12 months
Minnesota	$100-$50,000	no	5 days	12 months
Missouri	$200-$10,000	no	2 days	12 months
Montana	$0-$25,000	no	3 days	12 months
Nebraska	$0-$10,000	yes	3 days	24 months
Nevada	$0-$15,000	yes	5 days	12 months
New Jersey	$0-$25,000	no	90 days	24 months
New Mexico	$0-$12,500	no	30 days	12 months
New York	$0-$30,000†	yes	7 days	12 months
North Carolina (a)	$100-$20,000		3 days	24 months
North Dakota	$0-$25,000	no	3 days	12 months
Ohio	$0-$25,000	no	3 days	12 months
Oklahoma	$0-$10,000	no	3 days	12 months
Oregon	$250-$23,000	no	3 days	6 months
Pennsylvania	$0-$35,000	no	3 days	12 months
Rhode Island	$0-$25,000	no	10 days	24 months
South Carolina	$100-$3,000	no	2 days	6 months
Tennessee	$0-$5,000	no	2 days	12 months
Texas	$0-$25,000	no	3 days	6 months
Utah	$0-$25,000	**	7 days	12 months
Virgin Islands	up to $25,000	no	1 day	24 months
Virginia	$0-$15,000	no	5 days	24 months
Washington	$0-$15,000†	no	3 days	12 months
West Virginia	$0-$35,000	no	3 days	24 months
Wisconsin	$0-$40,000	no	5 days	12 months

(a) North Carolina's program is administratively established but not funded.
* Must report but no time limit specified
** No reference in statute
† Plus unlimited medical expenses

Source: U.S. Department of Justice, Office of Justice Programs, Bureau of Justice Statistics (BJS) 1987, update of *Victim/Witness Legislation: An Overview*. Originally prepared by BJS, July 1984, with assistance from National Organization for Victim Assistance.

Under most state laws, juvenile offenders do not commit "crimes." They commit *delinquent acts,* which are acts that would constitute crimes if committed by an adult. The trial phase of a juvenile case is an *adjudication hearing.* This means that the judge hears the evidence and determines whether the child committed the offense. The court may then take whatever action it deems to be in the child's best interests. The purpose is to rehabilitate, not punish, the child. The standard of proof is less rigid than the "beyond a reasonable doubt" standard of adult cases.

Juvenile courts usually hear cases involving persons between the ages of ten and 18. (The upper age may be lower in some states.) If the prosecution charges an older juvenile with a particularly serious or violent offense, the district attorney may request that an adult court try the juvenile as an adult.

Q. What is a parent's responsibility in juvenile cases?

A. Depending on the state where you live, you might be *liable* (legally responsible) for the acts of your child if you failed to supervise or control the child properly. For example, California recently passed a "gang parent" law that authorizes the arrest of parents of juvenile gang members who commit serious offenses. Similarly, if your teenage driver has an accident or commits a crime while driving the family car, the court may hold you responsible. One example may be the teenager driving while intoxicated, and possibly causing injuries to another.

WHERE TO GET MORE INFORMATION

Consult the "Where to Get More Information" sections at the end of the first two chapters for assistance.

The American Civil Liberties Union (ACLU) might be able to help if the prosecution charges you with a crime that involves civil or constitutional rights. Check your local telephone directory for the address and phone number. Call the national office at (212) 944-9800 or write to:

American Civil Liberties Union
132 West 43rd Street
New York, New York 10036

THE RIGHTS OF OLDER AMERICANS

THE RIGHT TO A JOB

In the past, most of us viewed 65 as the age of retirement. Today, more people are choosing to continue working well into their 70s. Many even change their careers later in life. The contributions of older workers testify to their vitality.

The *Age Discrimination in Employment Act* (ADEA) ensures that older workers receive equal and fair treatment in the workplace. It protects most workers 40 years and older from arbitrary age discrimination while on the job. It also supports their right to have a job for which they qualify. The ADEA does not cover employers who regularly employ less than 20 employees.

Besides the federal law, many states have passed similar, but stronger, laws.

The Rights of the Older Worker

Q. I thought I would have to retire at age 65. I hear that this is not true. Is there a mandatory retirement age?

A. No, the ADEA generally prohibits mandatory retirement by covered employers, pension plans, and seniority systems.

Q. If I become ill or disabled, must I retire?

A. The law protects you only against having to retire *just* because you are a certain age. If a "reasonable factor other than age" causes your employer to treat you in a way that is different from how it treats other employees, the ADEA does not protect you. So, if an illness or disability prevents you from doing your job satisfactorily, your employer may force you to retire.

However, other federal laws forbid discrimination against disabled people. This includes persons with certain illnesses, such as cancer. If the ADEA does not cover you, determine if other laws will protect you.

Your local office of the federal Equal Employment Opportunity Commission (EEOC) or a comparable state agency can provide details. An attorney with knowledge in this field also could help. There also may be a disability rights organization in your area that can provide information.

Workers Who May Be Forced to Retire

Employers may force a few types of workers to retire when they are 65 years of age or older. One group includes certain executives in important policy-making positions. These must be executives who will receive retirement benefits of at least $44,000 per year, not counting Social Security. Another group consists of fire fighters, police officers, and prison guards employed by state and local governments. A third group includes tenured professors. Many of these exceptions to the ADEA will expire in 1993.

Q. My employer says that I do not have to stop working at age 65. However, I will have to accept a job with less responsibility and less pay. Is this legal?

A. No, the ADEA also protects you in your present job situation. Your employer may not force you to take a less responsible job or accept a lower salary.

Q. What if my pension plan or seniority system says that I must retire before age 70? Is this legal?

A. No, with two exceptions, all workers may stay on the job no matter what their pension plan or seniority system says. The first exception applies to a few workers whom employers may force to retire, as discussed in the "Workers Who May Be Forced to Retire" article at left. The second one involves employees in jobs where age might be a *bona fide occupational qualification,* or BFOQ.

Q. My employer offers on-the-job training to all workers. However, because I am over 55, my employer does not want me to participate. My employer thinks I will leave the company soon. May my employer do this?

A. No, that is illegal. Besides protecting your right to keep your position regardless of age, the ADEA also protects your right to receive training to maintain your position and skills.

Q. May my employer prevent me from applying for another opening in the company because of my age?

A. No, your employer may not use your age to deny your right to transfer to a different job in the company.

Q. My employer passed over me for a promotion, which a younger person received. Is this legal?

A. Not if your employer passed over you because of your age. Employers covered by the ADEA may not discriminate in promotions solely because of age. However, you might have trouble proving that your age, not some other factor, was the cause.

Remember that age alone does not *entitle* you to promotions or to a specific job. Even though your employer has passed over you, your employer has not necessarily discriminated against you.

Q. What if my employer has a policy of not promoting anyone who is within five years of retirement?

A. Arbitrary, age-based promotion policies may be illegal. A policy of not promoting anyone within a certain number of years of retirement probably violates the law. So does a policy of not promoting anyone who fails to reach a certain level in the company by a certain age.

However, unless this policy is written down, you may find it hard to prove that such a policy exists.

How to Handle Age Discrimination in Hiring

Q. I want a new job. However, employers often tell me that I am too old for them to hire. Does the ADEA protect me?

A. Yes, the ADEA protects you from age discrimination in seeking a job and in keeping it. If the ADEA covers an employer, as it almost always does, it is illegal for that employer to discriminate in hiring strictly because of age. The law almost always entitles you to be considered equally with other applicants, regardless of age. The rare exceptions are where age is a bona fide occupational qualification for the job (see corresponding article at right). Your state's law also might protect you against age discrimination in getting a job.

However, proving discrimination is complex. It requires meeting certain standards of evidence. An attorney experienced in this field can help you evaluate your case properly.

Q. May a prospective employer ask me how old I am?

A. The ADEA does not specifically prohibit employers from asking your age. However, courts often consider it

Bona Fide Occupational Qualifications

The ADEA states that your employer may force you to retire when age is a "bona fide occupational qualification reasonably necessary to the normal operation of a particular business." Many people have questioned the definition of a "bona fide occupational qualification," or BFOQ. It may apply to workers whose jobs are especially physically demanding. This includes police officers, fire fighters, and correctional officers. For these specific occupations, the law will allow forced retirement age limits until 1993. After that the limits will expire.

Courts have been willing to accept BFOQs in certain cases. These involve employers that must protect public health and safety, and argue that aging brings some physical deterioration. An example would be airline pilots.

discriminatory for employers to ask your age directly or indirectly. (An indirect question might ask the year you graduated from high school.) An exception occurs in the rare cases where age is vital to the job. However, an employer *may* ask about your work experience, including how recent it is.

If you believe a prospective employer is asking about your age in order to discriminate, you may want to get legal advice about a possible age-discrimination charge.

Q. Is it legal for a "help wanted" ad to state that the employer prefers somebody of a specific age?

A. Not unless age is a bona fide occupational qualification. Employers may not place advertisements that discourage older workers from applying.

Overqualified or Discriminated Against?

At some point, an employer may say that you are overqualified for a job. Is this legal? It depends. Sometimes it might be reasonable to deny you a job because you have too much experience or education. For example, it is reasonable to assume that someone with a Ph.D. in education is overqualified for a position as a teacher's aide, since that position requires only two years of college education. In other cases, a court might decide that calling you "overqualified" is just an employer's pretext (excuse) to avoid hiring an older worker.

Q. I want to change careers. Do I have a right to a job in my new profession?

A. No, an employer does not have to hire you for a job for which you do not qualify. You should be given equal consideration with similarly qualified applicants, regardless of your age.

Suppose you apply for a job in computer programming, and the employer has offered to train employees on the job. Your age should not prevent you from being eligible for that job. The employer also may not use your age as a reason not to train you.

Q. Will I have trouble joining a labor union because of my age?

A. No, federal law says that only very small labor unions (those with fewer than 25 members) may bar someone because of age.

Q. May employment agencies "screen" job applicants based on their age?

A. No, the ADEA covers almost all employment agencies. They must refer you for any job for which you qualify.

Equal Treatment, Benefits, Pensions, and Job Security

Q. After an employer hires me, may the employer, because of my age, treat me in ways that are different from how it treats other workers?

A. No, under the law employers covered by the ADEA are not permitted to treat you differently because you are 40 years old or older. They may not give you less pay, different terms or conditions of employment, or a lower status job just because of your age. They also may not make you work part-time because you are older.

Q. Suppose I change my job late in life. Does my new employer have to give me the pension and benefits that a younger worker would receive?

A. Employee benefit plans are exempt from the ADEA as long as the plan is a "bona fide employee benefit plan such as a retirement, pension, or insurance plan which is not a subterfuge to evade the purposes of [the ADEA]." In a recent case, the U.S. Supreme Court interpreted this language to mean that employers can discriminate based on age in designing benefit packages so long as they were not trying to get around the ban on discrimination in hiring and firing. Before the Supreme Court case, the law was interpreted to mean that benefits for older workers could be different as long as employers spent equal amounts on older and younger workers' benefits. Now employers have much more leeway in providing benefits. Bills are pending in Congress to reinstate the "equal cost" rule. (See the "Law and the Workplace" chapter for more information on pensions.)

Q. My company recently laid off a lot of workers. Many of them were older than the company average. When the firm rehired workers, it rehired the younger employees first. Is this legal?

A. The ADEA does not allow covered employers to discriminate against older workers in layoffs and rehiring practices. (However, the employer might be able to do so if the company is following the terms of a bona fide seniority plan.) If your employer laid off or did not rehire a high proportion of older workers, you might have a reason to complain to the Equal Employment Opportunity Commission (EEOC).

Q. My employer just fired me because my boss says I was not doing a good job. I think it was because I am 62 and my boss wants to hire a younger person for less pay. How can I determine if my employer fired me because of my age?

A. The law does not protect older workers whom employers fire for "good cause." An employer may fire any worker, regardless of age, if there is a good reason.

Joke or Insult?

What could you do if your boss makes insulting remarks about your age? Federal law entitles you to fair, honest appraisals of your work. Your employer must give them without prejudice because of your age. Insulting remarks about your age, especially if they appear in your personnel file, could be evidence of illegal age discrimination.

If your boss makes the remarks orally, you must have witnesses to support your charge. Any remarks made to you will be subject to interpretation by other people. In other words, if your boss says it was "only a joke," you may not be able to prove otherwise. However, if you think you can, do not hesitate to pursue your rights. And remember, there is a precedent for even jokes being considered discriminatory. In the area of sex discrimination, "jokes" are definitely taboo. A court might find "jokes" about age evidence of discrimination.

If Forced Out Illegally, Look for Work

Should you look for another job if you think your employer has illegally fired you or forced you to retire? Yes, even though you may hope to get your former employer to take you back, you must look for another job. Otherwise, your former employer may be able to argue in court that you really are not willing or able to work.

If you cannot find a job and you have to start accepting Social Security benefits, you still will have a case. The important thing is to show that you *do* want to go on working. The best way to do that is to go out and look for a job.

Remember to document your job search. Do this by keeping copies of letters sent asking about employment, ads to which you responded, and a log of telephone conversations and interviews related to your job search.

In general, the standard is: Did your employer treat you, as an older worker, differently from the way your employer would have treated a younger worker? Suppose your employer fires you for absenteeism. That alone might not make up age discrimination. However, suppose your employer did not fire a younger worker who was absent as much as you were. Then you might be able to prove that your employer fired you because of your age.

What to Do About Job-Related Age Discrimination

Q. I believe I have been a victim of age discrimination. How do I file a charge?

A. You should file a charge with the Equal Employment Opportunity Commission (EEOC) in your area. EEOC employees receive special training about how to handle ADEA charges and how to advise workers filing charges. Like all other federal agencies, the listing for the EEOC appears under "U.S. Government" in the telephone directory.

Make the charge in writing. Give your name, age, and how the EEOC can reach you. Identify the company against which you are making the charge. Carefully describe the action you believe was discriminatory. The more specific you can be, the better.

In states that do not have age-discrimination laws, you must file this charge with the EEOC within 180 days of the act you believe was discriminatory. In states that do have such laws, you may file your *complaint* either with the state or with the EEOC. In these states, you have more time in which to go to the EEOC.

You may file your own age-discrimination lawsuit. However, you must still file charges of discrimination with both the state agency and the EEOC before going to court. The EEOC will tell you how to file your charge with the state.

Remember that you must *be prompt* about filing your charge. Call the EEOC as soon as possible after the act you believe was discriminatory.

Q. May my employer punish me if I file a charge with the EEOC?

A. No, federal law makes it illegal for your employer to retaliate against you for going to the EEOC.

Q. Is there anything else I can do?

A. Under the ADEA, you must wait 60 days after filing a charge with the EEOC before you may file your own lawsuit against your employer. You should not be in a hurry to take this step. Lawsuits can be expensive.

However, if you believe the EEOC is not pursuing your case strongly enough, consider filing your own lawsuit. If you are going to file your own lawsuit, you must do so within two years of the discriminatory act.

You also may "opt into" a case filed by someone else against your employer. However, if you believe your employer discriminated against you, do not wait for someone else to file a charge with the EEOC. You should go ahead and file your own charge.

Q. I believe my employer has discriminated against me because of my age. However, I really do not want to pursue a lawsuit. Do I have any other options?

A. Yes, you should try to negotiate a settlement with your employer. This could help avoid a lengthy lawsuit. In fact, the ADEA allows time, through the waiting period, for you to try to resolve your dispute through negotiation. Most state laws also require a waiting period.

Q. I think my company is discriminating against me as an older employee. However, I do not want to file a specific charge. What may I do?

A. The EEOC is permitted to investigate age discrimination even when nobody has filed charges against an employer. However, while the law does not require you to file a charge, you still must file a *complaint* with the EEOC in order to bring the matter to its attention. If desired, your identity may remain anonymous in this circumstance.

Q. I am not an older employee, but I think my company is discriminating against older workers. May I still file a charge?

A. No, you may not file a charge. However, you may file a *complaint* with the EEOC, as described above. Your identity will remain anonymous.

Q. What happens after I have filed a charge or complaint with the EEOC?

A. After you file a *charge,* the EEOC will try to mediate the dispute. It will try to straighten out the problem between you

EVIDENCE OF AGE DISCRIMINATION

The best evidence of age discrimination would be something in writing. Examples include a written policy, memos, or notations in personnel files. Another way to show age discrimination is through statistics showing a pattern of treating older workers differently. For example, statistics might show that an employer is more likely to hire or promote younger employees, or fire and lay off older employees.

In practice, however, age discrimination has been rather hard to prove in court. Generally, the burden of proof in age-discrimination cases lies with the person bringing charges.

and your employer without having to investigate or go to court.

If mediation does not work, the EEOC may investigate. After completing the investigation, the EEOC will decide if the employer has violated a federal law. If the answer is "yes," the agency may file suit on your behalf in federal court. Then government lawyers will represent you. If you have filed a private suit, it will automatically come to an end, and the government suit will replace it.

If you only have filed a *complaint,* the EEOC will investigate the conditions of the complaint. If the EEOC finds your complaint justified, it will act appropriately against the company.

Q. What will happen if I win my case?

A. The court will order the employer to make up to you what you lost through discrimination. This might include:

- Reinstatement in your former job, with your former salary and benefits;
- The awarding of back-pay for salary you did not receive while unemployed;
- A monetary award for damages;
- Placement in a new position if your charge concerned discrimination in promotion or job transfer; and
- Fringe benefits.

If you win your case, the company that discriminated against you may have to pay for your lawyer and other expenses, as well as for court costs.

Q. What if I am a federal employee and I see age discrimination happening?

A. In cases involving federal employees, the EEOC does not investigate or try to mediate. However, each federal agency has its own procedure for you to follow if you have an age-discrimination complaint. Again, it is important to act quickly and complain promptly. If you want to sue the government, you must first file a notice with the agency's EEO office—not the EEOC—and then wait 30 days.

THE RIGHT TO INCOME SECURITY

Older Americans naturally want to maintain their standard of living after retirement. Income maintenance plans include private pensions and pension rights for spouses. The Employee Retirement Income Security Act (ERISA) protects private pensions.

Private Pension Plans

Q. What is a private pension plan?

A. A pension is a program to provide money after retirement. Through a pension plan, an employer, an employee, or a union can set aside money to help the employee live after retiring from the job.

(continued)

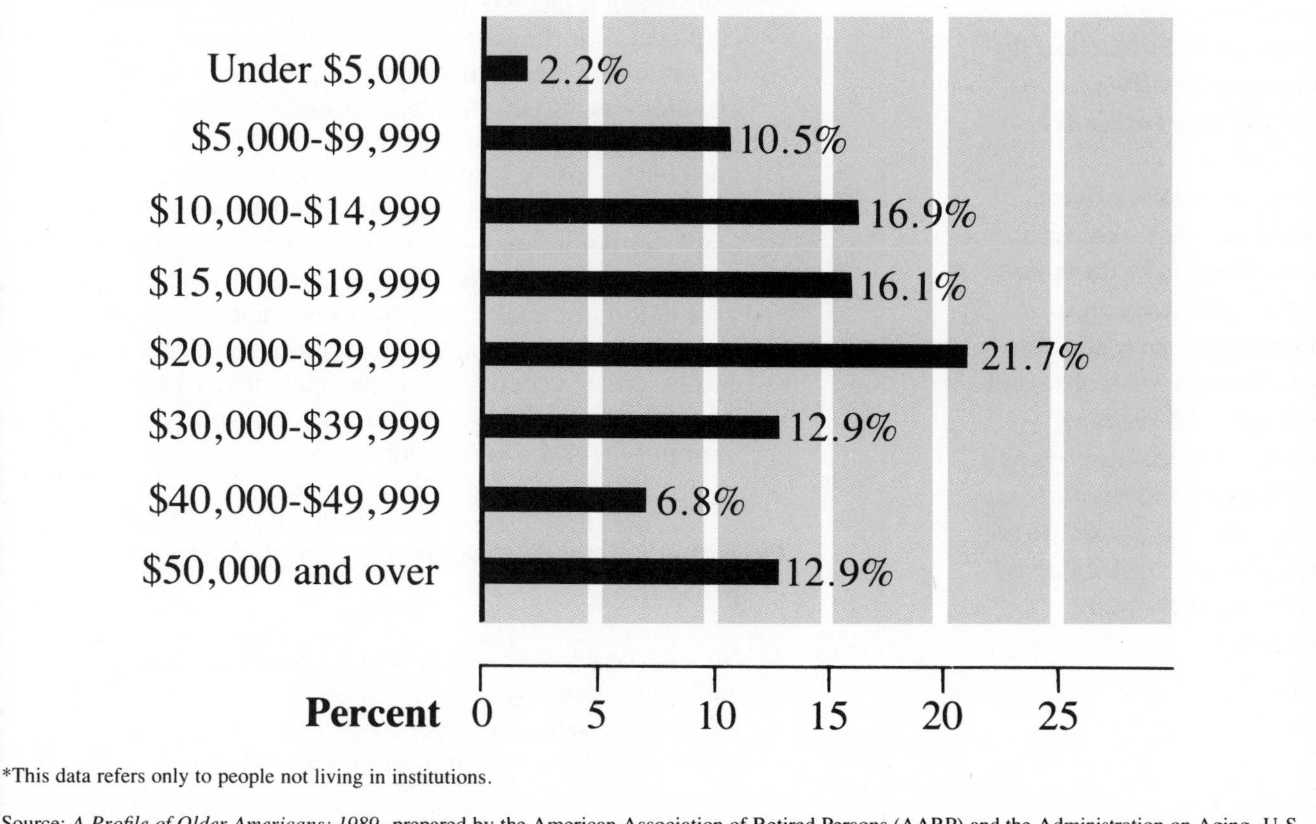

*This data refers only to people not living in institutions.

Source: *A Profile of Older Americans: 1989*, prepared by the American Association of Retired Persons (AARP) and the Administration on Aging, U.S. Department of Health and Human Services, based on data from the U.S. Bureau of the Census. Reprinted with permission of the AARP.

Pension Plan Participation

Your employer must allow you to participate in a pension plan if you meet certain qualifications. Generally, you must have worked for your employer at least one year before being allowed to participate. You also must have worked a certain number of hours in the year (usually 1,000). Usually you must be at least a certain age (often 21).

There are exceptions, however. For example, your employer does not have to allow you to participate in a pension established for a different category of worker. Thus, an employer does not have to allow a secretary to participate in a pension established for assembly-line workers.

Q. How is my private pension plan protected?

A. The Employee Retirement Income Security Act (ERISA) is the main law governing private pensions. Since 1975, ERISA has superseded almost all state laws covering pensions. ERISA deals with the following aspects of pension plans:

- Participation;
- Vesting, benefit accrual, and breaks-in-service;
- Funding;
- Administration of funds;
- Reporting and disclosure;
- Joint and survivor provisions; and
- Plan termination insurance.

ERISA sets legal minimums. While an employer's pension plan may provide more liberal terms, it must provide at least the terms set forth by ERISA.

However, despite amendments to ERISA, there are still many gaps in protection. All older Americans eligible for a private pension should fully understand their rights. They also should realize that the protection offered by ERISA does *not* apply to employees who retired before ERISA went into effect.

Q. How do pensions work?

A. In most plans, an employee, the employer, and sometimes a union each make a contribution, usually monthly, during the employee's working years. This money provides income for the employee after retirement. During the working years, the plan gathers and invests these contributions. When employees retire, they begin to receive a pension benefit, normally monthly, in the form of a check.

In other words, during your working years, each month the employer deducts a certain amount from your paycheck as your pension fund contribution. Your employer and perhaps your union also make a monthly contribution on your behalf. If you have worked enough years, when you retire the plan entitles you to receive a pension. The money you get depends on the amount of the contributions, the number of years you have put in, and your annual income.

Q. Is there a law that requires my employer to give me a pension?

A. No, employers do not have to set up a pension plan for employees. However, a plan covered by ERISA—whether established by an employer alone or jointly with a union—must meet certain minimum standards.

Q. What does "benefit accrual" mean?

A. *Benefit accrual* refers to the process of building up credits for pension benefits. For example, once you qualify for your employer's pension plan, each year of your employment may form a credit toward your pension. The plan may use these credits to determine the size of your pension benefit when you retire.

Q. What does "vesting" mean?

A. *Vesting* refers to a point in time. After that point, the plan may not deny employees' accrued benefits. Vesting usually occurs after a specified length of employment with the same employer.

Q. Does this mean the plan guarantees at least some pension money for me when I retire?

A. If you leave a job before you become vested in that company's pension plan, you will not be eligible for a pension from that employer when you retire. However, if you leave after you become vested, you should receive some pension, depending on your accrued credits.

Although you may have participated in a plan for several years, the plan probably will not vest until you have participated for a set amount of time.

Suppose you participate in a plan for four and one-half years, but the pension vests after five years. Then the plan does not entitle you to a pension. The only money that the plan entitles you to receive is money you paid into the pension plan directly (pension money taken directly out of your paycheck).

ERISA says that after 1989, pension plans must vest 100 percent after five years, although some do vest sooner. In addition, some plans may have "graded" (step-by-step) vesting, over seven years. Rules on vesting differ for plans in effect before 1989.

Q. What happens to my pension if I leave my job temporarily and then return?

A. It depends on how long you worked on the job and the length of your break. In general, the pension plan may not deprive you of credit that you have already earned if the break-in-service is shorter than the years you worked before the break. Suppose a pension plan covered you for four years and you now want to take off a year. You will not lose credit for those four years. However, if you take a break from the company for six years and then you return to that job, you may lose all the credit that you earned.

Taking a Break

If you had already become vested at the time of your break-in-service, you will not lose the pension benefits you have already accrued. ERISA protects your pension benefits affected by breaks-in-service. Under ERISA, if you are not vested, you may or may not lose credits, depending on the number of years worked both before and after the break-in-service. Another aspect is the number of hours worked each year. In general, ERISA requires your pension plan to give you at least partial credit for any year in which you worked 1,000 hours or more. If you work part-time or have had a break-in-service, ask for an explanation of your benefits from your employer.

Q. When do I start building benefits?

A. Normally, employees start building benefits as soon as they begin participating in a pension plan. ERISA requires an employer to give participating employees at least partial pension credit if they work 1,000 hours in a year.

Q. I want to change jobs. May I take my pension benefits with me to my new job?

A. That depends. Even with ERISA, you may not automatically transfer pension benefits if you change jobs. If you change jobs *before* your pension has vested, you usually lose all the benefits you built up in your old job. You have to start all over again with your new employer.

However, if you change jobs *after* your benefits have vested, ERISA entitles you to the entire amount of your vested benefits. You may:

- Put your vested funds in an IRA to avoid taxation;
- Transfer the funds to the new employer's pension plan if possible; or
- Form some other plan. (You may have to pay taxes on the money if you do not invest the funds in some type of pension or retirement program.)

Some unions have reciprocal arrangements that allow you to change employers and transfer your benefits.

Q. If I change jobs, may a pension plan exclude me because I am near retirement?

A. No, although sometimes you may have to work at least five years before being eligible for pension benefits. Also, a plan may still require you to meet vesting requirements.

Q. If I participate in a plan, how are my benefits figured?

A. The money you receive will depend on:

- Your plan;
- How many years you have worked;
- Your earnings when you worked;
- How old you are when you start receiving benefits; and
- Whether you are married.

Q. May my employer save money by firing me just before my pension vests?

A. ERISA protects you from being fired in order to deprive you of your pension. If you believe this happened to you, you have the right to challenge your employer's action. You may do this by filing a complaint with the U.S. Department of Labor or by filing a lawsuit in a state or federal court. However, you will have to prove that your employer fired you in order to deprive you of your pension and not for a valid reason.

Q. May my employer deprive me of pension benefits by changing my pension plan?

A. Under ERISA, an employer may not deprive you of benefits that have vested by switching plans or amending your present plan. However, your employer may deprive you of benefits not yet vested. Thus, two workers who vested in the company's pension plan at different years, under different plans, may receive different pensions. This may occur even if they retire the same year.

Q. May my employer deprive me of pension benefits by dropping the company's pension plan?

A. While an employer may end a pension plan, the employer may not avoid meeting pension plan obligations incurred while the plan was in effect. ERISA does not require an employer to offer a pension plan. However, ERISA does offer some protection to vested workers when a pension plan has been in effect. This protection varies depending on the type of benefit plan.

For example, ERISA has established the Pension Benefit Guaranty Corporation (PBGC). It protects certain benefits in specific types of funds. ERISA requires *defined-benefit* pension plans to pay insurance premiums to the PBGC. In return, the PBGC guarantees vested benefits up to a certain limit set by law.

The Retirement Equity Act (REA) offers additional protection. It says that an employer must offer workers the option of early retirement if a pension plan is to be ended. If the employee is already eligible for full retirement benefits under the pension plan, that employee will receive those benefits, even if the plan ends.

Q. I want to retire before the age of 65. Will this affect my pension?

A. It very well may affect your pension. Plans do not have to pay you a pension until you reach age 65, even if you retire early. Many pension plans will reduce your benefits by a certain percentage if you take them before the "normal" retirement age (usually 65).

Q. May I retire from my present job, find another job, and still receive benefits?

A. Yes, you may do this. If your pension has vested, you usually will keep getting benefits if you open a business or go to work full- or part-time. However, the plan may suspend payments if you go back to work for your former employer. Sometimes the payments also will stop if you go back to work in the same industry, trade, or geographical area.

Q. May I collect Social Security payments and my pension at the same time?

A. Yes, under most plans, you receive benefits besides Social Security. However, some plans do include a Social Security *offset*. This reduces your pension if you also receive Social Security. The first offset is legal. However, the plan may not reduce your pension benefits further if your Social Security benefits increase.

Q. What happens if another company takes over the company that employs me?

A. You should not lose your benefits. ERISA requires that all years of service with "employers maintaining the plan" must count toward your pension.

Getting Pension Plan Information

ERISA guarantees you the right to receive basic information about your plan. It must be written in language that is easy to understand. You should receive a booklet from your employer or union explaining what you have to do to get a pension. It also should explain the dollar amount of benefits paid by the plan.

Q. I want to know more about my pension benefits now, before I retire. What type of information must my plan tell me?

A. You have the right to know if your employer offers a pension plan for you, and if so, how much you can expect to receive when you retire. You have to ask for this information in writing, and you may ask for it once a year. Your plan may tell you that you have an accrued benefit of a certain amount, but you will not receive that benefit unless you work long enough to become vested.

Q. What facts about my pension benefits may I expect to receive when I retire?

A. You have a right to a statement from the plan telling you if you are entitled to a pension, and if so, how much you are entitled to receive at "normal" retirement age (usually 65).

This statement will not tell you how much the plan will reduce your pension if you take benefits before the normal retirement age or if you are married.

Q. I would like to know more about how my pension plan is investing its funds. Does the law entitle me to this information?

A. Yes, you have a right to know where your pension plan is investing the money, how well, and who is investing it. You should get a summary of this information every year. For complete details, you must ask in writing for a copy of the full annual report. The plan may charge you reasonable copying costs for the report.

Your plan's annual financial report is on file with the Labor Department. You can ask for information from the Division of Public Disclosure, Room N5507, U.S. Department of Labor, Washington, D.C. 20210. The telephone number is (202) 523-8771.

Q. What may I do if I do not like the way my plan is investing the money?

A. ERISA establishes certain strict standards. These aim to guarantee that plans will invest money wisely and do so only in the interest of employees and their spouses.

Chances are, however, that the plan will not violate ERISA even if you do not like the way your pension is investing the money. Even if you believe that the plan could invest the money much better somewhere else, the plan probably would still not violate ERISA.

However, if you believe the plan *is* violating ERISA's regulations, you may speak with an official of the U.S. Department of Labor. Or you may write to the Pension and Welfare Benefit Administration, Division of Technical Assistance and Inquiries, U.S. Department of Labor, 200 Constitution Avenue, N.W., Room N5658, Washington, D.C. 20210. The phone number for this office is (202) 523-8784. The U.S. Department of Labor also has offices in most major cities. The blue pages of your telephone directory will list the address and telephone number under "United States Government, Labor Department."

YOUR RIGHTS IN A NURSING HOME

Improving Treatment in a Nursing Home

If there is one common element uniting almost every older American, it probably is the fear of having to live in a nursing home. In recent years, federal and state governments have passed laws that regulate nursing homes. These laws try to assure that the nursing homes treat their patients well.

Q. What is a nursing home?

A. The term "nursing home" refers to at least three different types of living situations:

- *Skilled Nursing Facilities* (SNFs) are nursing homes that provide skilled nursing care by a registered nurse 24 hours a day. A physician is on staff as the medical director.
- An *Intermediate Care Facility* (ICF) provides medical and related care. A registered nurse does not necessarily provide such care. However, a registered nurse must be on duty at least eight hours a day, seven days a week. An ICF does not have to employ a medical director.
- A large number of institutions commonly called "nursing homes" are actually licensed as "board and care," "custodial care," or "domiciliary care" facilities. These institutions do not provide much in the way of medical care. However, they do provide room and board. They also furnish assistance in feeding, personal care, dressing, and similar personal actions. Occupants of these homes often are people who require supervision of their daily activities but otherwise are reasonably healthy.

Must Children Pay for Parents in Nursing Homes?

Many people believe that if patients in a nursing home cannot pay for their own care, their children may be legally required to cover these costs. That is not true. The only person legally responsible to help in the financial support is the spouse of the person staying in the nursing home. Also, if the nursing home resident is eligible for Medicaid, there are limits on the amount of support the spouse will be required to provide. Do not let a nursing home pressure a family member into taking on financial responsibility for the care of the nursing home resident.

Q. Has regulation improved the care in nursing homes?

A. Yes, it has helped, though it has not solved the problem. Care in nursing homes, regardless of type, ranges from highly competent and caring to terrible and abusive. Despite federal and state laws regulating nursing homes, unlicensed nursing homes continue to exist in most communities. These fall outside the scrutiny of nursing-home watchdog programs. Even homes that are subject to federal and state regulations are often badly monitored. They may not provide care that is high quality or even adequate.

Q. How well are board and care facilities regulated?

A. The state regulates licensed board and care facilities. Standards vary greatly from one area to another, as do costs.

Q. What can I do if I think a nursing home is not providing adequate care, or if I see actual abuse happening?

A. The most important thing you can do is to bring this issue to the attention of the regulatory agency and the nursing home ombudsman. Federal law provides for a nursing home ombudsman program in each state. Every nursing home should post details about the nursing home ombudsman.

Q. What can a nursing home ombudsman do?

A. The nursing home ombudsman will discuss your complaint and charges with you and then investigate. While the ombudsman program does not have powers of enforcement, it may help bring abuses to the attention of the proper authorities. Also, the ombudsman should act as an advocate for the nursing home residents. The ombudsman should make sure their rights to adequate care are protected.

To find out more about this program, and to report violations in providing residents access to the ombudsman, call your local (city, county, or state) agency on aging.

Q. My mother lives in a nursing home. I think she would function better if the home gave her more choices about what she could do. Examples could include which activities she wants to participate in, what clothes she wants to wear, and where she wants to go in the home. What may I do about it?

A. This is another area where the nursing home ombudsman may be of assistance. Perhaps the ombudsman may help you convey your concern to the nursing home director. The ombudsman also will be able to tell you if your requests are reasonable, considering the large number of regulations with which nursing homes must comply.

In addition, the nursing home may have a residents' council. Speak with a council member to see if somebody has previously addressed your concerns.

Q. What may I do if I think the nursing home is interfering with my rights?

A. You should contact your nursing home ombudsman and ask for help. In addition, you may have to get advice from a private attorney or a legal services agency. (See the first chapter, "When and How to Use a Lawyer.")

If you have trouble getting help, ask family members, other residents, or even visitors to assist you. Your need for nursing care should never infringe on your rights as a citizen.

THE RIGHTS OF IMPAIRED ELDERS

Accessibility in Housing

Q. I must use a wheelchair, and it is hard to maneuver in the kitchen of my apartment. Some changes would help me

Your Rights While Living in a Nursing Home

You will retain all your civil rights if you have to live in a nursing home. A nursing home may not require you to give up these rights simply because you need custodial care, supervision, or nursing care. What does this mean in reality? While you must obey the rules of the nursing home, you should not accept any rule that infringes on your legal rights. These include the rights:

- **To liberty;**
- **To make your own medical and care decisions;**
- **To have visitors;**
- **To practice your own religion;**
- **To seek legal counsel;**
- **To leave the nursing home if you choose;**
- **To get information about your care, including medical care;**
- **To see a doctor when you ask for one; and**
- **To manage your own money.**

Protecting Disabled Older Americans

As part of the aging process, older persons often become impaired or ill. This may limit their mobility. Sometimes they lose the ability to function independently.

Despite these limitations, impaired older persons do not lose their rights. The 1973 Federal Rehabilitation Act makes it illegal to discriminate against people with disabilities. It does not specifically single out older adults. This protection applies to disabled persons of all ages. In addition, two recent federal laws protect some specific rights of all disabled and impaired persons. These laws guarantee equal access to housing and voting.

cook and clean up, but my landlord does not want me to change anything. What may I do, short of moving?

A. The federal Fair Housing Amendments Act of 1988 gives renters the right to modify their apartments to meet their specific needs. This unlocks many opportunities for persons with physical and mental impairments.

For example, tenants may now install bathtub grab bars, "roll-under" sinks to accommodate wheelchairs, and handrails in hallways. Other possibilities include flashing lights for doorbells and thermostatic sensors on sinks.

Q. Who pays for these alterations?

A. The tenant pays for modifications to existing apartments. In addition, the apartment may have to be restored to its original condition when the tenant leaves. Some assistance may be available from your state or local rehabilitation department, as well as from voluntary organizations, such as clubs or churches.

Q. My wife uses a wheelchair. The developers of a new apartment complex that interests us do not want to install outside ramps or create wider hallways. Will this new housing bill help us?

A. Yes, the Fair Housing Amendments Act requires that all new multifamily housing be "adaptable." That means it must be modifiable for handicapped persons. This might mean building some apartments with wider doorways and hallways to handle wheelchairs. In addition, all new construction must be accessible to wheelchairs. However, many exceptions exist on this point.

Q. There is a new retirement complex for senior citizens under construction in our town. I want to move there. However, the developers said that because I use a walker, I could not rent an apartment. Will the new law help me?

A. The law may help, but it is too new to have received adequate testing in court. However, it might be used against some standard leases in housing for the elderly. Many new retirement centers offer housekeeping, transportation, and meals, but have leases that exclude people with mental and physical limitations. Such leases do not allow persons who use wheelchairs to rent. They also do not permit tenants who become disabled to remain in their apartments.

These leases appear to discriminate against people with impaired mobility who are otherwise fully able to live independently. In the future, courts may determine the legality of such clauses.

Accessibility in Voting

Q. It has become more and more difficult for me to get to polling places on election day to vote. Will I lose my right to vote if I do not participate in elections?

A. No, all citizens of legal age keep the right to vote, regardless of disabilities or handicaps. Generally, only people found incompetent by a court of law or convicted of a felony lose the right to vote.

Q. Because of a stroke, I must now use a wheelchair to get around. My polling place is downstairs at our local school, which has no elevator. How may I vote?

A. The federal Voting Accessibility for the Elderly and Handicapped Act calls for polling places accessible to everyone. However, the federal government does not strictly enforce the law. Disabled persons may continue to face difficulties.

Some common options to accessible polling places include curbside voting, allowing people to vote in an accessible polling place outside their home precinct, and using absentee ballots.

Q. My father is in a nursing home. May the nursing home deny him the right to vote?

A. No, federal law also ensures that residents of nursing homes are able to vote. Nursing homes must help residents exercise this right.

Q. Is there anything that I may do about discrimination against elderly or disabled people?

A. If you believe somebody has violated your rights because of your age or a disability, contact:

- Your state's department of human rights or human rights commission;
- Your city's human rights commission;
- The U.S. Justice Department office in your district;
- The department in your state that provides rehabilitation services; or

Mental Health and Housing

Suppose doctors have diagnosed your husband as having Alzheimer's disease. Then your landlord found out and refused to renew the lease on your apartment. Is this legal? No, the Fair Housing Amendments Act also outlaws discrimination against the mentally ill and the mentally impaired. Landlords may not turn away prospective renters because a family member has a mental handicap. A landlord may not refuse to rent an apartment to you because a person with Alzheimer's disease will be living with you.

This new law has led to community-based small group homes for younger mentally ill people. It also may lead to the creation of similar residential sites for older persons with mental impairments. These may be alternatives to large, institutional nursing homes.

- A lawyer specializing in discrimination law. (If you cannot afford a private lawyer, you may be able to get help through legal services or a law school legal-aid clinic.)

THE RIGHT TO REMAIN IN CONTROL OF YOUR LIFE

As we grow older, all of us face the possibility that one day we may become incapacitated. The time may come when we are no longer able to make our own decisions, manage our own financial affairs, or act on our own behalf.

When that happens, you and your property must be protected. It also is important that people honor your wishes wherever possible. How and where do you want to live? What decisions can you make? What decisions should you leave to someone else? Who do you want to make decisions for you? Several alternatives will ensure that people respect your wishes whenever possible. Through planning, the decisions made on your behalf can be those you would have made yourself.

Planning for Incapacity: The Use of Advance Directives

Q. What may I do to make sure that people consider my wishes if someday I become incapacitated?

A. Plan now to ensure that people respect your wishes after you have become incapacitated. Several tools, called *advance directives,* guarantee you a voice in your future. If incapacity strikes, these tools will tell other people how to care for you and your property.

Advance directives are similar to wills, except that they apply while you are still living. In a will, you name an executor (manager of your estate) and specify how you want your estate divided after your death. In an advance directive, you name a surrogate (replacement) decision-maker and specify the decisions you want made if you become incapacitated.

Three types of advance directives allow you to do this:

- Durable power of attorney;
- Durable power of attorney for health-care decisions; and
- Living will.

The details of creating these documents vary from one state to another. However, some general principles apply. The following sections discuss these principles.

Enforcing Your Right to Vote

To enforce your right to vote, contact the U.S. Justice Department or the state attorney general's office in your area. The blue pages of your telephone directory will list their phone numbers.

For details on how to exercise your right to vote when your voting place is inaccessible, call the local office of the League of Women Voters. If they are unable to help, call the local board of election commissioners, the county clerk's office, or the agency responsible for managing elections in your area.

Power of Attorney and Durable Power of Attorney

Q. What may I do to appoint a particular person to make decisions for me?

A. A power of attorney and a durable power of attorney offer two ways of giving someone authority to make decisions for you. Each meets different needs.

Q. What is a power of attorney?

A. A *power of attorney* is a written document. In it, you (the principal) grant certain powers to another person (the agent or "attorney in fact" or "power of attorney"). This enables the person to act on your behalf. A power of attorney may be very specific. It can limit the power of the agent to a specific act, such as selling your car for you or handling a particular financial transaction. Or the power may be very broad and without definition.

Note that a power of attorney also is one of the ways of referring to the *person* you have chosen to act for you. Thus, the same term can cover the legal document and the person.

Q. Why can't I just designate one of my daughters as my power of attorney now, while I am still mentally and physically fit? Then she may act for me if I ever become incapacitated or incompetent?

A. A simple power of attorney is not valid if you become incapacitated. However, if you have written a durable power of attorney before you become incapacitated, that document will be effective while you have a handicap.

Q. What exactly is a durable power of attorney?

A. A *durable power of attorney* is a special type of power of attorney. It remains effective even if you become incapacitated. It does not, however, remain effective after your death. That is, it does not replace an administrator or executor of your estate.

With a durable power of attorney, you may specify the type of care given to any dependent if you become incapacitated. Suppose you care for an elderly relative or a retarded child. Your durable power of attorney may continue that care if you become incapacitated. You also may use your durable power of attorney to make gifts to others while you are still alive but incapacitated.

Q. To whom should I give my authority by a power of attorney? Does the person have to be an attorney?

A. No, a power of attorney, regardless of type, does not have to be a lawyer. Your power of attorney or durable power of attorney should be someone who knows you well. After all, that person will make decisions for you. The person has to carry out your wishes and always act with your best interests in mind. The person may be a relative, a close friend, your personal attorney, or someone else you trust. If there is no one you trust with this power, it may be best not to draw up either of these advance directives.

Q. What if I do not want a power of attorney to take effect now, but only if I become disabled or incapacitated?

A. It may be possible to write your durable power of attorney so that it becomes effective *only* if you become incapacitated. People sometimes call this a *springing* power of attorney. However, the ability to write this type of durable power of attorney varies from one state to another. Consult a knowledgeable lawyer to find out what is required in your own state.

Q. Must I use a special form? Also, do I need a lawyer to write a durable power of attorney, including one for health-care decisions?

A. The laws authorizing durable powers of attorney vary between states. Therefore, you should consult a lawyer to make sure your durable power of attorney obeys your state's requirements. Some states require a special form, or at least a specific format. Certain states provide a sample form that allows you to check off the powers to be granted to the agent.

Q. My father has Alzheimer's disease. I would like him to appoint me his durable power of attorney, since he can no longer manage on his own. May he do this now or is it too late?

A. It may be too late. All advance directives, including the durable power of attorney and regular power of attorney, must be written while a person is still competent. This is why planning is so important.

However, just because doctors diagnose someone as having a specific disease does not mean that the patient is necessarily incompetent. Also, incompetency is not "global." That is, it does not affect all functions in the same way. Thus, even people in the early stages of a disease like Alzheimer's may be competent to make some types of decisions. They also may be more competent at certain times than at others.

Competency should be assessed on a case-by-case basis. Every consideration should be given to finding a way to increase a person's decision-making abilities.

Q. What if the durable power of attorney that I name does not want to be responsible for making these decisions for me?

A. You may not force that person to act. Always discuss your plans with the person you want to name as your durable power of attorney *before* executing the document.

Q. Who decides if I have a disability or not?

A. You can specify in your durable power of attorney how you wish to have your incapacity and mental status determined. These tests will show whether you are unable to make your own decisions or manage your own affairs. They also may help determine if you have regained capacity. The doctor or clinical psychologist who makes such evaluations should have experience in this area.

Durable Power of Attorney for Health-Care Decisions

Q. It sounds like a power of attorney is useful only for financial and property matters. What about my medical care?

A. Usually a power of attorney will handle financial and property issues. In recent years, some states have passed specific laws providing for durable powers of attorney for health-care decisions. In other states, this type of durable power of attorney can be written even without such laws.

A durable power of attorney for health-care decisions lets you pick someone to make medical decisions for you. That person may decide whether you will have surgery, what type of treatment you will receive, and in which nursing home you will be placed. These often are the same decisions that a "guardian of the person" might make for you. (A later section in this chapter discusses this in greater detail.) However, with a durable power of attorney for health-care decisions, you keep the right to pick the decision-maker. You also avoid the complicated procedures of guardianship and their expense. In addition, by naming a durable power of attorney for health-care decisions, you assure that your *own* wishes will be the basis for the decisions made on your behalf.

Revoking a Power of Attorney

If you change your mind about who you want as your power of attorney (durable or not), you may revoke the document. In fact, while you are competent, you may revoke a power of attorney at *any time* for any reason. Simply notify the person you have named to act on your behalf. For your protection, it is best to do this in writing. You also should notify any third parties with whom this person might have done business.

WHO PAYS FOR MEDICAL BILLS?

Does the person you choose to make decisions also become responsible for paying your medical bills? No, a durable power of attorney does not make the person financially responsible for any bills you incur. It simply appoints a substitute decision-maker.

For example, the durable power of attorney authorizes someone to admit you to a nursing home and arrange for paying your bills. However, that person is not personally responsible for these costs.

Many nursing-home contracts try to impose financial obligations through a *responsible party clause*. The person making decisions for you should be careful not to accept such liability. That person can do this by always signing a document as "John Doe's Attorney in Fact."

Q. How will my power of attorney for health-care decisions know what I would want done?

A. You and the designated person must thoroughly discuss your wishes *before* you design the durable power of attorney for health-care decisions. Your power of attorney must understand what choices you want made in different circumstances. For example, what sort of nursing home would you want to live in? Do you have a specific one in mind? What types of medical treatments would you *not* want to have? Would you want to have tube feedings or IVs sustain you? Discuss questions like these with your durable power of attorney before designing the document. Write down these wishes so that the durable power of attorney does not have to rely on memory.

Q. Why do I need someone else to make health-care decisions for me? I trust my doctor. Why can't I just rely on my doctor's judgment?

A. Doctors must make sure that their patients fully understand the treatment they are receiving and agree to it. The term for this is *informed consent*. Most routine treatments and examinations do not require special consent forms. However, broad or unusual treatments, including invasive (in-the-body) tests or operations, require specific consent. If the patient is unable to understand what the test is for, or what the surgery is and what risks it involves, a surrogate decision-maker must be appointed.

A durable power of attorney, specifying the person who is to make health-care decisions for you, protects your right to be informed. It also protects your right to refuse a treatment or operation, if that has been your declared wish in the past.

Q. I always take one of my children with me when I go to the doctor. Why can't my child make those decisions?

A. Usually consent by family members is acceptable. Some states even have family consent laws. However, if the family refuses their consent, or if there is an argument among family members, informal decision-making may not work. Thus, you should name your child as your durable power of attorney and specify that your child will make health-care decisions on your behalf. If you do not, a guardian of the person may have to be appointed. That would be both costly and time-consuming.

A durable power of attorney for health-care decisions assures that the family member *of your choice* will be consulted. If you do not want a specific family member involved, you may make that clear by appointing someone else.

Living Wills

Q. How is a durable power of attorney for health-care decisions different from "living wills"?

A. The durable power of attorney for health-care decisions allows another person to act as your substitute decision-maker. This person makes independent decisions based on what is in your best interests. These decisions are of many types. They may range from consent for hospitalization to consent for an operation or placement in a nursing home. If you discuss your wishes on these matters with the agent in advance, your agent will act according to your preferences.

In contrast, a *living will* is a specific document. It applies when you are terminally ill. It lists which specific medical treatments you wish to have or reject in your final illness.

Q. What is a living will?

A. A *living will* is an advance directive to help make health-care decisions for people at the end of life. It does not apply to all situations. However, it often ensures that people respect and follow your wishes about how you approach death.

Q. I believe I should be able to die with dignity. There are certain treatments I would want and some I do not want. Is there a way to make sure that this happens?

A. Yes, many states now have provisions for writing a living will. A living will lets you specify what types of life-prolonging treatments you wish to accept or reject if you become terminally ill. These include mechanical respirators, nasogastric tubes for feeding, and other forms of artificial life-support systems.

The treatments that qualify as artificial life-support may vary from one jurisdiction to another. A lawyer or other professional with experience in this area may help you determine what the limitations are in your state. Remember, you may use a living will to ask that health-care professionals use extraordinary efforts. It is not just to ask that they withhold such measures.

Q. Do I need an attorney to write a living will or may I do it myself?

A. Since requirements for drafting a living will vary from one state to another, you should consult a lawyer. You also should discuss your plans with your doctor.

When to Write a Living Will

You should write a living will—and update it—as you would a will dealing with your property. Do not wait until you are sick. Execute your living will while you are still competent.

A living will comes into play only if doctors expect you to die shortly. A terminal state can result from a stroke, auto accident, or long illness. Therefore, living wills are valuable documents for everyone, not just older adults.

Remember, although living wills address end-of-life issues, you always have the right to refuse or request any medical treatment, regardless of your condition.

It can be very hard to draft a living will that meets your state's requirements. For example, living wills need to be general enough to cover many different situations. However, they also must be specific about what you do and do not want done on your behalf. Achieving this balance can be difficult without the help of an experienced professional.

Most states require that a living will, like other wills, be witnessed and notarized. Model forms for living wills are available.

Q. Who is responsible for seeing that the conditions of my living will are met?

A. If you have executed a durable power of attorney, your substitute decision-maker also could see that people honor your end-of-life decisions. However, anyone may accept this responsibility for you. Or, if you are able, you could do it.

It is important that you share your wishes with your doctor and any specialists who are treating you. In fact, you should have a copy of your living will entered into your medical records. Share this information with others. Do not simply write a living will and then file it away without telling someone else about it.

Q. Does a court have to declare me incompetent before the doctors can use my living will?

A. No, you do not have to be found incompetent.

Living or Inter Vivos Trusts

Q. Are there advance directives that I can use to plan for estate management?

A. Yes, although we usually think of a trust as a legacy left to future generations, a trust may be used to manage your finances and investments while you are alive. By naming yourself as the beneficiary, you may ensure enough income to meet your needs.

Living trusts also are a way of ensuring that someone manages your estate properly, if you become incapacitated or simply do not wish to manage your own estate anymore. They are a way of planning for the proper handling of even routine financial affairs. A living trust may avoid the necessity of a guardian or conservator of the estate.

Staying Alive

What if you decide that you want extraordinary efforts exerted to keep you alive, once you have a terminal illness? May you revoke your living will? Yes, you may always change your living will or revoke it completely. You may do so either orally or in writing. If you revoke it, make sure that you withdraw all copies of the existing will. Also be sure to tell your doctor of your change of heart. Remember that you may use a living will to ask that your doctor use extraordinary efforts, not just to ask that such measures be withheld.

(continued)

Sample Living Will

The sample living will that follows is defined by statute for use in Illinois, but other states may have different laws. You would be well advised to consult with an attorney in your home state for the appropriate form.

Declaration

This declaration is made this _____ day of __________ (month, year). I, ____________________________________ , being of sound mind, willfully and voluntarily make known my desires that my moment of death shall not be artificially postponed.

If at any time I should have an incurable and irreversible injury, disease, or illness judged to be a terminal condition by my attending physician who has personally examined me and has determined that my death is imminent except for death delaying procedures, I direct that such procedures which would only prolong the dying process be withheld or withdrawn, and that I be permitted to die naturally with only the administration of medication, sustenance, or the performance of any medical procedure deemed necessary by my attending physician to provide me with comfort care.

In the absence of my ability to give directions regarding the use of such death delaying procedures, it is my intention that this declaration shall be honored by my family and physician as the final expression of my legal right to refuse medical or surgical treatment and accept the consequences from such refusal.

Signed ____

City, County and State of Residence ________________________

____

The declarant is personally known to me and I believe him or her to be of sound mind. I saw the declarant sign the declaration in my presence (or the declarant acknowledged in my presence that he or she had signed the declaration) and I signed the declaration as a witness in the presence of the declarant. I did not sign the declarant's signature above for or at the direction of the declarant. At the date of this instrument, I am not entitled to any portion of the estate of the declarant according to the laws of intestate succession or, to the best of my knowledge and belief, under any will of declarant or other instrument taking effect at declarant's death, or directly financially responsible for declarant's medical care.

Witness ____

Witness ____

Source: Reprinted with permission of West Publishing Co. from *1988 Supplement to Illinois Revised Statutes 1987,* State Bar Association Edition, copyright © 1989.

How a Living Trust Works

In a trust, a *trustee* holds property according to the terms of a written trust document. A *settlor* (the person establishing the trust) creates this document. It is for the benefit of one or more persons (the *beneficiaries*).

A will often sets up a trust that becomes effective after the death of the person establishing the trust. On the other hand, a living trust is effective during the lifetime of the settlor. In a living trust, the settlor and/or members of the settlor's family are the beneficiaries of the trust.

Q. Is there any way that I can use a living trust as an advance directive?

A. Yes. You may design a living trust so it takes effect only if you become incapacitated. In this way, you keep control over your affairs until the proper person determines that you are incompetent. As with a durable power of attorney, such a determination should be made by an experienced doctor or other professional.

Q. I always thought a trust simply paid an allowance to someone. If I need a trust because I cannot manage my own finances, how would this help me?

A. Some trust arrangements do just pay a sum to the beneficiary each month or each quarter (every three months). However, you may design a living trust in which the trustee handles many of the daily tasks of managing the estate, including paying bills and taxes. You may state in the trust agreement exactly what you want the trustee to do and how you want your assets managed.

Q. Is a living trust just for someone who is incompetent?

A. No. While a living trust is an excellent way for someone to plan and avoid the need for a guardian or conservator of the estate, a living trust also is ideal for anyone who wishes to turn over the financial management of his or her affairs to another person.

Q. My father has a lot of money in his estate, but he is becoming increasingly forgetful every week. May he still write a living trust?

A. Like all other advance directives, people must prepare living trusts before their competency comes into question. You may determine your father's ability to draft a trust agreement by having him completely evaluated. A lawyer may advise you about what standard of competency must be proven. If your father is not competent, he cannot draft a living trust or any other form of advance directive.

Q. May I decide that I want to change, or revoke, a living trust arrangement?

A. It depends on the type of trust. Before being declared incapacitated, you always may change or even revoke completely a revocable living trust document.

Q. How may I ensure that my trustee will properly manage my affairs after I become incapacitated?

A. Your trust instrument should contain specific instructions for managing your property. You should include a precise statement of what the trustee should do on your behalf.

Q. My wife and I hold most of our assets in common. May I still draft a living trust to protect my share of the estate?

A. Yes, but take care to ensure that the trust does not trespass on the rights or interests of your wife's portion of the estate. You may do this through careful drafting of the document and sound financial planning before incapacity.

Q. It sounds like a living trust is very complex. Who can help me decide if one is right for me?

A. It is best to consult with a lawyer or a trust officer familiar with living trusts to determine if one is right for you.

Representative Payees

Q. I do not have any income to turn over to a trust. All I have is my Social Security check. Would a living trust help me manage my money?

A. No, a living trust would not be the proper way to help you with your finances. However, in certain circumstances, a representative payee may take care of your daily expenses and manage your small income.

Q. What is a representative payee?

A. A *representative payee* is a person appointed by a government agency such as the Social Security Administration (SSA) or the Veterans Administration (VA). The payee manages your monthly income and ensures that your funds are spent for your benefit.

Q. What types of income may a representative payee manage?

A. A representative payee may only manage income from very specific sources. These are usually federal programs such as

WHO MAY BE A REPRESENTATIVE PAYEE?

Almost anyone may be a representative payee. However, the Social Security Administration has issued priorities about whom a government agency should appoint as a representative payee. The first priority includes your legal guardian, your spouse, or a relative. The reason is that these people have the strongest interest in seeing to your well-being and care. However, a government agency also may appoint a friend, especially if you are not

(continued)

Social Security, veterans benefits, black-lung benefits, and supplemental social insurance programs. If you have further income from other sources, a representative payee will not be appropriate for you.

You should check with a representative from your local Social Security or other government benefits office to find out if you are eligible and how to proceed.

Q. Must a court declare me incompetent before I can have a representative payee?

A. No, one advantage of a representative payee is that a court does not need to find you incompetent. However, you must have some sort of disability that prevents you from managing your own financial affairs. This may be a physical or mental disability. Although you will not need to go to court to have a representative payee appointed, you will need medical records of your disability.

Q. May I choose my representative payee before I become disabled?

A. No, since a government agency appoints a representative payee only when a disability exists, this option is not truly an advance directive. However, you may begin a representative payeeship on your own behalf. You also may choose your own payee. Since you do not have to be declared legally incompetent to have a representative payee, this alternative may help you avoid guardianship. It can protect your rights even if incapacity strikes.

Q. Do I need a lawyer to get a representative payee? Must I go to court first?

A. No, appointing a representative payee is informal and does not require a lawyer. It also does not need an appearance in court or any formal legal proceeding.

Q. I do not like the idea that someone else will be receiving my Social Security check. How may I be sure that they will not steal my money?

A. Supervising representative payees can be a problem. In principle, the representative payee must provide a detailed accounting to the agency paying the benefits. However, many exceptions exist. For example, spouses or institutional payees do not have to make such reports. Under some benefits programs, such as the VA, reporting requirements vary with the size of the benefit. There is not much you may do to protect yourself in such circumstances, except to plan for incapacity through other methods.

Q. If I regain my ability to control my own finances, may I dismiss a representative payee?

A. Yes, you may end a representative payeeship by showing that you have regained your capacity to manage your finances. There are several steps that you must follow. The first is to seek a doctor's certification that you are now able to manage your own financial affairs. You must then notify the government agency of your wish to dismiss the representative payee.

Because it is possible to end a representative payeeship, they are of great benefit to people whose disabilities result from illness or injuries from which they may recover.

Guardianship

Q. When should you seek a guardianship for someone who is no longer able to manage his or her own affairs?

A. People need a guardianship:

- If they need more protection than they may get from a durable power of attorney, or if no durable power of attorney has been authorized;
- If a living will is not applicable or does not exist; and
- If a representative payee is not possible or does not cover all the people's needs.

A *guardian* or *conservator* manages a person's financial affairs. The guardian or conservator also may make decisions about personal care.

Q. Is a guardianship a legal status, and does it take away rights?

A. Appointing a guardian requires a court procedure. It may cause you to lose many rights that you now enjoy. You may lose the right to marry, the right to vote, the right to hold a driver's license, and the right to make a will. Because of this, a guardianship usually is a last resort.

Q. What exactly is a guardian?

A. A guardian is a surrogate (substitute) decision-maker. A court of law chooses a guardian to make decisions for someone

(continued)

married or have no children. If there is no one who can serve as your representative payee, a public or nonprofit agency, such as a social-service organization, may serve on your behalf. A government agency also may appoint private agencies, but with less priority. In some areas, volunteer representative payee programs offer an alternative.

The Veterans Administration has a somewhat different set of priorities. Consult with the agency providing your benefits to find out who would be most appropriate.

Who Needs a Guardian?

Two basic types of people need guardians. They are people (1) who are incapable of making reasonable decisions for their financial affairs or personal care and (2) for whom less restrictive alternatives will not work. People with a physical or sensory handicap do not need guardians because of this fact alone. Nor do older people need guardians simply because of their advanced age.

A guardianship should relate to a serious inability to make decisions. It should not depend on preconceived (stereotypical) notions of old age, mental illness, or handicaps. In addition, it is always important to recognize a person's right to make foolish or risky decisions. These decisions by themselves do not mean that the person has a decision-making incapacity.

whom a court finds to be incompetent. A guardian may be responsible for someone's financial affairs, personal affairs, or both. The powers of a guardian may be very broad—in fact, they may be unrestricted—or they may be limited to certain areas of life.

Every state has laws regulating guardianships, although the language and procedures may vary. For example, some states use the term "conservator" to refer to someone appointed to manage another's financial affairs. On the other hand, a "guardian of the person" is responsible for the *personal* care and well-being of the incapacitated person. States often refer to the person who has a guardian as a "ward." The state also may refer to that person as "incompetent," "incapacitated," or "disabled."

Q. Who appoints a guardian?

A. A court of law appoints a guardian, after hearing evidence of a person's inability to make decisions. One important item of evidence is a doctor's report describing the incompetency.

In most states, the law specifies some form of due-process procedures. These try to protect a person from unfairly being declared incompetent. The procedures include notifying the allegedly incompetent person of the guardianship hearing. They also may involve making sure the person is at the hearing and appointing a lawyer to represent the person. However, the courts may not follow these procedures as strictly as they should.

Although guardianships take away many rights, they are sometimes necessary. You may not name a guardian for yourself *before* you need one. However, you may make your wishes known, in writing, and request that the court consider them. Again, let those who are close to you know your wishes in advance.

Obtaining a guardian for an incapacitated person is somewhat complex. The questions below should help you understand the procedure.

Q. How do I know if a person really cannot make decisions or is just acting foolishly?

A. You cannot tell by yourself. Have the person examined by a doctor or psychologist experienced in determining competency. The specialist should do a thorough examination to determine the person's physical and mental health. A person's decision-making may be impaired because of a physical cause that can be corrected.

Most states require a medical report that shows the person's incapacity. Check with a lawyer to see what your state specifies.

Q. If my elderly mother has a disability, how do I go about seeing that the court appoints a guardian?

A. It requires a court hearing. You probably will need a lawyer.

Generally a *petition* for guardianship must be filed and certain legal steps must be followed before the court may appoint a guardian. Usually the person who may need a guardian (in this case, your mother) receives a notice of the hearing. The court also must notify your mother of her rights. In many states, the court appoints an investigator to interview her and make a report to the court. This person is called a *guardian ad litem* or a *court investigator*.

At the hearing, a judge will review the petition, the court investigator's report, and the medical report. The judge also may ask the person filing the petition why the other person needs a guardian. In addition, the judge may want to ask the allegedly incompetent person some questions. The judge uses all this information to decide whether that person needs a guardian, and if so, who the guardian should be.

Unfortunately, there are still a large number of differences from one state to another. Consult a lawyer about your state's requirements.

Q. Is it hard to get a guardian appointed?

A. No, while it is time-consuming and often costly, it is not difficult to have a guardian appointed. In fact, courts grant most petitions for guardianships.

Q. What if someone thinks I need a guardian, and I do not want one?

A. Every state gives the allegedly incompetent person a chance to fight the petition for guardianship. If you do not think you need a guardian, you must inform the court of your desire to fight the guardianship. Usually you do this by appearing in court on the day of the hearing.

It is best to get your own lawyer to represent you at the hearing. If you cannot afford one, most states will have the court appoint one at the state's expense. If you cannot get to court, you may inform the court in writing of your wish to fight the petition. You should still hire a lawyer to represent you.

Q. This sounds very expensive. Who pays for a guardianship?

A. It can be expensive. The court charges fees for filing and court costs and for serving notice. Lawyer fees also can be

Who May Be a Guardian?

Laws vary from one state to another. In most states, the courts may appoint almost anyone as your guardian if the person meets legal requirements. Usually the court appoints the person filing the petition as the guardian. Most courts like to appoint a relative. They believe that family members will act in the best interests of the ward and know the ward best. However, the courts may appoint a friend or attorney, especially if no family members are available. The courts also may appoint multiple guardians, either with shared responsibilities or with responsibilities split between them. As a last resort, many states permit guardianships by a public or private agency.

high. If the court appoints a guardian of the estate, the estate often pays the guardian's fees. If there is no estate, the person filing the petition may have to pay for the costs of filing and serving notice. Poor people filing a petition sometimes can get legal help through legal-aid clinics or pro bono (free of charge) work by lawyers. As noted above, allegedly incompetent persons sometimes may get legal representation at the state's expense.

Q. May I specify who I want as my guardian?

A. Yes, but the court does not have an obligation to appoint this person. It is better if you write out your wishes in advance. You should do this as part of your general planning for incapacity. Sometimes the judge will ask incompetent people whom they would like as their guardian. However, the judge does not have to do so.

Q. May the court remove guardians?

A. Yes, but wards must prove that they are now competent to handle their own affairs. The court refers to the process for revoking a guardianship as a *restoration*. The ward begins this process through a lawyer or a written request to the judge.

It can be hard to have a guardian removed. Therefore, if someone's incapacity may be temporary, try some other form of protection before getting a guardianship. However, if no advance directives exist, it may be difficult to find an alternative.

A court also may remove a guardian who is not properly carrying out his or her responsibilities.

Q. What if I believe my elderly relative needs some help with her affairs. She is not totally incompetent. May a guardianship meet her needs?

A. In some states, you may appoint a guardian with only partial powers. The usual term for this is a *limited* guardianship. The legal requirements for a limited guardianship vary from one state to another.

All states, however, try to ensure that a guardianship is the "least restrictive" alternative. This means that the guardianship restricts the ward as little as possible, letting the ward do whatever the disability allows.

Suppose your relative can no longer manage her large estate, but she can handle her daily finances. The guardianship should let her keep control over everyday expenses. Or, let us say your relative needs a substitute decision-maker to place her in a nursing home. If she can say what type of nursing home she wants to live in, the decision-maker should honor those wishes.

Even when a limited guardianship is not feasible, the guardian may involve the ward in making decisions whenever possible.

Protecting Older Americans from Abuse and Exploitation

Q. What is elder abuse?

A. *Elder abuse* occurs when somebody neglects or abuses older people. The abuse can be physical or mental. Definitions of elder abuse differ from one state to another. Generally they include:

- *Physical abuse,* such as hitting, slapping, and shoving;
- *Sexual abuse,* including fondling, sexual intercourse, and forced intimate contact of almost any sort;
- *Verbal* and *psychological abuse,* such as screaming at the older person, calling the person names, and threatening the person;
- *Neglect,* which includes withholding food, shelter, medical care, medication, and other necessities from the older person; and
- *Restraint,* such as keeping the person locked up.

Also included in most states is *financial exploitation.* This can range from outright theft of funds from an older person to misuse of the older person's money. Cashing an older person's Social Security check and not using the funds for the person's care is one example. Many states also would consider misusing credit cards and joint funds as financial exploitation.

Recognizing the severity of this problem, every state now has specific elder abuse laws. You can get details on elder abuse laws and programs from your local area agency on aging or state unit on aging.

Q. Is elder abuse just a problem for very frail old people who live in nursing homes?

A. No, elder abuse is a real problem for many older people. Some victims of elder abuse are very frail and are unable to seek help on their own. However, many elder abuse victims are active older adults who cannot find a solution to this difficult problem.

Elder abuse can be a problem for both the rich and the poor. It does not strike only one race, social class, or economic standing.

Q. My son shares my apartment with me. Sometimes, when I forget things or get confused, he loses his temper, pushes me, and threatens to put me in a nursing home. Is this abuse?

A. Yes, that is elder abuse. Many types of elder abuse occur within the home. Even if the abuse only happens from time to time, it is still abuse. Seek help from your local unit on aging.

Q. My neighbor across the way is very old and sick. She depends on her daughter for shopping, cooking, and cleaning. However, her daughter often leaves the older woman without food and clean clothes. Is there anything I may do to help?

A. Yes, you may report this neglect to your local elder abuse reporting agency. This may be your state unit on aging (such as a department on aging or a human services department) or your local area agency on aging. You also may report the problem to a senior citizens' service agency.

You should not worry about being sued for making the report. Most states protect reporters acting in good faith. You may even make an anonymous report.

Spousal Abuse

Suppose your spouse often hits you and pushes you around. You are both over 65, and it is harder for you to run away from him or her. Is there anything you may do, especially after all these years?

You do not have to live with abuse, no matter what your age. Physical abuse is against the law, no matter whom it involves. It is no more legal for your spouse to hit you than for a stranger.

(continued)

Q. My son is using all my money to buy illegal drugs. He is also running up large charges on my credit cards. (His name is on my credit-card accounts and my bank accounts.) Since he is a co-owner of my home, I am afraid he will mortgage it or possibly even sell it to get more money. What may I do?

A. Even if your son has the legal right to access your funds, you may protect yourself from this type of financial exploitation. Go to the bank and ask a banker to help you transfer funds to new accounts that your son may not access. Write all your credit-card companies and ask them to remove your son's name from your accounts. Have them issue new credit cards to you.

Contact a lawyer to see what you must do to protect your home. If you cannot afford a lawyer, a legal-aid clinic may provide advice.

Finally, seek help for yourself and for your son from a local social-service agency. Many of them have experience in dealing with family difficulties of this sort. Do not allow your son's problems to overtake your own well-being and financial security.

Q. My son and daughter-in-law live with me in my home. They are living rent-free and give me no money for

household bills or food. I feel like they are taking advantage of me. Can someone help me?

A. You should not feel ashamed because your son and daughter-in-law are taking advantage of you. Nor should you feel obligated to give them all this help. Over 75 percent of all abusers are family members. The situation you describe is very common.

You may seek help from an elder abuse program operating in your area. They may provide counseling and other assistance to help you work out the problem.

LEGAL ASSISTANCE FOR OLDER PERSONS

Most of the time you would prefer to resolve disputes and manage affairs on your own. Sometimes, however, you will need expert help to protect your interests. Many older people already have lawyers who have helped them with legal issues in the past. Others will need to work with a lawyer for the first time. Still others will need help from a lawyer who is an expert about Social Security or age discrimination. The following section discusses problems unique to elderly people. For further information, read the first chapter, "When and How to Use a Lawyer."

Q. My 45-year-old son and I are co-owners of a condominium. We have had a falling out over some life-style issues. Do I need a lawyer to get me out of the joint ownership? How can my son and I resolve our differences?

A. You could hire a lawyer to help you dissolve the joint ownership of your condominium. However, there may be some other ways to resolve your difficulties.

Sometimes, problems that seem to be "legal" may be solved through other means. Many groups or individuals can help you handle personal problems. A psychotherapist or a social worker can suggest ways of dealing with your family problems. Some of these professionals now specialize in counseling for the elderly. You also can request such help from a social-service agency in your area. Your local area agency on aging can provide information on counseling.

Mediation is another possible means of resolving your dispute. It may be available through your local court or through a private mediator. Your local bar association also may be able to make a referral. For further information on mediation and other forms of alternative dispute resolution, see the first and second chapters in this publication.

(continued)

Fortunately, more and more police departments and courts are sensitive to domestic violence and are willing to help victims. If your spouse strikes you, call the police and file a complaint. You also may ask the police to help you find a domestic violence shelter. You may stay there if you wish to leave your abusive home. If you do not want to leave your home, you may seek an order of protection through the courts. With such an order, you may have your spouse removed from the home, even though he or she may be the owner. Find out what you can do by contacting a domestic violence assistance center or your area agency on aging.

Q. I am a retired electrician who continues to do small jobs for friends. I did some work for someone, but he refused to pay. I do not want to hire a lawyer to sue him, since the bill is only $200. Do I have any options?

A. Most states have special courts for small disputes. In "small claims" or "pro se" court, you can represent yourself, as long as your claim is under a certain dollar amount. Contact your local clerk of the court for more information.

Q. Are there any legal services that serve just older people?

A. Yes, older adults benefit from a wide variety of legal services programs offered through the Older Americans Act. There are also private sources such as bar association programs for the elderly and *pro bono* legal agencies with a special emphasis on the elderly. (Pro bono agencies operate for the good of the public and do not make a profit.)

Q. Do I need to be poor to get these legal services?

A. Some programs may be limited to people with low incomes. However, services offered through the Older Americans Act do *not* have income requirements.

You can find out more about legal services for the elderly by contacting your area agency on aging. Or you could try your local bar association or nearby law school legal clinics.

Q. I would like to speak with a lawyer about my estate. However, I am no longer able to leave my home. Are there legal services available to me?

A. Yes, if you are homebound, you can contact your local area agency on aging. If you live in a nursing home, you should speak with the nursing home ombudsman.

WHERE TO GET MORE INFORMATION

General Resources

For most older people, their main resource is their area agency on aging. It can supply details and referrals on many

Services Funded by the Older Americans Act

Funds from the Older Americans Act support a wide variety of legal services. These include help in writing wills for simple estates. Such services also offer help in preparing living wills and durable powers of attorney (discussed earlier in this chapter). Legal-aid programs for the elderly can help you get benefits from the Social Security Administration, including Medicare and Medicaid. They also will help you file claims and settle disputes with other public programs run by states and municipalities.

(continued)

topics. If you cannot find your local area agency on aging, contact your state agency on aging. Its address and phone number appear in the state government section of your telephone directory. Ask for a referral to your local area office.

Some municipalities and townships also have their own departments or commissions on aging. Look in the phone book or call your city or municipal general information number.

For more details on area agencies on aging, call (202) 484-7520, or write to:

National Association of Area Agencies on Aging
600 Maryland Avenue, S.W., Suite 208W
Washington, D.C. 20024

For information on state agencies on aging, call (202) 785-0707, or write to:

National Association of State Units on Aging
2033 K Street, N.W., Suite 304
Washington, D.C. 20006

Many associations promote the interests of older adults. The best known—and the largest—is the American Association of Retired Persons (AARP). You can join if you are over age 50. AARP has regional and local groups nationwide. Look in the telephone directory for the nearest group. Or to find one in your area, call (202) 872-4700, or write to:

American Association of Retired Persons
1909 K Street, N.W.
Washington, D.C. 20049

Other associations also promote the interests of older persons. They also provide information and education to senior citizens. These include:

National Council on the Aging
600 Maryland Avenue, S.W.
West Wing 100
Washington, D.C. 20024
(202) 479-1200

Older Women's League
730 11th Street, N.W., Suite 300
Washington, D.C. 20001
(202) 783-6686

National Council of Senior Citizens
925 15th Street, N.W.
Washington, D.C. 20005
(202) 347-8800

(continued)

The kinds of services offered vary from one area agency to another, as does the amount of help provided.

Most legal services programs for the elderly do not offer help in criminal matters or with civil suits. If you need this type of help you should contact your public defender's office, your state's attorney, or a pro bono service. In addition, legal services programs for the elderly also may not be able to represent you in guardianship proceedings.

Legal Aid for Elderly Persons

For information on the legal concerns of the elderly, besides the above resources, you also can contact your state or local bar association. Many bar associations publish handbooks on the legal rights of the elderly. In addition, you can obtain other information from:

American Bar Association
Commission on Legal Problems of the Elderly
1800 M Street, N.W., Suite 200
Washington, D.C. 20036
(202) 331-2297

National Senior Citizens Law Center
2025 M Street, N.W., Suite 400
Washington, D.C. 20036
(202) 887-5280

General Publications

Many booklets and pamphlets are available. Your area agency on aging, AARP, and the federal government offer many of them. For example, the Social Security Administration publishes many booklets on Social Security, Disability Insurance, SSI, and Medicare. You can obtain these from your local Social Security office. The Social Security Administration publications office also offers these booklets. For further information on these and other publications, call (800) 234-5772.

Credit

Many federal agencies enforce the Equal Credit Opportunity Act. However, you generally can direct questions to the Federal Trade Commission (FTC). To find out how to contact the FTC, see "Where to Get More Information" at the end of the "Consumer Credit" chapter.

Consumer Issues

The *Consumer's Resource Handbook* can help you locate the proper source of help for many different consumer problems.

t includes a directory of federal agencies. The handbook is .vailable free of charge from the Consumer Information Center-N, P.O. Box 100, Pueblo, Colorado 81002.

Also available from the Consumer Information Center is *'afety for Older Consumers.* This is an extensive checklist for inding and correcting fire and accident hazards around the .ome. It emphasizes the needs of the elderly. 29 pages. (1985) 'ublication 437W. 50 cents.

Education and Training

A wide variety of local and state agencies might be able to rovide details on educational and training programs for the lderly. For information about federal programs, you can direct uestions to the U.S. Department of Education. Or you also an contact the specific government agency, such as the U.S. Department of Labor, that provides funding for the particular rogram in which you are interested.

Elder Abuse

Elder abuse programs exist in many areas. For details, ontact your local area agency on aging or your state unit on ging. If you need immediate help, call the police. They have the ower to step in and investigate immediately. They also may have special senior citizen's unit.

Adult Protective Services: Programs in State Social Service gencies and State Units on Aging is a book that describes ate and national programs to fight the problem of elder abuse. is available from the National Association of State Units on .ging (NASUA) or the American Public Welfare Association APWA). For information on the book's cost and availability, ill or write NASUA at 2033 K Street, N.W., Suite 304, 'ashington, D.C. 20006, telephone (202) 785-0707 or APWA at 10 First Street, N.E., Suite 500, Washington, D.C. 20002, lephone (202) 682-0100.

Employment

You should direct questions regarding discrimination in the orkplace to a local office of the Equal Employment pportunity Commission (EEOC). Look in the "U.S. overnment" section of the telephone directory for a listing. If there is no local office near you, or if you want more details, call (202) 663-4900, or write to:

Equal Employment Opportunity Commission
1801 L Street, N.W., Room 9024
Washington, D.C. 20507

Other Rights Covered by the Age Discrimination Act

In general, you should direct questions about the Age Discrimination Act to the Office of Civil Rights in the Department of Health and Human Services. You can call the office at (202) 245-6671, or write to:

DHHS/Office of Civil Rights
Policy and Special Projects Staff
330 Independence Avenue, S.W.
Washington, D.C. 20201

Housing

The American Association of Homes for the Aging (AAHA) offers information on retirement housing. You can call (202) 296-5960, or write to:

American Association of Homes for the Aging
1129 20th Street, N.W., Suite 400
Washington, D.C. 20036

The American Association of Retired Persons (AARP) offers an excellent handbook called *Housing Options for Older Americans* (stock number D12063). For those considering a move to a long-term care facility, AARP also publishes *The Right Place at the Right Time: A Guide to Long-Term Care Choices* (stock number D12381). The telephone number and address for AARP's national headquarters are listed above.

For older Americans who remain in their home, AARP has another handy guide. *Home-Made Money: A Consumer's Guide to Home Equity Conversions* discusses how to benefit from the equity you have built up in your home. Order it from AARP Fulfillment, Home-Made Money, Department BHG, at the AARP national headquarters.

You can direct some housing questions to your local office of the U.S. Department of Housing and Urban Development (HUD). The national office of HUD offers information on problems unique to the elderly. For details on developing housing for the elderly, call (202) 755-5866, or write to:

Elderly Assisted Housing
Department of Housing and Urban Development
451 7th Street, S.W.
Washington, D.C. 20410

Another HUD office offers further help with housing problems of the elderly. For details, call (202) 755-5730, or write to:

Director, Office of Multifamily Housing Management
Department of Housing and Urban Development
451 7th Street, S.W.
Washington, D.C. 20410

Also contact your local (city or county) housing office for more information, since zoning and local ordinances vary widely.

Insurance

Your basic resources on insurance are your state's insurance ffice and a trusted insurance agent or lawyer.

Legal Assistance

You can get details on legal aid from various sources. Your rea agency on aging should be able to tell you about legal ervices funded by the Older Americans Act. Local or state bar ssociations can direct you to legal aid and pro bono services. ome bar associations also operate lawyer referral services. In ldition, a list of legal services providers is maintained by the merican Bar Association's Commission on Legal Problems of ie Elderly.

Living Wills

The Society for the Right to Die offers free living wills atching the legal requirements of each of the 41 states (and e District of Columbia) that have statutes on living wills. It fers free copies of its standard living will form for the nine states ithout laws on the subject. The Society includes instructions. urable power of attorney forms, where appropriate, are also available. Contact the Society at 250 West 57th Street, Suite 323, New York, New York 10107; telephone (212) 246-6973.

Pensions

One source of facts about pensions, particularly as the Employee Retirement Income Security Act (ERISA) affects them, is the Department of Labor (DOL). The DOL can provide a wide variety of literature and information on ERISA. For assistance, call (202) 523-8784, or write to:

Pension and Welfare Benefits Administration
U.S. Department of Labor
Division of Technical Assistance and Inquiries
Room N5658
200 Constitution Avenue, N.W.
Washington, D.C. 20210

Another resource is the Pension Rights Center. It is a public interest group that protects the pension rights of workers, retirees, and their families. To contact the center, call (202) 296-3776, or write to:

Pension Rights Center
918 16th Street, N.W., Suite 704
Washington, D.C. 20006

Powers of Attorney

AARP and the ABA's Commission on Legal Problems of the Elderly offer a booklet on health-care powers of attorney. Single copies are free. To order, write to:

AARP Fulfillment
(Stock Number D13895)
1909 K Street, N.W.
Washington, D.C. 20049

Retirement

Your area agency on aging should be able to refer you to local resources that will help you plan for retirement. The agency also should have free booklets on retirement-related subjects. Subjec

Bibliography SB-285, *Retirement,* is a listing of federal publications on retirement. For details, call (202) 783-3238, or write to:

Superintendent of Documents
U.S. Government Printing Office
Washington, D.C. 20402

Tax Benefits

The IRS is an excellent source of information on tax questions. The IRS's tele-tax service has recorded tax information on 140 topics. You can find the toll-free 800 number for your state by calling the IRS office in your area. Topics of interest to older persons include pensions and annuities, power of attorney information, lump-sum distributions, and Social Security and equivalent railroad retirement benefits.

In addition, IRS representatives are available to help you with your tax questions. Consult your local IRS office to find out about assistance by phone, by mail, or in person.

The IRS also publishes a number of free pamphlets dealing with common tax questions. They are available from your local IRS office. The basic Internal Revenue Service (IRS) publication for older Americans is Publication 554, *Tax Information for Older Americans.*

Other pamphlets of interest to older Americans include:

Self-Employed Retirement Plans (Publication 560)
Pensions and Annuity Income (Publication 575)
Individual Retirement Arrangements (IRAs) (Publication 590)
Pension General Rules (Publication 939)
Social Security Benefits and Equivalent Railroad Retirement Benefits (Publication 915)
Credit for the Elderly or the Disabled (Publication 524)
Tax Information for Handicapped and Disabled Individuals (Publication 907)

WILLS, TRUSTS, AND ESTATE PLANNING

INTRODUCTION

The term "estate planning" is a delicate way of saying "planning for your death." We all are a little squeamish about death, especially when we are the ones involved. This fear probably accounts for the fact that only around one out of every three Americans has a will. Yet it is time to take a deep breath and think about these matters. You should ignore your nervousness and start planning. If you do not, it may cause your friends, loved ones, and business associates a lot more grief when you die, in addition to what they will already be feeling about your death.

Important as planning for your death is, it is only half of estate planning. Your estate planning should cover the "now"—your present responsibilities. It also should include the "hereafter—your desire to protect those who will be alive after you have died.

The most cost-effective method of estate planning involves making gifts while you are still alive. If you keep your gifts below a certain amount, no taxes will be paid on them. By doing this, you may decrease the size of your taxable estate. This may save large amounts of taxes after your death.

Planning does not "cost" you. Rather, it pays—in results achieved, in dollar savings, and, most important, in peace of mind

Q. What are some examples of estate planning?

A. Estate planning allows you to provide for transfers of your property to your spouse, children, and others in the way you want. It also may do other things for you and your family:

- In your will, you may choose a guardian for your minor children if you have survived the other parent. By carefully using a trust and appointing a trustee, you may eliminate the need for bonds and court supervision of each minor child's property.
- You may select an executor of your estate in your will, and waive the usual requirement for a bond. In most states, choosing an independent executor will eliminate the need for bonds and the expense of court supervision of the settlement of your estate.
- You may choose to acknowledge or provide in other ways for a child (such as a stepchild or godchild) in whom you have an interest.
- After death, you may want your body to be given to medical science or to undergo cremation. If so, drawing up the proper documents in advance will carry out your wish. Similarly, you may want to limit your burial expenses or choose where to have your body buried.
- If you are the custodian for the assets of a child or grandchild under the Uniform Gift (or Transfers) to Minors Act, you may draw up a document appointing someone to succeed you. This avoids the cost of a court appointment. (This Act, which has been adopted in various forms in all states, permits you to select a custodian to receive and hold property for minor children. The custodian normally turns the property over to them when they reach the age of majority. The Act avoids the necessity of a court-appointed guardian.)
- Good planning also may enlarge your financial support of religious, educational, and other charitable causes. This may be done, either during your lifetime or upon your death.
- Other forms of planning concern preparing for the time when you can no longer take care of yourself. A living will deals with the treatment you want—or do not want—in your final illness, and may help your doctor, clergyman, and family in times of medical crisis. A "durable" health-care power of attorney lets you authorize someone to act on your behalf when you can no longer manage your own affairs. ("The Rights of Older Americans" chapter covers planning for incapacity.)

Q. What is an "estate"?

A. Your *estate* includes all your property. It consists of real estate and tangible personal property (such as your car). It also includes intangible (abstract) property like bank accounts, stocks, and pension benefits.

Q. When should I begin to plan my estate and will?

A. The time for planning is *now*. Do it while you have a clear head and possess all your faculties. The "Wills" section on the next page will discuss this further.

Q. Who else plays a role in planning my estate?

A. Successful estate planning normally involves a lawyer. It also may require an accountant, insurance adviser, or banker.

Q. Do I need to see a lawyer about estate planning?

A. It generally is advantageous to see a lawyer. In recent years, several books and "will kits" have become available. They claim to allow you to make your own will, though their quality varies. For very simple estates, a well-done book might let you make your will without hiring a lawyer. Simple estates involve little money and other assets, and transfer everything to only a few people.

However, wills made without the help of a lawyer often result in problems that are expensive to resolve. And, it is not always easy for a layperson to determine whether a given book or kit is up-to-date and thorough. Also, probate laws vary from one state to another.

In addition, the simplest wills are not always the best. Suppose you want to leave everything to your spouse, and you write that in a simple one-sentence will. Even assuming you have followed the required formalities, what happens if your spouse dies before you? Your simple will did not account for that. Also, leaving everything to your spouse could cost your children thousands of dollars in avoidable estate taxes (taxes on the privilege of transferring property to others after a person's death). Furthermore, the results of a mistake make writing your own will too risky for all but the simplest estates. A mistake could have your will tied up in probate, challenged, or even struck down.

Moreover, making a will does not have to cost much. Some law firms and legal clinics use computers to offer standardized "form" wills. They can easily adapt the form wills to many people's needs. This reduces the will-maker's legal bills. Most states now offer simplified probate procedures for small estates, reducing costs further. Some lawyers will not charge for an initial consultation. At that first visit they can tell you whether your estate is simple enough for you to make your own will.

TRANSFERRING YOUR ESTATE TO OTHERS

You may not distribute all your estate through your will. A will may transfer only part of it, called your *probate estate*. That usually consists of the real and personal property that you own solely in your name or in your name as a tenant-in-common with others.

It usually does not include certain rights and benefits (like pensions and life insurance). These rights normally must be handled outside the will. (You may control some of them by using a trust.) Depending on the form of ownership, property that you co-own with someone else may become your co-owner's property at the moment of your death, so your will may not affect it.

WILLS

Q. What is a will?

A. A *will* is a legal declaration (statement) that disposes of your property when you die.

Q. What are the main reasons for making a will?

A. A will allows you to distribute your property at the time of your death. It lets you do so in any manner you choose, except for the portion that you must leave to your spouse (discussed in the "Family Law" chapter) or the *forced heirship law* of Louisiana. (A later section in this chapter will discuss Louisiana's forced heirship law.) A will also allows you to choose the person, called an *executor* in most states, who will carry out the administration of your estate.

Q. Who may make a will?

A. Generally, any person of sound mind and memory, 18 years old or over, may make a will. Some states make exceptions to the age limit for military personnel. There also are exceptions for *emancipated* minors. These are minors who are married or who live away from home and support themselves.

Q. Do I need a will?

A. You may, especially if you have children, own a home or other property, or want to transfer your assets in ways that require a will. Even if you want to leave your property to the same people who would inherit it if you left no will, making a will should simplify administering your estate. That will save your family and friends a lot of time, trouble, and money.

Q. May I use a will to dispose of my property in any way I want?

A. In general, yes, you may do so. You may select the people to whom you want to leave your property. You also may leave them as much or as little property as you want. There are a few exceptions. For example, a surviving spouse may have the right to take a fixed share of the estate regardless of the will. Likewise, a will that makes no reference to one or more of your children may be void insofar as it applies to that child or those children under some states' *pretermitted*

DO YOU HAVE A WILL?

Everybody has heard about wills. However, most of us—70 percent, according to one estimate—do not have one. This section answers some common questions about wills. The law in this area varies according to the state you live in or the location of your property. Not all the details here will necessarily apply to your state. That is another reason to see a lawyer when planning your estate.

(unintentionally omitted) children statutes (discussed later in this chapter). Also, most states dislike conditions in wills that are bizarre, illegal, or against public policy.

Q. What does a will not cover?

A. Your will cannot cover properties that pass outside your probate estate. Examples are joint property (property you co-own with someone else, like a joint bank account) and life insurance that gets paid to a beneficiary (the person who will receive the money). Other examples include employee death benefits and other benefits similarly created by a contract.

Q. Will property in my name go to my heirs if I do not have a will?

A. It depends. Every state has laws that determine how to divide the probate estate of a person who dies with no will. These are the *laws of intestacy* or *descent and distribution laws.* However, other laws often determine how your property transfers after you die. (See the article on the next page.)

Uses of a Will

You may use a will to:

- **Dispose of property;**
- **Choose as the will's executor someone you have confidence in;**
- **Establish a trust to protect assets and save taxes;**
- **Give the executor and trustee power to spend income to meet the changing needs of children and other relatives; and**
- **Select someone to be the guardian of minor children.**

Q. Won't it cost me money to get a will drawn up? Is the cost of administering an estate greater with or without a will?

A. A skillfully drawn will reduces expenses by giving the executor the authority to act efficiently without unnecessary delay and expense. It may eliminate the need for a *surety bond* (a bond purchased at the expense of your estate to insure your executor's proper performance), thus saving the estate considerable expense. (Often a surety bond is called a *fidelity bond,* since its purpose is to protect the estate and its beneficiaries from misappropriation or misapplication of funds by the executor.) In many states, your will may direct that the involvement of the probate court can be kept to a minimum. If the will is *self-proved,* it may be possible to avoid a court hearing for its proof at which witnesses must testify. The *proof of will* is normally executed at the same time the testator (person making the will) signs the will. The witnesses generally need to have no further involvement in the matter. (A later section in this chapter discusses self-proved wills.)

Q. How does a will affect life insurance?

A. If a life insurance policy is payable to a beneficiary, the will of the insured does not affect the proceeds. However, the will may say who pays certain taxes on the proceeds. If the life insurance policy is payable to your estate, you may dispose of the proceeds in the will, like any other kind of property.

Q. My spouse already has a will. Do I need one too?

A. Yes, it is important that both spouses make separate wills.

Q. What if people do not want the gifts I leave them in my will?

A. Because of taxes or other reasons, sometimes the people who receive gifts *(bequests)* in a will do not want them. For example, if your son is bankrupt when you die, the law may entitle his creditors to be the first ones to access the money you leave him. He might want to give up the gift so that it will go to his sister, not his creditors.

Most states permit your heirs or other beneficiaries to *disclaim* (refuse) the inheritance or benefit. The Internal Revenue Code describes how a beneficiary may disclaim an interest in an estate for federal gift-tax and estate-tax purposes. Each state's law also defines how to disclaim for purposes of state inheritance taxes (which are state taxes on property that an heir or beneficiary under a will receives from a deceased person's estate).

Q. May a will help save taxes?

A. Yes. For example, if you set up a trust for the surviving spouse, you may minimize or eliminate taxes when the surviving spouse dies.

Q. When should I make my will?

A. You should do so while you are in good health and free from emotional stress. A will that someone hastily plans and drafts under pressure seldom does credit either to the maker or the planner. "Deathbed" wills often cause long lawsuits.

Writing and Maintaining Your Will

Q. I am going to my lawyer next week to write a will. What should I do before I go?

A. Planning for the visit can save you time and legal bills. Before going, find and organize all documents that show where your

Property That Passes Outside the Estate

Certain classes of property may pass outside the probate estate, because of other state laws or by contract. Examples include:

- **The portion of the community property owned by the surviving spouse;**
- **Property of any kind owned jointly with others with a right of survivorship;**
- **Property subject to a trust created by you during your lifetime;**
- **Annuities (regular payments) and other retirement benefits payable to beneficiaries other than your estate; and**
- **Life insurance proceeds paid to a named beneficiary.**

money and property is, what you spent on it, and who else owns it with you. This includes bank statements, insurance papers, employment benefit papers, deeds, business records, and tax records. Bring these documents with you.

You also should make two lists. First list what you have (property, money, and the like) and what your debts are. Then list where you want your property to go when you are dead. Include typewritten names and current addresses of anyone mentioned in your will or other estate documents.

Q. When do I need witnesses while writing my will?

A. All states require at least two witnesses to prove that a will is valid. In some states, the witnesses must testify in court. However, a growing number of states permit *self-proved wills.* These must be formally executed, with the signatures notarized and a self-proving *affidavit* (written statement of facts) attached. If you follow these requirements, the will may be admitted to probate without the testimony of witnesses or other proof.

MARRIAGE, DIVORCE, AND WILLS

In some states, a marriage revokes (cancels) a will. However, that does not happen *if* the will states that you made it with a specific marriage in mind and that the marriage shall not revoke it. In many states, divorce or dissolution of marriage revokes the provisions that benefit or involve the former spouse. This depends on your state's law.

Q. Who should be my witnesses?

A. They should be adults who have no potential conflict of interest. They should *not* be people who receive any gifts under the will or who might benefit from your death.

You do not need to bring witnesses with you to your lawyer's office. The lawyer and one or two of the lawyer's office employees usually will witness the signing.

Q. Where should I keep my will?

A. You should store it in a safe place. Examples include a safe deposit box, your lawyer's office, or your bank. Most jurisdictions permit you to keep the will at the probate court for a nominal fee. If you do store it in a safe deposit box, make sure someone else (certainly the executor) knows where it is and can obtain the will when you die. Sometimes the bank lacks permission to let anyone besides the deceased open the safe deposit box. Some state laws make it difficult to access the box after you have died. In those states, the will should not be kept in a safe deposit box.

Q. When does a will become effective?

A. A will takes effect only when two things happen. First, the will-maker (testator) must die. Second, the proper court (usually called a *probate court*) must accept the will as valid

Q. What if I write a will and change my mind? May I alter my will later?

A. Yes, you may change the provisions by writing an amendment (called a *codicil*) or by revoking the old will and writing a new one. However, you should not try to change the will by writing on or crossing out on the one you already signed. You must be mentally competent to make a codicil or revoke a will and make a new one.

In some states, there is another way of making parts of your will easily changeable. This can be important if your assets change often. It is called a *tangible personal property memorandum*, which will be discussed in detail after the following question.

Q. May I revoke my will?

A. Yes, you may make a new will revoking the old one. Or you may simply make a formal statement of revocation. Some states even permit oral revocations or revocations in which the will-maker destroys the will. However, many complex legal issues exist in this area. It is best to make a formal, written, and dated statement of revocation.

If you write a new will, include the date you sign and execute it. Also add a sentence stating that the new will revokes all previous wills. Otherwise, the court is likely to rule that the new will revokes the old one only where the two conflict. This could cause problems. When you execute the new will, it is a good idea to keep the old one in your files or leave it with your lawyer. Mark it "revoked, superseded by will dated _____." This provides a record in case any questions arise.

Q. How can a tangible personal property memorandum make it easier to change my will?

A. A *tangible personal property memorandum* (TPPM) is a separate handwritten document that you incorporate into the will "by reference." (This means that the will says something like "This will incorporates the provisions of a separate tangible personal property memorandum." Then the law regards the TPPM as part of the will.) The TPPM lists the date and the tangible personal property. Such property includes jewelry, artwork, and furniture. The TPPM also lists the people to whom you want the tangible personal property to go.

Most states recognize the validity of a TPPM. In states that do not recognize a TPPM, the executor usually will try to comply as closely as possible with your desires, as indicated by the TPPM.

Who Should Draft a Will?

Generally, a will must be written and witnessed in a special manner provided by law. Drafting a will usually requires learning, skill, and experience. The law does not require that only lawyers draft wills. However, it usually is a good idea to hire a lawyer to do your will. The complexities of many wills, and the many tax considerations involved, can make a lawyer's skill invaluable.

BASIC ELEMENTS OF A WILL

Wills do not have to follow a specific form. However, certain elements must be present to make a valid will. For example, it must show your intent to make the document your final word on what happens to your property. It other words, it must say that you really intend it to be a will and to revoke your prior wills.

With a few exceptions, the basic requirements for a valid will in all states are that:

- **The person making it (the *testator* or *testatrix,* if the person is female) must be of legal age;**
- **That person must be of sound mind;**
- **The will must follow certain formalities (that vary from one state to another);**
- **The will must be written;**
- **The testator must sign the will;**

(continued)

Q. When should I change my will?

A. It is a good idea to review your will every three to five years and update it as necessary. You should change your will to account for major changes in your life or financial situation. Examples are buying a new house, remarriage, moving to another state, a large increase (or decrease) in income, the birth of children, and the death of relatives. A well-drafted will makes provisions for these kinds of changes in your life. A TPPM makes it easier to make the changes.

Q. Are there other changes that affect a will?

A. Yes, you also have to watch out for *ademption.* This is what happens if you will something (say, your cats) to someone, but by the time you die, you no longer own any cats. Then the gift would fail completely. The beneficiary would not be entitled to, for instance, your parakeets. (A good will avoids this by using language like, "I give my dog, Spot, to my mother-in-law. However, if I do not own a dog, I give her any pet I do own at the time of my death.")

Types of Wills

Wills can be simple or complex. They can be used to achieve the wide range of family and tax objectives described in this chapter.

If a will provides for the outright distribution of assets, people usually call it a *simple will.* If the will sets up one or more trusts, it is a *testamentary trust will.* If it leaves some of the assets in a trust established before death, it is a *pour-over will.*

Unlike outright distribution, setting up a trust may ensure property management and minimize taxes. Certain pour-over and testamentary trust wills may protect surviving family members from creditors and from losing inherited property if the family member is later involved in a divorce.

Q. What is a holographic will?

A. A will that is entirely in the will-maker's own handwriting is a *holographic will.* About 20 states recognize the validity of such wills. However, sometimes it is hard to prove that the writer intended such a document to be a will. It also may be difficult to prove that the person wrote it at a certain time, and that it really was the statement of the person who supposedly wrote it. Therefore, holographic wills are not recommended to replace formally executed wills.

Q. What is an oral will?

A. *Oral wills* are wills that the maker spoke, but did not write down. Some states allow oral wills. However, they do so only in very limited circumstances. One example occurs when dying people, in their last illness, utter oral wills. Such wills (also called *nuncupative wills*) often are valid only to dispose of personal property.

Q. What is a joint will?

A. A *joint will* is one document that covers both a husband and wife (or any two people). These often are a big mistake, because they sometimes fail to distinguish the separate property of each individual will-maker. A joint will also can limit each spouse's ability to change his or her will after the death of one of them. This leaves the survivor with the risk of a lawsuit if he or she later makes a separate will benefiting persons other than those benefited by the joint will. And there can be adverse estate-tax consequences through the possible loss of the marital deduction.

Your Will and Your Children and Grandchildren

Q. What happens if I make a will, have another child, and then die before I can change my will to include that child?

A. It depends on the law of your state. Most states provide for a share of your property to go to such *pretermitted* (unintentionally omitted) children, unless your will expressly states that you have intentionally made no specific provision in your will for any offspring of yours who may later be born or adopted. This would often be the case if your will establishes or pours over to a family trust.

Q. What if I will some property to one of my children, but that child dies before I do?

A. A will may not make a gift to a dead person (although it may provide for the gift to go to the dead person's estate). Generally, if a beneficiary dies before you, the gift *lapses* (fails). It goes back into your estate.

However, many states have *anti-lapse* laws. These permit a gift to certain beneficiaries who die before you to pass on to those persons' descendants (children or grandchildren), unless the will expressly directs otherwise. Most states' anti-lapse laws apply only to certain beneficiaries. This very

(continued)

- **At least two disinterested (impartial) people who are competent to testify in court must be personally present at the signing of the will and then, in the presence of the testator and each other, sign the will as witnesses;**
- **The will must be properly *executed*. This means the will must state that the document is yours and that you signed it before witnesses, who then also signed it. In addition, this statement, which usually appears at the end of the will, must state the date and place of signing. There is only *one* fully executed will. Copies should *not* be signed, since no one will then know which is your last will.**

limited class of beneficiaries typically involves only surviving descendants. For example, the law might avoid a lapse only for direct descendants, not nephews or relatives by marriage. It is important to know your state's law in this area.

Things may be different if your will does not set out the gifts by name, but instead makes them to a class. For example, it might say, "I leave all my property in equal amounts to my children." Suppose you had three children when you made the will, and one dies before you do. Then the remaining two children will inherit one half, not one third, of your estate, even if the deceased child left children.

Q. Does the law treat adopted children the same as natural ones?

A. Generally, yes, unless you direct otherwise in your will.

Q. What about children from a previous marriage, stepchildren, or illegitimate children?

A. If your will states that gifts will go to your children (without declaring which ones), it will include children from all your marriages. However, suppose you marry someone with children from a previous marriage whom you do not formally adopt as your own. Then your bequest to your "children" does not include these stepchildren, unless your will specifically says so. In most states, a bequest to "children" includes only legitimate children and acknowledged illegitimate children.

Contested Wills

Q. What does it mean when a will is "contested"?

A. A will is contested when relatives who think they did not get a fair share from someone's will challenge it. The main grounds for will contests are that:
- The will was not properly executed;
- The will-maker lacked *testamentary capacity* (the ability to make a will). For example, he was senile when he left his estate to his cats;
- Somebody exerted undue influence on the will-maker. For instance, a sister held a gun to her dying brother's head, forcing him to leave his entire estate to her; or
- Someone committed fraud. For example, the corrupt brother retyped a page of the will to give him the Porsche collection.

How to Change a Will

An amendment to a will must be signed with the same formalities required for making a will. Such codicils must be dated so the court can tell whether you made them after your will.

***Never* add or cross out anything in your will. You must rewrite the will entirely or execute a codicil when you want to change it.**

In some states, the will may refer to a memorandum disposing of tangible personal property, such as furniture, jewelry, or automobiles. You may change this memorandum from time to time without the formalities of a will.

Q. Is my will likely to be contested? How may I prevent it?

A. You never can tell whether someone will contest your will. There is an old saying that you never really know someone until a will is read. However, the more closely your will follows legal requirements, the less likely a challenge will be successful. It is also another reason to update your will periodically.

You can take certain steps to reduce the chances of a will contest. One is by including a *no-contest* clause. In some states, this clause allows you to disinherit a beneficiary who contests the will. (Your lawyer can advise you just how far you may go with this.) If you use a living trust (discussed later in this chapter) with a pour-over will, you make it more difficult for family members to contest the validity of the trust. If the trust owns your assets before death (as a funded revocable trust), this prevents attacks from people whom you leave out of the will.

Q. What could happen if somebody contests my will?

A. A successful contest throws out the will, or at least part of it. The result is that your property would be distributed either according to your previous will or according to your state's intestacy laws (see the "If You Do Not Have a Will" section). Intestacy laws provide for your property to go to your spouse and blood relatives, in the percentages set by the state.

Probate

Q. What is probate?

A. Narrowly defined, *probate* is a court-supervised procedure that determines the validity of your will. *Probating the will* or *admitting the will to probate* refers to the process that decides whether your last will is your final statement disposing of your property. It also confirms the appointment of the person or bank you named to administer the estate.

People also use "probate" in the larger sense of *probating your estate*. Then "probate" means the process by which assets are (1) gathered; (2) applied to pay debts, taxes, and expenses of administration; and (3) distributed to the beneficiaries named in the will. Put bluntly, probate takes the ownership of your assets out of your dead hands and puts them into the hands of a living person or institution.

Probate affects some, but not all, of your assets. Nonprobate assets include things like joint property and life insurance paid to beneficiaries, as described above.

LIVING WILLS

Despite their name, these are not really wills at all. *Living wills* are a way of telling your doctor that you want—or do not want—certain medical techniques used to prolong your life during a terminal illness. Living wills do not dispose of property. That is why this chapter does not discuss them. See "The Rights of Older Americans" chapter for a discussion of living wills.

Steps in the Probate Process

Q. What happens if I have a will?

A. At death, your will normally *goes through probate*. Probate does not happen automatically after the funeral. Someone (the executor named in your will) must start the process.

Q. Who is the executor?

A. If you have a will, the *personal representative* for your estate is the *executor,* who is the person you appoint to administer your estate. This person is in charge of collecting your assets, administering your estate, and distributing your assets as provided in your will. This is an important job. Therefore, it is best for you to decide who will undertake it. You will make this decision by writing a will naming the executor you choose.

If you do not have a will, the probate court will appoint the personal representative for your estate. In most states, this person will be an *administrator*. However, the administrator basically will function the same as an executor.

Q. How does the executor calculate my assets?

A. After the court admits the will to probate, the executor files with the court an inventory of the estate assets. This lists the cash, property, and other items of value that you left behind. The executor also appraises (estimates) the value of all the estate's assets for the court. In addition, the executor lists any claims against the estate. For example, if the executor finds an IOU indicating that you owe money to your neighbor, the executor will put that in the list.

Q. Why is the choice of executor important?

A. The executor is responsible for collecting, preserving, and distributing assets. The executor also is responsible for estate tax filings and payments. If there is a loss in the value of the property, the executor could be liable. The beneficiaries (and sometimes a probate court) hold the executor accountable. Thus, the choice of an executor is important.

Q. Do executors get paid for their services?

A. The law entitles the executor to a reasonable fee (in some states, this is a fee fixed by law), unless the will provides otherwise. Your estate pays the fee.

Disinheriting Your Children

Except in Louisiana, the law does allow you to disinherit your children. However, you should specify which ones you want to disinherit or you will risk not accomplishing your goal. A child who simply is not mentioned may have a right to inherit under certain circumstances.

In a few states, you must leave the disinherited children a token amount, usually a dollar, to make sure they do not get a share against your wishes. The state of Louisiana is an exception to the general rule. It has a *forced heirship law,* entitling children to a minimum percentage of the estate. Any will provision to the contrary is void.

Q. Is property ever distributed while the will is in probate? Also, does the executor sell property to convert it to cash, or does the executor distribute the property as is?

A. Probate law encourages partial distributions during the probate period. Unless assets must be sold to raise cash to pay taxes and expenses, the executor may distribute them *in kind* (as is), rather than selling them. Contrary to popular belief, a well-prepared will allows the executor to begin helping the beneficiaries from the estate's assets right away.

Q. May more than one person serve as an executor?

A. Yes, one compromise is to appoint *coexecutors,* such as one personal friend and one person with business expertise. Or, to prevent family arguments, your will may have all your children serve as coexecutors.

Q. Are there any restrictions on the type of person who may be an executor?

A. The executor should *not* be a minor, convicted felon, or a noncitizen of the United States. Also, many state laws make it a good idea to pick an executor who is a legal resident of the state in which the estate will be administered.

Q. Does the executor have to be a lawyer?

A. No, but will-makers may choose lawyers as executors. And executors generally hire lawyers to perform some of the duties of administering the estate.

Q. Specifically, how will the executor administer my estate?

A. As soon as possible after your death, the executor will ask the court for *letters testamentary,* if you have a will. (The personal representative will ask the court for *letters of administration* if you do not have a will.) These letters from the court give the executor or personal representative the authority to administer your estate. These letters are the badge of authority. Bankers, lawyers, and business people insist on seeing them before turning over assets listed in your name to this stranger whom they probably have never met.

In most states, your executor also must advertise the fact of your death. The executor usually does this by placing a small notice in the newspaper. The purpose of this is so that creditors can become aware of your death and file claims (against your estate) with your executor.

Improving Probate's Reputation

Probate does not entirely deserve its bad reputation. Many states have streamlined and simplified their probate process for all estates unless somebody contests the will.

Most states have also adopted alternatives to probate procedures for families with small estates—for instance, $50,000 or less. These procedures may help save sometimes substantial court fees, lawyer fees, and executor fees. However, beware—when you add up all your assets (remember those intangibles), you will almost certainly turn out to be worth more than you think. You may not qualify for these alternatives.

THE EXECUTOR'S FUNCTION

The executor or personal representative does four things:

(1) Gathers all the assets of your estate;

(2) Assembles all bills, and pays all debts and estate taxes;

(3) Takes care of and invests the assets until they are paid out; and

(4) Pays out the balance of your estate according to your will, or, if you left no will, according to your state's intestacy laws.

Q. After making your death known and getting the letters testamentary, what does the executor do next?

A. The executor first pays all the debts, administration expenses, and taxes due from your estate. This includes filing a special federal estate-tax return within nine months after your death if your estate (including all insurance payable to the estate) exceeds $600,000 in value. Your executor also is expected to contest any claims for debts, expenses, and taxes that appear to be improper.

Then the executor distributes the remaining assets to the people or institutions as directed in your will. After doing everything required, the executor *closes the estate* by filing a form. It certifies that the executor has done everything the will and law require, and it confirms that the executor has finished taking care of the estate. The court and the beneficiaries have the opportunity to question whether the executor has performed adequately.

Q. What if the will does not specify how certain assets are to be distributed?

A. To handle any distributions that your will does not take care of, you may appoint a disinterested party as the sole executor, giving that person discretionary (judgmental) powers to decide who gets which assets. However, if you appoint an interested party—say, a family member—it may be wise to include a method for making these decisions. Examples are drawing for lots or arbitration by a third party. These methods may help avoid any abuse of discretion. They also will not place pressure on the executor.

Q. It takes some time to settle an estate. How does the family survive, financially speaking, until the executor distributes the assets?

A. Many states permit a family allowance to be paid to immediate family members while the long probate process continues. The executor also can distribute the income, as well as some of the assets, from the estate during this period if it is clear that the remaining property can pay all the estate's obligations.

Q. What is an independent executor?

A. About a dozen states permit the selection of an *independent executor*. After appraising and filing the inventory of assets with the probate court, this executor is free to administer the estate without the court intervening. That is why the state law refers to this person as an independent executor. This saves everyone time and trouble. However, the court may reenter the picture if someone challenges the independent executor's administration of the estate.

The independent executor has the power to do just about anything necessary to administer the estate. The independent executor may sue or be sued, and deny, pay, or settle other people's claims against your estate. The independent executor also may pay debts, taxes, and administration expenses. In addition, the independent executor may run your business (if part of the estate), and distribute your estate's assets to your beneficiaries according to your will. In some states, the independent executor may sell your property.

Q. What if the independent executor is a crook or an incompetent?

A. Any interested party (someone who stands to benefit from the estate) may demand an accounting. Then the independent executor must show the books and financial records for the estate. Courts remove independent executors who are guilty of theft or misconduct, or who become incompetent (for example, because of a stroke).

Q. What happens if the independent executor refuses to act?

A. An interested party may ask the court for an accounting and for distribution of the assets within a set period after the appointment of the independent executor. In most states, that period is at least a year.

Q. What is a reasonable fee for an executor seeing an uncontested will through probate?

A. The amount varies. You may state the amount of payment in the will. In any event, state law will often grant the executor a set percentage of the estate as a commission. For example, the executor may get three percent of all amounts paid and received in administering the estate.

Avoiding Probate

Q. Why do I want to avoid probate?

A. Books on how to avoid probate have sold very well in the past. That is no accident. Probate was once time-consuming

Whom Should You Appoint as Your Executor?

One approach is to appoint a person or bank with no potential conflict of interest—that is, an individual or institution who will not gain from the will. For this reason, many people avoid naming as executors their family members or people who are in business with them. This helps avoid fights and litigation between the executor and estate beneficiaries. The disadvantage of this approach is that nonfamily executors usually charge for their services. (They generally charge between two and five percent of the estate, depending on its size.) That might make it too expensive to hire such outsiders. So many people choose a friend or family member who will waive (refuse) the executor fee. Your lawyer can help you decide which course is best for you.

and costly. Heirs waited a long time for their property. When they got it, probate fees had reduced it.

Developments in recent years have lessened the need to avoid probate. Some states have simplified the procedures (such as the independent executor provisions). This has reduced or eliminated many inconveniences and charges.

Q. Are there new probate laws in a lot of states?

A. Yes, many states have new probate laws. Before the new laws, many people used probate avoidance techniques (including revocable trusts, discussed later) in states where probate was too slow and too costly. Since then, many states have adopted the Uniform Probate Code or have otherwise reformed their probate system.

The Code or new laws try to increase the privacy of family affairs and reduce or eliminate the surety/fidelity bond and appraisal costs. They also administer estates more quickly by having the executor and beneficiaries cooperate. In addition, they limit the court's involvement.

Laws in these states now offer less reason to avoid probate. Your lawyer can advise you of the probate system in your state (and in any other state in which you may own property).

Reasons to Avoid Probate

There are three primary reasons for minimizing the involvement of the probate court in your estate:

(1) Probate may take a long time—sometimes years;

(2) Probate is not private. The probate proceedings, including your will, become public records. The law often requires certain notices to appear in the newspaper; and

(3) Probate may be expensive. Your estate pays court fees, extra lawyer fees, and appraisal fees. Also, being in probate ties up your assets.

Q. What if my state does not have simplified probate procedures?

A. Probate is not all bad. However, if you live in a state that lacks simplified procedures, or if your estate does not qualify for them, there are ways to avoid probate, as noted in the answer to the following question.

Q. How may I avoid probate?

A. Someone must do the basic job of administering and accounting for assets. It does not matter whether an executor handles the estate in probate or whether you avoid probate.

You cannot avoid probate by simply not having a will. If you do that, the probate court will administer your estate through the even more awkward intestacy laws.

You may avoid probate by having a will to take care of the legal formalities *and* disposing of your property in some other way. The four most common ways of disposing of property and avoiding probate are through:

- Trusts;
- Gifts;
- Joint tenancy, also known as survivorship; and
- Contractual arrangements (such as life insurance and pensions).

If You Do Not Have a Will

Q. What happens if I die without a will?

A. The court will appoint a personal representative—the administrator. The administrator's job essentially is the same as the executor's. The only difference is that the court must supervise the activities of the administrator. This can be expensive and cause delay.

Q. How does the administrator administer the estate of a person who has died without a will?

A. Every state has *descent and distribution statutes* that, in effect, write your will for you. If you die *intestate* (without a will), your state's laws of descent and distribution will determine who receives your property. (These laws are also called *intestacy laws.*) The legal term for the order of people who receive your assets when you die intestate is *intestate succession.*

Q. How much does my spouse get if we have children and I die without a will?

A. The law commonly limits the surviving spouse to a one-half or one-third share.

Q. Do state laws normally give money to blood relatives rather than in-laws?

A. Yes, though these laws vary greatly. In general, intestacy laws prefer "blood" to "marriage." Your assets are more likely to go to a distant cousin whom you have never met than to your spouse's sister or your son's widow.

If there is no surviving spouse or children, other blood relatives become entitled to the property. The situation often becomes very complex.

Q. Does the law consider financial hardship?

A. No, the law is rigid and does not consider the needs or situation of the individual heirs. Suppose, for example, that you have a rich son who has never spoken to you since he stole your car. It is quite possible that he will get the same as the poor disabled son who is starting college.

(continued)

Who Gets Your Property if You Die Without a Will?

If there is no will, the court distributes the deceased's estate according to state law. This usually means it goes to the immediate family (the surviving husband or wife and children). If there is a spouse and no children, the spouse sometimes shares the estate with the parents of the deceased person. The law may distinguish between the deceased's real and personal property when the administrator distributes the property.

Most people assume that if someone dies without a will, the entire estate should go to the surviving spouse. Usually the law does *not* reflect this common belief. If someone dies without a will, state law may not provide the surviving spouse with an adequate means of support.

PROPERTY DISTRIBUTION AFTER DYING WITHOUT A WILL

The laws governing the distribution of property belonging to a person who dies intestate (that is, without a will) can be very complicated, reaching out to the descendants of the deceased's great-grandparents and even beyond.

The example below is based on the rules of descent and distribution in Illinois. It is offered only as a simplified version of the law. It is not intended to be representative of other states. This example merely demonstrates that the failure to leave a properly drawn will can lead to a distribution of property that is unintended by the deceased.

Survivors	Shares to Survivors of Illinois Intestate Deceased
Spouse; child or descendant	50 percent to spouse and 50 percent to child or descendant.
Child or descendant; no spouse	100 percent to child or descendant.
Parent; brother or sister; no spouse; no child or descendant	100 percent in equal shares among parents, brothers, and sisters. If only one parent survived the deceased, that parent receives a double share. Descendants of a deceased brother or sister take their ancestor's share, per stirpes.[1]
Grandparent or descendant of grandparent; no spouse; no child or descendant; no parent; no brother, sister, or descendant of brother or sister	50 percent to maternal grandparent, or if none, to descendant of maternal grandparent, and 50% to paternal grandparent, or if none, to descendant of paternal grandparent. If there is no grandparent and no descendant of a grandparent of one category, 100 percent to grandparent or descendant of grandparent of the other category.
Great-grandparent or descendant of great-grandparent; no grandparent or descendant of grandparent; no spouse; no child or descendant; no parent; no brother, sister, or descendant of brother or sister	Distribution to great-grandparent and descendant of great-grandparent is similar to example immediately above.
None of the above	100 percent to nearest kindred by rules of civil law.
No known kindred	100 percent to county.

[1]Descendants of a deceased child, brother, sister, grandparent, or great-grandparent take *per stirpes* the share that their ancestor would have taken. Suppose, for example, that the deceased (Grandparent A) had two children (Parents A and B), both of whom died before the deceased. In addition, one of the deceased's children (Parent A) left two children and the other child of the deceased (Parent B) left three children. In that case, the two children of Parent A would each take one half of their parent's share and the three children of Parent B would each take one third of their parent's share.

Source: Morton John Barnard, attorney, Gottlieb and Schwartz, Chicago, Illinois.

Q. Who will administer my estate if I die without a will?

A. The law designates who may administer the estate. It might not be the person you would have chosen. Also the law may require a surety (or fidelity) bond to be posted. (An earlier section in this chapter discusses this type of bond.) This adds another expense to the estate. It also reduces the amount of money that will go to your heirs.

Q. Does it complicate things if I die without a will and leave behind small children?

A. Yes, it does make matters more complex. Because you had no will, your minor children will inherit money from you. Since they are too young to handle the money themselves, someone will have to administer it for them—a court-appointed guardian.

If that person is a stranger chosen by the court, it may disturb the family. Also, that person's fees will reduce the size of the children's inheritance (when they reach the age of majority).

Regardless of whom the court appoints as guardian, that person may use the inheritance of a minor child for the child's support. However, the probate court usually must supervise this process. This adds complications that would not exist if you had made a will and provided for your children's funds to be held for them by a custodian under the Uniform Gift (or Transfers) to Minors Act or by a trustee.

Dying with No Will and No Relatives

This situation is unlikely. Most of us have some distant relatives, even if we do not know them. The state will do its best to find relatives of people who die intestate. However, if it cannot find any, your estate will become state property.

Transferring Property Without a Will

Q. Can't I just give away my property before I die?

A. It is not that simple. Gifts made while you are alive are *inter vivos gifts*. Gifts can save estate taxes to the extent that they transfer property within the annual gift tax exclusion of $10,000/$20,000 per recipient per year. (This exclusion is discussed in the "Tax Considerations" section that appears later in this chapter.) Gifts also can remove the property from the probate process. The real problem is that you do not know exactly when you will die, and you do not want to give away all your property and have nothing to live on. The tax aspects and effects on wills are secondary.

Larger gifts may be subject to federal gift taxes. You also may need to put in your will a statement that any gifts you have given anyone before you died are not "advances." If you fail to do that, the court may subtract the amount of the advance from the sum you left in the will. Suppose the month before you died you gave your son $10,000 toward college, and in the will you left him $25,000 without specifying that the college money was not an advance. Then the court might subtract the $10,000, and give him only $15,000.

Q. Is joint tenancy a substitute for a will?

A. Joint tenancy (discussed below and in the "Buying and Selling a Home" chapter) may sometimes be a useful method of transferring property at death. For example, it is a good way of transferring the family car or the family checking account. It also is a useful method of transferring the family home to a spouse. In other situations, especially those involving tax considerations, it sometimes may produce very unfortunate results.

Q. What can go wrong in a joint tenancy?

A. Several things can happen. A joint tenancy does not replace a will. For example, it does not cover what happens if the other joint tenant dies before you. Nor does it cover a common disaster, when both parties die at the same time.

Since joint tenancy property passes outside the will, having too much property in joint tenancy may disrupt the family estate plan reflected in the will. Joint tenancy also may produce unfortunate results when the "wrong" joint tenant dies first.

If you have substantial assets, and tax planning has already been done for your estate, it is advisable to consult a lawyer before deciding to put property in joint tenancy.

TRUSTS AND OTHER INSTRUMENTS

Q. What is a trust?

A. A *trust* is a legal instrument used to manage real or personal property. One person establishes it for the benefit of another. A trust usually involves three people:

(1) The *grantor* (the person who creates the trust, sometimes also known as the *settlor* or *donor*);
(2) The *trustee* (who holds legal title and manages the property for the benefit of the beneficiary); and
(3) The *beneficiary* (the person for whose benefit the property is held).

In a trust, a trustee holds property according to the provisions of a written trust document. This document

How to Set Up a Trust

Your lawyer can help you set up a trust. You may set up one in your will, or you may set up one by a trust agreement before you die.

A trust created by your will is a *testamentary trust*. In this type of trust, your will contains the trust provisions.

If you create a trust during your lifetime, you are the trust's *settlor*. This type of trust is a *living trust* or an *inter vivos trust*. The *trust agreement* or *trust declaration* contains the trust provisions. The provisions of that trust document (not your will or state law) can determine what happens to the property in the trust after you die.

(continued)

basically is a set of instructions to the trustee (like the instructions you leave for a baby-sitter). The trustee may be one or more persons or a corporate trust company or bank. The grantor sets up the trust for the benefit of one or more persons (the beneficiaries). Also, the grantor may be one of the trustees or one of the beneficiaries. In a revocable trust, it is common for the grantor to be the trustee or one of the trustees.

Trusts can be revocable or irrevocable. You may revoke (cancel) revocable trusts. You may not revoke irrevocable ones.

Either type of trust can manage property, help the grantor in the event of physical or mental incapacity, and dispose of property after the grantor's death.

Q. Do most trusts require a lawyer's help?

A. Yes, most trusts need an attorney. Trusts may range from very simple ones for limited purposes to very complex ones. The complicated ones may span two or more generations, provide tax benefits, and protect the family from creditors, including a divorcing spouse.

Q. What are the purposes of trusts?

A. Trusts may help you:

- Administer assets more effectively;
- Take care of your family (especially minor children) and others after your death or during an incapacitating illness or accident;
- Ensure privacy;
- Avoid probate;
- Protect your estate and beneficiaries from creditors; and
- Minimize taxes on your family's inheritance.

In effect, trusts to some extent may take the place of a will. That is, they may administer your property after your death, bequeath your property, and so on. However, you still may need a will to dispose of property not transferred to the trust during your life, coordinate the distribution of assets with the trust, and keep the estate out of reach of intestacy laws.

Q. Who should be my trustee?

A. The choice of the "right" trustee is critically important. A trust is only as effective as its trustee. You will have to decide whether the trustee should be a family member, a trusted financial adviser or lawyer, or a business associate. (See the discussion of executors that appeared earlier for some of the factors you should weigh. Also see the discussion of selecting a trustee in the "Living Trusts" section below.)

(continued)

In some states, financial institutions may have available standard short-form revocable trusts. They may set up these trusts for separate assets, such as a bank account or mutual fund shares. The trusts also may have separate beneficiaries.

Generally speaking, there are no tax advantages in a revocable trust, except those that also could be achieved by a skillfully drawn will. However, as discussed in this section, you may save considerable taxes by using an irrevocable trust.

WILLS, TRUSTS, AND ESTATE PLANNING

Trusts Are Not Only for the Wealthy

Many young parents with limited assets choose to create "standby" trusts either separately or in their wills. These are for the benefit of their children if both parents die before the children have come of age. Such trusts permit holding the trust estate (which often consists mostly of insurance proceeds) as a single undivided fund for supporting and educating minor children. The trust is divided among the children when the youngest has reached a specified age.

A will inflexibly divides property among children of different ages. If no trust is used, the property is divided among the children at the time of your death even though their needs may be different. The trust allows the children's needs to be taken into account by delaying the property division until all the children are "out of the nest."

Q. How may a trust protect my privacy more than a will?

A. When a person dies and the will is probated, it becomes a public document. The trust agreement generally is not filed with the probate court, even upon the death of the settlor of the trust. (In some states, a registration statement may have to be filed.) Since the trust is not a public document, it distributes trust property with more privacy than is possible through the usual probate procedures.

Q. Does a trust always save the estate some money in taxes?

A. No, a revocable trust intended to supplement or substitute for a will normally achieves only the same postdeath tax advantages as a skillfully drawn will. Probate reforms in some states have decreased the advantages of such a trust over a will.

Q. If I set up a trust and then move to another state, which state law applies?

A. State law governs trusts. If the trust involves real estate, the law of the state where the property is located applies. If the trust involves personal property, like a car or money, or most other things, the law of the state where the grantor lived at the time the trust was set up normally will control the trust. However, you may provide in your trust document (or your will) that the law of the state of your choice will control the disposition of your property.

Living Trusts

Q. What are living trusts?

A. A *living trust* allows you or someone you trust to own and manage your assets in a trust. The trust may benefit either you or someone else, usually your family.

Q. Why should I consider setting up a living trust?

A. A living trust provides management in case of incapacity. It also is one of the two main ways to avoid probate. (The other is joint tenancy or survivorship.)

Most people will need the help of a lawyer in creating a living trust. However, the legal bills could be about the same as what you will pay for having a lawyer write a complicated will. Also, you still avoid most of the costs of probate.

Q. How does a living trust work?

A. Your lawyer can best advise you on the details of setting up a living trust. Requirements vary with each state.

In general, you execute a document saying that you are putting certain assets in a trust for whomever you want to benefit. Most often, you name yourself and someone else as trustees of the trust (which makes you both grantor and trustee). If you do not have a cotrustee, you could name an alternate trustee to take over if you die or become incapacitated. You may have to change the ownership registration on some property, from your own name to the name of the trustees of the trust (for example, "John Smith, trustee of The John Smith Trust").

The living trust then provides that when you die, the trustee will distribute your assets to specified beneficiaries. This is similar to the instructions you would give to an executor in your will. For example, the trust could say, "At my death, my trustee is to give any car owned by the trust at my death to my son John, if he is then living . . . " and so on.

Q. Is it expensive to set up a living trust?

A. No, it is not very costly. A one-party living trust (described in the article on page 575 entitled "Whom Should You Appoint as the Trustee?") avoids trustee fees that you would otherwise have to pay to a bank or lawyer.

For most people, it probably is best to have a lawyer's help. You can save money by doing some research on your own and making a rough draft of the trust. That will minimize the billable time the lawyer spends on setting up the trust, thus reducing your legal costs. As with a will, ask your lawyer what documents you should bring with you. After collecting all the records, deeds, bank statements, and other required documents, make a list of what you have and where you want it to go when you die.

Q. What if I change my mind about how my assets should be distributed?

A. If you make the trust revocable and amendable (changeable), as most are, you may change it or rewrite the whole thing anytime.

A disadvantage of a revocable trust (as compared with an irrevocable trust) is that you must pay taxes on income from

Other Kinds of Trusts

Support trusts **direct the trustee to spend only as much income and principal (the main portion of the trust estate) as the trustee determines the beneficiary may require for his or her support.**

Discretionary trusts **permit the trustee to distribute income and principal among various beneficiaries as the trustee sees fit.**

Charitable trusts **allow the grantor to support some charitable purpose.**

Spendthrift trusts **are for people who the grantor believes would not be able to manage their own affairs—like an extravagant-spending spoiled child, or someone who is mentally incompetent. Such trusts also may be useful for beneficiaries who need protection from creditors.**

the trust assets. However, you probably would have had to do that anyway if you had not set up a trust.

Even an irrevocable trust does not avoid taxes. If it provides any benefit for the grantor or the grantor's spouse, it is not taxed separately. If it is taxed separately, it merely sets up a separate taxable entity that might be able to pay taxes at a lower rate, or shift the tax burden to the family beneficiary who receives distribution of the trust income. An irrevocable trust also may create a lot more paperwork.

However, an irrevocable living trust may help provide protection from creditors if certain rules are followed.

Q. If I set up a living trust, do I still need a will?

A. Yes, you do need one. The will takes care of unanticipated windfall assets or assets you failed to put into the trust. For example, it is very difficult to get every bit of property you own (such as furniture and clothing) into the trust. Some property is inappropriate for a trust for tax reasons (like certain stock options). Other property is inappropriate for legal reasons (like stock in a professional corporation).

However, since most of your assets will be in the trust, you still have the advantages of privacy and control. The will administration also will be much simpler, faster, and cheaper.

Finally, as a protection against someone contesting the validity of your trust, a pour-over will is essential.

The Advantages of a Living Trust

A living trust has four main advantages:

(1) It lets you—or someone else if you are not competent—control your assets during your life;

(2) It lets you avoid or minimize probate at your death;

(3) It may supplement or substitute for a complicated will by distributing your assets any way you want; and

(4) It reduces the chances of an expensive legal fight after you die. People challenge living trusts less often than they contest wills.

OTHER ESTATE ASSETS

Planning your estate does not stop with writing a will and setting up a trust. Most people have other benefits that those documents may not control. A good estate plan must take them into account.

Retirement Benefits and Annuities

Q. How does my employer's retirement plan fit into my overall estate strategy?

A. You may be entitled to receive some type of retirement benefit under an employee benefit plan offered by your employer. A deferred compensation or retirement benefit plan usually pays certain benefits to your beneficiaries if you die before reaching retirement age. After retirement, you may choose a benefit option that will continue payments after your death to one or more beneficiaries whom you select.

The law now orders that your spouse must receive annuities (periodic payments) from certain retirement benefit plans. You are permitted to reject the payment of these annuities only with your spouse's properly witnessed, signed consent.

The various payment options offered by your deferred compensation or retirement benefit plan will be treated differently for tax purposes. You should seek competent advice about the payment options available under your retirement plan and the tax consequences of each. Often you will want to name your revocable trust as the beneficiary to receive all your postdeath employee benefits.

Life Insurance

Q. While planning my estate, I realized that I must account for my life insurance. How may I do this?

A. If you have purchased life insurance on your own life, you may either:

(1) Designate one or more beneficiaries to receive the insurance proceeds upon your death; or

(2) Make the proceeds payable to your probate estate or to a trust created by you during your lifetime or by your will.

If the insurance proceeds are payable to your estate, they will be distributed as part of your estate according to the terms of your will. If you die without a will, the distribution will follow your state's laws of intestate succession. In either case, they will be subject to the claims of creditors (and they may be needlessly subjected to some states' inheritance taxes).

If the proceeds from your life insurance policy are payable to a trust, they will be held and distributed just like other trust assets. The insurance proceeds also may be free of creditors' claims. An irrevocable trust will not pay estate taxes on the proceeds if you transferred ownership of the insurance policies to the trust more than three years before your death.

Insurance proceeds that are payable to a minor child generally will require a court to appoint a legal guardian or conservator. You may avoid this by having a trust designated as beneficiary.

Whom Should You Appoint as the Trustee?

If you make yourself the trustee, you avoid having to pay trust fees. This *one-party* living trust means you do not need a bank or lawyer to be the trustee—and you will save money. If you do this, you should name a successor trustee to take over if you become incapacitated or after you die. This may be anyone you trust: a close friend, a grown child, your spouse, or your lawyer.

However, if you are using an irrevocable trust primarily to avoid taxes or for protection from creditors, you should not make yourself the trustee, as that may forfeit the tax and creditor protections otherwise made possible by an irrevocable trust.

Community Property

Q. I live in a community property state. How does this affect my estate after I die?

A. Under the laws of several states and Puerto Rico, most property acquired during the marriage by either spouse is held equally by husband and wife as *community property*. These states are Arizona, California, Idaho, Louisiana, Nevada, New Mexico, Texas, Washington, and Wisconsin. (Exceptions include property acquired through inheritance or as a gift.) This means that when one spouse dies, either the will or the laws of intestacy will transfer the deceased's half of the community property. The will does not affect the other half of the community property. That half belongs to the surviving spouse.

The first step is to determine what is community property and what is separate property. This is not always easy. The rules vary from one state to another.

Jointly Owned Property

Q. I am considering becoming a joint tenant in some property with another person. Will this affect my estate when I die?

A. Yes, it may have a large effect. If you own property with another person as *joint tenants with right of survivorship,* the property will pass directly to the joint tenant when you die. It will not be part of your probate estate. However, it will be part of your taxable estate.

Q. I am getting up in years. A friend suggested that I make my daughter a joint tenant on my checking account. Why would I want to do this?

A. People in old age often make their children or friends joint tenants on their bank accounts or stocks and bonds. They sometimes do this as a matter of convenience. It gives someone else access to the account to help pay bills.

However, when an older person dies, the property passes to the other person. The older person can specify in a will or other document that this is a "convenience" account and should not pass to the other person. This may (but will not necessarily) help. If it does not help, unplanned ownership of property often leads to unexpected and unwanted results. Also, the value of the property may be included in the taxable estate of a joint tenant who died before the

Arguments Over Joint Tenancy

Disputes, including lawsuits, are common between the estate of the original owner and the surviving joint tenant. Was the survivor's name added as a matter of convenience or management, or was a gift intended? In a community property state, property may become part of the estate of a spouse who never had an interest in the property. It depends on how the property's title was held.

An inadvertently created joint tenancy that passes property outright to a beneficiary, particularly to one's spouse, rather than to a tax-saving trust, may defeat the planning of a well-drawn will or trust plan.

(continued)

original owner. That deceased joint tenant never really "owned" the property. Perhaps that person did not even know that he or she had been a joint owner with the right of survivorship. Nonetheless, that person's estate could end up paying taxes on the property if it cannot demonstrate that the survivor contributed the funds.

Tax Considerations

Q. What is the impact of taxes on estates?

A. You may already know that the federal government imposes a maximum 28-percent or 33-percent income tax on your hard-earned dollars. What you may not know is that the federal government may tax that same money again when your estate eventually needs to transfer your wealth. This federal estate transfer tax, imposed when a person dies, may be as high as 60 percent. However, good estate planning may improve that picture considerably.

State inheritance taxes are imposed on the privilege of receiving property from someone else's estate. State estate taxes generally are imposed on the amount excluded from federal taxes. The taxes involved upon death are so complex that, for all but small to moderate estates, the tax advice of a lawyer is essential.

While it is possible that your state law of intestacy may distribute your property as you would wish, this may not result in the most favorable tax treatment. To reduce taxes, therefore, you must use the exemptions, deductions, and other planning opportunities provided in the tax laws. The next series of questions discusses some examples.

Q. What is the unified credit exemption?

A. The federal estate-tax laws now provide for a *unified credit*. This has the effect of exempting a part of a person's property (currently up to $600,000) from the federal estate tax.

This may seem to take care of all your tax worries, but do not be so sure. You may be worth more than you think. (Remember, there is life insurance and the value of your home and other property.) Prosperity and inflation combine to make a lot of estates liable for big taxes.

Your estate may include the family home, family farm, life insurance, household furnishings, benefits under employee benefit plans, and other items that produce no income while you are alive. In short, you may be "richer" than you think.

(continued)

Many of these problems also apply to institutional revocable trusts and "pay on death" forms of ownership of bank, broker, and mutual fund accounts and savings bonds. Effective planning requires knowledge of the consequences of each property interest and technique. You should avoid favoring the surviving joint tenant at the expense of other family members.

To the extent your estate exceeds $600,000, the federal estate-tax rates *start* at 37 percent. Many states also have significant inheritance or estate taxes.

Q. What is a marital deduction? How do I know if I qualify

A. Technical rules determine what property will qualify for a marital deduction and in what form it must be left to your spouse to qualify. Consult your lawyer before deciding whic property to leave to your surviving spouse, unless you are making the transfer as an outright gift.

Property qualifying for the marital deduction will be included in the taxable estate of the surviving spouse, except to the extent it has been consumed by the surviving spouse prior to death. Therefore, if the surviving spouse owns a lot of separate property, using the unlimited marital deduction may increase the combined tax paid by the two estates of both spouses. This has the effect of reducing the amount of property remaining for children, grandchildren, and other ultimate beneficiaries.

It also may be costly to leave the full marital deduction amount to your spouse when a smaller one would eliminate the federal estate tax payable on your death. This is becaus everything your spouse receives from you will be taxed in your spouse's estate, and you could be increasing your spouse's tax without saving your own estate any money. For this reason, it is a good idea to leave the $600,000 credit shelte amount in a way that does not qualify for the marital deduction. You could leave it to your children or others or to a trust for your spouse, as long as it is not a qualified marital deduction trust.

Your lawyer can design a marital deduction provision anc a family (i.e., credit shelter) trust that is for the benefit of your spouse. Using such a formula provides a marital deduction that exactly measures the amount necessary to maximize tax savings in each spouse's estate. Such a trust ca help you avoid having to make an uncomfortable choice between your spouse and your children in trying to reduce taxes.

OTHER EXEMPTIONS FROM TAXES

Federal and state taxes provide other exclusions and exemptions. For example, life insurance may be excluded from state inheritance and estate taxes in certain states, if you correctly arrange ownership and beneficiary designations before death.

Moreover, the federal estate-tax law gives an unlimited deduction for gifts to qualified charitable organizations. Most state tax laws contain similar provisions if the bequest is in the proper form.

Q. What are some examples of estate tax savings through gifts?

A. You may achieve some tax savings through carefully planne gifts. For example, you may use gifts to remove rapidly appreciating (increasing in value) property from your estate. Suppose you gave away stock that has grown rapidly in value. Then the amount it went up after the date of the gift—its appreciation in value—will be removed from your estate and will escape estate tax at your death.

You may use "annual exclusion" gifts (described below) to accumulate funds for a child's education and for many other purposes. Through inter vivos gifts that qualify for the annual exclusion (and certain exclusions for medical and tuition payments), you may reduce your estate to the tax-exempt level—currently $600,000.

Q. How much may I give away each year without paying gift taxes?

A. Since 1982, federal law has permitted you to give "annual exclusion" gifts of up to $10,000 per recipient per year tax-free. (The law allows married donors giving a gift as a couple to give $20,000 per recipient per year.) Even gifts exceeding these limits do not result in a gift tax until the cumulative total exceeds the $600,000 unified credit available. To apply the unified tax rate after your death, the government does not add predeath gifts up to this yearly limit back to your estate. This is so even if you made the gift within three years of your death, unless the gift was a life insurance policy. However, the value of your gifts in excess of the $10,000/$20,000 annual exclusion is added back to your estate for purposes of calculating the estate tax due.

Generally, only gifts made outright to people qualify for the exclusion. However, gifts involving trusts may qualify for the annual exclusion if the trust provisions meet certain technical requirements. You cannot keep the income on the property given as a gift or it will be taxed in your estate anyway.

Q. Are spouses allowed to give gifts to each other without paying gift taxes?

A. Yes, the law allows for tax-free gifts between spouses. The federal *gift tax marital deduction* is similar to the estate-tax marital deduction discussed above. Since 1981, property may be freely transferred between spouses (as long as the recipient spouse is a U.S. resident) without owing federal gift taxes. Spouses may use these tax-free gifts to shift assets so that each spouse may make full use of his or her unified credit exemption from federal estate taxes.

Q. What about gifts to charities? Are such gifts still tax deductible?

A. Gifts to qualified charities continue to be free of gift tax. They also are deductible from your income tax within certain liberal limits.

Taxes on Insurance Benefits

Q. Is there any advantage to making my insurance payable to somebody in particular, as opposed to my estate?

A. Yes, there may be a large difference in state (but not federal) taxes. Many states impose an inheritance or estate tax on the insurance proceeds payable to the estate. They do not, however, tax the insurance proceeds payable to a named beneficiary, including the trustee of either a living trust or a trust created by a will.

Insurance proceeds are subject to the federal estate tax if the dead person owned the policy or if that person has retained certain "incidents of ownership" regarding the policy. (*Incidents of ownership* simply indicate that the person had the usual attributes of an owner, such as the right to change the policy beneficiary, elect settlement options, take loans against the policy, surrender the policy for its cash value, and so on.) However, suppose the dead person had transferred complete ownership and control of the policy to another person more than three years before death. Then the proceeds of the policy after the death generally will not be subject to the federal estate tax.

The laws on the taxability of insurance proceeds are complex. Also, you should coordinate insurance with all other aspects of an estate plan.

POSTDEATH INCOME TAX PROBLEMS

Q. How may I limit the taxes my estate will have to pay?

A. Besides inheritance taxes, federal and state income taxes may apply to your property at death. The services of a lawyer—both before and after death—are critical to saving your estate both income and estate taxes. Your lawyer's advice may be invaluable in selling assets, timing the payment of expenses, and other matters of estate administration, as discussed below.

Selling Assets

Q. My father passed away earlier this year. Now the executor of his estate says that she must sell some of my father's

assets to pay certain expenses. Is this common? Will this affect the estate's taxes?

A. The answer to both questions is, yes. Death itself produces a large amount of extraordinary expenses. There are taxes to pay, expenses of administering the estate, and often the forced early payment of outstanding debts. To obtain the cash for such payments, the executor may have to sell assets. This may, in turn, trigger a capital gains tax at the time of the sale, but only on appreciation occurring *after* death. Assets held at death take a new income tax basis equal to their estate tax value, so typically assets sold by an executor reasonably soon after death will have little or no capital gain.

The assets selected for sale are critical. Choosing the right ones may defer the tax or accelerate it. It is important to make the right choice, keeping in mind present or future anticipated tax brackets.

Choices About Estate and Trust Administration

Q. I am getting totally confused. How will my estate and my trust affect the tax consequences of my death?

A. An estate and a trust each form a separate "taxpayer" for income tax purposes. The range of options available is broad. Timing the payment of estate expenses, and distributions under the will or trust, has critical tax implications.

Moreover, there are income tax options for Series E and H savings bonds, the filing of a joint return with the surviving spouse, and the deduction of medical expenses. There also are highly sophisticated techniques for timing of distributions to beneficiaries that may affect their income taxes and the estate's taxes. Again, see your lawyer or financial consultant for advice.

Q. Will the expenses of administering my estate be deductible from both my income-tax and estate-tax returns?

A. The expenses of administration may be either an income-tax or estate-tax deduction, but not both. Making this choice and timing the payments require both skill and the authority of a properly drafted will or trust document. You may even handle such expenses so that they are deductible directly or indirectly from the tax returns of the beneficiaries.

All this suggests that selecting a legal and tax adviser after death is only half the battle. No adviser can help if

Tax Consequences of Pension Plans

Payments under company deferred-compensation and pension plans produce a confusing range of possible choices. These may include a lump sum payment, installment payments, payments to an IRA, and the like, each with differing income tax results. Ask your lawyer or financial consultant for assistance with your particular situation.

the family member in charge (an executor, surviving spouse, or trustee) lacks power under the will or trust to make the proper tax choices.

Only a well-drafted trust or will can provide all the needed authority. Most states give the necessary authority by law, unless the person making the will provides otherwise. However, none of the laws cover all possible conflict of interest questions. Furthermore, no state laws eliminate the need for specific will clauses on distributing the family home, car, furnishings, and the like. Without such clauses, punitive income tax consequences may follow the distribution of such assets. Your estate will be hit with taxes also because of unplanned (and, after death, perhaps unplannable) final distribution of the residue of your estate.

Beneficiaries and Estate Taxes

Your beneficiaries may have to pay your estate's taxes. If not specified otherwise in your will, many states force the executor to charge everyone who receives anything from your estate a portion of the estate taxes. Other states provide that taxes will be taken out of the remainder of your estate. It is important to decide whether property you leave to your beneficiaries is meant to be depleted by estate taxes, or whether you mean for the estate taxes to be paid by your estate. Your will can provide for this in the way that best suits your own circumstances.

WHERE TO GET MORE INFORMATION

Your banker, lawyer, financial planner, and even some accounting firms offer advice on estate planning. "Self-help" books, tapes, kits, and computer software also try to help you understand estate planning. Some even help you do it yourself. These are available in law libraries and in most general libraries and bookstores.

However, what if you do not have a lawyer or financial adviser? Several public interest organizations will provide help or referrals for people who want to plan their estate.

To find a lawyer and learn about your state's laws, start with your state or local bar association. Bars often have brochures that tell you about your state's laws. Most bars offer referral services that can refer you to a lawyer. Since wills and estates are one of the basics of legal practice, there is no shortage of qualified lawyers to help you.

If your estate is small and your will is uncomplicated, a legal clinic may be able to help you for little charge. For-profit legal clinics write many wills. By using standard forms and paralegals they are able to prepare simple wills inexpensively. However, be sure that you need only a simple will. Not-for-profit legal clinics operated by law schools also may be able to prepare wills for little or no money.

If you are in your later years, you will find it easy to get help and referrals from your local area agency on aging. Many agencies feature "will days" on which lawyers come to the agencies to advise on estate planning. If you are an older U.S. citizen, you also will qualify for legal services under the Older Americans Act. Your area agency on aging can tell you how to obtain these services. (See "The Rights of Older Americans" chapter for further details.)

Older Americans also can get inexpensive materials and other assistance from the American Association of Retired Persons. You can find a local chapter in the telephone directory. Or you can contact the national organization at 1909 K Street, N.W., Washington, D.C. 20049. Its telephone number is (202) 872-4700.

People of any age with limited income may qualify for free or inexpensive legal services, including help in preparing a will. Check with your neighborhood justice center, or look under "Legal Services" in the government listings in your phone book.

Also, the probate courts in many states provide forms and sometimes information to the public about how to write and file the documents necessary to estate planning. Call your local probate court, and see what it has to offer.

Estates are taxed in some states. To find the rules in your state, contact your state revenue department.

The IRS is an excellent source of information on federal tax questions. The IRS's tele-tax service has recorded tax information on about 140 topics. You can find the toll-free 800 number for your state by calling the IRS office in your area. One of the tele-tax topics deals with estate taxes.

In addition, IRS representatives are available to help you with your tax questions. Consult your local office to find out about getting assistance by phone, by mail, or in person.

The IRS also publishes a number of free pamphlets dealing with common tax questions. *Tax Information for Survivors, Executors, and Administrators* (Publication 559) is of particular interest.

STATE BAR ASSOCIATIONS

Alabama State Bar
P.O. Box 671
Montgomery, AL 36101
(205) 269-1515

Alaska Bar Association
P.O. Box 100279
Anchorage, AK 99510
(907) 272-7469

State Bar of Arizona
363 N. 1st Ave.
Phoenix, AZ 85003
(602) 252-4804

Arkansas Bar Association
400 W. Markham
Little Rock, AR 72201
(501) 375-4605

State Bar of California
555 Franklin St.
San Francisco, CA 94102
(415) 561-8200

The Colorado Bar Association
1900 Grant St. #950
Denver, CO 80203
(303) 860-1115

Connecticut Bar Association
101 Corporate Place
Rocky Hill, CT 06067
(203) 721-0025

Delaware State Bar Association
706 Market St. Mall
Wilmington, DE 19801
(302) 658-5278

Bar Association of the District of Columbia
1819 H St., N.W.
12th Floor
Washington, D.C. 20006
(202) 223-6600

The District of Columbia Bar
1707 L St., N.W.
6th Floor
Washington, D.C. 20036
(202) 331-3883

The Florida Bar
650 Apalachee Parkway
Tallahassee, FL 32399
(904) 561-5600

State Bar of Georgia
800 The Hurt Building
Atlanta, GA 30303
(404) 527-8700

Hawaii State Bar Association
P.O. Box 26
Honolulu, HI 96810
(808) 537-1868

Idaho State Bar
P.O. Box 895
Boise, ID 83701
(208) 342-8958

Illinois State Bar Association
424 S. Second St.
Springfield, IL 62701
(217) 525-1760

Indiana State Bar Association
230 E. Ohio, 4th Floor
Indianapolis, IN 46204
(317) 639-5465

Iowa State Bar Association
1101 Fleming Building
Des Moines, IA 50309
(515) 243-3179

Kansas Bar Association
P.O. Box 1037
Topeka, KS 66601
(913) 234-5696

Kentucky Bar Association
West Main at Kentucky River
Frankfort, KY 40601
(502) 564-3795

Louisiana State Bar Association
601 St. Charles Ave.
New Orleans, LA 70130
(504) 566-1600

Maine State Bar Association
P.O. Box 788
Augusta, ME 04332-0788
(207) 622-7523

Maryland State Bar Association
520 W. Fayette St.
Baltimore, MD 21201
(301) 685-7878

Massachusetts Bar Association
20 West St.
Boston, MA 02111
(617) 542-3602

State Bar of Michigan
306 Townsend St.
Lansing, MI 48933-2083
(517) 372-9030

Minnesota State Bar Association
430 Marquette Ave.
Suite 403
Minneapolis, MN 55401
(612) 333-1183

Mississippi State Bar
P.O. Box 2168
Jackson, MS 39225-2168
(601) 948-4471

The Missouri Bar
P.O. Box 119
Jefferson City, MO 65102
(314) 635-4128

State Bar of Montana
P.O. Box 577
Helena, MT 59624
(406) 442-7660

Nebraska State Bar Association
P.O. Box 81809
Lincoln, NE 68501
(402) 475-7091

State Bar of Nevada
500 South 3rd St., #2
Reno, NV 89502-1085
(702) 382-0502

New Hampshire Bar Association
18 Centre St.
Concord, NH 03301
(603) 224-6942

New Jersey State Bar Association
One Constitution Square
New Brunswick, NJ 08901-1500
(201) 249-5000

State Bar of New Mexico
P.O. Box 25883
Albuquerque, NM 87125
(505) 842-6132

New York State Bar Association
One Elk St.
Albany, NY 12207
(518) 463-3200

North Carolina Bar Association
P.O. Box 12806
Raleigh, NC 27605
(919) 828-0561

North Carolina State Bar
P.O. Box 25908
Raleigh, NC 27611
(919) 828-4620

State Bar Association of
North Dakota
515½ E. Broadway
Suite 101
Bismarck, ND 58501
(701) 255-1404

Ohio State Bar Association
33 W. Eleventh Ave.
Columbus, OH 43201
(614) 421-2121

Oklahoma Bar Association
P.O. Box 53036
Oklahoma City, OK 73152
(405) 524-2365

Oregon State Bar
P.O. Box 1689
Lake Oswego, OR 97035
(503) 620-0222

Pennsylvania Bar Association
P.O. Box 186
Harrisburg, PA 17108
(717) 238-6715

Puerto Rico Bar Association
P.O. Box 1900
San Juan, P.R. 00903
(809) 721-3358

Rhode Island Bar Association
91 Friendship St.
Providence, RI 02903
(401) 421-5740

South Carolina Bar
P.O. Box 608
Columbia, SC 29202
(803) 799-6653

State Bar of South Dakota
222 E. Capitol
Pierre, SD 57501
(605) 224-7554

Tennessee Bar Association
3622 West End Avenue
Nashville, TN 37205
(615) 383-7421

State Bar of Texas
P.O. Box 12487
Austin, TX 78711
(512) 463-1463

Utah State Bar
645 S. 200 East
Salt Lake City, UT 84111
(801) 531-9077

Vermont Bar Association
P.O. Box 100
Montpelier, VT 05601
(802) 223-2020

Virginia Bar Association
701 E. Franklin Street, #1515
Richmond, VA 23219
(804) 644-0041

Virginia State Bar
801 E. Main St.
Ross Building, Suite 1000
Richmond, VA 23219
(804) 786-2061

Virgin Islands Bar Association
P.O. Box 4108
Christiansted, V.I. 00822
(809) 778-7497

Washington State Bar Association
500 Westin Building
2001 Sixth Ave.
Seattle, WA 98121-2599
(206) 448-0441

West Virginia Bar Association
P.O. Box 346
Charleston, WV 25322
(304) 342-1474

West Virginia State Bar
E-400 State Capitol
Charleston, WV 25305
(304) 346-8414

State Bar of Wisconsin
402 W. Wilson
Madison, WI 53703
(608) 257-3838

Wyoming State Bar
P.O. Box 109
Cheyenne, WY 82003-0109
(307) 632-9061

GLOSSARY

This glossary defines a number of terms in common legal use that generally are not understood by the average layperson. It does not include the obscure and the obvious, defining neither complex legal procedures that are little understood nor terms that generally are well understood by the public. The following definitions are not legal definitions of these terms. Most of them have very definite legal meanings that vary from one state to another. These are merely plain-English definitions intended to give you a general idea of the meanings.

A

abstract of title A chronological summary of all official records and recorded documents affecting the title to a parcel of real property.

accomplice A person who knowingly and voluntarily unites with the principal offender in a criminal act through aiding, abetting, advising, or encouraging the offender.

acquittal A verdict after a trial that a defendant in a criminal case has not been proven guilty beyond a reasonable doubt of the crime charged.

action Case, cause, suit, or controversy disputed or contested before a court of justice.

actus reus Proof that a criminal act has occurred.

additur An increase by a judge in the amount of damages awarded by a jury.

ademption Failure of a gift because the will-maker, by the time of death, no longer owns the property that the will-maker attempted to bequeath in the will.

adjudication Giving or pronouncing a judgment or decree. Also the judgment given.

ad litem A Latin term meaning for the purposes of the lawsuit. For example, a guardian "ad litem" is appointed to prosecute or defend a suit on behalf of an incapacitated person.

administration The process of collecting the estate's assets; paying its debts, taxes, expenses, and other obligations; and distributing the remainder as directed by the will.

administrator A personal representative, appointed by a probate court, who administers the estate of someone who dies without a will or leaves a will naming an executor who dies before the will-maker or who refuses to serve.

admissible evidence Evidence that can be legally and properly introduced in a civil or criminal trial.

adversary proceeding The legal procedure that features opposing parties; a contested proceeding. It differs from *ex parte proceeding.*

adversary system The trial methods used in the U.S. and some other countries. This system is based on the belief that truth can best be determined by giving opposing parties full opportunity to present and establish their evidence, and to test by cross-examination the evidence presented by their adversaries. All this is done under the established rules of procedure before an impartial judge and/or jury.

affiant A person who makes and signs an affidavit.

affidavit A written statement of fact given voluntarily and under oath. For example, in criminal cases, affidavits are often used by police officers seeking to convince courts to grant a warrant to make an arrest or a search. In civil cases, affidavits of witnesses are often used to support motions for summary judgment.

affirmative defense Without denying the charge, the defendant raises extenuating or mitigating circumstances such as insanity, self-defense, or entrapment to avoid civil or criminal responsibility.

affirmed In the practice of appellate courts, the word means that the decree or order at issue is declared valid and will stand as rendered in the lower court.

allegation The statement in a pleading of what a party expects to prove. For example, an indictment contains allegations of crimes against the defendant.

alternative dispute resolution Settling a dispute without a full, formal trial. Methods include *mediation, conciliation, arbitration,* and *settlement,* among others.

amicus curiae A friend of the court. One not a party to a case who volunteers to offer information on a point of law or some other aspect of the case to assist the court in deciding a matter before it.

answer The defendant's response to the plaintiff's allegations as stated in a complaint. An item-by-item, paragraph-by-paragraph response to points made in a complaint; part of the pleadings.

anti-lapse statute A state law that provides for a gift to go to the descendants of certain will beneficiaries who die before the will-maker dies.

appeal A request by the losing party in a lawsuit or criminal trial that the judgment be reviewed by a higher court.

appearance Coming into court. The formal act by which a defendant submits to the jurisdiction of a court.

GLOSSARY

ppellant The party who initiates an appeal. Sometimes alled a *petitioner.*

ppellate court A court having jurisdiction to hear appeals nd review a trial court's procedure.

ppellee The party against whom an appeal is taken. ometimes called a *respondent.*

rbitration A form of *alternative dispute resolution* in which he parties bring their dispute to a neutral third party and agree o abide by his or her decision. In arbitration there is a hearing t which both parties have an opportunity to be heard.)ecisions usually cannot be appealed.

rraignment In a criminal case, the proceeding in which an ccused person is brought before a judge to hear the charges iled against him or her and to enter a plea of guilty or not uilty. Sometimes called a *preliminary hearing* or *initial ppearance.*

rrest To take into custody by legal authority.

ssault Threat to inflict injury with an apparent ability to do o. Also, any intentional display of force that would give the ictim reason to fear or expect immediate bodily harm.

t issue The contested points in a lawsuit are said to be at issue."

ttachment A proceeding in which a creditor secures rights o real or personal property and holds it pending the outcome of a lawsuit.

ttorney-at-law An advocate, counsel, or official agent mployed in preparing, managing, and trying cases in the ourts. An officer in a court of justice who is employed by a arty in a cause to manage it for that party.

ttorney-in-fact A private person (who is not necessarily a awyer) authorized by another to act in his or her place, either or some particular purpose, as to do a specific act, or for the ransaction of business in general, not of legal character. This uthority is conferred by an instrument in writing, called a *etter of attorney,* or more commonly a *power of attorney.*

ttorney of record The principal attorney in a lawsuit, who igns all formal documents relating to the suit.

B

bail Money or other security (such as a *bail bond*) given to ecure a person's release from custody, which is at risk should he or she subsequently fail to appear before the court. "Bail" and "bond" are often used interchangeably.

bail bond An obligation signed by the accused to secure his or her presence at the trial. This obligation means that the accused may lose money by not properly appearing for the trial. Often referred to simply as *bond.*

bailiff A court attendant who keeps order in the courtroom and has custody of the jury.

bar Historically, the partition separating the general public from the space occupied by the judges, lawyers, and other participants in a trial. More commonly, the term means the whole body of lawyers.

bar examination A state examination taken by prospective lawyers in order to be admitted to practice law.

battery A beating, or wrongful physical violence. The actual threat to use force is an *assault*; the use of it is a battery, which usually includes an assault.

bench The seat occupied by the judge. More broadly, the court itself.

bench warrant An order issued by a judge for the arrest of a person.

beneficiary Someone named to receive property or benefits in a will. In a trust, a person who is to receive benefits from the trust.

bequeath To give a gift to someone through a will.

bequests Gifts made in a will.

best evidence Primary evidence; the best evidence available. Evidence short of this is "secondary." That is, an original letter is "best evidence," and a photocopy is "secondary evidence."

beyond a reasonable doubt The standard in a criminal case requiring that the jury be satisfied to a moral certainty that every element of a crime has been proven by the prosecution. This standard of proof does not require that the state establish absolute certainty by eliminating all doubt, but it does require that the evidence be so conclusive that all reasonable doubts are removed from the mind of the ordinary person.

bill of particulars A statement of the details of the charge made against the defendant.

bind over To hold a person for trial on bond (bail) or in jail. If the judicial official conducting a preliminary hearing finds probable cause to believe the accused committed a crime, the official will bind over the accused, normally by setting bail for the accused's appearance at trial.

booking The process of photographing, fingerprinting, and recording identifying data of a suspect. This process follows the arrest.

breach of contract A legally inexcusable failure to perform a contractual obligation.

brief A written statement prepared by one side in a lawsuit to explain to the court its view of the facts of a case and the applicable law.

GLOSSARY

burden of proof In the law of evidence, the necessity or duty of affirmatively proving a fact or facts in dispute on an issue raised between the parties in a lawsuit. The responsibility of proving a point—the burden of proof—is not the same as the standard of proof. *Burden of proof* deals with which side must establish a point or points; *standard of proof* indicates the degree to which the point must be proven. For example, in a civil case the burden of proof rests with the plaintiff, who must establish his or her case by such standards of proof as "a preponderance of evidence" or "clear and convincing evidence."

C

capital crime A crime punishable by death.

caption The heading on a legal document listing the parties, the court, the case number, and related information.

case law Law based on previous decisions of appellate courts, particularly the Supreme Court.

cause A lawsuit, litigation, or action. Any question, civil or criminal, litigated or contested before a court of justice.

cause of action The facts that give rise to a lawsuit.

caveat A warning; a note of caution.

certiorari A means of getting an appellate court to review a lower court's decision. The loser of a case will often ask the appellate court to issue a *writ of certiorari,* which orders the lower court to convey the record of the case to the appellate court and to certify it as accurate and complete. If an appellate court grants a writ of certiorari, it agrees to take the appeal. This is often referred to as *granting cert.*

challenge An objection, such as when an attorney objects at a *voir dire* hearing to the seating of a particular person on a jury, civil or criminal. It may be *challenge for cause* or *peremptory challenge.*

challenge for cause Objection to the seating of a particular juror for a stated reason (usually bias or prejudice for or against one of the parties in the lawsuit). The judge has the discretion to deny the challenge. This differs from *peremptory challenge.*

chambers A judge's private office. A hearing in chambers takes place in the judge's office outside of the presence of the jury and the public.

change of venue Moving a lawsuit or criminal trial to another place for trial, often because pre-trial publicity makes it difficult to empanel (assemble) an impartial jury.

charge to the jury The judge's instruction to the jury concerning the law that applies to the facts of the case.

charitable trust A trust set up to benefit a charity.

circumstantial evidence Evidence that merely suggests something by implication. One example is physical evidence, such as fingerprints, from which an inference can be drawn. Circumstantial evidence is indirect, as opposed to eyewitness testimony, which is direct.

citation A reference to a source of legal authority. Also, a direction to appear in court, as when a defendant is *cited* into court, rather than arrested.

civil actions Noncriminal cases in which one private individual or business sues another to protect, enforce, or redress private or civil rights.

civil procedure Process by which a civil case is tried and appealed, including the preparations for trial, the rules of evidence and trial conduct, and the procedure for pursuing appeals.

class action A lawsuit brought by one or more persons on behalf of a larger group.

clear and convincing evidence Standard of proof commonly used in civil lawsuits and in regulatory agency cases. It governs the amount of proof that must be offered in order for the plaintiff to prevail (win the case).

clemency or **executive clemency** Act of grace or mercy by the president or governor to ease the consequences of a criminal act, accusation, or conviction. It may take the form of *commutation* or *pardon.*

codicil An amendment to a will.

commit To send a person to prison, asylum, or reformatory pursuant (according) to a court order of *mittimus.*

common law Law arising from tradition and judicial decisions, rather than from laws passed by the legislature. The common law originated in England and has been followed as the law in most American jurisdictions. Also called *case law.*

commutation The reduction of a sentence, as from death to life imprisonment.

comparative negligence A legal doctrine by which acts of the opposing parties are compared to determine the liability of each party to the other, making each liable only for his or her percentage of fault. See also *contributory negligence.*

complainant The party who complains or sues; one who applies to the court for legal redress. Also called the *plaintiff.*

complaint The legal document that usually begins a civil lawsuit. It states the facts and identifies the action the court is asked to take.

conciliation A form of *alternative dispute resolution* in which the parties bring their dispute to a neutral third party, who elps lower tensions, improve communications, and explore ossible solutions. Conciliation is similar to *mediation,* but it ay be less formal.

oncurrent sentences Sentences for more than one violation hat are to be served at the same time, rather than one after the ther. Three five-year terms served concurrently add up to no ore than five years imprisonment. However, three five-year erms served consecutively impose a 15-year sentence. See also *umulative sentences.*

oncurring opinion An appellate court opinion by one or ore judges that agrees with the majority decision in the case, ut was reached for different reasons.

ondemnation The legal process by which the government nvokes its powers of *eminent domain* and takes privately wned real estate for public use, paying the owners just (fair) ompensation.

onsecutive sentences Successive sentences, one beginning at he expiration of another, imposed against a person convicted f two or more violations.

onservatorship Legal right given to a person to manage the roperty and financial affairs of a person deemed incapable of oing that for himself or herself. (See also *guardianship.* onservators have somewhat less responsibility than guardians.)

ontempt of court Willful disobedience of a judge's ommand or of an official court order.

ontinuance Postponement of a legal proceeding to a ater date.

ontract A legally enforceable agreement between two or ore competent parties made either orally or in writing.

ontributory negligence A legal doctrine that says if the laintiff in a civil action for negligence also was negligent, he or he cannot recover damages from the defendant for the efendant's negligence. Most jurisdictions have abandoned the octrine of contributory negligence in favor of *comparative negligence.*

conviction A judgment of guilt against a criminal defendant.

copyright The right to literary property, giving authors, composers, and other creators the sole right to reproduce and distribute their work for a limited period of time.

corpus delicti Body of the crime. The objective proof that a crime has been committed. It sometimes refers to the body of the victim of a homicide or to the charred shell of a burned house, but the term has a broader meaning. For the state to introduce a confession or to convict the accused, it must prove a corpus delicti, that is, the occurrence of a specific injury or loss and a criminal act as the source of that particular injury or loss.

corroborating evidence Supplementary evidence that tends to strengthen or confirm the initial evidence.

counterclaim A claim made by the defendant in a civil lawsuit against the plaintiff—in essence, a counter lawsuit within a lawsuit.

court costs The expenses of prosecuting or defending a lawsuit, other than the attorneys' fees. An amount of money may be awarded to the successful party (and may be recoverable from the losing party) as reimbursement for court costs.

cross-claim A claim by codefendants or coplaintiffs against each other and not against persons on the opposite side of the lawsuit.

cross-examination The questioning of a witness produced by the other side.

cumulative sentences Sentences for two or more crimes to run successively, rather than concurrently.

D

damages Money awarded by a court to a person injured by the unlawful act or negligence of another person.

decision The judgment reached or given by a court of law.

declaratory judgment A judgment that, without the need for enforcement, declares the rights of the parties or an interpretation of the law.

decree An order of the court. A final decree is one that fully and finally disposes of the litigation. An *interlocutory* decree is a preliminary order that often disposes of only part of a lawsuit.

defamation That which tends to injure a person's reputation. *Libel* is published defamation, whereas *slander* is spoken.

default A failure to respond to a lawsuit within the specified time. When a defendant does not respond in a timely fashion or does not appear at the trial, a *default judgment* is entered against the defendant.

defendant In a civil case, the person being sued. In a criminal case, the person charged with a crime.

demurrer A motion to dismiss a civil case because of the legal insufficiency of a complaint.

de novo Anew. A *trial de novo* is a new trial of a case.

deposition The testimony of a witness taken under oath in preparation for a trial.

descent and distribution statutes State laws that provide for the distribution of estate property of a person who dies without a will. Same as *intestacy laws.*

directed verdict An instruction by the judge to the jury to return a specific verdict.

direct evidence Proof of facts by witnesses who saw acts done or heard words spoken.

direct examination The first questioning of witnesses by the party on whose behalf they are called.

disbarment Form of discipline of a lawyer resulting in the loss (often permanently) of that lawyer's right to practice law. It differs from *censure* (an official reprimand or condemnation) and from *suspension* (a temporary loss of the right to practice law).

disclaim To refuse a gift made in a will.

discovery The pre-trial process by which one party discovers the evidence that will be relied upon in the trial by the opposing party.

dismissal The termination of a lawsuit. A *dismissal without prejudice* permits the suit to be filed again at a later time. In contrast, a *dismissal with prejudice* prevents the lawsuit from being filed later.

dissent An appellate court opinion setting forth the minority view and outlining the disagreement of one or more judges with the decision of the majority.

diversion The process of removing some minor criminal, traffic, or juvenile cases from the full judicial process, on the condition that the accused undergo some sort of rehabilitation or make restitution for damages. Diversion may take place before the trial or its equivalent, as when a juvenile accused of a crime may consent to probation without an admission of guilt. If the juvenile completes probation successfully—e.g., takes a course or makes amends for the crime—then the entire matter may be expunged (erased) from the record.

docket A list of cases to be heard by a court.

domicile The place where a person has his or her permanent, legal home. A person may have several residences, but only one domicile.

double jeopardy Putting a person on trial more than once for the same crime. It is forbidden by the Fifth Amendment to the U.S. Constitution.

due process of law The right of all persons to receive the guarantees and safeguards of the law and the judicial process. It includes such constitutional requirements as adequate notice, assistance of counsel, and the rights to remain silent, to a speedy and public trial, to an impartial jury, and to confront and secure witnesses.

E

elements of a crime Specific factors that define a crime, every element of which the prosecution must prove beyond a reasonable doubt in order to obtain a conviction. The elements that must be proven are (1) that a crime has actually occurred, (2) that the accused intended the crime to happen, and (3) a timely relationship between the first two factors. See also *actus reus* and *mens rea*.

eminent domain The power of the government to take private property for public use through *condemnation.*

en banc All the judges of a court sitting together. Appellate courts can consist of a dozen or more judges, but often they hear cases in panels of three judges. If a case is heard or reheard by the full court, it is heard en banc.

enjoin To require a person, through the issuance of an injunction, to perform or to abstain from some specific act.

entrapment A defense to criminal charges alleging that agents of the government induced a person to commit a crime he or she otherwise would not have committed.

equal protection of the law The guarantee in the Fourteenth Amendment to the U.S. Constitution that all persons be treated equally by the law. Court decisions have established that this guarantee requires that courts be open to all persons on the same conditions, with like rules of evidence and modes of procedure; that persons be subject to no restrictions in the acquisition of property, the enjoyment of personal liberty, and the pursuit of happiness, which do not generally affect others; that persons are liable to no other or greater burdens than such as are laid upon others; and that no different or greater punishment is enforced against them for a violation of the laws.

equity Generally, justice or fairness. Historically, equity refers to a separate body of law developed in England in reaction to the inability of the common-law courts, in their strict adherence to rigid writs and forms of action, to consider or provide a remedy for every injury. The king therefore established the court of chancery, to do justice between parties in cases where the common law would give inadequate redress. The principle of this jurisprudence (system of law) is that equity will find a way to achieve a lawful result when legal procedure is inadequate. Equity and law courts are now merged in most jurisdictions, though equity jurisprudence and equitable doctrines are still independently viable (capable of functioning).

escheat The process by which a deceased person's property goes to the state if no heir can be found.

escrow Money or a written instrument such as a deed that, by agreement between two parties, is held by a neutral third party *(held in escrow)* until all conditions of the agreement are met.

estate An estate consists of personal property (car, household items, and other tangible items), real property, and intangible property, such as stock certificates and bank accounts, owned in the individual name of a person on death. It does not include life insurance proceeds (unless the estate was made the beneficiary) or other assets that pass outside the estate (like joint tenancy assets).

estate tax Generally, a tax on the privilege of transferring property to others after a person's death. In addition to federal estate taxes, 18 states have their own estate taxes.

et al. And others.

exceptions Declarations by either side in a civil or criminal case reserving the right to appeal a judge's ruling upon a motion. Also, in regulatory cases, objections by either side to points made by the other side or to rulings by the agency or one of its hearing officers.

exclusionary rule The rule preventing illegally obtained evidence to be used in any trial.

execute To complete the legal requirements (such as signing before witnesses) that make a will valid. Also, to execute a judgment or decree means to put the final judgment of the court into effect.

executor A personal representative, named in a will, who administers an estate.

exhibit A document or other article introduced as evidence during a trial or hearing.

ex parte On behalf of only one party, without notice to any other party. For example, a request for a search warrant is an ex parte proceeding, since the person subject to the search is not notified of the proceeding and is not present at the hearing.

ex parte proceeding The legal procedure in which only one side is represented. It differs from *adversary system* or *adversary proceeding*.

ex post facto After the fact. The Constitution prohibits the enactment of ex post facto laws. These are laws that permit conviction and punishment for a lawful act performed before the law was changed and the act made illegal.

expungement Official and formal erasure of a record or partial contents of a record.

extradition The process by which one state surrenders to another state a person accused or convicted of a crime in the other state.

F

family allowance A small amount of money set aside from the estate of the deceased. Its purpose is to provide for the surviving family members during the administration of the estate.

felony A crime of a graver nature than a *misdemeanor,* usually punishable by imprisonment in a penitentiary for more than a year and/or substantial fines.

fiduciary A person having a legal relationship of trust and confidence to another and having a duty to act primarily for the other's benefit, e.g., a guardian, trustee, or executor.

finding Formal conclusion by a judge or regulatory agency on issues of fact. Also, a conclusion by a jury regarding a fact.

first appearance The initial appearance of an arrested person before a judge to determine whether or not there is probable cause for his or her arrest. Generally the person comes before a judge within hours of the arrest. Also called *initial appearance.*

fraud Intentional deception to deprive another person of property or to injure that person in some other way.

G

garnishment A legal proceeding in which a debtor's money, in the possession of another (called the *garnishee*), is applied to the debts of the debtor, such as when an employer garnishes a debtor's wages.

good time A reduction in sentenced time in prison as a reward for good behavior. It usually is one third to one half off the maximum sentence.

grand jury A group of citizens, usually numbering 23, who are assembled in secret to hear or investigate allegations of criminal behavior. A grand jury has the authority to conduct criminal investigations and to charge a crime by *indictment.* It also may have the power to issue a report, or *presentment,* without charging a crime.

grantor or **settlor** The person who sets up a trust.

guardian A person appointed by will or by law to assume responsibility for incompetent adults or minor children. If a parent dies, this will usually be the other parent. If both die, it probably will be a close relative.

guardianship Legal right given to a person to be responsible for the food, housing, health care, and other necessities of a person deemed incapable of providing these necessities for himself or herself. A guardian also may be given responsibility for the person's financial affairs, and thus perform additionally as a conservator. (See also *conservatorship.*)

H

habeas corpus A writ commanding that a person be brought before a judge. Most commonly, a writ of habeas corpus is a legal document that forces law enforcement authorities to produce a prisoner they are holding and to legally justify his or her detention.

harmless error An error committed during a trial that was corrected or was not serious enough to affect the outcome of a trial and therefore was not sufficiently harmful (prejudicial) to be reversed on appeal.

hearsay Evidence that is not within the personal knowledge of the witness but was relayed to the witness by a third party. Hearsay evidence generally is not admissible in court, although there are many exceptions under which it can be admitted.

holographic will A handwritten will.

hostile witness A witness whose testimony is not favorable to the party who calls him or her as a witness. A hostile witness may be asked leading questions and may be cross-examined by the party who calls him or her to the stand.

hung jury A jury that cannot reach a verdict.

I

immunity Grant by the court, in which someone will not face prosecution in return for providing criminal evidence. It differs from *sovereign immunity*.

impeachment of a witness An attack on the credibility (believability) of a witness, through evidence introduced for that purpose.

inadmissible That which under the rules of evidence cannot be admitted or received as evidence.

in camera In chambers, or in private. A hearing in camera takes place in the judge's office outside of the presence of the jury and the public.

independent executor A special kind of executor, permitted by the laws of certain states, who performs the duties of an executor without intervention by the court.

indeterminate sentence A sentence of imprisonment to a specified minimum and maximum period of time, specifically authorized by statute, subject to termination by a parole board or other authorized agency after the prisoner has served the minimum term.

indictment An accusation by a grand jury charging a person with a crime.

information Accusatory document, filed by the prosecutor, detailing the charges against the defendant. An alternative to an *indictment,* it serves to bring a defendant to trial.

infraction A violation of law not punishable by imprisonment. Minor traffic offenses generally are considered infractions.

inheritance tax A state tax on property that an heir or beneficiary under a will receives from a deceased person's estate. The heir or beneficiary pays this tax.

initial appearance In criminal law, the hearing at which a judge determines whether there is sufficient evidence against a person charged with a crime to warrant holding him or her for trial. The Constitution bans secret accusations, so initial appearances are public unless the defendant asks otherwise; the accused must be present, though he or she usually does not offer evidence. Also called *first appearance.*

injunction A measure by which a court usually orders a party to refrain from doing a particular act. A *preliminary injunction* is granted provisionally, until a full hearing can be held to determine if it should be made permanent.

instructions Judge's directions to the jury regarding the law in the case and the jury's authority to determine the facts and to draw inferences from the facts in order to reach a verdict. Also called *charge.*

intangible assets Nonphysical items such as stock certificates, bonds, bank accounts, and pension benefits that have value and must be taken into account in estate planning.

integrated bar Organized state bar association to which every lawyer in a state must belong in order to be permitted to practice in that state.

interlocutory Provisional; not final. An interlocutory order or an interlocutory appeal concerns only a part of the issues raised in a lawsuit.

interrogatories Written questions asked by one party of an opposing party for which written answers must be provided.

intervention An action by which a third person who may be affected by a lawsuit is permitted to become a party to the suit. Differs from the process of becoming an *amicus curiae.*

inter vivos gift A gift made during the giver's life.

inter vivos trust Another name for a *living trust.*

intestacy laws See *descent and distribution statutes.*

intestate Dying without a will.

intestate succession The process by which the property of a person who has died without a will passes on to others according to the state's descent and distribution statutes. If someone dies without a will, and the court uses the state's intestate succession laws, an heir who receives some of the deceased's property is an *intestate heir.*

irrevocable trust A trust that, once set up, the grantor may not revoke.

issue (1) The disputed point or question to which the parties to a case have narrowed their disagreement. It is a single material point that is affirmed by one side and denied by the other. When the plaintiff and the defendant have arrived at some point that one affirms and the other denies, they are said to be *at issue.* When the defendant has filed an answer denying all or part of the allegations of the complaint, the *issue has been joined* and the case is ready to be set for trial. (2) To send out officially (to issue an order).

J

joint and several liability A legal doctrine that makes each of the parties responsible for an injury liable for all the damages awarded in a lawsuit if the other parties responsible cannot pay.

joint tenancy A form of legal co-ownership of property (also known as *survivorship*). At the death of one co-owner, the surviving co-owner becomes sole owner of the property. *Tenancy by the entirety* is a special form of joint tenancy between a husband and wife.

judgment The final disposition of a lawsuit. *Default judgment* is a judgment rendered because of the defendant's failure to answer or appear. *Summary judgment* is a judgment given on the basis of pleadings, affidavits, and exhibits presented for the record without any need for a trial. It is used when there is no dispute as to the facts of the case and one party is entitled to a judgment as a matter of law. *Consent judgment* occurs when the provisions and terms of the judgment are agreed on by the parties and submitted to the court for its sanction and approval. A *judgment n.o.v.* is literally a judgment non obstante veredicto, which translates as *judgment notwithstanding the verdict*; it is a judge's decision to decide a case contrary to the verdict of the jury. It may be made in a civil or criminal case.

judicial review The authority of a court to review the official actions of other branches of government. Also, the authority to declare unconstitutional the actions of other branches.

jurisdiction The nature and scope of a court's authority to hear and/or decide a case. Also, the territory from which a court is authorized to hear cases.

jury A certain number of persons selected according to law and sworn to inquire into matters of fact and declare the truth about matters laid before them. A *grand jury* traditionally is composed of 23 people who decide whether the facts of a criminal case are sufficient to issue an indictment charging a person with a crime. A *petit jury* is an ordinary or trial jury, composed of six to 12 persons, which hears either civil or criminal cases.

jury commissioner The court officer responsible for choosing the panel of persons to serve as potential jurors for a particular court term.

justiciable Issues and claims capable of being properly examined in court.

L

lapsed gift A gift made in a will to a person who has died before the will-maker. If the state anti-lapse statute does not apply, the gift fails.

larceny Obtaining property by fraud or deceit.

leading question A question that suggests the answer desired of the witness. A party generally may not ask one's own witness leading questions. Leading questions may be asked only of hostile witnesses and on cross-examination.

legal aid Professional legal services available usually to persons or organizations unable to afford such services.

legislative history Background of action by a legislature, including testimony before committees, written reports, and debates on the legislation.

leniency Recommendation by the prosecutor to the judge regarding the sentence that may be imposed in a criminal case.

letters of administration Legal document issued by a court that shows an administrator's legal right to take control of assets in the deceased person's name.

letters testamentary Legal document issued by a court that shows an executor's legal right to take control of assets in the deceased person's name.

liable Legally responsible.

libel Published words or pictures that falsely and maliciously defame a person. Libel is published defamation; *slander* is spoken.

lien A legal claim against another person's property as security for a debt. A lien does not convey ownership of the property, but gives the lienholder a right to have his or her debt satisfied out of the proceeds of the property if the debt is not otherwise paid.

limine A motion requesting that the court exclude certain evidence that might prejudice the jury.

litigant A party to a lawsuit.

litigation A case, controversy, or lawsuit.

living trust A trust set up and in effect during the lifetime of the grantor. Also called *inter vivos trust.*

M

magistrate Judicial officer exercising some of the functions of a judge. It also refers in a general way to a judge.

mala in se "Evil in itself"—behavior that is universally regarded as criminal, such as murder.

mala prohibita "Wrong because prohibited"—behavior that is criminal only because a society defines it as such. An example is the manufacture of alcoholic beverages during Prohibition.

mandamus A writ issued by a court ordering a public official to perform an act.

manslaughter The unlawful killing of another without intent to kill; either voluntary—upon a sudden impulse, e.g., a quarrel erupts into a fistfight in which one of the participants is killed; or involuntary—during the commission of an unlawful act not ordinarily expected to result in great bodily harm, or during the commission of a lawful act without proper caution, e.g., driving an automobile at excessive speed resulting in a fatal collision. (See also *murder.*)

mediation A form of *alternative dispute resolution* in which the parties bring their dispute to a neutral third party, who helps them agree on a settlement.

memorialized In writing.

mens rea The "guilty mind" necessary to establish criminal responsibility.

Miranda warning Requirement that police tell a suspect in their custody of his or her constitutional rights before they question him or her. So named as a result of the *Miranda v. Arizona* ruling by the U.S. Supreme Court.

misdemeanor A criminal offense considered less serious than a *felony*. Misdemeanors generally are punishable by a fine or a limited local jail term, but not by imprisonment in a state penitentiary.

mistrial A trial that is terminated before a verdict is reached, either because of some extraordinary circumstance, because of a fundamental error prejudicial to the defendant (such as an improper drawing of jurors), or because of a *hung jury*.

mittimus The name of a precept (order) in writing, issuing from a court and directing the sheriff or other officer to convey a person to a prison, asylum, or reformatory, and directing the jailer or other appropriate official to receive and safely keep the person until his or her fate shall be determined by due course of law.

moot A moot case or a moot point is one not subject to a judicial determination because it involves an abstract question or a pretended controversy that has not yet actually arisen or has already passed. Mootness usually refers to a court's refusal to consider a case because the issue involved has been resolved prior to the court's decision, leaving nothing that would be affected by the court's decision.

motion An application for a rule or order, made to a court or judge.

murder The unlawful killing of a human being with malice aforethought (deliberate intent to kill). *Murder in the first degree* is characterized by premeditation; *murder in the second degree* is characterized by a sudden and instantaneous intent to kill or to cause injury without caring whether the injury kills or not. (See also *manslaughter*.)

N

negligence Failure to exercise the degree of care that a reasonable person would exercise under the same circumstances.

neighborhood justice center In many areas of the country, neighborhood justice centers help parties resolve their disputes outside the traditional justice system, through *arbitration, mediation,* or some other form of *alternative dispute resolution*.

next friend One acting without formal appointment as guardian for the benefit of an infant, a person of unsound mind not judicially declared incompetent, or other person under some disability.

no bill This phrase, endorsed by a grand jury on the written indictment submitted to it for its approval, means that the evidence was found insufficient to indict.

no-contest clause Language in a will that provides that a person who makes a legal challenge to the will's validity will be disinherited.

no-fault proceeding A civil case in which parties may resolve their dispute without a formal finding of error or fault.

nolle prosequi Decision by a prosecutor not to go forward with a charge of crime; it translates "I do not choose to prosecute." Also loosely called *nolle pros.*

nolo contendere A plea of no contest. In many jurisdictions, it is an expression that the matter will not be contested, but without an admission of guilt. In other jurisdictions, it is an admission of the charges and is equivalent to a guilty plea.

non compos mentis Not of sound mind.

notice Formal notification to the party that has been sued in a civil case of the fact that the lawsuit has been filed. Also, any form of notification of a legal proceeding.

nuncupative will An oral (unwritten) will.

O

objection The process by which one party takes exception to some statement or procedure. An objection is either sustained or overruled by the judge.

on a person's own recognizance Release of a person from custody without the payment of any *bail* or posting of bond.

one-day, one-trial jury service An innovation in many jurisdictions that requires a prospective juror to serve for only one day if he or she is not chosen for a jury, or for only one trial if chosen.

opinion The written decision of an appellate court. The *majority* or *plurality opinion* expresses the court's decision. A *concurring opinion* generally agrees with the majority, but usually states different or additional reasons for reaching the same conclusion. A *dissenting opinion* states the opinion of the judges who disagree with the majority. A *per curiam opinion* is an unsigned opinion "of the court."

order A written or oral command from a court directing or forbidding an action.

ordinance A local law adopted by a municipality.

overrule A judge's decision not to allow an objection. Also, a decision by a higher court finding that a lower court decision was in error.

P

pardon A form of *executive clemency* preventing criminal prosecution or removing or extinguishing a criminal conviction.

parens patriae The doctrine under which the court protects the interests of a juvenile.

parole The supervised conditional release of a prisoner before the expiration of his or her sentence. If the parolee observes the conditions, he or she need not serve the rest of his or her term.

party A person, business, or government agency actively involved in the prosecution or defense of a legal proceeding.

patent A government grant giving an inventor the exclusive right to make or sell his or her invention for a term of years.

peremptory challenge A challenge that may be used to reject a certain number of prospective jurors without giving a reason.

perjury The criminal offense of making a false statement under oath.

permanent injunction A court order requiring that some action be taken, or that some party refrain from taking action. It differs from forms of temporary relief, such as a *temporary restraining order* or *preliminary injunction.*

personal property Tangible physical property (such as cars, clothing, furniture, and jewelry) and intangible personal property, but not real property—that is, not land or rights in land.

personal representative The person who administers an estate. If named in a will, that person's title is an *executor*. If there is no valid will, that person's title is an *administrator*.

person in need of supervision Juvenile found to have committed a *status offense* rather than a crime that would provide a basis for a finding of delinquency. Typical status offenses are habitual truancy, violating a curfew, or running away from home. These are not crimes, but they might be enough to place a child under supervision. In different states, status offenders might be called *children in need of supervision* or *minors in need of supervision.*

petitioner The person filing an action in a court of original jurisdiction. Also, the person who appeals the judgment of a lower court. The opposing party is called the *respondent.*

plaintiff The person who brings a civil lawsuit. Also called the *complainant.*

plea In a criminal proceeding it is the defendant's declaration in open court that he or she is guilty or not guilty—the defendant's answer to the charges made in the indictment or information.

plea bargaining or **plea negotiating** The process through which an accused person and a prosecutor negotiate a mutually satisfactory disposition of a case. Usually it is a legal transaction in which a defendant pleads guilty in exchange for some form of leniency. It often involves a guilty plea to lesser charges or a guilty plea to some of the charges if other charges are dropped.

pleadings The written statements of fact and law filed by the parties to a lawsuit.

polling the jury The act, after a jury verdict has been announced, of asking jurors individually whether they agree with the verdict.

pour-over will A will that leaves some or all estate assets to a trust established before the will-maker's death.

power of attorney Formal authorization of a person to act in the interests of another person.

precedent A previously decided case that guides the decision of future cases.

preliminary hearing Another term for *arraignment.*

preliminary injunction Court order requiring action or forbidding action until a decision can be made whether to issue a permanent injunction. It differs from a *temporary restraining order.*

preponderance of the evidence Greater weight of the evidence, the common standard of proof in civil cases.

presentment Declaration or document issued by a grand jury that either makes a neutral report or notes misdeeds by officials charged with specified public duties. It ordinarily does not include a formal charge of crime. A presentment differs from an *indictment.*

pretermitted child A child born after a will is executed, who is not provided for by the will. Most states have laws that provide for a share of estate property to go to such children.

pre-trial conference A meeting between the judge and the lawyers involved in a lawsuit to narrow the issues in the suit, agree on what will be presented at the trial, and make a final effort to settle the case without a trial.

prima facie case A case that is sufficient—that is, has the minimum amount of evidence necessary to allow it to continue in the judicial process.

probable cause Sufficient legal reasons for allowing the search and seizure or the arrest of a person.

probate The court-supervised process by which a will is determined to be the will-maker's final statement regarding how the will-maker wants his or her property distributed. It also confirms the appointment of the personal representative of the estate. Probate also means the process by which assets are gathered; applied to pay debts, taxes, and expenses of administration; and distributed to those designated as beneficiaries in the will.

probate court The court with authority to supervise estate administration.

probate estate Estate property that may be disposed of by a will.

probation An alternative to imprisonment allowing a person found guilty of an offence to stay in the community, usually under conditions and under the supervision of a probation officer. A violation of probation can lead to its revocation and to imprisonment.

pro bono publico For the public good. Lawyers representing clients without a fee are said to be working pro bono publico.

pro se Person acting as his or her own attorney, whether or not he or she is a lawyer. Also, refers to small claims courts in some jurisdictions.

prosecutor A trial lawyer representing the government in a criminal case.

proximate cause The act that caused an event to occur. A person generally is liable only if an injury was proximately caused by his or her action or by his or her failure to act when he or she had a duty to act.

public defender Government lawyer who provides free legal defense services to a poor person accused of a crime.

Q

quash To vacate or void a summons, subpoena, etc.

R

real property Land, buildings, and other improvements affixed to the land.

reasonable person A phrase used to denote a hypothetical person who exercises qualities of attention, knowledge, intelligence, and judgment that society requires of its members for the protection of their own interest and the interests of others. Thus, the test of negligence is based on either a failure to do something that a reasonable person, guided by considerations that ordinarily regulate conduct, would do, or on the doing of something that a reasonable and prudent (wise) person would not do.

rebuttal Evidence disproving other evidence previously given or reestablishing the credibility of challenged evidence.

record All the documents and evidence plus transcripts of oral proceedings in a case.

re-direct examination Opportunity to present rebuttal evidence after one's evidence has been subjected to cross-examination.

redress To set right; to remedy; to compensate; to remove the causes of a grievance.

referee A person to whom the court refers a pending case to take testimony, hear the parties, and report back to the court. A referee is an officer with judicial powers who serves as an arm of the court.

rehearing Another hearing of a civil or criminal case by the same court in which the case was originally heard.

rejoinder Opportunity for the side that opened the case to offer limited response to evidence presented during the *rebuttal* by the opposing side.

remand To send a dispute back to the court where it was originally heard. Usually it is an appellate court that remands a case for proceedings in the trial court consistent with the appellate court's ruling.

remedy Legal or judicial means by which a right or privilege is enforced or the violation of a right or privilege is prevented, redressed, or compensated.

remittitur The reduction by a judge of the damages awarded by a jury.

removal The transfer of a state case to federal court for trial; in civil cases, because the parties are from different states; in criminal and some civil cases, because there is a significant possibility that there could not be a fair trial in state court.

replevin An action for the recovery of a possession that has been wrongfully taken.

reply The response by a party to charges raised in a pleading by the other party.

respondent The person against whom an appeal is taken. See *petitioner*.

rest A party is said to *rest* or *rest its case* when it has presented all the evidence it intends to offer.

return A report to a judge by police on the implementation of an arrest or search warrant. Also, a report to a judge in reply to a subpoena, civil or criminal.

reverse An action of a higher court in setting aside or revoking a lower court decision.

reversible error An error sufficiently prejudicial (harmful) to justify reversing the judgment of a lower court.

revocable trust A trust that the grantor may change or revoke.

revoke To cancel or nullify a legal document.

robbery Felonious taking of another's property, from his or her person or immediate presence and against his or her will, by means of force or fear. It differs from *larceny*.

rules of evidence Standards governing whether evidence in a civil or criminal case is admissible.

S

search warrant A written order issued by a judge that directs a law enforcement officer to search a specific area for a particular piece of evidence.

self-defense Claim that an act otherwise criminal was legally justifiable because it was necessary to protect a person or property from the threat or action of another.

self-incrimination, privilege against The constitutional right of people to refuse to give testimony against themselves that could subject them to criminal prosecution. The right is guaranteed in the Fifth Amendment to the U.S. Constitution. Asserting the right is often referred to as *taking the Fifth*.

self-proving will A will whose validity does not have to be testified to in court by the witnesses to it, since the witnesses executed an *affidavit* reflecting proper execution of the will prior to the maker's death.

sentence A court's determination of the punishment to be inflicted on a person convicted of a crime.

sentence report A document containing background material on a convicted person. It is prepared to guide the judge in the imposition of a sentence. Sometimes called a *presentence report*.

sequestration Keeping all the jurors together during a trial to prevent them from being influenced by information received outside the courtroom. Sequestered jurors usually are housed in a hotel, have their meals together, and are given edited copies of newspapers and magazines, all in an attempt to keep them free from outside influences.

sequestration of witnesses Keeping all witnesses (except plaintiff and defendant) out of the courtroom except for their time on the stand, and admonishing (cautioning) them not to discuss their testimony with other witnesses. Also called *separation of witnesses*. This prevents a witness from being influenced by the testimony of a prior witness.

service The delivery of a legal document, such as a complaint, summons, or subpoena, notifying a person of a lawsuit or other legal action taken against him or her. Service, which constitutes formal legal notice, must be made by an officially authorized person in accordance with the formal requirements of the applicable laws.

settlement An agreement between the parties disposing of a lawsuit.

settlor The person who sets up a trust. Also called the *grantor*.

slander False and defamatory spoken words tending to harm another's reputation, business, or means of livelihood. Slander is spoken defamation; *libel* is published.

small claims court A court that handles civil claims for small amounts of money. People often represent themselves rather than hire an attorney.

sovereign immunity The doctrine that the government, state or federal, is immune to lawsuit unless it gives its consent.

specific performance A remedy requiring a person who has breached a contract to perform specifically what he or she has agreed to do. Specific performance is ordered when damages would be inadequate compensation.

spendthrift trust A trust set up for the benefit of someone who the grantor believes would be incapable of managing his or her own financial affairs.

standing The legal right to bring a lawsuit. Only a person with something at stake has standing to bring a lawsuit.

stare decisis The doctrine that courts will follow principles of law laid down in previous cases. Similar to *precedent*.

status offenders Youths charged with the status of being beyond the control of their legal guardian—habitually disobedient, truant from school, or having committed other acts that would not be a crime if committed by an adult. They are not delinquents (in that they have committed no crime), but rather are *persons in need of supervision* (pins), *minors in need of supervision* (mins), or *children in need of supervision* (chins), depending on the state in which they live. Status offenders are placed under the supervision of the juvenile court.

statute of limitations The time within which a plaintiff must begin a lawsuit (in civil cases) or a prosecutor must bring charges (in criminal cases). There are different statutes of limitations at both the federal and state levels for different kinds of lawsuits or crimes.

statutory construction Process by which a court seeks to interpret the meaning and scope of legislation.

statutory law Law enacted by the legislative branch of government, as distinguished from *case law* or *common law*.

stay A court order halting a judicial proceeding.

stipulation An agreement by attorneys on both sides of a civil or criminal case about some aspect of the case; e.g., to extend the time to answer, to adjourn the trial date, or to admit certain facts at the trial.

strike Highlighting in the record of a case evidence that has been improperly offered and will not be relied upon.

subpoena A court order compelling a witness to appear and testify.

subpoena duces tecum A court order commanding a witness to bring certain documents or records to court.

summary judgment An order by a judge deciding a case in favor of one side on the basis of the pleadings, before trial and before or after a hearing. A judge issues a summary judgment upon determining there is no factual dispute to be determined by a jury.

GLOSSARY

summons A notice to a defendant that he or she has been sued and is required to appear in court. A *jury summons* requires the person receiving it to report for possible jury duty.

support trust A trust that instructs the trustee to spend only as much income and principal (the assets held in the trust) as needed for the beneficiary's support.

suppress To forbid the use of evidence at a trial because it is improper or was improperly obtained. See also *exclusionary rule*.

surety bond A bond purchased at the expense of the estate to insure the executor's proper performance. Often called a *fidelity bond*.

survivorship Another name for *joint tenancy*.

sustain A court order allowing an objection or motion to prevail (become effective).

T

tangible personal property memorandum (TPPM) A legal document that is referred to in a will and used to guide the distribution of tangible personal property.

temporary relief Any form of action by a court granting one of the parties an order to protect its interest pending further action by the court.

temporary restraining order A judge's order forbidding certain actions until a full hearing can be held. Usually of short duration. Often referred to as a *T.R.O.*

testamentary capacity The legal ability to make a will.

testamentary trust A trust set up by a will.

testator Person who makes a will (female: *testatrix*).

testimony The evidence given by a witness under oath. It does not include evidence from documents and other physical evidence.

third party A person, business, or government agency not actively involved in a legal proceeding, agreement, or transaction.

third-party claim An action by the defendant that brings a third party into a lawsuit.

title Legal ownership of property, usually real property or automobiles.

tort An injury or wrong committed on the person or property of another. A tort is an infringement on the rights of an individual, but not founded on a contract. The most common tort action is a suit for damages sustained in an automobile accident.

transcript The official record of all the testimony and events that occur during a trial or hearing.

trust A legal device used to manage property—real or personal—established by one person (the *grantor* or *settlor*) for the benefit of another (the *beneficiary*). A third person (the *trustee*) or the grantor manages the trust.

trust agreement or **declaration** The legal document that sets up a living trust. Testamentary trusts are set up in a will.

trustee The person or institution that manages the property put in trust.

V

vacate To set aside.

venire A writ summoning persons to court to act as jurors. Also refers to the people summoned for jury duty.

venue The proper geographical area—county, city, or district—in which a court with jurisdiction over the subject matter may hear a case.

verdict A conclusion, as to fact or law, that forms the basis for the court's judgment. A *general verdict* is a jury's finding for or against a plaintiff after determining the facts and weighing them according to the judge's instructions regarding the law.

voir dire Process of questioning potential jurors so that each side may decide whether to accept or oppose individuals for jury service.

W

waiver Intentionally giving up a right.

waiver of immunity A means authorized by statute by which a witness, before testifying or producing evidence, may relinquish the right to refuse to testify against himself or herself, thereby making it possible for his or her testimony to be used against him or her in future proceedings.

warrant Most commonly, a court order authorizing law enforcement officers to make an arrest or conduct a search. An affidavit seeking a warrant must establish probable cause by detailing the facts upon which the request is based.

will A legal declaration that disposes of a person's property when that person dies.

without prejudice A claim or cause dismissed without prejudice may be the subject of a new lawsuit.

with prejudice Applied to orders of judgment dismissing a case, meaning that the plaintiff is forever barred from bringing a lawsuit on the same claim or cause.

witness A person who testifies to what he or she has seen, heard, or otherwise experienced. Also, a person who observes the signing of a will and is competent to testify that it is the will-maker's intended last will and testament.

writ A judicial order directing a person to do something.

INDEX

A

B

INDEX

C

D

INDEX

INDEX

N

O

P

INDEX

U

V

W

Z